ESSENTIAL READINGS

ESSENTIAL READINGS

IN CANADIAN GOVERNMENT AND POLITICS

EDITED BY

PETER H. RUSSELL
FRANÇOIS ROCHER
DEBRA THOMPSON
LINDA A. WHITE

2010 / EMOND MONTGOMERY PUBLICATIONS / TORONTO, CANADA

Emond Montgomery Publications Limited
60 Shaftesbury Avenue
Toronto ON M4T 1A3
http://www.emp.ca/highered

Printed in Canada on recycled paper.
Reprinted October 2013.

We have attempted to request permission from and to acknowledge in the text all sources of previously published material. If we have inadvertently overlooked any acknowledgment, we offer our sincere apologies and undertake to rectify the omission in any future printings.

We acknowledge the financial support of the Government of Canada through the Canada Book Fund for our publishing activities.

Acquisitions and development editor: Mike Thompson
Supervising editor: Jim Lyons
Production editor: Sarah Gleadow
Proofreader: Jamie Bush
Text designer: Tara Wells
Cover designers: Stephen Cribbin & Simon Evers
Cover image: "Game Plan (Atlantic Canada)" painting courtesy of Peter Dykhuis (www.dykhuis.ca)
Front matter photographs: House of Commons (interior), "40th Parliament" courtesy of Library of Parliament—Roy Grogan; House of Commons (exterior), "Vote Culture" courtesy of S.E. Amesse (www.afimagesottawa.com).

Library and Archives Canada Cataloguing in Publication

Essential readings in Canadian government and politics / edited by Peter H. Russell ... [et al.].

ISBN 978-1-55239-317-8

1. Canada—Politics and government—Textbooks. I. Russell, Peter H.

JL75.E85 2010   320.971   C2009-905998-3

Contents

Part 3: Social and Political Diversity

Part 4: Federalism and Beyond

Part 5: The Courts and the Charter

Part 6: Ideologies and Identities

Preface

This project began with a brief conversation that took place, appropriately enough, on Parliament Hill, during which Emond Montgomery editor Mike Thompson suggested to Peter Russell the idea for this book.

It was immediately clear that while articulating the guiding principle was relatively easy—that is, a book that would pull together a broad selection of primary and secondary readings that one would want a student of Canadian politics to have some familiarity with—making the final selections was considerably more difficult, even if it remained an enjoyable exercise throughout. It must be conceded that another group of four scholars would have undoubtedly come up with a different list. And yet we think the selections represent a very solid introduction to the key issues and perspectives at the heart of Canadian politics, enhanced by a strong historical element that we think students will also greatly benefit from. We trust these pieces will spark lively discussions, and indeed there is also a worthwhile debate to be had about what other readings could, or should, have been included in this volume. No doubt in the coming years people will offer their suggestions for consideration in a future second edition, which we welcome. In the meantime, we hope readers will agree that this editorial team—a group with quite varied backgrounds and academic interests—has produced an appropriately diverse and engaging set of readings that do justice to the richness, nuance, and complexity of Canadian political life.

The publisher wishes to thank the following people for their assistance and input, whether formal or informal, during the conception and development of this project: Peter Aucoin (Dalhousie University), Stephen McBride (Simon Fraser University), Dennis Pilon (University of Victoria), Jennifer Smith (Dalhousie University), John von Heyking (University of Lethbridge), and Graham White (University of Toronto).

About the Authors

Peter H. Russell is a professor of political science (emeritus) at the University of Toronto

Francois Roçher is a professor and director of the School of Political Studies at the University of Ottawa

Debra Thompson is a PhD candidate in the Department of Political Science at the University of Toronto

Linda A. White is an associate professor in the Department of Political Science at the University of Toronto

Prime Ministers of Canada, 1867–Present

Election year	Prime Minister(s) following the election
1867	John A. Macdonald (Conservative)
1872	John A. Macdonald (Conservative)
1874	Alexander Mackenzie (Liberal)
1878	John A. Macdonald (Conservative)
1882	John A. Macdonald (Conservative)
1887	John A. Macdonald (Conservative)
1891	Macdonald / Abbott / Thompson / Bowell / Tupper (Conservative)
1896	Wilfrid Laurier (Liberal)
1900	Wilfrid Laurier (Liberal)
1904	Wilfrid Laurier (Liberal)
1908	Wilfrid Laurier (Liberal)
1911	Robert Borden (Conservative)
1917	Robert Borden / Arthur Meighen (Unionist)
1921	William Lyon Mackenzie King (Liberal)
1925	William Lyon Mackenzie King (Liberal) / Arthur Meighen (Conservative)
1926	William Lyon Mackenzie King (Liberal)
1930	R.B. Bennett (Conservative)
1935	William Lyon Mackenzie King (Liberal)
1940	William Lyon Mackenzie King (Liberal)
1945	William Lyon Mackenzie King / Louis St. Laurent (Liberal)
1949	Louis St. Laurent (Liberal)
1953	Louis St. Laurent (Liberal)
1957	John Diefenbaker (Conservative)
1958	John Diefenbaker (Conservative)
1962	John Diefenbaker (Conservative)
1963	Lester Pearson (Liberal)
1965	Lester Pearson / Pierre Trudeau (Liberal)
1968	Pierre Trudeau (Liberal)
1972	Pierre Trudeau (Liberal)
1974	Pierre Trudeau (Liberal)
1979	Joe Clark (Conservative)
1980	Pierre Trudeau / John Turner (Liberal)
1984	Brian Mulroney (Conservative)
1988	Brian Mulroney / Kim Campbell (Conservative)
1993	Jean Chrétien (Liberal)
1997	Jean Chrétien (Liberal)
2000	Jean Chrétien / Paul Martin (Liberal)
2004	Paul Martin (Liberal)
2006	Stephen Harper (Conservative)
2008	Stephen Harper (Conservative)

PART 1

Understanding Canada

Introduction

Canada has never been an easy country to understand. This is as true for its own people as for those who view it from the outside. It has never been a state based on a people with one language and one culture. From its founding in 1867 to the present day, the Canadian federation has been based on compromise and the accommodation of cultural and linguistic diversity. The writings included in this part mark critical milestones in the evolving nature of the different aspirations that have animated Canada's experience as a nation-state and the efforts to maintain its unity.

Part 1 begins with speeches by two of Canada's founding fathers, John A. Macdonald and George-Étienne Cartier. It was the partnership of these two leaders—one English Canadian and the other French Canadian—that made Confederation possible. In their speeches we can see the colonial nature of Canada's beginnings. Macdonald and Cartier share a strong allegiance to the British monarchical system and an equally strong distaste for what they view as the excesses of American democracy. But they differ in their aspirations for the federation they are founding. While Macdonald views federalism not as an ideal but as a pragmatic compromise and believes that the new federal parliament has been given "all the powers that are incident to sovereignty," Cartier emphasizes the deep cultural diversity that will give the new federation its distinctive identity.

The three items that follow their speeches show how these differing perspectives emerged as Canada became an independent federal state. The early 20th-century pamphlet written by Henri Bourassa, a staunch Canadian patriot in the Cartier mould, argues that Canada will best maintain its unity and its distinctiveness from the United States by fostering English–French dualism throughout Canada. By way of contrast, the instrumental tone of the Rowell-Sirois Royal Commission of Inquiry into the state of the federation following the Great Depression of the 1930s is much more in tune with the concerns of John A. Macdonald. The commission's conclusion is that the problems experienced by Canadian governments in dealing with the economic and social consequences of the depression demonstrated the need to strengthen the responsibilities and resources of the federal government. The centralizing trends that followed in the Second World War and post-war reconstruction prompted the government of Quebec to appoint the Tremblay Royal Commission to examine the constitutional issues raised by these centralizing developments. The Tremblay report calls for a return to the Quebecois understanding of Confederation being founded on a partnership between English and French Canadians. But, unlike Henri Bourassa earlier in the century, the Quebec commissioners believe the survival of the French-Canadian culture now depends entirely on Quebec.

The "Quiet Revolution" that capped Quebec's emergence as a secular and industrialized society dramatically radicalized the constitutional aspirations of much of francophone Quebec. Instead of calling for a return to the spirit of Confederation, Quebec political leaders in the 1960s mobilized support for a restructuring of the Canadian federation to properly reflect Quebec's place as one of Canada's founding peoples. Excerpts from a 1965 book by Daniel Johnson, leader of the Union Nationale party who would become premier of Quebec in 1966, indicate the challenge that will plunge Canada into a quarter century of mega constitutional politics. The title of Johnson's book, *Égalité ou Indépendence*, indicates the ultimatum that Quebec now poses to Canada. The Canadian who would lead Canada in responding to Quebec's challenge was another Quebecer, Pierre Elliott Trudeau. His essay on "Federalism, Nationalism, and Reason," published on the eve of his becoming prime minister of Canada, warns of the coming clash between Quebec nationalism and Canadian nationalism. Charles Taylor's essay on "Shared and Divergent Values" was written after the demise of the Meech Lake Accord. It looks back on the intense constitutional politics of the 1970s and '80s that resulted in the patriation of Canada's Constitution with a Charter of Rights and recognition of Aboriginal rights, but left old and new cleavages in the Canadian body politic.

Aboriginal peoples did not participate in Confederation. Although they continued to engage in a treaty-making process with Canada from Confederation to the early years of the 20th century, they were not acknowledged as partners in Confederation. References to them in Taylor's essay indicate that Canada's heavy season of constitutional politics afforded Aboriginal peoples an opportunity to place their aspirations on the country's constitutional agenda. The Royal Commission on Aboriginal Peoples (RCAP), appointed in 1991, was the first time a representative group of Aboriginal and non-Aboriginal Canadians had come together to consider the place of Aboriginal peoples in Canada. *People to People, Nation to Nation* is an overview of the commission's 1996 final report. It calls for rebuilding a relationship of Aboriginal peoples with Canada based on mutual respect, partnership, and fair sharing.

The final two writings included in this part reflect on how Canada may cope with unresolved constitutional issues and a population harbouring divergent senses of national identity. Both point to understanding Canada as a multinational democracy. Peter Russell's essay "Canada—A Pioneer in the Management of Constitutional Politics in a Multi-national Society," written in 2000 after the rejection of the Charlottetown Accord in the 1992 referendum and the narrow win for the federalist side in Quebec's 1995 referendum, considers the lessons to be learned from these mega constitutional failures about managing the process of constitutional change in deeply divided societies. James Tully's discussion of Canada as a multinational democracy places the Canadian experience in a larger international context. Tully draws on modern democratic theory to elucidate a set of principles for operating a multinational democracy such as Canada.

Further Suggested Reading

Janet Ajzenstat, Paul Romney, Ian Gentles, and William D. Gairdner, eds., *Canada's Founding Debates*. Toronto: University of Toronto Press, 1999.

Eugene Forsey, "The Crown and the Constitution." In *Freedom and Order*. Toronto: McClelland & Stewart, 1974.

Alain-G. Gagnon, ed., *Contemporary Canadian Federalism: Foundations, Traditions, Institutions*. Toronto: University of Toronto Press, 2009.

Alain-G. Gagnon and Raffaele Iacovino, *Federalism, Citizenship and Quebec: Debating Multinationalism*. Toronto: University of Toronto Press, 2007.

Roger Gibbins and Guy Laforest, eds., *Beyond the Impasse: Toward Reconciliation*. Montreal: Institute for Research on Public Policy, 1998.

John George Lambton (Earl of Durham), *The Durham Report*, 1839. New edition abridged by Gerald M. Craig. Montreal and Kingston: McGill-Queen's University Press, 2006.

Kenneth McRoberts, *Misconceiving Canada: The Struggle for National Unity*. Toronto: Oxford University Press, 1997.

Kenneth McRoberts and Dale Postgate, *Quebec: Social Change and Political Crisis*, revised edition. Toronto: McClelland & Stewart, 1988.

John Meisel, Guy Rocher, Arthur Silver, and Institute for Research on Public Policy (IRPP), eds., *As I Recall/Si je me souviens bien: Historical Perspectives*. Montreal: IRPP, 1999.

Peter H. Russell, *Constitutional Odyssey: Can Canadians Become a Sovereign People?* 3rd edition. Toronto: University of Toronto Press, 2004.

André Siegfried, *The Race Question in Canada*, 1907. Montreal and Kingston: McGill-Queen's University Press/Carleton Library Series, 1966.

Jeremy Webber, *Reimagining Canada: Language, Culture, Community and the Canadian Constitution*. Montreal and Kingston: McGill-Queen's University Press, 1994.

The Confederation Debates
in the Province of Canada

John A. Macdonald and George-Étienne Cartier (1865)

EDITORS' INTRODUCTION

Of the three colonies that came together in 1867 to form Canada—the Province of Canada (which combined what are now the provinces of Ontario and Quebec), New Brunswick, and Nova Scotia—Canada was the only one whose legislature conducted a full, detailed debate on the terms of the proposed federal union. This debate took place in Quebec City from early February to mid-March 1865. The debate was based on the 72 Resolutions agreed to by delegates from the British North American colonies at a conference held in Quebec City in October 1864. John A. Macdonald and George-Étienne Cartier were leading members of the "Grand Coalition" of Conservatives and Liberals that was formed in 1864 to govern the Province of Canada with the primary objective of settling its constitutional future. At the end of the debate a motion supporting the 72 Resolutions was adopted by a majority of 91 to 33. The majority in favour among members of the Legislative Assembly from Canada West (today's Ontario) was 56 to 6. Among members from Canada East (today's Quebec) it was 37 to 25. The 72 Resolutions, with a few changes agreed to at a conference in London that same year, became the basis of Canada's founding constitution, the British North America Act, *enacted by the Parliament of the United Kingdom in 1867.*

(Note to the reader: At the time, Hansard often recorded proceedings in third person.)

Legislative Assembly

Monday, February 6, 1865.

Attorney General Macdonald moved, "That an humble Address be presented to Her Majesty, praying that She may be graciously pleased to cause a measure to be submitted to the Imperial Parliament, for the purpose of uniting the Colonies of Canada, Nova Scotia, New Brunswick, Newfoundland, and Prince Edward Island, in one Government, with provisions based on certain Resolutions, which were adopted at a Conference of Delegates from the said Colonies, held at the city of Quebec, on the 10th October, 1864." He said: Mr. Speaker, in fulfilment of the promise made by the Government to Parliament at its last session, I have moved this resolution. I have had the honour of being charged, on behalf of the Government, to submit a scheme for the Confederation of all the British North American Provinces—a scheme which has been received, I am glad to say, with general, if not universal, approbation in Canada. The scheme, as propounded through the press, has received almost no opposition. While there may be occasionally, here and there, expressions of dissent from some of

4

the details, yet the scheme as a whole has met with almost universal approval, and the Government has the greatest satisfaction in presenting it to this House. ...

The subject, however, though looked upon with favour by the country, and though there were no distinct expressions of opposition to it from any party, did not begin to assume its present proportions until last session. Then, men of all parties and shades of politics became alarmed at the aspect of affairs. They found that such was the opposition between the two sections of the province, such was the danger of impending anarchy, in consequence of the irreconcilable differences of opinion, with respect to representation by population, between Upper and Lower Canada, that unless some solution of the difficulty was arrived at, we would suffer under a succession of weak governments—weak in numerical support, weak in force, and weak in power of doing good. All were alarmed at this state of affairs. We had election after election, we had ministry after ministry, with the same result. Parties were so equally balanced, that the vote of one member might decide the fate of the Administration, and of course of legislation for a year or a series of years. This condition of things was well calculated to arouse the earnest consideration of every lover of his country, and I am happy to say it had that effect. None were more impressed by this momentous state of affairs, and the grave apprehensions that existed of a state of anarchy destroying our credit, destroying our prosperity, destroying our progress, than were the members of this present House; and the leading statesmen on both sides seemed to have come to the common conclusion, that some step must be taken to relieve the country from the dead-lock and impending anarchy that hung over us. With that view, my colleague, the President of the Council, made a motion founded on the despatch addressed to the Colonial Minister, to which I have referred, and a committee was struck, composed of gentlemen of both sides of the House, of all shades of political opinion, without any reference to whether they were supporters of the Administration of the day or belonged to the Opposition, for the purpose of taking into calm and full deliberation the evils which threatened the future of Canada. ...

The report of that committee was laid before the House, and then came the political action of the leading men of the two parties in this House, which ended in the formation of the present Government. The principle upon which that Government was formed has been announced, and is known to all. It was formed for the very purpose of carrying out the object which has now received to a certain degree its completion, by the resolutions I have had the honour to place in your hands. As has been stated, it was not without a great deal of difficulty and reluctance that the Government was formed. The gentlemen who compose this Government had for many years been engaged in political hostilities to such an extent that it affected even their social relations. But the crisis was great, the danger was imminent, and the gentlemen who now form the present Administration found it to be their duty to lay aside all personal feelings, to sacrifice in some degree their position, and even to run the risk of having their motives impugned, for the sake of arriving at some conclusion that would be satisfactory to the country in general. The present resolutions were the result. And, as I said before, I am proud to believe that the country has sanctioned, as I trust that the representatives of the people in this House will sanction, the scheme which is now submitted for the future government of British North America. (Cheers.) ...

[W]e returned to Quebec, and then the Government of Canada invited the several governments of the sister colonies to send a deputation here from each of them for the purpose of considering the question, with something like authority from their respective governments. The result was, that when we met here on the 10th of October, on the first day on which we assembled, after the full and free discussions which had taken place at Charlotte-town, the first resolution now before this House was passed unanimously, being received with acclamation as, in the opinion of every one who heard it, a proposition which ought to receive, and would receive, the sanction of each government and each people. The resolution is, "That the best interests and present and future prosperity of British North America will be promoted by a Federal Union under the Crown of Great Britain, provided such union can be effected on principles just to the several provinces." It seemed to all the statesmen assembled—and there are great statesmen in the Lower Provinces, men who would do honour to any government and to any legislature of any free country enjoying representative institutions—it was clear to them all that the best interests and present and future prosperity of British North America would be promoted by a Federal Union under the Crown of Great Britain. And it seems to me, as to them, and I think it will so appear to the people of this country, that, if we wish to be a great people; if we wish to form—using the expression which was sneered at the other evening—a great nationality, commanding the respect of the world, able to hold our own against all opponents, and to defend those institutions we prize; if we wish to have one system of government, and to establish a commercial union, with unrestricted free trade, between people of the five provinces, belonging, as they do, to the same nation, obeying the same Sovereign, owning the same allegiance, and being, for the most part, of the same blood and lineage; if we wish to be able to afford to each other the means of mutual defence and support against aggression and attack—this can only be obtained by a union of some kind between the scattered and weak boundaries composing the British North American Provinces. (Cheers.) ...

I trust the scheme will be assented to as a whole. I am sure this House will not seek to alter it in its unimportant details; and, if altered in any important provisions, the result must be that the whole will be set aside, and we must begin *de novo*. If any important changes are made, every one of the colonies will feel itself absolved from the implied obligation to deal with it as a Treaty, each province will feel itself at liberty to amend it *ad libitum* so as to suit its own views and interests; in fact, the whole of our labours will have been for nought, and we will have to renew our negotiations with all the colonies for the purpose of establishing some new scheme. I hope the House will not adopt any such a course as will postpone, perhaps for ever, or at all events for a long period, all chances of union. All the statesmen and public men who have written or spoken on the subject admit the advantages of a union, if it were practicable: and now when it is proved to be practicable, if we do not embrace this opportunity the present favourable time will pass away, and we may never have it again. ...

The Conference having come to the conclusion that a legislative union, pure and simple, was impracticable, our next attempt was to form a government upon federal principles, which would give to the General Government the strength of a legislative and administrative union, while at the same time it preserved that liberty of action for the different sections which is allowed by a Federal Union. And I am strong in the belief that we have hit upon the happy medium in those resolutions, and that we have formed a scheme of government which unites the advantages of both, giving us the strength of a legislative union and the sectional freedom of a federal union, with protection to local interests. In doing so we had the advantage of the experience of the United States. It is the fashion now to enlarge on the defects of the Constitution of the United States, but I am not one of those who look upon it as a failure. (Hear, hear.) I think and believe that it is one of the most skillful works which human intelligence ever created; is one of the most perfect organizations that ever governed a free people. To say that it has some defects is but to say that it is not the work of Omniscience, but of human intellects. We are happily situated in having had the opportunity of watching its operation, seeing its working from its infancy till now. It was in the main formed on the model of the Constitution of Great Britain, adapted to the circumstances of a new country, and was perhaps the only practicable system that could have been adopted under the circumstances existing at the time of its formation. We can now take advantage of the experience of the last seventy-eight years, during which that Constitution has existed, and I am strongly of the belief that we have, in a great measure, avoided in this system which we propose for the adoption of the people of Canada, the defects which time and events have shown to exist in the American Constitution. In the first place, by a resolution which meets with the universal approval of the people of this country, we have provided that for all time to come, so far as we can legislate for the future, we shall have as the head of the executive power, the Sovereign of Great Britain. (Hear, hear.). ...

In the Constitution we propose to continue the system of Responsible Government, which has existed in this province since 1841, and which has long obtained in the Mother Country. This is a feature of our Constitution as we have it now, and as we shall have it in the Federation, in which, I think, we avoid one of the great defects in the Constitution of the United States. There the President, during his term of office, is in a great measure a despot, a one-man power, with the command of the naval and military forces—with an immense amount of patronage as Head of the Executive, and with the veto power as a branch of the legislature, perfectly uncontrolled by responsible advisers, his cabinet being departmental officers merely, whom he is not obliged by the Constitution to consult with, unless he chooses to do so. With us the Sovereign, or in this country the representative of the Sovereign, can act only on the advice of his ministers, those ministers being responsible to the people through Parliament. ...

Ever since the union was formed the difficulty of what is called "State Rights" has existed, and this had much to do in bringing on the present unhappy war in the United States. They commenced, in fact, at the wrong end. They declared by their Constitution that each state was a sovereignty in itself, and that all the powers incident to a sovereignty belonged to each state, except those powers which, by the Constitution, were conferred upon the General Government and Congress. Here we have adopted a different system. We have strengthened the General Government. We have given the General Legislature all the great subjects of legislation. We have conferred on them, not only specifically and in detail, all the powers which are incident to sovereignty, but we have expressly declared that all subjects of general interest not distinctly and exclusively conferred upon the local governments and local legislatures, shall be conferred upon the General Government and Legislature. We have thus avoided that great source of weakness which has been the cause of disruption of the United States. We have avoided all conflict of jurisdiction and authority, and if this Constitution is carried out, as it will be in full detail in the Imperial Act to be passed if the colonies adopt the scheme, we will have in fact, as I said before, all the advantages of a legislative union under one administration, with, at the same time the guarantees for local institutions and for local laws, which are insisted upon by so many in the provinces now, I hope, to be united. ...

As may be well conceived, great difference of opinion at first existed as to the constitution of the Legislative Council. In Canada, the elective principle prevailed; in the Lower Provinces, with the exception of Prince Edward Island, the nominative principle was the rule. We found a general disinclination on the part of the Lower Provinces to adopt the elective principle; indeed, I do not think there was a dissenting voice in the Conference against the adoption of the nominative principle, except from Prince Edward Island. The delegates from New Brunswick, Nova Scotia and Newfoundland, as one man, were in favour of nomination by the Crown. And nomination by the Crown is of course the system which is most in accordance with the British Constitution. We resolved then, that the constitution of the Upper House should be in accordance with the British system as nearly as circumstances would allow. An hereditary Upper House is impracticable in this young country. Here we have none of the elements for the formation of a landlord aristocracy—no men of large territorial positions—no class separated from the mass of people. An hereditary body is altogether unsuited to our state of society, and would soon dwindle into nothing. ...

I shall not go over the other powers that are conferred on the General Parliament. Most of them refer to matters of financial and commercial interest, and I leave those subjects in other and better hands. Besides all the powers that are specifically given in the 37th and last item of this portion of the Constitution, confers on the General Legislature the general mass of sovereign legislation, the power to legislate on "all matters of general character, not specifically and exclusively reserved for the local governments and legislatures." This is precisely the provision which is wanting in the Constitution of the United States. It is here that we find the weakness of the American system—the point where the American Constitution breaks down. (Hear, hear.) It is in itself a wise and necessary provision. We thereby strengthen the Central Parliament, and make the Confederation one people and one government, instead of five peoples and five governments, with merely a point of authority connecting us to a limited and insufficient extent. ...

There are numerous subjects which belong, of right, both to the Local and the General Parliaments. In all these cases it is provided, in order to prevent a conflict of authority, that where there is concurrent jurisdiction in the General and Local Parliaments, the same rule should apply as now applies in cases where there is concurrent jurisdiction in the Imperial and in the Provincial Parliaments, and that when the legislation of the one is adverse to or contradictory of the legislation of the other, in all such cases the action of the General Parliament must overrule, ex-necessitate, the action of the Local Legislature. (Hear, hear.) ...

In conclusion, I would again implore the House not to let this opportunity to pass. It is an opportunity that may never recur. At the risk of repeating myself, I would say, it was only by a happy concurrence of circumstances, that we were enabled to bring this great question to its present position. If we do not take advantage of the time, if we show ourselves unequal to the occasion, it may never return, and we shall hereafter bitterly and unavailingly regret having failed to embrace the happy opportunity now offered of founding a great nation under the fostering care of Great Britain, and our Sovereign Lady, Queen Victoria. (Loud cheers, amidst which the honourable gentleman resumed his seat).

The House, at eleven p.m., adjourned.

Legislative Assembly

Tuesday, February 7, 1865.

Attorney General Cartier rose to continue the debate on Confederation. ...

Everyone who knew anything of his past public course was aware that he was opposed to the principle of representation by population while Upper and Lower Canada were under one Government. He did not regret his opposition. If such a measure had been passed, what would have been the consequence? There would have been constant political warfare between Upper and Lower Canada. True it was that the members from Upper Canada, being in the majority, it might have been imagined they would have carried everything before them; but as far as justice to Lower Canada was concerned, such might not have been the case. The consequence of representation by population would have been that one territory would have governed another, and this fact would have presented itself session after session in the House, and day after day in the public prints. (Hear, hear.) The moment this principle had been conceded as the governing element, it would have initiated between the two provinces a warfare which would have been unremitting. (Hear, hear.) ...

In 1858 he first saw that representation by population, though unsuited for application as a governing principle as between the two provinces, would not involve the same objection if other partners were drawn in by a federation. In a struggle between two—one weak, and the other a strong party—the weaker could not but be overcome; but if three parties were concerned, the stronger would not have the same advantage; as when it was seen by the third that there was too much strength on one side, the third would club with the weaker combatant to resist the big fighter. (Cheers and laughter.) He did not oppose the principle of representation by population from an unwillingness to do justice to Upper Canada. He took this ground, however, that when justice was done to Upper Canada, it was his duty to see that no injustice was done to Lower Canada. He did not entertain the slightest apprehension that Lower Canada's rights were in the least jeopardized by the provision that in the General Legislature the French Canadians of Lower Canada would have a smaller number of representatives than all the other origins combined. ...

Confederation was, as it were, at this moment almost forced upon us. We could not shut our eyes to what was going on beyond the lines, where a great struggle was going on between two Confederacies, at one time forming but one Confederacy. We saw that a government, established not more than 80 years ago, had not been able to keep together the family of states which had broke up four or five years since. We could not deny that the struggle now in progress must necessarily influence our political existence. We did not know what would be the result of that great war—whether it would end in the establishment of two Confederacies or in one as before. However, we had to do with five colonies, inhabited by men of the same sympathies and interests, and in order to become a great nation they required only to be brought together under one General Government. The matter resolved itself into this, either we must obtain British North American Confederation or be absorbed into an American Confederation. (Hear, hear, and dissent.) ...

In our Federation the monarchical principle would form the leading feature, while on the other side of the lines, judging by the past history and present condition of the country, the ruling power was the will of the mob, the rule of the populace. Every person who had conversed with the most intelligent American statesmen and writers must have learned that they all admitted that the governmental powers had become too extended, owing to the introduction of universal suffrage, and mob rule had consequently supplanted legitimate authority; and we now saw the sad spectacle of a country torn by civil war, and brethren fighting against brethren. The question for us to ask ourselves was this: Shall we be content to remain separate—shall we be content to maintain a mere provincial existence, when, by combining together, we could become a great nation? It had never yet been the good fortune of any group of communities to secure national greatness with such facility. In past ages, warriors had struggled for years for the addition to their country of a single province. ...

Here, in British North America, we had five different communities inhabiting five separate colonies. We had the same sympathies, and we all desired to live under the British Crown. We had our commercial interests besides. It was of no use whatever that New Brunswick, Nova Scotia and Newfoundland should have their several custom houses against our trade, or that we should have custom houses against the trade of those provinces. In ancient times, the manner in which a nation grew up was different from that of the present day. Then the first weak settlement increased into a village, which, by turns, became a town and a city, and the nucleus of a nation. It was not so in modern times. Nations were now formed by the agglomeration of communities having kindred interests and sympathies. Such was our case at the present moment. Objection had been taken to the scheme now under consideration, because of the words "new nationality." Now, when we were united together, if union were attained, we would form a political nationality with which neither the national origin, nor the religion of any individual, would interfere. It was lamented by some that we had this diversity of races, and hopes were expressed that this distinctive feature would cease. The idea of unity of races was utopian—it was impossible. Distinctions of this kind would always exist. Dissimilarity, in fact, appeared to be the order of the physical world and the moral world, as well as in the political world. But with regard to the objection based on this fact, to the effect that a great nation could not be formed because Lower Canada was in great part French and Catholic, and Upper Canada was British and Protestant, and the Lower Provinces were mixed, it was futile and worthless in the extreme. Look, for instance, at the United Kingdom, inhabited as it was by three great races. (Hear, hear.) Had the diversity of race impeded the glory, the progress, the wealth of England? Had they not rather each contributed their share to the greatness of the Empire? Of the glories of the senate, the field, and the ocean, of the successes of trade and commerce, how much was contributed by the combined talents, energy, and courage of the three races together? (Cheers.) In our own Federation we should have Catholic and Protestant, English, French, Irish and Scotch, and each by his efforts and his success would increase the prosperity and glory of the new Confederacy. (Hear, hear.) He viewed the diversity of races in British North America in this way: we were of different races, not for the purpose of warring against each other, but in order to compete and emulate for the general welfare. (Cheers.) We could not do away with the distinctions of race. We could not legislate for the disappearance of the French Canadians from American soil, but British and French Canadians alike could appreciate and understand their position relative to each other. They were placed like great families beside each other, and their contact produced a healthy spirit of emulation. It was a benefit rather than otherwise that we had a diversity of races. ...

This scheme, he repeated, met with the approval of all moderate men. The extreme men, the socialists, democrats and annexationists were opposed to it. The French Canadian opponents of the project were, it appeared, afraid that their religious rights would suffer under the new arrangement. Fancy the celebrated *Institut Canadien*, of Montreal, under the lead of citizen Blanchet, taking religion under their protection! (Laughter.)

Mr. Dougall loudly proclaimed that the British Protestant minority would be entirely placed at the mercy of the French Canadians. He (Hon. Mr. Cartier) thought the arguments of the young French gentlemen belonging to the national democratic party who cried out that their religion and nationality would be destroyed, ought in all reason to be sufficient to satisfy the scruples and calm the fears of Mr. Dougall. The *True Witness*, which was also one of the enemies of the scheme, said that if it were adopted the French Canadians were doomed; while his brother in violence, the *Witness*, said that the Protestants were doomed. (Hear, hear, and laughter.) At a meeting recently held in Montreal on the subject, he (Hon. Mr. Cartier) observed that Mr. Cherrier had enrolled himself among the enemies of the project. Well, this fine quiet old gentleman announced that he had come out of his political retirement for the purpose of opposing Federation. All he (Hon. Mr. Cartier) could say was that he never knew Mr. Cherrier was a strong politician. However, it appeared that he had come out once more on the political stage for the purpose of opposing this villainous scheme, which was intended to destroy the nationality and religion of the French Canadians—all brought about by that confounded Cartier! (Laughter and cheers.)

Allusion has been made to the opinion of the clergy. Well he would say that the opinion of the clergy was for Confederation (Hear, hear.) Those who were high in authority, as well as those who occupied more humble positions, were in favour of Federation, not only because they saw in it so much security for all they held dear, but because it was just to their Protestant fellow-subjects as well, because they were opposed to political bickering and strife. This opposition to a state of political dissension and trouble was the general feeling of the clergy, and because they saw in Confederation a solution of those difficulties which had existed for some time, due regard being had to just rights, they were favourable to the project. The fact, however, was that when we saw such extreme opponents as Mr. Clerk, of the *True Witness*, Mr. Dougall, of the *Witness*, and the young gentlemen of the *Institut Canadien* combined to resist Confederation, because each party argued it would produce the most widely different results—we might look upon this fact, he repeated, as one of the strongest arguments in favour of Confederation. (Hear.) We had, on the other hand, all the moderate men, all that was respectable and intelligent, including the clergy, favourable to Federation. (Hear, hear, and oh, oh.) He did not, of course, mean to say that there were not respectable opponents to the project—what he did mean, however, was that it met general approval from the classes referred to. He was opposed, he might as well state most distinctly, to the democratic system which obtained in the United States. In this country of British North America we should have a distinct form of government, the characteristic of which would be to possess the monarchical element. When we had Confederation secured, there was not the least doubt but that our Government would be more respectable—that it would have more prestige, and command more respect from our neighbours. (Hear, hear.)

The French Language and the Future of Our Race

Henri Bourassa (1912)

EDITORS' INTRODUCTION

Henri Bourassa was a prominent Quebec politician and journalist. From the 1890s through the first half of the 20th century, he was the leading exponent of Canada as an independent Anglo-French nation. In 1910 he founded Le Devoir, *which has remained to this day one of Canada's most influential French-language newspapers. On June 28, 1912, he addressed the first Congrès de la langue française au Canada. The speech was published as a pamphlet in 1913, entitled "La langue française et l'avenir de notre race," and appears below in translation.*

Mr. President, Honourable Members, Ladies and Gentlemen,

It is difficult for me to believe that the organization of this magnificent congress did not have a discreet ulterior motive in giving me a topic that deals with the realm of the future. However, since I lay no claim to the gift of prophecy, I trust you will allow me to proceed with the forecasting of the future, relying on the teachings of the past and the lessons of the present day.

I have been asked to speak to you about the French language and its influence on the future of the race. If you will bear with me, we shall study the question from two points of view.

First of all we shall consider what the influence of the language may be on the future of the race itself; then we shall study the role of the language in the relations that must exist between the French race and the races that live with it on the American continent. ...

The 1867 Constitution and the Language

What are the exact terms of the Act of 1867? We do no need to discuss this tonight. All that is helpful to recall to those who have forgotten and to impress more strongly on their minds is that as far as federal laws and administration are concerned, the principle of absolute equality between the two languages is recognized to the letter; and that is enough. In fact if the law recognizes the principle, common sense as well as justice says that this principle must receive the sanction of all the means that are necessary to assure its application. In other words to suggest that under the authority of the 1867 constitution the rights of the French language exist only for Quebec is to say that the pact of 1867 was a trap, that Cartier, Macdonald, Brown, Howe and all the authors of this magnificent constitution were in league to deceive the people of Lower Canada!

As for me, I do not believe it; I think the true interpretation of the constitutional law that governs us is the one given it twenty-four years later by its chief author, Sir John A. Macdonald, in the memorable words the President of the Senate quoted the other day. I shall simply recall their content. It was that since 1867 in Canada there has no longer been a conquered race or a triumphant race, a ruling race or a subject race, but that on the contrary there is complete equality under the authority of the law itself for all that concerns the political, social, and moral rights of the two races, particularly for the public and private use of the two languages.

If French and English make up the double vocabulary of the Canadian people as a whole, how is it that there are narrow provincialists who affirm that any one of the legislatures of the Dominion of Canada can deprive the French-speaking citizens of any province of the means of giving their children knowledge and complete possession of this language in all the schools where their money is accepted just the same as the money of English-speaking people?

If the two languages are official, according to the very terms of the constitution, these languages have the right to coexist everywhere that the Canadian people lead a public life: at church, at school, in Parliament, in court, and in all public services. ...

Means of Preserving the Language—The Schools

I wish to speak to you this evening of only two means of assuring the permanence, life, and fruitfulness of the French language in Canada.

The first and most important of all is teaching, that is, the schools. In 1875, eight years after the inauguration of the constitution, Edward Blake—another great statesman who was not afraid of the truth, even when it was dangerous for him—proclaimed on the floor of the Commons that the principle of separate schools should be adopted all across Western Canada, so that the two races and two religious beliefs could teach as they chose, but with state aid; because, he said, this is the very principle on which the federal pact was arranged between Upper and Lower Canada. Between the French Canadians and the English Canadians, and between the Canadian Protestants and the Canadian Catholics; and if this principle is good for the Canada of old, it should be equally good for the Canada of the future.

Those in the English provinces who are opposed to the teaching of French in public and separate schools are really the violators of the fundamental spirit of the Canadian constitution; and those of our fellow countrymen who preach to us a doctrine of subservience and who say that it is monstrous to claim for the French language equal rights with the English language are violating the sprit of the constitution just as much. No, the pact drawn up by those two great statesmen Sir John A. Macdonald and Sir George-Étienne Cartier was not a pact of subservience; quite the opposite, it was a straightforward and honourable treaty, signed by the sons of two great nations that wished to join forces in order to end past divisions and hatreds for ever, so that from this fruitful union a great people might be born, conceived in justice.

Those in the English provinces who preach the exclusion of French and those in our French province who teach a lesson of subservience are both betraying the constitution and the faith sworn in it. ...

Towards French Sources

The second element necessary for the preservation of the language is to nourish it continually at the source from which it springs, at the only source that can assure its vitality and purity, that is, France. ...

But you will say that there is danger to our national unity. This nourishing at the sources of French thought can give rise to mental reservations and feelings of regret among the French Canadians; can isolate them from the British Empire and even from the Canadian Confederation. Those who talk like this show that they do not know the first thing about American history and are also ignorant of the human heart.

To think that by drawing intellectual light from the source that is France, or by seeking the nourishment the language needs, the French Canadian is going to become more French or less British or less Canadian is almost as sensible as believing that the cultured American wonders if he should not return to the Crown of England simply because he continues to read Shakespeare or Thackeray instead of nourishing his mind with the literature of the dime novels that fill the railway trains of the United States. The educated American is intellectually more English today than he was twenty-five years ago. He has learned that if he is to make gigantic material accomplishments by himself, to develop his territory, industry, and commerce in a really astonishing way, and to amaze the world with his political, industrial, and commercial vitality, he cannot ignore fifteen centuries of British civilization, from which he has drawn the best part of his blood and thought. But is he therefore less American, less devoted to his splendid homeland?

In the same way the French Canadian knows that if his language is not to become a dead language or a patois, as they call it in the "Parisian French" shops in Toronto, it must continue to find its nourishment in the homeland where it was formed.

A Canadian Literature

But if our language must become more and more French in form, it must become even more Canadian in content.

It must give birth to a Canadian literature, it must help us to write and read Canadian history, it must teach us to write well and to plead in favour of Canadian laws, and it must make us understand the spirit and the letter of the Canadian laws and constitution. And *Canadian* is not meant here in the narrow sense of our province or of our race, but in the complete and national meaning of this name that belongs to all the races that inhabit Canada. With the aid of this French language in an improved and living form we must seek out the origins of the English and American civilization; we must study the history of England and the United States; we must come to know the English and the Celts better and make ourselves better known to them.

Neither Isolation Nor Amalgamation

And this brings me to the second part of this study. I said that for the preservation and growth of the language we must bring ourselves closer to the intellectual life of France and at the same time *nationalize* our language along with all the other elements of our national life. Likewise when we define the scope of our claims we must keep in mind our situation with regard to the other races that share this land with us. We must be as wary of isolation as of assimilation. We cannot allow ourselves to be absorbed by any other race in Canada; but also we should not live like the Hebrews in Egypt, accepting the offer of seductive flesh-pots as compensation for their slavery. In Canada we must play the role of allies, brothers, associates. Therefore our duty forces us to investigate the ideas of those who fear and fight against the preservation and growth of the French language. Some see in this a danger to the unity of our faith and moral discipline; others an obstacle to national unity. ...

The French Language and the Upholding of Confederation

Not only does the maintaining of the French language offer no danger to the religious and national unity of the country, but I am sure that the preservation and expansion of the French language in each of the English provinces of Canada is the only positive moral guarantee of both the unity of the Canadian Confederation and the maintaining of the British institutions in Canada.

Human institutions are preserved only by the survival of the vital principles that fostered these institutions. I have proved that the Canadian Confederation is the result of a contract between the two races in Canada, French and English, based on equality and recognizing equal rights and reciprocal duties. Canadian Confederation will last only as long as this equality of rights is recognized as the basis of the public right in Canada, from Halifax to Vancouver.

At first glance it is difficult to explain the blindness of those who—and they are numerous—honestly want to bring about the gradual destruction of the French language, or the blindness of those more moderate people who agree to allow it to live on in the Province of Quebec, but strive to prevent its penetration elsewhere. However, this mentality is easily explained.

First of all their ignorance of history and the absence of any philosophy deprive the English-Canadian statesmen and journalists of really knowing the depths of the human soul and the concept of distant repercussions of events in the history of nations. They do not know the past, or they forget about it; and consequently their vision of the future is short-sighted and limited.

In the second place the habit of colonial servitude hampers them from seeing beyond the borders of the country they live in. Most Anglo-Canadians know only two countries, England and Canada; and many of them are hesitant to decide which of these is their real homeland.

Finally, the absence of an intellectual culture and the intense pursuit for wealth that permeates Canadian society as well as American society very often make us disregard the immense superiority of the latent moral forces that brood under the conspicuous brutal force. This is particularly true of politicians who seek driving powers of immediate interest.

There are some Anglo-Canadians who honestly believe that since the English language is the language of the mother country, it should also be the colony's. They seem to forget this very important fact: that the English language is the language not only of England, but also of the United States.

Our Relations with the United States

Please allow me a digression. The remarks I wish to make on this subject are not dictated by a feeling of animosity toward the great Republic. No, these racial hatreds, this habit of criticizing foreign peoples, are among the most obvious proofs of the limits of our public mentality and of our "colonialism." I admire the American people. They came at the appointed time in the design of Providence to offer their contribution to the harmony of nations. But I sincerely believe that in the true interests of America and the human race the United States and Canada must remain two separate nations. I am sure that the honest American opinion that does not fall prey to the temptations of greed in continually enlarging national territory is identical in this matter to the feelings of the Canadian people.

Now if Canada is to remain separate from the United States it is high time our fellow English Canadians opened their eyes and ears and broadened their outlook to realize that a real danger threatens the unity of the Canadian people and the preservation of its political existence. This danger is the slow but sure infiltration of Americanism that creeps into all the phases of our national, political, and social life.

Perhaps this will surprise you, but in reality Quebec, Champlain's old city, so French in its character, is more Canadian and more British than Montreal. Montreal is more Canadian and more British than Toronto. Toronto is more Canadian and more British than Winnipeg. Why? Because thanks to the predominance of the French language in Quebec City you have protected yourselves better from the American invasion than Montreal. Not only to the traveller passing through but also to the careful observer, that particularly "loyalist" city Toronto seems half won over to American ideas, to the American mentality, to American customs, to American speech, and to the American way of life; and this dangerous situation is to be feared far more than any commercial treaty or attack on the constitution, since it is the moral and personal winning over of the individuals who make up the nation. …

French Groups and Canadian Unity

However, the biggest obstacle that could be thrown up against the slow but sure conquest of the English provinces by American thinking—especially in the western provinces—would be the implanting in each of these provinces of French-Canadian groups that were as strong as possible. They could be given their own schools and French-speaking priests so that they could set up their own parishes and they would be like so many small Provinces of Quebec. In this way there would be men everywhere for whom the American ideal, the cult of the gold calf, the profits of commerce and industry, would not be the principal objective. There would also be the people in all parts of Canada who were behind the times, *dumb* enough— forgive me this word, gentlemen—to hold on to an ideal above that of wealth and success; people who would continue to do outside the Province of Quebec what they have done in the Province of Quebec for the last one hundred and fifty years: that is, keep the British institutions intact while at the same time claiming the right everywhere to express freely their thoughts on all political matters that concern Canada and the Empire.

3 The Rowell-Sirois Commission

Newton Rowell and Joseph Sirois (1940)

EDITORS' INTRODUCTION

In 1937 the Mackenzie King Liberal government established the Royal Commission on Dominion–Provincial Relations to conduct an inquiry into whether the balance of legislative responsibilities and fiscal resources between the central and provincial governments needed adjustments to deal with the challenges facing Canada as a modern industrial society. The chief justice of Ontario, Newton Rowell, was appointed to chair the commission. When Rowell became ill, Joseph Sirois, a Quebec notary, took over as chairman. The commission reported in May 1940.

Abstract of the Leading Recommendations

The Report which the Commission has prepared is the outcome of two-and-a-half years of carefully planned study. In the course of this period the Commission has held sessions in the capital of every province of Canada and at Ottawa. It has had the benefit of the collaboration of many of the provincial governments, of the evidence of federal and provincial civil servants, of representations made by a large number of organizations in every province of Canada. The Commission has given careful consideration to the requests and suggestions presented to it and has also, with the assistance of a very able research staff, instituted enquiries of its own into the financial, economic and social problems which came within the scope of its terms of reference.

The conclusions which the Commission has reached are, therefore, not sudden inspirations but the result of careful deliberation. The Commissioners consider it both remarkable and significant that on questions on which the most divergent views are widely and tenaciously held both by public men and by private citizens, they should have arrived at complete agreement. This agreement is not the result of compromise or of give and take but reflects a sincere unanimity of judgment on the great issues which confront the nation. Its significance is enhanced by the fact that the four Commissioners are men from different regions of Canada, men who differ widely in background and in training, as well as in general outlook; and it is also significant that the conclusions which they have reached are far from being the views which any one of them held at the outset of the inquiry. Whether or not the Report will be successful in presenting clearly and forcefully to others the considerations which have carried weight with the Commission, and in convincing others of the validity of the conclusions which the Commissioners have formed, the future alone can show. But in

Source: Excerpted from Book II of *The Report of the Royal Commission on Dominion–Provincial Relations.* Ottawa: Queen's Printer of Canada, 1940.

drawing attention to the changes which have taken place in their own views, in the light of the studies which have been made, the Commissioners hope that they may predispose others to peruse both the Report and the research studies which accompany it before arriving at their final opinion as to the merits of the recommendations which the Commission has made.

In the present summary the aim is to set out the principal recommendations embodied in the Report and to indicate briefly the reasons for them. At the heart of the problem lie the needs of Canadian citizens. These needs, whether material or cultural, can be satisfied only if all the provincial governments in Canada are in a position to supply those services which the citizen of today demands of them. The ability of provincial governments to meet the demands of their citizens depends in part on the constitutional powers which they enjoy, in part on their financial capacity to perform their recognized functions. The striking fact in the Commission's study of Canadian conditions is that many provinces, whose financial position is not the result of emergency conditions, are unable to find the money to enable them to meet the needs of their citizens. The basic problem before the Commission lies, therefore, in finding a way in which the financial position of the provinces could be improved and assured, without disastrous financial consequences to the Federal Government on whose efficient functioning all provinces are dependent. National unity and provincial autonomy must not be thought of as competitors for the citizen's allegiance for, in Canada at least, they are but two facets of the same thing—a sane federal system. National unity must be based on provincial autonomy, and provincial autonomy cannot be assured unless a strong feeling of national unity exists throughout Canada.

Some provincial governments explained to the Commission that they could pay their way, and perform their functions to their own complete satisfaction, if the Dominion were to assume this or that onerous service, or were to withdraw from this or that field of taxation, or were to increase their subsidies. But, on examination, it was found that a solution on these lines could not be generalized and that, while it might meet the needs of one or more of the provinces, it would do so at the cost of impairing the Dominion's finances, or of prejudicing the position of other provinces. The Commissioners were, therefore, compelled to dismiss any such solution as inadequate.

The Commission did, however, find one onerous function of government which cannot, under modern conditions, be equitably or efficiently performed on a regional or provincial basis. This function is the maintenance of those unemployed who are employable and of their dependents. In reaching this conclusion (which is amply supported by the Evidence and the research studies) the Commission merely confirmed conclusions which had been reached by earlier Commissions. So firmly is the Commission convinced of the validity of this conclusion that, even when it comes to consider the situation which will arise if its main recommendations are not implemented, it proceeds on the assumption that the relief of the unemployed who are able and willing to work will become a federal function. ...

There is, however, an important financial burden of which provincial governments can be relieved without any sacrifice of autonomy. This is the deadweight cost of their debt service. The burden taken up by the Dominion, if it were to assume this deadweight cost, would be less than the burden of which the provinces were relieved because, as maturities occurred, the debts could be refunded more advantageously by the Dominion than by the provinces. To this extent a saving would accrue to Canadian taxpayers. ...

In the case of one province this recommendation as to debt requires an important modification. The provincial debt of the Province of Quebec is low in comparison with the per capita debt other provinces, and is an unusually low fraction of the combined municipal and provincial debt of the Province. To meet this situation, which has arisen through the policy of this Province in imposing on municipalities onerous functions which are performed elsewhere by provincial government, the Commission has recommended that the Dominions should take over 40 per cent of the combined provincial and municipal net debt service in Quebec.

If the provinces are relieved, in accordance with this recommendation, of the deadweight burden to their debt, it is not unreasonable that they should surrender to the Dominion the subsidies, whatever their character, which they now receive. Prince Edward Island alone would give up subsidies more than equivalent to the deadweight cost of its debts and, as will be seen, this apparent loss will be more than made up in other ways. The abolition of the provincial subsidies will be in itself no inconsiderable reform, for their history (which is fully examined in the Commission's research studies) is long and tortuous. The subsidies have been based on no clear principles and it has been impossible to say whether or not different provinces have received equal treatment. Specious reasons have often been advanced, and not infrequently accepted, in support of readjustments in order to avoid the full implications of genuine reasons, and negotiations between the Dominion and the provinces have lacked the candour which is desirable in a democracy.

Up to this point the Commission's proposals, enormously beneficial as they would be to the provinces, would be very onerous to the Dominion. The Commission had, therefore, to consider how to provide the Dominion with sources of revenue which would enable it to carry its new burdens. This inquiry (as will be seen) was combined with the consideration of efficiency and equity in taxation specifically entrusted to the Commission. There could be no question of increasing the legal taxing powers of the Dominion since these are already unlimited. But the provinces, in return for the benefits which they would receive, and for further payments which the Commission finds it necessary to recommend, should be prepared to renounce some of the taxes which they employ (or are entitled to employ) at present. The Dominion, for its part, should be able and willing to refrain from competing with the provinces in respect of sources of revenue left to them and should leave the provinces free to collect these revenues in whatever way appears to them most efficient even if the method of indirect taxation should be involved.

Just as the assumption of provincial debts by the Dominion will lead to savings in interest from which taxpayers will benefit, so there are several taxes from which, if they are under unified control, as great a revenue can be obtained as at present with less hardship to the taxpayer. What is more important, a reorganization of these taxes, of a character which is possible only if they are under unified control, can remove many hindrances which in the recent past have been detrimental to the expansion of the national income (i.e., to the sum total of the incomes of all citizens of Canada). As this income expands, as the result of what may be fairly termed greater efficiency in taxation, the same revenue as at present can be obtained by taxes imposed at lower rates than those of today. The first of the taxes which the Commission recommends that the provinces should renounce is the tax on personal incomes. Not all provinces impose this tax. Those which get most revenue from it are often taxing incomes which other provinces think that they should have a share in taxing, because they are in part at least earned in them although they are received in those provinces in which investors live, or in which large corporations have their head offices. Nor is this all. The general equity of the whole Canadian tax system—and the Commission has been instructed to concern itself with equity as well as with efficiency in taxation—requires that the tax on personal incomes, which is one of the very few taxes capable of any desired graduation, should be used to supplement other taxes and should be uniform throughout Canada.

The second form of taxation which the Commission recommends that the provinces should forgo includes those taxes imposed on corporations which individuals or partnerships, carrying on the same business as the corporation, would not be required to pay, and taxes on those businesses which only corporations engage in. They include, therefore, the tax on the net income of corporations and a multitude of taxes devised to raise revenue from particular classes of corporations which a province cannot conveniently subject to a tax on net income. They do not include bona fide licence fees, the power to impose which would remain with the province. These provincial corporation taxes are peculiarly vexatious to those who pay them and particularly detrimental to the expansion of the national income. The cost of tax compliance is high. The tax is often payable by a corporation which has no net income. The tax is very likely to be a tax on costs rather than on profits. These taxes are also a frequent source of interprovincial jealousy. Great benefits may be expected if they are swept away and the equivalent revenue raised by federal taxes chiefly on corporate net income.

To ask the provinces to give up the entire revenue which they now derive from taxing corporations would, however, intensify a grievance of which the Commission received complaint in more than one province; for the Dominion would receive a tax on income which was in part derived from the depletion of irreplaceable natural wealth. It is clearly desirable that revenue of this character should be used for developmental work which will compensate for the damage which has been done to the resources of a province. The Commission has, therefore, recommended that the Dominion should pay over to the province concerned 10 per cent of the corporate income derived from the exploitation of the mineral wealth of the province. When what is required is the conservation of natural resources by maintaining their productivity, rather than compensation for depletion by new investment, the provinces are in a position to use their own taxing power.

The third tax which the Commission recommends that the provinces should forgo consists of various forms of succession duty. These differ from the income taxes in that they have not hitherto been used by the Dominion: but they are taxes to which the Dominion might at any time be compelled to resort. The use made of them by the provinces has given rise to bitter complaint because the provinces have not made equitable arrangements with one another so as to tax each item in an estate in one province only. The differences in rates between provinces, and the dangers of double taxation, seriously distort investment in Canada. The potential competition between provinces desirous of attracting wealthy residents has made it impossible to use these delicate instruments of taxation as a means for giving effect to social policies. Many provinces feel aggrieved because estates which have been built up by investment throughout the whole of Canada are taxed, not for national purposes, but for the benefit of strategically situated provinces.

If the Commission's recommendations stopped at this point, they would, instead of being enormously beneficial to the provinces, leave some of them in a parlous financial position.

After the provinces had, on the one hand, been relieved of the cost of unemployment relief and of the deadweight burden of their debt, and had, on the other hand, given up their right to impose personal income taxes, corporation taxes and succession duties, they would find themselves with far less variable expenditures than in the past and with less variable revenues. It is, therefore, possible to form an idea of the size of the probable surplus or deficit of each province. There is a purpose in making this calculation for, if a province were left with a prospective annual deficit, it would not be able to provide for the reasonable needs of its citizens unless it were able, without causing hardship, to increase the revenue which it derived from the sources remaining at its disposal, or to reduce its expenditures while still providing services equivalent to those provided by other provinces.

At this point there must be a refinement in the calculations. What is significant for the purposes of the Commission is the size of the surplus or deficit which would exist in a province if it were to provide the normal Canadian standard of services and impose taxation of normal severity. It is not the services which each province is at present providing, but the average Canadian standard of services, that a province must be put in a position to finance. It is not the revenue which its taxes yield at their present level which matters, but the revenue which it would derive from them if its people were as heavily taxed as Canadians in general. Just as in the case of debt it is necessary to take account of the fact that some provinces are more accustomed than others to provide services for their people through municipalities or other agencies instead of directly. The Commission has, therefore, attempted to compute, province by province, what the cost would be if the province and its municipalities taken together were to provide services on the Canadian standard. Adjustments have been made for the cost of the developmental services appropriate to the province, and for the weight of taxation in the province. The result has been that the Commission has been able to make a recommendation as to the amount, if any, which each individual province should receive from the Dominion annually to enable it to provide normal Canadian services with no more than normal Canadian taxation. The calculations involved were not easy and presented peculiar difficulties in Quebec because of the extent to which educational and social services in that Province are provided, not out of taxation, but by the Church. But the calculations have been made and the Commission recommends that each province found to be in need of such a payment should receive it by way of an annual National Adjustment Grant from the Dominion. This grant as originally fixed would be irreducible. The Commission recommends, however, that National Adjustment Grants should be re-appraised every five years. For special emergencies, which might arise in respect of any province (and which exist in one province today), special provision should be made, as it would be undesirable either to fix an annual grant in perpetuity on the basis of conditions that are transitory, or to fail to provide for serious emergencies. The Commission believes that these provisions will permit of the necessary elasticity in the financial relations between the provinces and the Dominion which has been lacking in the old subsidy system.

In order to assure all provinces of fair and equal treatment in the matter of grants, and in order to assure the general taxpayer that any new or increased grant is justified on the basis of the comparative need of the province concerned, it will be essential that all requests from the provinces with respect to grants should be examined as scientifically and objectively as possible. The Commission, therefore, recommends the establishment of a small permanent commission (which may be called the Finance Commission), assisted by an adequate technical staff, to advise upon all requests for new or increased grants, and to re-appraise the system of grants every five years.

The recommendations which have been described would, if implemented, safeguard the autonomy of every province by ensuring to it the revenue necessary to provide services in accordance with the Canadian standard. Every provincial government (including those whose position will be so good as to make adjustment grants unnecessary) would be placed in a better financial position than it is in today. And the financial position of every province would be immeasurably more secure than it is today. The Commission looks on this as its primary achievement. It is convinced that this fundamental problem must be faced and it has not been able to discover any alternative way in which it could be solved. The recom-mendations which the Commission has made must be judged as a whole. They cannot with fairness either to the provinces or to the Dominion be considered in isolation for any one of them taken alone might produce grotesque results. ...

It has been the aim of the Commission to frame proposals which will, if implemented, place jurisdiction over the social services in the hands of the governments most likely to de-sign and administer them, not merely with the greatest economy and the greatest technical efficiency, but with regard for the social, cultural and religious outlook of the various regions of Canada, which is essential to genuine human welfare. The financial proposals have been designed to enable every province of Canada to rely on having sufficient revenue at its com-mand in war-time as in peace-time, in years of adversity as in years of prosperity, to carry out the important functions entrusted to it. They are also designed to produce this result while leaving the fiscal powers of the Dominion as wide in fact as they have always been in law, so that it may direct the wealth of the nation as the national interest may require. If some such adjustment of Canadian economic life appeared sufficiently urgent to lead to the ap-pointment of the Commission in time of peace, how much more urgent is it in time of war? How much more urgent will it be in the critical transition from war to peace again?

The Report must face the verdict of public opinion and opinion is not the same in war as in peace. The Report was prepared with peace-time opinion in mind. But it is the hope of the Commission that the gravity of the hour will dispose people in all regions of Canada to take serious thought of their country's welfare and to look at the broad lines of the recom-mendations, keeping matters of detail in rational perspective. For the Report, while taking account of possibility of war as of any other emergency, was framed with a view to a future which will, it is hoped, be in the main one of peace, and it is on its merits with respect to this supposedly peaceful future that the Report must stand or fall. The Commission does not consider that its proposals are either centralizing or decentralizing in their combined effect but believes that they will conduce to the sane balance between these two tendencies which is the essence of a genuine federal system and, therefore, the basis on which Canadian na-tional unity can most securely rest.

Joseph Sirois
Chairman

The Tremblay Report

David Kwavnick (1954)

EDITORS' INTRODUCTION

The Tremblay Commission was established by the Duplessis government in Quebec in 1953 to conduct an inquiry into problems arising from what were seen as centralizing encroachments on the powers and resources granted to the provinces at the time of Confederation. Despite being given only a year in which to complete its work, the commission produced a massive five-volume report on the traditional culture of Quebec and the powers needed to secure it. The commission's report was prepared in French. Sections of its recommendations reproduced below are from an English translation edited by David Kwavnick in 1973.

General Outline and Summary of Recommendations

The constitutional imbroglio which has played a dominant part in Canada's recent history has appeared to be mainly fiscal and its most outstanding episodes have been in regard to taxes. But it has its origin in a fundamental divergence of opinion on the interpretation of Canadian federalism.

The situation which has gradually developed in this country, especially since the last war, is one whose control and remedy requires a re-examination of our attitudes towards the foundations of our constitutional and political system. There is not and there cannot be any question (despite suggestions from certain quarters) of a mere redistribution, through one method or another, of the funds required for the public administration. The real need is for a re-appraisal of the socio-political reality's lasting requirements, with a re-adjustment of the fiscal system made consequent thereto.

Therefore, we ourselves have sought to grasp the problem in its entirety. We are firmly of the belief that the entire constitutional system is bound up with the questions of taxes and of the allocation of taxes which, in turn, also involves the fundamental liberties and political lot both of the individual as a citizen, and of the two great cultural communities which make up our population.

To encompass the present situation in its true dimensions and in its profound causes, we have considered it our duty to study it first of all in the perspectives of history and according to the basic principles of political philosophy. For every human society is, in fact, a constantly evolving living complex whose state, at any given point of time, can only be understood by reference to the past and to a certain concept of order.

Source: Excerpted from *The Tremblay Report: Report of the Royal Commission of Inquiry on Constitutional Problems*, edited by David Kwavnick. Montreal and Kingston: McGill-Queen's University Press. Originally published by McClelland & Stewart, 1973. Reprinted by permission.

History

... The constitutional policy of the Province of Quebec has never, since 1867, departed from the strict federalist interpretation of the Constitution, nor from the proper juridical status and mutual relations of the parties constituting the Canadian state. It is its own best witness that it has taken seriously the agreement reached in 1867 and, in every circumstance, has done what was necessary to promote the sprit of that agreement in Canadian political life.

This fidelity to the federative principle it asserted resoundingly, and at the cost of heavy sacrifice, with regard to taxation and, notably, on the question of subsidies which is the central issue in the present federal-provincial controversy. ...

In a word—and this is the salient point to be gleaned from these pages of history—the attitude of the Province of Quebec in fiscal matters, as in all other matters of a constitutional nature, has never changed. It holds to an interpretation, according to the spirit of federalism, of the agreement reached in 1867.

THE PROBLEM OF CULTURE AND FEDERALISM

The Basic Question

Federalism and the problem of cultures are, to some degree, correlative. Here we touch the very root of the debate which has agitated Canadian opinion for years. The duality of cultures is the central premise of the Canadian political problem, no matter from what angle it may be approached. If the population were homogeneous, with the same religion, the same language, the same traditions and the same concept of order and of life, Canada might, especially in these days of swift and easy communications, satisfy the geographic and economic diversity of its vast territory with a modified federalism and even, in certain fields, with a fairly wide measure of administrative decentralization.

But such is not the case. Two great communities of differing origin and culture constitute its human components and each of them intends to live according to its own concepts and to preserve its own identity from one generation to another. The phenomenon is all the more ineradicable inasmuch as the difference in cultures almost exactly corresponds to the difference in religion. This fact has dominated the country's history for almost two centuries and it has conditioned all main stages of its constitutional evolution.

The Idea of Culture

Since this duality of cultures is the principle premise of the Canadian political problem, we have endeavoured to deal with it in its primary elements. We have therefore taken up and analyzed the basic ideas of culture, nation, society and state both *per se* and in their reciprocal relationships. We have attempted to isolate the predominating features of the two great Canadian cultures: what it is that distinguishes them and even what places them in opposition to each other. We have recalled the social consequences resulting from the opposition of cultures ever since the conquest in the province of Quebec; and finally, we have sought to define Quebec's special role within the Canadian Confederation, insofar as it constitutes the national focus of French-Canadian culture.

Federalism

Only federalism as a political system permits two cultures to live and develop side by side within a single state: that was the real reason for the Canadian state's federative form. Therefore we have studied federalism, first as a system of social organization resting on the four sociological and philosophical bases: the Christian concept of Man and society, the variety and complexity in social life, the idea of the common good, and the principle of every society's complementary functions. In the second place, we have studied federalism as a political and juridical system.

Competing Theses

According to the ideas held regarding the two major matters just mentioned, one either reaches the centralizing position habitually taken by the federal government or else one reaches the autonomist position which is traditionally that of the Province of Quebec.

As regards taxes, political economy, social policy and educational subsidies, these are the two theses which stand opposed. The federal government looks at Canada as a whole; it talks about "Canadian unity" without specifying whether it will be the product of group fusions or of their voluntary co-operation; of "Canadian culture" as if culture, which has Man himself as its object and has reference to a certain general concept of life, will allow no differentiation of inspiration or ways of life as between one group and another, of the "Canadian nation," as if the nation were not primarily and essentially a community of culture. Starting from there it considers it normal that, throughout the country, Canadians of every group should, for example, be subjected to the same system of social security and that the Constitution should be interpreted in the most centralizing way. Our chapters on the federal government's theories and practices on constitutional matters, with respect to education as well as in regard to economic, social and fiscal subjects clearly illustrate what we have just written. These bring to light the eminently practical effects of a whole series of concepts which, at first glance, might be considered essentially theoretical and speculative. As a matter of fact, the interpretation given, at the state level, to concepts such as culture, nation, society and citizenship expresses itself in laws, institutions and ways of life and thus tends either towards the conservation of a particular culture and the stimulation of its development or else it tends to undermine its capacity to perpetuate itself and, eventually, impoverishes its sources.

Federalism, as a political system, may vary according to the purposes for which it is intended. When its sole objective is to adapt the political system to the geographical and economic diversity of any given country, it can be more or less flexible and relaxed. On the contrary, if, within the framework of a single state, it aims at ensuring the parallel development of distinctive cultures, it is extensive and rigid.

Culture and the Sociological Milieu

Every particular culture needs a focus wherein to maintain and renew itself from generation to generation. That is to say, it requires a centre where each of its particulars, including language, traditions and ways of life must be currently necessary and a requisite for success to every person making up the collectivity. Thus, the required centre is one wherein the people who embody it may live according to their concepts, where they may express themselves freely according to their spirit and where they themselves ... may erect, according to their idea, the institutions necessary for the full expansion of individual and collective life. To fulfill its purpose and allow the cultural groups present within a single state to develop themselves according to their respective particularisms and thereby contribute to the prosperity of the whole, federalism must be broad enough to assure to each of them the political initiative in such functions of collective life as lie closest to the ideological, intellectual and social exigencies of the culture itself. By these we mean education, public charities, mutual assistance, labour and family organization, etc.

Despite the ambiguity of some of its sections, that is precisely what the Constitution of 1867 sought to bring about in Canada. Through its method of distributing powers, it assigned to the two orders of government those prerogatives which correspond to the objectives of cultural federalism. Since 1867, the Canadian reality has grown. It has become articulated and integrated but it has not changed insofar as its cultural components and its political requirements are concerned. And it is to these we must revert, no matter from what angle the state's structure and functioning may be studied. Without such a reference to the heart of the matter, technically efficient solutions may be found for this or that problem, but none will be found which will be politically just.

The Province of Quebec and French-Canadian Culture

If Anglo-Canadian culture is today spread throughout nine of the ten Canadian provinces and if it can count upon their organized life for its diffusion and renewal, French-Canadian culture on the other hand has only one real focus, and that is the Province of Quebec. This, then, is how the case of French Canada and of the Province of Quebec rests with regard to English Canada and the Canadian state. If, as is its legitimate ambition, Canada should eventually give birth to an authentic "nation" in whose midst the two groups will live in friendship, finding their full flowering in a co-operation made all the more fruitful because it is based on mutual trust, the role of the Province of Quebec, as national focus and primary political centre of one of the two groups, will be a truly great one, and one of which it must itself become aware, while the rest of the country has every interest not to under-estimate the importance of its role. ...

Recommendations

FEDERAL–PROVINCIAL RELATIONS

The Problem

In order to give a better idea of the direction and scope of our recommendations, we think it may be useful to re-state our problem's main elements. On the one hand:

1. The primary purpose of Canadian federalism is to allow the two great cultural communities which made up our population a) to live and develop themselves according to their respective particularisms and b) to co-operate in the building and progress of a common fatherland;

2. With regard to French-Canadian culture, the Province of Quebec assumes alone the responsibilities which the other provinces jointly assume with regard to Anglo-Canadian culture;
3. The Canadian reality, both economic and sociological, has undergone a profound transformation since 1867, but its cultural elements have not changed, so that the basic problem still remains the same.

Furthermore:

4. a) Transportation and integration of the economic and social complex have made economic stability one of the major political goals; b) ideas regarding the state's economic and social role have also evolved, with intervention by the state in the economy's functioning being today admissible, both in theory and in practice, while a new school of economists claims it can give it a scientific basis and standards;
5. Industrial concentration has created fiscal inequalities as between the provinces, and these should be remedied, as far as possible.

In the third place:

6. Control of the economy and equalization of fiscal conditions as between the provinces are the main reasons today invoked by the federal government as justifying its social as well as its fiscal policy. It considers both of these, over and above their special purposes, as being indispensable instruments of economic control. The federal government, moreover, relies on an interpretation of the Constitution according to which it is vested with the main economic powers, and possesses "unlimited" power to tax and "absolute" power to spend. Thus, it concludes that it alone can exercise all initiatives needed to control the economy, to maintain employment, and to equalize fiscal resources between the provinces. As a consequence, it seems to think that pursuit of economic and social goals has, in some way, priority over cultural objectives, and also that the federal government itself has similar priority over the provinces.

Such is the basic conflict of which the fiscal problem is the most visible manifestation. In short, it arises from a unitary non-federative interpretation of the Constitution and of the very notion of a state, and it arises also from a technically administrative but non-political concept of the state's role in economic and social affairs.

For our part, we hold that there is no opposition between the state's economic and social goals and its cultural objectives, and we believe that both of them can be effectively realized in a federative system, provided there is an awareness of the political nature of the problem and of the steps that must be taken in order to ensure a harmonious solution in a country as differentiated as Canada.

1. Politics, in the best sense of the word, has for its objective not merely welfare but good living, that is, the hierarchic totality of conditions needed for full assertion of human individuality. If it is true that the citizen serves the state, it is equally true that the state is in Man's service.
2. In a federative system, the state is composed of two orders, and not merely one single order of government, each of them acting by its own authority within its special domain but in coordination within the framework of constitutional law. Autonomy for

the component parts and co-ordination of policies are the conditions required to make this type of state efficacious, particularly in these days when the various functions of collective life are so fully integrated.

3. The institutions of communal life are the sociological expression of the culture, and one of its modes of renewal. Cultural policy and social policy are, therefore, only extensions of each other; they must have the same inspiration and they must be entrusted to the government which, being itself a participant in the culture, can best grasp its spirit and express it through laws.

4. The various kinds of taxes are in a qualitative relationship to the functions of collective life. In a federative state of the cultural type, they should be distributed between the orders of government according to the functions with which the latter are vested. Thus, since taxes on incomes have a direct incidence on persons and institutions, they should belong to the government on which cultural and social responsibility is incumbent. Since taxes on business operations and on the circulation of goods have a direct economic incidence and, if employed on the regional and local level, would tend to raise barriers within the same country, they should logically belong to that government which is vested with the larger economic responsibility and whose jurisdiction extends over the whole territory.

5. If equality of services between the several parts of a federative state is desirable, it cannot, however, be considered an absolute. Consequently, it cannot be established as a permanent system for the redistribution of funds nor, more especially, can it be sought to the detriment of the higher interests of one or more groups.

General Solution

RETURN TO THE CONSTITUTION

In our opinion, only a frank return to the Constitution can conciliate the principles enumerated above with the practical exigencies of Canadian politics today. We, therefore, recommend to the government of the Province of Quebec that it should invite the federal government and the governments of the other provinces, as constituent parts of the state, to undertake jointly a re-adaptation of the public administration according to the spirit of federalism. This re-shaping, carried out within the framework of the Constitution, would aim at re-interpreting its master-ideas in the four major provisions which a fiscal policy for our times, conforming both to federalism and to the state's general needs, ought to provide.

Two of these provisions, in their choice and arrangement of fiscal structures, imply options as to the principles from which Canadian policy should proceed.

5 Equality or Independence

Daniel Johnson (1965)

EDITORS' INTRODUCTION

Daniel Johnson was first elected as a Union Nationale member to the Quebec legislature in 1946. He served as a minister in the Duplessis government before becoming leader of the Union Nationale party in 1961. In 1965 he published Égalité ou indépendance *and had his party adopt it as its platform for constitutional reform. In 1966 he defeated Jean Lesage's Liberals and became premier of Quebec. Johnson's threat to lead Quebec to independence if Quebec could not achieve equality with the rest of Canada through constitutional reform led to the 1967 Confederation for Tomorrow Conference in Toronto. In February 1968, at the first of a long series of federal–provincial constitutional conferences, Johnson squared off with a newly appointed federal minister of justice, Pierre Elliott Trudeau.*

The Independence of Quebec

With assimilation definitively set aside, a status quo unable to satisfy anyone, us refusing to continue a policy of mending and interminable begging, there remain only two solutions: equality or independence, a new constitution or separation.

I think that we must not, *a priori*, reject the separatist solution. Because complete independence for Quebec, for reasons not dependent on itself, may become the only issue compatible with the survival and progress of the French Canadian nation. If others appear to be ready to sacrifice our culture, if need be, to save the Confederation, my attitude is completely different. Without animosity, however without bending, I must clearly state that Confederation is not an end in itself; and that if, after making every effort to make it equally habitable for our two cultural communities, we note that our efforts are in vain, the Confederation will seem to us unsalvageable. There are some who want to save Canada even at the expense of Quebec's autonomy. I, myself, am ready to save Quebec's autonomy even at the price of Confederation.

In saying this, I am only adapting to today's context a doctrine that was always part of my party. On at least two occasions, Mr. Duplessis repeated in the House what he had already proclaimed at the federal–provincial conference of 1950: "If they don't want to respect the pact of 1867, if they don't want us in the Confederation, the province of Quebec itself will take measures to survive." On December 1, 1959, one month before his death, Mr. Paul Sauvé also said this, speaking of a more equitable sharing of revenues: "I say with as much sincerity as I can muster, that if, in 1962, all the country's authorities do not realize that it is a question

Source: Excerpted and translated from Daniel Johnson, *Égalité ou indépendance. 25 ans plus tard à l'heure du lac Meech*. Montréal: VLB Éditeur, 1990. © VLB Éditeur. Reprinted by permission.

of life or death, I do not see how the Canadian Confederation will be able to continue to function."

I am thus not one of those who take separatists lightly. It really is too easy to go to Toronto or elsewhere and receive praise for saying, for instance, "Don't worry about Quebec separatists; they are nothing more than a handful of dreamers who want to build another Great Wall of China or another Berlin Wall outside their province."

Undoubtedly, there are extremists everywhere, but the separatists I know, and there are some in my very own party, have never had the thought that in our era, Quebec could be self-sufficient while ignoring the rest of the continent. Independence is not autarky, and those who confuse the two do so expressly to confuse things.

Every country, no matter the degree of liberation it may have achieved, must necessarily harmonize its economy with those of its surrounding neighbours. If it is independent, this will be done through treaties, agreements, and trade accords. Most importantly, this harmonizing must not always be done through others or according to the interests of others. It is to be the result of genuine cooperation.

The separatists, if I understand them, believe that, in the current state of things, this cooperation is no longer possible between the two communities that share Canada. They believe that political separation is a prerequisite for all future cooperation.

Those Who Fear Separatism

Certain politicians, in one language or the other, made speeches, some of which added further insult, in order to defeat separatism. I do not believe this is the correct method. Verbal violence appears to be as unjustifiable and inefficient as other forms of violence.

In my opinion, we will not prevent the dislocation of Canada by crusades and indictments. The weapon that must be used is that of comprehension and justice.

Why do some advocate total independence for Quebec? It is because they have had enough of begging and lame compromises. It is because they have lost their hope of feeling at home throughout Canada. It is because they want to leave their minority status, their situation of dependence.

Youth is impatient. It has a thirst for the absolute. Never will we be able to satisfy it with half-measures, crumbs or percentages of rights. It wants just solutions that are clear-cut and radical.

However, today as in the past, separatism to me does not necessarily appear as the only solution for now. In his recent work, *L'Option politique du Canada français* (*The Political Option of French Canada*), Philippe Garigue states that separatism would cause a split not only between English Canada and French Canada, but also within French Canada, because more than a million of us live outside Quebec. It is necessary to envision this event. Furthermore, as in 1791, separatism will not remove the problem of co-existence of two nations on one territory, since an important Anglophone minority, which has indisputable historical rights, also lives in our province.

Serious separatists are the first to recognize that Quebec could not live isolated anyway and that independence would not at all make the need for harmonious collaboration with the rest of the country and continent disappear. They say this: Let's become independent first and it will become much easier to establish in equality the conditions of such cooperation. This argument has weight. However, in the viewpoint created by the constitutional parliamentary committee, I prefer, for my part, before resorting to the ultimate recourse of separatism, to attempt all that can be attempted, so that the French Canadian nation can feel at home, as in a real homeland, in all of Canada.

It seems to me that we can attain equality through negotiation, without necessarily going as far as independence, which includes, needless to say, a certain number of risks that are quite difficult to evaluate.

With this in mind, I asked the constitutional committee, on May 13, 1964, to prepare a study on the consequences of independence.

Also, I continue to believe in the possibility of a dialogue and establishing in Canada a new constitution which would set up from the top, for the entire country, a truly bi-national body, where the agents of both cultural communities could work together, on equal footing, to manage their common interests.

I do not believe this exalting task to be beneath the moral and intellectual forces of Canadians of both cultures.

And in any case, it's this or separation.

The French Canadian nation, in development for the past three centuries, needs a climate of freedom to fully flourish. There cannot be cultural equality without cultural autonomy. And there cannot be cultural autonomy without political autonomy. The French Canadian nation must have a homeland. If it fails to happen politically from one ocean to the other, in a new, bi-national federalism, it will have no choice but to create an independent Quebec.

I know well that this is an extreme solution, a solution of last resort. It is a little bit like a strike. But for a union undertaking negotiation, it would not be wise at the start to exclude a strike option, even if it hopes to avoid it.

If secession became the only way for French Canadians to be themselves, to stay French, then it would not only be their right, it would be their duty to become separatists.

For my part, I have no doubt that, in this case, the Union Nationale will be the only party capable of achieving independence with order, with respect to individual freedoms and vested interests.

Canada or Quebec

This equality, will we attain it? The answer does not depend on us alone. This is why it appears premature to me to concern ourselves excessively now with the form of a new constitutional regime.

Before deciding on the container, let us decide on the content.

Some talk of a special status for Quebec, while remaining careful to not define what they mean by this. Here is a very convenient term that can mean almost anything. As I explained earlier, there are many examples of federations where some member states benefit from a special status. But I know of none that can apply exactly to the Canadian situation. Because this situation is unique.

Others speak of associated states. Interesting formula, but again, one should specify what one means by this, because all sorts of associations can exist. The minority shareholder is also an associate in a company.

What is important above all is to determine what the essential powers are for the affirmation of the French Canadian nation.

There are, for nations as much as for individuals, fundamental freedoms that are not to be begged for and which cannot be reason for compromises or underhanded dealings.

The right of self-determination, for the French Canadian nation, is of this order. It is a collective heritage that I consider fully acquired and I would never agree to renegotiate.

What we want is more than the powers that were accorded to us by the 1867 constitution.

What we want, in fact, is the right to decide for ourselves, or to have an equal part in decisions on all areas that concern our life as a nation.

After all, are we masters of our house when Ottawa alone governs everything concerning radio and television, media which are perhaps in our time the most efficient cultural instruments?

Are we masters of our house when Ottawa refuses to protect, with appropriate tariffs, the products of certain vital French Canadian industries?

Are we masters of our house when Ottawa can use immigration in a way to modify ethnic equilibrium, to the point of rendering us minorities in the State of Quebec?

Are we masters of our house when a decision of the Bank of Canada can affect the credit of our businesses, of our financial institutions and even of the State of Quebec?

Are we masters of our house when the federal tax department can skim the profits from the exploitation of natural resources which belong to the Quebec community and, through taxes on our companies, prevent us from planning our economy, according to our own needs?

Are we masters of our house when, through estate taxes, the federal government can encroach upon our civil code?

Are we masters of our house when nationalization is the only way to repatriate the taxes from our business into Quebec?

Are we masters of our house when the Supreme Court, of which the judges are all appointed by Ottawa, is the ultimate interpreter of our French code and the only tribunal to which we can submit our grievances against the federal government?

Here are the methods that Ottawa has to interfere directly into our national life. Here are the situations we must remedy if we want self-determination as a nation.

It is this I was thinking of when, in 1962, I adopted for the Union Nationale agenda an article that went like this:

> Draw up, in all areas, the master plans that will let the Quebec community flourish completely, following its own dreams and taking initiative for its own solutions, even if it requires demanding and obtaining participation from Ottawa as necessary for the realisation of these plans.

I admit it is not easy to obtain Ottawa's participation in initiatives favouring the growth of the Quebec community. But in which imbroglio would we throw ourselves into, if we were to, as required by the so-called repatriation formula, solicit participation from the other nine provinces?

Can you see the head of the state of Quebec undertaking a pilgrimage to each provincial capital to humbly beg each of the other Premiers to agree to have his legislature adopt a law allowing us, for example, to govern French radio and television?

Will we have to ask permission from another province, which population is barely half the size of Quebec City, to give priority to the French language in our national state?

Will we multiply by ten the difficulties the central government has already created? To what haggling will we have to bend to defeat the ten vetoes?

This is why I spoke of a straitjacket regarding the amendment formula that we disguise under the name of "repatriation formula." At a time when we feel the absolute necessity of expanding the powers of Quebec, it is not the time, it seems to me, to multiply the obstacles and to close the door on fruitful negotiations.

Federation, associated states, confederation, special status, republic, whatever it is, the new constitutional regime will have to give the French Canadian nation all the powers that are necessary to control its own destiny.

After three centuries of labour, our nation has earned the right to live freely. So much the better if it can feel at home from ocean to ocean. This implies that we are recognized as having complete equality. If not, we will have to have Quebec independence.

Canada or Quebec, wherever the French Canadian nation finds freedom, that is where home will be.

Quebec, March 1965.

Federalism, Nationalism, and Reason

Pierre Elliott Trudeau (1968)

EDITORS' INTRODUCTION
Pierre Trudeau was a leading Quebec intellectual who, along with Jean Marchand and Gerard Pelletier, was invited to join the federal Liberal Party and run for Parliament in 1965 to strengthen the Pearson Liberal government in facing the challenges arising from Quebec's "Quiet Revolution." His essay on federalism, nationalism, and reason is based on a paper he presented in 1964 to a joint meeting of the Canadian Political Science Association and the Canadian Law Teachers Association. It was included in Federalism and the French Canadians, *a collection of his writings edited by John Saywell and published in 1968, on the eve of his becoming leader of the Liberal Party and prime minister of Canada.*

State and Nation

The concept of federalism with which I will deal in this paper is that of a particular system of government applicable within a sovereign state; it flows from my understanding of state and nation. Hence I find it necessary to discuss these two notions in part I of this paper, but I need only do so from the point of view of territory and population. Essentially, the question to which I would seek an answer is: what section of the world's population occupying what segment of the world's surface should fall under the authority of a given state?

Until the middle of the eighteenth century, the answer was largely arrived at without regard to the people themselves. Of course in much earlier times, population pressures guided by accidents of geography and climate had determined the course of the migrations which were to spill across the earth's surface. But by the end of the Middle Ages, such migrations had run their course in most of Europe. The existence of certain peoples inhabiting certain land areas, speaking certain languages or dialects, and practising certain customs, was generally taken as data—*choses données*—by the European states which arose to establish their authority over them.

It was not the population who decided by what states they would be governed; it was the states which, by wars (but not "people's wars"), by alliances, by dynastic arrangements, by marriages, by inheritance, and by chance, determined the area of territory over which they would govern. And for that reason they could be called territorial states. Except in the particular case of newly discovered lands, the population came with the territory; and except in the unusual case of deportations, very little was to be done about it.

Source: Excerpted from *Federalism and the French Canadians*. Macmillan of Canada, 1968. Notes omitted. Reprinted by permission of the Estate of Pierre Elliott Trudeau. See http://www.trudeaufoundation.ca.

Political philosophers, asking questions about the authority of the state, did not inquire why a certain population fell within the territorial jurisdiction of a certain state rather than of another; for the philosophers, too, territory and population were just data; their philosophies were mainly concerned with discovering the foundations of authority over a *given* territory and the sources of obedience of a *given* population.

In other words, the purpose of Locke and Rousseau, not unlike that of the medieval philosophers and of the ancient Stoics, was to explain the origins and justify the existence of political authority *per se*; the theories of contract which they derived from natural law or reason were meant to ensure that within a given state bad governments could readily be replaced by good ones, but not that one territorial state could be superseded by another.

Such then was the significance of social contract and popular sovereignty in the minds of the men who made the Glorious Revolution, and such it was in the minds of those who prepared the events of 1776 in America and 1789 in France. As things went, however, the two latter "events" turned out to be momentous revolutions, and the ideas which had been put into them emerged with an immensely enhanced significance.

In America, it became necessary for the people not merely to replace a poor government by a better one, but to switch their allegiance from one territorial state to another, and in their own words, to

> declare, that these United Colonies, are, and of right ought to be, free and independent states; that they are absolved from all allegiance to the British crown, and that all political connection, between them and the state of Great Britain, is and ought to be totally dissolved; and that, as free and independent states, they have full power to levy war, conclude peace, contract alliances, establish commerce, and to do all other acts and things which independent states may of right do.

Here then was a theory of government by consent which took on a radically new meaning. Since sovereignty belonged to the people, if appeared to follow that any given body of people could at will transfer their allegiance from one existing state to another, or indeed to a completely new state of their own creation. In other words, the consent of the population was required not merely for a social contract, which was to be the foundation of civil society, or for a choice of responsible rulers, which was the essence of self-government; consent was also required for adherence to one territorial state rather than to another, which was the beginning of national self-determination.

Why the theory of consent underwent such a transformation at this particular time is no doubt a matter for historical and philosophical conjecture. ...

Consequently, it might be said that in the past the (territorial) state had defined its territorial limits which had defined the people or nation living within. But henceforth it was to be the people who first defined themselves as a nation, who then declared which territory belonged to them as of right, and who finally proceeded to give their allegiance to a state of their own choosing or invention which would exercise authority over that nation and that territory. Hence the expression "nation-state." As I see it, the important transition was from the *territorial state* to the *nation-state*. But once the latter was born, the idea of the *national state* was bound to follow, it being little more than a nation-state with an ethnic flavour added. With it the idea of self-determination became the principle of nationalities.

Self-determination did not necessarily proceed from or lead to self-government. Whereas self-government was based on reason and proposed to introduce liberal forms of government into existing states, self-determination was based on will and proposed to challenge the legitimacy and the very existence of the territorial states.

Self-determination, or the principle of nationalities (I am talking of the doctrine, for the expressions became current only later), was bound to dissolve whatever order and balance existed in the society of states prevailing towards the end of the eighteenth century. But no matter; for it was surmised that a new order would arise, free from wars and inequities. As each of the peoples of the world became conscious of its identity as a collectivity bound together by natural affinities, it would define itself as a nation and govern itself as a state. An international order of nation-states, since it would be founded on the free will of free people, would necessarily be more lasting and just than one which rested on a hodge-podge of despotic empires, dynastic kingdoms, and aristocratic republics. In May 1790, the Constituent Assembly had proclaimed: "La nation française renonce à entreprendre aucune guerre dans un but de conquête et n'emploiera jamais de forces contre la liberty d'aucun peuple."

Unfortunately, things did not work out quite that way. The French Revolution, which had begun as an attempt to replace a bad government by a good one, soon overreached itself by replacing a territorial state by a nation-state, whose territory incidentally was considerably enlarged. In 1789, the *Déclaration des droits de l'homme et du citoyen* had stated: "Le principe de toute souveraineté réside essentiellement dans la Nation. Nul corps, nul individu ne peut exercer d'autorité qui n'en émane expressément." But who was to be included in the nation? Danton, having pointed out in 1793 that the frontiers of France were designated by Nature, the French nation willed possession of that part of Europe which spread between the Rhine, the Pyrenees, the Atlantic Ocean, and the Alps. ...

The political history of Europe and of the Americas in the nineteenth century and that of Asia and Africa in the twentieth are histories of nations labouring, conspiring, blackmailing, warring, revolutionizing, and generally willing their way towards statehood. It is, of course, impossible to know whether there has ensued therefrom for humanity more peace and justice than would have been the case if some other principle than self-determination had held sway. In theory, the arrangement of boundaries in such a way that no important national group be included by force in the territorial limits of a state which was mainly the expression of the will of another group, was to be conducive to peaceful international order. In practice, state boundaries continued to be established and maintained largely by the threat of or the use of force. The concept of right in international relations became, if anything, even more a function of might. And the question whether a national minority was "important" enough to be entitled to independence remained unanswerable except in terms of the political and physical power that could be wielded in its favour. Why did Libya become a country in 1951 and not the Saar in 1935, with a population almost as great? Why should Norway be independent and not Brittany? Why Ireland and not Scotland? Why Nicaragua and not Quebec?

As we ask ourselves these questions, it becomes apparent that more than language and culture, more than history and geography, even more than force and power, the foundation of the nation is will. For there is no power without will. The Rocky Mountains are higher than the Pyrenees but they are not a watershed between countries. The Irish Sea and the Straits of Florida are much narrower than the Pacific Ocean between Hawaii and California, yet they are more important factors in determining nationhood. Language or race do not provide, in Switzerland or Brazil, the divisive force they are at present providing in Belgium or the United States.

Looking at the foregoing examples, and at many others, we are bound to conclude that the frontiers of nation-states are in reality nearly as arbitrary as those of the former territorial states. For all their anthropologists, linguists, geographers, and historians, the nations of today cannot justify their frontiers with noticeably more rationality than the kings of two centuries ago; a greater reliance on general staffs than on princesses' dowries does not necessarily spell a triumph of reason. Consequently, a present-day definition of the word "nation" in its juristic sense would fit quite readily upon the population of the territorial states which existed before the French and American revolutions. A nation (as in the expressions: the French nation, the Swiss nation, the United Nations, the President's speech to the nation) is no more and no less than the entire population of a sovereign state. (Except when otherwise obvious, I shall try to adhere to that juristic sense in the rest of this paper.) Because no country has an absolutely homogeneous population, all the so-called nation-states of today are also territorial states. And the converse is probably also true. The distinction between a nation-state, a multi-national state, and a territorial state may well be valid in reference to historical origins; but it has very little foundation in law or fact today and is mainly indicative of political value judgments.

Of course, the word "nation" can also be used in a sociological sense, as when we speak of the Scottish nation, or the Jewish nation. As Humpty Dumpty once told Alice, a word means just what one chooses it to mean. It would indeed be helpful if we could make up our minds. Either the juristic sense would be rejected, and the word "people" used instead (the people of the Soviet Union, the people of the United States; but what word would replace "national"? People's? Popular?); in that case "nation" would be restricted to its sociological meaning, which is also closer to its etymological and historical ones. Or the latter sense would be rejected, and words like "linguistic," "ethnic," or "cultural group" be used instead. But lawyers and political scientists cannot remake the language to suit their convenience; they will just have to hope that "the context makes it tolerably clear which of the two [senses] we mean."

However, for some people one meaning is meant to flow into the other. The ambiguity is intentional and the user is conveying something which is at the back of his mind—and sometimes not very far back. In such cases the use of the word "nation" is not only confusing, it is disruptive of political stability. Thus, when a tightly knit minority within a state begins to define itself forcefully and consistently as a nation, it is triggering a mechanism which will tend to propel it towards full statehood.

That, of course, is not merely due to the magic of words, but to a much more dynamic process which I will now attempt to explain. When the erstwhile territorial state, held together by divine right, tradition, and force, gave way to the nation-state, based on the will of the people, a new glue had to be invented which would bind the nation together on a durable basis. For very few nations—if any—could rely on a cohesiveness based entirely on "natural" identity, and so most of them were faced with a terrible paradox: the principle of national self-determination which had justified their birth could just as easily justify their death. Nationhood being little more than a state of mind, and every sociologically distinct group within the nation having a contingent right of secession, the will of the people was in constant danger of dividing up—unless it were transformed into a lasting consensus. ...

Nationalism and Federalism

Many of the nations which were formed into states over the past century or two included peoples who were set apart geographically (like East and West Pakistan, or Great Britain and Northern Ireland), historically (like the United States or Czechoslovakia), linguistically (like Switzerland or Belgium), racially (like the Soviet Union or Algeria). Half of the aforesaid countries undertook to form the national consensus within the framework of a unitary state; the other half found it expedient to develop a system of government called federalism. The process of consensus-formation is not the same in both cases. It is obviously impossible, as well as undesirable, to reach unanimity on all things. Even unitary states find it wise to respect elements of diversity, for instance by administrative decentralization as in Great Britain, or by language guarantees as in Belgium; but such limited securities having been given, a consensus is obtained which recognizes the state as the sole source of coercive authority within the national boundaries. The federal state proceeds differently; it deliberately reduces the national consensus to the greatest common denominator between the various groups composing the nation. Coercive authority over the entire territory remains a monopoly of the (central) state, but this authority is limited to certain subjects of jurisdiction; on other subjects, and within well-defined territorial regions, other coercive authorities exist. In other words, the exercise of sovereignty is divided between a central government and regional ones.

Federalism is by its very essence a compromise and a pact. It is a compromise in the sense that when national consensus on *all* things is not desirable or cannot readily obtain, the area of consensus is reduced in order that consensus on *some* things be reached. It is a pact or quasi-treaty in the sense that the terms of that compromise cannot be changed unilaterally. That is not to say that the terms are fixed forever; but only that in changing them, every effort must be made not to destroy the consensus on which the federated nation rests. For what Ernest Renan said about the nation is even truer about the federated nation: "L'existence d'une nation est … un plébiscite de tous les jours." This obviously did not mean that such a plebiscite could or should be held every day, the result of which could only be total anarchy; the real implication is clear: the nation is based on a social contract, the terms of which each new generation of citizens is free to accept tacitly, or to reject openly.

Federalism was an inescapable product of an age which recognized the principle of self-determination. For on the one hand, a sense of national identity and singularity was bound to be generated in a great many groups of people, who would insist on their right to distinct statehood. But on the other hand, the insuperable difficulties of living alone and the practical necessity of sharing the state with neighbouring groups were in many cases such as to make distinct statehood unattractive or unattainable. For those who recognized that the first law of politics is to start from the facts rather than from historical "might-have-been's," the federal compromise thus became imperative.

But by a paradox I have already noted in regard to the nation-state, the principle of self-determination which makes federalism necessary makes it also rather unstable. If the heavy paste of nationalism is relied upon to keep a unitary nation-state together, much more nationalism would appear to be required in the case of a federal nation-state. Yet if nationalism is encouraged as a rightful doctrine and noble passion, what is to prevent it from being used by some group, region, or province within the nation? If "nation algérienne" was a valid battle cry against France, how can the Algerian Arabs object to the cry of "nation kabyle" now being used against them?

The answer of course, is that no amount of logic can prevent such escalation. The only way out of the dilemma is to render what is logically defensible actually undesirable. The advantages *to the minority group* of staying integrated in the whole must on balance be greater than the gain to be reaped from separating. This can easily be the case when there is no real alternative for the separatists, either because they are met with force (as in the case of the U.S. Civil War), or because they are met with laughter (as in the case of the *Bretons bretonnisants*). But when there is a real alternative, it is not so easy. And the greater the advantages and possibilities of separatism, the more difficult it is to maintain an unwavering consensus within the whole state.

One way of offsetting the appeal of separatism is by investing tremendous amounts of time, energy, and money in nationalism, *at the federal level.* A national image must be created that will have such an appeal as to make any image of a separatist group unattractive. Resources must be diverted into such things as national flags, anthems, education, arts councils, broadcasting corporations, film boards; the territory must be bound together by a network of railways, highways, airlines; the national culture and the national economy must be protected by taxes and tariffs; ownership of resources and industry by nationals must be made a matter of policy. In short, the whole of the citizenry must be made to feel that it is only within the framework of the federal state that their language, culture, institutions, sacred traditions, and standard of living can be protected from external attack and internal strife.

It is, of course, obvious that a national consensus will be developed in this way only if the nationalism is emotionally acceptable to all important groups within the nation. Only blind men could expect a consensus to be lasting if the national flag or the national image is merely the reflection of one part of the nation, if the sum of values to be protected is not defined so as to include the language or the cultural heritage of some very large and tightly knit minority, if the identity to be arrived at is shattered by a colour-bar. The advantage as well as the peril of federalism is that it permits the development of a regional consensus based on regional values; so federalism is ultimately bound to fail if the nationalism it cultivates is unable to generate a national image which has immensely more appeal than the regional ones.

Moreover, this national consensus—to be lasting—must be a living thing. There is no greater pitfall for federal nations than to take the consensus for granted, as though it were reached once and for all. The compromise of federalism is generally reached under a very particular set of circumstances. As time goes by these circumstances change; the external menace recedes, the economy flourishes, mobility increases, industrialization and urbanization proceed; and also the federated groups grow, sometimes at uneven paces, their cultures mature, sometimes in divergent directions. To meet these changes, the terms of the federative pact must be altered, and this is done as smoothly as possible by administrative practice, by judicial decision, and by constitutional amendment, giving a little more regional autonomy here, a bit more centralization there, but at all times taking great care to preserve the delicate balance upon which the national consensus rests.

Such care must increase in direct proportion to the strength of the alternatives which present themselves to the federated groups. Thus, when a large cohesive minority believes it can transfer its allegiance to a neighbouring state, or make a go of total independence, it will be inclined to dissociate itself from a consensus the terms of which have been altered in its disfavour. On the other hand, such a minority may be tempted to use its bargaining strength to obtain advantages which are so costly to the majority as to reduce to naught the advantages to the latter of remaining federated. Thus, a critical point can be reached in either direction beyond which separatism takes place, or a civil war is fought.

When such a critical point has been reached or is in sight, no amount, however great, of nationalism can save the federation. Any expenditure of emotional appeal (flags, professions of faith, calls to dignity, expressions of brotherly love) at the national level will only serve to justify similar appeals at the regional level, where they are just as likely to be effective. Thus the great moment of truth arrives when it is realized that *in the last resort* the mainspring of federalism cannot be emotion but must be reason.

To be sure, federalism found its greatest development in the time of the nation-states, founded on the principle of self-determination, and cemented together by the emotion of nationalism. Federal states have themselves made use of this nationalism over periods long enough to make its inner contradictions go unnoticed. Thus, in a neighbouring country, Manifest Destiny, the Monroe Doctrine, the Hun, the Red Scourge, the Yellow Peril, and Senator McCarthy have all provided glue for the American Way of Life; but it is apparent that the Cuban "menace" has not been able to prevent the American Negro from obtaining a renegotiation of the terms of the American national consensus. The Black Muslims were the answer to the argument of the Cuban menace; the only answer to both is the voice of reason.

It is now becoming obvious that federalism has all along been a product of reason in politics. It was born of a decision by pragmatic politicians to face facts as they are, particularly the fact of the heterogeneity of the world's population. It is an attempt to find a rational compromise between the divergent interest-groups which history has thrown together; but it is a compromise based on the will of the people.

Looking at events in retrospect, it would seem that the French Revolution attempted to delineate national territories according to the will of the people, without reference to rationality; the Congress of Vienna claimed to draw state boundaries according to reason, without reference to the will of the people; and federalism arose as an empirical effort to base a country's frontiers on both reason and the will of the people.

I am not heralding the impending advent of reason as the prime mover in politics, for nationalism is too cheap and too powerful a tool to be soon discarded by politicians of all countries; the rising *bourgeoisies* in particular have too large a vested interest in nationalism to let it die out unattended. Nor am I arguing that as important an area of human conduct as politics could or should be governed without any reference to human emotions. But I would like to see emotionalism channelled into a less sterile direction than nationalism. And I am saying that within sufficiently advanced federal countries, the auto-destructiveness of nationalism is bound to become more and more apparent, and reason may yet reveal itself even to ambitious politicians as the more assured road to success. This may also be the trend in unitary states, since they all have to deal with some kind of regionalism or other. Simultaneously in the world of international relations, it is becoming more obvious that the Austinian concept of sovereignty could only be thoroughly applied in a world crippled by the ideology of the nation-state and sustained by the heady stimulant of nationalism. In the world of today, when whole groups of so-called sovereign states are experimenting with rational forms of integration, the exercise of sovereignty will not only be divided within federal states; it will have to be further divided between the states and the communities of states. If this tendency is accentuated the very idea of national sovereignty will recede and, with it the need for an emotional justification such as nationalism. International law will no longer be explained away as so much "positive international morality," it will be recognized as true law, a "coercive order ... for the promotion of peace."

Thus there is some hope that in advanced societies, the glue of nationalism will become as obsolete as the divine right of kings; the title of the state to govern and the extent of its authority will be conditional upon rational justification; a people's consensus based on reason will supply the cohesive force that societies require; and politics both within and without the state will follow a much more functional approach to the problems of government. If politicians must bring emotions into the act, let them get emotional about functionalism!

The rise of reason in politics is an advance of law; for is not law an attempt to regulate the conduct of men in society rationally rather than emotionally? It appears then that a political order based on federalism is an order based on law. And there will flow more good than evil from the present tribulations of federalism if they serve to equip lawyers, social scientists, and politicians with the tools required to build societies of men ordered by reason.

Who knows? Humanity may yet be spared the ignominy of seeing its destinies guided by some new and broader emotion based, for example, on continentalism.

Canadian Federalism: The Past and the Present

Earlier in this paper, when discussing the concept of national consensus, I pointed out that it was not something to be forever taken for granted. In present-day Canada, an observation such as that need not proceed from very great insight. Still, I will start from there to examine some aspects of Canadian federalism.

Though, technically speaking, national self-determination only became a reality in Canada in 1931, it is no distortion of political reality to say that the Canadian nation dates from 1867, give or take a few years. The consensus of what is known today as the Canadian nation took shape in those years; and it is the will of that nation which is the foundation of the state which today exercises its jurisdiction over the whole of the Canadian territory.

Of course, the will of the Canadian nation was subjected to certain constraints, not least of which was the reality of the British Empire. But, except once again in a technical sense, this did not mean very much more than that Canada, like every other nation, was not born in a vacuum, but had to recognize the historical as well as all other data which surrounded its birth.

I suppose we can safely assume that the men who drew up the terms of the Canadian federal compromise had heard something of the ideology of nationalism which had been spreading revolutions for seventy-five years. It is likely too that they knew about the Civil War in the United States, the rebellions of 1837–8 in Canada, the Annexation Manifesto, and the unsatisfactory results of double majorities. Certainly they assessed the centrifugal forces that the constitution would have to overcome if the Canadian state was to be a durable one: first, the linguistic and other cultural differences between the two major founding groups, and secondly the attraction of regionalisms which were not likely to decrease in a country the size of Canada.

Given these data, I am inclined to believe that the authors of the Canadian federation arrived at as wise a compromise and drew up as sensible a constitution as any group of men anywhere could have done. Reading that document today, one is struck by its absence of principles, ideals, or other frills; even the regional safeguards and minority guarantees are pragmatically presented, here and there, rather than proclaimed as a thrilling bill of rights. It has been said that the binding force of the United States of America was the idea of liberty, and certainly none of the relevant constitutional documents let us forget it. By comparison, the Canadian nation seems founded on the common sense of empirical politicians who had wanted to establish some law and order over a disjointed half-continent. If reason be the governing virtue of federalism, it would seem that Canada got off to a good start.

Like everything else, the Canadian nation had to move with the times. Many of the necessary adjustments were guided by rational deliberation: such was the case, for instance, with most of our constitutional amendments, and with the general direction imparted to Canadian law by the Privy Council decisions. It has long been a custom in English Canada to denounce the Privy Council for its provincial bias; but it should perhaps be considered that if the law lords had not leaned in that direction, Quebec separatism might not be a threat today: it might be an accomplished fact. From the point of view of the damage done to Quebec's understanding of the original federal compromise there were certainly some disappointing—even if legally sound—judgments (like the New Brunswick, Manitoba, and Ontario separate school cases) and some unwise amendments (like the B.N.A. No. 2 Act, 1949); but on balance, it would seem that constitutional amendment and judicial interpretation would not by themselves have permanently damaged the fabric of the Canadian consensus if they had not been compounded with a certain type of adjustment through administrative centralization.

Faced with provinces at very different stages of economic and political development, it was natural for the central government to assume as much power as it could to make the country as a whole a going concern. Whether this centralization was always necessary, or whether it was not sometimes the product of bureaucratic and political empire-builders acting beyond the call of duty, are no doubt debatable questions, but they are irrelevant to the present inquiry. The point is that over the years the central administrative functions tended to develop rather more rapidly than the provincial ones; and if the national consensus was to be preserved some new factor would have to be thrown into the balance. This was done in three ways.

First, a countervailing regionalism was allowed and even fostered in matters which were indifferent to Canada's economic growth. For instance, there was no federal action when Manitoba flouted the constitution and abolished the use of the French language in the legislature. ...

Second, a representative bureaucracy at the central level was developed in such a way as to make the regions feel that their interests were well represented in Ottawa. ...

Third, tremendous reserves of nationalism were expended, in order to make everyone good, clean, unhyphenated Canadians. Riel was neatly hanged to all who would exploit petty regional differences. The Boer War was fought, as proof that Canadians could overlook their narrow provincialisms when the fate of the Empire was at stake. Conscription was imposed in two world wars, to show that in the face of death all Canadians were on an equal footing. And lest nationalism be in danger of waning, during the intervals between the above events

Union Jacks were waved, Royalty was shown around, and immigration laws were loaded in favour of the British Isles. ...

In short, during several generations, the stability of the Canadian consensus was due to Quebec's inability to do anything about it. Ottawa took advantage of Quebec's backwardness to centralize; and because of its backwardness that province was unable to participate adequately in the benefits of centralization. The vicious circle could only be broken if Quebec managed to become a modern society. But how could this be done? The very ideology which was marshalled to preserve Quebec's integrity, French-Canadian nationalism, was setting up defence mechanisms the effect of which was to turn Quebec resolutely inward and backwards. It befell the generation of French Canadians who came of age during the Second World War to break out of the dilemma; instead of bucking the rising tides of industrialization and modernization in a vain effort to preserve traditional values, they threw the floodgates open to forces of change. And if ever proof be required that nationalism is a sterile force, let it be considered that fifteen years of systematic non-nationalism and sometimes ruthless anti-nationalism at a few key points of the society were enough to help Quebec to pass from a feudal into a modern era.

Technological factors could, practically alone, explain the sudden transformation of Quebec. But many agents from within were at work, eschewing nationalism and preparing their society to adapt itself to modern times. Typical amongst such agents were the three following: Laval's *Faculté des sciences sociales* began turning out graduates who were sufficiently well equipped to be respected members of the central representative bureaucracy. The *Confédération des travailleurs catholiques du Canada* came squarely to grips with economic reality and helped transform Quebec's working classes into active participants in the process of industrialization. The little magazine *Cité Libre* became a rallying point for progressive action and writing; moreover it understood that a modern Quebec would very soon call into question the imbalance towards which the original federal compromise had drifted, and it warned that English-Canadian nationalism was headed for a rude awakening; upholding provincial autonomy and proposing certain constitutional guarantees, it sought to re-establish the Canadian consensus on a rational basis.

The warnings went unheeded; Ottawa did not change. But Quebec did: bossism collapsed, blind traditionalism crumbled, the Church was challenged, new forces were unleashed. When in Europe the dynasties and traditions had been toppled, the new societies quickly found a new cohesive agent in nationalism; and no sooner had privilege within the nation given way to internal equality than privilege *between* nations fell under attack; external equality was pursued by way of national self-determination. In Quebec today the same forces are at work: a new and modern society is being glued together by nationalism, it is discovering its potentialities as a nation, and is demanding equality with all other nations. This in turn is causing a backlash in other provinces, and Canada suddenly finds herself wondering whether she has a future. What is to be done?

If my premises are correct, nationalism cannot provide the answer. Even if massive investments in flags, dignity, protectionism, and Canadian content of television managed to hold the country together a few more years, separatism would remain a recurrent phenomenon, and very soon again new generations of Canadians and Quebeckers would be expected to pour their intellectual energies down the drain of emotionalism. If, for instance, it is going to remain *morally wrong* for Wall Street to assume control of Canada's economy, how will it become *morally right* for Bay Street to dominate Quebec's—or for that matter, Nova Scotia's?

It is possible that nationalism may still have a role to play in backward societies where the *status quo* is upheld by irrational and brutal forces; in such circumstances, *because there is no other way*, perhaps the nationalist passions will still be found useful to unleash the revolutions, upset colonialism, and lay the foundations of welfare states; in such cases, the undesirable consequences will have to be accepted along with the good.

But in the advanced societies, where the interplay of social forces can be regulated by law, where the centres of political power can be made responsible to the people, where the economic victories are a function of education and automation, where cultural differentiation is submitted to ruthless competition, and where the road to progress lies in the direction of international integration, nationalism will have to be discarded as a rustic and clumsy tool.

No doubt, at the level of individual action, emotions and dreams will still play a part; even in modern man, superstition remains a powerful motivation. But magic, no less than totems and taboos, has long since ceased to play an important role in the normal governing of states. And likewise, nationalism will eventually have to be rejected as a principle of sound government. In the world of tomorrow, the expression "banana republic" will not refer to independent fruit-growing nations but to countries where formal independence has been given priority over the cybernetic revolution. In such a world, the state—if it is not to be outdistanced by its rivals—will need political instruments which are sharper, stronger, and more finely controlled than anything based on mere emotionalism: such tools will be made up of advanced technology and scientific investigation, as applied to the fields of law, economics, social psychology, international affairs, and other areas of human relations; in short, if not a pure product of reason, the political tools of the future will be designed and appraised by more rational standards than anything we are currently using in Canada today.

Let me hasten to add that I am not predicting which way Canada will turn. But because it seems obvious to me that nationalism—and of course I mean the Canadian as well as the Quebec variety—has put her on a collision course, I am suggesting that cold, unemotional rationality can still save the ship. Acton's prophecy, one hundred years ago, is now in danger of being fulfilled in Canada. "Its course," he stated of nationality, "will be marked with material as well as moral ruin, in order that a new invention may prevail over the works of God and the interests of mankind." This new invention may well be functionalism in politics; and perhaps it will prove to be inseparable from any workable concept of federalism.

Shared and Divergent Values

Charles Taylor (1991)

EDITORS' INTRODUCTION

Charles Taylor is one of Canada's most eminent philosophers. He was for many years a professor at McGill University, where he taught in both the philosophy and political science departments. Though Taylor is recognized internationally for his philosophical work, he has been engaged throughout his career in the political life of his country, most recently as a member of the Quebec Commission of Inquiry into Reasonable Accommodation (see reading 30 in this volume). His essay "Shared and Divergent Values" is his contribution to a volume of essays, entitled Options for a New Canada, *which considers the consequences for Canada of the failure to accommodate Quebec through the Meech Lake Accord.*

Are there divergences of value between the different regions of Canada? In a sense, these are minimal. There appears to be a remarkable similarity throughout the country, and across the French/English difference, when it comes to the things in life which are important. Even when it comes to the values that specifically relate to political culture, there seems to be broad agreement. About equality, nondiscrimination, the rule of law, the mores of representative democracy, about social provision, about violence and firearms, and a host of issues.

This was not always the case. Half a century ago, it seemed that there were serious differences between the two major groups as far as political culture was concerned. Pierre Trudeau wrote about this.[1] The ravages of Maurice Duplessis on the rule of law, which he seemed to be able to get away with—his treatment of Jehovah's witnesses and Communists—seemed to indicate that Quebec and French Canada had different views about the toleration of dissent. Some people were ready to believe that the two societies gave quite different values to the maintenance of unity around certain cherished truths and standards when these conflicted with the goods of tolerance, freedom, or permitted diversity. Not that the rest-of-Canada was all that liberal in those days. Various minorities and dissidents had a rough time. But the particular grounds for illiberalism were rather strikingly different in Quebec, seemingly organized around the values of a traditional, ultramontane Catholicism. They made the province stand out as exotic and disturbing in the eyes of other Canadians.

This difference has disappeared today. Partly one might say that French Canada has rejoined "English Canada"; more accurately one might say that the forces within Quebec that were always striving for a liberal society have won out. Perhaps it would be more insightful to say that both parts of Canada have been swept up into the liberal consensus that has become established in the whole western world in the wake of the World War II. As we shall

Source: Excerpted from *Options for a New Canada*, edited by Ronald L. Watts and Douglas M. Brown. Toronto: University of Toronto Press, 1991. Some notes omitted. Reprinted by permission.

see below, some English-speaking Canadians seem still to doubt this, to harbour a suspicion of Quebec's liberal credentials, but this is quite unfounded in the 1990s. Or rather, suspicions are in order, but just as they are about any other Atlantic society, for none of these is exempt from racism, chauvinism, and similar ills.

Ironically, at the very moment when we agree upon so much, we are close to breakup. We have never been closer to breakup in our history, although our values have never been so uniform. The road to uniformity goes beyond the ironing out of differences between the two major cultures. There has also been a steady erosion of urban-rural differences in outlook over the last half century. And the prodigious effect of modern communications has probably lessened all the various regional differences as well.

Why Canada?

So what is the problem? It emerges when you ask another kind of question, also in the realm of values in some broad sense. Not what do people cherish as good, but what is a country for? That is, what ought to be the basis of unity around which a sovereign political entity can be built? This is a strange question in a way; it is not one that would likely be asked in many countries. But it arises here because there are alternatives, and therefore a felt need for justification. These alternatives exist for us—in our understanding of our situation—even when they are not very likely, when they enjoy minimal support and are hardly in the cards politically. They can still exist as a challenge to self-justification because they existed historically, and we retain the sense that our existing arrangements emerge out of a choice that excluded them.

In Canada-outside-Quebec (COQ)[2] the alternatives are two: the country or bits of it could join, or could have joined the United States; and the bits could also have failed to join together—and indeed, could one day deconfederate again. So there are two existential questions for COQ which we can call the unity and distinctness questions respectively. For Quebec there is one big question, which is too familiar and too much on the agenda today to need much description. It is the issue of whether to be part of Canada or not; and if so, how. I stress that neither of the existential alternatives may be strong options in COQ today, but that does not stop them functioning as reference points for self-definition; as ways of defining the question: what do we exist for?

In a sense the existential questions of the two societies are interwoven. Perhaps COQ would not feel the need for self-definition, for an answer to the question, "What is Canada for?" to anything like the same degree if Quebec were not contemplating answering its existential question in a radical form. But once the country's existence is threatened in this way all the suppressed alternatives rise to the surface in the rest-of-Canada as well.

So what are the answers? It will be easier to set out the problem by taking "English Canada" first. The answer here used to be simple. Way back when it really fitted into our official name of "British North America," the distinctness question answered itself; and unity seemed to be the corollary of the drive for distinctness in face of the American colossus. But as the Britishness, even "Englishness" of non-Quebec Canada declines, this becomes less and less viable as an answer. We are all the Queen's subjects, but this seems to mean less to less people; and more awkwardly, it means quite a bit to some still, but nothing at all to others, and thus cannot be the basis of unity.

What binds Canada together outside Quebec is thus no longer a common provenance, and less and less a common history. But people find the bonding elements in political institutions and ways of being. This is not a total break from the old identity, because Britishness also defined itself largely in terms of political institutions: parliamentary government, a certain juridical tradition, and the like. The slide has been continuous and without a sharp break from the old to the new. There are even certain continuing elements, but the package is different.

Canadians feel that they are different from the Americans, because (a) they live in a less violent and conflict-ridden society. This is partly just a matter of luck. We do not have a history that has generated an undeclared, low-level race war continuously feeding itself in our cities. But it is also a matter of political culture. From the very beginning Americans have put a value on energetic, direct defense of rights, and therefore are ready to mitigate their condemnation of violence. There is more understanding of it south of the border, more willingness to make allowances for it. And this has something to do with the actual level of violence being higher there, as well as with a number of strange penchants of American society, such as that expressed in the powerful lobby for personal firearms. Canadians tend to put more value on "peace, order and good government." At least, this is how we see ourselves, which is perhaps what is important for our purposes; but there seems to be some truth in the perception.

As a consequence, there is more tolerance here of rules and restrictions that are justified by the need for order. With it there is more of a favourable prejudice (at least in English Canada), and a free gift of the benefit of the doubt to the police forces. Hence the relative absence of protest when the *War Measures Act* was invoked in 1970; hence also the strange reluctance of the Canadian public to condemn the RCMP, even after all the revelations of its dubious behaviour.

We might add that Americans' tolerance of conflict extends into the domain of law as well. They are more litigious than we are. They think that is a good thing, that it reflects well on them. No one should take any guff from anyone. We tend to deplore it. From an American point of view, we seem to have an endless appetite for guff. But perhaps the long-term effect of the 1982 Charter will be to diminish this difference.

Related to this first point, Canadians (b) see their political society as more committed to collective provision, over against an American society that gives greater weight to individual initiative. Appeals for reduced government can be heard from the right of the political spectrum in both countries, but the idea of what reduced government actually means seems to be very different. There are regional differences in Canada, but generally Canadians are proud of and happy with their social programs, especially health insurance, and find the relative absence of these in the U.S. disturbing. The fact that poverty and destitution have been left to proliferate in American cities as they have during the Reagan years is generally seen here as a black mark against that society. Canadian practice may not be as much better as many of us believe; but the important point is that this is seen as a difference worth preserving.

Thus these two answers, (a) *law and order* and (b) *collective provision*, help to address the distinctness question. They explain why we are and want to remain a distinct political unit. But what answers the unity question? Why be a single country, and what common goals ought to animate this country? In one sense, (a) and (b) can serve here as well, if one thinks (as many Canadians instinctively do) that we need to hang together in order to maintain this alternative political culture as a viable option in North America. And then (b) can be logically extended into one of the principal declared common objectives of the Canadian federation in recent decades: (c) the equalization of life conditions and life chances between the regions. The solidarity of collective provision, which within each regional society generates such programs as Medicare, can be seen as finding its logical expression in a solidarity of mutual help between regions.

And so Canadian federalism has generated the practices of large-scale redistribution of fiscal resources through equalization payments, and attempts have been made at regional development. This too contrasts with recent American practice and provides a further answer to the distinctness question. We perhaps owe the drive to equality to the fact that we have been confronted with existential questions in a way that our neighbours have not since 1865. The Canadian federal union has been induced to justify itself, and greater interregional solidarity may be one of the fruits of this underlying angst.

But this bonding principle has also been a worrying source of division, because it is widely seen as a locus of failed aspirations and disappointed expectations. The principles of *regional equality and mutual help* run against a perceived reality of central Canadian domination in the outlying regions, a grievous mismatch of promise and performance. ...

It is clear that this issue of regional equality is a very troubled one in Canada. That is because it is on one hand an indispensable part of the answer to the unity question; while on the other it seems to many so largely unrealized, and on top of it all, we agree less and less on what it actually means.

But even if things were going swimmingly in this domain, we still would not have a full answer to the unity question. English Canada has been becoming more and more diverse, less and less "English," over the decades. The fact that it has always been an immigrant society, i.e., one which functions through admitting a steady stream of new arrivals, on top of the fact that it could not aspire to make immigrants over to its original mould, has meant that it has *de facto* become more and more multicultural over the years. It could not aspire to assimilate the newcomers to an existing mould, because this was originally British, hence ethnic. In the United States, which has always operated on a strong sense that it incarnates unrivalled political institutions, the drive to make everyone American could proceed apace. It was never as clear what the Canadian identity amounted to in political terms, and insofar as it was conceived as British it could not be considered normative for new arrivals. First, it was only the identity of one part of the country, and second, it could not but come to be seen as one ethnic background among others.

Canadians have seen their society as less of a melting pot than the United. States; and there has been some truth in this. In contrast to the neighbour society, people have spoken of a Canadian "mosaic." So this has even become for some a new facet of their answer to the distinctiveness question, under the rubric (d) *multiculturalism*. This is also far from trouble-free. Questions are being posed in both the major cultures about the pace and even goals of integration, or assimilation of immigrants into the larger anglophone or francophone society. This is particularly troubling in Quebec, which has much less historic experience of assimilating immigrants and a much higher proportion of whose francophone population is *pure laine*.

This makes even more acute the need for a further point of unity, a common reference point of identity, which can rally people from many diverse backgrounds and regions. In a quite astonishing way, (e) the *Charter of Rights* has come to fill this role in English Canada in recent years. It is astonishing, because nine years ago it did not exist. Nor was there that much of a groundswell of support demanding its introduction before it became a bone of contention between federal and provincial governments in the run-up to the patriation of 1981–82. But the Meech Lake debate showed how important it has become in COQ not just as an additional bulwark of rights, but as part of the indispensable common ground on which all Canadians ought to stand. For many people, it has come in the space of a few years to define in part the Canadian political identity. And since in COQ the national identity has to be defined in terms of political institutions for reasons rehearsed above, this has been a fateful development.

Why Quebec?

How about Quebec? How can it go about answering its existential question? The terms are very different. In Quebec, there is not a distinctness issue. The language and culture by themselves mark us off from Americans, and also from other Canadians. Much of (a) to (e) is seen as a "Good Thing" in Quebec. Regarding (a)—law and order—people do not compare themselves a lot with the U.S., but there is no doubt that Quebecers are spontaneously on the side of law and order, and are even more horrified by internecine conflict than other Canadians. ...

Regarding (b)—collective provision—it goes without saying that people are proud of their social programs in the province, and want to keep them. Point (d)—multiculturalism—is more problematic. As a federal policy, multiculturalism is sometimes seen as a device to deny French-speaking minorities their full recognition, or even to reduce the importance of the French fact in Canada to that of an outsize ethnic minority. And within Quebec itself, the growing diversity of francophone society is causing much heartburn and anxiety. Point (c)—regional equality and mutual self-help—is generally supported in Quebec, and even (e)—the Charter was favourably seen until it came to be perceived as an instrument for the advancement of the uniformity of language regimes across the country. Even now its other provisions are widely popular.

But these do not go very far to answer the question, what is a country for? There is one obvious answer to this question, which has continued down through the decades for over two centuries: (f) you need a country to defend or promote the nation. The nation here was originally "la nation canadienne-française." Now without entirely abandoning the first formulation, it tends to be put as *la nation québécoise*. This does not betoken any change in ethnic identity, of course. It reflects rather a sense, which presents itself as realistic, but may be too pessimistic, that the really survivable elements of la nation canadienne-française are only to be found in Quebec.

But the real point here is that (f) makes the survival and/or flourishing of this nation/language one of the prime goals of political society. No political entity is worth allegiance that does not contribute to this. The issue: independent Quebec versus remaining in Canada turns simply on different judgements about what does contribute to this. ...

Equality of What?

[A] great area of conflict is between the demands of a special status for Quebec, and those of regional equality, once this is interpreted as requiring equality between the provinces. But whereas over the two models of liberalism there is really a genuine philosophic difference underlying all the misunderstanding, here there is still much mutual misperception and cross purposes.

For in fact, the two demands come out of quite different agendas, as has often been remarked. The demand for special status is usually one for assuming a wider range of responsibilities and hence for greater autonomy. The call for regional equality comes generally from those who feel that their interests have been given insufficient weight in federal policy-making, and hence aims for more clout in this process. One side wants to take a greater distance from the central government and legislature; the other wants a weightier place within these. That is why it has taken the form in recent years of a call for reform in federal institutions, notably the Senate.

So understood, these demands are not logically opposed. Of course, they can at many points get in each other's way. There has been a fear among provinces that look to a more active federal government to equalize conditions across the regions, that excessive powers to Quebec might end up weakening the power of the centre to act. This may indeed be, but it is not fated to do so. It is not the reflection of a logical conflict, such as that between equality of all provinces on one hand, and special powers for one of them on the other. The demands for special status and strong central government can possibly be made compatible. What has made this difficult in practice has been precisely the refusal to depart from uniformity. This has meant that any "concession" to Quebec has had to be offered to all the provinces. Fortunately, these have not always been taken up, and so we have evolved quite a considerable *de facto* special status for Quebec, as I remarked above. But it has never been possible to proceed in that direction openly and explicitly, because of the pressure for uniformity. In the Meech Lake Accord itself, designed to address the difficulties of Quebec, most of what was accorded to Quebec had to be distributed to all the others.

The language of "equality" between provinces has in fact been a source of confusion, screening the reality of what is at stake and making solutions more difficult. Equality is a notoriously difficult concept to apply, and depends on the respect one makes salient. It could be argued that Quebec needs powers that other provinces do not, to cope with problems and a vocation that other provinces do not have. Accordingly, this point could be seen as a move towards equality (to each province according to its tasks), not away from it. Moreover, the special status has nothing to do with having more clout at the centre. It involves something quite different.

All of this should encourage us to think that it may not be beyond human wit to fever a way to satisfy these different demands together. There are (a) provinces that want more say in the decisions of the federal government. There are others who, while not disinterested in this first goal are mainly concerned with (b) maintaining an active federal government as a force for economic and social equalization between regions. Then there is Quebec, which (c) wants the powers it thinks essential to the preservation and promotion of its distinct society.

To this we now have to add the aboriginal dimension. That means that our arrangements have to accommodate the need for forms of self-government and self-management appropriate to the different first nations. This may mean in practice allowing for a new form of jurisdiction in Canada, perhaps weaker than the provinces, but, unlike municipalities, not simply the creatures of another level of government.

Putting all this together will be very difficult. It will take much ingenuity and good will. Perhaps more of either than we possess. But the task will be utterly impossible if we persist in describing the problem in the misleading and often demagogic language of equality versus inequality of provinces. Put in these terms the problem is a false one, and the present importance of this formulation is a sign of our lack of lucidity and the decline of good will. It reflects the deep mutual suspicions that have come to cloud our political scene.

The game of multidimensional constitutional tug-of-war that we have been playing in Canada these past years has made our situation worse, partly by creating or strengthening unhealthy linkages, whereby aspirations that are, as such, perfectly compatible come to be seen as deadly rivals. Examples are the linkages made between linguistic duality and multiculturalism, or those between aboriginals and Québécois, or those between regional equality and the distinct society. It may already be too late to climb out of the skein of resentments and mutual suspicion, and it will take far-sighted and courageous leadership to do so. But it will also require that we see each others' aspirations for what they are, as free as possible from the rhetoric of resentment.

Levels of Diversity

Various solutions can be glimpsed beyond the present stalemate. One set would be based on a dualism in which Quebec would no longer be a federal unit just like the others. The other possible range would have as its basis a four- or five-region federalism decentralized enough to accommodate Quebec as a member on all fours with the rest. Either type of solution would have to accommodate difference in a way we have not yet succeeded in doing—at least openly and admittedly.

Can we do it? It looks bad, but I would like to close by saying a few words about what this might mean.

In a way, accommodating difference is what Canada is all about. Many Canadians would concur in this. That is why the recent bout of mutual suspicion and ill-will in the constitutional debate has been so painful to many of our compatriots. It is not just that the two sources of difference I have been describing are becoming more salient. Old questions may be reopened. To some extent Trudeau's remarkable achievement in extending bilingualism was made possible by a growing sympathy towards the French fact among political and social elites in CCQ. The elites pushed the bilingual process at a pace faster than many of their fellow citizens wanted. For many people lower down in the hierarchy, French was being "stuffed down their throats," but granted the elite-run nature of the political accommodation process in this country, they seemed to have no option but to take it.

During the Meech debate the procedures of elite negotiation came under sharp criticism and challenge. Moreover, the COQ elites were themselves split on how to respond to the new package, in a way they had not been on bilingualism. It was therefore not surprising that we began to see a rebellion against the accommodation of French. This might be the harbinger of greater resistance to come. Already one hears westerners saying that Canadian duality is an irrelevancy to them, that their experience of Canada is of a multicultural mosaic. The very bases of a two-language federation are being questioned again. This important axis of difference is under threat.

More fundamentally, we face a challenge to our very conception of diversity. Many of the people who rallied around the Charter and multiculturalism to reject the distinct society are proud of their acceptance of diversity. And in some respects rightly so. What is enshrined here is what one might call first-level diversity. There are great differences in culture and outlook and background in a population that nevertheless shares the same idea of what it is to belong to Canada. Their patriotism or manner of belonging is uniform, whatever their other differences, and this is felt to be a necessity if the country is to hold together.

This is far from accommodating all Canadians. For Quebecers, and for most French Canadians, the way of being a Canadian (for those who still want to be) is by their belonging to a constituent element of Canada, *la nation québécoise*, or *canadienne-française*. Something analogous holds for aboriginal communities in this country. Their way of being Canadian is not accommodated by first-level diversity. And yet many people in COQ are puzzled by the resulting sense of exclusion, because first-level diversity is the only kind to which they are sensitive, and which they feel they fully acknowledge.

To build a country for everyone, Canada would have to allow for second-level or "deep" diversity, where a plurality of ways of belonging would also be acknowledged and accepted. Someone of, say, Italian extraction in Toronto, or Ukrainian extraction in Edmonton, might indeed feel Canadian as a bearer of individual rights in a multicultural mosaic. His or her belonging would not "pass through" some other community, although the ethnic identity might be important to him or her in various ways. But this person might nevertheless accept that a Québécois, or a Cree, or a Déné, might belong in a very different way, that they were Canadian through being members of their national communities. And reciprocally, the Québécois, Cree, or Déné would accept the perfect legitimacy of the "mosaic" identity.

Is this utopian? Could people ever come to see their country this way? Could they even find it exciting and an object of pride that they belong to a country that allows deep diversity? Pessimists say no, because they do not see how such a country could have a sense of unity. The model of citizenship has to be uniform, or people would have no sense of belonging to the same polity. Those who say this tend to take the United States as their paradigm, which has indeed been hostile to deep diversity, and has sometimes tried to stamp it out as "un-American."

But these pessimists should bear in mind three things. First, deep diversity is the only formula on which a united federal Canada can be rebuilt, once we recall the reasons why we all need Canada—such as those above, i.e., law and order, collective provision, and regional equality and mutual self-help.

Second, in many parts of the world today, the degree and nature of the differences resemble Canada's rather than the United States. If a uniform model of citizenship fits better the classical image of the western liberal state, it is also true that this is a straightjacket for many political societies. The world needs other models to be legitimated, in order to allow for more humane and less constraining modes of political cohabitation. Instead of pushing ourselves to the point of breakup in the name of the uniform model, we would do our own and some other peoples a favour by exploring the space of deep diversity. To those who believe in according people the freedom to be themselves, this would be counted a gain in civilization.

In this exploration we would not be alone. Europe-watchers have noticed how the development of the Community has gone along with an increased breathing space for regional societies—Breton, Basque, Catalan—which were formerly threatened with the steamroller of the national state.

Finally, after dividing to form two polities with uniform citizenship, both successor-states would find that they had failed after all to banish the challenge of deep diversity; because the only way that they can do justice to their aboriginal populations is by adopting a pluralist mould. Neither Quebec nor COQ could succeed in imitating the United States, or the European national states in their chauvinist prime. Why not recognize this now, and take the road of deep diversity together?

Notes

1. "La Province de Québec au moment de la grève" in Pierre Trudeau (ed.), *La Grève de l'Amiante* (Montréal: les Éditions Cité Libre, 1956).

2. In Quebec we speak blithely of "English Canada," but the people who live there do not identify with this label. We need a handy way of referring to the rest of the country as an entity, even if it lacks for the moment political expression. In order to avoid the clumsy three-word hyphenated expression, I plan to use "COQ" henceforth in this paper. I hope the reader will not take this as a sign of encroaching barbarism, or Québécois self-absorption (although it might partake in small measure of both).

8 | People to People, Nation to Nation

Royal Commission on Aboriginal Peoples (1996)

EDITORS' INTRODUCTION

In the wake of the confrontation of Mohawk warriors with the Canadian Armed Forces at Oka and Kahnawake in the summer of 1990, the Mulroney government established the Royal Commission on Aboriginal Peoples. The commission was co-chaired by George Erasmus, Grand Chief of the Assembly of First Nations, and René Dussault, a Quebec judge. Its membership included leading members of the Inuit, Métis, and non-status Indian communities; Bertha Wilson, a retired Supreme Court of Canada justice; and Allan Blakeney, a former premier of Saskatchewan. The commission had a broad mandate to study and make recommendations on all aspects of the relationship between Aboriginal peoples and Canada. It began its work in 1991 and submitted its five-volume final report in 1996. "Looking Forward, Looking Back" is the opening section of a widely distributed summary of the commission's findings and recommendations, entitled People to People, Nation to Nation.

Looking Forward, Looking Back

After some 500 years of a relationship that has swung from partnership to domination, from mutual respect and co-operation to paternalism and attempted assimilation, Canada must now work out fair and lasting terms of coexistence with Aboriginal people.

The Starting Point

The Commission has identified four compelling reasons to do so:

- Canada's claim to be a fair and enlightened society depends on it.
- The life chances of Aboriginal people, which are still shamefully low, must be improved.
- Negotiation, as conducted under the current rules, has proved unequal to the task of settling grievances.
- Continued failure may well lead to violence.

CANADA AS A FAIR AND ENLIGHTENED SOCIETY

Canada enjoys a reputation as a special place—a place where human rights and dignity are guaranteed, where the rules of liberal democracy are respected, where diversity among peoples is celebrated. But this reputation represents, at best, a half-truth.

Source: Excerpted from *People to People, Nation to Nation.* Ottawa: Government of Canada, 1996.
See http://www.ainc-inac.gc.ca/ap/pubs/rpt/rpt-eng.asp#chp3.

A careful reading of history shows that Canada was founded on a series of bargains with Aboriginal peoples—bargains this country has never fully honoured. Treaties between Aboriginal and non-Aboriginal governments were agreements to share the land. They were replaced by policies intended to

... remove Aboriginal people from their homelands.
... suppress Aboriginal nations and their governments.
... undermine Aboriginal cultures.
... stifle Aboriginal identity. ...

THE LIFE CHANCES OF ABORIGINAL PEOPLE

The third volume of our report, *Gathering Strength*, probes social conditions among Aboriginal people. The picture it presents is unacceptable in a country that the United Nations rates as the best place in the world to live.

Aboriginal people's living standards have improved in the past 50 years—but they do not come close to those of non-Aboriginal people:

- Life expectancy is lower.
- Illness is more common.
- Human problems, from family violence to alcohol abuse, are more common too.
- Fewer children graduate from high school.
- Far fewer go on to colleges and universities.
- The homes of Aboriginal people are more often flimsy, leaky and overcrowded.
- Water and sanitation systems in Aboriginal communities are more often inadequate.
- Fewer Aboriginal people have jobs.
- More spend time in jails and prisons.

Aboriginal people do not want pity or handouts. They want recognition that these problems are largely the result of loss of their lands and resources, destruction of their economies and social institutions, and denial of their nationhood.

They seek a range of remedies for these injustices, but most of all, they seek control of their lives.

FAILED NEGOTIATIONS

A relationship as complex as the one between Aboriginal and non-Aboriginal people is necessarily a matter of negotiation. But the current climate of negotiation is too often rife with conflict and confrontation, accusation and anger.

Negotiators start from opposing premises. Aboriginal negotiators fight for authority and resources sufficient to rebuild their societies and exercise self-government—as a matter of right, not privilege. Non-Aboriginal negotiators strive to protect the authority and resources of Canadian governments and look on transfers to Aboriginal communities as privileges they have bestowed.

Frequent failure to come to a meeting of minds has led to bitterness and mistrust among Aboriginal people, resentment and apathy among non-Aboriginal people.

In our report, we recommend four principles for a renewed relationship—to restore a positive climate at the negotiating table—and a new political framework for negotiations. ...

RISK OF VIOLENCE

Aboriginal people have made it clear, in words and deeds, that they will no longer sit quietly by, waiting for their grievances to be heard and their rights restored. Despite their long history of peacefulness, some leaders fear that violence is in the wind.

What Aboriginal people need is straightforward, if not simple:

- Control over their lives in place of the well-meaning but ruinous paternalism of past Canadian governments.
- Lands, resources and self-chosen governments with which to reconstruct social, economic and political order.
- Time, space and respect from Canada to heal their spirits and revitalize their cultures.

> *We are getting sick and tired of the promises of the federal government. We are getting sick and tired of Commissions. We are getting sick and tired of being analyzed ... We want to see action.*
>
> *Norman Evans*
> *Pacific Métis Federation*

The Ghosts of History

Every Canadian will gain if we escape the impasse that breeds confrontation between Aboriginal and non-Aboriginal people across barricades, real or symbolic. But the barricades will not fall until we understand how they were built.

Studying the past tells us who we are and where we came from. It often reveals a cache of secrets that some people are striving to keep hidden and others are striving to tell. In this case, it helps explain how the tensions between Aboriginal and non-Aboriginal people came to be, and why they are so hard to resolve.

Canadians know little about the peaceful and co-operative relationship that grew up between First Peoples and the first European visitors in the early years of contact. They know even less about how it changed, over the centuries, into something less honourable. In our report, we examine that history in some detail, for its ghosts haunt us still.

The ghosts take the form of dishonoured treaties, theft of Aboriginal lands, suppression of Aboriginal cultures, abduction of Aboriginal children, impoverishment and disempowerment of Aboriginal peoples. Yet at the beginning, no one could have predicted these results, for the theme of early relations was, for the most part, co-operation.

The relationship between Aboriginal and non-Aboriginal people evolved through four stages:

- There was a time when Aboriginal and non-Aboriginal people lived on separate continents and knew nothing of one another.
- Following the years of first contact, fragile relations of peace, friendship and rough equality were given the force of law in treaties.
- Then power tilted toward non-Aboriginal people and governments. They moved Aboriginal people off much of their land and took steps to "civilize" and teach them European ways.

- Finally, we reached the present stage—a time of recovery for Aboriginal people and cultures, a time for critical review of our relationship, and a time for its renegotiation and renewal.

Many of today's malfunctioning laws and institutions—the *Indian Act* and the break-up of nations into bands, to name just two—are remnants of the third stage of our history. But there was honour in history, too; indeed, the foundations of a fair and equitable relationship were laid in our early interaction. ...

TREATY MAKING

Treaty making among Aboriginal peoples dates back to a time long before Europeans arrived. Aboriginal nations treated among themselves to establish peace, regulate trade, share use of lands and resources, and arrange mutual defence. Through pipe smoking and other ceremonies, they gave these agreements the stature of sacred oaths.

European traditions of treaty making date to Roman times, but in the seventeenth century, they took on new importance. They became the means for the newborn states of Europe to control their bickering and warfare—indeed, to end it for long periods. Treaties were a way of recognizing each other's independence and sovereignty and a mark of mutual respect.

In the colonies that became Canada, the need for treaties was soon apparent. The land was vast, and the colonists were few in number. They feared the might of the Aboriginal nations surrounding them. Colonial powers were fighting wars for trade and dominance all over the continent. They needed alliances with Indian nations.

The British colonial government's approach to the treaties was schizophrenic. By signing, British authorities appeared to recognize the nationhood of Aboriginal peoples and their equality as nations. But they also expected First Nations to acknowledge the authority of the monarch and, increasingly, to cede large tracts of land to British control—for settlement and to protect it from seizure by other European powers or by the United States.

The Aboriginal view of the treaties was very different. They believed what the king's men told them, that the marks scratched on parchment captured the essence of their talks. They were angered and dismayed to discover later that what had been pledged in words, leader to leader, was not recorded accurately. They accepted the monarch, but only as a kind of kin figure, a distant "protector" who could be called on to safeguard their interests and enforce treaty agreements. They had no notion of giving up their land, a concept foreign to Aboriginal cultures.

> *In my language, there is no word for "surrender." There is no word. I cannot describe "surrender" to you in my language, so how do you expect my people to [have] put their X on "surrender"?*
>
> Chief Francois Paulette
> Treaty 8 Tribal Council, Yellowknife, Northwest Territories

... The purpose of the treaties, in Aboriginal eyes, was to work out ways of sharing lands and resources with settlers, without any loss of their own independence. But the representatives of the Crown had come to see the treaties merely as a tool for clearing Aboriginal people off desirable land.

To induce First Nations to sign, colonial negotiators continued to assure them that treaty provisions were not simply agreed, but *guaranteed* to them—for as long as the sun shone and the rivers flowed.

> *The fact is that when the settlers came, the Indians were there, organized in societies and occupying the land as their forefathers had done for centuries. This is what Indian title means …*
>
> Supreme Court of Canada
> Calder v. Attorney General of British Columbia *(1973)*

Stage 4: Renewal and Renegotiation

Policies of domination and assimilation battered Aboriginal institutions, sometimes to the point of collapse. Poverty, ill health and social disorganization grew worse. Aboriginal people struggled for survival as individuals, their nationhood erased from the public mind and almost forgotten by themselves.

Resistance to assimilation grew weak, but it never died away. In the fourth stage of the relationship, it caught fire and began to grow into a political movement. One stimulus was the federal government's White Paper on Indian Policy, issued in 1969.

The White Paper proposed to abolish the *Indian Act* and all that remained of the special relationship between Aboriginal people and Canada—offering instead what it termed *equality*. First Nations were nearly unanimous in their rejection. They saw this imposed form of "equality" as a coffin for their collective identities—the end of their existence as distinct peoples. Together with Inuit and Métis, they began to realize the full significance of their survival in the face of sustained efforts to assimilate them. They began to see their struggle as part of a worldwide human rights movement of Indigenous peoples. They began to piece together the legal case for their continuity as peoples—nations within Canada—and to speak out about it.

They studied their history and found evidence confirming that they have rights arising from the spirit and intent of their treaties and the *Royal Proclamation of 1763*. They took heart from decisions of Canadian courts, most since 1971, affirming their special relationship with the Crown and their unique interest in their traditional lands. They set about beginning to rebuild their communities and their nations with new-found purpose.

> *The relationship between the government and Aboriginals is trust-like rather than adversarial, and … contemporary recognition and affirmation of Aboriginal rights must be defined in light of this historic relationship.*
>
> Supreme Court of Canada
> R. v. Sparrow *(1990)*

The strong opposition of Aboriginal people to the White Paper's invitation to join mainstream society took non-Aboriginal people by surprise. The question of who Aboriginal people are and what their place is in Canada became central to national debate.

A dozen years of intense political struggle by Aboriginal people, including appeals to the Queen and the British Parliament, produced an historic breakthrough. "Existing Aboriginal and treaty rights" were recognized in the *Constitution Act, 1982*.

This set the stage for profound change in the relationship among the peoples of Canada, a change that most governments have nevertheless found difficult to embrace.

The Way Forward

The policies of the past have failed to bring peace and harmony to the relationship between Aboriginal peoples and other Canadians. Equally, they have failed to bring contentment or prosperity to Aboriginal people.

In poll after poll, Canadians have said that they want to see justice done for Aboriginal people, but they have not known how. In the following chapters, we outline a powerful set of interlinked ideas for moving forward.

In the years since the White Paper, Canadian governments have been prodded into giving Aboriginal communities more local control. They have included more Aboriginal people in decision making and handed over bits and pieces of the administrative apparatus that continues to shape Aboriginal lives.

But governments have so far refused to recognize the continuity of Aboriginal nations and the need to permit their decolonization at last. By their actions, if not their words, governments continue to block Aboriginal nations from assuming the broad powers of governance that would permit them to fashion their own institutions and work out their own solutions to social, economic and political problems. It is this refusal that effectively blocks the way forward.

The new partnership we envision is much more than a political or institutional one. It must be a heartfelt commitment among peoples to live together in peace, harmony and mutual support.

For this kind of commitment to emerge from the current climate of tension and distrust, it must be founded in visionary principles. It must also have practical mechanisms to resolve accumulated disputes and regulate the daily workings of the relationship.

We propose four principles as the basis of a renewed relationship.

1. **Recognition**

   The principle of mutual recognition calls on non-Aboriginal Canadians to recognize that Aboriginal people are the original inhabitants and caretakers of this land and have distinctive rights and responsibilities flowing from that status. It calls on Aboriginal people to accept that non-Aboriginal people are also of this land now, by birth and by adoption, with strong ties of love and loyalty. It requires both sides to acknowledge and relate to one another as partners, respecting each other's laws and institutions and co-operating for mutual benefit.

2. **Respect**

   The principle of respect calls on all Canadians to create a climate of positive mutual regard between and among peoples. Respect provides a bulwark against attempts by one partner to dominate or rule over another. Respect for the unique rights and status of First Peoples, and for each Aboriginal person as an individual with a valuable culture and heritage, needs to become part of Canada's national character.

3. **Sharing**

The principle of sharing calls for the giving and receiving of benefits in fair measure. It is the basis on which Canada was founded, for if Aboriginal peoples had been unwilling to share what they had and what they knew about the land, many of the newcomers would not have lived to prosper. The principle of sharing is central to the treaties and central to the possibility of real equality among the peoples of Canada in the future.

4. **Responsibility**

Responsibility is the hallmark of a mature relationship. Partners in such a relationship must be accountable for the promises they have made, accountable for behaving honourably, and accountable for the impact of their actions on the well-being of the other. Because we do and always will share the land, the best interests of Aboriginal and non-Aboriginal people will be served if we act with the highest standards of responsibility, honesty and good faith toward one another.

> *The Six Nations of the Iroquois Confederacy have described the spirit of the relationship as they see it in the image of a silver covenant chain. "Silver is sturdy and does not easily break," they say. "It does not rust and deteriorate with time. However, it does become tarnished. So when we come together, we must polish the chain, time and again, to restore our friendship to its original brightness."*
>
> *Chief Jacob E. Thomas*
> *Cayuga First Nation, Haudenosaunee (Iroquois) Confederacy*

We propose that treaties be the mechanism for turning principles into practice. Over several hundred years, treaty making has been used to keep the peace and share the wealth of Canada. Existing treaties between Aboriginal and non-Aboriginal people, however dusty from disuse, contain specific terms that even now help define the rights and responsibilities of the signatories toward one another.

We maintain that new and renewed treaties can be used to give substance to the four principles of a just relationship.

Canada—A Pioneer in the Management of Constitutional Politics in a Multi-national Society

Peter H. Russell (2000)

EDITORS' INTRODUCTION

Peter Russell is a widely published scholar on constitutional, judicial, and Aboriginal politics. He taught political science at the University of Toronto from 1958 to 1996 and has served as president of the Canadian Political Science Association, the Canadian Law and Society Association, and the Churchill Society for the Advancement of Parliamentary Democracy. The following essay was originally presented at an international conference on constitutional reform in North America at the University of Augsberg in Germany.

It is Canada's fate to have become a pioneer in managing a very challenging type of constitutional politics. This is the constitutional politics of a democratic political community among whose people there are very different senses of national allegiance and identity. In such a society the big background issue of constitutional politics always is: can these people or peoples constitute a political community?

Canada's engagement in this kind of constitutional politics has come about not through rational choice or abstract philosophy. We have stumbled into this situation without fully realizing what we were doing. Even now many Canadians, perhaps even a majority—especially in "English Canada" and among new immigrants—would not accept my characterization of Canada as a multi-national society. They yearn for a Canada with a single sense of national identity. In effect, they yearn for a different Canada than the one in which they find themselves. Indeed, their very sense of unease about our disunity is an important element in Canada's constitutional restlessness.

In large measure we Canadians stumbled into the situation we find ourselves in through incomplete conquests. In the eighteenth century, the British did not complete their conquest of New France by expelling the Canadiens as they had earlier done with the Acadians. Nor did they carry through with a program of forced assimilation of French Catholics into their English/Protestant culture. Within 15 years of the conquest they recognized the conquered people's religion and civil law. The British did not do this out of any profound philosophical commitment to political or cultural pluralism. They did it mainly as a strategy for securing the loyalty of the Canadiens at a time when the Empire was threatened with rebellion in the

Source: *The Politics of Constitutional Reform in North America: Coping with New Challenges*, edited by Rainer-Olaf Schlutze and Roland Sturm. Opladen, Germany: Leske + Budrich Publishers, 2000. Reprinted by permission.

American colonies to the south. Nonetheless it was a decisive move towards a deeply pluralist Canada and Empire.

The absence of any commitment to cultural pluralism was evident again in the nineteenth century when British constitutionalists responded to rebellions in their two Canadian provinces. Lord Durham's plan was to assimilate the French Canadians into the English culture which he believed would soon dominate a reunited Canada. But the Québécois defeated this effort by surviving with their own sense of identity and forcing a federal constitutional solution with a province in which they as a majority would have enough political power to secure the essential elements of their distinct society.

The other incomplete conquest concerns the Indigenous peoples. In the seventeenth and eighteenth centuries the British (like the French) for military and commercial reasons entered into treaty-like agreements with Aboriginal nations. The Royal Proclamation of 1763 which set out British policy for governing the lands ceded by France at the end of the Seven Years War recognized the Indian nations' possession of territory outside the settled British colonies and laid down that settlement in this territory could take place only on lands that were sold or ceded by the Indians to the Crown. The Royal Proclamation, though often ignored in the nineteenth and twentieth centuries, survives as part of Canada's constitutional law. In 1982 its primacy was acknowledged in section 25 of the new *Canadian Charter of Rights and Freedoms*.

In Canada as in the United States once the settlers clearly had the upper hand militarily and demographically, treaty-like relations with Indigenous peoples gave way to colonial domination. Still there is an important difference between the two countries. In Canada right up into the twentieth century, treaties were the principal means for acquiring new lands from the Indians for settlement and economic development in much of Ontario, the western prairies, north-eastern British Columbia and part of the Northwest Territories. While the practical impact of these treaties was massive dispossession, nonetheless they did entail recognition by the incoming settler state of the Aboriginal signatories' nationhood and their collective ownership of traditional lands. The United States also made hundreds of treaties with Indian nations and through Chief Justice John Marshall's jurisprudence accorded Indian peoples the status of "domestic, dependent nations." However, soon after the Civil War, Congress abolished all future treaty-making. The American west was won from the Indians through brutal warfare rather than duplicitous treaties.

The continuity of treaty relationships with Aboriginal peoples in Canada has had important consequences for the present day. In the 1960s and 70s, a resurgence of Aboriginal nationalism induced the federal government to abandon its program of assimilation and resume the process of making agreements with native peoples who continue to occupy their traditional lands. Taking advantage of the constitutional restructuring brought on by Québec nationalism, Aboriginal peoples were able to have their rights, including treaty rights, recognized in the *Constitution Act* of 1982. Federal and provincial governments in Canada now recognize Aboriginal peoples as "First Nations" and are engaged, all across the country, in a process of negotiating self-government agreements with them, as well as with the Métis nation and Inuit peoples.

It is the persistence over centuries of the Québécois and the Indigenous peoples of Canada in insisting on their recognition as distinct peoples or nations that obliges Canada, if it is to survive with its present borders and population, to manage the constitutional affairs of a multi-national community. Let us be clear that what is at issue here is not simply a multi-cultural state but a multi-national state. Virtually every state in the world is in fact multi-cultural and acknowledges this, in varying degrees, in its laws and policies. Canada goes much further with multi-culturalism than most, extending financial support and encouragement to many ethnic minorities besides French-speaking Canadians and Aboriginal peoples. Functioning as a multi-national political community means something much more difficult and problematic than multi-culturalism. It means, in the Canadian case, acknowledging that two groups, French Canadians and Indigenous peoples, are not just cultural minorities but political societies with the special rights of homeland peoples to maintain political jurisdictions in which they can ensure their survival as distinct peoples.

Most of the Canadian citizens who belong to these "nations within" have a dual sense of national identity. In varying degrees most Aboriginal Canadians and French-speaking Québecers identify with Canada as well as with their own historic nations—though they may be reluctant to recognize Canada as "their nation." Alongside them, the majority of Canadians acknowledge Canada as their nation—their only nation—and in varying degrees despair of accommodating the "nations within." Managing the constitutional affairs of a population with such conflicting and incoherent notions of national identity is not just Canada's challenge but the challenge of many areas in the world today where some kind of national autonomy within a larger political community is the main alternative to the splintering of states or international conflict. That is why Canada's fortunes in dealing with this challenge bear watching.

Throughout its first century the Canadian federation had very few constitutional affairs to manage. The Confederation Constitution was based on an agreement between English and French Canadian politicians laden with ambiguity and conflicting expectations about the future of the federation. Indigenous peoples were included only as mute subjects of the new central government. Constitutional sovereignty—the power to amend the constitutional text—remained in the hands of the British Parliament. The federation grew and its structure evolved without any grand attempts to settle or accommodate constitutional differences. The main developments were the strengthening of provincial rights, a very strong commitment to a federal ethic, the confining of French Canada primarily to Québec, and concerted efforts by the federal government, despite the treaty process, to assimilate native peoples into what was fervently believed to be the superior culture of the Europeans.

Canadians did not become embroiled in constitutional politics until after World War II when federal politicians—French as well as English—moved by a sense of Canadian nationalism became determined to terminate Canada's constitutional colonialism and "patriate" the country's Constitution. They then confronted the unresolved ambiguities and differences about the nature of Canada as a political community. For transferring the power to amend the Constitution from Britain to Canada meant deciding who or what in Canada—which government or governments, which people or peoples—would be constitutionally sovereign. By the mid-1960s it was becoming clear that this grand issue—a mega issue in constitutional politics if ever there was one—would not be easy to resolve. A secular nationalism was also now moving many French Québecers to insist that patriation, the fulfillment of Canadian nationhood, should take place only if the position of Québec as the homeland of a nation within Canada was more strongly and explicitly secured in the Canadian Constitution. The result, of course, of this collision of nationalisms and constitutional visions was an entire generation of very heavy constitutional politics—what I have called "mega constitutional politics."

Fear not—I am not about to take you through the many chapters of this seemingly endless constitutional struggle—the Victoria Charter, Trudeau's initiatives, the 1980 Québec referendum, Patriation, the conferences with Aboriginal peoples, Meech Lake, the Charlottetown Accord, the 1995 Québec referendum and all of that. If you want details, there are many books written about all of these events, including one of my own (Russell 1993). (Indeed, I am in no position to complain about the struggle as I have truly dined out on it—in Canada and around the world). But I do wish to reflect on its outcome, and what we can learn from the experience about constitutionalism in societies that are deeply divided in a multi-national sense.

The first thing to observe is that after a generation of constitutional wrangling Canadians are no closer to resolving explicitly in formal constitutional terms the big issues that divide them. Important constitutional changes were made in 1982—patriation, a constitutional bill of rights and constitutional recognition of Aboriginal rights. But Prime Minister Trudeau's government forced these changes through over the opposition of Québec's provincial government and most of Canada's Aboriginal leaders. This led to the subsequent constitutional efforts—the inconclusive First Ministers' Conferences with Aboriginal leaders, the defeat of the Meech Lake Accord designed to accommodate Québec and the referendum defeat of the Charlottetown Accord designed to accommodate everyone. The miracle is not that this latter effort failed but that it came so close to succeeding!

At the end of all this, many observers of our constitutional scene would conclude that the Canadian political community is more deeply divided than it was at the beginning of this constitutional struggle. In the light of the nearly 50–50 split in the 1995 Québec referendum, the same might be said of Québec as a political community. And, as the Nisga'a Treaty with its provision for an Aboriginal nation to exercise a real share of law-making sovereignty in Canada runs into stiff opposition among non-Aboriginal Canadians, there is no sign of a clear consensus on the future of Aboriginal peoples in Canada. The one point on which Canadians are now constitutionally united is their exhaustion with contesting constitutional issues. It is this feeling of constitutional exhaustion that may in the end persuade Québec sovereignists not to proceed with yet another referendum. These failed efforts at reaching a constitutional consensus in Canada did succeed in changing one important feature of Canada's constitutional culture: they democratized it. Making the written Constitution the most important political issue in the country for a generation, talking about the Constitution as ideally a vision of our society, a mirror in which all Canadians can see themselves, a document inscribing what we are all about—all of this convinced the Canadian public that they must have a crucial say in making any important changes in the Constitution. Political elites may still play the lead role in negotiating and drafting constitutional proposals—that much of constitutional democracy remains intact. But for proposals for fundamental constitutional change to be legitimate in Canada they must now be ratified by the people voting in referendums.

This democratization of Canada's constitutional process has not been written into the country's Constitution—though it has been incorporated into the constitutional systems of Québec, the three western-most provinces and several Aboriginal nations. Nonetheless, I believe that for major constitutional changes in the structure of our federal institutions or the structure of the federation, in the status of Indigenous peoples, or in the *Charter of Rights and Freedoms*, a Canadian wide referendum would be a political imperative for all. For this reason Bruce Ryder and I in a paper on "Ratifying a Post-referendum Agreement on Québec Sovereignty" (Ryder/Russell 1997) argued that, if after a sovereignist win in a Québec referendum, federal, provincial and Aboriginal leaders negotiated an agreement on a fundamental change in Québec's constitutional status, their agreement would have to be submitted to a Canada-wide referendum.

At a very abstract philosophical level, a compelling case can be made for this democratization of the constitutional process: in a constitutional democracy, after all, shouldn't the people be sovereign and have the final say on their highest law, the Constitution? The trouble with applying this simple principle of popular sovereignty to a multi-national society like Canada is the absence of an agreement on who the sovereign people are or on how that will can be identified. Québec sovereignists would say the people of Québec are sovereign and a majority of them express the people's will. This view is repudiated by federalists within and outside Québec, many of whom would argue that some majority of Canadians—simple or extraordinary—is sovereign in Canada. Most Aboriginal people do not believe their nations ever surrendered their sovereignty—though they might have difficulty agreeing on how that sovereignty is expressed in the present context.

Thus in the Canadian case—and I would submit in other multi-national communities—that first step in the Lockean social contract whereby all consent to form a single sovereign people to be governed by an agreed upon political authority has not and may never be taken. In a setting such as this attempts at grand constitutional settlements are much more likely to exacerbate than to resolve societal conflict.

The recipe for managing constitutional affairs that this analysis yields is not one of constitutional *immobilisme*. One of the worst myths haunting Canada's constitutional affairs is that the only alternative to a grand resolution of constitutional issues is a constitutional deep-freeze. Through the 1990s since the demise of the Charlottetown Accord important changes have been taking place in the operation of our constitution. Changes in the roles and responsibilities of government in our federal system have occurred without formal constitutional amendment. Some of this was consolidated in a political agreement on the Social Union. The parties to this agreement were the federal government and all of the Canadian provinces except Québec. In this agreement, the provinces for the first time acknowledge the legitimacy of the federal government using its spending power to support initiatives in areas of exclusive provincial jurisdiction, and in exchange the federal government agrees to launch such shared-cost or block-funded programs only with the agreement of a majority of provincial governments.

Québec's non-participation in the Social Union agreement demonstrates the strength and limitation of this kind of change. In effect it underlines Québec's special status in the Canadian federation without requiring that Canadians agree on explicit recognition of this special status in the constitutional text—an agreement that would probably be impossible to secure.

Progress has also been made in reforming Aboriginal relations. The Royal Commission on Aboriginal Peoples—the first collaborative inquiry in world history of indigenous and non-indigenous people into the past, present and future of their mutual relationship—has mapped out the path to a post-colonial relationship through treaty-like agreements on land

and governance. Through such an agreement, Nunavut, the homeland of the Eastern Arctic Inuit, is now up and running as a new self-governing territory of Canada. Treaty negotiations on land and governance issues are currently under way at approximately 80 different "tables" in every part of Canada. The Supreme Court of Canada's 1997 decision in *Delgamuukw* confirming Aboriginal peoples' ownership and control of their traditional, unsurrendered lands gave strong legal backing to this modern treaty process.

Popular support for this process of recognizing Aboriginal nations as self-governing nations within Canada is, however, shaky. Many non-Aboriginal commentators in the popular media are shocked to learn that under the Nisga'a Agreement the Nisga'a people besides being citizens of Canada will be recognized as citizens of the Nisga'a nation and that the Nisga'a government will have supreme law-making authority on matters such as their own constitution, language and culture, the education of their children and the management of the 10% of their traditional lands and resources recognized in the Agreement as belonging to them. Similar provisions are contained in other agreements now being negotiated across the country. The Nisga'a people have ratified the agreement and a very unpopular British Columbian government has pushed it through the British Columbia legislature. It is now before the federal parliament which must also approve it before it becomes law. The Chrétien government having been a party to the treaty and with a majority in the House of Commons will ensure its safe passage, but not without an acrimonious political debate. If, as the opposition urged, the Nisga'a Agreement had been put to a referendum in B.C., it would very likely have been rejected. The Nisga'a agreement, the product of over twenty years of negotiations, is inevitably a compromise. It is bitterly attacked by native critics as giving up too much land and self-government, just as many non-Aboriginal Canadians question it for going too far the other way. In constitutional referendum campaigns fought through the mass media, nay-sayers have an easier time standing on the high ground of pure principle and scaremongering about change than do the defenders of grubby compromise.

Thus we Canadians limp along adjusting constitutional relationships in our multi-national political community without definitively settling the question of who or what we are, and without any clear popular consensus on the nature of the country expressed in the text of our constitution. The lesson we may have taught ourselves, and perhaps other deeply divided political communities, is that it is best not to try reaching a grand and explicit popular agreement on fundamental constitutional principles. As a number of our constitutional commentators have observed, abeyance and avoidance of intractable abstract questions such as the locus of sovereignty and the identity of the nation are conditions of constitutional peace in Canada. Of course, there are some who do not want peace. The most militant of these are the Québec sovereignists. They, by definition, do not accept that sovereignty should be shared. And despite constitutional exhaustion, they may yet force the issue. If they do have another referendum, and if they win it (whatever "winning" means), I am not sure what the final outcome will be—a totally independent Québec, a Québec in some new partnership relation with Canada or the status quo. However, I am fairly certain of one thing which is that in a newly configured Canada or an independent Québec with its present borders, as in Canada as it now is, sovereignty will in fact be shared among peoples, and there will once again be a need to practice the quiet and delicate constitutional arts of sharing sovereignty in a multi-national society.

Canada as a Multinational Democracy

James Tully (2001)

EDITORS' INTRODUCTION

James Tully is a Distinguished Research Professor at the University of Victoria. He has also taught at McGill University and the University of Toronto. Tully has gained worldwide recognition for his work in re-examining liberal political philosophy. He is also a leading scholar on democratic governance in an age of diversity, including the emergence of multinational states. In 2001, Tully and Professor Alain-G. Gagnon of McGill University co-edited the first full study of multinational democracies. Reproduced is a section of James Tully's introduction to that book.

The "Problematization" of the Constitutional Identity of a Multinational Society by Struggles over Recognition

A Multinational Society

Canada is described as a "free and democratic society" in section I of the Canadian *Charter of Rights and Freedoms*. For the purposes of this Introduction, a "multinational society" or "multinational democracy" is a type of "free and democratic society" which includes more than one "nation," or, more accurately, more than one "member" of the society demands recognition as a nation or nations. In the case of Canada, the present government of Quebec and many of the citizens demand recognition as a nation and the present leaders of the indigenous or "aboriginal" peoples and the majority of aboriginal people demand recognition as "first nations" or "indigenous peoples." For the sake of brevity, I will sometimes write simply that "Quebec" and the "aboriginal peoples of Canada" demand recognition as a nation and as first nations respectively. I mean by this shorthand that a majority of Quebecers and aboriginal people support these demands. A member of a multinational society that demands recognition as a nation may itself be a multinational society. Quebec, with eleven aboriginal peoples in and across its borders demanding recognition as first nations, is a multinational democracy.

To investigate the features of a free, multinational democracy let us start (not uncritically) from the classic liberal account of a reasonably plural, free and democratic society presented by John Rawls, in *Political Liberalism* (1996), and its careful and innovative extension by Anthony Laden, in *Reasonably Radical: Deliberative Liberalism and the Politics of Identity* (2001), to free and democratic, multicultural and multinational societies. Rawls and Laden

Source: Excerpted from *Multinational Democracies*, edited by Alain-G. Gagnon and James Tully. Cambridge: Cambridge University Press, 2001. Notes omitted. Reprinted with the permission of Cambridge University Press.

describe a free and democratic society as one that has a high degree of self-sufficiency and a place for all the main purposes of human life (Rawls 1996, pp. 40–3). A multinational society, like all free and democratic societies, meets these conditions. Moreover, a multinational society, like all free and democratic societies, is a fair system of social, political and economic cooperation in the broad and thick sense given to this phrase by Rawls. It is the congeries of democratic practices in which we acquire, exercise, question and modify our identities as national and multinational citizens (Rawls 1996, pp. 15–22, 41, 222, 269; Laden 2001, chs. 5–8).

"Cooperation" is more than socially coordinated action. "Cooperation is guided by publicly recognized rules and procedures that those cooperating accept and regard as properly regulating their conduct." Cooperation also involves the idea of "fair terms of cooperation"—"these are terms that every participant may reasonably accept, provided that everyone else likewise accepts them" (Rawls 1996, p. 16). The fair terms of cooperation apply to the basic structure of the society, to its political, economic and social institutions, and they are expressed in the constitutional principles of the society (Rawls 1996, pp. 257–8, 269–71; cp. SC 1998, paras. 50, 54). Accordingly, a demand for recognition as a nation or nations and its mode of institutional accommodation within a multinational society must be compatible with conditions of a fair system of social cooperation, or what the Supreme Court of Canada calls "unity," to be acceptable. Conversely, a demand for recognition is often supported by the claim that the prevailing terms of cooperation or unity are unacceptable in some respect, for example in the case of both Quebec and indigenous peoples.

A free and democratic society, whether multinational or uninational, is "free" in two relevant senses. The members of the society are free and the society as a whole is free. That is, the members of the society not only act democratically within the rules and procedures of cooperation; they also impose the rules on themselves and alter the rules and procedures democratically *en passant*. Such a society is "self-governing" or "self-determining," not in the radical sense that its members will into being the conditions of association. Rather, the members are free to either accept the conditions of association or enter into democratic negotiations to change the conditions that can be shown to be unjust; or, if the second of these options is blocked, to initiate the option to negotiate exit (SC 1998, paras. 83–105, 111–39). This is one of the most widely accepted principles of legitimacy in the modern world: for example, (1) of a liberal society as a fair system of social, political and economic cooperation, i.e. the rules are freely accepted and regarded as appropriate by the participants themselves (Rawls 1996, p. 16); (2) of "self-determination" as it is predicated of free societies or "peoples" in international law (SC 1998, paras. 111–39); and (3) of a free and democratic society in which the sovereign people or peoples impose the rules of the association on themselves as they obey those rules (Habermas 1998, pp. 49–74, 129–54, 253–64; Rawls 1996, pp. 396–409). The rules and procedures are neither imposed from the outside nor from an undemocratic element within. A member "nation" seeking recognition within the larger society itself will be free and democratic in these two senses as well, on pain of a performative contradiction (Tully 2000b).

A "nation" is a "people" with the right of self-determination. A multinational society is a "people" composed of peoples, a multi-peoples society or a multination. The multinational democracies studied in this volume have been recognized as self-determining, single nations or peoples by international law for centuries. The nations that demand recognition within multinational societies also and *eo ipso* demand recognition as "peoples." The terms "nations" and "peoples" have been used in overlapping ways over the last two hundred years and they are used interchangeably in discussions over, say, the Quebec "people" or "nation" and the "first nations" or "indigenous peoples." Since I wish to focus on the conditions of freedom and recognition in multinational societies, the concept of a people with the right of self-determination is appropriate, rather than the concept of a nation, which is appropriate for issues of nationalism.

A multinational society is usually but not always a federation. Israel and New Zealand, for example, are binational but not federal. I will concentrate on multinational federal societies because I wish to draw on Canada and because they are more complex than non-federal multinational societies. If we can clarify the main features of freedom and recognition in multinational federations, the non-federal cases should not be difficult. A federation is a society in which democratic self-government is distributed in such a way that citizens "participate concurrently in different collectivities" (SC 1998, para. 66)—in the democratic institutions of the society as a whole and of the federated members, such as provinces, states, nations or first nations. A "confederation," in contrast, is an association, not a society, in which citizens participate only in their "nation," not in the multinational confederation as a whole. The problem of multinational recognition in a confederation is correspondingly less complex and can be set aside for now.

Four Dimensions of Constitutional Identity

When a demand for the recognition of one or more nations or peoples arises in a multinational democracy, it "problematizes" the constitutional identity of the society. That is, the demand renders problematic the current (single-nation) constitutional identity of the society and proposes a change. Various solutions are then proposed to the problem in theory and practice. Looking back over fifty years of experience, three conflicting types of solution are standardly proposed around which citizens and governments mobilize: (1) defence of the status quo, with or without a degree of sub-constitutional change, (2) various forms of recognition of the nation or nations by changing the current constitutional identity, and (3) secession of the nation or nations and recognition as a new independent nation or nations, with or without some relation to the former society. As we see from the studies in this collection, each of the three types of strategic solution is defined by an evolving structure of argument which presents reasons for the justice and stability of its solution and the injustice and instability of the other two. Call the whole—including the reasons and causes of the demand, the proposals and solutions, the public discussions and negotiations, or refusals to negotiate, the amendments of the constitution and institutional changes, and the demands for recognition that this amendment in turn provokes—the "problematization" of the constitutional identity of a multinational democracy (Foucault 1984, p. 389 and Tully 1999b for the concept of problematization).

The "constitutional identity" of a multinational society, as of any free and democratic society, is its "basic constitutional structure," what I called above the publicly recognized and accepted rules and procedures by which the members of the society recognize each other and coordinate their cooperation. In the words of the Supreme Court of Canada, the constitution "embraces unwritten, as well as written rules," and includes "the global system of rules and principles which govern the exercise of constitutional authority" (Supreme Court 1998, para. 32). The constitution is the present system of rules of mutual recognition that gives a society its constitutional identity.

There are four major dimensions of the constitutional identity of a democratic society. First, a constitution recognizes the *members* of a society under their respective identities and enumerates their rights, duties and powers. For example, the Canadian constitution recognizes "citizens" with their rights, freedoms and duties, various types of "minorities" (linguistic, cultural, and individuals or groups disadvantaged because of race, ethnic origin, colour, religion, sex, age and mental or physical disability), "territories," "aboriginal peoples" and their rights, "provinces" with their legislative powers, the federation and its federal legislature, and the Canadian society as a whole. Second dimension, a constitution stipulates the *relations of governance* among the members, the rules and procedures that guide their conduct as members of a fair system of social cooperation (the totality of laws and regulations). Third, the constitution lays out a set of procedures and institutions of *discussion and alteration* of prevailing relations of governance over time. In Canada, these include the rights of public discussion, debate, assembly, voting, strike and dissent, courts, legislatures, procedures of federal-provincial renegotiation, the notwithstanding clause, treaty negotiations among first nations and federal and provincial governments, and procedures for amending the constitution. Fourth, the constitution includes the *principles, values and goods* that are brought to bear on the identification of members, the relations among them, and the discussion and alteration of their identities and relations over time. These principles, values and goods do not form a determinate and ordered set of principles of justice to which all the members agree. Rather, they are many, none is trump, different ones are brought to bear in different cases, and there is reasonable disagreement and contestation about which ones are relevant and how they should be applied in any case (SC 1998, paras. 49–54). Indeed, part of what makes the society free and democratic is reasonable disagreement among the members and their political traditions of liberalism, conservatism, socialism, republicanism, feminism, nationalism, multiculturalism, environmentalism and so on (Rawls 1999, pp. 140–3). These principles, values and goods comprise the public, normative warrants members appeal to in exchanging reasons over the justice and stability of their conflicting demands for and against recognition in any case (Rawls 1999, pp. 129–80; Laden 2001, chs. 5–7).

In cases of the recognition of nations in multinational societies, there are seven relevant principles. Following the Supreme Court, four principles are necessary (but not sufficient) to the "reconciliation of diversity with unity" in cases of multinationalism: the principles of federalism, democracy, the rule of law and constitutionalism, and the protection of minorities (SC 1998, paras. 32, 49, 55–82). In thin liberal democratic theories, two principles—democracy and rule of law—are said to be coequal and jointly sufficient for legitimacy (Habermas 1998, pp. 253–64). However, this is sufficient only for a subset of modern societies, those that are non-federal and do not acknowledge the protection of minorities as an independent principle.

In addition, three basic principles are indispensable to any free and democratic society: freedom, equality and distinctness. Free and equal are widely endorsed principles. By "freedom" I mean not only the freedoms associated with private autonomy (the freedom of the moderns), but also, and of primary concern in this case, the freedom associated with public autonomy, the democratic freedoms of members to participate in their society in the twofold sense explained in the section above. "Equality" includes not only the relatively uncontentious formal equality associated with thin liberal democracy, but also the substantive equality associated with thicker liberal societies (such as Rawls' "difference principle") and with social democracy (for example, social and economic rights for citizens and groups, and equalization transfers for provinces) (SC 1998, para. 64). Finally, it includes the equality of peoples. Members standardly disagree over the ranking, interpretation and application of these three aspects of equality.

Finally, members not only recognize each other as free and equal but also as the bearers of "distinct" or, as the Supreme Court puts it, "diverse identities" (SC 1998, paras. 43, 58, 59, 60, 74, 79–82). The freedom of expression of individual citizens, the principle of non-discrimination, equity policies, proportional representation, the protection of individual and group identities, languages and cultures, aboriginal rights, self-government and some federal arrangements (such as the special provisions for Quebec) are often justified in part by the principle of diversity or distinctness. Again, support varies and is contested, but public recognition of some forms of diversity and of "identity-related differences" is both unavoidable (language and culture being the most obvious examples) and good, either in itself or as a means to other goods, such as mutual respect.

PART 2

Representative Democracy

Introduction

Canadian democracy continues to be marked by its colonial heritage and by the gap between the theory and the actual practices of governance. One reason for this is that under the principle of parliamentary democracy (which stems from the Westminster tradition in the United Kingdom), and as that principle has evolved, executive power has increased, at the expense of legislative power. The result is that the prime minister and his office (the PMO) now have a greater capacity for action than ever before.

Historically, Parliament has been the basis for legitimizing political authority, and elections have been the means for the population to designate those who represent them; however, the strong party discipline and ministerial solidarity that characterize the Canadian political system largely limit the initiatives of members of Parliament who are not part of the executive. Moreover, Canada's electoral system, also of British heritage, has had a tendency to create majority governments, thus fostering the relative stability of Canadian governance. Additionally, the alternation between only two federal political parties, the Liberals and the Conservatives, contrasts sharply with territorial and societal representation in the parliamentary system. The result is an unequal representation of electoral preferences and an exacerbation of interregional tensions. The authors of the selections in this part will question the characteristics of the party system in Canada, the electoral system, and the manner in which the political system responds more or less appropriately to electoral expectations.

The first piece predates Confederation. It is a letter sent in 1858 to the Colonial Office in London, laying out a vision for Canada's governance. Many will be surprised to read that our Fathers of Confederation articulated to the British government a plan that was distinctly non-democratic in flavour, no doubt believing their campaign would be best served by distancing themselves from an American-style constitutional design.

Moving ahead to modern Canada, Alan C. Cairns discusses the major effects of the electoral system on the party system. Notably, he was one of the first to argue that political parties have not played an integrative role, nor have they answered Canadian expectations with regard to representation. The capacity of the party system to integrate different communities in Canada is compromised due to the effects of the electoral system, which reinforces the multiple divisions present within Canadian society. Adopting a different perspective that emphasizes broader social considerations, John Meisel explains why political parties are increasingly less capable of fulfilling their traditional functions, and furthermore, he examines how they have become impotent actors in relation to economic and social transformations.

In addition, the Cabinet is generally considered to be the centre of executive power. In a later piece, Donald J. Savoie calls this assumption into question. Rather, he argues that power has simultaneously escaped from the Cabinet and Parliament, as it has become increasingly concentrated in the hands of the prime minister and his immediate entourage. This concentration of power reinforces the prime minister's maneuverability, which resembles monarchical authority; this has a considerable impact on other dimensions of the state, notably the public service's performance, ministerial responsibility, and Parliament's capacity to hold the government accountable.

Lisa Young tackles the question of the advancement of responsible government, which was created out of the necessity to assure party cohesion and party discipline with the intent of reinforcing governmental stability. In this dynamic, the principle of responsible government and the functioning of political parties are mutually reinforcing. She suggests that the institutions of responsible government are less appropriate for responding to contemporary challenges than they were at the time of their installation in the 19th century. This is due to the fact that citizens now place more importance on representative government than on responsible government. This question was central to our political reality in early 2009, when the opposition parties sought to replace the minority government of Prime Minister Stephen Harper with a coalition government. Although this initiative was eventually aborted, it brought this important debate on the themes of responsible government versus representative government into the public domain. Writings by the late Eugene Forsey recall the role of the governor-general in the process of government dissolution, reminding us of the significance given to the notion of responsible government before the House of Commons. In an opinion piece published in the *Globe and Mail*, Tom Flanagan explains how the project of coalition government would go against democratic norms. In response, a group of academics drafted a letter that appeared in *Le Devoir* and the *Toronto Star*, maintaining that the procedures leading to the installation of such a government are consistent with the principle of responsible government. One could not find a better illustration of the conflicting interpretations of our form of democratic government.

Two pieces in this collection tackle a central question in political science, asking: "Who governs?" Grace Skogstad identifies the different sources and principles of political authority and evaluates their implications for effectiveness and legitimacy in contemporary Canada. The problem, she says, lies in the fact that citizens increasingly demand that political authorities take their points of view into account in a context where their power is increasingly diffused due to globalizing processes, and as authority shifts toward independent and private experts. Keeping with the subjects of governance and direct participation in collective rule making, Manon Tremblay and Linda Trimble interrogate the presence of women in politics. They compare the backgrounds, political experiences, and characteristics of men and women sitting in the House of Commons over the course of the 20th century, and demonstrate that gender continues to play a significant role. As the experience of women in politics continues to be different from that of men, they find there has not been much convergence. Apart from that, the Canadian electoral system continues to be hostile toward female candidates; once elected, they do not often occupy similar functions province-to-province, and their roles are often minimal.

Two pieces discuss the party system in Canada and its evolution. In "A New Canadian Party System," R.K. Carty, William Cross, and Lisa Young examine recent transformations and discuss a possible transition toward a new party system characterized by the rise of regional parties, regionalization of partisan politics, fragmentation of the electorate, democratization within each party, and increasing diversity between parties. From a political economy perspective, Janine Brodie and Jane Jenson are interested in the absence of a "pervasive class-based voting" process in Canadian politics. They highlight how claims between parties have had the effect of discrediting the centrality of class differences, which, though they remain at the heart of capitalist systems, have frequently been pushed into the background by political definitions that concentrate on tensions between linguistic, religious, and regional groups.

Further Suggested Reading

Louis Massicotte, "Electoral Reform in Canada." In André Blais, ed., *To Keep or to Change First Past the Post? The Politics of Electoral Reform.* Oxford and New York: Oxford University Press, 2008.

Matthew Mendelsohn and Andrew Parkin, "Introducing Direct Democracy in Canada." *Choices* 7(5). Montreal: Institute for Research on Public Policy, June 2001.

Henry Milner, *Making Every Vote Count: Reassessing Canada's Electoral System.* Peterborough, ON: Broadview Press, 1999.

Dennis Pilon, *The Politics of Voting: Reforming Canada's Electoral System.* Toronto: Emond Montgomery Publications, 2007.

Peter H. Russell, *Two Cheers for Minority Government: The Evolution of Canadian Parliamentary Democracy.* Toronto: Emond Montgomery Publications, 2008.

Donald Savoie, "The Federal Government: Revisiting Court Government in Canada." In Luc Bernier, Keith Brownsey, and Michael Howlett, eds., *Executive Styles in Canada: Cabinet Structures and Leadership Practices in Canadian Government.* Toronto: University of Toronto Press, 2005.

Leslie Seidle and Louis Massicotte, eds., *Taking Stock of Responsible Government in Canada.* Ottawa: Canadian Study of Parliament Group, 1999.

David E. Smith, *The People's House of Commons: Theories of Democracy in Contention.* Toronto: University of Toronto Press, 2007.

Jennifer Smith, "Democracy and the Canadian House of Commons at the Millennium." *Canadian Public Administration* 42(4), 1999.

11 "Not Derived from the People": Letter from the Fathers of Confederation to the British Colonial Secretary

Alexander Galt (1858)

EDITORS' INTRODUCTION

This letter, signed by three Fathers of Confederation but drafted primarily by Alexander Galt, contains what Peter Russell, in his book Constitutional Odyssey, *describes as "perhaps the most haunting lines in Canada's history." In their proposal to the Colonial Office in London, written just as the United States was moving inexorably toward a bloody civil war, Galt, George-Étienne Cartier, and John Ross took pains to point out that "the basis of Confederation now proposed differs from that of the United States in several important particulars. It does not profess to be derived from the people but would be the constitution provided by the imperial parliament, thus affording the means of remedying any defect."*

To British Colonial Secretary Edward Bulwer-Lytton.

London, 25th October, 1858.

Dear Sir Edward:

In the official communication which we have this day the honour to address to you, on the Confederation of the British North American provinces, we have felt it improper to offer any opinion upon the details which will form the subject of the proposed discussion by Delegates. It is also our duty not to cause embarrassment by advancing views which may yet have to be greatly modified. We venture, however, in compliance with your desire for a confidential communication on these points to suggest:

That the Federal Government should be composed of a Governor-General, or Viceroy, to be appointed by the Queen, of an Upper House or Senate elected upon a territorial basis of representation, and of a House of Assembly, elected on the basis of population, the Executive to be composed of ministers responsible to the legislature.

That the powers of the Federal legislators and Government should comprehend the Customs, Excise and all trade questions, Postal Service, Militia, Banking, Currency, Weights and Measures and Bankruptcy, Public Works of a National Character, Harbours and Lighthouses, Fisheries and their protection, Criminal justice, Public Lands, Public Debt and Government of unincorporated and Indian Territories. It will form a subject for mature deliberation whether the powers of the Federal Government should be confined to the points named, or should be extended to all matters and not specially entrusted to the local legislatures.

The Confederation might involve the constitution of a Federal Court of Appeal.

The general revenue, having first been charged with the expense of collection and civil government, to be subject to the payment of interest on the public debts of the Confederation to be constituted from the existing obligations of each—the surplus to be divided each year according to population. The net revenue from the Public Lands in each province to be its exclusive property, except in the case of the territories.

It may be expedient for a limited time to provide from the general revenue a certain fixed contribution for educational and judicial purposes until provision is made for the same by each member of the Confederation.

It will be observed that the basis of Confederation now proposed differs from that of the United States in several important particulars. It does not profess to be derived from the people but would be the constitution provided by the imperial parliament, thus affording the means of remedying any defect, which is now practically impossible under the American constitution. The local legislature would not be in a position to claim the exercise of the same sovereign powers which have frequently been the cause of difference between the American states and their general government. To this may be added that by the proposed distribution of the revenue each province would have a direct pecuniary interest in the preservation of the authority of the Federal Government. In these respects it is conceived that the proposed Confederation would possess greater inherent strength than that of the United States, and would combine the advantage of the unity for general purposes of a legislative union with so much of the Federation principle as would join all the benefits of local government and legislation upon questions of provincial interest. ...

G.E. Cartier.
JNO. Ross.
A.T. Galt.

12 The Electoral System and the Party System in Canada, 1921–1965

Alan C. Cairns (1968)

EDITORS' INTRODUCTION

Alan C. Cairns was a professor of political science at the University of British Columbia from 1960 to 1995, and a visiting scholar at numerous Canadian universities. He has published many works and articles on Canadian policy and the Constitution. He is an Officer of the Order of Canada and a Fellow of the Royal Society of Canada. This is a revised version of a paper presented in 1967 at the 39th annual meeting of the Canadian Political Science Association.

This paper investigates two common assumptions about the party system: (i) that the influence of the electoral system on the party system has been unimportant, or non-existent; and (ii) that the party system has been an important nationalizing agency with respect to the sectional cleavages widely held to constitute the most significant and enduring lines of division in the Canadian polity. Schattschneider, Lipset, Duverger, Key and others have cogently asserted the relevance of electoral systems for the understanding of party systems. Students of Canadian parties, however, have all but ignored the electoral system as an explanatory factor of any importance. The analysis to follow will suggest that the electoral system has played a major role in the evolution of Canadian parties, and that the claim that the party system has been an important instrument for integrating Canadians across sectional lines is highly suspect.

Discussion of the respective merits of single member constituency electoral systems and various systems of proportional representation is frequently indecisive because of an inability to agree on the values which electoral systems should serve. Advocates of proportional representation base their arguments on democratic fundamentalism. They simply argue that each vote should have equal weight, and that the distortion of the voters' preferences by single member constituency systems is no more to be justified than the use of false scales by a butcher. This idealistic argument is countered by the opponents of proportional representation with the assertion that executive stability is a more basic consideration, and that it is well served by the propensity of Canadian type systems to create artificial legislative majorities. This controversy will not concern us further.

Source: Excerpted from *Canadian Journal of Political Science*, vol. I, no. 1 (March 1968). Notes omitted. Reprinted by permisson.

It may be noted, however, that critical analysis of the single member constituency system encounters a cultural bias in the Anglo-Saxon world because of the pervasive hostility shown to systems of proportional representation, and the executive instability to which they allegedly contribute. Proportional representation has not been seriously considered as a possible alternative to the existing system. It exists in a limbo of inarticulate assumptions that it is responsible for the ills of the French political system, but it is given no credit for the sophistication and maturity of the Swedish political system.

Given this bias there is, no doubt, a tendency to transform a critique of the existing system into advocacy of proportional representation. The purpose of this paper, however, is not to advocate proportional representation, but simply to take a realistic look at some of the consequences of the prevailing system which have received insufficient attention. In any case, the habituation of Canadians to the existing system renders policy oriented research on the comparative merits of different electoral systems a fruitless exercise. ...

Approaches to a Theory of the Party System

This paper has suggested that the electoral system has been an important factor in the evolution of the Canadian party system. Its influence is intimately tied up with the politics of sectionalism which it has stimulated. Sectionalism in the party system is unavoidable as long as there are significant differences between the distribution of party voter support in any one section and the distribution in the country as a whole. The electoral system, however, by the distortions it introduces as it transforms votes into seats produces an exaggerated sectionalism at the level of representation. In view of this, the basic theme of the paper in its simplest form, and somewhat crudely stated, is that statements about sectionalism in the national party system are in many cases, and at a deeper level, statements about the politics of the single-member constituency system.

The suggested impact of the electoral system on the party system is relevant to a general theory of the party system but should not be confused with such a general theory. The construction of the latter would have required analysis of the import for the party system of such factors as the federal system, the relationship of provincial party organizations to the national party, the nature of the class system, the underlying economic and cultural bases for sectionalism, a parliamentary system of the British type, and many others. For this discussion all these have been accepted as given. They have been mentioned, if at all, only indirectly. Their importance for a general theory is taken for granted, as is the interdependencies they have with each other and with the electoral system. It is evident, for example, that the underlying strength of sectional tendencies and the weakness of class identification are interrelated with each other and with the electoral system as explanations of sectionalism in Canadian politics. For any one of these to change will produce a change in the outcomes which their interactions generate. We are not therefore suggesting that sectional tendencies are exclusive products of the electoral system, but only that that system accords them an exaggerated significance.

Concentration on the electoral system represents an attempt to isolate one aspect of a complex series of interactions which is only imperfectly understood and in the present state of our knowledge cannot be handled simultaneously with precision. In such circumstances the development of more systematic comprehensive explanations will only result from a dialectic between research findings at levels varying from that of individual voters through middle-range studies, such as Alford's recent analysis of class and voting, to attempts, such as those by Scarrow and Meisel, to handle a complex range of phenomena in one framework.

We can conclude that the capacity of the party system to act as an integrating agency for the sectional communities of Canada is detrimentally affected by the electoral system. The politicians' problem of reconciling sectional particularisms is exacerbated by the system they must work through in their pursuit of power. From one perspective it can be argued that if parties succeed in overcoming sectional divisions they do so in defiance of the electoral system. Conversely, it can be claimed that if parties do not succeed this is because the electoral system has so biased the party system that it is inappropriate to call it a nationalizing agency. It is evident that not only has the electoral system given impetus to sectionalism in terms of party campaigns and policy, but by making all parties more sectional at the level of seats than of votes it complicates the ability of the parties to transcend sectionalism. At various times the electoral system has placed barriers in the way of Conservatives becoming sensitively aware of the special place of Quebec and French Canada in the Canadian polity, aided the Liberals in that task, inhibited the third parties in the country from becoming aware of the special needs and dispositions of sections other than those represented in the parliamentary party, and frequently inhibited the parliamentary personnel of the major parties from becoming attuned to the sentiments of the citizens of the prairies. The electoral system's support for the political idiosyncrasies of Alberta for over two decades ill served the integration of that provincial community into the national political system at a time when it was most needed. In fact, the Alberta case merely illustrates the general proposition that the disintegrating effects of the electoral system are likely to be most pronounced where alienation from the larger political system is most profound. A particular orientation, therefore, has been imparted to Canadian politics which is not inherent in the very nature of the patterns of cleavage and consensus in the society, but results from their interplay with the electoral system.

The stimulation offered to sectional cleavages by the single-member constituency system has led several authors to query its appropriateness for national integration in certain circumstances. Lipset and Duverger have suggested that countries possessed of strong underlying tendencies to sectionalism may be better served by proportional representation which breaks up the monolithic nature of sectional representation stimulated by single-member constituency systems. Belgium is frequently cited as a country in which proportional representation has softened the conflict between the Flemish and the Walloons, and the United States as a country in which the single-member constituency system has heightened cleavages and tensions between north and south. Whatever its other merits, the single-member constituency system lacks the singular capacity of proportional representation to encourage all parties to search for votes in all sections of the country. Minorities within sections or provinces are not frozen out as they tend to be under the existing system. As a consequence sectional differences in party representation are minimized or, more accurately, given proportionate rather than exaggerated representation—a factor which encourages the parties to develop a national orientation.

Citizen Demands and Government Response

John Meisel (1976)

EDITORS' INTRODUCTION

John Meisel began teaching at Queen's University in 1949, where he is now professor emeritus. Over his career he has been interested in numerous aspects of Canadian politics, including parties, elections, political cohesion, national identity, Quebec politics, and Canadian culture. He has been chair of the Canadian Radio-television and Telecommunications Commission (1980–83) and president of the Royal Society of Canada (1992–95).

There is no absolute governability or ungovernability. Governability is always a function of tasks, both imposed from the outside and generated from the inside, and of capabilities, of both the elite and the masses.

—Joji Watanuki

Social science—like motorcars, hemlines and slang—is subject to the vicissitudes of fashion. The "in" thing, at one time, was to relate everything to Riesman's s curve and the other-directed personality; other periods were intrigued by Rostow's stages of economic growth, Hartzian fragment theory, Lijphart's consociationalism, or Bell's end of ideology. At the present time one of the mind-catching concerns stresses the so-called ungovernability of democracies and the related demand overload.

Most of these new perspectives have contributed to our understanding of social reality but none has provided completely satisfying insights—the recent agonizing over stresses in democratic polities being no exception. The "demand overload" thesis must therefore be examined and evaluated although, as I shall argue, it is not a completely persuasive perspective on our current discontents. The anxieties, jeremiads, philippics, and wails take innumerable forms and seem, at times, themselves to overload the mind with burdens of unrelieved gloom.

A thesaurus of the Cassandra-like chorus would have to include at least the following ideas: post-industrial society in the liberal democracies of the '70s is marked by a lack of purpose, an absence of community spirit, and a declining legitimacy of private and public authority. Technology has become a self-generating, uncontrollable force which has triggered a mindless, massive consumption of resources which if it continues unchecked, will drag mankind towards certain disaster. Citizens, partly because of the expansion of educational opportunities and growing affluence, incessantly generate ever more numerous and vehe-

Source: Excerpted from *Canadian Public Policy*, vol. 2, no. 4 (Autumn 1976). Notes omitted. Reprinted by permission.

mently articulated demands, the satisfaction of which is either impossible because of the unavailability of resources or because it requires a level of social control that people are no longer willing to accept. The decline in economic growth precludes the amelioration of conditions of the worst-off groups without adversely affecting the better-off. Political parties are less and less able to perform their traditional functions, governments are becoming impotent observers, and even abettors of disastrous social and economic developments, most notably at present, with respect to stagflation. The industrialized West's shocking profligacy and growing incapacity to reconcile dwindling resources with a stubbornly uncontrollable demographic explosion is beginning to endanger civilization as we have come to know it. Even the heat generated by industrial man ultimately threatens his survival (Beer, 1974; Bell, 1967; Bell, 1974; Crozier, Huntington and Watanuki, 1975; Heilbronner, 1975; Huntington, 1974).

From the viewpoint of a student of Canadian politics, satisfied to contemplate the world from a time perspective short of apocalyptic upheaval, these observations can be reduced to three groups of propositions:

(1) The lack of a sense of community, citizen duty and discipline, and the accompanying acquisitive particularism have resulted in people making unreasonable and impossibly high demands on governments;

(2) The demands are impossible to meet or dangerous for at least three reasons. (a) Resources are simply not adequate for their satisfaction and even their partial gratification may have crippling consequences for the effectiveness of the whole system. (b) Governments lack the decision-making capacity to deal with the plethora of demands and the ability to reconcile them into viable programs. (c) The excessive competition for favours among organized particular groups prevents the system from meeting critically important general interests of the community. This is exacerbated by the decline of political parties and by the new roles assumed by interest groups and the media.

(3) Among the drastic consequences of this system overload is the ungovernability of democracies: growing political and economic chaos, a further decline in civility, and the coming to an end of a system which, whatever its shortcomings, has done much to improve the quality of life of virtually all citizens.

How justified are these *cris de cœur*? ...

First, distinction must be made between socio-political forces common to all post-industrial democracies and those unique to Canada. ...

Second, we must also clearly differentiate between the two sides of our equation. It is the *relationship* between demands and capabilities which is crucial; one cannot evaluate one without bearing in mind the other.

Third, and we are at last getting into the substance of the case, the major change in western societies has been in their value systems. We have witnessed, and are witnessing, an epoch-making decline or transformation of traditional middle class values and their replacement by a new, still evolving, pattern of beliefs and priorities. Such critically important aspects of life as sex, family relations, as well as attitudes to work, authority, the state, and fellow man are all changing, often into paths diametrically opposed to previous directions. This volcanic upheaval affects political demands and behaviour, and since the direction of the change is *away* from the time-honoured middle class virtues, one must expect that the political consequences of the moral and ethical metamorphosis will offend those who evaluate public life from the viewpoint of an established middle class perspective.

In Canada, government is subject to changes additional to those just mentioned. Political values appear to be shifting, particularly with respect to the manner in which the federal and provincial spheres are viewed by the politically active population. Quebec independentism, western regionalism, and the assertion of local and regional rights throughout the country—not to mention the rights of the native peoples—are altering the atmosphere and context in which the respective levels of government can perform the tasks assigned them by the constitution and the services expected by their citizens. The governability of Canada is, in other words, being affected by a changing value system with respect to the very definition of the country and the relationship which should prevail among its people and its constituent parts. The resulting need for adjustments does not mean that Canada is becoming ungovernable but it points to the desirability of our fashioning political and administrative mechanisms suitable for coping with the current and impending situations.

Fourth, whatever the emerging shape of the class structure is likely to be—and it is too soon to be able to say—there is little doubt that the immediate future, at least, will increasingly be dominated by a new class.

The term "class" in the foregoing discussion, like much else in my argument, is perforce ill-defined. Without being able to pinpoint its exact meaning here I should elaborate by mentioning that I see a massive change occurring in post-industrial societies, involving a radical re-allocation of the powers and privileges of various social groups. This realignment is related to both the economic and occupational background of groups and to the values dominating life. The heretofore critical role of property in assuring power and privilege is not likely to disappear altogether but it is being increasingly overshadowed by technical knowledge, particularly skills related to the manipulation of people, and by closeness to the dominant decision-making sites in the private and public sectors. ...

Social classes have risen and fallen throughout the history of man and only the most myopic arrogance could lead us to reject the possibility that the present social structure may be undergoing profound change. There is considerable evidence to support the contention that we are living through an era witnessing the waning of the middle classes, as we have known them, and the emergence of a new class alignment. If our analysis is correct, if middle class values are giving way to new values, if the middle class is in the process of being replaced as a dominant force by a new class, then it would not surprise us to find that the equation between demands and the government response was also assuming new, as yet unanticipated, forms. In that event the countries heretofore supporting so-called democratic regimes may be evolving new ways of being governed, which is not to say that they are becoming ungovernable. Whether the new forms are democratic, in the conventional sense, remains to be seen and certainly depends on one's definition of democracy.

Canada offers a dramatic example of the trends we have noted and has probably given more visible signs of the privileged position of its mandarinate than have most liberal democracies. ...There has, in short, emerged a vast number of officials in both the private and public sectors, bolstered by powerful institutional bases, who exercise enormous influence on governmental decisions and on private life. They can be found not only in governments but in unions, educational institutions, health and social service agencies, research and consulting firms, in voluntary associations, even in professional and learned societies. Not infrequently they move from one such organization to another. And wherever they are, they play a critical role in the stimulation of demands.

And this brings us to my fifth point. Demands rarely arise in a spontaneous fashion in society. For needs to become wants, and wants demands, opinion leaders, animators, vanguards of the proletariat, or just plain elites have to mobilize their clientele. In Canada, many of the policies and programs which have undoubtedly contributed to strains in the system are traceable to what could be described as non-spontaneous, engineered, or created demands. It has always been thus, of course; what is changing is the extent or proportion of mobilization which is imposed from above and/or outside the groups directly affected. In our case, it is well known that the introduction of family allowances resulted from the Keynesian spell cast over our political and bureaucratic elites towards the end of the Second World War, reinforced by Gallup polls showing impressive CCF gains. Similarly, medicare, the LIP and OFY schemes, the indexing of pensions, the lavish terms of Canada's Unemployment Insurance Act or regional government were not introduced in response to the claims of existing beneficiaries. In some instances, in fact, the programs brought into being groups whose demands they allegedly met.

Another indication of the key role played in the articulation of demands by the newly emerging managerial class can be found in occupations like teaching or nursing, where the militancy or even unionization met resistance and became acceptable only after the organizational bureaucrats and activist leaders succeeded in persuading the majority of the desirability of pursuing confrontation tactics. Sometimes, as in the case of construction contracts preceding Expo or the Montreal Olympics, a highly opportunistic organizational style of the leadership, made possible by special circumstances, led to the establishment of national rates of pay far exceeding the hopes of those ultimately affected by them in faraway places.

I must stress that by citing the various foregoing examples in illustrating the extent to which demands are now created by public and private officials, I do not necessarily question the desirability of the programs or practices to which they have led. Some, I believe, are eminently worthy and others not. I approve of medicare and extensive social services and I welcome our public servants being generously (but *not* extravagantly) compensated; I deeply resent being converted to kilopascals by the whimsical decision of some bureaucratic, metric fanatic.

Having made a case, I hope, for the idea that demands and the governmental response cannot always be separated, that in a paradoxical sleight of hand, "responses" spawn demands, we must turn to the question of overload and non-governability. Have our new elites inside and outside the government released the kindly genie in Aladdin's lamp or have they unleashed the sorcerer's apprentice? I would reply affirmatively to both questions. Many of the new governmental outputs are clearly defensible and contribute to the improvement of the conditions of life of previously ill-favoured Canadians. On the other hand, some programs are wasteful and in many respects counter-productive; the overall performance of the government has been both inflationary and ineffective in reducing unemployment levels, particularly among certain sections of the population.

Sixth, without denying that we are beset by many of the foibles and even calamities identified by the pessimists, we can also admit to the presence of encouraging signs.

On the mass or public side, Canada seems much better off than its southern neighbour. Whereas in the USA students have observed a decline in electoral turnout, party identification, and a sense of efficacy, Canadian participation in elections remains essentially unchanged, a larger number of people identify with political parties and they do so more intensively than previously, although there is some inconclusive evidence suggesting that there appears to be a decline in the sense of citizen trust and in political effectiveness. At another level, we have taken imaginative steps to strengthen the citizens' capacity to participate in decision-making and so, presumably, to maintain or increase their sense of involvement: public funds are being made available to native peoples and environmental groups so that they can make more effective presentations to the Berger Commission (Berger, 1976: 5–7); the federal government experimentally subsidizes the Consumers Association of Canada, enabling it to challenge on more equal terms the corporate giants when they appear before regulatory agencies (Lewis, Jefferson, 1976), and changes in the laws affecting election costs have introduced some openness into party finance and have encouraged the financial participation of small donors (Paltiel, 1975). More generally, some scholars at least (Inglehart, 1971; Marsh, 1975) have produced evidence indicating that the "postbourgeois" values of young west Europeans are less self-seeking and more community responsive than older ones and that in the United States, contrary to the gloomsayers' argument, there is a growth of ideological politics and that "the dependent voter has been replaced by the responsive voter" (Pomper, 1975: 211).

These and similar glimmers of light may perhaps reflect no more than superficial and misleading palliatives: democratic politics in the eyes of many of its doubters on both the Left and the Right requires considerably more radical attention. But it is at least plausible to argue that the political process through which the mass public articulates and aggregates its demands is showing some signs of adjusting to emerging conditions, that participatory processes may emerge in which varieties of formerly excluded citizens can become involved in policy-making and that this experience may ultimately lead to a capacity for screening communal demands so as to assure that the most deserving problems are met without causing hardship to those who can ill afford them.

What about the other side: the elites and particularly those responsible for the governmental process? Do they offer any reassurance? At the risk of resembling witless Pollyanna I derive some cheer from speculating about the future of governments as well. As I have indicated above, I am convinced that governability as such is not, and never has been, an issue: *some* form of allocation of resources will continue to be made by the public sector and government will go on, probably responding differently to public needs than was the case in the heyday of middle class dominance. The question we thus confront is not whether governments can govern but in whose interests they do so. Even if massive inflation continues it is likely that *in the long run* the present middle and upper middle income groups will be most severely hit. As the economy stabilizes new policies will lead towards a new slicing of the pie. The administrative, technological elite will, as elites always do, itself benefit from the new order but other groups will also, of course, do comparatively well. The best organized, most effectively skilled, and the most strategically placed groups are likely to rise to new prominence and to new rewards.

This prospect does not fill me with alarm. The powerful managerial class, particularly in the public sector, embodies—and is likely to continue embodying—many of the best traditions of what is becoming the old order, including a strong sense of public duty and concern for excellence. While some of its technocratic elements may be disposed to taking a mechanistic, soulless approach to human problems, the administrative class in Canada has, as a whole, an impressive record of dedicated public service. Despite numerous recent gaffes, it can withstand comparison with its predecessors, particularly with what we might term the plutocratic, commercial and industrial-dominated elite. If compelled to choose between depending on the recommendations of the mandarins of the oil industry, for instance, or on those of the federal government, there would be no doubt about my choice. The constantly expanding responsibility of public, as distinct from private decision-making, irrespective of ownership, thus strikes me as an encouraging sign, despite its obvious dangers: it promises that publicly responsible allocative processes, rather than the selfishly manipulated market mechanisms, will increasingly affect outputs and ever more extensive areas of life.

On the other hand, those nurtured on middle class values are likely to feel greatly deprived in a world bereft of many of the previously established virtues. Adjustments of this sort are not easy, as the bourgeoisie in eastern Europe, for instance, has discovered, albeit under conditions vastly different from those likely to prevail here. But the process I have sketched is likely to take a very long time and to proceed almost unnoticed. We are well into it, without fully appreciating the degree to which this is already so.

To link the changing character of the relationship between citizen demands and government response to underlying secular changes in the social structure and to react sanguinely to them is not, of course, to deny that problems of adjustment exist. I have dwelled on one aspect of the matter in the hope of challenging dangerously stand-pat and even reactionary approaches to current tensions and dislocations. We cannot enter into a discussion of the available solutions here but should note that they can, and indeed should, be applied on several fronts. Richard Rose has correctly stressed that the "concept of overloaded government emphasizes that the contemporary crisis cannot be understood solely in terms of absolute properties of polity and society, but rather, by considering ratio relationships between different parts. Because overloading reflects a ratio there is more than one way in which to resolve stress" (Rose, 1975: 14). Rose further suggests that "politicians may find some hope in considering that the Chinese ideograph for 'crisis' can also be translated as 'opportunity,'" and identifies four fronts on which action can occur: increasing resources, improving government institutions, improving the impact of government programs, and reducing expectations (Rose, 1975: 15–16). Which options receive the greatest attention will depend on the values, attitudes, and skills of the new mandarin class. The first thing we need to do—and this is by far the most important point of my argument—is to learn more than we know about ongoing changes within the middle class and about its relations to other sectors of society. Another thing is clear: the most promising strategy is not to expend energy on making the present and future differ as little as possible from the past but to make the future avoid past errors. The need everywhere is to keep breaking down the constantly present and re-emerging elite-mass barriers. In Canada we must also make additional efforts to reduce obstacles impeding free and equal centre–periphery interaction, whether this dimension is conceived spatially or in terms of social and economic power.

14 Prorogation Revisited: Eugene Forsey on Parliament and the Governor General

Eugene Forsey and Helen Forsey (1984, 2009)

EDITORS' INTRODUCTION

Eugene Forsey was both a public official and an experienced commentator on Canadian political life. He taught at McGill, Carleton, and Waterloo universities. His political engagement began with the CCF, then within the Liberal Party of Canada, which led to his being nominated a senator in 1970. He was considered to be an expert on constitutional issues, especially the reserve powers of the Crown. His daughter, Helen Forsey, is a writer and activist based in rural Eastern Ontario and Newfoundland's Avalon Peninsula.

Below is the text of a document, typed and signed by my father, Eugene Forsey, the late Senator and constitutional expert. Dated August 15, 1984, it was among the papers I retrieved from his office and apartment after his death in 1991. It sets out very clearly the role of the Governor General "if no party gets a clear majority in the election."

The principles Eugene Forsey outlines in this paper apply directly to Mr. Harper's outrageous action last month in asking the Governor General to prorogue Parliament, and to the Governor General's action in granting his request. He has his hypothetical Governor General tell the Prime Minister:

> "Prime Minister, responsible cabinet government means government by a cabinet with a majority in the House of Commons. I don't know whether you have such a majority. No one knows. The only way to find out is by summoning Parliament and letting it vote … It is not for me to decide who shall form the Government. But it is for the House of Commons. I cannot allow you to prevent the House of Commons from performing its most essential function. To permit you to do that would be to subvert the Constitution. I cannot allow you to usurp the rights of the House of Commons."

The specific scenario outlined in my father's document differs slightly from the present case in that the 40th Parliament did meet—however briefly—after the October election, and did—however unwisely—pass the Speech from the Throne. But the principle remains the same. The Prime Minister and the Governor General prevented the House of Commons from performing its "most essential function": deciding who should govern.

Source: rabble.ca; sourced January 19, 2009. Reprinted by permission of Helen Forsey.

It's all very well to say they only "delayed" that decision. If so, they had no business doing anything of the sort. As my father argued so compellingly in his many writings on the subject, any action taken to prevent the House of Commons from voting and possibly bringing the government down is a travesty of democracy. The classic example was the "King-Byng affair" of 1926, when Prime Minister Mackenzie King asked Lord Byng, the Governor General, to dissolve Parliament while a vote of non-confidence was pending.

In 1926, Mackenzie King wanted the critical vote "delayed" in order to hold a fresh election and use the campaign to hoodwink the electorate into putting him back into office. In 2008, Stephen Harper wanted the vote in the House "delayed" in order to keep hold of the reins of power, mount a massive propaganda war against the opposition at taxpayers' expense, and hope for political amnesia to set in over the holidays. Whether in the form of dissolution or prorogation, such "delay" constitutes a subversion of the Constitution, a usurpation of the rights of the House of Commons.

My father actually anticipated a rather similar use of prorogation to prevent Parliament from carrying out its responsibilities. And he stated what should happen in such a case:

> "The only protection against such conduct is the reserve power of the Crown, the Governor General, to refuse such prorogation or dissolution, and, if necessary, to dismiss the Government which advised such prorogation or dissolution."

It doesn't get much clearer than that.

***

Note: *I have copied the document here as he typed it himself, with his formatting and underlining. The only change I have made is to flag with asterisks three segments that are less directly relevant to our current situation, and place them at the end. Those three segments, while not essential to the basic argument in the current context, give a taste of the rigorousness and thoroughness with which my father pursued, analyzed and documented all such matters.*—Helen Forsey

Position of the Governor General If No Party Gets a Clear Majority in the Election

I have been asked what the Governor General does if no party gets a clear majority (more than half the seats in the House of Commons) in the general election.

I. The answer is, "Nothing."

The incumbent Prime Minister has a choice between two courses:

a) He can resign. The Governor General then sends for the Leader of the Opposition, and asks him to form a government.

b) He (the incumbent Prime Minister) can meet the new House of Commons. If it supports him, he remains in office. If it defeats him, he resigns, and the Governor General sends for the Leader of the Opposition.

This is what happened in Britain in 1886, 1892 and 1924.* In Canada, in 1926, Mackenzie King (who had been defeated in his own constituency, as had eight of his Ministers) had come out of the election of 1925 with 101 seats to the Conservatives' 116 (in a House of 245). He met the new House, and, till late in June, was sustained by it.

The Government in office, even if it has fewer seats than the official Opposition, is entitled to meet the new House, and let it decide whether to keep that Government in or throw it out.

There is no reason at all for any intervention by the Governor General. Indeed, any such intervention would be grossly improper.

It is not the business of the Governor General to decide who should form the Government. It is the business of the newly elected House of Commons.**

II. If no party gets a clear majority in the election, and the incumbent Government decides not to resign (as it has a perfect right to do) but attempts to carry on for an extended period without meeting the new House (financing the country's business by means of Governor General's special warrants, as provided for in the *Financial Administration Act*, Section 23), then, at some point, Her Excellency would have the right, indeed the duty, to insist that Parliament should be summoned; the right, the duty, to refuse to sign any more special warrants till it was summoned. She would have to say:

> "Prime Minister, responsible cabinet government means government by a cabinet with a majority in the House of Commons. I don't know whether you have such a majority. No one knows. The only way to find out is by summoning Parliament and letting it vote. If you will not advise me to summon Parliament forthwith, then I shall have to dismiss you and call on the Leader of the Opposition. It is not for me to decide who shall form the Government. But it is for the House of Commons. I cannot allow you to prevent the House of Commons from performing its most essential function. To permit you to do that would be to subvert the Constitution. I cannot allow you to usurp the rights of the House of Commons."

I have said, "for an extended period," and "at some point." What period? What point?

There can be no precise answer. How many grains make a heap? But if, let us say, for three months, or four, or five, or six, the newly elected Parliament had not been summoned, at some point there would most certainly be a public outcry:

> "Here! What's going on? Responsible government means government by a cabinet with a majority in the House of Commons. Has this Government, which is spending millions of public money, a majority in the House of Commons? The only way to find out is to summon Parliament and let the House vote. If this Government won't advise that action, then we'd better get a Government that will, and get it quick, and it's the duty of the Governor General to see that we do get it. Her action is our only protection against a gross violation of the very essence of our Constitution."

I must emphasize that the courts could do absolutely nothing.

I must emphasize also that, in law, the Government could stay in office, and finance the ordinary business of government by Governor General's special warrants, for a very long time. True, it would have to summon Parliament within twelve months of the last sitting of the previous Parliament. But, having done so, it could then prorogue it, after a session of a few hours, and repeat the performance a year later. (Indeed, it could dissolve Parliament after a session of only a few hours, as Mr. King did on January 25, 1940.)

The only protection against such conduct is the reserve power of the Crown, the Governor General, to refuse such prorogation or dissolution, and, if necessary, to dismiss the Government which advised such prorogation or dissolution.***

(signed) Eugene Forsey
August 15, 1984

* In each case (Salisbury in 1886 and 1892, Baldwin in 1924. Salisbury was defeated in the newly elected House in 1886 and 1892, and Baldwin Salisbury was defeated in the newly elected PHouse in 1924.)

** Immediately after the election of 1972, when for a few days, it looked as if the Conservatives would have 109 seats to the Liberals' 107, there was a considerable chorus of voices claiming that the Governor General should call on the Conservative leader, Mr. Stanfield, to form a Government. This would have necessitated his dismissing Mr. Trudeau. Every constitutional authority would agree that there could be circumstances which would warrant the Governor General's exercising his "reserve power" to dismiss a Government. But no constitutional authority would say this was one of such circumstances.

If, in 1972, Mr. Stanfield had in fact won 109 seats to Mr. Trudeau's 107, the Governor General would have had no warrant whatever, no right whatever, to usurp the authority of the House of Commons to decide which of the two should be Prime Minister.

If the Governor General, after the election of 1925, had dismissed Mr. King and called on Mr. Meighen to form a Government, then, when the new House met, it might have defeated Mr. Meighen, and the Governor General would have been compelled to call on Mr. King. Meanwhile, the welkin would have rung, and properly so, with denunciations of the unconstitutionality of His Excellency's intervention, his usurpation of the rights of the House of Commons.

If, after the election of 1972, the Governor General had dismissed Mr. Trudeau and called on Mr. Stanfield, exactly the same results could have followed.

*** If anyone questions the word "millions" above, in relation to Governor General's special warrants, he or she need only look up the official records for the occasions when such warrants have been used (during an election) to finance the ordinary business of government to the tune of hundreds of millions of dollars. I myself heard Mr. Michener, a few years back, tell a Senate Committee that he had once signed a single special warrant for hundreds of millions (it was either $200,000,000 or $400,000,000; I can easily, if need be, find the precise figure in the Proceedings of the Committee).

I must also emphasize that we have, in Canada, nothing like the United Kingdom's Army and Air Force Annual Act, and that, since 1896, it has never been the custom to make the voting of interim Supply by Parliament a condition precedent to a dissolution of Parliament.

15 The Party System

Janine Brodie and Jane Jenson (1990)

EDITORS' INTRODUCTION

Janine Brodie teaches in the Department of Political Science at the University of Alberta. She holds a Canada Research Chair in Political Economy and Social Governance, and has published widely on questions of gender equality, political representation, citizenship, social policy, globalization, and transformations in governance. Jane Jenson is a professor of political science at the Université de Montréal, holds a Canada Research Chair in Citizenship and Governance, and is a member of l'Institut d'études européennes (IEE) at the same university. Her more recent works examine issues of citizenship and social policy.

Canada's federal party system provides a somewhat perplexing case for students of politics in liberal democracies. Some sociological theory, drawing on western European experience in particular, predicts that as changes in social structure induced by urbanization and industrialization occur, the traditional electoral cleavages of religion, language and region are eroded by the politics of class. In so-called "modernized" party systems, a class cleavage differentiates the electoral support base of the parties as well as their major policies. From this perspective, the Canadian federal party system does not appear to have "modernized." Instead, religion, language and especially region continue to differentiate the Canadian electorate's support for political parties. Studies of federal voting behaviour consistently depict an electorate which does not divide its support for political parties according to occupational position or even according to the location which voters think they occupy in a status ranking. In addition, the programs and policies of the two major parties reveal few differences in the class interests that they claim to protect and advance. Both depict themselves as guardians of the "national interest." As a result, they are most clearly distinguished by the differences in electoral support that they gain from Canada's major language groups and regions.

This is not to say that Canadian electoral politics has not witnessed at least some of the symptoms of a modernizing party system. From the earliest years, there have been social democratic or socialist parties active in the federal party system. Yet, all these parties, including the New Democratic Party, have never enjoyed anything near a majority of the support of their supposed constituency, the Canadian working class. Rather, the Liberal party gains more votes from workers than does the self-styled social democratic party, the NDP.

Source: Excerpted from "The Party System" by Janine Brodie and Jane Jenson. In *Canadian Politics in the 1990s*, 3rd edition, edited by M.S. Whittington and G. Williams. Toronto: Nelson, 1990. Reprinted by permission of the authors.

Students of Canadian political parties do not agree on how to explain or even describe this perplexing feature of our party system. One kind of study simply attempts to categorize the members of the federal party system so that they can be compared. For example, some typologies describe the federal party system according to the number of parties competing within it. Yet, even at this most elementary level of categorization, there is minimal agreement. Does Canada have a two-party system, since only the Liberals and Progressive Conservatives stand any reasonable chance of forming a government? Or, has there been four-party system (until 1980) because there were four competitors which consistently won seats in Parliament? Or, should we count two-and-a-half parties, acknowledging the persistence of the NDP despite its remote chance of forming a national government? These questions have all been answered in the positive by students of party politics.

Another body of literature characterizes the federal parties according to their organization and electoral orientations. Here again, there is little consensus. Most observers agree, however, that there is a noteworthy difference between the two major parties and the NDP and its predecessor, the Co-operative Commonwealth Federation (CCF). The two major parties are generally described as cadre parties, pragmatic parties, or parties seeking consensus, while the CCF/NDP is depicted as a mass party and a party of program, principle, or protest. Nevertheless, regardless of the basis of categorization, none of these typologies explains the anomalies of the federal party system, especially its apparent inability to "modernize" in predicted ways.

Party and Class in Canada

There are several popular explanations for the absence of pervasive class-based voting in federal politics. This absence has been attributed, by different authors, to the cultural cleavage between French and English Canada and the consequent lack of a sense of nation, to the conflict between central and peripheral regions, and to constitutional biases which encourage regionalism. A familiar theme, however, is the notion that Canadian politics never has been characterized by class conflict because such conflict is irrelevant. Economic and geographic conditions, it is argued, have defused potentially divisive economic cleavages by promoting population movement and social mobility. A further deduction made by such observers is that Canada is a "middle-class" society where material and social benefits are widely shared and, thus, Canadian politics need not be affected by either class conflict or ideology. Partisan debate can focus on the other issues.

Another suggestion about why class-based electoral politics has not flourished in Canada is based on observations about the nature of the federal parties themselves. Sometimes coupled with the "middle-class" view of Canadian society, this perspective describes the Liberals and Conservatives as "brokers," offering the electorate an aggregation and accommodation of the myriad of potentially conflicting interests that inevitably arise in any society. The parties' only concern, according to this analysis, is to accommodate diverse interests sufficiently to build an electoral coalition large enough to capture power. Instead of organizing the electorate around class interests, the major parties are said to engage in a politics of moderation which minimizes differences and restrains divisive tendencies. It is further argued that a beneficial consequence of such brokerage parties is that they can knit together diverse interests in a polity which is otherwise weakly integrated.

As appealing as the middle-class and brokerage theses may be, there are a number of factors which potentially challenge their validity as explanations of the absence of class voting. First, and most obviously, Canada is not and never was a "middle-class" society. In recent years, in fact, the distribution of wealth has grown even less equal. Similarly, there are ample reasons to question the accuracy of the brokerage conception of federal politics. If the major parties are solely concerned with accommodating social conflicts, then the federal party system is witness to their failures. For decades, large regionally-based third parties have occupied their own space on the partisan landscape, citing the neglect and biases of the "brokerage parties" as their reason for entering the electoral fray. Their existence suggests that not all interests are equally accommodated by the two major parties.

Finally, there is little evidence to suggest that brokerage parties are neutral and non-class-based organizations. Their major sources of campaign financing, their patterns of recruitment of members and candidates, and their policy orientations all suggest that the Liberals and Progressive Conservatives have a decidedly status quo and frankly pro-capitalist bent. Yet, paradoxically, these class parties find much of their electoral support among workers. Thus, we return to the question: why is there so little evidence of class-based voting in Canada's federal party system?

To begin answering, it is helpful to return and re-examine the original prediction about the "inevitability" of class-based electoral politics in industrial societies. The principal assumption underlying the prediction is that there is a direct relationship between economic and partisan development. This view of the organization of class relations in liberal democracies arises from economistic Marxist analyses as well as from political sociology's observation that labour or socialist parties and class-based voting emerged and endured in industrialized countries. This formulation is also predicated on a further assumption—notably, that voters' political demands, attitudes and behaviour automatically reflect their class position.

According to these assumptions, electoral politics, organized around a class cleavage, will be concerned primarily with questions of control over economic production and distribution. In this view, competition between classes will lead to the general partisan organization of the bourgeoisie, and those supporting the interests of the bourgeoisie, into one party, and workers, and those supporting the interests of workers, into another. Partisan competition is thus assumed to develop between those who have, according to the rules of the private economy, control over the production process and its profits and those who have, according to the laws of liberal democracy, some control over the production process through the state.

The deduction that workers will be organized into one party and the bourgeoisie into another, however, is not the only one possible starting from an initial assumption about the political importance of classes in liberal democratic politics. In fact, what history has demonstrated in the last century of the joint development of capitalism and liberal democracy is the following: while capitalism has proceeded in all countries in similar directions toward centralization, monopolistically large corporations, and an increase in state intervention in the economy, partisan expression of class conflict has differed widely in the several countries. Students of political sociology who have taken a rather deterministic view of the relationship between economic development and partisan organization, by and large, have been unable to explain the many variations of electoral politics in advanced capitalist countries. This is perhaps because they have tended to minimize the effects of specific national and historical contexts as well as the combined impact of elections, ideologies and political parties themselves in structuring partisan and class relations.

Historically, mass political parties came into being when franchise reform created large numbers of voters who had not previously participated in electoral politics. The way this integration occurred was important in structuring the subsequent partisan organization of class relations because parties primarily (though not exclusively) provided the electorate with a *definition of politics*. They defined the content of politics and the meaning of political activity by shaping an ideology. Most generally, *political parties have a major role in shaping the interpretation of what aspects of individuals' lives should be considered political, how politics should be conducted, what the boundaries of political discussion most properly may be, and what kinds of conflicts can be resolved through the electoral process.* From the vast array of tensions, differences, and inequalities characteristic of an society, parties are crucial to the selection of those which will be defined as political alternatives in the electoral process and thereby shape how the electorate will divide against itself. Whether a problem is considered to be a religious, economic or political question is set by this definition. This role of parties is profoundly important because *before* electoral cleavages come into being a definition of what is political must exist.

Elections are events of conflict and competition, but the substance of electoral politics is not automatically given. For example, politics may be described as the expression of conflict between classes or between ethnic groups or as the aggregation of individual preferences. Economic conditions, such as the level of industrialization, set parameters around the range of organization which is possible in any society, but they can never guarantee that particular classes will be politically active. Subordinate classes will not spontaneously recognize the political implications of their disadvantaged location in capitalist relations of production and vote according to their class position. Members of particular occupational sectors in capitalist society, whether they are farmers, blue-collar workers or office workers, do not and will not act cohesively as a class until they become aware that they are members of a class. The nurturing of this awareness demands, as a prerequisite, ideological and organizational activity. Classes as active and self-conscious social actors must be created, and, in turn, the extent to which they live politically as classes is largely the extent to which they behave as classes in elections.

At a very minimum, class-based voting must be preceded by the development of a class-based organization which challenges existing definitions of politics which interpret social and political relations in non-class terms. If the existence, characteristics and partisan implications of class conflict are exposed by the activities of a well-developed trade-union movement of a powerful and influential party of the left, then there will be evidence, at the level of voting, of class-based politics. Without these prior conditions, class cleavages will be submerged, distorted and rarely visible in voting behaviour.

Since the late nineteenth century, socialist parties have existed which have defined politics as the expression of conflict between classes and not as neutral aggregations of individual or group preferences. They have precipitated a conflict over definitions of politics as well as government policies. The existence of such a debate over definitions means that voters have been offered alternative bases for electoral alignment, and some of these threaten the very existence of one or more of the bourgeois parties. Not surprisingly, then, such parties struggle hard to maintain and recreate a definition of politics which denies the centrality of class differences and relations in capitalist systems. Time and again, confronted with a class-based definition of politics advanced by socialist parties, bourgeois parties have retorted that this definition is inappropriate and that politics is really about race or religion, and moreover that politics is not about conflict at all but about finding consensus so that the capitalist system can be managed successfully to the benefit of all.

If alternative ways of organizing the electorate are possible under the same economic conditions, and the nature of this organization affects the manner in which classes and individuals behave in electoral politics, we begin to see a way of unraveling the perplexity of the Canadian party system. The extent to which capitalist relations of production are debated politically depends in large part on how successfully either socialist or bourgeois parties organize the electorate behind their respective points of view. If politics is defined as conflict between language groups, it is more difficult to unite for partisan action members of the same class who have different linguistic backgrounds. In other words, some political cleavages are likely to be incompatible with others, as the dominance of one cleavage generally inhibits the growth of others. By examining this contest over the definition of politics, it is possible to arrive at a better understanding of the background to the contemporary Canadian party system, which is divided along lines of language and region.

16 The Rise of Court Government in Canada

Donald J. Savoie (1999)

EDITORS' INTRODUCTION

Donald J. Savoie teaches at the Université de Moncton. Since 2004 he has held the Canada Research Chair in Public Administration and Governance, and during 2004–5, he was Director of Research and Senior Advisor to Justice John Gomery's Commission of Inquiry into the Sponsorship Program and Advertising Activities in the Government of Canada. He has published widely on questions of public policy, regional development, public administration, and federalism. The following piece was originally presented as the Presidential address to the Canadian Political Science Association at the Université de Sherbrooke in June 1999.

In 1956, C.B. Power, a senior minister in the Mackenzie King government, observed with deep concern that the war years had strengthened the prestige and power of Cabinet at the expense of Parliament.[1] Power's concerns, as history has shown, were well founded. Ned Franks has stated that "unquestionably Parliament has become a less prominent place for major political announcements and debates, and the decline is continuing."[2] In this article, I argue that Cabinet has joined Parliament as an institution being bypassed, that it is clear that effective power no longer resides with the prime minister acting in concert with his "elected Cabinet colleagues."[3] Court government has taken root in Canada. By this I mean that in the late 1990s, effective power rests with the prime minister and a small group of carefully selected courtiers. These include key advisors in his office, two or three senior cabinet ministers (notably the minister of finance), carefully selected lobbyists, pollsters and other friends in court, and a handful of senior public servants.

In the latter part of the twentieth century, Canadians witnessed major changes in the way they were governed. The changes were neither sudden nor, for the most part, introduced with much fanfare. They were gradual, which may explain why they attracted little notice. The public debate in Canada since the late 1960s focused on actual or proposed constitutional changes and not on the internal machinery of government. In any event, changes to the machinery of government rarely, if ever, enjoy much media or public profile. Yet the evolution of the machinery of government, particularly within the federal government, has had far-reaching consequences for the public service, public policy, Canadian federalism and, ultimately, for Canadians themselves.

Source: Excerpted from *Canadian Journal of Political Science*, vol. 32, no. 4 (December 1999). Some notes omitted. Reprinted by permission.

This article challenges long-established conventions or understandings about how our government works. Gordon Robertson, former secretary to the Cabinet, stated in 1971 that in our system "ministers are responsible. It is their government."[4] The Privy Council Office, in its 1993 publication on the machinery of government, argued that "we operate under the theory of a confederal nature of decision making where power flows from ministers."[5] I maintain, to the contrary, that power no longer flows from ministers, but from the prime minister, and unevenly at that.

The above speaks to the evolution of how policies are struck and decisions are made in Ottawa. J.S. Dupré argued that "institutionalized" Cabinet replaced the "departmentalized" Cabinet in the late 1960s and early 1970s. Individual ministers and their departments lost a great deal of autonomy to full Cabinet, or to shared knowledge and collegial decision making.[6] This era did not last very long before court government started to take root. To be sure, information was gathered at the centre. However, it was gathered for the benefit of the prime minister and a handful of senior advisors operating in the Privy Council Office (PCO) and the Prime Minister's Office (PMO), not for collegial decision making. Court government took root in Ottawa under Pierre Trudeau and, if anything, it grew stronger under both Brian Mulroney and Jean Chrétien. ...

The way to govern in Ottawa—at least since Trudeau—is for prime ministers to focus on three or four priority issues while always keeping an eye on Quebec and national unity concerns. Tom Axworthy, former principal secretary to Pierre Trudeau, in his appropriately titled article, "Of Secretaries to Princes," wrote that "only with maximum prime ministerial involvement could the host of obstacles that stand in the way of reform be overcome ... [the prime minister] must choose relatively few central themes, not only because of the time demands on the prime minister, but also because it takes a herculean effort to coordinate the government machine."[86] To perform a herculean effort, a prime minister needs carefully selected individuals in key positions to push the agenda. Cabinet, the public service as an institution, or even government departments, are not always helpful. For example, Trudeau established an ad hoc group of officials at the centre to pursue his 1983 peace initiative "largely because of the skepticism of the Department of External Affairs."[87]

The result is that important decisions are no longer made in Cabinet. They are now made in federal-provincial meetings of first ministers, during "Team Canada" trade visits abroad, where first ministers can hold informal meetings, in the Prime Minister's Office, in the Privy Council Office, in the Department of Finance, in international organizations and at international summits. There is no indication that the one person who holds all the cards, the prime minister, and the central agencies which enable effective political authority to reside at the centre, are about to change things. In Canada, there is little in the way of internal institutional checks to inhibit or thwart the prime minister. Prime ministers Margaret Thatcher of Britain and Bob Hawke of Australia were tossed out of their offices before their mandates were finished. Their own parliamentary caucuses showed them the door. This would be unthinkable in Canada. Even at the depths of Mulroney's unpopularity, there was no indication that his caucus was about to boot him out of office. In any event, in Canada the caucus holds no such power. In Britain, prime ministers must still deal with powerful ministers who have deep roots in their party and well-established party policies and positions on many issues. In Australia, the prime minister must contend with an elected and independent Senate.

In Canada, national unity concerns, the nature of federal-provincial relations and the role of the mass media tend, in a perverse fashion, to favour the centre of government in Ottawa. The prime minister's court dominates the policy agenda and permeates government decision making to such an extent that it is only willing to trust itself to overseeing the management of important issues. In a sense, the centre of government has come to fear ministerial and line department independence more than it deplores line department paralysis. As a result, court government is probably better suited to managing the political agenda than is cabinet government. The prime minister decides, at least within the federal government, who has standing at court.

But this is not without significant implications for national political institutions and, ironically, for Canadian federalism. Indeed, from a long-term perspective, court government may not be as effective as the courtiers might assume. The fact is that the prime minister and a handful of courtiers can hardly fully appreciate, let alone accommodate, the regional factor in policy making.

Notes

1. C.G. Power, "Career Politicians: The Changing Role of the M.P.," *Queen's Quarterly* 63 (1956), 488–89.

2. C.E.S. Franks, "The Decline of the Canadian Parliament," *The Hill Times* (Ottawa), May 25, 1998, 15.

3. See Denis Smith, "President and Parliament: The Transformation of Parliamentary Government in Canada," in Thomas A. Hockin, ed., *Apex of Power: The Prime Minister and Political Leadership in Canada* (2nd ed.; Scarborough: Prentice-Hall, 1977), 114. See also David E. Smith, "Bagehot, the Crown and the Canadian Constitution," this JOURNAL 28 (1995), 619–35.

4. Gordon Robertson, "The Changing Role of the Privy Council Office," *Canadian Public Administration* 14 (1971), 497.

5. Canada, *Responsibility in the Constitution* (Ottawa: Privy Council Office, 1993).

6. See J.S. Dupré, "The Workability of Executive Federalism in Canada," in H. Bakvis and W. Chandler, eds., *Federalism and the Role of the State* (Toronto: University of Toronto Press, 1987), 238–39.

86. Axworthy, "Of Secretaries to Princes," 247.

87. Ibid., 262.

17 Value Clash: Parliament and Citizens After 150 Years of Responsible Government

Lisa Young (1999)

EDITORS' INTRODUCTION

Lisa Young has taught in the Department of Political Science at the University of Calgary since 1996. Her publications include writings on Canadian political parties, women's participation in politics, interest groups and social movements, and the regulation of electoral finance.

Canadian society has undergone remarkable change since 1848. It is not surprising that the institutions and practices that emerged to govern a scattered, predominantly agrarian population in the nineteenth century have come under unfavourable scrutiny by the 30 million mainly urban, educated, affluent Canadians adapting to post-industrial economic conditions in an interdependent global economy and society. That the basic design of Canadian parliamentary institutions has changed little during a period in which there has been profound social change and the Canadian state has expanded exponentially attests to the durability of the idea of responsible government. That said, Parliament and the practices surrounding responsible government have throughout this century come under critical scrutiny from a variety of sources.

The advent of responsible government in Canada created an imperative for cohesive, disciplined political parties to support stable governments. The development of political parties in Canada has reflected that imperative. As a consequence, responsible government and political parties are inextricably linked in the Canadian experience. As Canadians have grown dissatisfied with the quality of democracy in the country, they have laid the blame squarely on Parliament and the parties that structure it. Over the past three decades, Parliament and political parties have both become increasingly unpopular, as citizens' discontent with the Canadian political process has mounted.

The institutions of responsible government are less appropriate to contemporary Canadian society than they were to the social structures of 1848. The modern Canadian electorate is increasingly unwilling to accept a politics in which important decisions are made

Source: Excerpted from "Value Clash: Parliament and Citizens After 150 Years of Responsible Government" by Lisa Young. In *Taking Stock of Responsible Government in Canada*, edited by Leslie Seidle and Louis Massicotte. Ottawa: Canadian Study of Parliament Group, 1999. Some notes omitted. Reprinted by permission.

behind closed doors and a political elite that appears unresponsive to citizens' views and dismissive of their deliberative capacities. Popular discontent in the contemporary era focuses not so much on questions of governance, but rather on issues of representativeness, responsiveness and accountability of elected representatives. In the eyes of significant segments of the electorate, responsible government stands in the way of representative government.

This paper examines two dimensions of the representational crisis of responsible government. The first dimension is the failure of the political system to adequately represent the changing interests and identities of the Canadian electorate. This is, in large part, a failure of the Canadian party system but it also stems from certain aspects of party discipline and solidarity. The second dimension of this representational crisis centres on the capacity of Parliament to reflect the views of Canadians. This populist critique lays the blame on party discipline and calls for more direct citizen involvement in political decision-making.

Three arguments will be developed in this paper. First, the representational demands that have been placed on Canadian parties have become increasingly complex; the institutions and practices surrounding responsible governments in Canada have made the task of accommodating these representational demands all the more difficult. Second, responsible government (particularly in its Canadian variant) assumes a deferential populace. Such deference is, however, in short supply in contemporary Canada. As a result, serious tensions have emerged. Third, much of the popular discontent with Parliament stems from a disjuncture that is built into the Canadian practice of responsible government. Parties are the crucial unit within the political system, yet the electoral system and the formal workings of Parliament are all predicated upon the fiction that individual Members of Parliament enjoy sufficient autonomy to represent the interests and opinions of their constituents in a meaningful way. As the electorate grows less deferential, this disjuncture becomes less tenable. Although there are no easy solutions to remedy Canadians' discontent with their governing institutions, any proposed remedies must take into account and try to lessen this disjuncture between formal arrangements and political realities. ...

Institutional Reform

Although the source of Canadians' dissatisfaction with Parliament and responsible government does not lie entirely with the institutions themselves, some institutional reforms warrant serious consideration. There is a clear disjuncture between the formal arrangements employed in Canadian elections, in which voters cast a ballot for an individual MP, not a party, and the organization of Parliament, in which tightly disciplined parties structure the parliamentary process. Institutional reforms designed to lessen this disjuncture may lessen the scope of citizen discontent.

Within Parliament, reforms that create a more meaningful role for individual Members of Parliament warrant serious consideration. Replicating the British practice of loosening the confidence convention so that strict party discipline is required only on the most significant pieces of legislation would be a positive move. It would adapt the practice of responsible government as it has evolved in Canada to allow for some independence of backbench MPs on policy issues of importance to their constituents. Once in place, such a practice is likely to loosen the cultural constraints of party discipline, as backbenchers become accustomed to a greater degree of independence. Such a reform would also require the governing party to consult more extensively with its backbench to ensure that legislation had the requisite support. This could, in time, increase the responsiveness of government to citizens' views. By increasing the autonomy of individual Members of Parliament, the capacity of these individuals to represent—and to be seen to be representing—the interests of their constituents or of non-territorially organized groups like women also increases. In this sense, such a reform would respond to the perceived representational deficit in the contemporary system.

The disjuncture between the electoral and parliamentary systems could be substantially resolved by adopting a different electoral system. The first-past-the-post system employed in Canada barely recognizes the existence of political parties. Citizens vote not for a political party, but for an individual candidate who, if elected, is to represent the view of all her or his constituents in Ottawa. Some form of proportional representation (PR) or hybrid of PR and single member plurality system would lessen this disjuncture. Voters would be able to cast a ballot not for an individual, but for a party, or for both an individual and a party. This would make a situation like the current parliament—a Liberal majority government elected with the support of only 38 per cent of voters—impossible. It would also lessen the highly regionalized results produced by the current system. Kent Weaver has demonstrated that even a small number of seats elected through a PR top-up system designed to ensure some measure of proportionality between the votes received and seats won would substantially decrease the regionalized character of electoral outcomes that have tended to leave some regions unrepresented in governing parties.[52] Such a reform is also likely to lend itself to the election of greater numbers of women and minority candidates.[53] In short, electoral reform would alleviate representative deficits for both territorially-based and non-territorial groups.

Conclusion

When first granted, responsible government represented a victory for the advocates of democracy who had campaigned for it. In contrast to the previous practice of representative government, responsible government was without question more democratic, as it gave the electorate's representatives genuine authority. Responsible government and the practices that emerged around it in Canada were appropriate to the social conditions and political culture of the day. Canadian society was predominantly rural, localist and hierarchically organized. Such conditions favoured a form of democracy in which local notables were sent to Parliament to represent the interests of a relatively homogenous and generally deferential community. In the contemporary era, however, citizens' expectations and demands for representation are difficult to accommodate within the confines of responsible government.

Before a coherent discussion of prescriptive reforms can begin, it is first necessary to develop a clearer understanding of the sources of citizen discontent and the growing populism that accompanies it. Further research is needed to determine to what extent this discontent is unique to Canada and related to institutional design. At present, it is difficult to determine whether the Canadians who say that they want to participate directly in policy decisions would, in fact, be willing to assume the demands of citizenship in such a regime. The research from American states which use ballot initiatives should serve a cautionary tale in this regard.

That said, it is clear that the disjuncture between the formal electoral arrangements in which voters cast a ballot for an MP, not a party, yet parties form the only meaningful structures within Parliament, must be lessened. Certain reforms would move in this direction. First, replicating the British practice of loosening party discipline on some votes would be a step in the right direction. Second, adopting a different type of electoral system would do a great deal to resolve this disjuncture.

Notes

52. Kent Weaver, "Improving Representation in the Canadian House of Commons," *Canadian Journal of Political Science* 30 (3): 473–512.

53. See Lisa Young, "Electoral Systems and Representative Legislatures," *Canadian Parliamentary Review* 21 (3): 12–14.

18 A New Canadian Party System

R. Kenneth Carty, William Cross, and Lisa Young (2002)

EDITORS' INTRODUCTION

R. Kenneth Carty teaches in the Department of Political Science at the University of British Columbia, and is a past president of the Canadian Political Science Association. He is considered a leading expert on Canadian party politics and has published widely in that field, with a frequent emphasis on comparative approaches.

William Cross is the Hon. Dick and Ruth Bell Chair for the Study of Canadian Parliamentary Democracy in the Department of Political Science at Carleton University. He has published on Canadian institutions and the way in which civil society interacts with party politics and legislatures.

Lisa Young has taught in the Department of Political Science at the University of Calgary since 1996. Her publications include Advocacy Groups *(with Joanna Everitt) and* Feminists and Party Politics.

Introduction

The 1993 Canadian general election represented a disruption of unprecedented proportions in the patterns of Canadian party politics. Rather than returning things to normal, the outcome of the 1997 general election appeared to signal a longer-term change in these patterns. This chapter uses a model of party change based on David Smith's and R. Kenneth Carty's historical accounts of party system transition to evaluate the dynamics of change in all aspects of the party system during the last decade.[1] Our analysis, which shows that the contemporary era of change resembles earlier patterns of transition, enables us to sketch a profile of an emerging fourth party system in Canada.

The Canadian Party System: Background

"Party System" is an elusive concept. At its simplest, it encompasses the constellation of parties present in the system. Theoretical accounts of party systems and changes in them that are based in the Western European experience tend to classify party systems according to the number of parties or the relative ideological location or competitive position of the parties.[2]

Source: Excerpted from "A New Canadian Party System" by Kenneth Carty, William Cross, and Lisa Young. In *Political Parties, Representation, and Electoral Democracy in Canada*, edited by William Cross. Oxford: Oxford University Press via UBC Press, 2002. Some notes omitted. Reprinted by permission of UBC Press.

Until 1993, the number of parties in the Canadian system changed little, and the two major parties remained dominant. Because of this stability, Canadian scholars have taken a more finely tuned approach to studying the party system, creating classifications based on such variables as organizational features, representative capacity, campaign styles and available modes of communication, and the prevailing styles of politics and governance. Such studies have identified three party systems and their intervening periods of transition since Confederation. This chapter focuses on the current transformation.[3]

The Canadian tradition, typified by historical accounts of the three Canadian party systems, defines the first party system, from Confederation to 1917, as highly localist and dependent on patronage to hold the parties together. The parties were based in the parliamentary caucus, which retained the power to select the leader. The second system, which spanned the years from 1921 to 1957, was characterized by a politics of regional brokerage. Extra-parliamentary parties became more significant, but strong regionally based ministers dominated their party organizations. The third party system, from 1963 on, has been an era of pan-Canadian politics. Extra-parliamentary parties became more important, but the advent of television and the professionalization of politics ensured that the party leader remained the central figure in party affairs.

Two periods of transition marked the time between the first and second and then the second and third party systems. These periods followed "considerable social and demographic changes in the basic structure of the electorate. Both ... helped break old electoral alignments and patterns of political organization, making it easier for new systems of partisan mobilization to emerge. In both cases the Liberals were then left best placed to establish and epitomize the new system."[4]

To evaluate the extent to which the contemporary disruption in the party system constitutes another fundamental transition, we analyse changes in the four crucial functions of political parties: representation and accommodation of society's interests, democratic organization, the contesting of elections, and governing. During each of the past periods of transition identified by Smith and Carty, there has been evidence of change in each of these four areas. So if the current period is again one of transition, we would expect to see change in each. That analysis allows us to identify five features that define the emerging fourth party system: the rise of two new federal parties—the Bloc Québécois and Reform (now Canadian Alliance); increased regionalization of the party system; fragmentation of the electorate; democratization within the parties; and greater diversity among the parties. ...

A New Canadian Party System

Having examined changes in four functions of Canadian parties—representation/accommodation of societal interests, institutionalization of democratic practices, election fighting, and governing—we are led to conclude that the Canadian party system is once again in transition. This latest transition may be significantly different from its predecessors, for it is not clear that the Liberals and Conservatives will once again manage to transform themselves and find a way to dominate national politics in the fourth Canadian party system as they did in the first three.

Although there are substantial continuities between the third party system and the system that is now taking shape, five distinguishing characteristics of the emerging system can be identified. Most immediately evident is the entry of two new parties that have eclipsed both the Conservatives and the NDP in Parliament. Closely related to this is a highly regionalized pattern of party competition. Compounding the fragmentation that results from greater regionalization is the increasing use of private and highly segmented campaign communications, which effectively breaks up the mass national electorate that formed the basis for the pan-Canadian appeals of the third party system. The participatory demands of an assertive citizenry contributed to the decline of the third party system and have left a mark on the emerging system as all the parties have tried to become more internally democratic. Finally, the emerging system is characterized by new diversity in the societal basis, ideology, and internal organizations of the parties that constitute it.

Two New Parties

The first and most readily apparent defining characteristic of the emerging party system is a change in the cast of characters. Whereas the old party system was dominated by the Liberal and Conservative parties, with the NDP as a perpetual third party, the emerging party system encompasses a very different set of parties. This situation presents a serious threat to the Liberal and Conservative parties' historic domination of Canadian politics. Although it is not clear which of these parties will persist and which may fade away or merge, it is evident that the Liberals and Conservatives no longer enjoy the security of being the dominant parties in a relatively stable party system.

With the breakdown of the Mulroney coalition in 1993, large segments of the electorate in Alberta, British Columbia and Quebec opted to support regionally based parties certain to be in opposition. In the West, this was part of a well-established pattern: since the First World War, Alberta voters have supported majority governments on only three occasions. In each case (1958, 1984, and 1988), Alberta voters did not change their patterns of support; rather, the rest of the country came to them. This willingness of a plurality of Alberta voters to be excluded from governing coalitions, coupled with an apparent satisfaction at having their views represented by a regional party, suggests that little will deter former Reform supporters in Alberta and parts of British Columbia from supporting the Canadian Alliance. For the foreseeable future, then, the Canadian Alliance is likely to remain a significant presence in Canadian politics.

By the same token, it is difficult to imagine a scenario in which the Bloc Québécois entirely disappears in the immediate future. Committed sovereignists remain a significant force in Quebec politics, and these voters are unlikely to support the Liberals or Conservatives. Without a leader from Quebec at the helm, the Conservatives appear unlikely to win the support of soft sovereign voters. This leaves sovereignist voters with only two viable options: voting for the Bloc or not voting at all. Barring significant changes on the constitutional front, the Bloc appears a more or less permanent feature of the emerging system.

Even if the Bloc and Canadian Alliance do not survive the transition into the new party system, they will have played a significant role in shaping the system in general and the practices of the other parties in the system. The continued presence of these two regionally based parties will ensure that political competition remains highly regionalized. Moreover, a central dynamic of the emerging system is one that pits the new regional parties against the older parties, which are trying to maintain their pan-Canadian scope and basis of support.

Reform's populism and claims of internal democracy have forced the other parties to respond with reforms to their internal organization.

Regionalization

A second and related defining characteristic of the emerging party system is greater regionalization, both in the basis of party support and in the patterns of campaigning. This trend is due to the entry of two regional parties and the breakdown of the pan-Canadianism of the old system. The long-standing cleavage in Canadian politics between the centre and the periphery has now become vividly captured within the party system, the two new and radically decentralist parties being pitted against the older pan-Canadian parties.

In both 1993 and 1997, national elections were anything but national. In the 1993 campaign, the two regionally based parties' unanticipated surge in strength caught the old parties by surprise, and their familiar, pan-Canadian strategies proved to be unsuited to the new kind of campaign. In 1997 the old parties were better prepared, and both the Conservatives and New Democrats ran regionally targeted campaigns. And the Liberals, as the only party to compete aggressively in all parts of the country, prepared different strategies and messages for each region. What developed, essentially, were five distinct regional party systems, each with its own campaign and political dynamics.

It is no coincidence that the party system became far more regionalized in the immediate aftermath of the failure of the constitutional rounds of the late 1980s and early 1990s. The electorate's rejection of the Charlottetown Accord in a national referendum marked the end of the era of uncontested executive federalism in which regional conflicts were brokered, not within the governing party, but rather within the first ministers' conference. In the emerging party system, regional claims are being made within the party system, with regionally based parties increasingly acting as representatives of regional interests in the national political arena.

Fragmentation of the Electorate

Although the regionalization of party competition is the most readily apparent face of the fragmentation of the national political debate, technological advances have allowed a further fragmentation. New communication technologies, coupled with increasingly rich sources of socio-demographic data, have allowed parties to make their appeals to the electorate in increasingly targeted and private ways. Rather than a mass appeal to the Canadian electorate through network television, parties are able to communicate with votes through direct mail, over the telephone, or through the Internet, delivering a message targeted to the voters' demographic group or general interests. As this sort of political communication proliferates, the national discussion of politics during an election campaign will increasingly be replaced by a series of highly focused, private conversations. When coupled with the regional dynamics of campaigns, this trend is contributing to the end of pan-Canadian mass appeals.

Democratization

Among the factors contributing to the demise of the third party system was the rising assertiveness and populism of the Canadian electorate. Once largely content to defer to the decisions of political elites, Canadians have increasingly come to distrust political institutions and the people who run them, and are calling for a direct voice for citizens in political decisions. These changing attitudes created significant pressures for change in the political system writ large and in each of the political parties. As a result, we have seen changes to both the party system and internal practices of the parties. This populist discontent is manifested most clearly by the emergence of the Reform party, which criticized both the structure of Canadian political institutions and the top-down practices of the old parties. Reform/Canadian Alliance has attempted, with some success, to conduct its internal party affairs in such a manner as to demonstrate its commitment to populist and democratic principles. This has prompted the other parties to respond, most notably by changing their method of leadership selection to some variation on universal membership voting. This shift represents the essence of the changing norms of internal party democracy because it will allow more party members an opportunity for direct, unmediated participation in what may be the party's most important decision.

Greater Diversity Among Parties

The final distinguishing characteristic of the emerging party system is a much enhanced diversity in the societal basis, ideology, and internal organization of the parties. In the third party system, there was remarkable uniformity among the three major parties in their efforts to develop or maintain a pan-Canadian focus, their efforts to promote inclusiveness through representational quotas of various kinds, and even their internal organization.[30] Unlike its predecessor, the new party system is characterized by considerable diversity among the parties. The first source of this is the division between the new, regionally based parties with their decentralist views and the old, pan-Canadian parties with their continuing attachment to the central government. The second, and related, source of diversity is the new parties' rejection of the basic principles of pan-Canadianism: bilingualism, multiculturalism, and the politics of accommodation. The third source of diversity lies in different conceptions of representation: Reform/Canadian Alliance explicitly rejects the old parties' efforts to promote inclusion by recognizing difference and has eschewed the old parties' practice of providing representational guarantees. The conservatives have followed suit in their reforms to their internal party practices.

Certainly, this new diversity of principle and form presents a profound challenge to the kind of party politics and, in fact, the kind of governance Canadians have been accustomed to in the past half century. For many, this challenge is understood as a threat to the Canada and the way of life they value highly. Much more is at stake in Canadian party politics than has been in a long time. The shape of the emerging party system will ultimately affect the politics of coming decades, and it is clear that many fundamental principles of the governing regime will be contested by the new political actors.

Conclusion

According to the criteria we set out, it is evident that the Canadian party system is in transition. Some elements of the contemporary transition fit tidily into the historical patterns. The pressure for internal party democracy and the consequent change in the method of selecting the leader are precise parallels for developments during earlier transitions. And changes in campaign communication technologies appear to hold the same transformative promise as did radio and television in earlier transitions, although this is less clear.

Other elements of the contemporary transition appear somewhat different than earlier transitions. Most notably, this is the first transition in which the fate of one of the two historic parties that have long governed Canada appears in question. Although the place of the Liberal party within the party system has changed little, it is not clear that the Conservative party will survive the current transition intact. This is also the first transition in which the party system is considered to be threatened by alternative modes of political representation—interest groups and social movement organizations. Even though the threat may not be as great as it appears, it is noteworthy that the easy primacy of parties on the Canadian political landscape seems in question.

Notes

1. David Smith, "Party Government, Representation and National Integration in Canada," in P. Aucoin, ed., *Party Government and Regional Representation in Canada* (Toronto: University of Toronto Press, 1985); and R.K. Carty, "Three Canadian Party Systems: An Interpretation of the Development of National Politics," in Hugh Thorburn, ed., *Party Politics in Canada*, 7th ed. (Scarborough: Prentice-Hall, 1996).

2. Theoretical models of changes in party systems that are more closely related to the party systems of Western Europe can be found in Maurice Duverger, *Political Parties* (London: Methuen, 1954) and Giovanni Sartori, *Parties and Party Systems* (Oxford: Oxford University Press, 1976).

3. It should be noted at the outset that when party systems in Canada change, much remains the same. At least until 1993, no change in the party system deposed the Liberal and Conservative parties from their place as the two major parties in the system. Through all these transitions, the tension between local and national parties has remained constant. Moreover, the fundamental role of parties—contesting elections, selecting leaders, and nominating candidates—has remained remarkably stable since Confederation. Change has characterized the role of minor parties in the system, the dynamics of competition, the patterns of internal party organization, and the ways in which elections are fought.

4. Carty, "Three Canadian Party Systems," 142.

30. The NDP diverged somewhat from the other two parties with its ties to organized labour and its slightly different mechanism for leadership selection, but beyond these differences the parties were remarkably similar. This similarity, we have argued, contributed to the downfall of the third party system, as it left too many interests and perspectives unrepresented.

Who Governs? Who Should Govern?: Political Authority and Legitimacy in Canada in the Twenty-First Century

19

Grace Skogstad (2003)

EDITORS' INTRODUCTION

Grace Skogstad is a professor of political science at the University of Toronto and a past president of the Canadian Political Science Association. She is interested in Canadian agrarian policy and has published numerous articles on public policy and the decision-making process. The following piece was originally presented as the Presidential Address to the Canadian Political Science Association in Halifax in 2003.

Who governs? Who should govern? These empirical and normative questions are at the heart of the discipline of political science. In democracies, the question directs us to our beliefs and practices regarding the exercise of legitimate political authority. Why do we obey the rules and decisions to which those in authority collectively bind us? The answer is clear. We obey, first, because we believe that those who make legally enforceable decisions have a right to do so; and second, because we believe the decisions themselves—the public policies—are socially desirable. In representative democracies, those who exercise authority do so with public consent, having been freely chosen in elections and subject to mechanisms of accountability that ensure that they roughly reflect the public's will and preferences. This much about the exercise of political authority in Canada is obvious.[1]

What is less often appreciated is that this conception of political authority, which vests authority and legitimacy in elected state officials, is not the only model to be found in contemporary governing practices. Canadians juggle a plurality of conceptions of political authority. Alongside the still dominant, state-centred model of representative democracy, three other models co-exist. They are, first, expert authority whereby those with superior knowledge are expected to deliver efficacious outcomes; second, market-based or private authority, as vested in economic and other private actors to regulate certain activities; and third, popular authority or the idea that "the people" should directly decide issues that concern them.

This article elaborates upon these competing sources and principles of political authority, and assesses their implications for effective and legitimate governing in contemporary Canada. This account highlights some of the factors, and in particular, political cultural shifts

Source: Excerpted from *Canadian Journal of Political Science*, vol. 36, no. 5 (December 2003). Some notes omitted. Reprinted by permission.

and developments in the global economy, that have lent momentum to alternatives to the Weberian (1994) state-centred model of political authority. The argument is not that the competitors to state-centred political authority are new models on the Canadian landscape. Both expert authority and popular authority have long historic roots in Canadian political discourse and governing practices. Rather, my argument is that the co-existence of these various models of political authority at this particular historic juncture presents significant challenges to governing in Canada.

To see the conundrum created by their co-existence, it is helpful to recognize that legitimacy has both an input and output component. Political authority enjoys input legitimacy when individuals believe that those who make legally enforceable decisions have a right to do so. In democracies, input legitimacy is sourced in procedures that allow citizen preferences to enter into the political process. Political authority enjoys output legitimacy when the outputs of governing—public policies and other decisions—meet social standards of acceptability and appropriateness. While legitimation standards differ across societies and over time, output legitimacy generally captures the belief that decisions and policy outcomes promote the common welfare of the political community through effective problem-solving and distributive justice. As Fritz Scharpf (1999: 12) observes, in democratic states "input- and output-oriented legitimacy co-exist side by side, reinforcing, complementing, and supplementing each other." It is the combination of input legitimacy—that is, procedural legitimacy—and output legitimacy—that is, substantive legitimacy—that leads individuals to feel a sense of obligation to obey collectively binding decisions even when they conflict with their own preferences.

The dilemma that confronts Canadian governments is that the state-centred model of political authority has been weakened in terms of both its input and output legitimacy. On the input side, there is evidence of a domestic cultural shift that includes a desire on the part of Canadians for a more direct role in policy making. Governments have incentives to respond to this demand, for example, by veering towards a popular authority model, like participatory democracy. Simultaneously, developments in the global political economy lend legitimacy to expert and private authority to an unprecedented degree. On the output legitimacy side, the capacity of Canadian governments to deliver policy outcomes consistent with the expectations of Canadian citizens is narrowed. The developments associated with the globalizing political economy maximize efficiency and undermine values of transparency, accountability and social justice. However, these values are the very ones by which Canadians judge the legitimacy of their governments' actions.

The challenge, then, for Canadian governments is to find a way to manoeuvre within this terrain of conflicting domestic and international normative standards of governing procedures (input legitimacy) and policy outcomes (output legitimacy). Governments have met this challenge by shrinking the public sphere and vacating ground to private authority. What is the effect on governments' output legitimacy? The results are mixed. Governments have also made a concerted effort to reach out to societal actors to get their input into decision making. Segments of the public have been brought more directly into policy formulation. Do these initiatives shore up the input legitimacy of governments? They have the potential to do so. Ultimately, however, if input and output legitimacy are to reinforce and complement one another, the state-centred model must be retained and reformed. Reform of Canada's institutions of representative democracy is the best guarantee for the pursuit of the collective goals, and accountable and transparent government, that Canadians value. ...

Canadians themselves appear to recognize that there is no real substitute to state-centred political authority when it comes to delivering effective policy outcomes. We prefer elected governments as our primary agent for achieving our collective goals (Bricker and Greenspon, 2001: 321; Graves, 1999: 43, 4 8). The professional survey analyst, Frank Graves (1999: 42), argues that "Governments still enjoy legitimacy in terms of the power citizens think they should wield" and, further, "Canadians do not call for a reduction in government power." Nevitte (2002: 28) himself acknowledges that "the broad swath of the population is not deeply dissatisfied with the way democracy works in Canada. " At the same time, however, Canadians, like those in other Westminster systems (Aucoin, 1995), are demanding more accountability of governments between elections. And we want, according to survey data (Bricker and Greenspon, 2001: 81), decision-making processes that are more open and transparent.

If there is no real substitute to state-centred political authority when it comes to delivering policy outcomes that are likely to pass tests of output legitimacy, it is weak input legitimacy that is a problem. Grafting elements of popular authority onto representative democracy appears to be the necessary corrective to shore up the input legitimacy of governing. Mechanisms of participatory democracy, like policy networks that give representatives of society formal or informal rights of participation, cannot substitute for state-centred governing because of their representational inadequacies. Governing through policy networks is unlikely to be as inclusive of the public as are even badly apportioned legislative chambers in simple plurality electoral systems.

However, as a supplement to representative democracy, participatory democracy can enhance its input legitimacy. The discussion between specialist and generalist publics, between elites and non-elites, that takes place in public forums like hearings of parliamentary committees and the Citizens' Dialogue organized by the Romanow royal commission on health care, is often polemical and self-interested. Nonetheless, its public character has the potential to yield important benefits in terms of legitimizing governing. Fritz Scharpf (1999: 20) observes that when policy debates are conducted in public and pluralistically open forums, a wider range of issues, interests and policy options is likely to be considered. Public deliberation, he argues, checks self-interested behaviour because: "It simply would not do to justify publicly a political demand or policy proposal on purely self-regarding grounds ... self-interest is forced to masquerade as public interest, at which point the possibility of contestation allows competing interests or public-interested critics to challenge such claims" (Scharpf, 2000: 118). Not all public discussion and debate will enhance the legitimacy of decision making. But when it is conducted in a way that allows citizens to make sense of what is happening, then it has considerable potential to do so.

These possibilities for learning and understanding presented by properly structured public debate[10] also show a way to integrate expert, popular, and state-centred models of authoritative policy making. Most of us would not want policies to regulate the risk of a new technology to be made in disregard of scientists' best calculations of its risk. Efficacious policies in this sphere derive from credible scientific knowledge. At the same time, scientists will likely only be able to convince a sceptical public that the risks are manageable through an open dialogue and debate. The answer to the question posed earlier about how to resolve the imbroglio over the authoritative basis of regulating genetically modified products must be, at least in the first instance, a government-structured public debate open to all interested parties. That deliberative process is a requisite step in the decision-making process but cannot usurp the decision-making role of elected officials. Input legitimacy necessitates the public debate; output legitimacy requires that elected officials take decisions and be held to account for them.

As for market-based authority, how can it be integrated with popular and state-based authority models in a way consistent with Canadian norms of openness and accountability? One way is by private economic actors responding to Canadians' demand to be more directly accountable for their actions (Bricker and Greenspon, 2001: 319–20). Where self-initiated accountability is not forthcoming, the second option is for governments to make it mandatory. In the instance of GM products, if private authority cannot satisfy Canadians' labeling demands, governments will have little option but to make it mandatory. In short, it is the state again that must be the ultimate authority in reconciling conflicts between market-based and popular authority.

State-centred authority remains our best bet for effective and legitimate governing in Canada. To capitalize on that bet, however, our representative institutions must be reformed to become more authentic chambers of representation and deliberation. A full discussion of what these reforms might entail would include the electoral system and party discipline. Replacing the simple plurality, single-member electoral system with one incorporating principles of proportional representation would strengthen the numerical position of opposition parties vis-à-vis the governing party. Arguably, as well, it would enhance the quality of representation in the legislative and executive chambers by resulting in a more diverse and more experienced body of elected members. Loosening party discipline would allow for this more plural universe of views to be openly articulated and championed. The greater likelihood of coalition government under a system of proportional representation would increase the incentives for not only aggregative politics but likely deliberative politics as well. Depending on the model of PR chosen, these salutary effects could be achieved without diminishing the capacity for effective governing (Massicotte, 2001). Others will disagree about the priority of these two reforms and their effects for effective and legitimate governing. The point remains: if Canadians' answer to the questions of "Who should govern?" and "Who governs?" are to be one and the same, the practices of representative democracy in Canada must be brought into better alignment with the value Canadians place on open, transparent and accountable governing.

Notes

1. This article does not address the issue of the legitimacy of the distribution of political authority within the Canadian federal state or the 1982 *Constitution Act*.

10. The growing literature on deliberative democracy provides both theoretical and empirical insight into the conditions that enable deliberation that can promote understanding and even consensus on thorny policy issues. See Chambers (2003) for an overview.

20 Still Different After All These Years? A Comparison of Female and Male Canadian MPs in the Twentieth Century

Manon Tremblay and Linda Trimble (2004)

EDITORS' INTRODUCTION

Manon Tremblay has taught at the School of Political Studies, University of Ottawa, since 1992. The primary focus of her work is gender and politics. In 2006, she received the Prix de la Présidence de l'Assemblée nationale for her book, Québécoises et représentation parlementaire.

Linda Trimble teaches at the Department of Political Science at the University of Alberta, and has published on media representations of female politicians, gender and politics in Canada, and news coverage of Canadian national elections.

Early studies of women's participation in Canadian politics showed key differences in the social and political backgrounds of male and female politicians. Notably, the academic and professional qualifications of female legislators are more modest than those of male legislators, and this is also the case for their experience within political parties more generally. For example, women elected to political office were less likely than their male counterparts to be lawyers. This observation sparked the idea that to gain credibility in political institutions, women had to be more like men by acquiring the attributes male politicians held. More recent studies of women elected to political office indicate that women have indeed responded to this analysis; today, women politicians are as educated as men, they have entered the professions in numbers equal to those of men and they are just as involved in their communities. Some studies go further, suggesting that women have exceeded their male counterparts in some socio-demographic areas and in their political and electoral progress.[1] What accounts for this apparent convergence between women and men in politics? Have women changed over the years, or have the characteristics of both men and women shifted over time?

There are reasons to believe differences between male and female politicians persist into the twenty-first century. While Canadian women have made great progress in recent years regarding education, the legal profession and political party experience, there are still major disparities between men and women. For example, in 1997, the average income for women

Source: Excerpted from *The Journal of Legislative Studies*, vol. 10, no. 1 (Spring 2004). Some notes omitted. Reprinted by permission.

was 62 per cent of that of men, which means that they may have had jobs that paid less and were less flexible and, consequently, they had to wait longer to acquire the resources, namely financial and support networks, to enter politics.[2] However, men may be at a greater disadvantage than women in some respects, such as ministerial responsibilities. The need for first ministers to fill cabinet posts according to regional, gender, linguistic and other types of group-based representation, coupled with the fact that cabinets are shrinking, may give elected women an edge when it comes to executive positions.

This article explores these questions by comparing the backgrounds, political experiences and social characteristics of men and women who served in the Canadian House of Commons during the twentieth century. It challenges a number of assumptions about the convergence of men's and women's federal political careers in Canada. While on some measures male and female members of parliament (MPs) no longer differ, in other respects they remain distinct or have even become more divergent over time. Thus a straightforward linear model of initial polarisation between the genders followed by a period of convergence resulting in harmonisation receives only partial support from this study. Gender continues to act as a causal variable shaping the characteristics and careers of federal politicians, but its effects are complex and multi-dimensional. ...

As mentioned earlier, men's career profile in federal politics has changed over time. As in the case of female MPs, this change reflects the evolution of the Canadian party system. As we move from cohort to cohort, fewer male candidates seek a first mandate in the House of Commons under a party that was in power when parliament was dissolved. In the past, fewer male MPs were given parliamentary and ministerial responsibilities than they are today. All in all, female politicians have changed over the years, but so have their male colleagues, and it is not possible to claim that the women have simply brought themselves into line with the men. In general, there are differences between the federal political careers of women and men, but there are also numerous areas of similarity. The idea that female and male politicians were polarised in the past and now share a similar profile cannot explain the complexity of their parliamentary careers. Lastly, the women involved in politics in the past are not necessarily the same as the women in today's political arena, but this is also true for men. Over time, women have developed a career profile in federal politics that does not simply mirror men's experiences. Brodie's assertion that a full understanding of women's political career paths requires comparisons of women with other women is supported by these findings.[69] In effect, comparisons by sex alone cannot reveal all of the complex subtleties, and by incorrectly assuming that the experiences of male politicians are universal, current political concepts allow for a monolithic and simplistic depiction of women's experiences as a mere deviation from those of men.

Conclusion

The purpose of this article was to examine how women's involvement in federal parliamentary activities has changed in the twentieth century, and to compare it with a sample of male MPs. This examination was based on two inter-related hypotheses distilled from existing studies of women's participation in Canadian politics: firstly, that the former polarisation of female and male politicians has given way to harmonisation; and, secondly, that harmonisation has occurred because women's profiles have changed to become more like those of men. This study found that the idea of a past polarisation and current harmonisation between women and men does not fully reflect women's experiences in federal parliamentary activities in the twentieth century, as only three of the 16 variables selected support this model. Furthermore, this model received less than and/or roughly the same support as the other explanations; for example, the idea that male and female legislators were more alike in the past and now diverge in their backgrounds and experiences (past harmonisation/current polarisation) explains changes in three of the 16 variables selected. The model of a long-standing and ongoing polarisation between women and men in the House of Commons was also dispelled. Male and female MPs are remarkably similar in their attributes and career paths. The model of past and ongoing harmonisation receives the strongest support: eight of the 16 variables making up the three axes of socio-demographic profile, political and party experience and federal political career. It must therefore be concluded that there is no single prevailing model to explain the evolution of women's involvement in Canadian federal parliamentary activities in the twentieth century. This evolution is influenced by the diversity and complexity of the women's backgrounds and the paths they choose. It cannot be evaluated according to absolutes or locked into a linear model that moves it from polarisation to harmonisation.

Nor is there a single model to describe the evolution of women elected to the House of Commons as a group, from one cohort to another; in some ways, the women most recently elected to the Lower House resemble their predecessors and, in other ways, they are different. However, a strong pattern is evident from the data: for nine of the 16 variables measured, today's MPs are significantly different from the women who came before them. The first women elected to the Commons and today's representatives differ in terms of education, the province of representation, the type—urban or rural—of the riding where first elected, the party affiliation at the time of election, the means by which they were first elected (general or by-election), the number of years in the Commons, parliamentary and ministerial responsibilities, and, finally, the reasons for withdrawing from federal political life. Since female politicians do not evolve in isolation, these changes are often explained by changes in Canadian society itself. For instance, women now have greater access to higher education, contemporary Canadian society is more urbanised than in years past, women are politicians in their own right and do not need to be stand-ins for male family members. Furthermore, to understand why so many female MPs in the third cohort received parliamentary responsibilities, we have to consider issues of visibility and representation, as well as the primacy of constitutional negotiations during that era, all topics of great importance to the Mulroney governments.

Men also changed from cohort to cohort, and in a frequency similar to that of women: the men serving in the Commons today differ from their predecessors in terms of nine of the 16 variables selected. Therefore, it is probably incorrect to interpret—as do Arend and Chandler[70]—women's involvement in Canadian parliamentary activity (especially federally) based on a theory that, in the twentieth century, women adopted men's socio-demographic profile as well as their experiences within the parties and electorally. It seems better to picture a mutual convergence of women and men, rather than women becoming more like men.

A single model cannot account for women's involvement in federal parliamentary activities. Studies conducted so far—especially recent ones—have focused on a substantive understanding rather than a descriptive understanding of women's political representation.

However, at a time when women occupy one out of every five seats in the Canadian House of Commons, we need more research into socio-demographic characteristics, as well as their electoral progress and advancement within the parties, so that we can better understand not only the profiles and paths associated with electoral success, but also the complexities of women's descriptive and substantive representation in Canadian federal politics.

According to Hannah Fenichel Pitkin, when the time to reflect on the nature of political representation comes "(w)e may ask what a representative does, what constitutes the activity of representing. Or we may ask what a representative is, what he [sic] must be like in order to represent."[71] This latter meaning is descriptive; it favours what the elected person is, rather than what s/he does (or substantive representation). The primary focus of representation is, thus, *who* the representative is or should be instead of *what* s/he does or should do. This implies that by her mere presence in the House of Commons, a female MP "represents" women. Williams develops this rationale by suggesting a link between "standing for" and "acting for" women's representation when she asserts:

> even though the experiences and perspectives of marginalized group members [women] are themselves diverse, the social positions of group members are sufficiently similar that there are good reasons to believe that members of marginalized groups, *on average*, are more likely to represent the concerns and interests of citizens from those groups than are nonmembers.[72]

However, as the results of this study show, on the one hand women MPs constitute a diversified group, and on the other they share many traits with their male counterparts. Thus, since women parliamentarians are quite diverse, and since female and male MPs are quite similar, are political women the best women's representatives from a substantive perspective?

Notes

1. J.H. Black and L. Erickson, "Similarity, Compensation or Difference? A Comparison of Female and Male Office-Seekers," *Women and Politics*, 21/4 (2000), pp. 1–38.

2. Statistics Canada, *Women in Canada 2000: A Gender-Based Statistical Report* (Ottawa: Minister of Industry, 2000).

69. Brodie, *Women and Politics in Canada*, p. 11.

70. Arend and Chandler, "Which Distinctiveness?"

71. H.F. Pitkin, *The Concept of Representation* (Berkeley, CA: University of California Press, 1967), p. 59.

72. M.S. Williams, *Voice, Trust, and Memory: Marginalized Groups and the Failings of Liberal Representation* (Princeton, NJ: Princeton University Press, 1998), p. 6.

21 Only Voters Have the Right to Decide on the Coalition

Tom Flanagan (2009)

EDITORS' INTRODUCTION

Tom Flanagan teaches at the Department of Political Science at the University of Calgary. He has been a long-time strategist and political adviser to Stephen Harper, and served as senior communications adviser for the federal Conservative party in the 2006 election that brought Harper to power, having also served as Harper's chief of staff while he was leader of the official opposition. He is a senior fellow with The Fraser Institute *and author of several books including* Harper's Team *and* First Nations? Second Thoughts. *The following opinion piece appeared at the height of the national debate that raged over the possible formation of a coalition government.*

The Globe and Mail
January 9, 2009

Defenders of the Liberal-NDP-Bloc Québécois coalition argue that, if the Conservative government's budget is defeated in the House of Commons, the Governor-General should invite the Liberal Leader to form a cabinet with some posts allocated to the NDP. There is no need for another election, they say, because together the three coalition partners hold a majority of the seats in the House, and the Bloc has agreed not to bring down a Liberal-NDP government for at least 18 months.

The coalition's apologists glory in the supposed fact that Canada's Constitution is not democratic. Responsible government, they say, means only that the cabinet has to maintain majority support in the House; it doesn't mean the voters have a voice. Canadians, in their view, are just deluded if they think Canada is a democracy.

Obviously, the apologists didn't pay attention in Political Science 101. Here's why they're wrong.

Canada has inherited the antiquated machinery of responsible government from the pre-democratic age of the early 19th century, when most people couldn't vote and political parties were only parliamentary cliques. But a lot has happened since Benjamin Disraeli last took tea with Queen Victoria.

Canada changed from a constitutional monarchy to a constitutional democracy as the franchise was extended to all adults and political parties became national in scope. That evolution was recognized in 1982 in the Charter of Rights and Freedoms. Section 1 charac-

Source: *The Globe and Mail*, January 9, 2009. Web edition. Reprinted by permission.

terizes Canada as "a free and democratic society," and Section 3 grants the right to vote to "every citizen of Canada."

In its 1998 decision on the secession reference case, the Supreme Court of Canada emphasized that democracy was one of "the underlying principles animating the whole of the Constitution."

The most important decision in modern politics is choosing the executive of the national government, and democracy in the 21st century means the voters must have a meaningful voice in that decision. Our machinery for choosing the executive is not prescribed by legislative or constitutional text; rather, it consists of constitutional conventions—past precedents followed in the light of present exigencies. The Supreme Court has said it will expound these conventions but will not try to enforce them. The virtue of relying on conventions is that they can evolve over time, like common law, and can be adapted to the new realities of the democratic age.

That means that, in the area of choosing the executive, the Constitution, for all practical purposes, is whatever the Governor-General says it is; there is no appeal from vice-regal decisions. But that doesn't mean the Governor-General is a free agent; she has a responsibility to make her decisions within the Constitution, including those "underlying principles" identified by the Supreme Court.

How, then, should Michaëlle Jean decide if the government is defeated over the budget? Arguably, a new election would be called for, even though it would only be five months after the last election. Gross violations of democratic principles would be involved in handing government over to the coalition without getting approval from voters.

Together, the Liberals and the NDP won just 114 seats, 29 fewer than the Conservatives. They can be kept in power only with the support of the Bloc, whose raison d'être is the dismemberment of Canada. The Liberals and NDP have published the text of their accord but not of their agreement with the Bloc.

The coalition partners, moreover, did not run on a platform of forming a coalition; indeed, the Liberals' Stéphane Dion denied that he would make a coalition with the NDP. In countries where coalition governments are common, parties reveal their alliances so that citizens can know how their votes will affect the composition of the executive after the election. In stark contrast, those who voted for the Liberals, NDP or Bloc in the last election could not possibly have known they were choosing a Liberal-NDP government supported by a secret protocol with the Bloc.

Put it all together, and you have a head-spinning violation of democratic norms of open discussion and majority rule. The Governor-General, as the protector of Canada's constitutional democracy, should ensure the voters get a chance to say whether they want the coalition as a government. They haven't yet had that chance.

22 What Happens Next If PM Loses Vote on Coming Budget?

Various Authors (2009)

EDITORS' INTRODUCTION

Numerous professors from various Canadian universities signed this opinion page letter, which appeared in The Toronto Star *and* Le Devoir. *Its goal was to address widespread public misunderstanding of how Parliament functions, and it also served to counter Tom Flanagan's interpretation of events then occurring in Ottawa, which was published two weeks earlier (see the previous reading in this section). The signatories are all recognized experts in constitutional law and Canadian politics.*

Following the fiasco that ended with Harper proroguing Parliament, some of Canada's top legal minds walk us through the rules of the House. Politicians and public, take heed.

The Toronto Star
January 23, 2009

In light of the recent events, it has become clear that many Canadians are unfamiliar with some of the basic rules of our constitutional democracy. In a recent Ipsos Reid poll, 51 per cent of participants mistakenly thought Canadians directly elect their prime minister. We feel it is our duty, as constitutional scholars, to clarify the rules governing the appointment of government.

After a general election, the Governor General of Canada normally asks the leader of the party that has gathered a majority of seats in the House of Commons to become the prime minister and to form a government.

According to the principle of responsible government, the government must enjoy the confidence of the House of Commons in order to govern legitimately.

Our Constitution requires that the prime minister and the cabinet, not being elected directly by the people, enjoy the support of a majority of the elected members of Parliament. In our parliamentary system, it is precisely this support that gives the government its democratic legitimacy. Without this democratic support, the prime minister and his cabinet have none.

When the general election does not return a majority of seats to any one party, the governor general will then have to appoint as prime minister a Member of Parliament who is able to gather enough support to sustain the confidence of the House for a reasonable period of time.

Source: *Toronto Star*, January 23, 2009. Web edition. Reprinted by permission.

If the person who was prime minister prior to the dissolution of the House has not yet resigned and it is unclear which party or parties could gather sufficient support from MPs to lead a government after a fresh election, the governor general may let that person try to govern until it is made clear he or she does not enjoy the support of the House. In a minority situation, the prime minister cannot claim to have "won" a right to govern. At best, he or she can claim to have the right to try to sustain the confidence of the House.

When a minority government loses the confidence of the House, the governor general is no longer bound by the advice of the prime minister. The governor general must then exercise what is known as her "personal prerogatives." She may dissolve Parliament and call for a new election or, if the elections have been held relatively recently (opinions range between six and nine months), she may invite the leader of another party to attempt to form a government that would enjoy the confidence of the House.

The same may be true if the prime minister of a minority government were to request a dissolution of the House early after an election. In fact, certain authorities, such as Eugene Forsey, even claim that "(I)f a government asks for dissolution whilst a motion of censure is under debate, it is clearly the Crown's duty to refuse."

While in our parliamentary system, as is the case in the Commonwealth in general, the governor general (or the person fulfilling a similar role in other jurisdictions) may offer the opposition leader the opportunity to form the government in such circumstances, other parliamentary systems give the opposition the right to form a new government (i.e. Spain's and Belgium's constitutions). In the case of Germany, the constitution even makes it an obligation in certain circumstances.

Such rules are meant to avoid creating an incentive for minority government prime ministers to make successive calls for elections until one party gathers sufficient support to form a majority government. Successive elections can be quite disruptive, if only because without a functioning Parliament to vote on matters of supply, unelected officials are forced to adopt special measures to pay for the operations of government.

When the governor general exercises her personal prerogatives and decides whether or not to dissolve Parliament or call on the opposition parties to form a new government, she must act in a judicial manner, with total impartiality. In such circumstances, she must be guided by her duty to protect the Constitution and, in particular, the principles of democracy and responsible government.

It is our opinion that in the event of a non-confidence vote or a request for dissolution of Parliament after only 13 sitting days of the House of Commons, the governor general would be well-advised to call on the leader of the opposition to attempt to form a government.

This would be most appropriate in the circumstances where that leader has already gathered the assurance that he would enjoy the support of a majority of votes on any issue of confidence for the next year or so. The principle of democracy would be protected insofar as the new government would enjoy the support of a majority of the elected officials.

This would ensure the stability of our political system.

The Authors

This article was submitted by professors from the following universities:

Université de Montréal: Stéphane Beaulac, law; Karim Benyekhlef, law; François Chevrette, law, honorary dean

University of Ottawa: Denis Boivin, law; John H. Currie, law; Sébastien Grammond, law, acting dean; Martha Jackman, law; François J. Larocque, law; Errol P. Mendes, law; Charles-Maxime Panaccio, law; David Robitaille, law; Sophie Thériault, law

Université du Québec à Montréal: Pierre Bosset, law; Rachel Chagnon, law; Hugo Cyr, law; Lucie Lemonde, law; Jean-Pierre Villaggi, law

York University: Barbara Cameron, political science

Simon Fraser University: Duncan Cameron, political science; Andrew Heard, political science

University of Saskatchewan: Mark Carter, law

Université de Moncton: Michele L. Caron, law

Queen's University: C.E.S. (Ned) Franks, political science, emeritus professor

University of Calgary: Jennifer Koshan, law

McGill University: Roderick A. Macdonald, law; F.R. Scott, constitutional and public law

Dalhousie University: Dianne Pothier, law

University of Toronto: Denise Réaume, law; Peter H. Russell, political science; Lorne Sossin, law

Osgoode Hall Law School: Bruce Ryder, François Tanguay-Renaud

University of British Columbia: Brendan Naef, Ph.D. candidate in law; Margot Young, law

Université Laval: Maxime Saint-Hilaire, Ph.D. candidate in law

Wilfrid Laurier University: David Docherty, political science, dean of arts

University of Windsor: Heather MacIvor, political science

University of Victoria: Dennis Pilon, political science; Jeremy Webber, law, honorary dean

University of Manitoba: Paul G. Thomas, political science

PART 3

Social and Political Diversity

Introduction

Canada has a worldwide reputation for diversity, tolerance, and multiculturalism. Legislation and numerous policies at all levels of government protect our rights as citizens of Canada and seek to prevent discrimination based on race, ethnicity, gender, sexual orientation, and ability. However, these endeavours have been the products of political struggles. They are the culmination of long processes in which racial and ethnic minorities, women, sexual minorities, and Aboriginal peoples have fought to attain the full rights of citizenship. Canadian history is marked by political events that have been instrumental in the creation of a society in which all people—no matter what race, ethnicity, gender, or sexual orientation—are protected from unequal treatment. Undoubtedly, racism, sexism, and other forms of discrimination still exist in Canada; the selections in this part demonstrate both how far we have come and the challenges that remain.

Race, Ethnicity, and Multiculturalism

The first section of this part considers the evolution of attitudes and policies toward racial and ethnic minorities in Canada. It begins with a selection from *Strangers at Our Gates* by J.S. Woodsworth, a quintessential example of the anti-immigrant sentiment that characterized decades of Canadian history, from the imposition of a head tax on Chinese immigrants in 1885 to the immigration policies that restricted non-white immigration between 1924 and 1962.

The next three selections situate the birth of Canadian multiculturalism within the French–English cleavage of Canadian society between the 1960s and 1980s. First, the Royal Commission on Bilingualism and Biculturalism's investigation into the status of French Canadians and the use of the French language in Canadian society spurred many important political developments, such as the *Official Languages Act* of 1969. However, it also had to answer to "other" ethnic Canadians, who felt their contributions to the development of Canada were overlooked within the English–French debate. These concerns were directly addressed in the second selection, the 1971 "Statement on Multiculturalism" by Prime Minister Pierre Trudeau. In this speech to the House of Commons, Trudeau advocated the official recognition of Canadian multiculturalism within a bilingual framework, eloquently arguing that diversity and pluralism were part of Canadian identity, not oppositions to it. However, some Quebeckers perceived this move as an attempt to diminish their claim to being a distinct society within Canada. This perspective is explored in Guy Rocher's piece, which is a direct response to Trudeau's statement.

The next group of readings consider coming to terms with Canada's racist past and working toward improving our multicultural future. During the Second World War, the Canadian government ordered the internment of thousands of Japanese Canadians in British Columbia. These people of Japanese descent, most of whom were born in Canada, also had their houses confiscated and property seized. Brian Mulroney's official apology in 1988 for the internment of Japanese Canadians along Canada's West Coast was an important symbolic gesture which acknowledged that the internment was driven far more by racist anti-Asian sentiment than by the purported threat to national security. The selection from Rhada Jhappan and Daiva Stasiulis also reaches into the past, highlighting the various policies and legal actions used to regulate and control racial minorities and Aboriginal peoples in the hopes of ensuring that Canada remained a white settler society. The third selection on this theme is by one of Canada's top scholars of multiculturalism, Will Kymlicka. He contends that Canada's policy of multiculturalism has merit and will ultimately lead to more positive ethnocultural relations among groups.

Though we have clearly improved upon the mistakes and injustices of the past, this is not to say that racism, discrimination, and intolerance have been fully eradicated from Canadian society. The final selection is from "Building the Future: A Time for Reconciliation," the recent report on accommodation practices in Quebec by Charles Taylor and Gérard Bouchard. The report was commissioned in response to growing hostilities toward racial and ethnic minorities in Quebec, and attempts to come to terms with an increasingly diverse population as it collides with Quebec's distinct society.

Aboriginal Peoples

The second group of readings in this part concerns Canada's relationship with its First Peoples. The history of this relationship is largely characterized by government coercion, colonization and subjugation. Section 91(24) of the *British North America Act* gave the federal government jurisdiction over "Indians and lands reserved for Indians," and in 1876 the government consolidated all legislation concerning Native peoples into the *Indian Act*, the first element of a massive regulatory regime designed to manage Indian lives from cradle to grave.

The first selection is Canada's 1969 Statement on Indian Policy, presented to the House of Commons by then Minister of Indian Affairs Jean Chrétien. Influenced by the civil rights movement in the United States that demanded equality for all, this policy proposed the eradication of the "special treatment" for Aboriginal peoples, which in the government's view was the ultimate cause of their disadvantage. The White Paper, as it is commonly called, proposed eliminating the *Indian Act*, abolishing Indian status, dismantling the Department of Indian Affairs, and handing control of Indian affairs to provincial governments in order to create a more equal and just society. The unintended consequence of the White Paper was the mass mobilization of Aboriginal peoples against any attempt to disintegrate the special historical relationship they had with the Crown. Within a matter of weeks of the tabling of the White Paper, Harold Cardinal had published *The Unjust Society*, our second selection in this part. Cardinal's book attacks the Trudeau government's betrayal of Aboriginal peoples after months of supposed consultation. This book, along with the "Red Paper" that Natives published in response to the government's White Paper, helped create intense political pressure from Aboriginal peoples, which eventually forced the government to retreat from its position.

Though Aboriginal policy has undeniably come a long way—from attempts at forced assimilation to the recognition of Aboriginal people's inherent right to self-government—there is still much work to be done. The last three readings in this section provide three different viewpoints from Aboriginal scholars on the challenges their communities face on the road ahead. Legal scholar John Borrows argues that indigenous and Canadian legal traditions need not be mutually exclusive; rather, First Nations can attain rights and recognition within the Canadian political community. Clem Chartier traces the historical and legal path of Métis land rights and self-government. In contrast to John Borrows' piece, Taiaiake Alfred's calls for indigenous resistance against an inherently colonial Canadian state.

Gender and Sexuality

Women's rights have come a long way in Canada. In the first third of the 20th century, women fought for the right to vote, to hold public office, and to be considered "persons" under the law. The latter third of the century began with the Royal Commission on the Status of Women's landmark recognition of the pervasiveness of gender inequality in Canadian society. As this first selection demonstrates, the commission's inquiry examined the disadvantaged status of women and recommended steps to be undertaken by the federal government to alleviate gender discrimination in society. A number of selections in this section underline the fact that disadvantage can be manifested in a number of ways. In the realm of the formal institutions of legislatures and the judiciary, women remain underrepresented and face unique challenges to gaining access to what has historically been considered an "old boys club." Two selections in this part examine these issues: Jane Arscott and Linda Trimble address the lack of women politicians, and Madam Justice Bertha Wilson considers the role of women judges in Canada.

Formal politics is also supplemented by unofficial politics—interest groups, social movements, and the ways in which the everyday lives of women are affected by gender disadvantage. It is important to recognize, however, that the category of "women" is problematic—we cannot and should not assume that all women mobilize for the same reasons or face the same kinds of discrimination. Mary Ellen Turpel's article, written in response to the 20th anniversary of the Report of the Royal Commission on the Status of Women, criticizes the mandate and recommendations of the report as conceptually and culturally inappropriate for First Nations women. Similarly, Himani Bannerji's deconstruction of Canadian multiculturalism suggests the extent to which women of colour are excluded and marginalized.

This part would certainly not be complete without reference to the struggles of gays and lesbians for equality in Canada. The legalization of same-sex marriage in 2005 was certainly a victory that originated from decades of uphill struggles and strategic lobbying for full citizenship rights. Legal battles have been fought in order for sexual orientation to be included as grounds of discrimination under section 15 of the *Canadian Charter of Rights and Freedoms*, to permit same-sex couples to adopt children, to have equal access to social benefits such as pensions plans, and even to allow a gay high school student to bring his partner to the prom. The excerpt from Miriam Smith's book *Lesbian and Gay Rights in Canada* highlights the evolution of gay and lesbian political activism in Canada in the last decades of the 20th century.

Further Suggested Reading

Race, Ethnicity, and Multiculturalism

Yasmeen Abu-Laban and Christina Gabriel, *Selling Diversity: Immigration, Multiculturalism, Employment Equity and Globalization.* Peterborough, ON: Broadview Press, 2002.

Constance Backhouse, *Colour-Coded: A Legal History of Racism in Canada, 1900–1950.* Toronto: University of Toronto Press, 1999.

Neil Bissoondath, *Selling Illusions: The Cult of Multiculturalism in Canada.* Toronto: Penguin, 1994.

Linda Cardinal, "Language and the Ideological Limits of Diversity in Canada." *Journal of Multilingualism and Multicultural Development* 26(6), 2005.

François Houle, "Canadian Citizenship and Multiculturalism." In Pierre Boyer, Linda Cardinal, and David Headon, eds., *From Subjects to Citizens: A Hundred Years of Citizenship in Australia and Canada.* Ottawa: University of Ottawa Press, 2004.

Genevieve Fuji Johnson and Randy Enomoto, eds., *Race, Racialization, and Antiracism in Canada and Beyond.* Toronto: University of Toronto Press, 2007.

Charles Taylor, "The Politics of Recognition" in Amy Gutmann, ed., *Multiculturalism: Examining the Politics of Recognition.* Princeton, NJ: Princeton University Press, 1994.

Aboriginal Peoples

Alan Cairns, *Citizens Plus: Aboriginal Peoples and the Canadian State.* Vancouver: UBC Press, 2000.

Glen Coulthard, "Subjects of Empire: Indigenous Peoples and the 'Politics of Recognition' in Canada." *Contemporary Political Theory* 6(4), 2007.

Delgamuukw v. British Columbia, [1997] 3 SCR 1010.

Tom Flanagan, *First Nations? Second Thoughts.* Montreal and Kingston: McGill-Queen's University Press, 2000.

Martin Papillon, "Aboriginal Quality of Life Under a Modern Treaty: The Experience of the James Bay and Northern Quebec Agreement." *Choices* 14(9). Montreal: Institute for Research on Public Policy, August 2008.

Daniel Salée, "The Quebec State and Indigenous Peoples." In Alain-G. Gagnon, ed., *Québec: State and Society*, 3rd edition. Peterborough, ON: Broadview Press, 2004.

Gender and Sexuality

Sylvia Bashevkin, *Welfare Hot Buttons: Women, Work and Social Policy Reform.* Toronto: University of Toronto Press, 2002.

Alexandra Dobrowolsky, *The Politics of Pragmatism: Women, Representation, and Constitutionalism in Canada.* Toronto: Oxford University Press, 2000.

Edwards v. Canada (Attorney General), [1930] AC 124 (the "Persons" case).

Egan v. Canada, [1995] 2 SCR 513.

Joyce Green, "Canaries in the Mines of Citizenship: Indian Women in Canada." *Canadian Journal of Political Science* 34(4), 2001.

R. v. Morgentaler, [1988] 1 SCR 30.

Reference Re: Same Sex Marriage, [2004] 3 SCR 698, 2004 SCC 79.

Ayelet Shachar, "Feminism and Multiculturalism: Mapping the Terrain." In A.S. Laden and D. Owen, eds., *Multiculturalism and Political Theory.* Cambridge: Cambridge University Press, 2007.

Women's Legal Education and Action Fund (LEAF), *Equality and the Charter: Ten Years of Feminist Advocacy Before the Supreme Court of Canada.* Toronto: Emond Montgomery Publications, 1996.

Lisa Young, *Feminists and Party Politics.* Vancouver: UBC Press, 2000.

23 Strangers Within Our Gates

J.S. Woodsworth (1909)

EDITORS' INTRODUCTION

James Shaver Woodsworth (1874–1942) was a leading Methodist social reformer and the first leader of the Co-operative Commonwealth Federation (CCF), which would later become the NDP. Though he spent most of his life as an advocate for the poor, the working class, and farmers, his attitudes toward non-whites and Natives were representative of many British Canadians of the time: Asians and blacks were "essentially non-assimilable elements [that] are clearly detrimental to our highest national development, and hence should be vigorously excluded."

The Problem of Immigration

Immigration and transportation are the two questions of greatest importance to Canada. From the situation, extent and character of the country, transportation must always be one of the leading factors in industrial and commercial development. But as men are greater than things, so immigration is greater than transportation. Canada has many problems, but they all dwindle into insignificance before the one great, commanding, overwhelming problem of immigration. Of vital importance to us are the character, the welfare and the development of the peoples who are to be the people of Canada. ...

Just at this stage Canada becomes a field for immigration. Just when restriction leagues are being formed in the United States and rigid immigration laws are being enacted, Canada adopts a "progressive immigration policy," and puts forth every effort to secure immigrants. It is true that our relations with the Mother Land are such that we are receiving a large number of Britishers. But we are also receiving immigrants from all parts of Europe—that is, we are taking our place side by side with the United States as the Old World's dumping ground. As the sluices are closed there, the flood will be diverted to Canada, whatever the policy of the Government may happen to be. As the free lands are taken in the United States, and the pressure of population begins to be felt, the flood will flow in upon us as surely as water finds its level. ...

Source: Excerpted from *Strangers Within Our Gates, or Coming Canadians* by J.S. Woodsworth. Toronto: Doreen Stephen Books, 1909.

When it is considered how slow is the natural increase in a nation—that is, the excess of births over deaths—it becomes evident what an enormous strain is being put upon our institutions. We, as Canadians, must do in one year what under normal conditions would be spread over many years. Fancy a mother with her own baby to care for adopting half a dozen other babies—some of them, too, of very uncertain tempers!

Fancy a family increased suddenly by the presence of several strange children! What a problem to feed and clothe them—to train them and educate them—to instill into them the family traditions and impart to them the family spirit!

English and Russians, French and Germans, Austrians and Italians, Japanese and Hindus—a mixed multitude, they are being dumped into Canada by a kind of endless chain. They sort themselves out after a fashion, and each seeks to find a corner somewhere. But how shall we weld this heterogeneous mass into one people? That is our problem. ...

Restriction of Immigration

But if we had provision for thorough examination, what standard should we require? In addition to those already in the list of the prohibited, persons of poor physique, persons mentally deficient, the hopelessly incapable, the morally depraved—these surely should be excluded. In this matter our sympathies are divided. We pity the poor man or woman or child who cannot come up to the standard. There may be exceptional cases in which such people would "do well" in Canada. But we cannot but think that we must protect the highest interests of our own land. Each country should be forced to care for its own criminals, paupers and diseased. To relieve any country of the burden is only to delay the application of measures that will abolish the conditions which produce these classes.

But there is here a larger question—the advisability or the justifiability of excluding not merely certain individuals, but certain classes. There is the live question of the Orientals on the Pacific Coast. The Chinese, Japanese and Hindus are—or the majority of them are—physically and mentally "fit." They are in no sense paupers or incapables. Indeed, one of the most frequent and serious charges against them is that they are able to drive out other labour. Should they be excluded—if so, on what grounds? Much has been said on both sides. There is, no doubt, a national prejudice that should be overcome. On the other hand, the expression, "This is a white man's country," has deeper significance than we sometimes imagine.

The advocates for admission argue that we ought not to legislate against a particular class or nation, and that the Orientals are needed to develop the resources of the country. Their opponents believe that white labourers cannot compete with Orientals, that the standard of living will be lowered, and white men driven out, and they claim that a nation has the right to protect itself.

Needless to say, the economic aspects are those that really divide men on this subject, for, generally speaking, capitalists and employers are ranged against the labour party. Perhaps in the early stages of development, Chinese labour was necessary. Perhaps, for some time, the presence of a limited number of Orientals may be advantageous. But it does seem that the exclusionists are right in their contention that labourers working and living as the Orientals do, will displace European labourers. It is generally agreed that the two races are not likely to "mix." Ultimately, then, the question resolves itself into the desirability of a white caste and a yellow, or black caste, existing side by side, or above and below, in the same country. We confess that the idea of a homogeneous people seems in accord with our democratic institutions and conducive to the general welfare. This need not exclude small communities of black or red or yellow peoples. It is well to remember that we are not the only people on earth. The idealist may still dream of a final state of development, when white and black and red and yellow hall have ceased to exist, or have become merged into some neutral gray. We may love all men and yet prefer to maintain our own family life. …

We, in Canada, have certain more or less clearly defined ideals of national well-being. These ideals must never be lost sight of. Non-ideal elements there must be, but they should be capable of assimilation. Essentially non-assimilable elements are clearly detrimental to our highest national development, and hence should be vigorously excluded.

24 Royal Commission on Bilingualism and Biculturalism

A. Davidson Dunton and André Laurendeau (1967)

EDITORS' INTRODUCTION

The Royal Commission on Bilingualism and Biculturalism, often referred to as "The B&B Commission," was established in 1963 by Prime Minister Lester B. Pearson with an original mandate "to inquire into and report upon the existing state of bilingualism and biculturalism in Canada and then recommend what steps should be taken to develop the Canadian Confederation on the basis of an equal partnership between the two founding races." However, partly due to pressure from Ukrainian Canadians, the commission also examined "the contribution made by other ethnic groups to the cultural enrichment of Canada and the measures which should be taken to safeguard that contribution." The commission's report was delivered in several stages between 1965 and 1970. The excerpt below is from the 1967 book entitled The Official Languages.

Equal Partnership or "Le Principe d'Égalité"

The languages and cultures of this country can be thought of in many different ways. However, our mandate clearly states the problem in terms of equality: it postulates an "equal partnership between the two founding races" ("le principe de l'égalité entre les deux peuples fondateurs"). As we understand our mandate, this equality should be the equal partnership not only of the two peoples which founded Confederation but also of each of their respective languages and cultures. What we are aiming for, then, is the equal partnership of all who speak either language and participate in either culture, whatever their ethnic origin. For us the principle of equal partnership takes priority over all historical and legal considerations, regardless of how interesting and important such considerations may be. ...

Equality from the Individual Point of View

Just as the equality of all before the law cannot do away with all inequalities (notably those of intelligence, courage, health, and education), equality between the two dominant languages and cultures cannot mean absolute equality of the members of both groups. The point at issue is essentially equality of opportunity, but a *real equality of opportunity*—an

Source: Excerpted from *Royal Commission on Bilingualism and Biculturalism*. Ottawa: Government of Canada, 1967.

equality ensuring that the fact of speaking English or French would be neither a help nor a handicap to a person seeking entry into the institutions affecting our individual and collective life.

We have deliberately outlined this ideal in absolute terms, which some people will consider over-simplified, in order to emphasize the great gap which separates the cultural groups. The members of a privileged group living under almost perfect conditions are tempted to take their situation for granted and not to stop to consider what others are missing. Members of the underprivileged group may reach a greater or lesser degree of alienation, and so become unaware of their cultural underdevelopment or of the hybrid nature of their culture, not to mention the inferiority complex which so often inhibits them and makes them feel inadequate.

Some analyses in this Report will show that cultural equality, as understood here, hardly exists between Canada's two main language groups. Indeed, if the facts are examined in the light of the norms that we have suggested, one may be tempted to despair of establishing the conditions for equality which form the main theme of this Report. At the very least, we must be realistic. We have no intention of proposing the impossible; it will never be possible for the members of the two main cultural groups to enjoy the advantages described above throughout the country on an equal footing. We first must see to what extent the wide gulf between current reality and an ideal cultural equality can be reduced. Inevitably in some areas there will be a striking gap between the state of affairs described and the recommendations offered for its reform. Political decisions cannot rapidly or radically change a long-standing state of affairs or old ways of thinking. We are sufficiently aware of this fact not to propose arbitrary measures based on abstract theory rather than on realities. A realistic approach avoids the possibility of unrealistic expectations among members of the minority; it also invites breadth of vision from the majority, which should be more aware than before that it will in any case always be in a privileged position. ...

The principle of equality implies respect for the idea of minority status, both in the country as a whole and in each of its regions. Within the provinces or small administrative entities, both Anglophones and Francophones live in some cases as a majority, in some cases as a minority. Since the English-speaking population is larger across the country, its members are less often in the minority; but they are the minority in some areas, especially in the province of Quebec. The Francophones are usually in the minority outside Quebec. In either case, however, the principle of equality requires that the minority receive generous treatment.

This proposal may seem Utopian, but is it really so? Recognizing the rights of a linguistic minority does not reduce those of the majority: with a little good will, the rights of both can be exercised without serious conflict, as is clearly demonstrated by the examples of Switzerland and Finland. In other words, a majority does not abdicate when it resolves to take a minority into consideration; it remains the majority, with the advantages its situation implies, while at the same time demonstrating its humanity.

This is political wisdom too. The history of countries with more than one language and culture shows how often rigid attitudes held by majorities have made common life difficult, if not impossible. The use of force, in any circumstances, results in either revolt or submission. Besides, for the majority to hold back from acts within its power or to allow events it would be able to prevent, out of respect for the minority, is not a product of weakness but a step forward in civilization. In this spirit too will we approach the matter of the other minorities.

We must work to develop and consolidate existing situations where they provide the possibility of establishing a certain equilibrium between the two communities. We know that Anglophones form the majority in nine of the ten provinces of Canada; Francophones the majority in Quebec. This is a state of affairs which should be turned to account. Indeed, the concentration of more than 4,000,000 Francophones in a single province is the only factor which gives some reality, at the outset, to the concept of equal partnership. Quebec constitutes an environment where the aspirations and the needs of four out of five Francophones in Canada can be satisfied. The mere fact of this concentration leads to a spontaneous French way of life and makes that way of life easier to organize. This is why we believe the place of the Québécois in the French fact in Canada will in practice have to be recognized much more than it is today; we are thinking particularly of the world of work, in the federal public sector and in the private sector. But there is also a political aspect: Quebec is the only province where French-speaking Canadians are in the majority and the English-speaking in the minority. Here the weight of numbers favours the Francophones, and it is a powerful lever. They can exercise a preponderant influence in their own province; they can also make themselves heard by the rest of the country, especially in the federal Parliament, and thus take an active part in the life of Canada. Of course there are risks involved. The problem can be succinctly formulated. How can we integrate the new Quebec into present-day Canada, without curbing Quebec's forward drive and, at the same time, without risking the breaking up of the country?

All these facts combine to give Quebec a leading role in promoting the French language and culture in Canada, whatever may be the political solution finally adopted. This conclusion is in the nature of things; it is not the outcome of ideology or some messianic notion. In this sense it is an obvious and incontrovertible fact that Quebec is not "a province like the others."

25 Statement on Multiculturalism

Pierre Elliott Trudeau (1971)

EDITORS' INTRODUCTION

Many attribute the birth of multiculturalism to Prime Minister Pierre Trudeau. In this speech to the House of Commons in 1971, Trudeau advocates the official recognition of Canadian multiculturalism for the first time, suggesting that diversity and pluralism are integral parts of Canadian identity. Though some government programming followed this statement, the Canadian government did not pass the Multiculturalism Act *until 1988. However, this original invocation of the idea of a multicultural Canada had powerful symbolic value.*

House of Commons

Friday, October 8, 1971

ROUTINE PROCEEDINGS
Canadian Culture

Announcement of Implementation of Policy of Multiculturalism Within Bilingual Framework

Right Hon. P.E. Trudeau (Prime Minister): Mr. Speaker, I am happy this morning to be able to reveal to the House that the government has accepted all those recommendations of the Royal Commission on Bilingualism and Biculturalism which are contained in Volume IV of its reports directed to federal departments and agencies. Hon. members will recall that the subject of this volume is "the contribution by other ethnic groups to the cultural enrichment of Canada and the measures that should be taken to safeguard that contribution."

Volume IV examined the whole question of cultural and ethnic pluralism in this country and the status of our various cultures and languages, an area of study given all too little attention in the past by scholars.

It was the view of the royal commission, shared by the government and, I am sure, by all Canadians, that there cannot be one cultural policy for Canadians of British and French origin, another for the original peoples and yet a third for all others. For although there are two official languages, there is no official culture, nor does any ethnic group take precedence over any other. No citizen or group of citizens is other than Canadian, and all should be treated fairly.

The royal commission was guided by the belief that adherence to one's ethnic group is influenced not so much by one's origin or mother tongue as by one's sense of belonging to

Source: *House of Commons Debates.* 3rd Session, 28th Parliament, vol. VIII. Ottawa: Government of Canada, 1971.

the group, and by what the commission calls the group's "collective will to exist." The government shares this belief.

The individual's freedom would be hampered if he were locked for life within a particular cultural compartment by the accident of birth or language. It is vital, therefore, that every Canadian, whatever his ethnic origin, be given a chance to learn at least one of the two languages in which his country conducts its official business and its politics.

A policy of multiculturalism within a bilingual framework commends itself to the government as the most suitable means of assuring the cultural freedom of Canadians. Such a policy should help to break down discriminatory attitudes and cultural jealousies. National unity if it is to mean anything in the deeply personal sense, must be founded on confidence in one's own individual identity; out of this can grow respect for that of others and a willingness to share ideas, attitudes and assumptions. A vigorous policy of multiculturalism will help create this initial confidence. It can form the base of a society which is based on fair play for all.

The government will support and encourage the various cultures and ethnic groups that give structure and vitality to our society. They will be encouraged to share their cultural expression and values with other Canadians and so contribute to a richer life for us all.

In the past, substantial public support has been given largely to the arts and cultural institutions of English-speaking Canada. More recently and largely with the help of the royal commission's earlier recommendations in Volumes I to III, there has been a conscious effort on the government's part to correct any bias against the French language and culture. In the last few months the government has taken steps to provide funds to support cultural educational centres for native people. The policy I am announcing today accepts the contention of the other cultural communities that they, too, are essential elements in Canada and deserve government assistance in order to contribute to regional and national life in ways that derive from their heritage yet are distinctively Canadian.

In implementing a policy of multiculturalism within a bilingual framework, the government will provide support in four ways.

First, resources permitting, the government will seek to assist all Canadian cultural groups that have demonstrated a desire and effort to continue to develop a capacity to grow and contribute to Canada, and a clear need for assistance, the small and weak groups no less than the strong and highly organized.

Second, the government will assist members of all cultural groups to overcome cultural barriers to full participation in Canadian society.

Third, the government will promote creative encounters and interchange among all Canadian cultural groups in the interest of national unity.

Fourth, the government will continue to assist immigrants to acquire at least one of Canada's official languages in order to become full participants in Canadian society. ...

In conclusion, I wish to emphasize the view of the government that a policy of multiculturalism within a bilingual framework is basically the conscious support of individual freedom of choice. We are free to be ourselves. But this cannot be left to chance. It must be fostered and pursued actively. If freedom of choice is in danger for some ethnic groups, it is in danger for all. It is the policy of this government to eliminate such danger and to "safeguard" this freedom.

26 The Ambiguities of a Bilingual and Multicultural Canada

Guy Rocher (1972)

EDITORS' INTRODUCTION

In awarding him their Molson Prize in the Social Sciences and Humanities, the Canada Council said this of Guy Rocher of the Université de Montréal: "[He] is a scholar, a teacher, a visionary and a builder. As a scholar, he has been a pioneer in the sociology of education, law and medical ethics both nationally and internationally. His extraordinary scientific production continues to grow with each passing year. As a teacher, he has trained tens of thousands of sociology students in Canada and throughout the world through his teachings and publications of an exemplary lucidity and clarity of thought. As a visionary and builder, he was an instigator and designer of the educational, social and cultural modernization of contemporary Quebec."

In the following excerpt, Rocher analyzes the consequences of the Trudeau government's unveiling of its multiculturalism policy in October 1971.

This official stand of the Canadian government constitutes an important innovation: it breaks with the image of a unitary country as well as with that of a bicultural one. Moreover, it is an innovation which has substantial practical consequences, realized in the form of the investment of millions of dollars in various programs designed to support Canadian cultural diversity.

The Bases for This New Position

Let us attempt to pursue in somewhat greater depth the analysis of this evolution of the Canadian government's view. Apart from the political, or even electoral, aims which were imputed to the Trudeau government, how does the government justify its innovation?

It seems to me that, in contrast to the Pearson government and the Commission on Bilingualism and Biculturalism, the image of Canada put forward by the Trudeau government has a new foundation or a new base. The Laurendeau-Dunton Commission and the Pearson government position was based on a point of view which was both historical and sociological. The concept of two nations was supported by two facts, one historical and the other socio-

Source: Excerpted from Guy Rocher, "Les ambiguïtés d'un Canada bilingue et multicultural," *Revue de l'Association canadienne d'éducation de langue française*, vol. 1, no. 3 (septembre 1972). Translated in *Cultural Diversity and Canadian Education: Issues and Innovations*, edited by John R. Mallea and Jonathan C. Young. Ottawa: Carleton University Press/McGill-Queen's University Press, 1984. Reprinted by permission.

logical. First, it was seen that, historically, the country originated in two communities—anglophone and francophone—which provided the principal social and political structures still in evidence. Secondly, it was recognized that new Canadians integrate with one or the other of these two communities, both from the linguistic and from the cultural standpoint, even though they may maintain links with the culture of the country from which they or their forefathers emigrated.

In contrast, the Trudeau government's position relies on what I would call psycho-sociological foundations. The document of October 8, 1971 expresses it as follows:

> One of man's fundamental needs is a feeling of belonging, and much of our contemporary social malaise—among all age groups—exists because this need has not been met. Ethnic groups are by no means the only means of satisfying this need to belong, but they have played a very-important role in Canadian society. Ethnic pluralism can help us to overcome or to avoid the homogenization or depersonalization of a mass society. Vital ethnic groups can give second-, third- and later-generation Canadians the feeling that they are linked to the traditions and peoples of various parts of the world and various periods of time.

The ethnic community thus appears to the Trudeau government as one of the primary groups able to fulfill contemporary man's need for identity and security, and to counter the anonymity and anomie of the mass society.

It is also through an appeal to social psychology that the document explains how multiculturalism can simultaneously serve Canadian unity; "The greater our feeling of security in a given social context, the more we are free to explore our identity outside this context. Ethnic groups give people a feeling of belonging which enables them to face society better than they could as isolated individuals. Fidelity to one's own culture does not necessarily, and does not usually, diminish the even greater fidelity towards the collectivity and towards the country."

This distinction between the historico-sociological foundations and the psycho-sociological foundations of an image of Canada may seem theoretical. However, it does indeed appear to be at the source of two very different concepts of Canada. The first emphasizes the central role of two original communities, to which is grafted the cultural impact of all the other ethnic groups. The second emphasizes instead the multiplicity of the ethnic groups, their absolute cultural as well as political equality, within the framework of Canada's official bilingualism.

The Dangers Inherent in This Position

I now wish to develop the reasons why I feel this concept of Canadian society to be ambiguous, faulty and dangerous in its longer-term implications. I have three principal objections:

Bilingualism

First, the distinction between language and culture constitutes one of the most debatable basic implications of the Trudeau government's position. Official bilingualism for Canada is thus detached from the cultural support upon which it relied up to now. In particular, official bilingualism, which as is known only too well, has practically no sociological roots since the majority of Canadians, whether anglophone or francophone, are not bilingual, takes on a very artificial character. Within the new context of multiculturalism, the fragile Canadian bilingualism likely risks being only a vestige of a past which can easily be abandoned or possibly denied. Bilingualism could have had some meaning inasmuch as it symbolized the marriage of two linguistic and cultural communities within Canadian Confederation. But when this idea of two cultural communities is abandoned in favour of Canada's multicultural nature, bilingualism becomes an abstraction, the symbol of a past which no longer corresponds to the present. Under these conditions, it can be foreseen that maintaining a bilingualism with such shallow roots will be found to be more and more difficult. In setting aside the historical basis for biculturalism, one will soon find no reason to maintain an artificial bilingualism. It may then be that Canada can be defined just as well as a unilingual country, or as a country where four, five or six languages are official.

It is not necessary to go far afield to find the ambiguities of bilingualism in a multicultural context; they appear in the Trudeau government statement of October 8, 1971. While proclaiming the distinction between language and culture, the Trudeau government announced that it would "take measures with a view to supplying educational materials for a non-official language. … Acquiring the language of one's forefathers is an important part of the development of a cultural identity." Here we see the Trudeau government recognize the link between language and culture, after denying this same link when it was a question of biculturalism and bilingualism. Furthermore, the federal government announced that it would do something for non-official languages which it has never done in establishing French in education outside Quebec. The logical outcome of the policy set out by the Trudeau government is the imminent establishment of multilingualism to replace bilingualism.

In Montreal, there already exists the kind of bilingualism which the policy of multiculturalism will lead to. Among new Canadians, the bilingualism currently practised is English–Greek, English–Italian, English–German bilingualism; English–French bilingualism is almost non-existent.

National Identity

The second important reservation which I have with respect to multiculturalism is that I do not believe it constitutes the basis for a nation. The Canadian nation, as defined by the Trudeau government, no longer has a central cultural core which is clearly identifiable. Canada would be a sort of microcosm or meeting-place for all the nations of the world, represented here by groups of greater or lesser numerical size, all having an equal right to recognition and financial support of the Canadian government. Canada probably could have been greatly enriched if it had been able to maintain the idea of two cultural communities serving as poles for groupings of the other ethnic groups. Instead of this, there is proposed to us a nebulous sort of image constituted by an undefined number of different cultures, which the Trudeau government would wish to see interact but to which it proposes no common denominator.

I perceive a sense of failure in this stance taken by the Trudeau government: it is recognized that there is no Canadian culture, either anglophone or francophone. Whereas the idea of biculturalism put forward the image of a Canada with a certain internal structure, the concept of multiculturalism offers us the absence of a national culture as its program. I wonder what kind of nation can really exist on a basis which is so fluid and so noncommittal.

The Francophone Community

Finally, I wish to emphasize very briefly that, for the French-Canadian community, this new multicultural policy is a large step backwards which has as yet, I think, gone unrecognized by French Canadians. For several generations, French Canadians have struggled to gain a recognition of a bilingualism which would not only be a recognition of French as an official language, but at the same time a recognition of the French-Canadian community as the counterpart of the English-Canadian community in the Canadian sociological structure. By detaching bilingualism from biculturalism, the Trudeau government betrays all the hopes which French Canadians could have placed in bilingualism as they perceived it; that is, closely linked to the biculturalism of which it was both a symbol and an essential condition.

Of the two main linguistic and cultural communities, anglophone and francophone, it is obviously the francophone community which will suffer the most from this new multicultural policy, and which can feel threatened by it. In reality, since the anglophone community is predominant everywhere but in Quebec, and even there is also very powerful, it will necessarily remain the centre of attraction for all the other ethnic cultures. On the other hand, in this new context the francophone community will see its position and its status decline rapidly. With economic forces already acting to its disadvantage, it will become more and more secondary in the midst of all the other cultures which will compose the new Canadian mosaic.

It is my personal belief that, as French Canadians become aware of this new situation, the Quebec separatist option will appear to be a desirable solution to an increasing number of French Canadians. I fear that the cultural fragmentation proposed to us by the October 1971 declaration of the Canadian government will in fact prove a plan for destroying Canadian Confederation. A multicultural Canada offers too few chances for the future survival and flourishing of the French-Canadian culture. The creation of an independent francophone Quebec will then appear to be the one final chance for a North American francophone nation whose future is inevitably uncertain.

27 Apology to Japanese Canadians

Brian Mulroney (1988)

EDITORS' INTRODUCTION

Brian Mulroney's official apology for the internment of Japanese Canadians along Canada's West Coast was the result of years of lobbying. The apology itself was an important symbolic gesture as an official acknowledgment of the injustice that had occurred. The redress settlement also included payment of $21,000 to all surviving internees, a reinstatement of citizenship to those who were deported following the end of the Second World War, and a $24 million contribution to the establishment of the Canadian Race Relations Foundation.

House of Commons

Thursday, September 22, 1988

ROUTINE PROCEEDINGS
Visible Minorities

Japanese Canadians Interned During World War II—National Redress

Right Hon. Brian Mulroney (Prime Minister): Mr. Speaker, nearly half a century ago, in the crisis of wartime, the Government of Canada wrongfully incarcerated, seized the property, and disenfranchised thousands of citizens of Japanese ancestry. We cannot change the past. But we must, as a nation, have the courage to face up to these historical facts.

The issue of Japanese-Canadian redress is one which I raised in the House of Commons more than four years ago with the Prime Minister of the day when I was Leader of the Opposition. I said then in this House:

> There is a world of difference between regret and a formal apology. Canadians of Japanese origin had their rights trampled upon. The reputation of this country was besmirched.

Since then, Mr. Speaker, the present Government has sought a settlement with the Japanese-Canadian community to put things right between them and their country; to put things right with the surviving members of the Japanese-Canadian wartime community of 22,000 persons; to put things right with their children, and ours, so that they can walk together in this country, burdened neither by the wrongs nor the grievances of previous generations.

It is fitting that representatives of the National Association of Japanese Canadians are present in the visitors' gallery on this solemn occasion because today I have the honour to

Source: *House of Commons Debates.* 2nd Session, 33rd Parliament, vol. XV. Ottawa: Government of Canada, 1988.

announce, on behalf of the Government of Canada, that a comprehensive redress settlement has been reached with the National Association of Japanese Canadians on behalf of their community.

Some Hon. Members: Hear, hear!

Mr. Mulroney: Perhaps the most important element of this redress is the official acknowledgement of the wrongs of the 1940s. But redress must go beyond words and laws—important as they are for our present understanding and our future actions. The Minister of State for Multiculturalism and Citizenship (Mr. Weiner) will be announcing the details of the settlement, and I pay special tribute today to his skill and resolve in this matter, and to the Secretary of State (Mr. Bouchard) who, immediately after his swearing in as a Minister of the Crown, made the resolution of this important moral issue a matter of the highest priority for him and his colleagues. In a special way, I readily acknowledge the strong moral leadership on this particular question and, indeed, others, that has long been provided by the Hon. Member for Vancouver South (Mr. Fraser), the very distinguished Speaker of the House of Commons.

Some Hon. Members: Hear, hear!

Mr. Mulroney: Mr. Speaker, I think all Members of the House know that no amount of money can right the wrong, undo the harm, and heal the wounds. But it is symbolic of our determination to address this issue, not only in the moral sense but also in a tangible way. In that spirit, we will accept applications for the granting of Canadian citizenship to eligible persons of Japanese ancestry who were expelled from Canada or had their citizenship revoked during these years. We will also accept requests for the clearing of names of eligible persons of Japanese ancestry who were convicted of violations under the War Measures Act—thankfully now gone from our texts of law in Canada—and the National Emergency Transitional Powers Act.

As well, in commemoration of all who suffered these injustices, we will establish a Canadian Race Relations Foundation to foster racial harmony and cross-cultural understanding in Canada.

[*Translation*] Mr. Speaker, not only was the treatment inflicted on Japanese-Canadians during the War both morally and legally unjustified, it went against the very nature of our country, of Canada. We are a pluralistic society. We each respect the language, opinions and religious convictions of our neighbour. We celebrate our linguistic duality and our cultural diversity. We know that the strength of our country lies in the collective energies of its regions. We are tolerant people who live in freedom in a land of abundance. That is the Canada of our ancestors. That is the Canada our ancestors worked to build. That is the kind of country we want to leave our children, the Canada of the Charter of Rights and Freedoms, the new Official Languages Act and the Canadian Multiculturalism Act. A Canada that at all times and in all circumstances works hard to eliminate racial discrimination at home and abroad.

[*English*] A Canada, Mr. Speaker, that is able to face up to the mistakes of the past, and so become better prepared to face the challenges of the future.

I am tabling at this time the specific terms of the Government's historic agreement with the National Association of Japanese Canadians. I will meet later this morning with the

President of the National Association of Japanese Canadians and some of his colleagues who are with him today to formalize this special agreement.

Most of us in our own lives have had occasion to regret certain things that we have done. Error is an ingredient of humanity, so too is apology and forgiveness. We all have learned from personal experience that as inadequate as apologies are they are the only way we can cleanse the past so that we may, as best we can, in good conscience face the future.

I know that I speak for Members on all sides of the House today in offering to Japanese Canadians the formal and sincere apology of this Parliament for those past injustices against them, against their families, and against their heritage, and our solemn commitment and undertaking to Canadians of every origin that such violations will never again in this country be countenanced or repeated.

Some Hon. Members: Hear, hear!

28 The Fractious Politics of a Settler Society: Canada

Daiva Stasiulis and Radha Jhappan (1995)

EDITORS' INTRODUCTION

In this piece Stasiulis and Jhappan explore the implications of Canada's development as a "white settler society" and its effects on the autonomy of Aboriginal peoples, immigrants, racial minorities and women, paying particular attention to the racial and gendered hierarchies that have characterized much of Canadian history.

Contemporary Politics: Symbolic Re-ordering of Ethnic and National Identities

The current politics surrounding racial and ethnic diversity in contemporary Canada is a lesson in how settler societies and the legitimacy of assumed racial/ethnic hierarchies eventually come undone. The struggles of First Nations, Québec sovereignists, racial/ethnic minorities and women for symbolic recognition and claims on state resources (or in some cases, separate states) have severely undermined the assumptions about race and gender of the British white settler colonization model. Aboriginal, Québec and ethnic/racial minority politics also illustrate the practical impossibility of integrating divergent ethnocultural identity claims within the same political, territorial, administrative and institutional framework (Salée, 1994a).

Irreconcilable ethnocultural claims are perhaps posed most acutely by the confrontation in claims of francophone Québeckers and First Nations people within the province of Québec. The development of Québec nationalism is complex and has been tied to many divergent projects of social reform ranging across the political spectrum. Prior to the 1960s, Québec represented a primarily agrarian society, dominated by Roman Catholic clergy and controlled by a Montréal-based English elite. The past 35 years, beginning with the so-called Quiet Revolution of the 1960s, have seen the modernization of the Québec state and economy. Francophone Québeckers, in the flush of newly awakened nationalism, sought to overturn the fact that in a province where 80 per cent of the population was francophone, the language of higher education, management, finance, business and labour relations was English.

Source: Excerpted from *Unsettling Settler Societies: Articulations of Gender, Race, Ethnicity and Class*, edited by Daiva Stasiulis and Nira Yuval Davis. London: Sage Publications, 1995. Reprinted by permission.

They therefore set about building a virtual state within the Canadian state through the considerable powers permitted to provincial governments under federalism.

Provincial autonomy and linguistic distinctiveness have provided francophone Québeckers with the political apparatus, state intellectuals and resources to assert their ethnocultural distinctiveness, build a Québec bourgeoisie and lay their claims to political sovereignty. The territorial focus of Québecois nationalism on Québec and its state also stemmed from the fact that the population of French descent is becoming a receding minority in Canada as a whole (23 per cent in 1991). To ensure the survival of language, the core strategy of Québec nationalists has been to make Québec a unilingual society. To this end, francophone Québeckers have sought controls on immigration policy to maximize the number of French-speaking immigrants, and have passed laws that restrict the rights of children to English-language education, legislate the language of work and erase all public manifestations of English or languages other than French in commercial signage.

The memory of "the Conquest," printed on every Québec licence plate (*Je me souviens* or "I remember"), continues to mythologize the defeat of the Québec nation at a time when francophones are economically and politically an empowered majority in that province. Currently, an economistic nationalism dominates the public agenda of Québec which articulates the desire of the francophone Québec business elite to better position itself first in the North American and then in the global market (Salée, 1994b). Powerful Québec capitalists have "come to look on the Canadian market, and their cultural and political links with the English Canadian business class, as a historical left-over, a relic of a time when they, as Québecois, were the hewers of wood and drawers of water" (Ignatieff, 1993: 114). Similarly, Québec mass media, educational institutions and popular culture refer to Québec exclusively when referring to society in general: "Books have been published on 'Québec mushrooms' or 'Québec small game,' as if there were frontiers for morels and rabbits!" (Gagnon, 1994: 3).

Contemporary francophone Québec identity: that draws selectively on traditional imagery of a rural and colonized past, yet exudes the confidence of Québec's captains of industry, is not coterminous with all those who occupy Québec. As Salée (1994b: 15) has observed, this imagined community of a "founding nation" excludes those identities that are frequently discounted (immigrants), silenced (First Nations; those at the economic margins such as the poor, youth and many women), or oppositional (the Anglo Québec "conquerors"). However, it is Aboriginal political claims that pose the major threat to francophone Québec's claims for special recognition.

Several issues have brought Québec nationalism into conflict with the nationalism of particular First Nations—hydroelectric development, the role of the Québec police in the armed confrontation with Mohawk warriors at Kanesatake and Kahnawake (or Oka) in the summer of 1990 (York and Pindera, 1991), and constitutional negotiations (Jhappan, 1993). For the Québec government, the James Bay hydroelectric project is a central symbol of Québec's modernization and represents the core of its competitive advantage in the North American economy; for the Cree, it is an invasion in their homeland (Ignatieff, 1993: 124–5).

The claims of First Nations in Québec (and Canada as a whole) to self-determination and self-government, an adequate territorial base and control over resources rest on inherent rights "since time immemorial." If recognized by the Canadian government, such claims made by representatives of Aboriginal peoples across the country would mean a fundamental restructuring of the Canadian federation to accommodate entirely new governments and sovereign territories. In Québec, First Nations' aspirations "delegitimize the very foundations upon which Québec has built its claims for special status within the Canadian federation" (Salée, 1994a: 4). In fact, bitter animosity was activated between Aboriginal leaders and Québec politicians during the constitutional reform process of 1991–2, when the former finally succeeded in displacing the "two founding nations" mythology with a new construct, "three founding nations" (Jhappan, 1993: 238–42).

Of course, Québec has not been the only province to deny Aboriginal territorial and political claims; all of the provinces have abrogated aboriginal rights with the result that there are outstanding claims all over the country. Indeed, in some ways, up to the 1990s, Québec's legislative Native policy, especially under Parti Québecois (sovereignist) governments in the 1970s and 1980s, has been more progressive than that of most other provinces (Gourdeau, 1993). ...

Whereas the Québecois see themselves as oppressed *vis-à-vis* "English Canada," Aboriginal peoples have been oppressed by both. Unlike francophone Québeckers, who have at their disposal a provincial state which provides substantial legislative and institutional autonomy, as well as significant economic power, Aboriginal peoples do not have the bargaining power to force concessions from *either* the provincial *or* the federal states. Moreover, the particular history of marginalization of Aboriginal peoples, the institutionalized and societal racism levelled at them for several hundred years, their geographic dispersion and, crucially, the fact that they, unlike Québec, are claiming ownership of lands all over the country are factors which put them in a vastly inferior bargaining position *vis-à-vis* both Québec and the rest of Canada.

Despite such an overwhelming imbalance of power, Aboriginal peoples in Canada have employed a range of strategies in pursuit of their claims, some of which have brought important victories. A series of legal challenges in the 1980s and 1990s, for example, have won declarations from the highest courts that Aboriginal and treaty rights are pre-existing legal rights which must be honoured or disposed of with the consent of the First Nations concerned (Jhappan, 1991). Such legal advances have been complemented by several historic political innovations, most notably the creation of Nunavut, a settlement of an Inuit land claim which will give the Inuit self-government over one-fifth of Canada's land mass in the eastern Arctic by 1999. It must be noted, however, that these victories are largely localized to specific tribal groups. While others may be empowered by them, in general Aboriginal peoples still suffer from ingrained discriminatory practices, and find themselves at the top of virtually every index of socio-economic distress.

The racial and ethnic heterogeneity of the settler population and the continued importance of immigration in Canada have led to a dramatic reshaping of the racial and ethnic composition of the population. In the 1991 census, of a population of 27 million, the proportion of Canadians of (single) "other" origins was 31 per cent, higher than the proportions of British (21 per cent), French (23 per cent), Aboriginal (1.7 per cent) or combined origins (rounded percentages, 1991 Canadian Census). Notwithstanding their relative numbers, however, the politics of the "others"—non-British, non-French and non-Aboriginal groups—are far less destabilizing insofar as they do not take the form of demands for self-determination, autonomous political or administrative institutions, or separate territory and control of resources (Salée, 1994a: 2). The struggles of racial, ethnocultural and immigrant minorities in Canada have encompassed a broad range of issues speaking to the aspirations of these minorities for equity, protection from discrimination and symbolic recognition of the reality of ethnic and racial pluralism. These include anti-racist, affirmative action and fair immigration and refugee campaigns, and efforts to bring racial and ethnic democracy within the institutions of the public service, law enforcement, education, representative political institutions, trade unions and women's movements.

The geographical dispersion and heterogeneity of minority groups makes them far less cohesive in their demands upon the state, and hence easier to ignore. The symbolic recognition of these groups' presence in Canada has chiefly taken the form of multiculturalism policies and agencies developed at the level of the national and most provincial states. Multiculturalism policy (as distinguished from the socio-demographic reality of ethnic diversity) arose as a result of protests by ethnic minorities over the settler society construct of a "bilingual and bicultural" Canada, reflected in cultural and official language state policies. Since its establishment as official federal government policy in 1971, the central tenet of multiculturalism has been the promotion of racial/ethnic harmony and equality through respecting individuals' cultural differences.

Since the mid-1980s, popular and elite opinion on multiculturalism has become increasingly negative and developed into a virtual assault on the existence of the policy and its assumptions (Abu-Laban and Stasiulis, 1992). After a brief period whereby the administrative and legislative status of the policy had been elevated, the federal government in 1993 abruptly submerged the federal multiculturalism bureaucracy into an amorphous new department called Heritage Canada (Tepper, 1994: 103).

Although the arguments for rejecting multiculturalism are themselves diverse, there is little question that increasing numbers of Canadians are willing to discard government policies that promote a "cultural mosaic." The policy has long attracted vocal opposition from Québec, where francophone Québeckers have claimed that multiculturalism denies the cultural integrity of Québec society, and by relativizing culture, masks the "national question" that has otherwise dominated federal politics (Rocher, 1973; Labelle, 1991). Members of ethnic and racial minorities have faulted the policy for its failure to alleviate racism or discrimination, for ghettoizing ethnocultural communities' justice and equity concerns, and for handicapping the movement of "ethnics" into the mainstream (Abu-Laban and Stasiulis, 1992: 376–8).

The inextricable link of multiculturalism to immigration (the source for diversity) also means that the growing hostility to multiculturalism since the mid-1980s expresses the abhorrence of many white Canadians to the predominantly third world origins of most immigrant newcomers. The broad wave of deindustrialization that has gutted Canada's (Ontario-Québec) industrial heartland since the early 1980s, financial deregulation, the accompanying corrosion of the welfare state, and the further decline in Canadian living standards associated with NAFTA are trends which have heightened the anxiety of many groups. The result has been a backlash against so-called "minorities" by those whose majority or dominant status is perceived as under economic or cultural threat, and whose politics draw on a refurbished arsenal of images and metaphors associated with the racial/gender/class order of the white settler colony.

Putting Multiculturalism into Perspective

Will Kymlicka (1998)

EDITORS' INTRODUCTION

The following reading is excerpted from "Putting Multiculturalism into Perspective," which is the title of a chapter in Will Kymlicka's book Finding Our Way: Rethinking Ethnocultural Relations in Canada. *In these passages, Kymlicka defends multiculturalism as a positive force that leads toward, not away from, the integration of immigrants into Canadian society.*

The Immigrant Response to Nation-Building

The historical evidence, both in Canada and abroad, shows that the capacity and motivation to undertake such an ambitious nation-building project is found only in non-immigrant national minorities. Immigrant groups have responded in a very different way to state nation-building policies. They have typically accepted the expectation that they will integrate into the dominant societal culture. They have not objected to requirements that they and their children learn an official language, and that they participate in common institutions operating in that language.

Why have immigrants historically accepted integration? One reason is that they have already voluntarily left their own cultures with the expectation of integrating into a different national society. That's just what it means to immigrate; if they found the idea of integrating into another culture repugnant, they would not have chosen to leave their homelands.[12] Moreover, since most arrive in Canada as individuals or families, rather than as entire communities, immigrants typically lack the territorial concentration or corporate institutions needed to form a linguistically distinct society alongside the mainstream society. To try to recreate such a distinct parallel society would require tremendous support from the host society—support that host governments are reluctant to offer.

In both of these respects, immigrants are very different from national minorities, for whom nation-building threatens a culturally distinct society that already exists and has functioned for generations. Historically, the nationalist option has been neither desirable nor feasible for immigrants, and in fact there are very few (if any) examples in the Western democracies of immigrant groups forming nationalist movements for self-government or secession. In short, faced with the choice between integration and fighting to maintain a

---

Source: Excerpted from *Finding Our Way: Rethinking Ethnocultural Relations in Canada* by Will Kymlicka. Oxford: Oxford University Press, 1998. Some notes omitted. Reprinted by permission of the author.

distinct societal culture, immigrant groups in Canada have historically chosen the former, while national minorities have chosen the latter.

In some other countries, however, the situation is more complex. The extent to which immigrant groups have been allowed or encouraged to integrate varies considerably. Whereas in Canada it is easy for immigrants to become full citizens regardless of their race, religion, or ethnic origin, in many parts of the world, including some Western democracies, they are much les welcome, and it is far more difficult for them to acquire equal citizenship. Where immigrants are subject to severe prejudice and legal discrimination—and hence where full equality within the mainstream society is unachievable—it is possible that some may come to question the goal of integration.[13]

Similarly, the extent to which national minorities have been able to maintain separate cultures varies form country to country. National minorities that have been subject to long periods of highly coercive policies of assimilation, such as the Bretons in France, have eventually lost most or all of their institutions and traditions of self-government. As a general rule, however, in Western democracies dominant cultures have had far less success integrating national than immigrant groups. While national minorities have resisted integration into the common culture and sought to protect their separate existence by consolidating their own societal cultures, immigrants have accepted the expectation of integration.

Is Multiculturalism Separatist?

Is there any reason to think that multiculturalism is changing this pattern? Does it repudiate the principles and policies promoting integration, and instead treat immigrant groups as if they were national minorities? Some critics think so. According to Richard Gwyn, "logically" the policy of multiculturalism entails that "the doctrine of self-governing territories as applied now to native people could be extended to all identity groups."[14] In reality, nothing could be further from the truth.

Consider any of the sorts of programs commonly associated with multiculturalism, whether curriculum reform in public schools (e.g., revising the history and literature curricula to give greater recognition to the historical and cultural contributions of ethnocultural minorities; bilingual education programs for the children of immigrants at the primary level), or institutional adaptation (revising work schedules or dress-codes so as to accommodate the religious holidays and practices of immigrant groups; adopting workplace or school harassment codes prohibiting racist comments; guidelines from the broadcasting regulator, the Canadian Radio-television and Telecommunications Commission [CRTC], on ethnic stereotypes), or public education programs (anti-racism educational campaigns; cultural diversity training for police, social workers, or health-care professionals), or cultural development programs (funding ethnic festivals and ethnic studies programs; providing mother-tongue literacy courses for adult immigrants), or affirmative action (preferential treatment of visible minorities in access to education, training, or employment).

This list goes well beyond the confines of the federal government's official policy of multiculturalism. Many of these programs fall under the jurisdiction of other federal departments (e.g., employment equity; broadcasting guidelines), or other levels of government (school curricula), and, strictly speaking, are not part of Canada's "multiculturalism" policy. On the other hand, since the federal policy was explicitly intended to serve as a model and catalyst for other departments and other levels of government, it is perhaps not inappropriate to consider all of these as loosely related to "multiculturalism."

Since each of the above programs raises its own unique issues, it would be misleading to talk about "the impact of multiculturalism" in general, as if all of them had the same motivations and consequences. Even so, it is important to note that *none* of these programs—either individually or in combination—involves anything close to a program of nation-building, or the "logic of self-governing territories." None of them involves creating Spanish-language army units, or Vietnamese-language universities. And none of them involves creating new political units that would enable Ukrainians to exercise self-governing powers in the area of government employment or immigration. Nor have any such measures been demanded by these immigrant groups. ...

The fact is that existing multiculturalism policies have not created *any* of the public institutions needed to create and sustain a separate societal culture for the Chinese, the Somalis, or any other immigrant group. None of the academic, political, or economic institutions that would enable an immigrant group to participate in modern life through their mother tongue have been created. If (unlike the Hutterites) Somali Canadians or Ukrainian Canadians or Vietnamese Canadians want to have access to the opportunities made available by modern society, they must do so within the economic, academic, and political institutions of either the anglophone or the francophone societal culture in Canada.

This should not be surprising, because multiculturalism has not replaced any of the broader panoply of government policies and structures that promote societal integration. It is still the case that immigrants must learn to speak one of the official languages to gain citizenship, or graduate from high school, or find government employment, or gain professional accreditation. These are the basic pillars of government-supported integration within liberal democracies, and none of them has in any way been eroded by multiculturalism policies. Nor was multiculturalism intended to erode them.

In fact, multiculturalism could not have been intended to enable or encourage immigrants to become national minorities, like the Québécois or Aboriginal peoples. Gwyn's claim that the logic of multiculturalism means that "the doctrine of self-governing territories as applied now to native people could be extended to all identity groups" is nonsensical. It would be inherently contradictory for government to encourage immigrant groups to form their own societal cultures (via multiculturalism policies) while simultaneously insisting (via education, employment, and citizenship policies) that immigrants must learn to speak one of the official languages fluently in order to gain citizenship, graduate from school, find government employment, or acquire professional licensing or trade certification.

And even if the government had somehow adopted this contradictory set of goals, the amount of money spent on multiculturalism is so miniscule that it would have no discernible effect when weighed against all the government spending that promotes integration. The 20 million dollars spent on multiculturalism programs is a drop in the bucket compared with the billions of dollars spend on policies that directly or indirectly promote integration.

So the idea that multiculturalism policies are first steps on the road to separate public institutions is multiply bizarre. These policies have not in fact created such institutions, nor could they have been intended to do so without undermining firmly entrenched policies regarding citizenship, education, and employment; and in any event the funding they receive is so small that it could not hope to create a fraction of the institutions needed for such a separatist goal.

Of course it is still possible to fear that some leaders of ethnic groups hope multicultural-ism policies will provide a springboard to a more comprehensively separatist policy. If so, however, both the hope and the fear are in vain, for they massively underestimate the sort of support needed to create and sustain a separate societal culture. It makes more sense simply to accept the obvious: there is no rational basis for the fear that multiculturalism policies will be used to enable immigrant groups to sustain their own societal cultures. This fear is a mirage, without any basis in reality. There is no evidence from any of the major Western immigrant countries that immigrants are seeking to form themselves into national minorities, or to adopt a nationalist political agenda.

Notes

12. Obviously this doesn't apply to refugees. People who flee their homeland to avoid persecution cannot be said to have chosen to immigrate. While their subjective motivations differ from those of immigrants, however, their objective circumstances within Canada are similar in terms of the feasibility of nation-building. Like immigrants, they arrive as individuals or families, and so lack the territorial concentration or corporate institutions needed for nationalist mobilization.

13. For example, if the German government persists in making it difficult for long-term Turkish residents (and their children and grand-children) to gain citizenship, one would expect Turks to press for greater powers of self-government, so that they can create and perpetuate a separate and self-governing society alongside the German society to which they are denied entry. But this is not the preference of the Turks, who, like immigrants in other liberal democracies, want to become full and equal participants in German society. The historical record suggests that forms of self-government will be sought by immigrant groups within liberal democracies only if they face unjust barriers to their full integration and participation in the mainstream society.

14. Gwyn, *Nationalism Without Walls* (Toronto: McClelland and Stewart, 1995): 156.

30 Bouchard-Taylor Report on Accommodation Practices in Quebec

Gérard Bouchard and Charles Taylor (2008)

EDITORS' INTRODUCTION

The Consultation Commission on Accommodation Practices Related to Cultural Differences was established in February 2007 with a mandate that included taking stock of accommodation practices in Quebec, conducting extensive consultations, and formulating recommendations to the government to ensure that accommodation practices conform to the pluralistic, democratic, and egalitarian values of Quebec society. As the report authors noted in their introduction, "As was readily apparent in the fall of 2007, Quebecers are divided. This is the very first observation arising from the public and private consultations that we conducted. It is also apparent from the findings of surveys conducted in recent years. Quebecers are divided over accommodation but also over most of the questions pertaining to it." They add that "[we] well know that not everyone will agree with our conclusions," but stress that "the time has come for reconciliation."

Summary of the Full Report

I. Mandate and Investigation

A. MANDATE

On February 8, 2007, Québec Premier Jean Charest announced the establishment of the Consultation Commission on Accommodation Practices Related to Cultural Differences in response to public discontent concerning reasonable accommodation. The Order in Council establishing the Commission stipulated that it had a mandate to: *a)* take stock of accommodation practices in Québec; *b)* analyse the attendant issues bearing in mind the experience of other societies; *c)* conduct an extensive consultation on this topic; and *d)* formulate recommendations to the government to ensure that accommodation practices conform to Québec's values as a pluralistic, democratic, egalitarian society.

We could have broached the Commission's mandate in two ways, i.e. in a broad sense or in a narrow sense. The narrower sense would consist in confining the Commission's inves-

Source: Excerpted from *Building the Future: A Time for Reconciliation*. Report by Gérard Bouchard and Charles Taylor for The Consultation Commission on Accommodation Practices Related to Cultural Differences (CCAPRCD). Quebec City: Government of the Province of Quebec, 2008.

tigation to the strictly legal dimension of reasonable accommodation. The second approach would be to perceive the debate on reasonable accommodation as the symptom of a more basic problem concerning the sociocultural integration model established in Québec since the 1970s. This perspective called for a review of interculturalism, immigration, secularism and the theme of Québec identity. We decided to follow the second course in order to grasp the problem at its source and from all angles, with particular emphasis on its economic and social dimensions. The school-to-work transition and professional recognition, access to decent living conditions and the fight against discrimination are indeed essential conditions for ensuring the cultural integration of all citizens into Québec society.

B. OUR INVESTIGATION

The Commission had at its disposal a budget of $5 million, which enabled it to carry out a number of activities. We commissioned 13 research projects carried out by specialists from Québec universities. A number of research instruments were developed, including a typology designed to classify the arguments in the briefs submitted and the e-mails that we analysed. We organized 31 focus groups with individuals from different milieus in Montréal and the regions. We held 59 meetings with experts and representatives of sociocultural organizations. We also set up an advisory committee comprising 15 specialists from various disciplines.

As for the public consultations, we commissioned four province-wide forums, organized by the Institut du Nouveau Monde, in which over 800 people participated. The Commission held sessions in 15 regions, in addition to Montréal, for a total of 31 days of hearings. The public responded very generously to our appeal by submitting more than 900 briefs. We read all of these texts and discussed them with their authors during 328 hearings, during which we heard testimony from 241 individuals. In the centres where hearings were held, we organized 22 evening citizens' forums open without restriction to the public and broadcast live or pre-recorded by a number of television networks, which attracted a total of 3 423 participants. Each forum, which lasted for nearly three hours, afforded, on average, 40 participants from all social backgrounds to take the floor and express their opinions. Between August 2007 and January 2008, the Commission also operated a Website that afforded the public opportunities to engage in exchanges (over 400,000 visits). ...

II. Sources of the Accommodation Crisis

A. A CRISIS OF PERCEPTION

After a year of research and consultation, we have come to the conclusion that the foundations of collective life in Québec are not in a critical situation. Our investigation did not reveal to us a striking or sudden increase in the adjustments or accommodation that public institutions allow, nor did we observe that the normal operation of our institutions would have been disrupted by such requests, which is eloquently confirmed by the very small number of accommodation cases that ends up before the courts.

We also observed a certain discrepancy between practices in the field, especially in the education and health sectors, and the feeling of discontent that has arisen among Quebecers. An analysis of debate on the question of accommodation in Québec reveals that 55% of the cases noted over the past 22 years, i.e. 40 cases out of 73, were brought to the public's attention during the period March 2006 to June 2007 alone. The investigation of the cases that received the most widespread media attention during this period of turmoil reveals that, in 15 of 21 cases, there were striking distortions between general public perceptions and the actual facts as we were able to reconstitute them. In other words, the negative perception of reasonable accommodation that spread in the public often centred on an erroneous or partial perception of practices in the field. Our report describes several cases that confirm this conclusion.

B. ANXIETY OVER IDENTITY

Sudden media enthusiasm and rumours contributed to the crisis of perception, although they alone cannot explain the current of dissatisfaction that spread among a large portion of the population. The so-called wave of accommodation clearly touched a number of emotional chords among French-Canadian Quebecers in such a way that requests for religious adjustments have spawned fears about the most valuable heritage of the Quiet Revolution, in particular gender equality and secularism. The result has been an identity counter-reaction movement that has expressed itself through the rejection of harmonization practices. Among some Quebecers, this counter-reaction targets immigrants, who have become, to some extent, scapegoats. What has just happened in Québec gives the impression of a face-off between two minority groups, each of which is asking the other to accommodate it. The members of the ethnocultural majority are afraid of being swamped by fragile minorities that are worried about their future. The conjunction of these two anxieties is obviously not likely to foster integration in a spirit of equality and reciprocity.

We can conclude that Quebecers of French-Canadian ancestry are still not at ease with their twofold status as a majority in Québec and a minority in Canada and North America. However, we should also point out that a number of Western nations are experiencing malaises that resemble those expressed during debate on accommodation. A comparison of the situation in Québec with that in several European countries reveals that a number of fears that may be warranted elsewhere are not necessarily justified here.

III. Social Norms

One of the key sources of anxiety mentioned during our consultations concerns the putative absence of guidelines to handle accommodation or adjustment requests. However, over the years, Québec society has adopted an array of norms and guidelines that form the basis of a "common public culture." In our report, we allude to these reference points that must guide the process of evaluating requests, with particular emphasis on the social norms that would benefit from clarification, more specifically as regards integration, intercultural relations and open secularism.

A. REASONABLE ACCOMMODATION AND CONCERTED ADJUSTMENT

The field of harmonization practices is complex and there is more than one way to define and delineate it. Among the criteria, we have decided to give priority to the framework for handling requests, which leads us to distinguish between the legal route and the citizen route.

Under the legal route, requests must conform to formal codified procedures that the parties bring against each other and that ultimately decree a winner and a loser. Indeed, the courts impose decisions most of the time. The legal route is that of reasonable accommodation. Requests follow a much different route under the second path, which is less formal and relies on negotiation and the search for a compromise. Its objective is to find a solution that satisfies both parties and it corresponds to concerted adjustment.

Generally speaking, we strongly favour recourse to the citizen route and concerted adjustment, for several reasons: *a)* it is good for citizens to learn to manage their differences and disagreements; *b)* this path avoids congesting the courts; and *c)* the values underlying the citizen route (exchanges, negotiation, reciprocity, and so on) are the same ones that underpin the Québec integration model. In quantitative terms, we have noted, moreover, that most requests follow the citizen route and only a small number rely on the courts.

Moreover, our investigation revealed that, in the case of both the citizen route and the legal route, the fear of a domino effect is unfounded. Indeed, several criteria allow us to evaluate accommodation or adjustment requests. Such requests may be rejected if they lead to what jurists call undue hardship, i.e. an unreasonable cost, a disruption of the organization's or the establishment's operations, the infringement of other people's rights or the undermining of security or public order. A number of public institutions have already sought inspiration in the legal guideline of undue hardship to define evaluation methods that take into account their distinctive features. We also observed that many milieus have acquired solid expertise in the realm of intercultural relations and harmonization practices.

B. INTERCULTURALISM

Often mentioned in academic papers, interculturalism as an integration policy has never been fully, officially defined by the Québec government, although its underlying principles were formulated long ago. This shortcoming should be overcome, all the more so as the Canadian multiculturalism model does not appear to be well adapted to conditions in Québec.

Generally speaking, it is in the interests of any community to maintain a minimum of cohesion. It is subject to that condition that a community can adopt common orientations, ensure participation by citizens in public debate, create the feeling of solidarity required for an egalitarian society to function smoothly, mobilize the population in the event of a crisis, and take advantage of the enrichment that stems from ethnocultural diversity. For a small nation such as Québec, constantly concerned about its future as a cultural minority, integration also represents a condition for its development, or perhaps for its survival.

That is why the integrative dimension is a key component of Québec interculturalism. According to the descriptions provided in scientific documentation, interculturalism seeks to reconcile ethnocultural diversity with the continuity of the French-speaking core and the preservation of the social link. It thus affords security to Quebecers of French-Canadian origin and to ethnocultural minorities and protects the rights of all in keeping with the liberal tradition. By instituting French as the common public language, it establishes a framework in society for communication and exchanges. It has the virtue of being flexible and receptive to negotiation, adaptation and innovation.

C. OPEN SECULARISM

Liberal democracies, including Québec, all adhere to the principle of secularism, which can nonetheless be embodied in different systems. Any secular system achieves some form of balance between the following four principles: 1. the moral equality of persons; 2. freedom of conscience and religion; 3. the separation of Church and State; and 4. State neutrality in respect of religious and deep-seated secular convictions.

Certain systems impose fairly strict limits on freedom of religious expression. For example, France recently adopted restrictive legislation governing the wearing of religious signs in public schools. There are three reasons why we believe that this type of restrictive secularism is not appropriate for Québec: a)it does not truly link institutional structures to the outcomes of secularism; b) the attribution to the school of an emancipatory mission directed against religion is not compatible with the principle of State neutrality in respect of religion and non-religion; c) the integration process in a diversified society is achieved through exchanges between citizens, who thus learn to get to know each other (that is the philosophy of Québec interculturalism), and not by relegating identities to the background.

Open secularism, which we are advocating, seeks to develop the essential outcomes of secularism (first and second principles) by defining institutional structures (third and fourth principles) in light of this objective. This is the path that Québec has followed historically, as witnessed by the Proulx report, which also promotes open secularism.

IV. Harmonization Practices: Elements of a Policy

In light of the social norms that we delineate in our report, we are proposing a number of general key directions aimed at guiding the interveners and individual Quebecers concerned by harmonization practices. However, it is important to note that adjustment requests must be evaluated on a case-by-case basis and that there may be exceptions to general rules.

1. Pursuant to the norms and guidelines that we are formulating, adjustment requests that infringe gender equality would have little chance of being granted, since such equality is a core value in our society. In the health care sector as in all public services, this value disqualifies, in principle, all requests that have the effect of granting a woman inferior status to that of a man.

2. Coeducation is an important value in Québec society but it is not as fundamental as gender equality. As a general guideline, coeducation should, however, prevail everywhere possible, for example when students are divided into classes, in swimming classes, and so on.

3. As for prayer rooms in public establishments, our position reflects the opinion that the Commission des droits de la personne et des droits de la jeunesse adopted on February 3, 2006. The opinion states that educational establishments are not obliged to set up permanent prayer rooms. However, it is entirely in keeping with the spirit of adjustments to authorize for the purpose of prayer the use of rooms that are temporarily unoccupied. Certain exceptions are made in the case of penitentiaries, hospitals or airports since the individuals who must remain there are not free to visit a church if they so desire.

4. Still in keeping with the notion of the separation of Church and State, we believe that the crucifix must be removed from the wall of the National Assembly, which, indeed, is the very place that symbolizes the constitutional state (a reasonable alternative would be to display it in a room devoted to the history of Parliament). For the same reason, the saying of prayers at municipal council meetings should be abandoned in the many municipalities where this ritual is still practised. On the other hand, the installation of an erub does not infringe the neutrality of the State and thus may be authorized provided that it does not inconvenience other people.

5. The same reasoning leads to respect for dietary prohibitions and to allow in class the wearing of an Islamic headscarf, a kippah or a turban. The same is true of the wearing of the headscarf in sports competitions if it does not jeopardize the individual's safety. It should be noted that all of these authorizations promote integration into our society.

6. Applicants who are intransigent, reject negotiation and go against the rule of reciprocity will seriously compromise their approach, e.g. this would be true of a student who refused any compromise concerning dress to participate in a swimming class.

7. Requests must seek to protect or restore a right. Thus, we believe that non-Christian religious holidays are legitimate since they rectify an inequality. Conversely, requests must not infringe other people's rights. This criterion forbids the exclusion of certain scientific works in a classroom library or opposition by a parent to a blood transfusion necessary for his child's survival.

8. In keeping with the aim of the education system, students must not be exempted from compulsory courses. However, a student may be authorized to abandon a music course for another equivalent course in the case of an optional activity.

V. An Evolving Québec

Regardless of the choices that our society makes to meld cultural differences and contemplate a common future, such choices will be largely doomed to failure if several conditions are not present.

1. Our society must combat underemployment, poverty, inequality, intolerable living conditions and various forms of discrimination.

2. French-speaking Québec must not succumb to fear, the temptation to withdraw and reject, nor don the mantle of a victim. It must reject the scenario of inevitable disappearance, which has no future.

3. Another mistake would be to conceive the future of pluriethnicity as so many juxtaposed separate groups perceived as individual islets, which would mean replicating in Québec what is the most severely criticized in multiculturalism.

4. French-Canadian Quebecers have unpleasant memories of the period when the clergy wielded excessive power over institutions and individuals. It would be unfair that this situation leads them to direct at all religions the painful feeling inherited from their Catholic past.

5. Quebecers of French-Canadian origin must also be more aware of the repercussions on minority groups of their anxieties. Minority groups have undoubtedly been alerted recently by the image of an ethnocultural majority that is apparently unsure of itself and subject to outbursts of temper.

However, several factors seem to bode well for the edification of a promising future. The upcoming generations are displaying considerable openness in their way of perceiving and experiencing intercultural relations. A number of recent surveys have not revealed a clear rift between Montréal and the regions from the standpoint of perceptions of accommodation. Reliable studies reveal that, contrary to certain perceptions, the Montréal area is not ghettoized. We believe that the process of edifying a common identity is firmly under way in numerous areas that must be emphasized, i.e. the use of French, the sharing of common values, the promotion of a Québec collective memory, intercommunity initiatives, civic participation, artistic and literary creation, and the adoption of collective symbols. In keeping with the rule of law and the imperatives of pluralism, the identity that we are edifying must be able to develop as a citizen culture, and all Quebecers must be able to invest in it, recognize themselves in it and develop in it.

VI. *Priority Recommendations*

To conclude, our recommendations focus on five key themes:

1. First of all, they call for a definition of new policies or programs pertaining to interculturalism (legislation, a declaration or a policy statement) and secularism (a proposed white paper).
2. Several recommendations are linked to the central theme of integration and focus primarily on: *a)* recognition of immigrants' skills and diplomas; *b)* francization programs; *c)* the need for more sustained efforts to regionalize immigration; and *d)* the need for enhanced coordination between government departments.
3. From the standpoint of intercultural practices and mutual understanding, our recommendations highlight: *a)* the need for broader training of all government agents in public institutions, starting with the schools, because of the role they play in socialization and *b)* the need to further encourage community and intercommunity action projects.
4. In keeping with the harmonization policy formulated in our report, our recommendations are intended to foster the accountability of interveners in the citizen sphere (public and private agencies) by ensuring that they have received adequate training. We are asking the government to ensure that the practical knowledge acquired in institutions be recorded, promoted and disseminated in all of the milieus concerned.
5. Another priority field is the fight against inequality and discrimination. Our recommendations in this respect focus primarily on: *a)* the under-representation of ethnic minorities in the government; *b)* the urgency of combating the numerous forms of discrimination, Islamophobia, anti-Semitism and the racism to which racialized groups, especially Blacks, are subject; *c)* the support to be offered immigrant women; *d)* the need to increase the resources of the Commission des droits de la personne et des droits de la jeunesse; and *e)* the strengthening of economic and social rights in the Québec Charter.

31 "The White Paper": Statement of the Government of Canada on Indian Policy

Jean Chrétien (1969)

EDITORS' INTRODUCTION

In a 1969 speech about the government's proposed White Paper, Prime Minister Pierre Trudeau sums up the government's stance with the following statement: "[A]boriginal rights, this really means saying, 'We were here before you. You came and you took the land from us and perhaps you cheated us by giving us some worthless things in return for vast expanses of land and we want to re-open this question. We want you to preserve our aboriginal rights and to restore them to us.' And our answer—it may not be the right one and may not be one which is accepted but it will be up to all of you people to make your minds up and to choose for or against it and to discuss with the Indians—our answer is 'no.'"

Presented to the First Session of the Twenty-eighth Parliament by the Honourable Jean Chrétien, Minister of Indian Affairs and Northern Development, June 1969.

Foreword

The Government believes that its policies must lead to the full, free and non-discriminatory participation of the Indian people in Canadian society. Such a goal requires a break with the past. It requires that the Indian people's role of dependence be replaced by a role of equal status, opportunity and responsibility, a role they can share with all other Canadians.

This proposal is a recognition of the necessity made plain in a year's intensive discussions with Indian people throughout Canada. The Government believes that to continue its past course of action would not serve the interests of either the Indian people or their fellow Canadians.

The policies proposed recognize the simple reality that the separate legal status of Indians and the policies which have flowed from it have kept the Indian people apart from and behind other Canadians. The Indian people have not been full citizens of the communities and

Source: Excerpted from *Statement of the Government of Canada on Indian Policy*. Department of Indian Affairs and Northern Development. Ottawa: Government of Canada, 1969.

provinces in which they live and have not enjoyed the equality and the benefits that such participation offers.

The treatment resulting from their different status has been often worse, sometimes equal, and occasionally better than that accorded to their fellow citizens. What matters is that it has been different.

Many Indians, both in isolated communities and in cities, suffer from poverty. The discrimination which affects the poor, Indian and non-Indian alike, when compounded with a legal status that sets the Indian apart, provides dangerously fertile ground for social and cultural discrimination.

In recent years there has been a rapid increase in the Indian population. Their health and education levels have improved. There has been a corresponding rise in expectations that the structure of separate treatment cannot meet.

A forceful and articulate Indian leadership has developed to express the aspirations and needs of the Indian community. Given the opportunity, the Indian people can realize an immense human and cultural potential that will enhance their own well-being, that of the regions in which they live and of Canada as a whole. Faced with a continuation of past policies, they will unite only in common frustration.

The Government does not wish to perpetuate policies which carry with them the seeds of disharmony and disunity, policies which prevent Canadians from fulfilling themselves and contributing to their society. It seeks a partnership to achieve a better goal. The partners in this search are the Indian people, the governments of the provinces, the Canadian community as a whole and the Government of Canada. As all partnerships do, this will require consultation, negotiation, give and take, and co-operation if it is to succeed.

Many years will be needed. Some efforts may fail, but learning comes from failure and from what is learned success may follow. All the partners have to learn; all will have to change many attitudes.

Governments can set examples, but they cannot change the hearts of men. Canadians, Indians and non-Indians alike, stand at the crossroads. For Canadian society the issue is whether a growing element of its population will become full participants contributing in a positive way to the general well-being or whether, conversely, the present social and economic gap will lead to their increasing frustration and isolation, a threat to the general well-being of society. For many Indian people, one road does exist, the only road that has existed since Confederation and before, the road of different status, a road which has led to a blind alley of deprivation and frustration. This road, because it is a separate road, cannot lead to full participation, to equality in practice as well as in theory. In the pages which follow, the Government has outlined a number of measures and a policy which it is convinced will offer another road for Indians, a road that would lead gradually away from different status to full social, economic and political participation in Canadian life. This is the choice.

Indian people must be persuaded, must persuade themselves, that this path will lead them to a fuller and richer life. Canadian society as a whole will have to recognize the need for changed attitudes and a truly open society. Canadians should recognize the dangers of failing to strike down the barriers which frustrate Indian people. If Indian people are to become full members of Canadian society they must be warmly welcomed by that society.

The Government commends this policy for the consideration of all Canadians, Indians and non-Indians, and all governments in Canada.

Summary

1. Background

The Government has reviewed its programs for Indians and has considered the effects of them on the present situation of the Indian people. The review has drawn on extensive consultations with the Indian people, and on the knowledge and experience of many people both in and out of government.

This review was a response to things said by the Indian people at the consultation meetings which began a year ago and culminated in a meeting in Ottawa in April.

This review has shown that this is the right time to change long-standing policies. The Indian people have shown their determination that present conditions shall not persist.

Opportunities are present today in Canadian society and new directions are open. The Government believes that Indian people must not be shut out of Canadian life and must share equally in these opportunities.

The Government could press on with the policy of fostering further education; could go ahead with physical improvement programs now operating in reserve communities; could press forward in the directions of recent years, and eventually many of the problems would be solved. But progress would be too slow. The change in Canadian society in recent years has been too great and continues too rapidly for this to be the answer. Something more is needed. We can no longer perpetuate the separation of Canadians. Now is the time to change.

This Government believes in equality. It believes that all men and women have equal rights. It is determined that all shall be treated fairly and that no one shall be shut out of Canadian life, and especially that no one shall be shut out because of his race.

This belief is the basis for the Government's determination to open the doors of opportunity to *all* Canadians, to remove the barriers which impede the development of people, of regions and of the country.

Only a policy based on this belief can enable the Indian people to realize their needs and aspirations.

The Indian people are entitled to such a policy. They are entitled to an equality which preserves and enriches Indian identity and distinction; an equality which stresses Indian participation in its creation and which manifests itself in all aspects of Indian life.

The goals of the Indian people cannot be set by others; they must spring from the Indian community itself—but government can create a framework within which all persons and groups can seek their own goals.

2. The New Policy

True equality presupposes that the Indian people have the right to full and equal participation in the cultural, social, economic, and political life of Canada.

The government believes that the framework within which individual Indians and bands could achieve full participation requires:

1   that the legislative and constitutional bases of discrimination be removed;
2   that there be positive recognition by everyone of the unique contribution of Indian culture to Canadian life;

3 that services come through the same channels and from the same government agencies for all Canadians;
4 that those who are furthest behind be helped most;
5 that lawful obligations be recognized;
6 that control of Indian lands be transferred to the Indian people

The Government would be prepared to take the following steps to create this framework:

1 Propose to Parliament that the Indian Act be repealed and take such legislative steps as may be necessary to enable Indians to control Indian lands and to acquire title to them.
2 Propose to the governments of the provinces that they take over the same responsibility for Indians that they have for other citizens of their provinces. The take-over would be accompanied by the transfer to the provinces of federal funds normally provided for Indian programs, augmented as may be necessary.
3 Make substantial funds available for Indian economic development as an interim measure.
4 Wind up that part of the Department of Indian Affairs and Northern Development which deals with Indian Affairs. The residual responsibilities of the Federal Government for programs in the field of Indian affairs would be transferred to other appropriate federal departments.

In addition, the Government will appoint a Commissioner to consult with the Indians and to study and recommend acceptable procedures for the adjudication of claims.

The new policy looks to a better future for all Indian people wherever they may be. The measures for implementation are straightforward. They require discussion, consultation, and negotiation with the Indian people—individuals, bands, and associations—and with provincial governments.

Success will depend upon the co-operation and assistance of the Indians and the provinces. The Government seeks this co-operation and will respond when it is offered.

3. The Immediate Steps

Some changes could take place quickly. Others would take longer. It is expected that within five years the Department of Indian Affairs and Northern Development would cease to operate in the field of Indian affairs; the new laws would be in effect and existing programs would have been devolved. The Indian lands would require special attention for some time. The process of transferring control to the Indian people would be under continuous review.

The Government believes this is a policy which is just and necessary. It can only be successful if it has the support of the Indian people, the provinces, and all Canadians.

The policy promises all Indian people a new opportunity to expand and develop their identity within the framework of a Canadian society which offers them the rewards and responsibilities of participation, the benefits of involvement and the pride of belonging.

32 The Unjust Society

Harold Cardinal (1969)

EDITORS' INTRODUCTION

Harold Cardinal was a long-time leader of the Indian Association of Alberta and a founding member of the National Indian Brotherhood (the predecessor of the Assembly of First Nations). Only 24 years old when he wrote The Unjust Society, *he was also the principal author of the "Red Paper"—also known as "Citizens Plus"—which was the Aboriginal response to the government's White Paper, and which has been widely credited with forcing the government to abandon its proposed policy. The title of Cardinal's book is a direct reference to Prime Minister Trudeau's earlier promise of a "Just Society."*

The Buckskin Curtain

The Indian-Problem Problem

The history of Canada's Indians is a shameful chronicle of the white man's disinterest, his deliberate trampling of Indian rights and his repeated betrayal of our trust. Generations of Indians have grown up behind a buckskin curtain of indifference, ignorance and, all too often, plain bigotry. Now, at a time when our fellow Canadians consider the promise of the Just Society, once more the Indians of Canada are betrayed by a programme which offers nothing better than cultural genocide.

The new Indian policy promulgated by Prime Minister Pierre Elliott Trudeau's government, under the auspices of the Honourable Jean Chrétien, minister of Indian Affairs and Northern Development, and Deputy Minister John A. MacDonald, and presented in June of 1969 is a thinly disguised programme of extermination through assimilation. For the Indian to survive, says the government in effect, he must become a good little brown white man. The Americans to the south of us used to have a saying: "The only good Indian is a dead Indian." The MacDonald-Chrétien doctrine would amend this but slightly to, "The only good Indian is a non-Indian."

The federal government, instead of acknowledging its legal and moral responsibilities to the Indians of Canada and honouring the treaties that the Indians signed in good faith, now proposes to wash its hands of Indians entirely, passing the buck to the provincial governments.

Small wonder that in 1969, in the one hundred and second year of Canadian confederation, the native people of Canada look back on generations of accumulated frustration under

Source: Excerpted from *The Unjust Society: The Tragedy of Canada's Indians* by Harold Cardinal. Edmonton: Hurtig Publishers, 1969.

conditions which can only be described as colonial, brutal and tyrannical, and look to the future with the gravest of doubts.

Torrents of words have been spoken and written about Indians since the arrival of the white man on the North American continent. Endless columns of statistics have been compiled. Countless programmes have been prepared for Indians by non-Indians. Faced with society's general indifference and a massive accumulation of misdirected, often insincere efforts, the greatest mistake the Indian has made has been to remain so long silent.

As an Indian writing about a situation I am living and experiencing in common with thousands of our people it is my hope that this book will open the eyes of the Canadian public to its shame. In these pages I hope to cut through bureaucratic doubletalk to show what it means to be an Indian in Canada. I intend to document the betrayals of our trust, to show step by step how a dictatorial bureaucracy has eroded our rights, atrophied our culture and robbed us of simple human dignity. I will expose the ignorance and bigotry that has impeded our progress, the eighty years of educational neglect that have hobbled our young people for generations, the gutless politicians who have knowingly watched us sink in the quicksands of apathy and despair and have failed to extend a hand.

I hope to point a path to radical change that will admit the Indian with restored pride to his rightful place in the Canadian heritage, that will enable the Indian in Canada at long last to realize his dreams and aspirations and find his place in Canadian society. I will challenge our fellow Canadians to help us; I will warn them of the alternatives.

I challenge the Honourable Mr. Trudeau and the Honourable Mr. Chrétien to reexamine their unfortunate policy, to offer the Indians of Canada hope instead of despair, freedom instead of frustration, life in the Just Society instead of cultural annihilation. ...

"As Long as the Rivers Run ... "

With Forked Tongue

Everyone who has watched a late late movie on television sooner or later has found himself half-sleeping through one of the old-time westerns. Inevitably, at some point in the thriller a beaten travesty of Indian leadership draws his blanket around his shoulders and solemnly intones, "White man speaks with forked tongue." Even Indians laugh at a cliché like that, but their laughter is a little strained; the truth the phrase still tells, still rankles.

Our people believe very little the white man says, even today, because the white man continues to speak with forked tongue. Individual white men may not have to lie; they may, like the minister for Indian Affairs, his deputy minister, even our prime minister, be pedantically consistent in their own public statements about Indian policy. But when the position they have taken is a complete denial of promises the Canadian government once made to us and has always upheld (though never fulfilled), then their position, their statements represent an entire society's lie—the betrayal of the Indian people.

Our people no longer believe. It is that simple and it is that sad. The Canadian government can promise involvement, consultation, progressive human and economic development programmes. We will no longer believe them. The Canadian government can guarantee the most attractive system of education. We will not believe them. They can tell us their beautiful plans for the development of local self-government. We will shrug our disbelief.

The government can create a hundred national Indian advisory councils to advise us about our problems. We will not listen to them. We will not believe what they say. The federal bureaucrats can meet with us one thousand times a year, but we will suspect their motives. We will know they have nothing new to say. We will know they speak with forked tongue.

After generations of endless frustration with the Canadian government, our people are tired and impatient. *Before* the Canadian government tries to feed us hypocritical policy statements, more empty promises, more forked tonguistics, our people want, our people, the Indians, demand just settlement of all our treaty and aboriginal rights. Fulfillment of Indian rights by the queen's government must come before there can be any further cooperation between the Indians and the government. We demand nothing more. We expect nothing less.

Yes, the prime minister roused our hopes with his talk of a compassionate and just society. Then his minister for Indian Affairs told us our problems would vanish if we would become nice, manageable white men like all other Canadians. Just recently, the prime minister himself flicked the other fork of his tongue. In a speech in Vancouver, Mr. Trudeau said, "The federal government is not prepared to guarantee the aboriginal rights of Canada's Indians." Mr. Trudeau said, "It is inconceivable that one section of a society should have a treaty with another section of a society. The Indians should become Canadians as have all other Canadians."

Have other Canadians been led to this citizenship over a path of broken promises and dishonoured treaties?

To the Indians of Canada, the treaties represent an Indian Magna Carta. The treaties are important to us, because we entered into these negotiations with faith, with hope for a better life with honour. We have survived for over a century on little but that hope. Did the white man enter into them with something less in mind? Or have the heirs of the men who signed in honour somehow disavowed the obligation passed down to them? The Indians entered into the treaty negotiations as honourable men who came to deal as equals with the queen's representatives. Our leaders of that time thought they were dealing with an equally honourable people. Our leaders pledged themselves, their people and their heirs to honour what was done then.

Our leaders mistakenly thought they were dealing with an honourable people who would do no less than the Indians were doing—bind themselves, bind their people and bind their heirs to honourable contracts.

Our people talked with the government representatives, not as beggars pleading for handouts, but as men with something to offer in return for rights they expected. To our people, this was the beginning of a contractual relationship whereby the representatives of the queen would have lasting responsibilities to the Indian people in return for the valuable lands that were ceded to them.

The treaties were the way in which the white people legitimized in the eyes of the world their presence in our country. It was an attempt to settle the terms of occupancy on a just basis, legally and morally to extinguish the legitimate claims of our people to title to the land in our country. There never has been any doubt in the minds of our people that the land in Canada belonged to them. Nor can there have been any doubt in the mind of the government or in the minds of the white people about who owned the land, for it was upon the basis of white recognition of Indian rights that the treaties were negotiated. Otherwise, there could have been nothing to negotiate, no need for treaties. In the language of the Cree Indians, the Indian reserves are known as *the land that we kept for ourselves* or *the land that we did not give to the government*. In our language, *skun-gun*.

When one party to an agreement continually, ruthlessly breaks that agreement whenever it suits his purpose, the other partner cannot forever be expected to believe protestations of faith that accompany the next peace offering. In our society, a man who did not keep his part of a fair bargain, a man who used tricks and shady deals to wriggle out of commitments, a man who continually spoke with a forked tongue became known as a crook. Indians do not deal with cheats.

Mr. Chrétien says, "Get rid of the *Indian Act*. Treat Indians as any other Canadians." Mr. Trudeau says, "Forget the treaties. Let Indians become Canadians." This is the Just Society? To the Indian people, there can be no justice, no just society, until their rights are restored. Nor can there be any faith in Mr. Trudeau, Mr. Chrétien, the government, in white society until our rights are protected by lasting, equitable legislation.

As far as we are concerned our treaty rights represent a sacred, honourable agreement between ourselves and the Canadian government that cannot be unilaterally abrogated by the government at the whim of one of its leaders unless that government is prepared to give us back title to our country.

Our rights are too valuable to surrender to gallic or any other kind of rhetoric, too valuable to be sold for pieces of gold. Words change; the value of money fluctuates, may even disappear; our land will not disappear.

We cannot give up our rights without destroying ourselves as people. If our rights are meaningless, if it is inconceivable that our society have treaties with the white society even though those treaties were signed by honourable men on both sides, in good faith, long before the present government decided to tear them up as worthless scraps of paper, then we as a people are meaningless. We cannot and we will not accept this. We know that as long as we fight for our rights we will survive. If we surrender, we die.

Currently, this lack of faith in our government, this feeling that our government speaks with a forked tongue is called a credibility gap. The credibility gap between white society and Indian, between our government and our people must be closed. Our lack of faith in the federal government has far-reaching implications. As long as our rights are not honoured, and as long as the government continues to make it clear it has no intention of honouring them, then we must continue to be apprehensive about new plans such as the Chrétien policy to abolish the *Indian Act* and to do away with the Indian Affairs branch of the government. We will be fearful of any attempt by the federal government to turn over to provincial governments responsibility for Indian Affairs. We will be certain that the federal government is merely attempting to abandon its responsibilities. Provincial governments have no obligations to fulfill our treaties. They never signed treaties with the Indians. We could not expect them to be concerned with treaty rights. In our eyes, this new government policy merely represents a disguised move to abrogate all our treaty rights. This is our government speaking once again with forked tongue.

Until such time as the federal government accepts and protects our rights with abiding legislation, we will oppose and refuse to participate in any federal–provincial schemes that affect our rights.

33 Aboriginal Rights and Land Issues: The Métis Perspective

Clément Chartier (1985)

EDITORS' INTRODUCTION

Clément Chartier is a Métis lawyer, activist, politician, and writer. After having worked in the provincial government of Saskatchewan, he opted for a more activist approach to securing Métis rights, taking on positions in a number of Métis and indigenous political bodies at both the national and provincial levels. He is currently president of the Métis National Council.

Legal terms relating to the rights of the aboriginal peoples of Canada have often been used interchangeably. "Aboriginal title," "Indian title," "native title," "usufructuary rights," and "aboriginal rights" have at one time or another been used to attempt to describe the rights the colonizers felt aboriginal peoples possessed.

In the early 1500s, after America became known to the Europeans, several writers and theologians spoke on behalf of the Indian peoples. They stated that Indians, although heathens and non-Christians, nevertheless were capable of ownership of land and had sovereignty over their territories. Spain, Portugal, France, and England did not accept these views, but nevertheless found it useful to recognize some of the rights possessed by the aboriginal inhabitants. They also quickly realized that the Americas were vast and that they need not fight over them. They essentially came to a gentleman's agreement: whoever got to a piece of land first could claim it for his sovereign. The principal right remaining for the aboriginal people was the right to continue the peaceful enjoyment of their way of life and the use of their territories.

In the early 1800s the United States Supreme Court began to define this theory as the "doctrine of discovery." Basically, this meant that the country that arrived first could claim it for its king or queen. In order to perfect their title, the discoverers had to settle the land. They further stated that the aboriginal peoples had a right to continue using the land until they either gave up that right or were conquered. That is how the concept of aboriginal title or rights was created. There is still no clear, definitive statement to be made about what exactly is covered by the term "aboriginal title." It is clear that hunting, trapping, and fishing are some of the aboriginal rights that exist. In Canada, the privy council in the *St Catherine's Milling* case (1888) stated that aboriginal title was merely a usufructuary right and that Indian peoples did not own the land. They went on to state that they did not have to describe

---

Source: From *The Quest for Justice: Aboriginal Peoples and Aboriginal Rights*, edited bt Menno Boldt, J. Anthony Long, and Leroy Little Bear. Toronto: University of Toronto Press, 1985. Reprinted by permission.

what those usufructuary rights were. (A usufruct is the right to use the property of another to one's own advantage so long as the property is not altered or damaged.)

In the *Calder* case (1973) the Supreme Court of Canada also stated that it did not have to define what aboriginal title was composed of. The judgments of Chief Justice Hall and Justice Judson addressed aboriginal title in a cursory fashion. The chief justice held that the Nishga still had valid aboriginal title:

> ... *this is not a claim to title in fee but is in the nature of an equitable title or interest ... a usufructuary right to occupy the lands and to enjoy the fruits of the soil, the forest and the rivers and streams which does not in anyway deny the Crown's paramount title as it is recognized by the law of nations. Nor does the Nishga claim challenge the Federal Crown's right to extinguish that title. Their position is that they possess a right of occupation against the world except the Crown and that the Crown has not to date lawfully extinguished that right.*

Justice Judson, ruling that the aboriginal title of the Nishga had been extinguished, expressed the following opinion with respect to Indian title: "... the fact is that when the settlers came, the Indians were there, organized in societies and occupying the land as their forefathers had done for Centuries. This is what Indian Title means and it does not help one in the solution of this problem to call it a 'personal or usufructuary right.'"

However, the Federal Court-Trial Division, in the *Baker Lake* case (1979), said that although the Inuit of Baker Lake retained valid aboriginal title, they did not own minerals below the surface. Basically, the court stated that aboriginal title relates only to hunting, trapping, and fishing—elements of a traditional life-style—and that uranium mining and Inuit hunting at Baker Lake could continue jointly. The decision was not appealed.

Briefly stated, the legal position in Canada at present is that the crown has the underlying title to the land and the aboriginal peoples have merely a "possessory" right, that is, a right to the use of the land. ...

It should be noted at this time that the term "Indian" was used both in the royal proclamation and in the Constitution Act, 1867. However, neither document defined the term. In the *Re Eskimos* case (1939) the Supreme Court of Canada ruled that the term "Indian" as used in the Constitution Act, 1867, included the Eskimos (Inuit). It is the opinion of the Métis National Council and the Association of Métis and Non-status Indians of Saskatchewan as well as some legal scholars that the Métis are also included in the category of "Indian." The opinion that it is not necessary to be defined as an Indian under the Indian Act to be a constitutional "Indian" is based on the fact that the current Indian Act still excludes the Inuit despite the ruling in *Re Eskimos*.

Support for this proposition can also be found in the Constitution Act, 1982. Section 35(2) defines aboriginal peoples as the "Indian, Inuit and Métis peoples of Canada." In *Re Eskimos*, Justice Kerwin stated that "the majority of authoritative publications and particularly those that one would expect to be in common use in 1867, adopt the interpretation that the term 'Indians' includes all the Aborigines of the territory subsequently included in the Dominion." That the Métis are Indians (constitutionally) also finds support in section 31 of the Manitoba Act, 1870, which expressly recognized that the Métis shared in the Indian title to land. This legislation was subsequently given constitutional force by the British North America Act, 1871. There can be no further doubt with respect to this issue; the Manitoba Act, 1870, is now included in schedule 1 of the Constitution Act, 1982. ...

The first piece of legislation to refer specifically to the Métis people was the Manitoba Act, 1870, which provided for the distribution of lands "towards the extinguishment of the Indian Title to the lands in the Province." By section 31 the government set aside 1,400,000 acres to be divided among the children of the half-breed heads of families residing in Manitoba at the time of the transfer, "in such mode and on such conditions as to settlement or otherwise, as the Governor General in Council may from time to time determine." The government allowed gross injustices to be perpetrated against the half-breed people through the implementation of a grant and scrip system, leaving the half-breeds landless and in abject poverty which persists to this day. In 1879, the Dominion Lands Act extended this attempted unilateral extinguishment of rights to the rest of the Northwest Territories, although the provisions were not implemented until the 1885 War of Resistance at Batoche.

The Manitoba Métis Federation has challenged as unconstitutional subsequent federal and provincial legislation allowing this injustice to take place. The federation is seeking a declaration that the federal and provincial legislation purporting to extinguish their rights is outside the legislative competence of both levels of government.

A brief overview of the implementation of this form of so-called extinguishment will help in understanding the injustices suffered by the Métis. While treaties with the Indians set apart communal tracts of land and recognized other rights, the scrip issued to the half-breeds was for a specific amount of land which was fully alienable. In addition, by this method of unilateral dealing, the government of Canada also purported to extinguish all aboriginal title rights possessed by the Métis, including the right to hunt. As a consequence of this imposed scrip system, most of the land fell into the hands of speculators.

The Canadian government, in dealing with the Métis, issued land and money scrip. Land scrip was a certificate describing a specified number of acres and naming the person to whom the land was granted. Only that person could register the scrip in exchange for the land selected. Because they lacked information and knowledge about the land scrip system most Métis never registered the scrip; most registrations were done by opportunistic speculators and swindlers, who would appear at the registry office with any aboriginal person who was readily available. To facilitate the transaction, the speculator would have a transfer or quit-claim signed by the unwitting Métis or else would forge his signature, usually an X.

Money scrip was in essence a bearer bond. It was easily negotiable for money, goods, services, or land. Anyone who presented it would be able to redeem it in exchange for dominion land, which at the time was selling at one dollar per acre. Money scrip was introduced after a considerable amount of lobbying by speculators who stood to gain in their dealings with Métis who had no experience or familiarity with such transactions. Both money and land scrip were redeemable at one dollar per acre. After a number of years, however, the price of land and the value of land scrip increased. Thus, money scrip became less desirable.

Both land and money scrip could only be used for dominion lands in surveyed areas. Scrip was only issued to the Métis in what are now the provinces of Manitoba, Saskatchewan, and Alberta, although a limited amount was given to Métis who had moved to the northern United States. This was so even though a portion of Treaty 8 covered the northeast portion of British Columbia. Because scrip could only be applied against surveyed land, a significant number of Métis were immediately at a disadvantage. For example, in the 1906 Treaty 10 area of northern Saskatchewan, 60 percent of the scrip issued was land scrip. To this day there is virtually no surveyed land in that area. As a consequence, the Métis of northern

Saskatchewan were deprived of their land base and their opportunity to acquire ownership of land. With respect to the Northwest Territories, when Treaty 11 was entered into in 1921, the Métis were allotted a cash grant of $240 rather than land or money scrip.

Researchers for the Association of Métis and Non-status Indians of Saskatchewan have documented evidence that of the scrip issued, one-third was land scrip and two-thirds money scrip, for a total of 31,000 certificates or 4,030,000 acres (these figures are based on 80 percent of the known remaining files). Over 90 percent of the scrip was delivered into the hands of banks and speculators. The banks received over 52 percent of the issued scrip. The Department of the Interior, which was responsible for the scrip program, facilitated the transfer of scrip to corporations and individual speculators by keeping scrip accounts for them.

Although scrip was meant to be used for land only, the notes were used for other purposes. Because of the desperate and destitute situation of the Métis, scrip was often sold for cash, bringing the equivalent of twenty-five cents on the dollar or acre in 1878, and rising to five dollars per acre for land scrip in 1908. The majority of scrip, however, was sold for approximately one-third of its face value. Scrip was also exchanged for farm animals, implements, seed, food, and other supplies.

Most of this speculative activity took place outside the area covered by the Manitoba Act, 1870. Therefore, the constitutional implications of section 31 of that act did not apply. Nevertheless, there is a line of thought that holds that all aboriginal peoples in Rupert's Land and the Northwest Territories had their aboriginal title constitutionally entrenched by virtue of section 146 of the Constitution Act, 1867. That section provided for the entry into confederation of those two areas, and decreed that "the provisions of any Order-in-Council in that behalf shall have the effect as if they had been enacted by the Parliament of the United Kingdom of Great Britain and Ireland."

On 19 November 1869, the Hudson's Bay Company surrendered its charter to the crown. Following the negotiations between the provisional government and the Canadian government, the British Parliament passed an order-in-council on 23 June 1870 making Rupert's Land a part of Canada effective 15 July 1870. Section 14 of that order-in-council stated that "any claims of Indians to compensation for lands required for purposes of settlement shall be disposed of by the Canadian Government in communication with the Imperial Government; and the company shall be relieved of all responsibility in respect of them." Also incorporated into the order-in-council were addresses to the queen by the Senate and the House of Commons. The first one, dated December 1867, asked for the transfer of Rupert's Land to Canada: "Upon the transference of the territories in question to the Canadian Government, the claims of the Indian tribes to compensation for lands required to purposes of settlement will be considered and settled in conformity with the equitable principles which have uniformly governed the British Crown in its dealings with the aborigines." The order-in-council does not specifically refer to half-breeds, although it does refer to "aborigines"; it was issued after the Manitoba Act expressly recognized the half-breeds right to land under Indian title.

In the *Paulette* case (1973) Mr. Justice Morrow, then of the Northwest Territories Supreme Court, was of the opinion that the provisions or conditions of the order-in-council had "become part of the Canadian Constitution and could not be removed or altered except by Imperial Statute." But for the provisions found in section 31 of the Manitoba Act, 1870, it is clear that the Canadian Parliament is precluded from dealing unilaterally with the aboriginal title of the aboriginal people covered by the order-in-council, that is, those aboriginal people living within the area covered by the Hudson's Bay Company charter. Any doubt about the referential incorporation of the order-in-council under the provisions of section 146 can arguably be laid to rest by the specific inclusion of the order-in-council as the Rupert's Land and the North Western Territory Order under schedule 1 of the Constitution Act, 1982.

It is argued by the Métis National Council and the Association of Métis and Non-status Indians of Saskatchewan that the action of the federal government, coupled with its knowledge of the fraud that was being perpetrated, was illegal, immoral, and inequitable, and that the aboriginal title of the Métis remains unextinguished.

Also of concern to the Métis is the Constitution Act, 1930, which ratified the Natural Resources Transfer Agreements between the provinces of Manitoba, Saskatchewan, and Alberta and the federal government. By these agreements the provinces were given ownership and control of the natural resources within their boundaries. Contained in the agreements is a provision that the provinces would allow "Indians" to continue hunting, trapping, and fishing for food on all unoccupied crown lands and lands to which they have a right of access. This constitutional provision cuts down the aboriginal and treaty right to hunt, trap, and fish for commercial purposes. The places of hunting are also restricted. It is of great concern to the Métis and non-status Indians that the term "Indians" is not defined. In a judgment rendered on 20 July 1978, the Saskatchewan Court of Appeal ruled that the term "Indian" as used in the agreement did not include the accused, a non-treaty, non-status Indian. This decision prevented all aboriginal people not entitled to be registered under the Indian Act from exercising their right to hunt, trap, and fish, even for food. This decision was not appealed and the issue has still not been resolved.

It is the belief of the Métis that the long-standing denial of our rights, economic deprivation, poverty, and the displacement of our people have to be rectified in a manner that is meaningful to us. We require a cultural, social, economic, and political regeneration as well as an adequate land base and resource rights. The concept of Métis nationalism and accepted principles of international law indicate that these goals can be reached through political expression and in a spirit of goodwill. Our right to self-determination is on a higher plane than the legal fiction of aboriginal title. As a nation of aboriginal people, we have a right to a homeland and self-government no less than the Palestinians or the blacks of South Africa. This right is a right of choice, a right to choose statehood, assimilation, or anything in between. The Métis have chosen to exercise this right within the Canadian federation, and will seek to have it acknowledged in all forthcoming constitutional conferences. It must always be kept in mind that the conferences are for the purpose of identifying and defining all the rights of aboriginal peoples, not merely their aboriginal and treaty rights.

The Métis will insist on a charter of rights, which will be in addition to the current recognition and affirmation of our existing aboriginal rights. This charter will provide the legal basis for a third level of government for and by aboriginal people, and by implication will necessarily alter the current jurisdictional division of powers under sections 91 and 92 of the Constitution Act, 1867, including section 91(24) respecting Indians and the lands reserved for the Indians. The Métis, while not rejecting aboriginal title, are striving for the entrenchment of our right to self-determination. The primary attributes of that right are a land base and Métis self-government.

Recovering Canada: The Resurgence of Indigenous Law

John Borrows (2002)

EDITORS' INTRODUCTION

This is an excerpt from Recovering Canada, *the culmination of almost a decade of writings by legal scholar John Borrows, who is so well regarded within the Aboriginal law community that his scholarship has been cited in Supreme Court cases. Rather than conceptualizing Canadian and Aboriginal legal traditions as juxtaposed, Borrows argues that Canadian law stands to benefit greatly from Aboriginal traditions, culture, and legal concepts.*

With or Without You: First Nations Law in Canada

Much of the history of Canadian law concerning Aboriginal peoples is often seen as conflictual, a contest between ideas rooted in First Nations, English, American, and international legal regimes in which one source of law must become ascendant. Courts taking this view have frequently refused to apply First Nations law, preferring to recognize the common law as the sole or pre-eminent source of law in Canada. I will argue that it is unnecessary for courts to approach the interpretation of Aboriginal rights as though each source of law was in competition with the others. The Supreme Court of Canada has defined Aboriginal rights in such a way that these sources can often be harmonized, and need not obstruct each other. As Brian Slattery has pointed out, Canadian law applying to First Nations is an autonomous body of law, not fully bound to any one of the legal systems identified above. It "bridges the gulf" between First Nations and European legal systems by embracing each without forming a part of them. While it is true that legal doctrines from Britain, the United States, and the international community (or, for that matter, First Nations) have had a persuasive influence on the development of Canadian law, the body of case law dealing with Aboriginal issues is, in the end, "indigenous" to Canada. Thus, while Canadian law dealing with First Nations may borrow legal notions from various Aboriginal and non-Aboriginal cultures, it is also a uniquely Canadian amalgam of many different legal orders. It is therefore incumbent upon Canadian judges to draw upon Indigenous legal sources more often and more explicitly in deciding Aboriginal issues. ...

Source: Excerpted from *Recovering Canada: The Resurgence of Indigenous Law* by John Borrows. Toronto: University of Toronto Press, 2002. Notes omitted. Reprinted by permission.

Taking the Court ... Seriously: Sources of Law in Canadian Aboriginal Rights Jurisprudence

Since the pre-existing rights of First Nations can often function alongside western legal principles, the task for the courts is to find more appropriate terminology to describe Aboriginal rights. Ultimately this requires recognizing a category of Canadian law to receive First Nations law. The judiciary has already taken steps in this regard by noting that First Nations law protects sui generis interests. Sui generis is a Latin term meaning "forming a kind by itself; unique, literally of its own particular kind," or class. In defining Aboriginal rights as unique, the judiciary has acknowledged that it cannot use conventional common law doctrines alone to give them meaning. Aboriginal rights have always been regarded as different from other common law rights. They do not wholly take their source or meaning from the philosophies that underlie the Western canon of law. Although equal in importance and significance to other rights, Aboriginal rights are different because they are held only by Aboriginal people in Canadian society. A sui generis approach to interpreting Aboriginal rights is appropriate because, in some respects, Aboriginal peoples are unique within the wider Canadian population. The existence of this doctrine suggests the possibility that Aboriginal rights stem from alternative sources of law that reflect the unique historical presence of Aboriginal peoples in North America.

While the sui generis doctrine of Aboriginal rights places significant emphasis upon Aboriginal difference, it does not ignore the similarities between Aboriginal and non-Aboriginal peoples. A legal doctrine focused exclusively upon the differences between Aboriginal and non-Aboriginal people would distort the reality both of Crown-Aboriginal relations and Aboriginal peoples' lives. Aboriginal and non-Aboriginal people have developed ways of relating to one another which, over the centuries, have produced numerous similarities between the various groups. Moreover, Aboriginal and non-Aboriginal people often share interests in the same territories, ecosystems, economies, ideologies, and institutions. While imperfect, and often skewed to the disadvantage of Aboriginal people, these points of connection cannot be ignored. The sui generis doctrine expresses the confidence that there are sufficient similarities between the groups to enable them to live with their differences. Under this doctrine, points of agreement can be highlighted and issues of difference can be preserved to facilitate more productive and peaceful relations. The sui generis doctrine reformulates similarity and difference and thereby captures the complex, overlapping, and exclusive identities and relationships of the parties.

In describing Aboriginal rights as sui generis, the court observed that an Aboriginal right "derives from the Indian's historic occupation and possession of their tribal lands." This interpretation takes account of the fact that "when the settlers came, the Indians were there, organized in societies and occupying the land as their forefathers had done for centuries." As stated in *Van der Peet*, "[A]boriginal rights [exist] ... because of one simple fact: when Europeans arrived in North America, [A]boriginal peoples were already here, living in communities on the land, and participating in distinctive cultures, as they had for centuries." In that case, the Supreme Court was perhaps at its clearest in holding that Aboriginal rights arise from the traditional laws and customs of Aboriginal peoples. Lamer C.J.C. held that, just as Aboriginal rights cannot be categorized using conventional common law doctrines alone, neither can they be defined using only Indigenous legal principles. Their essence lies in their bridging of Aboriginal and non-Aboriginal legal cultures. The court thus found that Aboriginal rights are a "form of intersocietal law that evolved from long-standing practices linking the various communities." This view was supported by drawing from Professor Walters's writings. The court stated: "The challenge of defining [A]boriginal rights stems from the fact that they are rights peculiar to the meeting of two vastly different legal cultures; consequently there will always be a question about which legal culture is to provide the vantage point from which rights are to be defined ... a morally and politically defensible conception of rights will incorporate both legal perspectives." Therefore, the sui generis conception of Aboriginal rights exists to respect and incorporate the presence of Canada's two vastly different legal cultures. A sui generis approach will place "equal weight" on each perspective and thus achieve a "true reconciliation" between the cultures.

This same point was recognized in *R. v. Delgamuukw*, where the court wrote, "what makes [A]boriginal title sui generis is that it arises before the assertion of sovereignty." Chief Justice Lamer furthered this point by writing that Aboriginal title "is also sui generis in the sense that its characteristics cannot be completely explained by reference to either the common law rules of real property or to the rules of property found in [A]boriginal legal systems. As with other [A]boriginal rights, it must be understood by reference to both common law and [A]boriginal perspectives." This formulation of Aboriginal title gives legal recognition and force to the systems by which First Nations organized themselves, "with a legal as well as a just claim to retain possession" of their territory "and to use it according to their discretion." Since Aboriginal organization and occupation of land is dependent on the existence of Indigenous laws, these laws become a source of Aboriginal rights. The fact that the sui generis interest in land has its roots in Aboriginal law means that these laws must form a part of the contemporary meaning of Aboriginal rights. Because Aboriginal legal systems of occupancy were not irretrievably interrupted or altered by the reception of the common law, there is a continuity of First Nations legal relationships "in the lands they traditionally occupied prior to European colonization, [which] both pre-dated and survived the claims to sovereignty" by non-Native peoples. In this way, the sui generis formulation of Aboriginal rights attests to the continued existence of First Nations law.

Finally, the pre-existing and contemporary status of Indigenous law was made very plain by the Supreme Court of Canada in *Mitchell v. M.N.R.* In declaring the source of Aboriginal rights Chief Justice McLachlin wrote that "English law ... accepted that the Aboriginal peoples possessed pre-existing laws and interests, and recognized their continuation ..." As such, she held, "[A]boriginal interests and customary laws were presumed to survive the assertion of sovereignty, and were absorbed into the common law as rights." McLachlin C.J.C.'s declaration that Aboriginal laws secured the protection of the common law following the assertion of sovereignty by the Crown demonstrates why Aboriginal laws may be held to exist despite the intervention of foreign (non-Aboriginal) legal systems. The common law (and since 1982 constitutional law) status of Indigenous law is what makes possible the submission that Aboriginal laws have relevance in contemporary legal disputes.

Since one source of Aboriginal rights is "the relationship between common law and pre-existing systems of [A]boriginal law," Canadian courts and lawmakers charged with developing Aboriginal rights law must grapple with First Nations laws and legal perspectives. Creating law that accounts for both parties' legal perspectives makes sense in the context of Aboriginal and treaty rights litigation because these disputes involve the interaction of legal interests from Aboriginal and non-Aboriginal societies. The use of First Nations law in these instances creates an effective check on inappropriate analogies drawn from other legal sources. The application of Indigenous law by Canadian courts helps to ensure that interactions between the Crown and First Nations are perceived as being fair. It can counteract the powerful influence of non-Aboriginal laws in the development of sui generis principles and help to ensure that this law is as impartial and free of bias as possible. Thus, the explicit reception of Aboriginal perspectives and principles more firmly establishes an autonomous body of law that bridges Aboriginal and non-Aboriginal legal cultures. The sui generis doctrine allows for this *intermingling* of common law and Aboriginal conceptions. Such symmetry allows for the recognition of Aboriginal difference while building strong ties of cooperation and unity between Aboriginal and non-Aboriginal people.

Given that First Nations laws continue to give meaning and content to Aboriginal rights and form a part of the "laws of Canada," reference to these laws in Canadian law recognizes a foundational and unifying principle in Aboriginal rights jurisprudence. Indigenous laws have "always constituted an integral part of their distinctive culture ... for reasons connected to their cultural and physical survival," and they constitute a principled reference point in the interpretive framework of Aboriginal rights. Since Indigenous laws are integral to the exercise of Aboriginal rights they must be implied into the very fabric of this unique jurisprudence. In considering the existence of any Aboriginal right, it is necessary to recognize that such rights are manifestations of an integral and overarching phenomena. A pervasive and unifying principle that underpins the existence of Aboriginal rights is the existence of Indigenous law and legal perspectives. By inquiring into the First Nations legal viewpoint which gives meaning to particular Aboriginal rights, courts can approach these cases on a more principled and global basis, while retaining their fact- and site-specific context. When courts incorporate Indigenous laws into Canadian Aboriginal rights law they give fuller meaning to them as sui generis interests. ...

Epilogue: At the Beginning

Tradition ... cannot be inherited, and if you want it you must obtain it by great labour

The question of how to implement the reception of First Nations law more fully in Canadian law is just beginning to unfold. Full respect for and acceptance of First Nations law will not be easy to accomplish, even though there is legal precedent that would allow it as well as strong and clear evidence of existing Indigenous law. The contemporary dynamics of political, economic, and social power place the common law in a superordinate position relative to Indigenous law. Lawyers and judges trained in conventional legal reasoning are bound to encounter difficulties in interpreting Indigenous law because they are accustomed to looking to reported cases to assist them in defining and applying the law. It will be a great challenge to present First Nations laws to decision makers unfamiliar with non-European cultures. Changing the cultural power of conventional Western law will also be difficult. Legal principles derived from communities outside the cultural mainstream often encounter daunting obstacles before they are accepted.

Bias and prejudice will also be hard to overcome; despite recent case law, some people will continue to believe that First Nations laws are inferior. This problem has arisen in the

United States, where tribal law is more prominent. It is exemplified in the following account of the Chief Justice of the Navajo Court speaking to a six-state conference of judges on the meaning of "Indian traditional law" or "Indian common law." After Chief Justice Yazzie spoke, "Jim Zion, our court solicitor, dashed outside for a cigarette. He overheard two Wyoming judges talking about what I had to say. The first judge said, 'What did you think of Chief Yazzie's presentation on Navajo common law?' The second laughed and said, 'He didn't mention staking people to anthills.'" Inappropriate caricatures of First Nations will inevitably persist for many years, and prejudices rooted in racial and cultural bias will continue to suppress the legitimacy and acceptance of First Nations law. The unique characteristics of Indigenous law, moreover, will make its reception into Canadian common law more complex. As a result, it may take longer for these laws to enjoy the same respect accorded to other categories of the common law.

Yet there are mechanisms currently in place that would allow for the communication, proof, interpretation, reception, and application of First Nations law. Ethnography, recorded precedent, learned treatises, judicial notice, expert testimony, and skilled advocates can all assist judges in this venture. Properly trained lawyers of all cultures would conceivably be able to learn and articulate First Nations law, given appropriate access to, and support from, the community they represent. Among this cadre of lawyers are legally trained members of First Nations. Many of these people are bicultural and/or bilingual and have learned law from their Elders as well as from Canadian legal and academic institutions. They can interpret Western common law precedent, but they also know where to find resolutions to the same questions within First Nations customary or common law. They have access to an alternative source of knowledge and their contributions can help courts resolve troublesome issues. They can bridge the gulf between First Nations and European legal systems and help to make the law truly intersocietal. ...

First Nations legal traditions are strong and dynamic and can be interpreted flexibly to deal with the real issues in contemporary Canadian law concerning Aboriginal communities. Tradition dies without such transmission and reception. Laying claim to a tradition requires work and imagination, as particular individuals interpret it, integrate it into their own experiences, and make it their own. In fact, tradition is altered by the very fact of trying to understand it. It is time that this effort to learn and communicate tradition be facilitated, both within First Nations and between First Nations and Canadian courts. There is persuasive precedent in Canadian law recognizing the pre-existence of Aboriginal rights and their associated laws. Furthermore, the courts have created an opportunity to receive these laws into Canadian law by analogy and through sui generis principles. These principles must be allowed to influence the development of law in Canada. When First Nations laws are received more fully into Canadian law, both systems will be strengthened. As both an Anishinabek and Canadian citizen, it is my hope that Canada will not disregard the promise of respect that Canadian law holds for First Nations. Canadian legal institutions will soon determine if First Nations law will continue with or without them.

35 Wasáse: Indigenous Pathways of Action and Freedom

Taiaiake Alfred (2005)

EDITORS' INTRODUCTION

Taiaiake Alfred is a professor of Indigenous Governance at the University of Victoria. He writes that "Wasáse" is an ancient war ritual, a ceremony of unity, strength, and commitment to action. It is through the ethical and political vision of the Wasáse that the Onkwehonwe, *the original peoples, can regenerate themselves and reconnect with their cultures and communities.*

First Words

There are many differences among the peoples that are indigenous to this land, yet the challenge facing all Onkwehonwe is the same: regaining freedom and becoming self-sufficient by confronting the disconnection and fear at the core of our existences under colonial dominion. We are separated from the sources of our goodness and power: from each other, our cultures, and our lands. These connections must be restored. Governmental power is founded on fear, which is used to control and manipulate us in many ways; so, the strategy must be to confront fear and display the courage to act against and defeat the states power.

The first question that arises when this idea is applied in a practical way to the situations facing Onkwehonwe in real life is this: How can we regenerate ourselves culturally and achieve freedom and political independence when the legacies of disconnection, dependency, and dispossession have such a strong hold on us? Undeniably, we face a difficult situation. The political and social institutions that govern us have been shaped and organized to serve white power and they conform to the interests of the states founded on that objective. These state and Settler-serving institutions are useless to the cause of our survival, and if we are to free ourselves from the grip of colonialism, we must reconfigure our politics and replace all of the strategies, institutions, and leaders in place today. The transformation will begin inside each one of us as personal change, but decolonization will become a reality only when we collectively both commit to a movement based on an *ethical* and *political* vision and consciously reject the colonial postures of weak submission, victimry, and raging violence. It is a political vision and solution that will be capable of altering power relations and rearranging the forces that shape our lives. Politics is the force that channels social, cultural,

---

Source: Excerpted from *Wasáse: Indigenous Pathways of Action and Freedom* by Taiaiake Alfred. Peterborough, ON: Broadview Press, 2005. Reprinted by permission.

and economic powers and makes them imminent in our lives. Abstaining from politics is like turning your back on a beast when it is angry and intent on ripping your guts out.

It is the kind of politics we practise that makes the crucial distinction between the possibility of a regenerative struggle and what we are doing now. Conventional and acceptable approaches to making change are leading us nowhere. Submission and cooperation, which define politics as practised by the current generation of Onkwehonwe politicians, are, I contend, morally, culturally, and politically indefensible and should be dismissed scornfully by any right-thinking person and certainly by any Onkwehonwe who still has dignity. There is little attention paid in this book to the conventional aspects of the politics of pity, such as self-government processes, land claims agreements, and aboriginal rights court cases, because building on what we have achieved up until now in our efforts to decolonize society is insufficient and truly unacceptable as the end-state of a challenge to colonialism. The job is far from finished. It is impossible to predict what constraints and opportunities will emerge, but it is clear that we have not pushed hard enough yet to be satisfied with the state's enticements. Fundamentally different relationships between Onkwehonwe and Settlers will emerge not from negotiations in state-sponsored and government-regulated processes, but only after successful Onkwehonwe resurgences against white society's entrenched privileges and the unreformed structure of the colonial state.

As Onkwehonwe committed to the reclamation of our dignity and strength, there are, theoretically, two viable approaches to engaging the colonial power that is thoroughly embedded in the state and in societal structures: armed resistance and non-violent contention. Each has a heritage among our peoples and is a potential formula for making change, for engaging with the adversary without deference to emotional attachments to colonial symbols or to the compromised logic of colonial approaches. They are both philosophically defensible, but are they both equally valid approaches to making change, given the realities of our situations and our goals? We need a confident position on the question as to what is the right strategy. Both armed resistance and non-violent contention are unique disciplines that require commitments that rule out overlapping allegiances between the two approaches. They are diverging and distinctive ways of making change, and the choice between the two paths is the most important decision the next generation of Onkwehonwe will collectively make.

This is the political formula of the strategy of armed resistance: facing a situation of untenable politics, Onkwehonwe could conceivably move toward practising a punishing kind of aggression, a raging resistance invoking hostile and irredentist negative political visions seeking to engender and escalate the conflict so as to eventually demoralize the Settler society and defeat the colonial state. Contrast this with the strategic vision of nonviolent contention: Onkwehonwe face the untenable politics and unacceptable conditions in their communities and confront the situation with determined yet restrained action, coherent and creative contention supplemented with a positive political vision based on re-establishing respect for the original covenants and ancient treaties that reflect the founding principles of the Onkwehonwe-Settler relationship. This would be a movement sure to engender conflict, but it would be conflict for a positive purpose and with the hope of recreating the conditions of coexistence. Rather than enter the arena of armed resistance, we would choose to perform rites of resurgence.

These forms of resurgence have already begun. There are people in all communities who understand that a true decolonization movement can emerge only when we shift our politics from articulating grievances to pursuing an organized and political battle for the cause of our freedom. These new warriors understand the need to refuse any further disconnection from their heritage and the need to reconnect with the spiritual bases of their existences as Onkwehonwe. Following their example and building on the foundation of their struggles, we have the potential to initiate a more coordinated and widespread action, to reorganize communities to take advantage of gains and opportunities as they occur in political, economic, social, and cultural spheres and spaces created by the movement. There is a solid theory of change in this concept of an indigenous peoples' movement. The theory of change is the lived experience of the people we will encounter in this book. Their lives are a dynamic of power generated by creative energy flowing from their heritage through their courageous and unwavering determination to recreate themselves and act together to meet the challenges of their day.

A common and immediate concern for anyone defending the truth of their heritage is the imperative to repel the thrust of the modern state's assault against our peoples. The Settlers continue to erase our existences from the cultural, social, and political landscape of our homelands. Onkwehonwe are awakening to the need to move from the materialist orientation of our politics and social reality toward a restored spiritual foundation, channelling that spiritual strength and the unity it creates into a power that can affect political and economic relations. A true revolution is spiritual at its core; every single one of the world's materialist revolutions has failed to produce conditions of life that are markedly different from those which it opposed. Whatever the specific means or rationale, violent, legalist, and economic revolutions have never been successful in producing peaceful coexistence between peoples; in fact, they always reproduce the exact set of power relations they seek to change, rearranging only the outward face of power …

Outright assaults and insidious undermining have brought us to the situation we face today, when the destruction of our peoples is nearly complete. Yet resurgence and regeneration constitute a way to power-surge against the empire with integrity. The new warriors who are working to ensure the survival of their people are not distracted by the effort to pass off as "action" any analysis of the self-evident fact of the defeat of our nations. They don't imagine that our cause needs further justification in law or in the public mind. They know that assertion and action are the urgencies; all the rest is a smokescreen clouding this clear vision.

The experience of resurgence and regeneration in Onkwehonwe communities thus far proves that change cannot be made from within the colonial structure. Institutions and ideas that are the creation of the colonial relationship are not capable of ensuring our survival; this has been amply proven as well by the absolute failure of institutional and legalist strategies to protect our lands and our rights, as well as in their failure to motivate younger generations of Onkwehonwe to action. In the face of the strong renewed push by the state for the legal and political assimilation of our peoples, as well as a rising tide of consumerist materialism making its way into our communities, the last remaining remnants of distinctive Onkwehonwe values and culture are being wiped out. The situation is urgent and calls for even more intensive and profound resurgences on even more levels, certainly not moderation. Many people are paralyzed by fear or idled by complacency and will sit passively and watch destruction consume our people. But the words in this book are for those of us who prefer a dangerous dignity to safe self-preservation.

People have always faced these challenges. None of what I am saying is new, either to people's experience in the world or to political philosophy. What is emerging in our communities is a renewed respect for indigenous knowledge and Onkwehonwe ways of thinking. This book hopes to document and glorify this renewal, in which Onkwehonwe are linked in spirit and strategy with other indigenous peoples confronting empire throughout the world. When we look into the heart of our own communities, we can relate to the struggles of peoples in Africa or Asia and appreciate the North African scholar Albert Memmi's thoughts on how, in the language of his day, colonized peoples respond to oppression: "One can be reconciled to every situation, and the colonized can wait a long time to live. But, regardless of how soon or how violently the colonized rejects his situation, he will one day begin to overthrow his unliveable existence with the whole force of his oppressed personality."[1] The question facing us is this one: For us today, here in this land, how will the overthrow of our unliveable existence come about? ...

Wasáse is spiritual revolution and contention. It is not a path of violence. And yet, this commitment to non-violence is not pacifism either. This is an important point to make clear: I believe there is a need for morally grounded defiance and non-violent agitation combined with the development of a collective capacity for self-defence, so as to generate within the Settler society a reason and incentive to negotiate constructively in the interest of achieving a respectful coexistence. The rest of this book will try to explain this concept (an effort the more academically inclined reader may be permitted to read as my theorizing the liberation of indigenous peoples).

My goal is to discover a real and deep notion of peace in the hope of moving us away from valuing simplistic notions of peace such as certainty and stability for these are conceptions that point only to the value of order. Some readers may find themselves confused by the seeming contradictions in my logic and question how "peace" can be the orienting goal of this warrior-spirited book, wondering if perhaps a concept like "justice" may be more to the point and truer to the spirit of a book that takes a war dance as its emblem. But justice as a liberatory concept and as a would-be goal is limited by its necessary gaze to the politics, economics, and social relations of the past. However noble and necessary justice is to our struggles, its gaze will always be backward. By itself, the concept of justice is not capable of encompassing the broader transformations needed to ensure coexistence. Justice is one element of a good relationship; it is concerned with fairness and right and calculating moral balances, but it cannot be the end goal of a struggle, which must be conceived as a movement from injustice and conflict through and beyond the achievement of justice to the completion of the relationship and the achievement of peace.

The old slogan, "No justice, no peace," is a truism. We must move from injustice, through struggle, to a mutual respect founded on the achievement of justice and then onward towards peace. Step by step. Lacking struggle, omitting respect and justice, there can and will be no peace. Or happiness. Or freedom. These are the real goals of a truly human and fully realized philosophy of change.

Peace is hopeful, visionary, and forward-looking; it is not just the lack of violent conflict or rioting in the streets. That simple stability is what we call order, and order serves the powerful in an imperial situation. If peace continues to be strictly defined as the maintenance of order and the rule of law, we will be defeated in our struggle to survive as Onkwehonwe. Reconceptualized for our struggle, peace is being Onkwehonwe, breaking with the disfiguring and meaningless norms of our present reality, and recreating ourselves in a holistic sense. This conception of peace requires a rejection of the state's multifaceted oppression of our peoples simultaneously with and through the assertion of regenerated Onkwehonwe identities. Personal and collective transformation is not instrumental to the surging against state power, it is the very means of our struggle.

Memmi, who was so powerful in his exposure of colonial mentalities at play during the Algerian resistance against French colonialism, spoke of the fundamental need to cure white people, through revolution, of the disease of the European they have collectively inherited from their colonial forefathers. I believe his prescription of spiritual transformation channelled into a political action and social movement is the right medicine. ...

The thoughts and vision I am offering through these words are rooted in the cultural heritage of Anówarakowa. And proudly so! They are not compromises between indigenous and non-indigenous perspectives; nor are they attempts to negotiate a reconciliation of Onkwehonwe and European cultures and values. These words are an attempt to bring forward an indigenously rooted voice of contention, unconstrained and uncompromised by colonial mentalities. A total commitment to the challenge of regenerating our indigeneity, to rootedness in indigenous cultures, to a fundamental commitment to the centrality of our truths—this book is an effort to work through the philosophical, spiritual, and practical implications of holding such commitments.

These commitments require the reader to challenge critically all of his or her artificial and emotional attachments to the oppressive colonial myths and symbols that we have come to know as our culture. I know that this is asking people to wander into dangerous territory; disentangling from these attachments can also feel like being banished, in a way. But stepping into our fear is crucial, because leaving the comfort zone of accepted truth is vital to creating the emotional and mental state that allows one to really learn.

It is a new approach to decolonization. Less intense, or less threatening, ideas about how to make change have proven ineffective from our perspective. I believe it is because they are bound up in and unable to break free from the limiting logic of the colonial myths that they claim to oppose. The myths' symbols and embedded beliefs force aboriginal thinking to remain in colonial mental, political, and legal frameworks, rendering these forms of writing and thinking less radical and powerless against imperialism. The reflections, meditations, teachings, and dialogues that form the core of this book are indigenous and organic: they emerge from inside Onkwehonwe experiences and reflect the ideas, concepts, and languages that have developed over millennia in the spaces we live, among our peoples. I want to bring the heritage and truth of Anówarakowa to a new generation and to engage passionately with indigenous truths to generate powerful dynamics of thought and action and change. I did not write this book *about* change, I wrote it from *within* change. I wrote it with the plain intent of instigating further contention. My hope is that people who read these words will take from them a different way of defining the problem at the core of our present existence, one that brings a radically principled and challenging set of ideas to bear on how to remake the relationship between Onkwehonwe and Settler.

A big part of the social and political resurgence will be the regeneration of Onkwehonwe existences free from colonial attitudes and behaviours. Regeneration means we will reference ourselves differently, both from the ways we did traditionally and under colonial dominion. We will self-consciously recreate our cultural practices and reform our political identities by drawing on tradition in a thoughtful process of reconstruction and a committed reorganization of our lives in a personal and collective sense. This will result in a new conception of what it is to live as Onkwehonwe. This book is my contribution to the larger effort to catalyze and galvanize the movements that have already begun among so many of our people. Restoring these connections is the force that will confront and defeat the defiant evil of imperialism in this land. We need to work together to cleanse our minds, our hearts, and our bodies of the colonial stain and reconnect our lives to the sources of our strength as Onkwehonwe. We need to find new and creative ways to express that heritage. I wrote this book as an Onkwehonwe believing in the fundamental commonality of indigenous values; yet I wrote it from within my own experience. I aim to speak most directly to other Onkwehonwe who share my commitments and who are travelling the same pathway. These words are offered in the spirit of the ancient Wasáse, which was so eloquently captured by my friend Kahente when I asked her to tell me how she understood the meaning of the ritual:

> There is a spiritual base that connects us all, and it is stimulated through ceremony. The songs and dances that we perform are like medicine, *Ononkwa*, invoking the power of the original instructions that lie within. In it, we dance, sing, and share our words of pain, joy, strength, and commitment. The essence of the ancestors' message reveals itself not only in these songs, speeches, and dances but also in the faces and bodies of all who are assembled. This visual manifestation shows us that we are not alone and that our survival depends on being part of the larger group and in this group working together. We are reminded to stay on the path laid out before us. This way it strengthens our resolve to keep going and to help each other along the way. It is a time to show each other how to step along that winding route in unison and harmony with one another. To know who your friends and allies are in such struggle is what is most important and is what keeps you going.

If non-indigenous readers are capable of listening, they will learn from these shared words, and they will discover that while we are envisioning a new relationship between Onkwehonwe and the land, we are at the same time offering a decolonized alternative to the Settler society by inviting them to share our vision of respect and peaceful coexistence.

Note

1. Albert Memmi, *The Colonizer and the Colonized* (Boston, MA: Beacon Press, 1991) 120.

36 Royal Commission on the Status of Women in Canada

Royal Commission Report (1970)

EDITORS' INTRODUCTION

Commissioned by the government of Lester B. Pearson in 1967, the mandate of the Royal Commission on the Status of Women was to examine the situation of women in Canadian society and make policy recommendations to the federal government. The commission's report in 1970 is widely considered to be a landmark in the struggle for women's equality in Canada.

Criteria and Principles

In a dozen succinct words the Universal Declaration of Human Rights has clarified the issue of the rights of women: "All human beings are born free and equal in dignity and rights."

Canada is, therefore, committed to a principle that permits no distinction in rights and freedoms between women and men. The principle emphasizes the common status of women and men rather than a separate status for each sex. The stage has been set for a new society equally enjoyed and maintained by both sexes.

But practices and attitudes die slowly. As we travelled across the country, we heard of discrimination against women that still flourishes and prejudice that is very much alive. It became abundantly clear that Canada's commitment is far from being realized.

We have been asked to inquire into and report upon the status of women in Canada and we have done so in the light of certain principles. A general principle is that *everyone is entitled to the rights and freedoms proclaimed in the Universal Declaration of Human Rights.* We have examined the status of women to learn whether or not they really have these positive rights and freedoms both in principle and in practice. Some of our recommendations should establish a measure of equality that is now lacking for men as well as for women.

Explicit in the Terms of Reference given us by the Government is our duty to ensure for women equal opportunities with men. We have interpreted this to mean that equality of opportunity for everyone should be the goal of Canadian society. The right to an adequate standard of living is without value to the person who has no means of achieving it. Freedom to choose a career means little if the opportunity to enter some occupations is restricted.

Source: Excerpted from *Final Report of the Royal Commission on the Status of Women in Canada.* Ottawa: Government of Canada, 1970. Notes omitted.

Our Terms of Reference also imply that *the full use of human resources is in the national interest*. We have explored the extent to which Canada develops and makes use of the skills and abilities of women.

Women and men, having the same rights and freedoms, share the same responsibilities. They should have an equal opportunity to fulfil this obligation. We have, therefore, examined the status of women and made recommendations in the belief that *there should be equality of opportunity to share the responsibilities to society as well as its privileges and prerogatives*.

In particular, the Commission adopted four principles: first, *that women should be free to choose whether or not to take employment outside their homes*. The circumstances which impede this free choice have been of specific interest to our inquiry. Where we have made recommendations to improve opportunities for women in the work world, our goal has not been to force married women to work for pay outside of the home but rather to eliminate the practical obstacles that prevent them from exercising this right. If a husband is willing to support his wife, or a wife her husband, the decision and responsibility belong to them.

The second is that *the care of children is a responsibility to be shared by the mother, the father and society*. Unless this shared responsibility is acknowledged and assumed, women cannot be accorded true equality.

The third principle specifically recognizes the child-bearing function of women. It is apparent that *society has a responsibility for women because of pregnancy and child-birth, and special treatment related to maternity will always be necessary*.

The fourth principle is that *in certain areas women will for an interim period require special treatment to overcome the adverse effects of discriminatory practices*. We consider such measures to be justified in a limited range of circumstances, and we anticipate that they should quickly lead to actual equality which would make their continuance unnecessary. The needs and capacities of women have not always been understood. Discrimination against women has in many instances been unintentional and special treatment will no longer be required if a positive effort to remove it is made for a short period.

With these principles in mind, we have first looked at women in Canadian society. Within this perspective we have gone on to consider the position of women in the economy, the education they receive, their place in the family and their participation in public life. We have considered the particular implications of poverty among women, conditions of citizenship and aspects of taxation, and the Criminal Code as it affects the female offender. ...

Canadian Women and Society

Social Change

The democratization of education has greatly affected the aspirations and expectations of Canadian women. Little by little, the doors of nearly all educational institutions have been opened to them over the last hundred years. In 1967, female graduates made up about a third of the 27,533 Canadian graduates in arts, pure science and commerce, and more than half the 7,590 graduates in education, library science and social work. And yet many fields of learning still remain substantially male preserves with only token female representation; fewer than five per cent of the 1,796 graduates in law and theology, fewer than 12 per cent of the graduating medical doctors and about six per cent of the graduating dentists in 1967 were women. Moreover, institutions of higher learning have yet to adapt their general plans and structures to the needs of married women.

In the face of deep-rooted functional change, marriage and the family persist as an institution of particular importance to women. The importance of family is due to the need of human beings, whether children or adults, to "belong" in a close social relationship with others. Functions of the family, however, which wives used to perform—such as the education of children, treatment of illness and care of the aged—are now undertaken increasingly by private or public institutions. Today 90 per cent of Canadian women marry and live in families and, because of the longer life span, may remain married for an average of 40 years. Divorce is now increasing and many divorced women remarry.

The Cultural Mould

...[Many philosophers and most theologians] postulated the existence of an inferior feminine "nature," in opposition to that of man. Aristotle's theory that a women's role in conception is purely passive was accepted for centuries. It was not until the second half of the nineteenth century that scientists demonstrated that both parents made equivalent contributions to a child's biological inheritance.

The three principle influences which have shaped Western society—Greek philosophy, Roman law, and Judeo-Christian theology—have each held, almost axiomatically, that woman is inferior and subordinate to man and requires his domination. This attitude still persists today; for example, in most religions, a woman cannot be ordained or authorized to be a spiritual leader.

On the basis of ancient concepts, it has been all too easy to divide assumed male and female functions and psychological traits into separate, opposing categories. These categories, or stereotypes, have by no means disappeared from popular belief and thinking about the nature of women and men. Women are expected to be emotional, dependent and gentle and men are thought to possess all the contrary attributes: to be rational, independent and aggressive. These are the qualities assumed to be suitable for women in the closed world of the home, husband and children, and for men in the outside world of business, the professions or politics. The stereotypes and the models of behaviour derived from this assumption do not necessarily correspond to the real personalities of a great number of men and women. ...

In Canada as elsewhere, the cultural mould has been imposed upon and accepted by many women and tends to confuse discussions on the subject of the status of women. Several briefs pointed this out: "Women, too, in large part still believe that a woman's place is in the home, at least while her children are young." "The all-too-prevalent opinion, common amongst women as well as men, that women with the odd exception are less ambitious, timid, less capable, and less well-organized than men, is fallacious, if closely examined."

During the 1968 public hearings of the Commission, two Canadian daily newspapers published questionnaires "for Men Only" in order to obtain a sampling of men's opinions on the question of women. Such surveys are usually affected by different kinds of bias: for example, the sampling might not be representative of the whole population. Nevertheless they are not meaningless even though the results have to be interpreted with care. In these samplings the results showed, generally, traditional opinions. Many of the respondents declared that women tended to find more discrimination than in fact existed and that Canada did not need a Royal Commission on the Status of Women. More than half the replies received by the *Toronto Star* declared that woman's place is in the home. In the survey by *Le Devoir*, majority opinion favoured a male rather than a female superior on the job. Most respondents were of the opinion that women lack the emotional control demanded for combining a career with marriage and motherhood. On the other hand, the young men who responded to *Le Devoir*, and the husbands of working wives who replied to the *Toronto Star*, wanted greater liberty for Canadian women. Answers received by the *Toronto Star* were almost unanimous in their view that gainfully employed women should be legally responsible for the support of their families, and that they should be required, if necessary, to pay alimony in cases of divorce.

The feeling that women who have equal financial resources should have responsibilities equal to those of men may mark an important evolution of attitudes. The stereotype of the man as the sole family breadwinner yields to the new picture of the wife as his economic partner. Yet woman remains mainly identified with her old role as housewife. When people try to reconcile these two different images—the traditional woman and the actual woman who is many-faceted, as a man is, and who often works for pay—the stereotype is not always discarded. ...

The stereotype of the ideal woman has its effect upon Canadian women. It appears that many women have accepted as truths the social constraints and the mental images that society has prescribed, and have made these constraints and images part of themselves as guides for living. This theory could partly explain why some women are little inclined to identify themselves with the collective problems of their sex and tend to share the conventional opinions of society. Social scientists have noted a similar phenomenon in their study of certain minority groups, or people treated as inferior. Their members often fail to identify with their own group. This is particularly true of individuals who cross the border separating them from the majority and who then adopt its attitudes and standards.

The concept of the psychological minority offers one possible interpretation of the effects upon women of stereotyping. Women do not, in fact, constitute a social group since they are found everywhere and in all classes. They cannot be isolated, as a collectivity, from the other members of society with whom they live in close relation. They cannot, moreover, be described as a demographic minority in society as a whole, though they are often a minority in the world of work and politics. But, according to some writers, a psychological minority group is an aggregation whose collective destiny depends on the good will or is at the mercy of another group. They—the members of a psychological minority—feel and know that they live in a state of dependency, no matter what percentage they may be of the total population.

Stereotypes are perpetuated by the mass media. Day after day, advertising reinforces and exploits stereotypes to achieve greater sales by repeating the idea that the "real" woman and the "real" man use this or that product. Although men as well as women are stereotypes, the results may be more damaging for women since advertising encourages feminine dependency by urging women not to act but to be passive, not to really achieve but to live out their aspirations in the imagination and in dreams.

Woman is often presented as a sex object, defined as a superficial creature who thinks only of her appearance, who sees herself mainly in terms of whether she is attractive to men. She conforms to the beauty and youth standards which men are said to want of her. In a study prepared for the Commission, it was found that over 89 per cent of the women pictured in Canadian newspapers and magazines are less than 35 years of age. As presented by the advertiser, women are hardly ever associated with intelligence, sincerity, culture, originality or talent. Instead, they are depicted as being young, elegant and beautiful. "The mass media must in some way be encouraged to change their emphasis. ...."

At least 30 of the briefs received by the Commission protested against the degrading, moronic picture of woman thus presented. These briefs objected to woman, in advertisements, being shown as fragile, without depth or reality, and obsessed by her desire to please masculine hero-figures as artificial as herself. Repetition is a "hidden persuader" in advertising, an especially effective tool influencing children and young girls to aspire to constraining models and low ideals. When women are shown in active pursuits, these activities are in the order of polishing furniture and preparing food. Some women's magazines contribute to the exaltation of housework as a fine art and very often persuade women that to conform to the image of housewife *par excellence* is a duty and that not to conform signifies inadequacy. Housework is rarely viewed in these publications, and in advertising, for what it is: a necessary task that is performed in order to make the family comfortable.

Stereotypes pass naturally from one generation to the next. Whatever sex-linked biological determinants of personality there may be, no one yet seems to have isolated them clearly, or surely. However, the standards and models of behaviour taught either explicitly or by example in the family begin to affect boys and girls from their earliest childhood. ...

Expressed opinion is one thing—actual behaviour may be another. Despite their traditional point of view, as shown by these studies, young people are living lives that increasingly differ from those of their parents. Well over half the Canadian population is under the age of 30 and not all are conforming to all the old patterns. Some of them commonly express dissatisfaction with—and freely question—customs and institutions long taken for granted. And it cannot be assumed that the once accepted roles of men and women will be exempt. The behaviour of many young people, for example, in their choice of dress, music and lifestyle, may tell as much about their attitudes as their responses to formal surveys.

The role of women will necessarily change as society itself evolves. In making our recommendations, we have tried to take into account what may be in store for Canadians in the years to come. Predictions about what life will be like in the future are increasingly being used as tools for better understanding of changes in present society. ...

The future of our country will be determined substantially by the direction we Canadians choose to take now. If women are to be able to make full use of their capabilities, help is needed from the whole society. Even so, women themselves must work for change: "... women are the best helpers of one another. Let them think; let them act; till they know what they need. We only ask of men to remove arbitrary barriers. Some would like to do more. But I believe it needs that Woman show herself in her native dignity to teach them how to aid her; their minds are so encumbered by tradition."

Plan for Action

Conclusion

Even in the interval since the establishment of this Commission, there have been signs of change in public attitudes toward many of the problems with which we have been concerned. But the pace is not sufficiently rapid, and there is little public awareness of the extent to which an improvement in the status of women is required or of the over-all impact on society which such a change would bring. At issue is the opportunity to construct a human society free of a major injustice which has been part of history.

The extension of "woman's place" to all areas of society is part of the world-wide process of democratization. What we have recommended deals only with a few pressing and immediate problems. But what we have in mind is a releasing of positive and creative forces to take on still larger human tasks. Men, as well as women, would benefit from a society where roles are less rigidly defined.

To set the stage for this better employment of human capacities, equality of opportunity for women is a fundamental first step. The effect of our recommendations is likely to be more far-reaching than any one recommendation would indicate. The total impact will be considerably greater than the sum of the changes we propose. But the Commissioners are aware that true equality of opportunity for women and men can only result from radical changes in our way of life and in our social organization and probably must go as far as an equal sharing by parents in the care of their children and a complete reorganization of the working world.

The nine-to-five working day and full-time employment are neither sacred nor are they guarantees of efficiency. Productive efficiency may indeed have to yield its place as the sole criterion of employment practices. Human values may assume greater importance. Many rigid constraints that are part of today's economic world may be relaxed, to the benefit of all.

We may begin to question why banks, the post office, doctors and dentists are available only during the hours when everyone else is at work. Why is employment so rigidly structured that additional education is almost inaccessible? Should not the educational system stress the need to adapt to a changing society rather than to conform to the habits of yesterday? Flexibility may be introduced in many aspects of social organization as a consequence of the need to establish equality for women. Canada can afford to experiment boldly.

Women, as they seek equality, must contend with a society conceived and controlled by men. They require a high degree of resolution to disregard present barriers and to attain the positions which best reflect their ability. But existing structures are not sacrosanct; women must be aware that they are entering a world that can be changed. And men, as they recognize women's claim to equality, may welcome an opportunity to examine Canada's institutions in a new light.

We have indicated some of the characteristics of the society that could emerge. The magnitude of the changes that must be introduced does not dismay us, but we are dismayed that so much has been left undone. In terms of Canada's commitments and the principles on which a democracy is based, what we recommend is no more than simple justice.

37 Will Women Judges Really Make a Difference?

Bertha Wilson (1990)

EDITORS' INTRODUCTION

*In her 2001 biography of Madam Justice Bertha Wilson (*Judging Bertha Wilson: Law as Large as Life*), Ellen Anderson begins the book's preface with a description of the "firestorm of controversy" that greeted Wilson in 1990 after she gave a speech at Osgoode Hall Law School entitled "Will Women Judges Really Make a Difference?" The group REAL Women attempted to have her removed from the Supreme Court, on the grounds that the questions posed in her speech violated her oath of impartiality.*

When I was appointed to the Supreme Court of Canada in the Spring of 1982, a great many women from all across the country telephoned, cabled, or wrote to me rejoicing in my appointment. "Now," they said, "we are represented on Canada's highest court. This is the beginning of a new era for women." So why was *I* not rejoicing? Why did *I* not share the tremendous confidence of these women?

First came the realization that no one could live up to the expectations of my well-wishers. I had the sense of being doomed to failure, not because of any excess of humility on my part or any desire to shirk the responsibility of the office, but because I knew from hard experience that the law does not work that way. Change in the law comes slowly and incrementally; that is its nature. It responds to changes in society; it seldom initiates them. And while I was prepared—and, indeed, as a woman judge, anxious—to respond to these changes, I wondered to what extent I would be constrained in my attempts to do so by the nature of judicial office itself.

In the literature which is required reading for every newly appointed judge, it is repeatedly stated that judges must be both independent and impartial, that these qualities are basic to the proper administration of justice and fundamental to the legitimacy of the judicial role. The judge must not approach his or her task with preconceived notions about law or policy, with personal prejudice against parties or issues, or with bias toward a particular outcome of a case. Socrates defined the essential qualities of a judge in the following manner: "Four things belong to a judge: to hear courteously, to answer wisely, to consider soberly, and to decide impartially. ..."[1]

Source: Excerpted from "Will Women Judges Really Make a Difference?" *Osgoode Hall Law Journal*, vol. 28, no. 3 (2000). This paper was originally presented at the Fourth Annual Barbara Betcherman Memorial Lecture, Osgoode Hall Law School, February 8, 1990. Some notes omitted.

But what has all this got to do with the subject: "Will women judges really make a difference?" It has a great deal to do with it, and whether you agree or not will probably depend on your perception of the degree to which the existing law reflects the judicial neutrality or impartiality we have been discussing. If the existing law can be viewed as the product of judicial neutrality or impartiality, even although the judiciary has been very substantially male, then you may conclude that the advent of increased numbers of women judges should make no difference, assuming, that is, that these women judges will bring to bear the same neutrality and impartiality. However, if you conclude that the existing law, in some areas at least, cannot be viewed as the product of judicial neutrality, then your answer may be very different.

Two law professors at New York University, Professor John Johnston and Professor Charles Knapp, have concluded, as a result of their studies of judicial attitudes reflected in the decisions of judges in the United States, that United States judges have succeeded in their conscious efforts to free themselves from habits of stereotypical thought with regard to discrimination based on colour[16] However, they were unable to reach a similar conclusion with respect to discrimination based on sex, finding that American judges had failed to bring to sex discrimination the judicial virtues of detachment, reflection, and critical analysis which had served them so well with respect to other areas of discrimination. They state: "'Sexism'—the making of unjustified (or at least unsupported) assumptions about individual capabilities, interests, goals and social roles solely on the basis of sex differences—is as easily discernible in contemporary judicial opinions as racism ever was."[17]

Professor Norma Wikler, a sociologist at the University of California, has reviewed a number of other studies of judicial attitudes conducted by legal researchers and social scientists. These studies confirm that male judges tend to adhere to traditional values and beliefs about the natures of men and women and their proper roles in society. The studies show overwhelming evidence that gender-based myths, biases, and stereotypes are deeply embedded in the attitudes of many male judges, as well as in the law itself. Researchers have concluded that gender difference has been a significant factor in judicial decision-making, particularly in the areas of tort law, criminal law, and family law. Further, many have concluded that sexism is the unarticulated underlying premise of many judgments in these areas, and that this is not really surprising having regard to the nature of the society in which the judges themselves have been socialized. ...[18]

So, where do we stand in Canada on this matter? As might be expected, feminist scholars in Canada have over the past two decades produced a vast quantity of literature on the subject, some of it very insightful, very balanced, and very useful, and some of it very radical, quite provocative, and probably less useful as a result.

But all of it, it seems, is premised, at least as far as judicial decision-making is concerned, on two basic propositions: one, that women view the world and what goes on in it from a different perspective from men; and two, that women judges, by bringing that perspective to bear on the cases they hear, can play a major role in introducing judicial neutrality and impartiality into the justice system.

Taking from my own experience as a judge of fourteen years' standing, working closely with my male colleagues on the bench, there are probably whole areas of the law on which there is no uniquely feminine perspective. This is not to say that the development of the law in these areas has not been influenced by the fact that lawyers and judges have all been men. Rather, the principles and the underlying premises are so firmly entrenched and so fundamentally sound that no good would be achieved by attempting to re-invent the wheel, even if the revised version did have a few more spokes in it. I have in mind areas such as the law of contract, the law of real property, and the law applicable to corporations. In some other areas of the law, however, a distinctly male perspective is clearly discernible. It has resulted in legal principles that are not fundamentally sound and that should be revisited when the opportunity presents itself. Canadian feminist scholarship has done an excellent job of identifying those areas and making suggestions for reform. Some aspects of the criminal law in particular cry out for change; they are based on presuppositions about the nature of women and women's sexuality that, in this day and age, are little short of ludicrous.

But how do we handle the problem that women judges, just as much as their male counterparts, are subject to the duty of impartiality? As was said at the outset, judges must not approach their task with preconceived notions about law and policy. They must approach it with detachment and, as Lord MacMillan said, purge their minds "not only of partiality to persons, but of partiality to arguments."[24] Does this then foreclose any kind of "judicial affirmative action" to counteract the influence of the dominant male perspective of the past and establish judicial neutrality through a countervailing female perspective? Is Karen Selick, writing recently in the *Lawyers Weekly*, correct when she argues that offsetting male bias with female bias would only be compounding the injustice?[25] Does the nature of the judicial process itself present an insuperable hurdle so that the legislatures rather than the courts must be looked to for any significant legal change?

In part this may be so. Certainly, the legislature is the more effective instrument for rapid or radical change. But there is no reason why the judiciary cannot exercise some modest degree of creativity in areas where modern insights and life's experience have indicated that the law has gone awry. However, and this is extremely important, it will be a Pyrrhic victory for women and for the justice system as a whole if changes in the law come only through the efforts of women lawyers and women judges. The Americans were smart to realize that courses and workshops on gender bias for judges, male and female, are an essential follow-up to scholarly research and learned writing. In Canada, we are just beginning to touch the fringes. ...

I return, then, to the question of whether the appointment of more women judges will make a difference. Because the entry of women into the judiciary is so recent, few studies have been done on the subject. Current statistics show that just over 9 percent of federally appointed judges are women;[28] it is reasonable to assume that more women will be appointed to the Bench as more women become licensed to practice law. Will this growing number of women judges by itself make a difference?

The expectation is that it will, that the mere presence of women on the bench will make a difference. In her article "The Gender of Judges," Suzanna Sherry (an Associate Law Professor at the University of Minnesota) suggests that the mere fact that women are judges serves an educative function; it helps to shatter stereotypes about the role of women in society that are held by male judges and lawyers, as well as by litigants, jurors, and witnesses.[29]

Judge Gladys Kessler (former President of the National Association of Women Judges in the United States) defends the search for competent women appointees to the bench. She says: "But the ultimate justification for deliberately seeking judges of both sexes and all colors and backgrounds is to keep the public's trust. The public must perceive its judges as fair, impartial and representative of the diversity of those who are being judged."[30] Justice Wald has expressed similar sentiments. She believes that women judges are indispensable to the public's confidence in the ability of the courts to respond to the legal problems of all classes of citizens.[31]

Dianne Martin, a criminal lawyer writing in the *Lawyers Weekly*, sees another way in which the presence of women on the bench is helpful and constructive. It is easier, she says, for women lawyers to appear as counsel before a woman judge. She says the "difference is that you are 'normal'—you and the judge have certain shared experiences and a shared reality that removes, to a certain extent, the need to 'translate' your submissions into 'man talk' or a context that a male judge will understand."[32] The woman judge does not see you as "out of place" or having "something to prove by appearing in a courtroom arguing a case before her."[33] ...

Some feminist writers are persuaded that the appointment of more women judges will have an impact on the process of judicial decision-making itself and on the development of the substantive law. As was mentioned earlier, this flows from the belief that women view the world and what goes on in it from a different perspective from men. Some define the difference in perspective solely in terms that women do not accept male perceptions and interpretations of events as the norm or as objective reality. Carol Gilligan (a Professor of Education at Harvard University) sees the difference as going much deeper than that. In her view, women think differently from men, particularly in responding to moral dilemmas. They have, she says, different ways of thinking about themselves and their relationships to others.[37] ...

Gilligan's work on conceptions of morality among adults suggests that women's ethical sense is significantly different from men's. Men see moral problems as arising from competing rights; the adversarial process comes easily to them. Women see moral problems as arising from competing obligations, the one to the other; the important thing is to preserve relationships, to develop an ethic of caring. The goal, according to women's ethical sense, is not seen in terms of winning or losing but, rather, in terms of achieving an optimum outcome for all individuals involved in the moral dilemma. It is not difficult to see how this contrast in thinking might form the basis of different perceptions of justice.

There is merit in Gilligan's analysis. In part, it may explain the traditional reluctance of courts to get too deeply into the circumstances of a case, their anxiety to reduce the context of the dispute to its bare bones through a complex system of exclusionary evidentiary rules. This is one of the characteristic features of the adversarial process. We are all familiar with the witness on cross-examination who wants to explain his or her answer, who feels that a simple yes or no is not an adequate response, and who is frustrated and angry at being cut off with a half-truth. It is so much easier to come up with a black and white answer if you are unencumbered by a broader context which might prompt you, in Lord MacMillan's words, to temper the cold light of reason with the warmer tints of imagination and sympathy.

Gilligan's analysis may also explain the hostility of some male judges to permitting intervenors in human rights cases. The main purpose of having intervenors is to broaden the context of the dispute, to show the issue in a larger perspective or as impacting on other groups not directly involved in the litigation at all. But it certainly does complicate the issues to have them presented in polycentric terms.

Professor Patricia Cain, in her article "Good and Bad Bias: A Comment on Feminist Theory and Judging," says:

What we want, it seems to me, are lawyers who can tell their clients' story, lawyers who can help judges to see the parties as human beings, and who can help remove the separation between judge and litigant. And, then, what we want from our judges is a special ability to listen with connection before engaging in the separation that accompanies judgment.

Obviously, this is not an easy role for the judge—to enter into the skin of the litigant and make his or her experience part of your experience and only when you have done that, to judge. But we have to do it; or at least make an earnest attempt to do it. Whether the criticism of the justice system comes to us through Royal Commissions, through the media, or just through our own personal friends, we cannot escape the conclusion that, in some respects, our existing system of justice has been found wanting. And as Mr. Justice Rothman says, the time to do something about it is *now*.

One of the important conclusions emerging from the Council of Europe's Seminar on Equality between Men and Women held in Strasbourg last November is that the universalist doctrine of human rights must include a realistic concept of masculine and feminine humanity regarded as a whole, that human kind *is* dual and must be represented in its dual form if the trap of an asexual abstraction in which *human being* is always declined in the masculine is to be avoided. If women lawyers and women judges through their differing perspectives on life can bring a new humanity to bear on the decision-making process, perhaps they *will* make a difference. Perhaps they will succeed in infusing the law with an understanding of what it means to be fully human.

Notes

1. J.K. Hoyt, *The Cyclopedia of Practical Quotations*, rev'd ed. (New York: Funk & Wagnalls, 1896) at 330.

16. J.D. Johnston & C.L. Knapp, "Sex Discrimination by Law: A Study in Judicial Perspective" (1976) 46 N.Y. U. L. Rev. 675.

17. *Ibid.* at 676.

18. N.J. Wikler, "On the Judicial Agenda for the 80s: Equal Treatment for Men and Women in the Courts" (1980) 64 *Jud.* 202.

24. Shientag, *supra*, note 4 at 62.

25. K. Selick, "Adding More Women Won't End Bias in Justice System" (1990) 9:35 *Lawyer's Weekly* 7 at 7.

28. Canadian Centre for Justice Statistics, *Profile of Courts in Canada, 1987–1988* (Ottawa: Supply and Services Canada, 1989).

29. S. Sherry, "The Gender of Judges" (1986) 4 *Law & Inequality* 159 at 160.

30. As quoted in J.E. Scott, "Women on the Illinois State Court Bench" (1986) 74 *Ill. B.J.* 436 at 438.

31. P.M. Wald, "Women in the Law" (1988) 24:11 *Trial* 75 at 80.

32. D. Martin, "Have Women Judges Really Made a Difference?" (1986) 6:14 *Lawyers Weekly* 5 at 5.

33. *Ibid.*

37. See C. Gilligan, *In a Different Voice: Psychological Theory and Women's Development* (Cambridge, Mass.: Harvard University Press, 1982).

38 Patriarchy and Paternalism: The Legacy of the Canadian State for First Nations Women

Mary Ellen Turpel (1993)

EDITORS' INTRODUCTION

In this reading, Mary Ellen Turpel (Aki-Kwe) assesses the Royal Commission on the Status of Women in Canada 20 years later, criticizing it for failing to address the unique challenges faced by First Nations women and challenging all feminists to question the extent to which their goals and aspirations are truly universal.

Reflections on the Royal Commission Report: Equality Is Not Our Starting Point

The underlying thesis behind the mandate for the Royal Commission of 1967 was a commitment to ensure that women enjoy equal opportunities with men in Canadian society. The central idea in this thesis, while arguably appropriate and supportable for non-aboriginal women in Canada, is inappropriate conceptually and culturally for First Nations women. First Nations communities, and in particular the communities of my heredity, the Cree community, are ones which do not have a prevailing ethic of equal opportunity for men and women in this sense. It is important in the Cree community to understand the responsibilities of women and of men to the community. Equality is not an important political or social concept. Other First Nations people have the same attitude toward equality.[11] As Skonaganleh:rá, a Mohawk woman, explains of her perspective:

> I don't want equality. I want to go back to where women, in aboriginal communities, were complete, where they were beautiful, where they were treated as more than equal—where man was helper and woman was the centre of that environment, that community. So, while I suppose equality is a nice thing and while I suppose we can never go back all the way, I want to make an effort at going back to at least respecting the role that women played in communities.

Source: Excerpted from "Patriarchy and Paternalism: The Legacy of the Canadian State for First Nations Women" by Mary Ellen Turpel. *Canadian Journal of Women and the Law*, vol. 6, no. 1 (1993). An earlier version of this article was presented at the conference "Women and the Canadian State" in Ottawa, November 1, 1990. Some notes omitted. Reprinted by permission.

As Osennontion, another Mohawk woman, adds:

To me, when these women, who call themselves "feminist" or get called "feminist," talk about equality, they mean sameness. They appear to want to be the *same* as a man. They want to be treated the same as a man, make the same money as a man ... and, they consider all women, regardless of origin, to be the same, to share the same concerns. I, for one, maintain that aboriginal women are *different*, as are the women who are burdened with such labels as immigrant women, or visible minority women. I certainly do not want to be a "man!"

Equality is simply not the central organizing political principle in our communities. It is frequently seen by our Elders as a suspiciously selfish notion, as individualistic and alienating from others in the community. It is incongruous to apply this notion to our communities. We are committed to what would be termed a "communitarian" notion of responsibilities to our peoples, as learned through traditional teachings and our life experiences. I do not see this communitarian notion as translating into equality as it is conventionally understood.

In this regard, I should note that the traditional teachings by our Cree Elders instruct us that Cree women are at the centre of the Circle of Life. While you may think of this as a metaphor, it is in fact an important reality in terms of how one perceives the world and how authority is structured in our communities. It is women who give birth both in the physical and in the spiritual sense to the social, political, and cultural life of the community. It is upon women that the focus of the community has historically been placed and it was, not surprisingly, against women that a history of legislative discrimination was directed by the Canadian State. Our communities do not have a history of disentitlement of women from political or productive life. This is probably the most important point for feminists to grasp in order to appreciate how State-imposed gender discrimination uniquely affected First Nations women. I have found that it is difficult for white feminists to accept that patriarchy is not universal. ...

Because of the special position of Cree women, discrimination by the Canadian State through the Indian Act, and other initiatives, has been potentially lethal. Gender discrimination was cleverly directed (in a Machiavellian sense) against First Nations women because the legislators identified that if they could assimilate women, First Nations peoples would be most easily and effectively assimilated. In so attempting to assimilate us, the State introduced the norm of discrimination on the basis of sex: it was exported from your culture to our culture. Fortunately, we have resisted the attempt to assimilate the First Nations, although we now face a situation in which we must fight against patriarchy both inside and outside of our communities. That legislation has had the continued effect of dividing our communities, dividing our families, dividing our homes. It has broken down our matriarchal tribal support network. A First Nations woman cannot necessarily look to her mother, grandmother, or older aunties to help her because she may have been forced to leave the community through discrimination. Moreover, she may now have trouble reconnecting because of her experiences in a foreign culture, because poverty has led her to equate being a First Nations person with being worthless, and because of lost self-esteem due to racism commonly experienced outside the community. She may also be excluded because her Indian Act-elected government will not let her return.

Our family structures have been systematically undermined by the Canadian State in every way imaginable—forced education at denominational residential schools, imposed male-dominated political structures, gender discrimination in determining who is to be recognized as an "Indian," and the ongoing removal of First Nations children by child welfare authorities. It is difficult for us to look to this State for any change when the presence of the State has been synonymous with a painful dividing of our houses. We have had to struggle against these State-imposed or sanctioned initiatives. At the same time, we have had to react to and struggle with the internal imprint of State-enforced patriarchy on our men and on our political structures. Some of our men have lost touch with their sense of responsibility to women. They have been taught that patriarchy is the ideology of the civilized, and they have tried to act accordingly. However, this cannot mean we abandon our men. They too have been abused and oppressed by the Canadian State.

Some aboriginal leaders now believe that it is a sign of advancement not to have women involved in political discussions because, after all, that is the lesson they have learned by observing how the Canadian State operates. Women are to be relegated to a "private" sphere; men are public actors. This is a great community challenge for us. However, this challenge is not synonymous with the challenge of equal opportunity with men. As Osennontion shares:

> In addition to all of the responsibilities ... perhaps the most daunting for women, is her responsibility for the men—how they conduct themselves, how they behave, how they treat her. She has to remind them of their responsibilities and she has to know when and how to correct them when they stray from those.
>
> At the beginning, when the "others" first came here, we held our rightful positions in our societies and held the respect due us by the men, because that's the way things were then, when we were following our ways. At that time, the European woman was considered an appendage to her husband, his possession. Contact with that European male and the imposition of his ways on our people, resulted in our being assimilated into those ways. We forgot our women's responsibilities and the men forgot theirs.

Despite the imposition of patriarchy on our communities, our teachings still instruct us that the responsibility of men is, first and foremost, to be the woman's helper, to be the supporter of women (not in an economic sense of division of labour), because this means being the supporter of the people. A commitment to this role in our communities is not translatable into the world of equal opportunity of women with men. These are different paths, different conceptions of cultural and genderal identity we are attempting to "walk" ("walk" means to follow or exemplify).

It is essential that you separate two concepts which are at the foreground here so as not to be confused. On the one hand, it is important to understand the position that First Nations women occupy both historically and in the real contemporary sense, in some of our communities, particularly those which are matriarchal, and to appreciate how this position was attacked by the Canadian State.[18] On the other hand, it is essential not to confuse First Nations women's suppressed status as a result of Canadian State policy of State-imposed legal definitions and institutional structures in the Indian Act, with a reaction translatable into a desire to have what White women or men have in this society. The former is patriarchy, the latter is paternalism. Both were imposed upon us as communities and individuals. We do not want continued patriarchy nor do we want paternalistic prescriptions for our future paths. We want to extricate ourselves from these debilitating forces. At the same time, it is wholly distracting and irresponsible for us to place the blame for First Nations women's experiences at the feet of First Nations men.

From our perspective, just as there are a variety of First Nations peoples, so too are there a variety of cultural perspectives in our teachings on men and women. The perspective of First Nations women is one which does not enable one to look at equal opportunity without looking at the larger political climate for our beliefs, our existence within (or at the margins of) Canadian society. In other words, before we can consider these debates about gender equality, what about our claims to cultural equality? What about your role in our problems and, more importantly, what is your role in developing solutions to the problems faced in First Nations communities? Before imposing upon us the logic of gender equality (with White men), what about ensuring for our cultures and political systems equal legitimacy with the Anglo-Canadian cultural perspective which dominates the Canadian State?

In a speech to the Conference on Women and the Canadian State,[19] the Honourable Mary Collins, Minister Responsible for the Status of Women and the Association of National Defence, suggested that women must work to eliminate the "culture of violence" by men against women. In this regard, she was referring specifically to domestic violence. To First Nations people, the expressions "culture of violence" and "domestic violence" not only have their customary connotation of violence by men against women but also mean domestic (that is, Canadian State) violence against the First Nations. A "culture of violence" also conjures up for a First Nations person the image of a dominant Canadian culture that tolerates and even sanctions State violence against First Nations peoples. To have lived through the summer of 1990, with the spectacle of police and army intervention in Mohawk communities (with the arguably full complicity of the federal government) is to have a real sense of the other signification of "domestic violence."

What violence has this State done to the First Nations? More importantly for the feminist movement, is this violence connected to the culture of violence men exhibit toward women? Can a State which uses violence in this way preach about eliminating violence in the home? These interpretations and concerns we have obviously cannot be boxed into the category of "gender." Gender as an isolated category is useful, primarily, to women who do not encounter racial, cultural, or class-based discrimination when they participate in Canadian society. Moreover, to look only to an objective of equality with men is clearly insufficient for First Nations women's struggles and continued identities because this cannot encompass our aspirations as cultures. I cannot separate my gender from my culture. I am not a woman sometimes and Cree at others. I am both because both are intertwined in the way I experience and understand the world. It is only for the purposes of preparing papers like this one that, in trying to grasp the category of gender, I even reflect upon separating one from the other.

My interpretation of the objective of ensuring equal opportunity with men as expressed in the Royal Commission mandate implies equal opportunity for First Nations women with non-aboriginal (so-called White) men. I would suggest that this is an inappropriate starting point because, as I have been suggesting, First Nations women have different roles and responsibilities *vis-à-vis* men. Moreover, I do not see it as worthwhile and worthy to aspire to, or desire, equal opportunity with White men, or with the system that they have created. The aspirations of White men in the dominant society are simply not our aspirations. We do not want to inherit their objectives and positions or to adopt their world view. To be perfectly frank, I cannot figure out why non-aboriginal women would want to do this either. Maybe I have missed something in the discussions, and ask you to help me understand why this could be construed as what you want. I realize that your desires are probably quite diverse.

However, I was troubled by my participation in the Conference on Women and the Canadian State because I did not hear women vigorously challenge this assumption in the mandate of the Royal Commission *Report*. I do not want to look to White men as the starting point to define an agenda or to assess our predicament. Is there somewhere else to look? I think there is another place, at least for First Nations communities.

The Royal Commission *Report* adopted, in its criteria and principles section, an interpretation of the Commission's mandate to mean that "equality of opportunity for everyone should be the goal of Canadian society." In fairness to the Commissioners who prepared the 1970 document, there was a statement in the *Report* that throughout the hearings, First Nations peoples urged that the Commission not adopt a view of their aspirations as defined by non-aboriginal people living somewhere else in Canada, (i.e., the South), that their aims and goals should not be established by outside authorities or those who are not part of their culture. Unfortunately, the Commissioners did not take this demand seriously enough, nor did they consider its implications in light of their mandate or conclusions. Consequently, they were not capable of understanding the significance of First Nations women's different positions on equality, and the set of concerns regarding the State which went beyond gender.

What are the implications of the mentality which suggests that the goal for society is equality with (White) men? To me, to be a First Nations person in Canada means to be free to exist politically and culturally (these are not separate concepts): to be free to understand our roles according to our own cultural and political systems and not according to a value system imposed upon us by the Indian Act for over 100 years, nor by role definition accepted in the Anglo-European culture. This means that men are not, and therefore cannot be, the measure of all things.

As noted earlier, the First Nations community of my heredity never viewed women as naturally inferior, or, with a little help, equal to a certain status which men have already achieved. For the *Report* to look at us with the assemblage of assumptions of the dominant society is to ignore our existence as peoples with distinct cultural viewpoints and political aspirations. It does violence to our understanding of the central role of women in our communities. Moreover, it does violence to us by marginalizing us and relegating our place to somewhere outside of your conceptions of meaningful membership in Canadian society. It makes us feel as though if we reject what White men have "achieved," we reject being part of this society.

The Royal Commissioners were evidently trying to help, particularly by making certain findings such as those relating to poverty as a lifestyle for First Nations women in Canada. In this regard, it is distressing to look back on the generation since the *Report*, and to realize that First Nations women live in the same cycle of poverty today that they lived in 20 years ago, if not worse. Even the Supreme Court of Canada has recently pronounced that in light of the constitutional position of First Nations peoples in Canada, First Nations women living on a reserve may not have (and in reality do not have) protection for matrimonial property.

At least one Royal Commissioner was genuinely concerned with the extent to which he was capable of understanding the situation of First Nations women. In a separate submission he suggested that:

> The privations endured by these people [First Nations people] in many areas—health, education, standards of living—are shocking. Undoubtedly, we all feel that every means should be

taken to improve conditions for this neglected group of Canadians. However, the subject is outside the Commission's terms of reference. Furthermore, the Commission is not qualified to deal with the complex problems which arise when attempting to introduce social and economic changes in cultures which are so very different from ours. *Goodwill in these matters is often, and sometimes quite rightly, interpreted as a form of paternalism or as a more or less conscious attempt to destroy these cultures.* I very much fear that some of the recommendations (Nos. 90–97) advanced by the Commission in this section may have been drawn up a little too hastily.

There were no First Nations people who sat as Royal Commissioners for this study. While the Royal Commission *Report* is laudable to some women, it was inadequate in that it was unable to seriously consider First Nations women's concerns. A separate study was, and is, definitely required. However, as Paulo Freire notes, "we cannot enter the struggle as objects in order to later become subjects." We must not be objects in the study and objects in the solutions to our problems. I often feel, particularly as a law teacher interacting with materials involving First Nations peoples written by those without direct knowledge, that our problems have been studied enough, especially in the object-mode of analysis. We need to turn our minds to a mutually-agreed upon framework within which to resolve our relations with the State. We no longer need to be objects, nor do we need well-intentioned paternalism or projections of what we should become. First Nations women's concerns were marginalized in the *Royal Commission Report on the Status of Women in Canada*. The few findings which were made regarding First Nations women lacked context or vision as to a future path for meaningful change. They were not by us, for us. They were a projection of an assessment of our needs, yet they did not take up in earnest the context of patriarchy and paternalism which are our shackles. ...

Gender discrimination against First Nations women in the Indian Act is clearly more significant when juxtaposed against the cultural backdrop of First Nations history and State oppression. The Royal Commission *Report* confirms to me how White men and women have constructed a concept of gender equality which denies the experience of First Nations peoples' lives and which cannot grasp the magnitude of our experience of gender discrimination. We need to start a discussion which does not include a pre-conceived notion of gender equality. We need dialogue on cultural equality and an openness to other views on the roles and responsibilities of people to their communities. Perhaps on the 20th anniversary of the *Report*, we can identify how the feminist agenda, as defined and exemplified by this *Report* and accepted by the feminist movement, was insensitive to First Nations women and how this is a problem to be met in the future.

Notes

11. In the Mi'kmaq language, the term for equality means to bring one down to the level of other people. This is an interesting juxtaposition with Canadian legal formulations.

18. Women do, despite the influence of patriarchy and paternalism, run First Nations communities. They, for the most part, run the band offices, health programs, education boards, and other community-based institutions.

19. University of Ottawa, 1 November 1990.

39 Lesbian and Gay Rights in Canada: Social Movements and Equality-Seeking

Miriam Smith (1999)

EDITORS' INTRODUCTION

In this historical examination of lesbian and gay politics and lobby efforts in Canada, Smith simultaneously highlights the challenges faced by a fragmented social movement and the legal successes achieved over 25 years of political activism.

From Gay Liberation to Rights Talk

The relationship between sociological change and political change is complex. The difference in the meaning frame and strategies of the lesbian and gay rights movement before and after the Charter is not a question of the presence or absence of equality-seeking. It is a question of differences between *types* of equality-seeking, critically, between an interpretative frame of gay liberation and the rights-talk meaning frame of the post-Charter period. In the seventies, the gay liberation movement viewed equality-seeking as part of a transformative social vision of sexual freedom that sought to undermine traditional sex, gender, and family roles, to erase the stigma attached to sexual preference, to liberate the full sexual potential (gay/straight/bisexual) of everyone; and to eliminate the very categorization of sexual preference or "sexual orientation." Gay liberation as a transformative vision of political and social change was part of the counter-culture of the sixties; many of its early adherents were participants in the youth revolt of the period and had experience in other counter-cultural movements, including leftist politics. The transformative vision of gay liberation was decidedly postmodern in its disavowal of categories and stable subjects; it wanted to deconstruct and subvert the most private realm of all, the realm of sexuality. Yet, at the same time, the gay liberation movement was premised on the politicization of sexual identity and, as such, sought to create awareness and self-consciousness, to mobilize lesbians and gay men in a common cause and to build organizations and institutions that would serve the communities. The movement faced an uphill task in convincing lesbians and gay men to share in a common sense of social and political identity. As Chapter 2 demonstrated, many, if not most, lesbians chose to participate in the women's movement during the seventies rather than in the male-dominated gay liberation movement. In the major urban centres, the lesbian and

---

Source: Excerpted from *Lesbian and Gay Rights in Canada: Social Movements and Equality-Seeking, 1971–1995* by Miriam Smith. Toronto: University of Toronto Press, 1999. Reprinted by permission.

gay male worlds usually functioned separately from each other socially and, to a great extent, politically as well. Furthermore, the gay liberation movement faced a tension that is common to progressive social movements. On the one hand, the transformative vision of gay libera-tion was premised on the abolition of gay and straight as meaningful categories. On the other hand, the gay liberation movement was premised on the politicization of lesbian and gay identity. Similarly, the Marxian socialist movement in the nineteenth century sought to overthrow capitalism, to establish a society in which the working class would no longer be exploited, and ultimately to destroy the very categories of worker and capitalist. Yet the po-litical mobilization of the working-class behind the socialist vision required the creation of a sense of working class political identity and the establishment of organizations and insti-tutions based on that identity.

Equality-seeking in the seventies was pursued within the meaning frame of gay liberation, using the political opportunity structure of the time, human rights codes and commissions. Activists of this period did not believe that legal or political changes would secure lesbian and gay freedom in the absence of a mass movement of lesbians and gays, which could re-inforce and support rights claims that might be secured in law. Rights claims under the law were not seen as separate from politics. Rather, equality-seeking was deployed as a strategy and a meaning frame in order to build a sense of lesbian and gay political identity, to mobi-lize the lesbian and gay constituency and to develop the networks and organizations of the gay liberation movement. Gay liberation was aimed as much at lesbians and gay men them-selves as it was at the wider society or the state. The achievement of legal or political changes was rightly viewed as unlikely during this period. Yet the small and financially precarious gay liberation groups used litigation as part of a broad repertoire of strategies that included lobbying governments, running candidates for Parliament, and holding demonstrations. As in Scheingold's view of rights as political resources, equality-seeking was used to legitimate gay liberation as a movement, to politicize lesbian and gay grievances, and to demonstrate the gap between liberal democratic values and the daily realities of lesbian and gay oppres-sion. In this sense the gay liberation movement was engaged in challenging the dominant codes of society, one of the key functions of social movements according to Melucci and Castells. The source of the meaning frame of gay liberation during its initial period was the protest frame provided by the U.S. civil rights movement, along with the concrete political opportunities afforded by the development of human rights codes in many jurisdictions. The extent to which civil rights functioned as a master frame can be seen in the terminology of the period, which characterized the template of equality-seeking as "the civil rights strat-egy" and squarely placed this framework within the broader context of equality-seeking by other movements, such as the women's movement.

In contrast, the meaning frame of rights talk generated by the Charter removes rights from their social and political context and sees rights claims entrenched in law as the main substantive goal of the lesbian and gay rights movements. The achievement of legal change, rather than building a lesbian and gay network and organizations is the goal. Rights talk is thus premised on the definition of law as the only form of politics while gay liberation as-sumed that success before the law is secondary to other political goals. The meaning frame of rights talk has important political consequences: rights talk in the post-Charter period is devoid of any larger social and political vision. With the partial exception of the CLGRO, which continues to call itself a gay liberation organization, no transformative social and political vision animates current lesbian and gay rights organizations in federal jurisdiction; rather, the public presentation of rights talk rests on the implicit assumption of formal equality rights in which lesbians and gays will be treated as part of the mainstream of Canadian society with the same rights and obligations as other Canadians in respect of their families and relationships.

Political Opportunity and Meaning Frames

The change in the political opportunity structure of Canadian political institutions represented by the entrenchment of the Charter has had substantial effects on the cultural frame, mobilizing structures, and strategies of the lesbian and gay rights network. With respect to the mobilizing structures of the movements, the Charter has led to the creation of new groups (the Same Sex Benefits Committee, gay and lesbian employee groups both within and without the trade union structure, LEGIT, EGALE) in reaction to the potential for litigation created by section 15. However, the Charter has had little impact on the specific forms of organization that are deployed by these new groups. The lesbian and gay rights network was decentralized and fragmented in the 1970s and early eighties, prior to the entrenchment of the Charter, and it remains decentralized and fragmented in its wake. The impact of a newly created political opportunity, the opening afforded for lesbian and gay rights mobilization that was created by the Charter, was insufficient to generate a coherent pan-Canadian organization or umbrella group that could legitimately claim to represent lesbians and gays in all areas of Canada. The only group with any pretensions to a "national" role, EGALE, has been repeatedly criticized for its alleged lack of contact with the lesbian and gay world outside Ottawa. The lesbian and gay communities have failed to mobilize their resources in the direction of this type of organizational effort and the federal state, which has provided core organizational funding for other collective actors, has not been inclined to provide such funding for lesbian and gay rights groups.

The Charter has had its greatest impact on the interpretive framework of the lesbian and gay rights network and on the strategies of equality-seeking. This impact, like the impact of any change in the political opportunity structure, must be estimated in terms of the history of the movement. The original cultural frame of the gay liberation movement predated the Charter. The Charter subsequently initiated a change that entailed a shift from one form of equality-seeking to another, from the deployment of rights as political resources, which were part of a broader strategy of building the movement and its organizations, to one of the pursuit of legal change as the overriding goal, or, as I have termed it here, from gay liberation to rights talk. In turn, the strategies that have been used in pursuit of legal change have tended to undermine the possibilities of developing the mobilizing structures of the movement. Rights talk, precisely because it separates law from politics, privileges an apolitical approach to litigation in which the goal is to win cases rather than to use them to mobilize the grass roots of the movement around the symbolic politics of rights claiming. Rights talk reinforces the fragmentation of the mobilizing structures of the lesbian and gay rights network by privileging the role of experts, especially lawyers, in the pursuit of rights claims before the courts and renders the development of pan-Canadian structures difficult. The Canadian lesbian and gay rights movement *might* have moved away from gay liberation ideology by the nineties even without the Charter, although the brief career of Queer Nation and the ideology and tactics of AIDS activism in Canada suggest that there is still considerable support for liberatory ideology and "in-your-face tactics" at the grass-roots level and on AIDS issues. For the lesbian and gay groups in federal jurisdiction, however, the *specific interpretative framework* that emerged in the eighties and nineties would not have developed without the Charter. Directions in social movement activism cannot simply be read as objective reflections of sociological changes. After all, sociological changes could have pushed the movement in many different directions in the post-gay liberation period. Queer Nation and ACT UP emerged in the same sociological setting as EGALE. The gay liberation movement in Canada had moved decisively away from equality-seeking and litigation by 1980; the fact that the movement's state-directed activism turned toward litigation and toward the specific interpretative framework of rights talk in the late eighties and nineties cannot be explained without reference to the Charter's impact.

From a comparative perspective, even when changes in the political opportunity structure are relatively major by the standards of advanced capitalist democracies, the impact of such changes on social movements must be considered in terms of their ideological and organizational histories. The political opportunity structure plays an important role in explaining the evolution of social movement ideology and discourse over time. In relatively stable capitalist democracies, such as Canada, political institutions form a key aspect of the political opportunity structure. Transnational strategies and the global political culture of lesbian and gay politics have played a peripheral role in the story of lesbian and gay equality-seeking in Canada to date. The state has not been decentred; even in a globalizing context, states provide the essential parameters of the human rights regimes for equality-seeking social movements. The Canadian state is not irrelevant for the lesbian and gay rights movement in Canada; the movement focused on obtaining policy goods from the state from the very beginning, even if, in the early period, such attempts were aimed at politicizing the lesbian and gay constituency as much as actual policy success. In the eighties and nineties, the lesbian and gay rights movement has concentrated on the achievement of policy changes, many of which would have concrete material consequences for lesbian and gay citizens. Like many other social movements (the women's movement, the disability rights movement), the lesbian and gay rights movement has not embraced postmaterialist goals; rights claims in the eighties and nineties have material implications, especially in the case of relationship recognition issues. All of this suggests that the archetypal "new social movement" that is often depicted in the literature as focused on culture and community rather than on the state and material interests has been overdrawn and is not sufficiently grounded in the empirical realities of social movement organizing in the context of advanced capitalist democracies. Finally this work also demonstrates that, beyond shaping the strategies and chances for success of movements aiming to influence the state, the political opportunity structure may also influence the actual values and goals of social movements, the very demands that they make of the state, and the way in which these demands are framed to the state, to their own members, and to the wider society. Once established, institutions such as the Charter create new paths for social movements that shape the discourse, values, and self-understandings of movement actors.

40 The Dark Side of the Nation

Himani Bannerji (2000)

EDITORS' INTRODUCTION

Situated within feminist Marxism, Bannerji provides a critical perspective on Canadian identity and the place of non-white women in the Canadian social fabric. This excerpt is an example of "third wave" feminist scholarship, which emphasizes that conceptions of a universal experience of womanhood are unrepresentative of the experiences of non-white women.

The Paradox of Diversity: The Construction of a Multicultural Canada and "Women of Colour"

The Name of the Rose, or What Difference Does It Make What I Call It

The two ways in which the neutral appearance of the notion of diversity becomes a useful ideology to practices of power are quite simple. On the one hand, the use of such a concept with a reference to simple multiplicity allows the reading of all social and cultural forms or differences in terms of descriptive plurality. On the other, in its relationship to description it introduces the need to put in or retain a concrete, particular content for each of these seemingly neutral differences. The social relations of power that create the difference implied in sexist-racism, for example, just drop out of sight, and social being becomes a matter of a cultural essence (Bannerji, 1991). This is its paradox—that the concept of diversity simultaneously allows for an emptying out of actual social relations and suggests a concreteness of cultural description, and through this process obscures any understanding of difference as a construction of power, Thus there is a construction of a collective cultural essence and a conflation of this, or what we are culturally supposed to be, and what we are ascribed with, in the context of social organization of inequality. We cannot then make a distinction between racist stereotypes and ordinary historical/cultural differences of everyday life and practices of people from different parts of the world. Cultural traits that come, let us say, from different parts of the third world are used to both create and eclipse racism, and we are discouraged from reading them in terms of relations and symbolic forms of power. The result is also an erasure of class and patriarchy among the immigrant multi-cultures of others, as they too fall within this paradox of essentialization and multiplicity signified by cultural diversity of official multiculturalism. In fact, it is this uncritical, de-materialized, seemingly

Source: Excerpted from *The Dark Side of the Nation: Essays on Multiculturalism, Nationalism, and Gender* by Himani Bannerji. Toronto: Canadian Scholars' Press, 2000. Some notes omitted. Reprinted by permission.

de-politicized reading of culture through which culture becomes a political tool, an ideology of power which is expressed in racist-sexist or heterosexist differences. One can only conclude from all this that the discourse of diversity, as a complex systemically interpretive language of governing, cannot be read as an innocent pluralism.

The ideological nature of this language of diversity is evident from its frequent use and efficacy in the public and official, that is, institutional realms. In these contexts its function has been to provide a conceptual apparatus in keeping with needs which the presence of heterogeneous peoples and cultures has created in the Canadian state and public sphere. This has both offset and, thus, stabilized the Canadian national imaginary and its manifestation as the state apparatus, which is built on core assumptions of cultural and political homogeneity of a Canadianness. This language of diversity is a coping mechanism for dealing with an actually conflicting heterogeneity, seeking to incorporate it into an ideological binary which is predicated upon the existence of a homogeneous national, that is, a Canadian cultural self with its multiple and different others (see Bannerji, 1997). These multiple other cultural presences in Canada, interpreted as a threat to national culture which called for a coping, and therefore for an incorporating and interpretive mechanism, produced the situation summed up as the challenge of multiculturalism. This has compelled administrative, political and ideological innovations which will help to maintain the status quo. This is where the discourse of diversity has been of crucial importance because this new language of ruling and administration protects ideologies and practices already in place. It is postulated upon pluralist premises of a liberal democratic state, which Canada aspires to be, but also adds specific dimensions of legitimation to particular administrative functions. ...

The Essence of the Name, or What Is to Be Gained by Calling Something Diversity

In order to understand how the concept of diversity works ideologically, we have to feed into it the notion of difference constructed through social relations of power and read it in terms of the binaries of homogeneity and heterogeneity already referred to in our discussion on multiculturalism. It does not require much effort to realize that diversity is not equal to multiplied sameness, rather it presumes a distinct difference in each instance. But this makes us ask, distinctly different from what? The answer is, obviously, from each other and from whatever it is that is homogeneous—which is an identified and multiplied sameness, serving as the distinguishing element at the core in relation to which difference is primarily measured. The difference that produces heterogeneity suggests otherness in relation to that core, and in social politics this otherness is more than an existential, ontological fact. It is a socially constructed otherness or heterogeneity, its difference signifying both social value and power. It is not just another cultural self floating non-relationally in a socio-historical vacuum. In the historical context of the creation of Canada, of its growth into an uneasy amalgam of a white settler colony with liberal democracy, with its internally colonized or peripheral economies, the definitions and relations between a national self and its other, between homogeneity and heterogeneity, sameness and diversity, become deeply power ridden.[17] From the days of colonial capitalism to the present-day global imperialism, there has emerged an ideologically homogeneous identity dubbed Canadian whose nation and state Canada is supposed to be.

This core community is synthesized into a national we, and it decides on the terms of multiculturalism and the degree to which multicultural others should be tolerated or accommodated. This "we" is an essentialized version of a colonial European turned into Canadian and the subject or the agent of Canadian nationalism. It is this essence, extended to the notion of a community, that provides the point of departure for the ideological deployment of diversity. The practice is clearly exclusive, not only of third world or non-white ethnic immigrants, but also of the aboriginal population. Though often described in cultural linguistic terms as the two nations of anglophones and francophones, the two nations theory does not include non-whites of these same language groups. So the identity of the Canadian "we" does not reside in language, religion or other aspects of culture, but rather in the European/North American physical origin—in the body and the colour of skin. Colour of skin is elevated here beyond its contingent status and becomes an essential quality called whiteness, and this becomes the ideological signifier of a unified non-diversity. The others outside of this moral and cultural whiteness are targets for either assimilation or toleration. These diverse or multicultural elements, who are also called newcomers, introducing notions of territoriality and politicized time, create accommodational difficulties for white Canadians, both at the level of the civil society, of culture and economy, and also for the ruling practices of the state. An ideological coping mechanism becomes urgent in view of a substantial third world immigration allowed by Canada through the 1960s up to recent years (see Eliott & Fleras, 1992). This new, practical and discursive/ideological venture, or an extension of what Althusser has called an ideological state apparatus, indicates both the crisis and its management. After all, the importation of Chinese or South Asian indentured labour, or the legally restricted presence of the Japanese since the last century, did not pose the same problems which the newly arrived immigrants do (see Bolaria & Li, 1988). As landed residents or apprentice citizens, or as actual citizens of Canada, they cannot be left in the same limbo of legal and political non-personhood as their predecessors were until the 1950s. Yet they are not authentic Canadians in the ideological sense, in their physical identity and culture. What is more, so-called authentic Canadians are unhappy with their presence, even though they enhance Canada's economic growth. Blue ribbon Hong Kong immigrants, for example, bring investments which may be needed for the growth of British Columbia, but they themselves are not wanted. But they, among other third world immigrants, are here, and this calls for the creation of an ideology and apparatus of multiculturalism (with its discourse of a special kind of plurality called diversity) as strategies of containment and management. ...

In the very early 1980s, Prime Minister Pierre Trudeau enunciated his multicultural policy, and a discourse of nation, community and diversity began to be cobbled together. There were no strong multicultural demands on the part of third world immigrants themselves to force such a policy. The issues raised by them were about racism, legal discrimination involving immigration and family reunification, about job discrimination on the basis of Canadian experience, and various adjustment difficulties, mainly of child care and language. In short, they were difficulties that are endemic to migration, and especially that of people coming in to low income jobs or with few assets. Immigrant demands were not then, or even now, primarily cultural, nor was multiculturalism initially their formulation of the solution to their problems. It began as a state or an official/institutional discourse, and it involved the translation of issues of social and economic injustice into issues of culture (see Kymlicka 1995).

Often it was immigrant questions and quandaries *vis à vis* the response of the so-called Canadians that prompted justificatory gestures by the state. These legitimation gestures were more directed at the discontented Canadians than the discriminated others. Multicultural-ism was therefore not a demand from below, but an ideological elaboration from above in which the third world immigrants found themselves. This was an apparatus which rear-ranged questions of social justice, of unemployment and racism, into issues of cultural di-versity and focused on symbols of religion, on so-called tradition. Thus immigrants were ethnicized, culturalized and mapped into traditional/ethnic communities. Gradually a po-litical and administrative framework came into being where structural inequalities could be less and less seen or spoken about. Antiracism and class politics could not keep pace with constantly proliferating ideological state or institutional apparatuses which identified people in terms of their cultural identity, and converted or conflated racist ascriptions of difference within the Canadian space into the power neutral notion of diversity. An increase in threats against third world immigrants, the rise of neo-nazi white supremacist groups and ultra conservative politics, along with a systemic or structural racism and anti-immigration and anti-immigrant stances of political parties, could now be buried or displaced as the immi-grants' own cultural problem. Politics in Canada were reshaped and routed through this culturalization or ethnicization, and a politics of identity was constructed which the immi-grants themselves embraced as the only venue for social and political agency. ...

Through the decades from the 1960s, political developments took place in Canada which show the twists and turns in the relationship between third world immigrants and the state.[22] With the disarray of left politics in the country and growth of multicultural ideology, all political consciousness regarding third world immigrants has been multiculturalized. These cultural/ethnicized formulations were like chemical probes into a test tube of solution around which dissatisfactions and mobility drives of the others began to coalesce. Wearing or not wearing of turbans, publicly funded heritage language classes, state supported islamic schools modelled on the existence and patterns of catholic schools, for example, provided the profile of their politics. They themselves often forgot how much less important these were than their full citizenship rights, their demand for jobs, non-discriminatory schools and work places, and a generally non-racist society. Differentiated second or third class citi-zenships evolved, as a non-white sub-working class continued to develop. Their initial will-ingness to work twice as hard to get a little never materialized into much. Instead a mythology developed around their lack of success, which spoke of their shifty, lazy work habits and their scamming and unscrupulous use of the welfare system. This is especially ironic since they often came from countries, such as those in the West Indies, from which Canada continues to bring substantial profits. But this story of neo-colonialism, of exploitation, racism, dis-crimination and hierarchical citizenship never gains much credibility or publicity with the Canadian state, the public or the media. This reality is what the cultural language and politics of diversity obscures, displaces and erases. It is obvious that the third world or non-white immigrants are not the beneficiaries of the discourse of diversity. ...

Multiculturalism as an official practice and discourse has worked actively to create the notion and practices of insulated communities. Under its political guidance and funding a political-social space was organized. Politically constructed homogenized communities, with their increasingly fundamentalist boundaries of cultures, traditions and religions, emerged from where there were immigrants from different parts of the world with different cultures and values. They developed leaders or spokespersons, usually men, who liaised with the state on their behalf, and their organizational behaviour fulfilled the expectations of the Canadian state. New political agents and constituencies thus came to life, as people sought to be politically active in these new cultural identity terms. So they became interpellated by the state under certain religious and ethnically named agencies. Hardheaded businessmen, who had never thought of culture in their lives before, now, upon entering Canada, began using this notion and spoke to the powers that be in terms of culture and welfare of their community. But this was the new and only political playing field for "others" in Canada, a slim opportunity of mobility, so they were/are willing to run through the multicultural maze. What is more, this new cultural politics, leaving out problems of class and patriarchy, appealed to the conservative elements in the immigrant population, since religion could be made to overdetermine these uncomfortable actualities, and concentrated on the so-called culture and morality of the community. Official multiculturalism, which gave the conservative male self-styled representatives *carte blanche* to do this, also empowered the same male leaders as patriarchs and enhanced their sexism and masculinism. In the name of culture and god, within the high walls of community and ethnicity/women and children could be dominated and acted against violently because the religions or culture and tradition of others supposedly sanctioned this oppression and brutality. And as politically and ideologically constituted homogenized cultural essences which are typed as traditional, such as muslim or sikh or hindu communities, violence against women could go on without any significant or effective state intervention. ...

The result of this convergence between the Canadian state and conservative male representatives or community agents has been very distressing for women in particular. Between the multicultural paradigm and the actuality of a migrant citizen's life in Canada, the gap is immense. Among multiculturalists of both the communitarian and the liberal persuasion Canada is a nation space which contains different "races" and ethnicities, and this presence demands either a "politics of recognition" (Taylor, 1992) or a modified set of individual and group rights. But for both groups this diversity of others or difference between Canadian self and other has no political dimension. It speaks to nothing like class formation or class struggle, of the existence of active and deep racism, or of a social organization entailing racialized class production of gender. The history of colonization is also not brought to bear on the notions of diversity and difference. So, the answer to my original question—what is to be gained from a discourse of diversity and its politics of multiculturalism?—lies in just what has actually happened in Canadian politics and its theorization, what I have been describing so far, namely in the erasure and occlusion of social relations of power and ruling. This diversified reification of cultures and culturalization of politics allows for both the practice and occlusion of heterosexism and racism of a narrow bourgeois nationalism. This means the maintenance of a status quo of domination. Many hard socio-political questions and basic structural changes may now be avoided. People can be blamed for bringing on their own misfortunes, while rule of capital and class can continue their violence of racism, sexism and homophobia. ...

Conclusion

Diversity as discourse, with its constellation of concepts such as multiculturalism, ethnicity, community, and so forth, becomes an important way in which the abstract or formal equality of liberal democracy, its empty pluralism, can gain a concreteness or an embodiment. Through it the concept of citizenship rids itself of its emptiness and takes on signals of a particularized social being or a cultural personhood. The sameness implied in the liberal notion citizenship is then stencilled onto a so-called diverse culture, and offers a sense of concrete specificity. This purported plurality with pseudo-concreteness rescues class democracy, and does not let the question of power relations get out of hand. Differences or diversities are then seen as inherent, as ontological or cultural traits of the individuals of particular cultural communities, rather than as racist ascriptions or stereotypes. This helps the cause of the status quo and maintains ascribed and invented ethnicities, or their displaced and intensified communal forms. The discourse of diversity makes it impossible to understand or name systemic and cultural racism, and cultural racism, and its implication in gender and class.

When concreteness or embodiment is thus ideologically depoliticized and dehistoricized by its articulation to the discourse of diversity, we are presented with many ontological cultural particularities which serve as markers of ethnicity and group boundaries. Since these ethnic communities are conceived as discrete entities, and there is no recognition of a core cultural-power group, a dispersion effect is introduced through the discourse of diversity which occludes its own presumption of otherness, of being diverse, and which is predicated upon a homogeneous Canadian identity. It is with regard to this that diversity is measured, and hides its assumptions of homogeneity under the cover of a value and power neutral heterogeneity. Thus it banishes from view a process of homogenization or essentialization which underpins the project of liberal pluralism.

Ultimately then, the discourse of diversity is an ideology. It has its own political imperatives in what is called multiculturalism elaborated within the precincts of the state. It translates out into different political possibilities within the framework of capitalism and bourgeois democracy, and both communitarian liberals and liberals for individual rights may find it congenial to their own goals. Politics of recognition, an ideology of tolerance, advocacy of limited group rights, may all result from adopting the discourse of diversity, but what difference they would actually make to those people's lives which are objects of multicultural politics, is another story.

Notes

17. On the racialized nature of Canada's political economy as a white settler colony, and its attempts to retain features of this while installing itself as a liberal democracy, see Bolaria and Li (1988).

22. For example, the change in immigration policy from the "family reunification" programme to a primarily skills based one shifts the demography of Canada. It brings a kind of immigrant, perhaps from Eastern Europe, who does not pose the problem of "race."

Still Counting

Linda Trimble and Jane Arscott (2003)

EDITORS' INTRODUCTION

In spite of the significant strides made toward women's equality in Canada, Arscott and Trimble demonstrate that women are only "halfway to equal" in terms of political representation in federal and provincial legislatures. They affirm that an "electoral glass ceiling" is firmly in place; women's representation has reached a plateau at about 20 percent of seats. Arscott and Trimble illustrate that, though progress has been made, there remains a significant distance yet to cover.

A Gendered Leadership Gap

What are we to make of the push to advance equality for women over the years? Because progress has been made in some areas but not others, the results are mixed. Women's equality has not come nearly as far or as fast as many of us would like to see. After decades of women's movement activity, policy-making to raise the status of women, and concerted political action, men still hold a disproportionate share of the top jobs in public life, thus revealing the persistence of a gendered leadership gap, with pernicious effects. Women regularly receive less in wages, status, and high-ranking positions than they have earned. International studies have confirmed the existence of such gendered leadership gaps around the world. This phenomenon produces social, economic, and political shortfalls, with serious implications for the quality of democratic deliberation. As a result, democratic deficits—gaps or flaws in the democratic political system that diminish its effectiveness and legitimacy—have emerged.

Two democratic deficits in particular have still to be addressed. One is the underrepresentation of women in public life. Were it not for the legacy of sex bias, women and men would be expected to hold roughly equal numbers and varieties of top jobs in public life as in the rest of society. This is not the case. Many fewer women than men hold high-ranking political positions. As political columnist Hugh Winsor summarizes the point: "Expect lots of gender correctness from this Prime Minister [Chrétien] on the easy files. But when it comes to real muscle, the guys have got it and they are going to keep it." Second, leadership positions continue to go almost exclusively to men, a gender bias that occurs despite clear evidence that sex-based discrimination is both real and powerful. Further deficits affecting the well-being and political legitimacy of democracy itself will occur if the underrepresentation deficit and the gendered leadership deficit are not corrected. The election of political representatives to institutions of representative government is an integral component of

Source: Excerpted from *Still Counting: Women in Politics Across Canada* by Linda Trimble and Jane Arscott. Peterborough, ON: Broadview Press, 2003. Notes omitted. Reprinted by permission.

democracy, for elected political institutions foster popular sovereignty, political equality and freedom, and popular consultation.

Many people see nothing wrong with outcomes that disproportionately elect men. They say men are more interested in politics and public life than women. Some go so far as to argue, as does Canadian Alliance strategist Tom Flanagan, that men are better suited to political leadership than are women. From the outset it is important to make clear that such positions do not stand up under careful examination. In a free and democratic society such as Canada aspires to be, principles of fairness and equity demand that women as well as men be leaders in public life. It is a matter of "simple justice" Why, then, does it remain so difficult for women to take their rightful place as leaders in Canadian society? Because systematic sexism, old biases, conventional practices, and current arrangements of political power are difficult to disrupt, never mind topple. …

The Count Begins

Accounts of women's progress in electoral representation generally began in 1970 when the Royal Commission on the Status of Women (RCSW) systematically raised questions for the consideration of Parliament. This influential body, appointed in 1967, brought the matter to public view and did so in a manner that provided a reference point for subsequent research. The staff of the RCSW set out to measure women's presence in public life. The first problem they encountered was that data on gender in public life were not collected, because gender was not considered to be relevant; woman's sphere was the private or domestic realm, not the public world of the economy and politics. In the political sphere, women did not count, and, in any case, few were present to be counted. Moreover, none of the commissioners or other staff members had any involvement in electoral politics on which to draw for insights into the sort of information that ought to be gathered.

What to do? Women and politics had to be prominent in the Royal Commission's report because political participation had been the first item listed on its mandate. But there was next to nothing to be said about women's electoral success, as there had been precious little of it. In 1967 there were five women senators out of 100, two women MPs out of 264 seats in the Commons, one woman in a cabinet of 25, and an unknown number of female legislators in assemblies in the provinces and territories across the country. There had never been a woman speaker, federal party leader, prime minister, justice of the Supreme Court, governor general, lieutenant-governor, or other highly placed woman parliamentarian. No matter what they counted, it was clear women held fewer than 2 per cent of the top jobs associated with public life. Putting pencil to paper, the RCSW's final tally indicated that women figured as less than 1 per cent of all candidates for election to provincial and federal legislatures.

In the end, the commissioners developed a view of political life that went beyond electoral representation to emphasize participation in public life in general. They expanded their inquiry to various kinds of appointments controlled by the federal government, including nominations to the Senate, to the bench on federal courts, boards of Crown corporations, and federal agencies. Many of these same positions are listed on the Table of Precedence, which is used to establish the relative importance of offices that serve the government of Canada. …

In the end, the RCSW recommended the election of more female representatives by appealing to political parties to involve women at all levels of political participation. They recommended, too, that the federal government demonstrate leadership in selecting women for appointments, most certainly to the Senate and also to government-controlled boards and positions—in short, to top jobs. As we will see, no such change occurred. It took another 15 years before women approached the 10 per cent level of representation in federal politics, longer in some provinces and territories. Ten per cent representation by women was by no means certain even 30 years later in several jurisdictions in Canada. Because the increase has been so gradual and over so long a period, it was perhaps unavoidable that the women who did succeed in getting elected and appointed to top jobs would be considered as firsts worth talking about almost exclusively for their novelty value. ...

Including More, and More Diverse, Women: Progress from 1970 to 2000

Journalists writing in the immediate aftermath of the RCSW report pointedly asked, "Where are the women?" and "Why aren't there more of them?" *Chatelaine* magazine noted prior to the federal election of 1971 that female MPs were a rarer breed than whooping cranes (one woman, 56 birds). Like the birds, women politicians did not become extinct; far from it, as so many were qualified for the job. And the diversity of the species increased with the enfranchisement of Aboriginal and ethnic minority women, occurring as it did variously from the late 1940s to the late 1960s. In 1972, *Chatelaine* editor Doris Anderson declared that there were lots of "good women willing and able to run. (In our October issue last fall, without half trying, we turned up 105 of them.)" The photograph *Chatelaine* published of the potential candidates had few visible minority women among their number. Over time, the number of women and the diversity of candidates' heritage and life experience has increasingly been a matter for public discussion. ...

Counting Matters: The More Elected, the More Selected

It appears that remarkable progress had been made in a relatively short period in the mid-1980s. Following the election of the Mulroney government in 1984, many more Conservative women were elected than ever before, and, for the first time, women comprised almost 10 per cent of the membership of the House of Commons. Numbers were slightly lower at the subnational level, as there were only 50 women legislators out of 647 in provincial and territorial legislatures across the country (7.7 per cent). However, women politicians had been elected in more than token numbers, and women's political representation thus could finally be considered a serious subject for academic inquiry. In 1985, the first two books analyzing women in federal politics were published.

But what happens when we broaden the analysis of women's presence in public life, as did the RCSW, to include appointed positions? In the year following the 1984 federal general election, there were 12 women senators out of 101 (12 per cent) and 6 women in a cabinet of 39 (15.4 per cent). In 1985, no women represented the Crown or sat in the speaker's chair. (In the preceding 15 years there had been three women lieutenant-governors, one woman governor general, and one woman speaker, Jeanne Sauvé, who occupied the post from 1980 to 1984.) In 1985, there were no female federal party leaders and no women prime ministers, justices of the Supreme Court, or premiers. Women had broken the 10 per cent level federally, but most of the top jobs associated with public life continued to elude them entirely.

Women count in electoral politics, as in life in general, when their presence creates general public expectations about what they merit. To count is to matter. It means being important, worthy of being taken into account. When something comes to matter that did not matter before, it may be necessary to go back and search out that which previously was overlooked as being of no significance. When new matters emerge, gathering evidence is part of the effort required to dignify the phenomenon with appropriate understanding. When women were absent from elected political office, there was no expectation that they would head up government departments, hold ambassadorships, represent Canada on international bodies, sit on the bench, or become premier or prime minister. As long as women were absent from legislatures, they were invisible to those who make such appointments. They were seen to have no claim to the honours and public profile that grateful nations can bestow on their worthy citizens.

In Canada, women have been regarded as meritorious in society in proportion to their presence in public life. Moreover, the primary indicator of merit used in this country has long been women's capacity to get themselves elected. This social fact is a political convention that appears in no policy document but which plays out as the recurrent theme explaining why women continue to be excluded from equal shares of high-profile public positions. There appears to be an unwritten rule that women earn prominence in public life in direct proportion to their capacity to win election, expand their presence in the government party caucus, and "earn" cabinet posts. For more than 30 years, this attitude has been used to support the political convention we describe as "the more elected, the more selected": the more women legislators are elected, the more they are likely to be selected for political appointments.

Collecting the numbers of women elected and appointed to top jobs shows a strong correlation between women's level of representation in the House of Commons, seats in cabinet, and their profile in the public service and on the federal bench. The trend that becomes immediately apparent is that as the federal general elections go for women, so goes the nation. In Chapter 6 we show an even more specific correlation between women's presence in the government caucus and the number of cabinet positions awarded.

The significance of tracking women's electoral performance (which is one of the most important career paths to leadership positions in politics) can be established in two ways. First, anecdotal evidence supports the existence of a political convention of earned electoral entitlement that can be backed up with empirical evidence. The memoirs and personal papers of women aspirants to political jobs express their frustration that they could not make the power-holders of the day understand that they had earned the position they sought. Their demands for consideration were routinely deflected, with remarks, like the one received by Pauline Jewett when she asked Lester B. Pearson for a post in his government's cabinet. They already had one woman (Judy LaMarsh), she was told.

In February 2002, a quarrel broke out between Prime Minister Jean Chrétien and Carolyn Bennett, Chair of the Status of Women Caucus for the Liberals. Although we discussed the dispute in Chapter 1, the story is worth mentioning again here because it so clearly illustrates the "more elected, the more selected" phenomenon. Bennett publicly criticized the underrepresentation of women after a major shuffle resulted in one fewer position for women at the cabinet table. The prime minister chastised her for pointing out the inequity in public. He defended the government's record of appointing women to top jobs, pointing to a governor general, a Supreme Court justice, and eight lieutenant-governors (six of whom served at the same time). An article published in the *National Post* indirectly defended the prime minister by observing that the percentage of women in the new cabinet (23 per cent) actually exceeded the percentage of women in the House of Commons (20.6 per cent). In other words, in the newly constituted Chrétien cabinet, women got slightly more than they deserved. Election to Parliament has been taken as a measure of women's "deservingness" for key appointments.

The second technique for measuring this phenomenon is provided by the Table of Precedence of Canada, an official ranking of positions of importance in the government of Canada overseen by the Department of Heritage. Our analysis of the Tables, at 15-year intervals, examines the increased representation of women in key public positions. Does the growth in women's electoral presence occur at the same time as advances in other measures of women's representation such as membership in the Senate, cabinet appointments, and high-profile appointments representing the Crown?

Table 2.6 makes it clear that women's position in cabinet, in government, in most federally controlled, high-level appointments is strongly influenced by the number of women elected. No women, no status. Twenty per cent elected equals about 20 per cent of prestigious positions, nothing more, sometimes less. Not only is the correlation strong, it has operated for decades.

At one level it has been generally known that this is the case. Demonstrating that the more women elected federally results in more top jobs in public life shows government policy being directed by the heavy hand of political convention and past practice. The empirical data—the hard, consistent evidence—reveals that this phenomenon indeed has existed for more than 30 years. The convention of the more elected, the more selected shows no signs of changing in the near future. Is this the best way of deciding what Canadian women merit? Probably not. So long as women's electoral representation has been steadily increasing, so has women's share of the most powerful political posts. However, what happens if the electoral project stalls, as we argue it has in Chapter 3? The marked progress that occurred between 1970 and 1985 and the steady but gradual increases that characterized 1985–2000 have indeed slowed to a near standstill. What, then, can women expect? Will there be fewer top jobs for women and a corresponding lack of further improvement in increasing women's presence in public life?

We maintain that a plateau in political representation by women has already been reached. There has been a leveling off in women's electoral representation, a trend discussed more thoroughly in Chapter 3. Based on past experience this halt in further progress bodes ill for women's aspirations for equality and fairness in Canada, at least in the short term. What do these trends forecast for women's status in society more generally? What place will women have in political representation and public life 15 years hence?

Table 2.6: Tables of Precedence for Canada, 1970, 1985, 2000[1]

Rank	Position	1970	1985	2000
1–5	1-Gov Gen., 2-PM, 3-Chief Justice, 4-Speaker Senate, 5-Speaker HoC	0/5	1/5	3/5
6	Ambassadors, High Commissioners, Ministers, Plenipotentiary[2]	—	—	—
7	Members of the Cabinet[3]	0/30	6/39 [15%]	10/36 [27.8%]
8	Leader of the Opposition	0/1	0/1	0/1
9	Lieutenant-Governors	0/10	2/10	6/10
10	Members of the Queen's Privy Council, not of the Cabinet	3/101 [3.0%]	10/175 [5.7%]	30/224 [13.4%]
11	Representatives of Major Religious Denominations	—	—	—
12	Premiers of the Provinces	0/10	0/10	0/10
13–16	Justices of the Supreme Court, Justices of highest courts of each Prov. and Terr., Judges of other superior courts in the provs. and terrs.	N/A	N/A	N/A
17	Members of the Senate	4/88 [4.5%]	12/101 [11.8%]	33/93 [35.5%]
18	Members of the House of Commons	1/264 [0.4%]	27/282 [9.5%]	62/301 [20.6%]
19	Consuls-General of countries without diplomatic representation	N/A	N/A	N/A
20	Chief of the Defence Staff	0/1	0/1	0/1
21	Members of the Executive Councils, Provincial, within their Provinces	[~2.5%]	[~8.3%]	[~25%]
22–24	Speaker of the Legis. Council in Provs., Members, Speaker of Leg. Assemblies	—	—	—
	Members of Legislative Assemblies within their Provinces	15/639 [2.3%]	67/647 [10.3%]	165/738 [22.3%]
Total	**Elected and Appointed Representatives of Canada**	**27/1313** [2.1%]	**102/1365** [7.5%]	**359/1720** [20.9%]

[1] Effective dates 19 December 1969, 1 March 1985, and 1 April 1999.

[2] Our count is a best case: two women ambassadors in 1970 (B.M. Meagher, High Commissioner to Kenya and Uganda, and Pamela Ann McDougall, Ambassador to Poland) out of 121, 0/85 in 1985, and unknown for 2000. Women's representation in the Foreign Service needs further study.

[3] Not counted in the tabulation because listed again under Members of Parliament.

A key concern of this book is the complacency surrounding women's underrepresentation in political life. As a matter of public policy do Canadians need any longer to be concerned about counting the number of women who get elected to high public office? The answer offered here is a resolute "Yes." But in 1991 another Royal Commission, this one on Electoral Reform and Party Financing (RCERPF), concluded the answer to this question was "No," that policy interventions were no longer necessary to secure women's place in electoral politics. The RCERPF argued that, once 20 per cent representation had been achieved federally, this level of participation would be sufficient to keep the upward momentum going to sustain further improvements to electoral representation by women. This minimum was achieved in the federal general election of 1997 as well as in many provincial and territorial jurisdictions. It would seem that women's numbers among the country's legislators is no longer a problem. The once hot topic concerning how to get more women elected to top jobs no longer has any place on the public agenda even at election time. So, does this mean the problem of women's underrepresentation in political life has been solved?

Our answer is, "Hold on. Not so fast." Important issues that affect women's full participation in the life of the nation remain much as before, and these still need to be given their due. Our data provide a base of information from which to predict what the political status of women is likely to be by the time we approach the centenary of (some) women's electoral participation in 2015. Unless unforeseen events intervene to shake the roots of Canadian society, the patterns from the past remain the best predictor of what is to come.

Consider the following: in the 1970s the conclusion drawn by the RCSW was that women had to be encouraged to participate more directly and effectively in political life to demonstrate their worthiness for government appointments. By 1985 what progress had been made still barely reached the 10 per cent level, and then only on the prime indicator of electing women to the House of Commons. At the millennium 15 years later, 20 per cent representation by women had been reached, again not uniformly in legislatures across the country but only in the House of Commons. Given the evidence, much of which is presented in the next chapter, there is no strong reason to believe that significant progress will be made in the next 15 years. We expect 2015 to bring the level of representation in elected positions to about 26 per cent. If Senate appointments for women continue in the current vein, it is possible that women will comprise 40 per cent of the Upper House by 2015. Symbolic representation for women will thereby far outstrip women's access to positions of political power and policy spaces where key decisions are made.

Women in Canada hold less than half of the top jobs that would be theirs were it not for the political convention that women will only merit more of these positions when they earn them through the ballot box. Although the data come almost entirely from the federal scene, our work comparing provincial and territorial jurisdictions to the situation federally leads us to hypothesize that the trend probably holds more universally than the evidence provided here. As this and the remaining chapters show, the pattern that emerges is crystal clear: prevailing attitudes, political conventions, and practices have established 20 per cent, and little more, as women's share. When it comes to matters of leadership of governing political parties, competitive political parties, senior cabinet posts, and national honours, men continue to be selected for four out of every five posts. Historically, the numbers have circumscribed what women actually got as their share in public life.

PART 4

Federalism and Beyond

Introduction

The 1867 *British North America Act* outlines the powers and responsibilities of the two orders of government in Canada, which are the federal parliament and the provincial legislatures. If the general institutional set-up was clear for the Fathers of Confederation, the intents and purposes behind the creation of Canada remain an object of debate. The central government has always displayed an important capacity to intervene in the economy, but since the end of the Second World War, the provinces have become increasingly active in the realms granted to them by the Constitution (social affairs, municipalities, education, health, and so on).

Nevertheless, the development of the welfare state in the post-war years has translated into higher state intervention. The federal government sought, successfully, to intervene in several areas considered to be exclusively provincial jurisdictions, notably in the health and social service spheres. The two orders of government now operate in nearly every domain of social, economic, and cultural activity. Many consider the initial division of powers to be obsolete. The numerous initiatives of the federal and provincial governments have become intertwined to the point where it has become difficult to differentiate between the responsibilities of each. This dynamic creates a multitude of conflicts between the federal and provincial governments.

This part of *Essential Readings* addresses two different but complementary themes. The first relates to federal–provincial relations, the second to questions of constitutional politics in Canada. One might conclude that the constitutional debates that erupted at the end of the 1960s, the repatriation of the Constitution in 1982 (without Quebec's consent), the failures of Meech Lake and the Charlottetown Accords in 1990 and 1992 respectively, and the adoption of the *Clarity Act* in 1999–2000, all illustrate not only the contradictory interests of political actors, but also the opposing visions of the Canadian political community, and the conflicting understanding of what Canadian federalism is supposed to achieve.

Intergovernmental Relations

Three of the readings in this first section examine the impact of federalism on the functioning of Canadian society. For Donald V. Smiley, a radical reform of governmental institutions in Canada has appeared, since the 1970s, to be the price of guaranteeing the survival of the federal system in Canada. He recalls that federalism supports, and is supported by, multiple geographically concentrated diversities, and provincial governments have become the principal institutions for their expression. The main conflicts characterizing the federal system emphasize questions of redistribution of wealth through equalization, of perpetually contested national economic policies, and of the stakes relating to the Canadian cultural duality. He proposes institutional modifications seeking to more adequately reflect the Canadian diversity in order to better represent attitudes and territorial interests.

Alan C. Cairns underlines that the federal government was unable to acquire new powers at the expense of the provinces due to the fact that the Canadian political system is haunted by the question of national unity, and its operation reveals a bias favouring the provinces. He emphasizes that Canadian federalism is a function not of society but of the Constitution; and more importantly, of governments that operate in the Constitutional framework, looking out for their own self-interest.

Richard Simeon and Ian Robinson insist on the fact that federalism is simultaneously an ensemble of institutional structures and a characteristic of society that takes into account multiple identities. They discuss these dimensions and show how they are at the heart of changes undertaken (and political contestations) during the last few decades.

The other two readings in this section explore specific issues in more detail. Stéphane Dion, former federal Minister of Intergovernmental Affairs from 1996 to 2003, argues that the Canadian government did not adopt a centralist approach and never encroached on provincial jurisdictions. On the contrary, he suggests that the process required is one of reinforcing governmental capacity to work in close collaboration. In his piece, Martin Papillon demonstrates how Aboriginal peoples' claims represent incredible challenges for the institutions of Canadian federalism. Although they achieve a certain form of recognition within the political system, the subordination of Aboriginal peoples, reinforced by the process of "internal colonization," is difficult to overturn because they have no formal status as partners within the federation. This furthermore exacerbates the conflicts in an institutional context that continues to exclude them.

Constitutional Politics

The second section tackles the theme of constitutional politics and, specifically, the conflict between the government of Quebec and the Canadian government. The issue of Quebec sovereignty was at the centre of political attention from the beginning of the 1970s to the end of the 1990s. Many political initiatives were taken either to justify or to counter, if not thwart, this political project. The first selection revisits arguments put forward by the Parti Québécois, first elected in 1976, which justify the necessity to modify the political status of Quebec and to opt for a different form of association with the "rest of Canada." This PQ White Paper insists upon the limits of the federal system and its form, which would create a new understanding between Quebec and Canada.

The failure of the 1980 referendum on sovereignty-association ended with the repatriation of the Constitution without Quebec's consent. A newspaper account from November 1981, along with public statements made by Pierre Elliott Trudeau and René Lévesque after what was known as "the night of the long knives," provide a very good indication of the heated political atmosphere of this era.

A second referendum took place in Quebec in 1995 and a very thin majority of Quebec voters (50.58 percent, with only 54,288 more ballots in favour of the No option) pronounced their desire to stay within Canada. After having been harshly criticized for lacking a viable strategy during the Quebec referendum, then Prime Minister Jean Chrétien asked the Supreme Court to provide a ruling on the constitutionality of a unilateral secession. In an opinion that surprised many (*Reference re Secession of Quebec*, [1998] 2 SCR 217), the highest court of the country concluded that if a province sought to separate from Canada, a clear majority on a clear question would translate into an obligation to negotiate with all Canadian partners. Several months later, the Canadian government adopted the *Clarity Act*. The government of Quebec responded to this legislative initiative by adopting its own law, asserting Quebec's fundamental right to decide their future for themselves, without exterior interference. François Rocher and Nadia Verrelli analyze the meaning of the Supreme Court's reference and the *Clarity Act* and address the issues they pose for Canadian constitutional democracy. They contend that the Supreme Court and the federal government based their reasoning on a false dichotomy between notions of ambiguity and clarity. Alain Noël, for his part, argues that an option for Quebecers, in the wake of recent constitutional reform initiatives, is to accept Canada in its actual form, given the impossibility of a constitutionally valid exit strategy.

The last two readings discuss non-constitutional changes or institutional arrangements that allow Canadian federalism to evolve without modifying the fundamental law of the country. If mega-constitutional debates are over, Peter Russell suggests, recent innovations demonstrate that Canadian federalism is capable of adjusting to contemporary challenges. Hence, this would represent a return to a more pragmatic approach, in the Burkean tradition, rather than a contractual approach à la John Locke, which is what characterized the rhetoric of the constitutional debate. Finally, Sujit Choudhry examines the debate regarding the federal spending power in emphasizing the conflict between the constitutional logic of the 19th century, and the fiscal practices of federalism in the 20th and 21st centuries.

Further Suggested Reading

David Cameron and Richard Simeon, "Intergovernmental Relations in Canada: The Emergence of Collaborative Federalism." *Publius* 32(2), 2002.

Audrey Doerr, "Public Administration: Federalism and Intergovernmental Relations." *Canadian Public Administration* 25(4), 1982.

Jacques Frémont, "La face cachée de l'évolution contemporaine du fédéralisme canadien." In Gérald A. Beaudoin, et al., eds., *Le fédéralisme canadien de demain : réformes essentielles/Federalism for the Future: Essential Reforms*. Montreal: Wilson and Lafleur, 1998.

Government of Canada, "Social Union Framework Agreement: An Agreement Between the Government of Canada and the Governments of the Provinces and Territories," February 1999.

Samuel V. LaSelva, "Federalism as a Way of Life: Reflections on the Canadian Experiment." *Canadian Journal of Political Science* 16(2), 1993.

W.R. Lederman, "Unity and Diversity in Canadian Federalism." *Canadian Bar Review* LIII, 1975.

Jacques Parizeau, Concession speech following second Quebec referendum, October 30, 1995.

François Rocher, "The Quebec–Canada Dynamic or the Negation of the Ideal of Federalism." In Alain-G. Gagnon, ed., *Contemporary Canadian Federalism: Foundations, Traditions, Institutions*. University of Toronto Press, 2009.

Claude Ryan, "L'égalité est-elle possible?" *Journal of Canadian Studies* 1(2), August 1966.

F.R. Scott, "The Special Nature of Canadian Federalism." *Canadian Journal of Economics and Political Science* 13, 1947.

42 The Structural Problem of Canadian Federalism

Donald V. Smiley (1971)

EDITORS' INTRODUCTION

Donald Smiley taught political science at Queen's University (1954–55), the University of British Columbia (1959–70), the University of Toronto (1970–76), and at York University from the 1970s until his death in 1990. He is considered to be one of the most distinguished specialists in constitutional politics and Canadian federalism, themes on which he has published numerous books and articles.

This paper suggests that a radical restructuring of the institutions of the Government of Canada *may* be the price for the survival of the Canadian federal system. I emphasize *may* because I have no overriding confidence that the pervasive particularisms of the Canadian community, in particular those which divide Quebec from the rest of Canada, can much longer be contained within a federal framework. On the other hand, while constitutional discussion continues a case can be made for considering as yet unexplored alternatives.

The scheme for constitutional reform presented by the federal government to the first of the Constitutional Conferences in February 1968 did suggest significant reform in the structure and workings of central institutions:

> Discussions on the division of powers should take place, in the opinion of the Government of Canada, after the constitutional conferences have considered the other principal elements of the Constitution—the rights of individual Canadians, including linguistic rights, and the central institutions of federalism. We say this because provincial interests and the interests of Canada's two linguistic groups are not and cannot be represented simply through the device of transferring powers from the federal government to provincial governments. These interests are and must be reflected as well in constitutional guarantees and in the central institutions of federalism. It follows that a balanced judgement as to the powers required by the provincial governments for the primary purpose of protecting linguistic or provincial interests can only be made in the perspective of the constitutional guarantees and the representation of such interests in the central organs of government. To jeopardize the capacity of the federal government to act

Source: Excerpted from *Canadian Public Administration*, vol. 14, no. 3 (September 1971). Some notes omitted.

for Canada, in the name of protecting linguistic and provincial rights, when what is essential could be accomplished through constitutional guarantees and the institutions of federalism, would be to serve Canadians badly. Furthermore, the division of powers between orders of government should be guided by principles of functionalism, and not by ethnic considerations. Such principles can best be applied after issues concerning the protection of linguistic rights have been settled.[1]

Mr. Pearson's statement was perceptive in its recognition that the Canadian constitutional system could not deal effectively with the country's diversities exclusively through the division of powers between Ottawa and the provinces. There was in this formulation the judgment, or the hope, that if the institutions of the central government gave a fuller recognition to linguistic and cultural duality the pressures of Quebec toward autonomy could be lessened. However, the then prime minister's plan showed an almost exclusive preoccupation with this duality to the neglect of other particularisms. Further, the federal statement referred to only a limited number of institutions of the central government—the Senate, the Supreme Court, the public service and the national capital—and failed to consider the House of Commons and the cabinet and the relation between these bodies and other organs of government. At any rate, the federal authorities soon dropped their elaborate plan for reviewing the constitution in stages.

In general terms, a federal system of government sustains and is sustained by geographically-based diversities.[2] People in the states, regions or provinces have from the first to develop attitudes, traditions and interests both specific to these areas and significant for politics and government. The master-solution of federalism to the problem of territorial diversity is to confer jurisdiction over those matters where diversity is most profound and most divisive to state or provincial governments. However, in the interdependent circumstances of the contemporary world there can be no complete hiving off of such matters. What economists call "spillovers" of state or provincial policies are so ubiquitous that a matter of jurisdiction which concerns only the residents of particular regions will not be of crucial importance even to them. Enough integration on national lines to secure the continuing survival of the federation will almost eventually bring about demands that the national government take steps towards country-wide standards of services, taxation burdens and economic opportunities even where such actions involve federal involvement in matters within the constitutional jurisdiction of the states or provinces. There is another kind of conflict involving territorial particularisms which the federal division of powers is not able to resolve: those situations where the various states and regions impose contradictory demands upon the national government. In summary then, a constitutional division of powers between national and regional governments by itself cannot under modern circumstances resolve problems caused by geographical diversities. The stability of political systems is overwhelmingly a matter of the relation between the internal conflicts of these systems and their institutional capacity to give authoritative resolution to such conflicts.[3] If conflicts are not numerous or profound the institutions and procedures for handling such differences need be neither elaborate nor effective. The opposite is of course true. Obviously too, the institutional structures condition the kinds of conflicts that arise for resolution and in turn are conditioned by these conflicts.

It is the argument of this paper that in the Canadian federal system territorial particularisms have come to find outlets almost exclusively through the provinces. This situation has come about largely as a result of the working of the institutions of the central government which from time to time operate so as to deny provincial and regional interests an effective share in central decision-making. Thus these interests turn to the provinces and continue to do so even after future circumstances provide them with more power in the central government. Canada is now experiencing a number of profound domestic conflicts where the contending forces follow territorial lines along with a relative institutional incapacity for giving authoritative resolution to these conflicts.

The Substance of the Present Conflicts

The major conflicts in Canadian politics along territorial lines are the following.

1. *Those related to interprovincial and interregional equalization by the federal government.* In recent years equalization has been extended much beyond the Rowell-Sirois recommendation that each province should have at its disposal adequate revenues to provide services at national average levels without imposing on its citizens taxation at rates above the national average. Equalization now involves a complex of federal and federal-provincial programs to encourage economic growth and enhance economic opportunities in the less favoured parts of Canada, particularly in Quebec and the Atlantic provinces.

2. *Those related to national economic policies.* The traditional economic cleavages between central Canada and the peripheral provinces to the east and west of the heartland remain, even though the peripheral economies—and in particular those of western Canada—have become more diversified. These continuing conflicts involve national trade, transportation and monetary policies as well as newer differences with respect to the development and sale of natural resources.

3. *Those relating to cultural duality in Canada.* The response of the provinces with English-speaking majorities to the French fact in Canada is most positive in those with large French-speaking minorities and least so where this minority is small. These differences are evident whether the claims of duality are expressed through recognition of the two official languages, some sort of special arrangement for Quebec or support for constitutional revision.

If we classify the interests and policies of the provinces toward each of these areas of conflict the result is something like that shown in Table 1. In these terms, Quebec and the western provinces are ranged against each other on each of the axes of conflict. This conflict is more marked in the case of Alberta and British Columbia than in Saskatchewan or Manitoba. These two latter provinces are on the borderline between "have" and "have not" provinces and if favourable economic circumstances should push them toward the former category the country would be clearly divided on the issue of interprovincial equalization by the Ottawa River.

Table 1

	Contending Provinces		Provinces Whose Attitudes Are Ambiguous
Interprovincial equalization	Quebec and the Atlantic provinces	Ontario Alberta BC	Saskatchewan Manitoba
National economic policies	Quebec Ontario	Atlantic and western provinces	
Cultural duality	Quebec Ontario New Brunswick	BC Alberta Saskatchewan Newfoundland	NS Manitoba PEI

There appears to be an emergent conflict involving provincial and regional particularisms in respect to economic nationalism. Influences toward nationalism can be expected to be more insistent at the federal level than at the provincial. From about the mid-1950s onward the provincial governments have assumed major responsibilities for attracting foreign capital for development and have shown little concern whence such capital comes.[4] It can be expected that economic nationalism will come to have some influences on the politics and policies of some if not all of the provinces but it seems likely that these influences will be weaker at the provincial than at the federal level. More generally, it seems almost certain that the incidence of nationalistic sentiments and interests will vary significantly among the various provinces and regions. ...

Conclusion and Recommendations

It may be that Canada is governable, if at all, only by adherence to John C. Calhoun's principle of the concurrent majority which "gives to each division or interest through its appropriate organ either a concurrent voice in making and executing the laws or a veto on their execution."[23] The concurrent majority principle might of course be embodied in the operation of federal–provincial relations and to some degree this has come to be so. However, as I have argued, Canada cannot be governed effectively by these means. To be realistic, the predisposition of British parliamentary institutions is against institutional restraints on the powers of government. Thus, although these institutions in Canada as elsewhere have proved very flexible, their thrust, in Calhoun's terms, is toward the rule of the numerical rather than the concurrent majority.

The following implications of my general argument are made in a very tentative way.

1. Any restructuring of federal institutions to give territorial particularisms a more effective outlet should recognize other diversities than those of Anglophone and Francophone. In the past decade the dominant currents of thought and policy in central Canada have emphasized cultural and linguistic duality to the neglect of other attitudes and interests which divide Canadians. The price of this neglect is the resurgence of regionalism in the western provinces. While such a formulation is inevitably somewhat arbitrary, it appears to me that a five-region division of Canada corresponds fairly closely with continuing territorial diversities which merit recognition as such in the institutions of the federal government.

2. Unless and until the government of Canada ceases to operate within British parliamentary traditions, the Senate can play only a restricted role in representing geographically delimited interests whatever changes are made in the way members of this body are appointed or in its functions. So long as the prime minister and his important ministers sit in the House of Commons and must retain the continuing support of a majority in that House to retain office, the Senate will remain in a secondary position.

3. A strong case can be made for the explicit recognition of representative bureaucracy in the federal government. Such an alternative does not imply that civil servants are primarily ambassadors of such territorial interests. W.R. Lederman has made an argument for regional quotas on the Supreme Court of Canada in terms which have direct relevance to the federal bureaucracy.[24] Professor Lederman rejects in the name of the tradition of judicial independence that members of a final court of appeal are—or should be—the delegates of the government which appointed them. However, he asserts:

> The [regional] quotas are necessary and proper because Canada is a vast country differing in some critical ways region by region. There are common factors but there are unique ones too. If we ensure that judges are drawn from the various regions ... we ensure that there is available within the Court collective experience and background knowledge of all parts of Canada. In judicial conferences and other contacts within the Court membership, the judges are able to inform and educate one another on essential facts and background from their respective parts of Canada.[25]

4. In terms of Professor Gow's bold proposals,[26] a strong case can be made for a radical restructuring of the federal cabinet and departments of government to make these institutions more effectively representative of regional and cultural interests. One of his suggestions is that the cabinet should "consist of ten to twelve ministers: five regional ministers and others drawn from External Affairs, Finance and a few other departments."[27] The regional minister's deputy "would be a regional minister stationed in a central location within the area served by the minister. He would be the eyes and ears of the minister in the region reporting to him on any matter having to do with the coordination of the activities of the federal departments with one another, or with provincial or municipal departments."[28] Several of the departments with field staffs should have an assistant deputy minister stationed in each of the five regions of Canada. "They would have coordinate standing with the most senior of existing assistant deputies. With such a status, it would be necessary that conflicts between a regional and functional or occupational point of view would be resolved at the level of the deputy minister and minister."

5. Consideration should be given to the reform of the electoral system. In such a reform it seems to me that the first consideration should be to ensure that the regional composition of parties in the House of Commons conforms more closely to their respective regional strengths in popular votes than is the case under the existing electoral law.

6. In broader terms, the kinds of reforms I am suggesting are advanced by measures which attenuate the dominance of the prime minister over his own cabinet and caucus and of the governing party over the House of Commons. Thus an increase in the independence and effectiveness of parliamentary committees is to be welcomed. A case can be made for increasing the number of free votes in the House of Commons and for a rule by which a government would be required to resign only after defeat on an explicit vote of confidence.

There should be a reversal of the current trend toward giving the majority in the House the power to determine the time allowed to debate particular measures. Some attenuation of the power of the Prime Minister to obtain a dissolution would be desirable. The effective and continuing representation of all important regional interests is clearly incompatible with the degree of dominance of the federal political system by the office of the prime minister that we are now experiencing.

The kinds of reforms I am suggesting would move our political institutions to be more like those of the United States. For this reason alone these recommendations might well be thought unworthy of consideration by Canadians. However, I have nowhere suggested an American-type separation of executive and legislative powers at the federal level. Responsible parliamentary government is a flexible instrument and, if I understand the circumstances of a century ago, the Fathers of Confederation believed it compatible with the highly localized incidence of federal power. It is perhaps more reasonable to argue that the present unsatisfactory results of federal-provincial interaction are at least as palatable as a constitutional system where many crucial political decisions are regulated by regional concurrent majorities at the federal level. On the other hand, the existing regime appears to me to be reducing the sphere in which the national government can act without provincial constraints to a dangerously restricted scope. If my argument is even broadly accurate, the solution—if there is one—is to make federal institutions more effectively representative of territorially-based attitudes and interests.

Notes

1. *Federalism for the Future*, Ottawa, Queen's Printer, 1968, pp. 34–8.

2. William S. Livingston, *Federalism and Constitutional Change*, Oxford, 1956, chap. 1.

3. Donald V. Smiley, "Canadian Federalism and the Resolution of Federal-Provincial Conflict," in F. Vaughan, P. Kyba and P. Dwivedi, eds., *Contemporary Issues in Canadian Politics*, Toronto, Prentice-Hall, 1970, pp. 48–66.

4. For some of the results see the series of case studies by Philip Mathias, *Forced Growth*, Toronto, James Lewis and Samuel, 1971.

23. John C. Calhoun, *A Disquisition on Government*, American Heritage series edition, Indianapolis, New York, Bobbs-Merrill, 1953.

24. W.R. Lederman, "Thoughts on Reform of the Supreme Court of Canada," *Background Papers and Reports*, Vol. II, Ontario Advisory Committee on Confederation, Queen's Printer, Toronto, 1970, pp. 306–8.

25. *Ibid.*, p. 307.

26. Gow, "Canadian Federal Administration and Political Institutions." See particularly part V.

27. *Ibid.*, p. 181.

28. *Ibid.*, p. 169.

43 The Governments and Societies of Canadian Federalism

Alan C. Cairns (1977)

EDITORS' INTRODUCTION
Alan C. Cairns was a professor of political science at the University of British Columbia from 1960 to 1995 and a visiting scholar at numerous Canadian universities. He published many books and articles on Canadian policy and the Constitution. He is an Officer of the Order of Canada and a Fellow of the Royal Society of Canada. An earlier version of this text was presented as the Presidential Address to the Canadian Political Science Association in Fredericton in June 1977.

> If you marry the Spirit of your generation you will be a widow in the next.
>
> —Dean Inge

The Canadian political system, now in its second century, can no longer be taken for granted. It is altogether possible, some would say probable, and some would say desirable, that major institutional change, not excluding the fragmentation of Canada, is on the immediate horizon. It is therefore an opportune time to reflect on the century-long interaction between government and society in Canada. I use the word "reflect" advisedly, for this is not the type of interaction about which hard statements can be confidently made.

The impact of society on government is a common theme in the study of democratic polities. Less common is an approach which stresses the impact of government on the functioning of society. I have chosen the latter for the guiding theme of my remarks, because I am convinced that our approach to the study of Canadian politics pays inadequate attention to the capacity of government to make society responsive to its demands. ...

The reaction against traditional political science, with its alleged overemphasis on the formal, legal aspects of the polity at the expense of the social forces which worked it, was given striking emphasis for students of federalism in W.S. Livingston's famous assertion in 1956 that "Federalism is a function not of constitutions but of societies."[1] The dynamic of the system was to be sought not in government, or in features of the constitution, but in society. In the elaboration of this sociological perspective political systems are seen as superstructures devoid of autonomy, and lacking independent coercive and moulding power *vis-à-vis* their environment.

Two decades before the appearance of Livingston's seminal piece, the depression of the thirties produced a great outburst of federalist literature, or, more properly, anti-federalist

Source: Excerpted from *Canadian Journal of Political Science*, vol. 10, no. 4 (December 1977). Some notes omitted. Reprinted by permission.

literature, in English Canada, which presupposed "The Obsolescence of Federalism."[2] This literature viewed the central government as the fortunate and necessary beneficiary and provincial governments as the hapless victims of overwhelmingly powerful socioeconomic forces. In essence, it was argued that technological interdependence and the evolution of a national market made centralized leadership necessary for planning purposes, and destroyed the sociological basis for the vitality and meaningful survival of the provinces. Provincial governments, considered out of tune with fundamental requirements and urgent imperatives rooted in society and economy, apparently had no resources adequate to stay the execution decreed for them by scholars with the future in their bones.

The centralization predicted in the thirties seemed firmly and securely in place in the forties, and for much of the fifties. It was explained in 1957 by Professor J.A. Corry as a product of technological necessity. Corry, responding to prevailing interpretations of the nature and direction of socioeconomic change, produced a polished epitaph for any significant future role for provincial governments. The growth of "giant corporations, national trade associations, and national trade unions" created a nationalizing of sentiment among elites who backed the central government and thus contributed to the centralization of authority in Ottawa. The most a province could hope for, he asserted, "is freedom for minor adventure, for embroidering its own particular patterns in harmony with the national design, for playing variant melodies within the general theme. ... [I]t is everywhere limited in the distance it can go by having become part of a larger, although not necessarily a better, scheme of things."

To the distress of a later generation of liberal-left critics of federalism, Corry's prediction of a nationalization of politics and the continuing centralization of authority in federal hands proved premature. For John Porter, writing in the mid-sixties, when the centralizing impulse born of depression, war, and post-war reconstruction had faded, the federal system was little more than a pious fraud devoid of real meaning for the citizenry, and sustained by academics with a vested interest in their esoteric knowledge of the system's functioning, and by political and bureaucratic elites happy to place federal roadblocks in the way of class politics. To Porter, reiterating an argument widely employed in the thirties, the "conditions of modern industrial society and international relations ... [made] it ... almost essential that the central government acquire power at the expense of the provincial ... governments."[5] Canada, however, was relatively exempt from this necessary and beneficial trend. The cause of this regrettable backwardness was located in the political system with its exaggerated obsession with national unity, and its bias in favour of provincial rights. Reduced to essentials, Porter's position was simply that the class cleavage, based on the economic system, was the true, natural, and dynamic cleavage, while regional cleavages stimulated and fostered by the political system were fundamentally artificial, meaningless, and accordingly undeserving of respect. A well-functioning, modern political system, in marked contrast to the existing federal system, would serve, above all else, as an instrumentality for the expression of creative politics founded on the class struggle of advanced industrial society, with regional considerations shunted to the sidelines. This may be called the sociologist's ideal political system, for it awards primacy to his subject matter.

The unavoidable briefness of my remarks obviously does not do justice to the complexity and diversity of the extensive literature on Canadian federalism, and inevitably oversimplifies the views of those few writers mentioned above. What I have tried to do is to highlight their relative failure to perceive the degree of autonomy possessed by governments and the ongoing capacity of the federal system to manufacture the conditions necessary for its continuing survival. Where such is partially noted, as it is by Porter, the admission is grudging and is accompanied by pejorative adjectives which cloud the analysis.

In a sense, Livingston's plea to search for the determinants of a changing federalism in society, not constitutions, was not needed in Canada. From the mid-thirties to the present we have not lacked sociological approaches to federalism. The weakness of our understanding lies elsewhere, in a failure to treat government with appropriate seriousness. The remainder of this paper is an attempt to redress the balance by arguing, contrary to Livingston, that federalism, at least in the Canadian case, is a function not of societies but of the constitution, and more importantly of the governments that work the constitution.

The great mystery for students of Canadian federalism has been the survival and growth of provincial governments, particularly those of English Canada. Sociologically-focussed inquiries, with Quebec as an implicit model, have looked for vital, inward-looking provincial societies on which governments could be based and, finding none, have been puzzled why these governmental superstructures, seemingly lacking a necessary foundation, have not faded away.

The sociological perspective pays inadequate attention to the possibility that the support for powerful, independent provincial governments is a product of the political system itself, that it is fostered and created by provincial government elites employing the policy-making apparatus of their jurisdictions, and that such support need not take the form of a distinct culture, society, or nation as these are conventionally understood. More specifically, the search for an underlying sociological base, whatever its nature and source, as the necessary sustenance for viable provincial political systems, deflects us from considering the prior question of how much support is necessary. Passivity, indifference, or the absence of strong opposition from their environment may be all that provincial governments need in order to thrive and grow. The significant question, after all, is the survival of provincial governments, not of provincial societies, and it is not self-evident that the existence and support of the latter is necessary to the functioning and aggrandisement of the former. Their sources of survival, renewal, and vitality may well lie within themselves and in their capacity to mould their environment in accordance with their own governmental purposes.

In the analysis of contemporary party systems much has been made of the extent to which today's parties represent the historic residue of the cleavages of yesteryear. In the Canadian case the freezing of party alternatives fades into insignificance compared with the freezing by the federal system of initially five and now eleven constitutionally distinct and separate governments. The enduring stability of these governments contrasts sharply with the fluctuating fortunes of all parties and the disappearance of many. Governments, as persisting constellations of interests, constitute the permanent elements of the Canadian polity which, thus far, have ridden out the storms of social, economic, and political change.

The decision to establish a federal system in 1867 was a first-order macro decision concerning the basic institutional features of the new polity. It created competitive political and bureaucratic elites at two levels of government endowed with an impressive array of jurisdictional, financial, administrative, and political resources to deploy in the pursuit of their objectives. The post-Confederation history of Canadian federalism is little more than the record of the efforts of governing elites to pyramid their resources, and of the uses to which they have put them. Possessed of tenacious instincts for their own preservation and growth, the governments of Canadian federalism have endowed the cleavages between provinces, and between provinces and nation which attended their birth, with an ever more comprehensive political meaning.

The crucial, minimum prerequisites for provincial survival and growth have been the preservation of jurisdictional competence, and of territorial integrity. In terms of the former, it is notable that explicit change in the constitutional responsibilities of the two levels of government has been minimal, in spite of strong centralizing pressure on occasion. The division of powers has been altered to federal advantage only three times, in each of which unanimous provincial consent was obtained, and in two of which provincial paramountcy was respected. Provincial pressure has ensured the *de facto* acceptance of the principle that the concurrence of all provincial governments is necessary for any amendment which would reduce their formal constitutional authority. Even in their periods of greatest weakness provincial governments steadfastly resisted and thwarted all efforts to accord explicit constitutional recognition to a more flexible amendment procedure dealing with the division of powers. By their self-interested obstinacy they preserved their basic bargaining power for the future, and formally protected the jurisdictional integrity essential for subsequent increases in their governmental potency. ...

A federal system of governments, supported by parties and pressure groups which parallel the governmental structure, and infused with conflicting federal and provincial visions of economy and society held by competing political and bureaucratic elites, requires a language of political debate appropriate to its fundamental political concerns. Hence, the dominant political language since Confederation has been geared to the making of claims and counterclaims by the federal and provincial spokesmen for territorially-defined societies. In an indirect way, and with the passage of time, the federal language of political discourse became a vehicle for the standard normative controversies which concern modern political systems, questions dealing with equality, the socioeconomic rights of citizens, and social justice. Inevitably, however, the pressure of existing language contributed to the clothing of new controversies in federal garments and their emergence in claims on behalf of provincial communities and governments, or charter members, or founding races, or the national interest as defined by Ottawa.

Clearly, the political language of federalism, and the federal political system with which it is intertwined, have encouraged a politics in which provincial particularisms have been accorded special prominence. Provincial governments as the claimants for, and recipients of federal bounty, have acted as surrogates for the communities they govern. In the dialectical process of federal provincial controversies, the claims of provincial governments encounter the rival claims of the central government with its constitutional authority to speak for all Canadians, for the national community stretching from Bonavista to Vancouver Island. The political incentives for the federal government to couch its claims in the language of individual citizen rights and obligations engender a direct conflict with provincial claims on behalf of territorially-based communities, the reconciliation of which is worked out in the federal process.

Formerly, many of these conflicts derived sustenance from specific clauses in the British North America Act, from the terms of admission of individual provinces to the federal system, or from certain alleged intentions of the Fathers relating to the rights of particular provinces or communities. The resultant language of political debate was fundamentally stabilizing in its emphasis on rights and claims which presupposed continuing membership in an ongoing political system. Under the impact of the constitutional crisis of the past two decades, essentially precipitated by the changed objectives of Quebec political elites, and the concomitant allocation of the political decisions of 1867 to a distant and irrelevant past, the language of political debate has undergone a dramatic change. The historic, rooted language of the various versions of the compact theory has virtually disappeared, as have other backward-looking justifications which appealed to a common past. They have been replaced by a confusion of newly-developing political languages, more nakedly power-seeking, which reflect the ambitions of some political elites to refashion their position, inside or outside the federal system, as the past fades into insignificance, and the induced obligation for other elites to respond in kind. In Quebec the forward-looking language of national self-determination has replaced the traditional elite emphasis on prescriptive rights derived from history and the constitution. The new attitude was graphically expressed by Claude Morin when he was deputy minister of federal-provincial affairs in the Lesage government. "Quebec's motto is: We're through fooling around! It seems ridiculous to me to invoke the Constitution. It is like invoking St. Thomas."[68]

The destruction of a customary historical language was accelerated by the recent process of constitutional review which downgraded the Canadian constitutional heritage and promised new beginnings which it failed to deliver. The present language situation is clearly in flux as disputants talk past each other, rather than to each other. No new linguistic paradigm in which debate can be couched has emerged. Linguistic instability and federal instability reinforce each other.

The political language of federalism, a language for the conducting of political competition and cooperation between territorially-based groups and their governments, is necessarily hostile to the nation-wide politics of class. The politics and language of class assume that the conditioning effects of capitalism have washed out identities and political perspectives based on socialization into provincial frames of reference. This has not yet happened. In spite of the auspicious depression circumstances of its birth, its early antipathy to the provinces, and its long-standing attempts to create a new politics and language of class at the national level, the CCF and its successor the NDP have made only minor dents in the nonclass language of federalism.

For nearly half a century left-wing academic analysis has stressed the allegedly inexorable logic of capitalist development in producing class polarization and a modern class-based politics, described as "creative politics" by its more recent exponents. Indeed, by constant repetition this perspective has become the time-honoured traditional language of a dissenting minority which updates the old arguments and the standard predictions decade after decade. Elections and surveys have been carefully monitored since the thirties in numerous attempts to detect the always imminent emergent trend of class mobilization and polarization, the assumed hallmarks of a maturing economy. The failure of reality to conform to the canons of this version of social science has evoked fulminations against federalism, and an adroit use of the concept of false consciousness. These have had minimal impact on the nonclass world view of elites and masses involved in the political world of federalism. The political language of territorially-based group competition derived from the federal system, and socialized into the consciousness of political actors since Confederation, has prevailed over the twentieth-century challenge from the weakly-developed language of class based on the economy. ...

By implication this paper has suggested that to look at the literature of Canadian federalism historically makes clear how much has been a response to particular climates of academic and intellectual opinion, how much has been characterized by an anti-federalist mentality, and how the wish has too frequently fathered the thought. Studies of Canadian politics have suffered from a disciplinary mobilization of bias which grossly underestimates the autonomy of elites, the weight of government, and the moulding effect of institutions on political behaviour. A form of sociological reductionism common to North American political scientists has stressed society at the expense of the polity and either devalued, ignored, or denied an autonomous role for government. Democratic assumptions have elicited analyses which focus on the popular impact on government and neglect the reverse. Egalitarianism has had similar effects by undervaluing and underweighting the extent, significance, and unavoidability of elite discretion. Further, the search for class politics has entailed a stress on elections, an excessive interest in parties, and a deflection of attention from the overriding reality of government.

Developments in comparative politics have played a part in our miseducation. The evanescence and crumbling of political systems in the post-independence states of the Third World have contributed to a brutal awareness of the fragility of political structures incompatible with the historic social systems they confront. The study of the latter and their impact on the polity has elicited a strong sociological thrust in Third-World studies. However, the sociological perspective appropriately applied to the "soft states" of Africa, Asia, and Latin America has been uncritically and inappropriately extended to the study of the highly-institutionalized political systems of the western world. Finally, the weakly-developed idea of the state in the English-speaking world has reduced the visibility of government, and, no doubt, contributed to the academic underestimation of its central political role. Accordingly, the enterprise of assessing the creative, formative, and coercive capacities of government, authority, and institutions requires us to overcome the biases of sociological reductionism, democratic mythology, egalitarian levelling, incorrect Third-World analogies, and the disciplinary errors to which they contribute. Success in the enterprise will provide much-needed understanding of "the reality of structures, the extent of their 'grip' over society, and the true importance of constitutions in shaping behaviour."

Notes

1. *Federalism and Constitutional Change* (Oxford: Clarendon Press, 1956), 4.

2. The title of a famous 1939 article by Harold J. Laski, reprinted in A.N. Christensen and E.M. Kirkpatrick (eds.), *The People, Politics, and the Politician* (New York: Holt, 1941).

5. *The Vertical Mosaic* (Toronto: University of Toronto Press, 1965), 380.

68. Cited in Donald V. Smiley, *The Canadian Political Nationality* (Toronto: Methuen, 1967), 80.

Collaborative Federalism in an Era of Globalization

Stéphane Dion (1999)

EDITORS' INTRODUCTION

Stéphane Dion was a professor in the Department of Political Science at the University of Montreal from 1984 until 1996. After his election to the House of Commons as a Member of Parliament, he was Minister of Intergovernmental Affairs under Prime Minister Jean Chrétien (1997–2003) and then Minister of the Environment for Prime Minister Paul Martin (2004–6), after which he became the leader of the Liberal Party of Canada from December 2006 to December 2008.

Governance in Canada is taking on forms that are less hierarchical and that are based more on cooperation and mutual trust. This trend can be seen within governmental institutions, in relations between governments and the private and voluntary sectors, and in relations among governments themselves.

The auditor general wrote in his report this year that "[c]ollaborative arrangements, also called partnering, are increasingly being used in federal program and service delivery as a management tool and to share power and authority with the government's partners in making decisions. In our view, they have the potential to be an innovative, cost-effective and efficient way of delivering programs and services."

I share the auditor general's point of view. The Canadian federation is evolving towards greater cooperation and consensus-building, while still respecting the constitutional jurisdictions of each order of government, rather than towards extensive centralization in favour of the federal government or extensive decentralization in favour of the provincial governments.

Canadians want greater intergovernmental cooperation. According to an Ekos poll conducted in November 1997, an absolute majority of Canadians (58%) prefer closer cooperation between governments, without major transfers of power, compared with 25% who would like to see a major decentralization to provincial governments, and 15% who want a major shift of activities to the federal government. Even in Quebec, supporters of intergovernmental cooperation (50%) outnumber supporters of either decentralization (39%) or centralization (7%).

This tendency towards a greater collaboration faces opposition. Some of this opposition, for example, comes from proponents of centralization, who believe that the Government of

Source: Excerpted from *Collaborative Government: Is There a Canadian Way?* edited by Susan Delacourt and Donald G. Lenihan. Toronto: Institute of Public Administration of Canada, 1999. Reprinted by permission.

Canada ought to regain a greater role in a number of areas that are now in the hands of the provincial governments.

After briefly reviewing the arguments in favour of centralization, I will show how the Government of Canada is not following this course of action. Its approach, in fact, is cooperation and consultation with the provincial and territorial governments. I will be looking at this issue from four angles: 1) budgetary policy; 2) new policies introduced by the federal government in recent years; 3) the Social Union Framework Agreement; and 4) foreign policy.

Is the Federation Too Decentralized?

It has long been said that Canada is too decentralized and that the power of the provincial governments is excessive and a barrier to rational governance. This criticism of the decentralized nature of our federation is adapted to the flavour of the month, to the concepts in fashion in the market of ideas.

In the 1960s, in the heyday of the Keynesian movement, it was said that provincial autonomy was preventing Canada from adopting rational economic planning.

Today, the concept currently in fashion is globalization, meaning the internationalization of markets, the increasing importance of international agreements, and the growing trend towards supranational management. The proponents of centralization are now saying that the commercial, cultural and environmental issues currently being negotiated on the international scene are playing an increasingly extensive and important role and are increasingly cutting across provincial jurisdictions. In this context, the Canadian government is seemingly between a rock and a hard place: it must centralize, but this means taking over responsibilities now under provincial jurisdiction.

To illustrate this theory, I could refer to a federalist author who advocates centralization, but instead, I will use a more paradoxical case, that of former Quebec Premier Jacques Parizeau.

Unlike other spokespersons of the independence movement, Mr. Parizeau does not subscribe to the untenable thesis that Canada is centralized. He acknowledges that Canada is decentralized. In a statement on 28 February 1999, for example, he affirmed that "Canadian federalism is about the most decentralized in the world, along with Switzerland."

Mr. Parizeau, however, maintains that Canada *must* become centralized, because decentralization is a form of governance that has become irrational and ineffective, ill-adapted to modern constraints. He has been defending this idea since the late 1960s. It was in a speech in Banff on 17 October 1967 that he brought it up for the first time.

At that time, he described Canada as having turned into a "blind alley," because decentralization had "gone much too far." The excessive power of the provinces was, he argued, preventing the federal government from enforcing "rational planning": "A country should not be allowed to balkanize decision-making to the extent that exists now."

One can thus see a striking parallel between this advocate of Quebec independence and the pro-Canada advocates of centralization, who mistakenly see the strength of our provincial governments as a hindrance to rational governance.

In 1967, economic planning was the fashionable argument advanced to support the perceived need for centralization. It was asserted that centralization was somehow the key to economic prosperity. Three decades later, it is quite clear that events have proved this prophecy wrong: Canada did not centralize, yet it continued to perform strongly.

Of course we have serious problems to solve, including poverty, pollution and economic weaknesses in some sectors; at the same time, the successes speak for themselves. Canada is currently ranked first in the world by the UN Human Development Index; third in terms of business climate, by the Economist Intelligence Unit; fifth in terms of economic competitiveness, by the World Economic Forum; fifth in terms of government efficiency, by the National Bureau of Economic Research; and sixth in terms of honesty of commercial and governmental practices, by Transparency International. Not bad for a federation that some claim is doomed to deadlock because of decentralization!

But this won't last, the centralizers keep telling us. Centralization is coming, this time for good, driven by globalization. Here, once again, is Mr. Parizeau, who very recently repeated in almost the same words his bleak diagnosis of 1967. This time, however, he tied it to globalization rather than to economic planning, when he said, "If the federal government is to be able to retain the powers of a genuine government and to set policies, it is imperative that it centralize what is an extraordinarily decentralized federation" (28 February 1999).

Canada will either centralize or it will wither. Such is the message of the prophets of centralization. It is a message that has remained unchanged and unchanging for decades but that has adapted to the flavour of the month. It will be proven as wrong in the future, as it has been in the past. In fact, the ability of our governments to work together will be enhanced. Our decentralized federation, based on solidarity of its citizens and cooperation among its governments, is perfectly equipped to deal with the issues related to globalization.

Budgetary Policy

The Government of Canada believes in the virtues of our decentralized federation. In the last two federal budgets, the government's first targets for reinvestment were transfers to the provincial governments. Thirty-eight per cent of new spending in the 1998–1999 budget was allocated directly to the provinces, as was 68% of the 1999–2000 budget.

In addition, during the period of cuts, from 1993–1994 to 1998–1999, the finance minister made smaller reductions to cash and tax-point transfers to the provinces (7.4%) than to direct spending by the federal government (10.8%). During that period, equalization payments were spared any reduction, which helped the less wealthy provinces.

Rather than centralization, the evolution of our budgetary federalism reflects the will of the Government of Canada to provide the provincial and territorial governments with financial assistance so that they can enhance their capacity to take action and implement their own policies.

New Policies Put in Place by the Federal Government

The federal government is determined to implement flexible policies that make it possible to pursue Canada-wide objectives, while taking into account the diversity of the country.

The Infrastructure Program has thus been a model of federal–provincial–municipal cooperation. The National Child Benefit was designed to allow the federal government to help the provincial governments design different policies rather than forcing them all to do the same thing. The new, more stringent measures regarding young offenders set out in the Act in Respect of Criminal Justice for Young Persons will be optional, available to those attorneys general who wish to use them. The legislation on electronic commerce and the protection of personal information will complement, rather than replace, the provincial laws in provinces where there is similar legislation, as is the case today in Quebec.

The framework for negotiating job-training agreements allows the provincial governments to choose between co-management models and more extensive autonomy. The environmental harmonization agreement promotes cooperation in a sector where both orders of government have very weighty responsibilities.

Even the much-discussed Millennium Scholarships program cannot be described as a step towards centralization. The Government of Canada has long been helping Canadians financially to give them better access to provincial educational institutions, without interfering in education in any way. Mr. Mulroney's government, for example, of which Mr. Bouchard was a member, introduced the Canada Scholarships.

The important thing is to avoid any unnecessary duplication, in a spirit of consensus-building. The prime minister of Canada has said that he is willing to work in accordance with the method proposed unanimously by Quebec's national assembly. It should be noted that in the United States, 75% of public student assistance comes from the federal government, and in Germany it is 65%.

The Social Union Framework Agreement

The Social Union Framework Agreement reflects the need for the two orders of government to work together, while respecting their constitutional jurisdictions. It should facilitate the establishment of common objectives for health, postsecondary education and social services, while building on the diversity of experiences.

The agreement commits governments to working together to eliminate harmful or unreasonable barriers to the mobility of Canadians. Governments will exchange knowledge so as to learn more from one another. They will consult one another on their respective priorities and opportunities for cooperation. They will notify one another before implementing major changes and will strive to avoid duplication while clarifying their roles and responsibilities. They will use a dispute-prevention and -resolution mechanism based on joint negotiations and the participation of third parties to determine the facts or obtain the services of mediators. They are also committed to cooperating more effectively with aboriginal peoples throughout Canada.

The framework agreement places new requirements for cooperation and consultation on the federal government in exercising its spending power. Canada, the federation where the federal spending power is already used the least and the resulting transfers to provinces have the fewest conditions, is developing unprecedented mechanisms so as to base that spending power on cooperation among governments.

So how does all of that fit in with predictions of centralization brought about by globalization? Clearly, not very well. On the contrary, it represents a new and promising approach for managing interdependence.

Foreign Policy and Intergovernmental Consultation

Our provincial, federal and territorial governments cooperate very actively in matters of foreign policy. In all international negotiations, the Government of Canada ensures that Canada's negotiating positions reflect the expressed interests of the provincial governments. Mechanisms for consultation with the provincial governments have been in place for many years, work in an exemplary fashion, and may rightly be envied by the members of other federations.

For a number of years now, when meetings deal with issues under their jurisdiction, representatives of the provincial governments have been invited to participate in the Canadian delegations at UN meetings (on the environment, the status of women, and social development, for example), at OECD sectoral meetings, or at general and sectoral UNESCO conferences.

This Canadian intergovernmental cooperation has yielded excellent results on the international scene. Throughout the Uruguay Round negotiations, which led to the creation of the World Trade Organization, the Canadian negotiators kept provincial representatives fully informed and consulted them on Canada's negotiating positions. This cooperative, pragmatic approach enabled our negotiators to secure effective protection for cultural industries under the General Agreement on Trade in Services (GATS).

This same intergovernmental cooperation has allowed Canada to negotiate a host of rights and obligations under the Canada-United States Free Trade Agreement, NAFTA, and the Canada-Chile Free Trade Agreement. These include cultural exemptions that allow the federal and provincial governments to maintain or adopt policies to promote our cultural industries.

Conclusion

I am not claiming that everything is perfect in our federation. We still need to improve the way our governments work together, both at home and on the international scene.

Despite this, however, the way in which Canada manages to express its rich diversity, with a single voice, is a winning formula as we face the challenges associated with globalization.

Clearly, few countries are better positioned than ours is in taking on this global world. Canada is a respected country that has an excellent reputation based on the quality of its diplomats and its vast network of embassies. It has successfully combined cohesion with extensive diversity. It comprises provinces and territories with complementary strengths, two official languages that are international languages, and two legal systems, common law and civil law, that allow it to speak the legal language of the vast majority of countries. It has close connections with Europe, the Americas and Asia, with a multicultural population that opens up opportunities in every corner of the world.

We must not reject the decentralized nature of our federation. On the contrary, we must build on our exceptional capacity to pursue shared objectives, at home and abroad, strengthened by the diversity of our experiences.

It is true that our federation sometimes produces friction between governments and headaches for federal and provincial politicians and bureaucrats. In the long run, however, our federation produces a synergy that allows us to more effectively promote the economic, cultural and other interests of all Canadians, within Canada and around the world.

45 The Dynamics of Canadian Federalism

Richard Simeon and Ian Robinson (2004)

EDITORS' INTRODUCTION

Richard Simeon teaches in the Department of Political Science at the University of Toronto. His interests and writing have focused on federalism, public policy, and the Canadian Constitution. From 1983 to 1985, he was a Research Coordinator (Institutions) for the Royal Commission on the Economic Union and Canada's Development Prospects (the Macdonald Commission). He has also served with several Government of Ontario advisory groups.

Ian Robinson teaches at the Residential College, University of Michigan in Ann Arbor. He has been working on issues related to labour and globalization, with a particular focus on North America. In 1990 he published, with Richard Simeon, State, Society, and the Development of Canadian Federalism.

Introduction

Federalism is the most visible and distinctive element in Canadian political life. More than in most other advanced industrial countries, our politics have been conducted in terms of the conflicts between regional and language groups and the struggles between federal and provincial governments. Many of our most important political issues—from the building of the postwar welfare state to the energy wars in the 1970s to the constitutional wars of the 1980s and 1990s to the crisis in health care in this decade—have been fought in the arena of federal-provincial relations and shaped by the institutions of the federal system. The very structure of Canadian federalism, with its ebb and flow of power between federal and provincial governments, has been at the heart of our political debates. Indeed, for many observers, what makes Canada distinct is the highly decentralized character of its federal system.

We can think of federalism in several ways. Federalism refers, first, to a particular set of governing institutions (the classic definition comes from Wheare 1964). It is a system in which political authority is divided between two or more constitutionally distinct orders or levels of government. Each has a set of constitutional powers; each has an independent base of political legitimacy in the electorate. In Canada, we talk of federal and provincial governments. Municipal governments are also important in the lives of Canadians, but they do not have independent constitutional status. On the other hand, Aboriginal governments may one day constitute a "Third Order of Government," parallel to federal and provincial governments (Royal Commission on Aboriginal Peoples 1993).

Source: Excerpted from *Canadian Politics*, 4th edition, edited by James Bickerton and Alain-G. Gagnon. Peterborough, ON: Broadview Press, 2004. Reprinted by permission.

Several other elements are central to the design of federal institutions (Watts 1996). There is the *constitution,* which sets out *the division of powers* and the relationships among the governments. In the Canadian context, there has been increasing debate about whether it is necessary for all provinces to have identical powers ("symmetrical federalism") or whether powers can either formally or informally vary according to the needs and characteristics of individual provinces, as in the case of Quebec ("asymmetrical federalism") (Smiley and Watts 1985). Most federal constitutions also create a Supreme Court, one of whose central purposes is to act as umpire between levels of government, and an *amending formula* establishing procedures for altering the division of powers. Since one of the central characteristics of all federal systems is the wide range of shared and overlapping responsibilities (*"interdependence"*), federal institutions also include a set *of mechanisms of intergovernmental relations* (first ministers' conferences and the like) through which the governments deal with each other. Associated with these mechanisms is a complicated set *of fiscal arrangements,* dividing up the revenue pie, financing shared responsibilities, and assisting the poorer provinces through equalization payments. Almost unique among federal countries, Canada is largely lacking in one other institution—that is, a *second chamber* in the national Parliament explicitly designed to represent the states or provinces within central decision-making. Unlike the American Senate or the German Bundesrat, the Canadian Senate has conspicuously failed to play this role, thus forcing struggles within our federal system to be worked out in relations between governments which sometimes take on the character of international negotiations or "federal–provincial diplomacy" (Simeon 1972).

Federalism, then, is at heart an *institutional structure.* Along with Westminster-style cabinet government and, since 1982, the Charter of Rights and Freedoms, it is one of three institutional pillars of Canadian government. Each of these pillars embodies a somewhat different conception of democracy; they coexist in a dynamic tension.

Second, federalism can be seen as *a characteristic of the society.* We talk of Canada as a "federal society" (Livingston 1956). By that we mean the salience of differences that are organized and expressed largely on the basis of region or territory. Such differences may be rooted in language, history, and culture or in differences of economic interest. They interact strongly with the institutional dimension of federalism: Canada has federal institutions largely because of the initial differences in interest and identity among the founding provinces. But federal institutions, in turn, perpetuate these regional differences and reinforce Canadians' tendency to see politics in regional terms.

Third, federalism is underpinned by *multiple identities.* Citizens are members of both the national community, embodied in the national government, and of provincial communities reflected in their provincial governments. If the balance falls too far to one side, there remains little to hold the system together in the face of demands for provincial independence; if it falls too far the other way, there is little to prevent the aggrandizement of federal power and movement towards a unitary state. Federalism is thus about the coexistence of multiple loyalties and identities; it is about divided authority, "national standards" and provincial variation, "self-rule" and "shared rule," "coming together" and "coming apart." Finding the right balance between these is the trick. Much survey evidence confirms that Canadians are, indeed, federalists in this sense, valuing both their national and their provincial identities (Graves *et al.,* 1999; Cutler and Mendelsohn 2001).

Federalism is often justified as a means by which different regional/ linguistic communities can live together in a single state. On the one hand, it helps preserve local communities by assuring them the opportunity to manage their own affairs through their provincial government; on the other hand, it allows them to pursue their common interests through the federal government. Federalism thus combines "*shared rule* through common institutions and *regional self rule* for the governments of constituent units" (Watts 1996: 7).

Other ideas have also been used to justify federalism. In the American political tradition, federalism is seen, along with the Bill of Rights and the separation of powers between president and legislature, as a way to check and limit excesses of governmental power. ...

In this chapter, we will talk about all three dimensions of Canadian federalism. Our focus is primarily on what drives the federal system and what accounts for the changes that we have seen over time. In this sense, for the most part we treat federalism as a *dependent variable*. What explains, for example, the relative balance of power and influence between federal and provincial governments? What explains the nature and level of conflict or disagreement among them? What accounts for the ways they manage their interdependence?

Relative to other federations, Canada is one of the most decentralized, in terms of political authority, powers, and financial resources. The relationship between governments is more often seen as an equal partnership than as a hierarchy. It is also more competitive and adversarial than in most other federations.

We can also look at federalism as an *independent variable*. Here we focus on the consequences of federalism. Does federalism make a difference? What are its effects on public policy or the structure of identities? Do some groups or interests benefit by federalism; are others weakened? How does federalism structure our party system or the role and strategies of interest groups? ...

To see federalism as an independent variable quickly shades into a third kind of question: evaluation or judgement. Does federalism contribute to the quality of Canadian democracy? To making public policy that is timely and effective? To the successful management of the diverse social groups that make up the Canadian population?

On all these dimensions, federalism seems to point in two directions. It offers the democratic virtues of government closer to the people and to local needs, but the closed nature of much intergovernmental decision-making has led many to complain of a "democratic deficit" (Simeon and Cameron 2002). It suggests effective ways to balance national and regional concerns in public policy, but again it can be criticized for slowing policy responses in areas where the responsibilities of governments overlap—the "joint decision trap" (Scharpf 1988). Finally, federalism does provide valuable tools for accommodating differences, providing regional and linguistic minorities with provincial governments they can use to pursue their own interests and resist control by the national majority. But, at the same time, federal institutions help institutionalize and perpetuate these same divisions (Simeon and Conway 2001).

Evaluative questions quickly spill over into questions about reform. Many elements of the federal system have been and remain hotly contested in Canadian politics. And the stakes have been high: at some times even the very survival of the country. Traditionally, reform efforts stressed the operation of federal structures such as fiscal arrangements, the division of powers, and the amending formula. Since the 1960s, however, the issues have become more fundamental: the place of Quebec in the federal system and whether it should have distinct status or powers; Senate reform to accommodate better in Ottawa the interests of the smaller provinces; self-government for Aboriginal peoples in the federal system; and the implications of federal arrangements for disadvantaged groups such as women and the disabled, many of whom have felt neglected by one or another aspect of federalism (Russell 1992).

Explanatory Models

Scholars have used a number of models or theories to explain how the federal system works and how it changes over time. *Societal* explanations view political institutions and policies as fundamentally shaped by the social and economic environment in which they are embedded. The "causal arrow" runs from society to the state. Within this category, there are further subdivisions. *Political economy* sees economic factors as the primary driving forces of political phenomena. There are many variants of this idea, some emphasizing international economic forces, others domestic factors (Stevenson 1977). Scholars point to such things as the economic imperatives that drove the impulse to unite in a federal system in the first place, the variations in regional economies as central sources of conflict, the impact of the Great Depression of the 1930s on the federal system, and the *need* to reshape federalism in order to build the postwar Keynesian welfare state. Contemporary exponents of these approaches stress how changes in the global political economy, especially the economic integration of North America, reshape domestic economic and political forces, including federalism (Courchene 1992).

Societal explanations also explore the social and cultural foundations of federalism, including French-English relations and the relations between the different regions and provinces. Thus, the presence of Quebec ensured that the Canadian union would be federal, and the political effects of its "Quiet Revolution" in the 1960s fuelled the debates of the 1970s and 1980s. Western alienation was exacerbated by the "energy wars" of the 1970s, leading to demands for greater provincial power and greater provincial constraints on national decision-making.

Along with these regional and linguistic divisions are other divisions in Canadian society that are not necessarily territorially concentrated. Class conflicts play an important role, as the federal system needed to respond to the policy agenda (greater recognition of trade unions, a stronger welfare state) of workers, unionists, and political parties such as the Co-operative Commonwealth Federation and the New Democratic Party (Porter 1965). More recently other identities, for example, women and ethnic Canadians, have gained greater political prominence and in so doing have mounted major challenges to the functioning of Canadian federalism, with its institutions predicated largely on territory (Cairns 1991).

All these approaches argue that the federal state is a product of underlying social forces. In recent years many writers, especially Alan Cairns (1977, 1979), have turned that model around. The causal arrow, they argue, runs the other way: the state and its leaders shape, mould, and manipulate society. What governments do is not a product simply of external pressures, but of the ambitions, skills, resources, and ideologies of the bureaucratic and political authorities who occupy formal positions. Again, there are variants of this institutional, or "state-centred," approach. Some emphasize the interests of political elites, especially their desire to preserve and enhance their own power. Public criticism of the Meech Lake Accord in 1987 and the Charlottetown Accord in 1992 as illegitimate deals concocted behind closed doors by self-serving first ministers reflected this idea. The conduct of intergovernmental relations is often criticized as being more concerned with governments protecting their turf, and winning political credit while shifting blame, than it is with the substantive issues of public policy.

A more benign institutional explanation is simply that all institutions, including federalism, enshrine their own internal logic and thus help structure political life—empowering some groups and weakening others, making some kinds of strategies successful and others unsuccessful (Simeon 1975). Thus, in Canada, federalism entrenches and institutionalizes the territorial divisions and blurs and weakens other divisions, such as class. It leads to a politics especially preoccupied with linguistic and regional conflict and with intergovernmental relations.

No single approach can possibly account for the evolution of the federal system over more than a century. We bring together elements of both societal and state-centred approaches, and we focus on the *interaction* between them. The causal arrow flows both ways. In particular we emphasize the impact of economic and social forces in setting the basic context within which federalism operates. But how these forces are channelled and expressed, and how successful they will be, is in turn greatly influenced by the federal structure and by the choices made by individual leaders.

We begin with the Confederation settlement, then trace the period from 1867 to the 1920s, showing how centralized federalism, based in part on the extension to Canada of the British colonial model, was replaced by a more province-centred and classical form of federalism. Then we look at the crises that faced Canadian federalism in the Great Depression and World War II, followed by the development of the Keynesian welfare state through *cooperative federalism*. The period from 1960 to 1982 saw the intensification of federal-provincial conflict, driven first by Quebec nationalism and later by the resurgence of provincialism, especially in the West. We call this *competitive federalism*. Following 1982, we trace the conflicting pressures on federalism engendered on the one hand by the continuing need to resolve regional and linguistic tensions and on the other by the need to respond to newly mobilized social forces, armed with the Charter of Rights and Freedoms, which challenged many aspects of federal politics. This was the period of *constitutional federalism*. Woven through these social divisions were profound economic changes, which also challenged many elements of contemporary federalism. By the late 1990s, after the failures of constitutional federalism, attention turned to alternative ways to adapt and modernize the federation and to the development of new ways for provincial and federal governments to work collaboratively on economic and social issues (Lazar 1998). We call this emerging pattern *collaborative federalism*. As we shall see, change is seldom moving in one direction, and the economic and social pressures are not always synchronized. ...

Conclusion

Federalism, it has been said, is a "process" rather than a steady state. This has been abundantly true of Canadian federalism throughout its history, as the governments and institutions that make it up have responded to changing circumstances and shifting policy agendas. We conclude with a few of the current and future challenges that the system faces.

1. *Alleviating the "democratic deficit."* How can intergovernmental relations be rendered more open and transparent to citizens? This could involve opening the process to more citizen participation or strengthening the role that parliaments and legislatures play in debating and scrutinizing the conduct of intergovernmental relations.
2. *Alleviating the "policy deficit."* Here the concerns are: how to shift federal-provincial debates from often sterile debates over turf and status to a greater concern for the substance of issues. Behind that is the question of how to find the right balance between "national standards" that will apply across the whole country, and the variations in policy that federalism is designed to encourage. And there is the further question of whether effective policy is more likely to emerge from close collaboration between governments or through more vigorous and open competition and debate between them.

    Another continuing challenge is getting the roles and responsibilities—and the financial resources to pay for them—right. Provinces have recently complained of a "fiscal imbalance," arguing that the chief areas of growing government spending lie largely in their jurisdiction, while Ottawa has more access to revenues. The solution, they say, is not in greater use of the federal spending power to act in areas of provincial jurisdiction, but to move more taxing powers to the provinces.
3. *Accommodating difference.* Many of the difficulties in reconciling East and West, French- and English-speakers in Canada lie not in federalism itself, but in larger elements of our institutional structure discussed elsewhere in this book: an ineffective Senate; an electoral system that exaggerates regional differences; a regionally fragmented party system; and a parliamentary system that is dominated by the executive, leaving little room for individual MPs to speak for their local interests. This analysis suggests that simply improving the institutions of intergovernmental relations is insufficient. With respect to Quebec, the continuing question is how much "asymmetry"—whether formal or informal—is possible or desirable in the Canadian federation.
4. *From federalism to multilevel governance.* Traditionally, Canadians have seen federalism as concerning federal and provincial governments. But Canadians are also greatly affected by two other orders of government—local or municipal government and Aboriginal governments. Local governments provide a vast array of services, yet are constitutionally subordinate to the provinces. Local governments—especially the large urban areas that are the centres of economic growth and multiculturalism—are now calling for greater recognition and authority, for greater financial resources, and for seats at the intergovernmental table. Whether, and how, they will be integrated into the Canadian pattern of multilevel governance is an important question for the future. The same is true for Aboriginal governments. The idea that they would constitute a "Third Order" of government in Canada was included in the 1993 Charlottetown Accord and was a central recommendation of the Royal Commission on Aboriginal Peoples (RCAP), but it has not been enacted. Nevertheless court decisions and political negotiations are moving towards self-government, and critical questions remain about how they will relate to both federal and provincial governments in the future.

46 Canadian Federalism and the Emerging Mosaic of Aboriginal Multilevel Governance

Martin Papillon (2007)

EDITORS' INTRODUCTION

Martin Papillon teaches at the School of Political Studies at the University of Ottawa. His research focuses on the policies and rights of Aboriginal peoples, federalism and intergovernmental relations in Canada, citizenship and diversity, as well as social policy.

In the past thirty-five years, Aboriginal peoples[1] have mounted a fundamental challenge to the institutions of Canadian federalism. They have adopted the language of recognition and national self-determination to reassert their political status and to question the legitimacy and authority of Canadian governments over their lands and communities. Following the analytical framework proposed in this volume, this chapter discusses and assesses the performance, effectiveness, and legitimacy of Canadian federalism in light of these challenges. How, and to what extent, have the institutions and processes of Canadian federalism responded to Aboriginal claims for greater recognition and political autonomy? Ten years ago the Royal Commission on Aboriginal Peoples (RCAP) proposed a fundamental reconfiguration of Aboriginal-state relations in which Aboriginal governments would form a third order of government in the federation. Are current dynamics conducive to the development of such a relationship?

There are significant obstacles to the recognition of Aboriginal governing institutions as coequal partners in the federation. Deeply embedded assumptions about state sovereignty, as well as institutions and practices inherited from colonial policies, have proven highly resistant to change. Moreover, the diversity in socio-economic and demographic conditions of Aboriginal communities, not to mention the particularities of each nation's historical relationship with the Canadian state, complicates the picture for advocates of an Aboriginal order of government.

That being said, significant changes have taken place over the past few decades in the dynamics of Aboriginal, federal, provincial, and territorial relations. In addition to the constitutional recognition of Aboriginal and treaty rights, new treaties and self-government

Source: Excerpted from "Canadian Federalism and the Emerging Mosaic of Aboriginal Multilevel Governance" by Martin Papillon. In *Canadian Federalism: Performance, Effectiveness, and Legitimacy*, 2nd edition, edited by Herman Bakvis and Grace Skogstad. Toronto: Oxford University Press, 2007. Some notes omitted. Reprinted by permission.

agreements have proven to be a significant platform from which some Aboriginal nations and communities have rebuilt their governing capacities. As Frances Abele and Michael Prince argued in the previous edition of *Canadian Federalism* (2002: 228), less visible but nonetheless significant changes have also taken place in the dynamics of policy-making and policy implementation between Aboriginal organizations and governments and their federal, provincial, and territorial counterparts. These changes have led to the development of a complex and highly diverse mosaic of multilevel governance relations. It is increasingly through such multilevel exercises that Aboriginal organizations and governments are asserting their authority and legitimacy, and reconfiguring the landscape of Canadian federalism. The extent to which this process of incremental changes is conducive to larger shifts in the structure of Canadian federalism over the long run is, however, a matter of debate.

Aboriginal Peoples and Canadian Federalism: Facing the Legacy of Colonialism

Aboriginal peoples are the descendents of the populations that lived in what is now North America prior to the arrival of European settlers. Like all colonized societies, Aboriginal peoples in Canada are facing a state that was imposed upon them by external powers. As elsewhere, the dominant society simply imposed its conception of sovereignty and claimed exclusive jurisdiction over the territory. In the process, Aboriginal peoples, who initially engaged in nation-to-nation treaty relations with the Crown, were absorbed into the dominant political order without their consent. This process of "internal colonization" is now well documented (RCAP, 1996, vol. 1), from the initial stage of diplomatic alliances and treaty making to the processes of land confiscation, cultural assimilation, and dismantlement of traditional forms of government. Indigenous societies became "domesticated" and "dependent" nations, as Chief Justice John Marshall of the United States Supreme Court famously stated. Aboriginal peoples now seek to liberate themselves from this process, reassert their status as distinct political entities, and redefine their relationship with the Canadian federation accordingly. There are, however, a number of challenges in addressing the legacy of colonialism.

A Multi-faced Reality

Aboriginal people represent approximately 3.4 per cent of the Canadian population. They are highly diverse: of the 1,066,500 individuals who identified with an Aboriginal group in the 2001 census, 63 per cent identified as North American Indians (First Nations), 31 per cent as Métis, and 6 per cent as Inuit. In addition, there are between 40 and 60 distinct Aboriginal nations in Canada today, according to the Royal Commission on Aboriginal Peoples (RCAP, 1996, vol. 2), each with its own traditions, history, language, and sense of collective identity. To further complicate things, 50 per cent of the Aboriginal population now lives in urban centres. As Figure 14.1 suggests, Aboriginal people form a significant proportion of the population only in the northern territories, Saskatchewan, and Manitoba.

Aboriginal people also face important social and economic challenges, largely as a result of past policies designed to accelerate their assimilation into the Canadian mainstream. As the comparative data in Table 14.1 indicate, while improving in certain areas, the Aboriginal

Figure 14.1
Geographic Distribution of the Aboriginal Population

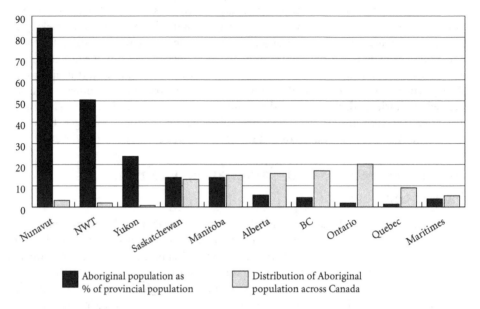

Source: Statistics Canada (2003).

population's socio-economic conditions are still significantly worse than those of the average Canadian.[5] The average income of Aboriginal families is 28 per cent lower than that of non-Aboriginal Canadians. Fifty-five per cent of Aboriginal individuals living in cities live in poverty, compared to 24 per cent for all Canadians. These conditions are compounded by demographic trends; the Aboriginal population is younger and growing faster than the Canadian average. A chronic housing crisis and a lack of basic infrastructure, such as sewage and drinking water, also negatively affect the living conditions of the Aboriginal population in many remote areas.

Aboriginal peoples also vary considerably in their status and institutional relationships with the Canadian state. For one, while all Aboriginal peoples were recognized as having the same rights under the Constitution Act, 1982, it is important to recognize that not all have a treaty-based relationship with the Crown. The result is significant variations in the land and governance regime of each nation. In addition, while most First Nations come under the regime of the federal Indian Act, Inuit and Métis do not. The federal government also distinguishes between First Nations who are considered "status" Indians, and thus entitled to certain benefits under the Act, and non-status Indians, who fall outside the Act and live mostly in urban areas. These legal distinctions, despite their somewhat arbitrary nature, tend to reinforce political divisions amongst Aboriginal peoples.

These differences in conditions, status, and entitlements have significant repercussions for Aboriginal peoples and their relationship with Canadian federalism. Clearly, there is not one single Aboriginal reality to be addressed with a single set of solutions. This reality is further compounded by the fact that Aboriginal peoples do not necessarily all share the same

Table 14.1 Socio-economic Conditions of the Aboriginal Population in Canada

	Aboriginal Population	Canadian Population
Median age	24.7	37.7
Population growth (annual rate)	1.8%	.7%
Average household income	$21,296	$29,769
Low-income families	31.2%	12.9%
Secondary diploma (15 & over)	55%	70%
University degree	6%	15%
Single-parent families	32% on reserve 46% in urban areas	17%
Life expectancy at birth	Men: 68.9 Women: 76.3	Men: 76.3 Women: 81.5

Sources: Statistics Canada (2003); Indian and Northern Affairs Canada (2004).

conception of their relationship with the Canadian state. While some simply reject Canadian sovereignty over their traditional lands, others, especially the Inuit and Métis, have historically been less reluctant to accept the authority of the Canadian Constitution. Aboriginal populations living in urban settings also often have very different viewpoints and interests than those living in remote areas, where control over the land and natural resources is a key element of ongoing conflicts with the state. Within each community there are also often conflicting views between "traditionalists," who seek to reassert traditional lifestyle, values, and governing practices, and those who focus on the modernization of socio-economic and political structures as a key element of the project of autonomy.

The Constraining Nature of Canadian Federalism

In addition to their diverse realities, Aboriginal peoples also face significant challenges related to the institutions of Canadian federalism. Although the Royal Proclamation of 1763 recognized the status of Aboriginal nations as distinct political entities, no Aboriginal representatives were invited to the Charlottetown and Quebec conferences of 1864, where the foundations of the Canadian federation were established. As a result, they never consented, explicitly or implicitly, to the division of authority over the land and peoples that resulted from the Constitution Act, 1867. Instead, they effectively became an object of federal jurisdiction according to section 91(24) of the Act, which confers on the federal Parliament the power to legislate over "Indians and Land reserved for Indians." The institutions of Canadian federalism thus have very little, if any, legitimacy from an Aboriginal perspective. The initial exclusion of Aboriginal peoples from those institutions created a number of constraints that still limit their political aspirations in the Canadian context.

Most significantly, while authority in a federation is divided between orders of governments, the doctrine of state sovereignty is still deeply entrenched in the British-inspired Canadian parliamentary system. There is no space in the Canadian federation for the expression of political authority outside the two constitutionally recognized orders of government. As a result, from a strictly positivist constitutional perspective, Aboriginal governments' authority can only be delegated from the federal and provincial Parliaments. Aboriginal peoples, supported by many legal scholars and Aboriginal rights advocates, reject this conception of sovereignty and argue instead that they have an *inherent* right to self-government, that is a right that emanates not from the Constitution, but from their historical presence—as politically organized peoples—on the land (Macklem, 2001; RCAP, 1996, vol. 2). As we will see in the second part of this chapter, the principle of an inherent Aboriginal right to self-government has been accepted by the federal government and most provinces, but its implementation in practice still faces significant institutional resistance.

Without formal status as federal partners, Aboriginal peoples and their governments also have no statutory voice in the shared institutions of "intrastate federalism," such as the federal Parliament, the Cabinet, or the Supreme Court, other than what their demographic weight calls for. They also have had historically only limited access to the important mechanisms of "interstate federalism" associated with the growing web of intergovernmental processes and institutions that characterize the Canadian federation. This lack of access to key institutions and processes of Canadian federalism reinforces their weak legitimacy and certainly affects their performance and effectiveness in addressing Aboriginal claims.

The division of powers in the Canadian federation has also contributed to what are often tense relations between Aboriginal peoples and provinces (Long and Bold 1988). Especially relevant in the Canadian context is provincial authority over public lands and natural resources. Provinces have naturally sought to maximize local economic development, mainly through natural resource extraction, often without much regard for Aboriginal rights and interests. Highly visible conflicts over hydroelectric developments, forestry and fisheries, or over developments on public lands for which the title is still contested by an Aboriginal group, regularly make headlines in Canadian media and contribute to divisions and a high degree of mistrust between the Aboriginal population and non-Aboriginal Canadians.[8]

Finally, Aboriginal people have also long been, and continue to be, victims of the competitive nature of Canadian federalism, especially with regards to the provision of social programs and services. Paradoxically, the issue here is not so much who *can*, but rather who *must* exercise its legislative authority. Again, the conflict revolves around the interpretation of section 91(24) of the Constitution Act, 1867. As we have seen, the federal government initially interpreted its responsibilities restrictively and excluded Inuit, Métis, and non-status Indians from the Indian Act regime. But even for those covered by the Indian Act, the federal government has on numerous occasions sought to transfer its responsibilities for the provision of services to provinces.[9] The latter, though reluctant to allow federal interventions in their areas of jurisdiction, have always insisted on the federal government's responsibility for the provision of social programs to the Aboriginal population. As a result, a significant number of Aboriginal individuals, especially off-reserve Indians and Métis, have fallen into a jurisdictional gap and for a long time were simply ignored by both orders of government. Even today federal and provincial authorities tend to interpret their respective responsibilities in relation to Aboriginal people more or less liberally depending on the interests at stake. Jurisdictional uncertainties add to an already complex policy challenge in developing long-term, coordinated solutions to Aboriginal socio-economic conditions.

We can thus conclude that in addition to lacking legitimacy as a result of Aboriginal people's exclusion at the time of the creation of the federation, Canadian federalism has not been a particularly effective conduit for addressing the legacy of colonialism. Nor has it historically performed well as a unifying system of governance. In fact, the institutions and processes of Canadian federalism have exacerbated conflicts with Aboriginal people and have contributed significantly to the reproduction of the system of exclusion inherited from the colonial period. Reconciling the Canadian federal system with Aboriginal claims to self-determination is thus not a simple task. ...

Conclusion: An Emerging Mosaic of Multilevel Governance Relations

The relationship between Aboriginal peoples and Canadian federalism remains uncertain and tentative. The initial exclusion of Aboriginal peoples from the federal compact still looms large today, affecting not only the legitimacy but also the performance and effectiveness of the institutions and processes of Canadian federalism as they try to address the difficult colonial legacy. Although Canadians are often perceived to be more supportive of Aboriginal rights than their Australian or American counterparts, this support has not led to a radical reconfiguration of Canadian federalism along the lines proposed by the RCAP and proponents of treaty federalism. Multiple factors work against such a significant reform of Canadian federalism, most significantly the institutional resilience of existing practices and conceptions of state sovereignty and governmental authority. The profound diversity, demographic situation, and socio-economic conditions of Aboriginal peoples also compound these difficulties. So does the fiscal dependency of Aboriginal governments on their federal and provincial counterparts.

That being said, significant shifts have taken place in the constitutional framework and institutions of Canadian federalism. As we have seen, these shifts remain very much a work in progress. The extent and meaning of Aboriginal rights are still being defined through the courts as well as through public and academic debates. Despite the recent developments in treaty negotiations, federal and provincial authorities still impose significant limits on both the process and the substance of agreements. The status of the self-governing structures slowly emerging from such processes varies considerably from one agreement to the other, and their viability largely depends on the willingness of both federal and provincial authorities to put resources and goodwill into implementing each agreement. In this respect, Canadian federalism has performed rather poorly, as the specific responsibilities and obligations of the federal and provincial governments often remain unclear. The participation of Aboriginal organizations in mechanisms of executive federalism raises a new set of issues in terms of legitimacy and accountability, as their status in such processes remains largely ad hoc and uncertain. The rejection of the Kelowna Accord by the newly elected Conservative government also raises concerns regarding the effectiveness of intergovernmental mechanisms in addressing pressing social and economic issues in Aboriginal communities that cut across the boundaries of federal and provincial jurisdictions.

As I have suggested, it is perhaps in the emerging dynamics of multilevel governance in the negotiation of policy implementation that Aboriginal, federal, and provincial relations have changed most significantly. This change may not affect the constitutional status of Aboriginal peoples, but Aboriginal governments now play a growing role in the development and implementation of policies, and as a result consolidate their capacity and legitimacy both within the communities and in their relations with federal and provincial authorities. Aboriginal governance is now increasingly being played out in multiple venues. If the federal government has kept the upper hand with its constitutional authority and fiscal capacity, provinces now play an increasing role as a result of their involvement in treaty negotiations and in the process of administrative devolution to Aboriginal governments and organizations. Aboriginal governments have been increasingly proactive in developing their intergovernmental capacity, and engage with their federal and provincial counterparts in policy negotiations. In other words, Aboriginal governance is less and less a unidirectional, top-down affair and is increasingly becoming a multilevel, trilateral reality.

This emerging trilateral, multilevel governance regime is far from uniform, as the context, status, needs, and expectations, as well as political clout of Aboriginal nations vary considerably. Different self-government agreements, land bases, and provincial positions in relation to Aboriginal peoples also affect the nature and dynamics of multilevel governance. It is perhaps more accurate to talk of a mosaic of multilevel governance relations between Aboriginal nations and their federal and provincial counterparts, each with its own institutional framework *and* evolving dynamics. While it does not create a formal third order of governments *or* a parallel treaty-based federal structure, this emerging multilevel mosaic offers what can, in effect, be defined as an alternative way for Aboriginal peoples to reshape their relationship with Canadian federalism. In this perspective, change is not coming from above, through formal constitutional processes, but rather from below, through the consolidation of Aboriginal governments' capacity and legitimacy in exercises of governance. Only time will tell whether this changing dynamic can eventually lead to a more efficient and legitimate relationship between the Canadian federation and Aboriginal peoples.

Notes

1. Following the practice in the Canadian literature, the term "Aboriginal peoples" in this text refers to Métis and Inuit peoples as well as First Nations (still often referred to as Indians). Distinctions among the three are made when necessary.

4. Of major Canadian cities, Winnipeg has the largest Aboriginal population, with 56,000 persons, accounting for 8 per cent of its population.

5. A 2004 report of the United Nations Human Rights Commission suggests that while Canada was 7th on the UN Human Development Index for that year, Aboriginal peoples living in Canada would rank 48th on the list of 174 countries.

8. There is no space here for an exhaustive list of recent conflicts, but one can think of the 1990 Oka crisis in Quebec, the 1995 standoff at Ipperwash Provincial Park and the 2006 land dispute in Caledonia, Ontario, as examples of land disputes that turned sour. The recent conflicts over the fisheries in the Maritimes and British Columbia are examples of disputes over natural resources.

9. The infamous *White Paper on Indian Policy* of 1969 notably proposed such transfer.

47 Quebec–Canada: A New Deal

Government of Quebec (1979)

EDITORS' INTRODUCTION

The Parti Québécois' (PQ) White Paper was made public in 1979, one year before the 1980 referendum which asked that Quebeckers provide their government with a mandate to negotiate the terms of a new agreement between Quebec and Canada. This document introduces how the PQ presented notions of association and sovereignty to its citizens, as well as the mechanisms that would be put in place in order to realize the PQ's project.

If we are really looking for a new agreement between Quebec and the rest of Canada, it is absolutely essential to replace federalism by another constitutional formula.

This search for a new formula must be carried out with due consideration for the fundamental, legitimate preoccupations of Quebecers, who want to communicate and talk directly and freely with their neighbours and with other nations, who do not want to destroy Canada or to be completely separate from it, who wish to improve their situation, and who are determined to see that the changes to come are made democratically and without disorder.

The Government of Quebec fully shares and endorses these preoccupations.

The Way of the Future

Thinking of the future the Government of Quebec proposes a constitutional formula which would replace the present federal system and at the same time respect the legitimate feelings of Quebecers toward Canada. This new system, while freeing Quebec from Ottawa's domination, would not break up an economic community that extends from the Atlantic to the Pacific; it would ensure for Quebec a maximum of autonomy while maintaining the natural interdependence and the historical and human links that exist between Quebec and the rest of Canada; it would enable Quebec to institute the measures that it lacks at present, without forcing the other provinces to accept responsibilities they do not feel they need. This new system would provide permanent solutions to the many problems engendered by relations between Quebec and Ottawa over the years.

Source: Excerpted from the English translation of *La nouvelle entente Québec–Canada. Proposition du gouvernement du Québec pour une entente d'égal à égal : La souveraineté-association.* Quebec City: Government of Quebec, 1979.

Of the two roads open to Quebecers—a federalism whose fundamental renewal is to all intents and purposes impossible because it would contradict the very nature of federalism, and a new agreement between Quebec and Canada capable of reconciling political autonomy and economic interdependence—the Government of Quebec has chosen the latter, sovereignty-association, a contemporary expression of Quebec's continuity, in brief a new deal.

The Modern Phenomenon of Association

The recent history of international relations shows that federalism can no longer be regarded as the only formula capable of reconciling the objectives of autonomy and interdependence. Although it was fashionable in the past century, the federal formula must now give way to associations between sovereign countries. While no new federations are being created, economic associations are on the increase on every continent. ...

These various associations of sovereign states are distinguished from one another by the nature of their activity and the degree of their integration, as well as by the history of relations between the member states and their various characteristics: population, culture, political system, etc.

The European communities are probably the most advanced examples of economic integration. Their activity is primarily economic, but it also spills over into social policy and scientific policy, among other areas. The economic union between Belgium and Luxembourg, and the Benelux countries, which appeared before the European Economic Community, are part of the European movement toward economic integration, while preserving a certain cohesion of their own within the Nine. As for the European Free Trade Association, its economic links are rather weak.

On the other hand, the Nordic Council and the Association of Southeast Asian Nations, while not as completely integrated, have a much more diversified activity.

Basing itself firmly on the historical trend of Quebec thinking, which has always sought to redefine relations between Quebec and the rest of Canada on a more egalitarian basis, the Government of Quebec proposes this type of modern formula of association between sovereign countries to ensure for Quebecers a better control of their own affairs, without shattering the Canadian economic framework.

Association in equality may take many forms: far more flexible than federalism, it is more easily adapted to the realities of countries that resort to it, and the degree of association will depend on whether cooperation is to be limited to certain fields or maximum advantage is to be taken of a broader economic community.

Modern economic associations are generally the result of cooperation between individual countries and entirely sovereign nations, which have agreed to pool some of their powers. In such cases, integration is based on the sovereignty of the partners. In our case, however, economic integration already exists and it is the sovereignty of the partners that must be established. The point of departure is different but the aim is identical.

The Implications of Sovereignty

The idea of sovereignty is clearly defined in international law: it is, in general terms, the power to make decisions autonomously, without being subject in law to any superior or exterior power, which implies that the sovereign state has full jurisdiction over a given territory. Sovereignty ensures complete autonomy, in the sense that the state enjoys full legal freedom in all fields; its authority is exercised to the exclusion of any other within the limits of its territory; and it can be present in the community of nations. ...

The Special Character of the Quebec–Canada Relationship

The examples cited above show the great variety in the types of association entered into by many sovereign peoples throughout the world; no less different are the historical circumstances that led these people to such varied solutions. Quebec too has evolved in circumstances that are specific to it, circumstances which, while they have certain analogies with some of the cases cited above, cannot be reduced to any one of them. The institutions and the functioning of the future association between Quebec and Canada must reflect what is specific to each of the communities.

Most of the countries now grouped in various associations enjoyed sovereignty long before they joined together, while those that associated a few decades ago did so at a time when the state did not yet occupy as large a place in the economic activity of nations. On the one hand, Quebec has not yet gained its sovereignty, while on the other hand, the institutions of the state, because of the size of their expenditures at all levels of government, play a considerable economic and social role in Quebec as well as in the rest of Canada.

Given the situation of our two communities, and because the economic space that Canada and Quebec share must be both preserved and developed, the Quebec government wants to propose to the rest of Canada that the two communities remain in association, not only in a customs union or a common market but in a monetary union as well. Thus Canada can be preserved intact as an economic entity, while Quebec can assume all the powers it needs as a nation to ensure its full development. Replacing federalism by association will, in effect, maintain economic exchange, but the nature of political and legal relations between Quebec and Canada will be changed.

The Proposal

For a proper understanding of the formula proposed by the Government of Quebec, we will describe how it will function by examining the powers that will be exercised by Quebec and specifying the extent of the association between Quebec and Canada; we will also say a word about the Quebec–Canada community structures that must be provided for.

We hasten to state that the changes described here will not occur overnight after the Referendum, but will be, can only be, the result of negotiations between Quebec and Canada, negotiations that will be started as a result of a positive answer in the Referendum. In the next chapter we will explain how the proposed formula will be gradually implemented.

A. Sovereignty

Through sovereignty, Quebec would acquire, in addition to the political powers it already has, those now exercised by Ottawa, whether they were assigned to the federal government under the British North America Act of 1867 or whether it assumed them since that time, directly or indirectly.

Sovereignty is the power to levy all taxes, to make all laws and to be present on the international scene; it is also the possibility to share freely, with one or more states, certain national powers. Sovereignty for Quebec, then, will have a legal impact on the power to make laws and to levy taxes, on territorial integrity, on citizenship and minorities, on the courts and various other institutions, and on the relations of Quebec with other countries.

For each of these subjects, the government wishes to define as clearly as possible the position it intends to adopt in its negotiations with the rest of Canada.

- Laws and Taxes—The only laws that will apply on Quebec's territory will be those adopted by the National Assembly, and the only taxes that will be levied will be those decreed by Quebec law. In this way, there will be an end to the overlapping of federal and Quebec services, which has been so often denounced, thereby enabling Quebec to control the totality of its fiscal resources. Existing federal laws will continue to apply as Quebec laws, as long as they are not amended, repealed or replaced by the National Assembly.

- Territory—Quebec has an inalienable right over its territory, recognized even in the present Constitution, which states that the territory of a province cannot be modified without the consent of that province. Moreover, since the agreements were reached on James Bay, there no longer is any lien on any part of the Quebec territory. In becoming sovereign, Quebec, as is the rule in international law, will thus maintain its territorial integrity. Moreover, it would be desirable for Quebec to regain the advantages that would normally come to it from its geographical position, putting an end to the uncertainties that have surrounded the issue of jurisdiction over the Gulf of St. Lawrence, Labrador and the Arctic regions.

- Citizenship—The Quebec government gives its solemn commitment that every Canadian who, at the time sovereignty is achieved, is a resident of Quebec, or any person who was born there, will have an automatic right to Quebec citizenship; the landed immigrant will be able to complete residency requirements and obtain citizenship. The Parliament of Canada will have to decide whether Canadians who become Quebec citizens may maintain their Canadian citizenship as well. Quebec, for its part, would have no objection. Any person who is born in a sovereign Quebec will have the right to Quebec citizenship; the same will hold true for any person born abroad of a father or mother who has Quebec citizenship. Quebec citizenship will be recognized by a distinct passport, which does not rule out the possibility of an agreement with Canada on a common passport, since the two states will have close relations, of a community nature, that may cover many subjects. Canadian citizens will enjoy the same rights in Quebec as Quebec citizens enjoy in Canada. The acquired rights of foreign nationals will also be fully recognized.

- The Minorities—The government pledges that Quebec's Anglophone minority will continue to enjoy the rights now accorded it by law, and that other communities in Quebec will be given the means to develop their cultural resources. The Amerindian and Inuit communities, if they so desire, will be in full possession on their territory of institutions that maintain the integrity of their societies and enable them to develop freely, according to their own culture and spirit. As for Francophone minorities in Canada, Quebec intends to fulfil its moral responsibilities towards them, as it has started to do, for that matter, despite its limited means.

- The Courts—Naturally, the Quebec courts will be the only ones to administer justice in Quebec. All judges will be appointed in accordance with Quebec laws, and judges who are now on the bench will remain in their functions. However, a joint court, constituted through the treaty of association between Quebec and Canada, will have the power to interpret this treaty and decide on the rights that result from it.
- External Relations—Quebec will continue to be bound by the treaties to which Canada is now a signatory. It may withdraw from them should the occasion arise according to the rules of international law. Consequently, Quebec will respect the agreement on the St. Lawrence Seaway and will become a full partner in the International Joint Commission. As for alliances such as NATO and NORAD, Quebec will respect its responsibilities and offer its contributions in accordance with its aims. In order to fully play its role on the international scene and defend its interests, Quebec will ask to be admitted to the United Nations and to its specialized agencies. Finally, while developing its relations and its cooperation with Francophone countries, Quebec will consider remaining a member of the British Commonwealth.

B. Association

In today's world no nation, great or small, can live in isolation. Interdependence, considering the economic advantages that it brings, far from being as constraining as some seem to think, can on the contrary result in enriching forms of cooperation and interaction, and thus improve the present and future lot of the societies taking part.

Quebec has never wanted to live in isolation: from the start it has accepted interdependence. However, it wishes to ensure that it will be directly involved in determining the terms of this interdependence.

To this end, the Quebec government intends to offer to negotiate with the rest of Canada a treaty of community association, whose aim will be, notably, to maintain the present Canadian economic entity by ensuring continuity of exchange and by favouring, in the long run, a more rapid and better balanced development of each of the two partners.

This treaty will have an international status and will bind the parties in a manner and for a term to be determined. It will define the partners' areas of common activity and confirm the maintenance of an economic and monetary union between Quebec and the rest of Canada. It will also determine the areas where agreement on goals will be considered desirable. Finally, it will establish the rules and institutions that will ensure the proper functioning of the Quebec–Canada community, and determine its methods of financing.

48 "The Night of the Long Knives"

Newspaper Report (1981)

EDITORS' INTRODUCTION

The federalists' victory during the 1980 Quebec referendum paved the way for intense negotiations, which culminated in the conclusion of an agreement between the federal and provincial governments, with the exception of Quebec. This newspaper article from that week in November 1981 recalls the context and circumstances encompassing this agreement that permitted the repatriation and amendment of the Canadian Constitution in 1982. The article is followed by public statements from Prime Minister Pierre Elliott Trudeau and Quebec's Premier René Lévesque, made in the immediate aftermath of the agreement, which clearly express the opposing sentiments of that epoch. Such sentiments continue to mark Canadian politics to this day.

Secret, all-night talks behind historic accord

Friday, November 6, 1981
By Robert Sheppard, Globe and Mail Reporter

OTTAWA—The pressure-pot atmosphere of four days in a closed room, plus the prospect of a referendum battle on the charter of rights, produced a historic constitutional agreement yesterday among Canada's 11 first ministers.

The makings of the deal—involving substantial tradeoffs on the charter of rights to limit the power of the courts—evolved from a number of bargaining moves and political pacts, some planned, some accidental, and a secret "kitchen meeting" between influential ministers from the federal Government, Ontario and Saskatchewan.

The basis for yesterday's agreement was a late-hour compromise paper from six provinces that was put on the table by Newfoundland's Brian Peckford.

It had been worked on all night by officials from six delegations, but some of the essential ingredients of the package had been discussed the night of the Supreme Court decision five weeks ago by three veterans of the constitutional battle—Attorneys-General Roy Romanow of Saskatchewan, Roy McMurtry of Ontario and Jean Chrétien of the federal Government—over a bottle of scotch at Mr. Chrétien's Ottawa home.

The essence of the deal was confirmed by these three again in an exchange of written notes in a fifth-floor kitchen at the Government Conference Centre Wednesday night when it appeared that the whole project might fall apart.

Source: *The Globe and Mail*, November 6, 1981.

The dynamics that set up the final political accommodation yesterday began Wednesday morning when Premiers William Bennett of B.C. and Allan Blakeney of Saskatchewan put forward their own compromise positions, thereby beginning the eventual disintegration of the so-called Gang of Eight.

However, according to key insiders, the final straw that set up the deal and allowed the various provinces to abandon their Quebec ally came only after Premier René Lévesque of Quebec unexpectedly threw his support behind Prime Minister Pierre Trudeau's casual suggestion to hold a referendum on the issue of the charter of rights.

None of the other premiers wanted a referendum and so Mr. Lévesque's solo move made it easier for the rest to meet the Prime Minister's bottom-line demand on language rights, ministers from several key provinces said.

The sudden interest in the referendum proposal by the two long-time political foes nearly scuppered the careful plans of some of the more moderate premiers.

Interestingly, while the Trudeau referendum offer had been floated earlier in the private sessions, Mr. Lévesque waited until Wednesday to express his agreement, after two of the dissenting premiers had indicated their particular compromise proposals. "Quebec got very angry and I guess it began to feel pushed out," a key provincial official said. "So the idea of a referendum to settle the issue must have seemed to it like a good fight. It was all very cathartic for the group as a whole." Later that morning in the private conference room, Quebec Intergovernmental Affairs Minister Claude Morin angrily turned on the Saskatchewan delegation and accused them of forcing the issue with their compromise paper. He said Quebec would have no choice but to retaliate by saddling the country with a referendum.

Here then, according to a number of federal and provincial sources, is how the events of the past two days unfolded:

Wednesday, November 4th

At the breakfast meeting of the eight provinces most strongly opposed to the Trudeau initiatives, Premier Bennett informed his colleagues he planned to commit British Columbia to a constitutional commitment to provide minority-language education rights.

Over the previous weeks, in a number of delicate and sometimes deliberately vague conversations with the federal side, Mr. Bennett and his staff had come to realize that the issue of language rights was the Prime Minister's bottom line. (On Tuesday, Mr. Bennett had taken another compromise position to the Prime Minister on behalf of the Gang of Eight that went only as far as calling for opting-in on education rights. Mr. Trudeau had exploded angrily, telling the premiers they were being duped by Quebec.) At the Wednesday breakfast meeting, Premier Blakeney of Saskatchewan also said he was going to put forward a proposal of his own that would entrench the principle of minority-language education rights but provide for no enforcement by the courts.

The Blakeney proposal, which some members of his delegation felt was only a last-chance effort to keep the various parties talking, was actually in large part a Saskatchewan-Ontario project. This had a peculiar effect on Mr. Trudeau, some players said privately, because he sensed he might be losing his main ally, Ontario's William Davis.

In some respects, the Blakeney proposal played down the minority-language education rights and played up the more universal rights in the controversial charter. This contrasted with the Bennett proposal of the same day, which did almost the opposite, forcing the Prime Minister toward making a difficult political choice between linguistic rights and fundamental rights for all Canadians to win more support for his project.

Throughout the day the referendum option dominated the discussion and those seeking an immediate pact were losing hope.

The Prime Minister said at one point the referendum offer was his bottom line, "take it or leave it," and he left those in the room with the impression that if they did not go along he would be making the offer publicly to at least ease the concerns of British MPs.

Toward the end of the afternoon, Premier Peckford said he had a final offer he wanted to place on the table the next day and then distributed it in synopsis form to the other ministers.

The federal Justice Minister had torn off a small yellow paper from a memo pad the day before and written down four possible options Ottawa might endorse. Having given this to his Saskatchewan counterpart, he called him aside Wednesday afternoon and said dejectedly: "It looks like it's all over. What can you do?" The two, along with Mr. McMurtry repaired quietly to a small kitchen on the fifth floor of the conference centre. Taking out the scrap of paper, Mr. Romanow circled the most likely option. "Can you buy that?" Mr. Chrétien asked. "Yeah, there's something there." And that was the nucleus of the deal.

At 9:30 that night, the premiers and officials from Alberta, Newfoundland and Saskatchewan met in Mr. Blakeney's suite at the Chateau Laurier Hotel to consider a two-page document Mr. Peckford had drawn up in his suite.

They were joined later that night by Premier Angus MacLean of Prince Edward Island and officials from Nova Scotia and British Columbia. A serious drafting effort went on until nearly 4 a.m. Thursday, making it the second all-night session for Saskatchewan officials.

Meanwhile, across town, Mr. Romanow, Mr. McMurtry, Premier Davis and Michael Kirby, secretary to the federal Cabinet for federal–provincial relations, were meeting on their own, in telephone contact with the others, as were Quebec officials across the river in Hull.

A large part of these meetings dealt with the "notwithstanding clause," which allows legislatures to pass specific legislation notwithstanding the provisions of the charter of rights. (This idea had been presented to Prime Minister Trudeau on Tuesday—while the Gang of Eight met throughout the afternoon—by the Ontario ministers. And Mr. Trudeau had taken to calling the proposal "the McMurtry formula.") Mr. Romanow returned to the Chateau and persuaded Mr. Peckford to include the notwithstanding clause in his proposal, some sources say.

Thursday, November 5th

The drafting of the Peckford proposal had been completed only a few hours before the eight provinces had their regular breakfast conference in advance of yesterday's final day.

Although Quebec officials had been informed generally about the nature of the proposal, Premier Lévesque left no doubt he wanted no part in it.

Although Mr. Lévesque has repeatedly said he would provide educational services for the English minority in Quebec if the other provinces provided French-language services on a reciprocal basis, he was angry about being "constitutionally blackmailed" into such a commitment, he told his fellow premiers.

As well he did not like the proposal of not providing financial compensation to any province that opted out of future change, a condition that was necessary to gain Ontario support.

The drafters of the Peckford proposal had also omitted the new constitutional guarantees for aboriginal treaties, on the insistence of B.C. and Alberta, two provinces where native land claims have been heating up in recent years.

At the meeting of the 11 first ministers, there was some initial discussion about the referendum proposal and then the topic turned to the Peckford paper. Some premiers objected to the Prime Minister's invitation that they speak first on the issue. However, he insisted on hearing them out before he replied. His reply, when it came, was strangely conciliatory, given the often-bitter sessions of the previous days.

The tenor of the Prime Minister's remarks indicated to the premiers that he was indeed ready to strike a deal, Mr. Peckford told reporters later.

Mr. Trudeau said he had some minor objections to the package, but he felt there was common ground. He asked that the proposal include the so-called sunset law, which would have legislatures reaffirm the "notwithstanding clauses" every five years or they would expire, and this was almost immediately accepted.

The proposal was given to federal drafters to work on while the first ministers continued their discussions and a new clause, inviting native leaders to the next round of constitutional talks, was added at that point and agreed to.

Mr. Lévesque raised the question of Quebec's traditional veto and said he could not agree with the proposal if there was no change in the mobility section and if financial compensation for provinces opting out (which he said was his quid pro quo for signing the provincial accord formula) was not re-included.

Mr. Trudeau would not agree to either request, although he said he would be willing to discuss further the drafting of the mobility rights section.

Mr. Lévesque also said Ottawa could not impose the charter or new amending formula without the agreement of the Government of Quebec or a reference to the people of Quebec and called on the Prime Minister to submit the proposal to a referendum there. The answer was a stony no.

There was also a discussion about an opting-in formula for the provision of minority-language educational rights, which nine of the provinces agreed to provide and Quebec refused.

The opting-in clause was dropped from the initial proposal. It was left to the federal Government to decide whether to use the London card to impose it on that province at this point or leave it open for some time in the future.

After 3½ hours in private session, the first ministers re-entered the public conference room and announced their agreement.

"I am happy to report that a consensus has been reached"

Excerpt from Public Statement by Prime Minister Pierre Trudeau, Friday, November 6, 1981

Pierre Trudeau: Well, when we met Monday morning, I suggested that we had a short but a difficult agenda; that we had to ask ourselves if we wanted patriation, if we wanted an amendment formula, and if we wanted a charter.

I am happy to report, on behalf of the conference, that a consensus has been reached on those three areas—and I will deal very briefly with them, each in turn, because I realize that we are anxious to attend to other business. ...

On the amendment formula, we have also reached a consensus. It is, roughly stated, the accord formula reached last April by the premiers, the eight premiers meeting on April 16, I believe. It is essentially that accord formula, with one subtraction—important, I know for Quebec—which I will return to later. But, in essence, I think the main part of that accord formula is the one that Canadians will have as their amendment formula to their constitution.

On the charter, we have a charter. It is not the charter, not exactly the one that was processed through the House of Commons and Senate during several months, but we have a charter of which Canadians can be proud and of which, I hope, we will still be able to say it is probably the best charter in the world. ...

I have one regret. I put it on the record. I will not return to it. I have the regret that we have not kept in the amending formula a reference to the ultimate sovereignty of the people as could be tested in a referendum. ...

If I understand correctly, Quebec can unfortunately not sign this accord along with the other 10 because, they told us this morning, it was unacceptable to remove the compensation clause from the amending formula.

That is, a province which chooses not to accept an amendment would not have a constitutional guarantee of receiving compensation. ...

The second reason they gave us for not signing this accord was the mobility clause allowing Canadians from diverse provinces to go to live or work in others. We think this concept is essential to the notion of one Canada where Canadians can work where they wish, but we put into the text ... a formula which would allow provinces suffering from a higher unemployment rate than the national average to protect themselves through special legislation. There, too, I say to Quebec that our door is not closed. If we can find other formulae to accommodate the justifiable worries of a province, be it Quebec or any other, we are ready to study new texts on this.

The third reason for which Quebec cannot sign this accord, as we understand it, is that we don't expressly say that the clause which will henceforth oblige the nine English provinces to give their French minorities education in their own language—and I say in passing, I think it is a noble day for Canada that we have finally recognized that the French minorities will be constitutionally protected—we heard from the Quebec Premier that he cannot accept the same for Quebec. ...

But it is clear that, as a Canadian Government, we cannot take a position in the constitution where we protect French minorities but not the English minority in Quebec. I am speaking still of schooling.

So those are the three points on which we have reached a fundamental and, I think, extraordinarily opportune agreement—nine provinces and the federal Government. And those are my views on what can still be done in the future. A constitution is entrenched. It is not written in stone for all time, and I hope that in the weeks and, if necessary, months to come we will still be able to persuade our colleagues from Quebec to do in the constitution what in fact historically has always been done in Quebec since the beginning of Confederation, to treat their Anglophone minorities in the school system equitably.

I am convinced it can be done, and therefore, though there is one sad note in this conclusion, I am hopeful that with good will, and in the interests of Canada and of its peoples, we will very soon be able to make this accord unanimous.

"Quebec finds itself alone"

Excerpt from Public Statement by Quebec Premier René Lévesque, Friday, November 6, 1981

René Lévesque: Gentlemen, following this hymn to harmony of Mr. Davis, I must say that I sincerely regret that Quebec now finds itself today in a position which has almost become one of the fundamental traditions of the Canadian federal regime: Quebec finds itself alone. It will be up to the Quebec people to draw their conclusions.

I arrived here on Monday with a mandate—voted with the unanimity of all parties in the Quebec National Assembly—asking the federal Government and asking, of course, our colleagues around the table, but first and foremost the Government that was the author of the resolution before the House of Commons, to give up the unilateral character of this project and to give up imposing in any way on the rights and duties of the Quebec National Assembly without its consent. Because behind the National Assembly, we have the people of Quebec who hold the power. I also stressed the fact that the federal Prime Minister and his Government were thus acting without any explicit mandate, without any type of mandate from the citizens, not only of Quebec but of the rest of the country, and, in this respect, the apparent offer of compromise which was so spectacularly made yesterday morning—that is the referendum offer—appeared to be interesting, because in substance it would have been a democratic manner of breaking the deadlock, of giving all citizens who are the only source of power—and no one around this table has equivalent power—an opportunity to have their say. And it was at the same time the only federal proposal that would comply with the mandate we had been given by the Quebec National Assembly.

By yesterday afternoon, the federal Prime Minister did his best to destroy the offer as he entered into greater detail. However, if Mr. Trudeau was serious, was sincere and honest, he could renounce imposing on us this project, on the people of Quebec, in a way which is still unilateral in our perspective. He could maintain the idea of a referendum; nothing prevents him from doing so—he does not need the agreement of anyone around this table to do so. Without this, as far as we are concerned, we must note that Mr. Trudeau has deliberately chosen, in order to obtain the support of English Canada, a step which imposes forcefully on Quebec a decrease in its rights and duties without its consent, whereas all parties represented in the National Assembly have already unanimously rejected this formula. …

Finally, with respect to our exclusive jurisdiction over education, we have been given the right not to accept its imposition. But by removing four lines of the project put forward this morning in the closed section, we introduce an element of permanent blackmail on Quebec respecting the eventual renouncing of its exclusive right to decide what it will do in the area of culture, its very identity and access to schools ultimately. I heard earlier intentions of good will expressed by the federal Prime Minister in this area. He said that we could take the time to make adjustments, seek better formulae. I can assure you that I'm going to do my best. ...

This morning, before leaving the meeting, I asked two final questions of the Prime Minister and of our colleagues gathered here. The questions are as follows: first, you proposed yesterday that if we did not arrive at a consensus, this federal proposal would not be implemented, either with respect to the amending formula or to the charter of rights, without the support of the majority of the Quebec people, because in the referendum formula you put forward yesterday ... based on the four main regions, of which Quebec is one. Today, of course, you have the agreement, Mr. Prime Minister, of the other provinces on a proposed resolution, but you do not have Quebec's agreement. Therefore, you do not have in any way a consensus in the sense that you deemed it was necessary in the referendum perspective which you yourself defined. Would you be ready to commit yourself not to imposing this project until it has been submitted to the people of Quebec and accepted in the majority? The reply was in the negative. Of course, we maintain the right to consult the Quebec people. ...

To conclude, I do want to thank all of you for the time we have spent together. I did have the impression that this was a co-operation that might have become permanent. ...

Once again Quebec is the odd man out. All of this is rather sad. I don't think it's sad only for Quebec; perhaps it is even sadder for Canada. This means another hardening of the regime, as far as we are concerned. The federal regime feels like a straitjacket to us, and this seems like a tightening of it to us because we will see our powers and guarantees reduced and they were already very insufficient. There is no possibility for a self-respecting Quebec government to accept such a development. The present Quebec Government ... will never accept this. We will never accept a reduction of our power, the taking away of our traditional and fundamental powers, without our consent. And I repeat that we will take all the means left at our disposal to prevent this from happening.

Quebec Secession Reference

Supreme Court of Canada (1998)

EDITORS' INTRODUCTION
Eleven months after the referendum on sovereignty, which took place in Quebec on October 30, 1995, the federal government led by Prime Minister Jean Chrétien asked the Supreme Court to provide a ruling on the legality of a Quebec unilateral declaration of independence. The Court made its reference public on August 20, 1998.

The following is the judgement delivered by THE COURT:

Introduction

[1] This Reference requires us to consider momentous questions that go to the heart of our system of constitutional government. ...

[2] The [questions] posed by the Governor in Council ... [read] as follows:

1. Under the Constitution of Canada, can the National Assembly, legislature or government of Quebec effect the secession of Quebec from Canada unilaterally?
2. Does international law give the National Assembly, legislature or government of Quebec the right to effect the secession of Quebec from Canada unilaterally? In this regard, is there a right to self-determination under international law that would give the National Assembly, legislature or government of Quebec the right to effect the secession of Quebec from Canada unilaterally?
3. In the event of a conflict between domestic and international law on the right of the National Assembly, legislature or government of Quebec to effect the secession of Quebec from Canada unilaterally, which would take precedence in Canada? ...

The Operation of the Constitutional Principles in the Secession Context

[83] Secession is the effort of a group or section of a state to withdraw itself from the political and constitutional authority of that state, with a view to achieving statehood for a new territorial unit on the international plane. In a federal state, secession typically takes the form of a territorial unit seeking to withdraw from the federation. Secession is a legal act as much as a political one. By the terms of [the question] of this Reference, we are asked to rule on the legality of unilateral secession "[u]nder the Constitution of Canada." This is an

Source: Excerpted from Supreme Court of Canada, *Reference re Secession of Quebec*, [1998] 2 SCR 217.

appropriate question, as the legality of unilateral secession must be evaluated, at least in the first instance, from the perspective of the domestic legal order of the state from which the unit seeks to withdraw. As we shall see below, it is also argued that international law is a relevant standard by which the legality of a purported act of secession may be measured.

[84] The secession of a province from Canada must be considered, in legal terms, to require an amendment to the Constitution, which perforce requires negotiation. The amendments necessary to achieve a secession could be radical and extensive. Some commentators have suggested that secession could be a change of such a magnitude that it could not be considered to be merely an amendment to the Constitution. We are not persuaded by this contention. It is of course true that the Constitution is silent as to the ability of a province to secede from Confederation but, although the Constitution neither expressly authorizes nor prohibits secession, an act of secession would purport to alter the governance of Canadian territory in a manner which undoubtedly is inconsistent with our current constitutional arrangements. The fact that those changes would be profound, or that they would purport to have a significance with respect to international law, does not negate their nature as amendments to the Constitution of Canada.

[85] The Constitution is the expression of the sovereignty of the people of Canada. It lies within the power of the people of Canada, acting through their various governments duly elected and recognized under the Constitution, to effect whatever constitutional arrangements are desired within Canadian territory, including, should it be so desired, the secession of Quebec from Canada. As this Court held in the *Manitoba Language Rights Reference*, ... "[t]he Constitution of a country is a statement of the will of the people to be governed in accordance with certain principles held as fundamental and certain prescriptions restrictive of the powers of the legislature and government." The manner in which such a political will could be formed and mobilized is a somewhat speculative exercise, though we are asked to assume the existence of such a political will for the purpose of answering the question before us. By the terms of this Reference, we have been asked to consider whether it would be constitutional in such a circumstance for the National Assembly, legislature or government of Quebec to effect the secession of Quebec from Canada unilaterally.

[86] The "unilateral" nature of [Quebec secession] is of cardinal importance and we must be clear as to what is understood by this term. In one sense, any step towards a constitutional amendment initiated by a single actor on the constitutional stage is "unilateral." We do not believe that this is the meaning contemplated by [the reference question], nor is this the sense in which the term has been used in argument before us. Rather, what is claimed by a right to secede "unilaterally" is the right to effectuate secession without prior negotiations with the other provinces and the federal government. At issue is not the legality of the first step but the legality of the final act of purported unilateral secession. The supposed juridical basis for such an act is said to be a clear expression of democratic will in a referendum in the province of Quebec. This claim requires us to examine the possible juridical impact, if any, of such a referendum on the functioning of our Constitution, and on the claimed legality of a unilateral act of secession.

[87] Although the Constitution does not itself address the use of a referendum procedure, and the results of a referendum have no direct role or legal effect in our constitutional scheme, a referendum undoubtedly may provide a democratic method of ascertaining the views of the electorate on important political questions on a particular occasion. The demo-

cratic principle identified above would demand that considerable weight be given to a clear expression by the people of Quebec of their will to secede from Canada, even though a referendum, in itself and without more, has no direct legal effect, and could not in itself bring about unilateral secession. Our political institutions are premised on the democratic principle, and so an expression of the democratic will of the people of a province carries weight, in that it would confer legitimacy on the efforts of the government of Quebec to initiate the Constitution's amendment process in order to secede by constitutional means. In this context, we refer to a "clear" majority as a qualitative evaluation. The referendum result, if it is to be taken as an expression of the democratic will, must be free of ambiguity both in terms of the question asked and in terms of the support it achieves.

[88] The federalism principle, in conjunction with the democratic principle, dictates that the clear repudiation of the existing constitutional order and the clear expression of the desire to pursue secession by the population of a province would give rise to a reciprocal obligation on all parties to Confederation to negotiate constitutional changes to respond to that desire. The amendment of the Constitution begins with a political process undertaken pursuant to the Constitution itself. In Canada, the initiative for constitutional amendment is the responsibility of democratically elected representatives of the participants in Confederation. Those representatives may, of course, take their cue from a referendum, but in legal terms, constitution-making in Canada, as in many countries, is undertaken by the democratically elected representatives of the people. The corollary of a legitimate attempt by one participant in Confederation to seek an amendment to the Constitution is an obligation on all parties to come to the negotiating table. The clear repudiation by the people of Quebec of the existing constitutional order would confer legitimacy on demands for secession, and place an obligation on the other provinces and the federal government to acknowledge and respect that expression of democratic will by entering into negotiations and conducting them in accordance with the underlying constitutional principles already discussed.

[89] What is the content of this obligation to negotiate? At this juncture, we confront the difficult inter-relationship between substantive obligations flowing from the Constitution and questions of judicial competence and restraint in supervising or enforcing those obligations. This is mirrored by the distinction between the legality and the legitimacy of actions taken under the Constitution. We propose to focus first on the substantive obligations flowing from this obligation to negotiate; once the nature of those obligations has been described, it is easier to assess the appropriate means of enforcement of those obligations, and to comment on the distinction between legality and legitimacy.

[90] The conduct of the parties in such negotiations would be governed by the same constitutional principles which give rise to the duty to negotiate: federalism, democracy, constitutionalism and the rule of law, and the protection of minorities. Those principles lead us to reject two absolutist propositions. One of those propositions is that there would be a legal obligation on the other provinces and federal government to accede to the secession of a province, subject only to negotiation of the logistical details of secession. This proposition is attributed either to the supposed implications of the democratic principle of the Constitution, or to the international law principle of self-determination of peoples.

[91] For both theoretical and practical reasons, we cannot accept this view. We hold that Quebec could not purport to invoke a right of self-determination such as to dictate the terms of a proposed secession to the other parties: that would not be a negotiation at all. As well,

it would be naive to expect that the substantive goal of secession could readily be distinguished from the practical details of secession. The devil would be in the details. The democracy principle, as we have emphasized, cannot be invoked to trump the principles of federalism and rule of law, the rights of individuals and minorities, or the operation of democracy in the other provinces or in Canada as a whole. No negotiations could be effective if their ultimate outcome, secession, is cast as an absolute legal entitlement based upon an obligation to give effect to that act of secession in the Constitution. Such a foregone conclusion would actually undermine the obligation to negotiate and render it hollow.

[92] However, we are equally unable to accept the reverse proposition, that a clear expression of self-determination by the people of Quebec would impose no obligations upon the other provinces or the federal government. The continued existence and operation of the Canadian constitutional order cannot remain indifferent to the clear expression of a clear majority of Quebecers that they no longer wish to remain in Canada. This would amount to the assertion that other constitutionally recognized principles necessarily trump the clearly expressed democratic will of the people of Quebec. Such a proposition fails to give sufficient weight to the underlying constitutional principles that must inform the amendment process, including the principles of democracy and federalism. The rights of other provinces and the federal government cannot deny the right of the government of Quebec to pursue secession, should a clear majority of the people of Quebec choose that goal, so long as in doing so, Quebec respects the rights of others. Negotiations would be necessary to address the interests of the federal government, of Quebec and the other provinces, and other participants, as well as the rights of all Canadians both within and outside Quebec.

[93] Is the rejection of both of these propositions reconcilable? Yes, once it is realized that none of the rights or principles under discussion is absolute to the exclusion of the others. This observation suggests that other parties cannot exercise their rights in such a way as to amount to an absolute denial of Quebec's rights, and similarly, that so long as Quebec exercises its rights while respecting the rights of others, it may propose secession and seek to achieve it through negotiation. The negotiation process precipitated by a decision of a clear majority of the population of Quebec on a clear question to pursue secession would require the reconciliation of various rights and obligations by the representatives of two legitimate majorities, namely, the clear majority of the population of Quebec, and the clear majority of Canada as a whole, whatever that may be. There can be no suggestion that either of these majorities "trumps" the other. A political majority that does not act in accordance with the underlying constitutional principles we have identified puts at risk the legitimacy of the exercise of its rights.

[94] In such circumstances, the conduct of the parties assumes primary constitutional significance. The negotiation process must be conducted with an eye to the constitutional principles we have outlined, which must inform the actions of *all* the participants in the negotiation process.

[95] Refusal of a party to conduct negotiations in a manner consistent with constitutional principles and values would seriously put at risk the legitimacy of that party's assertion of its rights, and perhaps the negotiation process as a whole. Those who quite legitimately insist upon the importance of upholding the rule of law cannot at the same time be oblivious to the need to act in conformity with constitutional principles and values, and so do their

part to contribute to the maintenance and promotion of an environment in which the rule of law may flourish.

[96] No one can predict the course that such negotiations might take. The possibility that they might not lead to an agreement amongst the parties must be recognized. Negotiations following a referendum vote in favour of seeking secession would inevitably address a wide range of issues, many of great import. After 131 years of Confederation, there exists, inevitably, a high level of integration in economic, political and social institutions across Canada. The vision of those who brought about Confederation was to create a unified country, not a loose alliance of autonomous provinces. Accordingly, while there are regional economic interests, which sometimes coincide with provincial boundaries, there are also national interests and enterprises (both public and private) that would face potential dismemberment. There is a national economy and a national debt. Arguments were raised before us regarding boundary issues. There are linguistic and cultural minorities, including aboriginal peoples, unevenly distributed across the country who look to the Constitution of Canada for the protection of their rights. Of course, secession would give rise to many issues of great complexity and difficulty. These would have to be resolved within the overall framework of the rule of law, thereby assuring Canadians resident in Quebec and elsewhere a measure of stability in what would likely be a period of considerable upheaval and uncertainty. Nobody seriously suggests that our national existence, seamless in so many aspects, could be effortlessly separated along what are now the provincial boundaries of Quebec. As the Attorney General of Saskatchewan put it in his oral submission:

> A nation is built when the communities that comprise it make commitments to it, when they forego choices and opportunities on behalf of a nation, ... when the communities that comprise it make compromises, when they offer each other guarantees, when they make transfers and perhaps most pointedly, when they receive from others the benefits of national solidarity. The threads of a thousand acts of accommodation are the fabric of a nation. ...

[97] In the circumstances, negotiations following such a referendum would undoubtedly be difficult. While the negotiators would have to contemplate the possibility of secession, there would be no absolute legal entitlement to it and no assumption that an agreement reconciling all relevant rights and obligations would actually be reached. It is foreseeable that even negotiations carried out in conformity with the underlying constitutional principles could reach an impasse. We need not speculate here as to what would then transpire. Under the Constitution, secession requires that an amendment be negotiated. ...

[100] The role of the Court in this Reference is limited to the identification of the relevant aspects of the Constitution in their broadest sense. We have interpreted the questions as relating to the constitutional framework within which political decisions may ultimately be made. Within that framework, the workings of the political process are complex and can only be resolved by means of political judgments and evaluations. The Court has no supervisory role over the political aspects of constitutional negotiations. Equally, the initial impetus for negotiation, namely a clear majority on a clear question in favour of secession, is subject only to political evaluation, and properly so. A right and a corresponding duty to negotiate secession cannot be built on an alleged expression of democratic will if the expression of democratic will is itself fraught with ambiguities. Only the political actors would have the information and expertise to make the appropriate judgment as to the point

at which, and the circumstances in which, those ambiguities are resolved one way or the other. ...

[102] The non-justiciability of political issues that lack a legal component does not deprive the surrounding constitutional framework of its binding status, nor does this mean that constitutional obligations could be breached without incurring serious legal repercussions. Where there are legal rights there are remedies, but ... the appropriate recourse in some circumstances lies through the workings of the political process rather than the courts.

[103] To the extent that a breach of the constitutional duty to negotiate in accordance with the principles described above undermines the legitimacy of a party's actions, it may have important ramifications at the international level. Thus, a failure of the duty to undertake negotiations and pursue them according to constitutional principles may undermine that government's claim to legitimacy which is generally a precondition for recognition by the international community. Conversely, violations of those principles by the federal or other provincial governments responding to the request for secession may undermine their legitimacy. Thus, a Quebec that had negotiated in conformity with constitutional principles and values in the face of unreasonable intransigence on the part of other participants at the federal or provincial level would be more likely to be recognized than a Quebec which did not itself act according to constitutional principles in the negotiation process. Both the legality of the acts of the parties to the negotiation process under Canadian law, and the perceived legitimacy of such action, would be important considerations in the recognition process. In this way, the adherence of the parties to the obligation to negotiate would be evaluated in an indirect manner on the international plane.

[104] Accordingly, the secession of Quebec from Canada cannot be accomplished by the National Assembly, the legislature or government of Quebec unilaterally, that is to say, without principled negotiations, and be considered a lawful act. Any attempt to effect the secession of a province from Canada must be undertaken pursuant to the Constitution of Canada, or else violate the Canadian legal order. However, the continued existence and operation of the Canadian constitutional order cannot remain unaffected by the unambiguous expression of a clear majority of Quebecers that they no longer wish to remain in Canada. The primary means by which that expression is given effect is the constitutional duty to negotiate in accordance with the constitutional principles that we have described herein. In the event secession negotiations are initiated, our Constitution, no less than our history, would call on the participants to work to reconcile the rights, obligations and legitimate aspirations of all Canadians within a framework that emphasizes constitutional responsibilities as much as it does constitutional rights. ...

Summary of Conclusions

[149] The Reference requires us to consider whether Quebec has a right to *unilateral* secession. Those who support the existence of such a right found their case primarily on the principle of democracy. Democracy, however, means more than simple majority rule. As reflected in our constitutional jurisprudence, democracy exists in the larger context of other constitutional values such as those already mentioned. In the 131 years since Confederation, the people of the provinces and territories have created close ties of interdependence (eco-

nomically, socially, politically and culturally) based on shared values that include federalism, democracy, constitutionalism and the rule of law, and respect for minorities. A democratic decision of Quebecers in favour of secession would put those relationships at risk. The Constitution vouchsafes order and stability, and accordingly secession of a province "under the Constitution" could not be achieved unilaterally, that is, without principled negotiation with other participants in Confederation within the existing constitutional framework.

[150] The Constitution is not a straitjacket. Even a brief review of our constitutional history demonstrates periods of momentous and dramatic change. Our democratic institutions necessarily accommodate a continuous process of discussion and evolution, which is reflected in the constitutional right of each participant in the federation to initiate constitutional change. This right implies a reciprocal duty on the other participants to engage in discussions to address any legitimate initiative to change the constitutional order. While it is true that some attempts at constitutional amendment in recent years have faltered, a clear majority vote in Quebec on a clear question in favour of secession would confer democratic legitimacy on the secession initiative which all of the other participants in Confederation would have to recognize.

[151] Quebec could not, despite a clear referendum result, purport to invoke a right of self-determination to dictate the terms of a proposed secession to the other parties to the federation. The democratic vote, by however strong a majority, would have no legal effect on its own and could not push aside the principles of federalism and the rule of law, the rights of individuals and minorities, or the operation of democracy in the other provinces or in Canada as a whole. Democratic rights under the Constitution cannot be divorced from constitutional obligations. Nor, however, can the reverse proposition be accepted. The continued existence and operation of the Canadian constitutional order could not be indifferent to a clear expression of a clear majority of Quebecers that they no longer wish to remain in Canada. The other provinces and the federal government would have no basis to deny the right of the government of Quebec to pursue secession, should a clear majority of the people of Quebec choose that goal, so long as in doing so, Quebec respects the rights of others. The negotiations that followed such a vote would address the potential act of secession as well as its possible terms should in fact secession proceed. There would be no conclusions predetermined by law on any issue. Negotiations would need to address the interests of the other provinces, the federal government, Quebec and indeed the rights of all Canadians both within and outside Quebec, and specifically the rights of minorities. No one suggests that it would be an easy set of negotiations.

[152] The negotiation process would require the reconciliation of various rights and obligations by negotiation between two legitimate majorities, namely, the majority of the population of Quebec, and that of Canada as a whole. A political majority at either level that does not act in accordance with the underlying constitutional principles we have mentioned puts at risk the legitimacy of its exercise of its rights, and the ultimate acceptance of the result by the international community.

[153] The task of the Court has been to clarify the legal framework within which political decisions are to be taken "under the Constitution," not to usurp the prerogatives of the political forces that operate within that framework. The obligations we have identified are binding obligations under the Constitution of Canada. However, it will be for the political actors to determine what constitutes "a clear majority on a clear question" in the circum-

stances under which a future referendum vote may be taken. Equally, in the event of demonstrated majority support for Quebec secession, the content and process of the negotiations will be for the political actors to settle. The reconciliation of the various legitimate constitutional interests is necessarily committed to the political rather than the judicial realm precisely because that reconciliation can only be achieved through the give and take of political negotiations. To the extent issues addressed in the course of negotiation are political, the courts, appreciating their proper role in the constitutional scheme, would have no supervisory role.

[154] We have also considered whether a positive legal entitlement to secession exists under international law in the factual circumstances contemplated by Question 1, i.e., a clear democratic expression of support on a clear question for Quebec secession. Some of those who supported an affirmative answer to this question did so on the basis of the recognized right to self-determination that belongs to all "peoples." Although much of the Quebec population certainly shares many of the characteristics of a people, it is not necessary to decide the "people" issue because, whatever may be the correct determination of this issue in the context of Quebec, a right to secession only arises under the principle of self-determination of peoples at international law where "a people" is governed as part of a colonial empire; where "a people" is subject to alien subjugation, domination or exploitation; and possibly where "a people" is denied any meaningful exercise of its right to self-determination within the state of which it forms a part. In other circumstances, peoples are expected to achieve self-determination within the framework of their existing state. A state whose government represents the whole of the people or peoples resident within its territory, on a basis of equality and without discrimination, and respects the principles of self-determination in its internal arrangements, is entitled to maintain its territorial integrity under international law and to have that territorial integrity recognized by other states. Quebec does not meet the threshold of a colonial people or an oppressed people, nor can it be suggested that Quebecers have been denied meaningful access to government to pursue their political, economic, cultural and social development. In the circumstances, the National Assembly, the legislature or the government of Quebec do not enjoy a right at international law to effect the secession of Quebec from Canada unilaterally.

[155] Although there is no right, under the Constitution or at international law, to unilateral secession ... this does not rule out the possibility of an unconstitutional declaration of secession leading to a *de facto* secession. The ultimate success of such a secession would be dependent on recognition by the international community, which is likely to consider the legality and legitimacy of secession having regard to, amongst other facts, the conduct of Quebec and Canada, in determining whether to grant or withhold recognition. Such recognition, even if granted, would not, however, provide any retroactive justification for the act of secession, either under the Constitution of Canada or at international law.

50 The Clarity Act

Government of Canada (2000)

EDITORS' INTRODUCTION

The Parliament of Canada adopted Bill C-20 in June 2000. This bill, An Act to give effect to the requirement for clarity as set out in the opinion of the Supreme Court of Canada in the Quebec Secession Reference, *is better known as the* Clarity Act. *This legislation outlined the circumstances in which the Government of Canada could undertake a negotiation with the secession of one province.*

Preamble

WHEREAS the Supreme Court of Canada has confirmed that there is no right, under international law or under the Constitution of Canada, for the National Assembly, legislature or government of Quebec to effect the secession of Quebec from Canada unilaterally;

WHEREAS any proposal relating to the break-up of a democratic state is a matter of the utmost gravity and is of fundamental importance to all of its citizens;

WHEREAS the government of any province of Canada is entitled to consult its population by referendum on any issue and is entitled to formulate the wording of its referendum question;

WHEREAS the Supreme Court of Canada has determined that the result of a referendum on the secession of a province from Canada must be free of ambiguity both in terms of the question asked and in terms of the support it achieves if that result is to be taken as an expression of the democratic will that would give rise to an obligation to enter into negotiations that might lead to secession;

WHEREAS the Supreme Court of Canada has stated that democracy means more than simple majority rule, that a clear majority in favour of secession would be required to create an obligation to negotiate secession, and that a qualitative evaluation is required to determine whether a clear majority in favour of secession exists in the circumstances;

WHEREAS the Supreme Court of Canada has confirmed that, in Canada, the secession of a province, to be lawful, would require an amendment to the Constitution of Canada, that such an amendment would perforce require negotiations in relation to secession involving at least the governments of all of the provinces and the Government of Canada, and that those negotiations would be governed by the principles of federalism, democracy, constitutionalism and the rule of law, and the protection of minorities;

WHEREAS, in light of the finding by the Supreme Court of Canada that it would be for elected representatives to determine what constitutes a clear question and what constitutes a clear majority in a referendum held in a province on secession, the House of Commons,

Source: Government of Canada, Bill C-20. Adopted by Parliament June 29, 2000.

as the only political institution elected to represent all Canadians, has an important role in identifying what constitutes a clear question and a clear majority sufficient for the Government of Canada to enter into negotiations in relation to the secession of a province from Canada;

AND WHEREAS it is incumbent on the Government of Canada not to enter into negotiations that might lead to the secession of a province from Canada, and that could consequently entail the termination of citizenship and other rights that Canadian citizens resident in the province enjoy as full participants in Canada, unless the population of that province has clearly expressed its democratic will that the province secede from Canada;

NOW, THEREFORE, Her Majesty, by and with the advice and consent of the Senate and House of Commons of Canada, enacts as follows:

House of Commons to consider question

1. (1) The House of Commons shall, within thirty days after the government of a province tables in its legislative assembly or otherwise officially releases the question that it intends to submit to its voters in a referendum relating to the proposed secession of the province from Canada, consider the question and, by resolution, set out its determination on whether the question is clear.

Extension of time

(2) Where the thirty days referred to in subsection (1) occur, in whole or in part, during a general election of members to serve in the House of Commons, the thirty days shall be extended by an additional forty days.

Considerations

(3) In considering the clarity of a referendum question, the House of Commons shall consider whether the question would result in a clear expression of the will of the population of a province on whether the province should cease to be part of Canada and become an independent state.

Where no clear expression of will

(4) For the purpose of subsection (3), a clear expression of the will of the population of a province that the province cease to be part of Canada could not result from:

   (*a*) a referendum question that merely focuses on a mandate to negotiate without soliciting a direct expression of the will of the population of that province on whether the province should cease to be part of Canada; or

   (*b*) a referendum question that envisages other possibilities in addition to the secession of the province from Canada, such as economic or political arrangements with Canada, that obscure a direct expression of the will of the population of that province on whether the province should cease to be part of Canada.

Other views to be considered

(5) In considering the clarity of a referendum question, the House of Commons shall take into account the views of all political parties represented in the legislative assembly of

the province whose government is proposing the referendum on secession, any formal statements or resolutions by the government or legislative assembly of any province or territory of Canada, any formal statements or resolutions by the Senate, any formal statements or resolutions by the representatives of the Aboriginal peoples of Canada, especially those in the province whose government is proposing the referendum on secession, and any other views it considers to be relevant.

No negotiations if question not clear

(6) The Government of Canada shall not enter into negotiations on the terms on which a province might cease to be part of Canada if the House of Commons determines, pursuant to this section, that a referendum question is not clear and, for that reason, would not result in a clear expression of the will of the population of that province on whether the province should cease to be part of Canada.

House of Commons to consider whether there is a clear will to secede

2. (1) Where the government of a province, following a referendum relating to the secession of the province from Canada, seeks to enter into negotiations on the terms on which that province might cease to be part of Canada, the House of Commons shall, except where it has determined pursuant to section 1 that a referendum question is not clear, consider and, by resolution, set out its determination on whether, in the circumstances, there has been a clear expression of a will by a clear majority of the population of that province that the province cease to be part of Canada.

Factors for House of Commons to take into account

(2) In considering whether there has been a clear expression of a will by a clear majority of the population of a province that the province cease to be part of Canada, the House of Commons shall take into account:

    (*a*) the size of the majority of valid votes cast in favour of the secessionist option;

    (*b*) the percentage of eligible voters voting in the referendum; and

    (*c*) any other matters or circumstances it considers to be relevant.

Other views to be considered

(3) In considering whether there has been a clear expression of a will by a clear majority of the population of a province that the province cease to be part of Canada, the House of Commons shall take into account the views of all political parties represented in the legislative assembly of the province whose government proposed the referendum on secession, any formal statements or resolutions by the government or legislative assembly of any province or territory of Canada, any formal statements or resolutions by the Senate, any formal statements or resolutions by the representatives of the Aboriginal peoples of Canada, especially those in the province whose government proposed the referendum on secession, and any other views it considers to be relevant.

No negotiations unless will clear

(4) The Government of Canada shall not enter into negotiations on the terms on which a province might cease to be part of Canada unless the House of Commons determines,

pursuant to this section, that there has been a clear expression of a will by a clear majority of the population of that province that the province cease to be part of Canada.

Constitutional amendments

3. (1) It is recognized that there is no right under the Constitution of Canada to effect the secession of a province from Canada unilaterally and that, therefore, an amendment to the Constitution of Canada would be required for any province to secede from Canada, which in turn would require negotiations involving at least the governments of all of the provinces and the Government of Canada.

Limitation

(2) No Minister of the Crown shall propose a constitutional amendment to effect the secession of a province from Canada unless the Government of Canada has addressed, in its negotiations, the terms of secession that are relevant in the circumstances, including the division of assets and liabilities, any changes to the borders of the province, the rights, interests and territorial claims of the Aboriginal peoples of Canada, and the protection of minority rights.

⁵¹ Bill 99

National Assembly of Quebec (2000)

EDITORS' INTRODUCTION

On December 7, 2000, in response to the Clarity Act, *the National Assembly of Quebec adopted Bill 99,* An Act respecting the exercise of the fundamental rights and prerogatives of the Québec people and the Québec State. *This law reiterated the political and judicial principles that constitute the underpinnings of Québécois society and democracy.*

An Act Respecting the Exercise of the Fundamental Rights and Prerogatives of the Québec People and the Québec State

WHEREAS the Québec people, in the majority French-speaking, possesses specific characteristics and a deep-rooted historical continuity in a territory over which it exercises its rights through a modern national state, having a government, a national assembly and impartial and independent courts of justice;

WHEREAS the constitutional foundation of the Québec State has been enriched over the years by the passage of fundamental laws and the creation of democratic institutions specific to Québec;

WHEREAS Québec entered the Canadian federation in 1867;

WHEREAS Québec is firmly committed to respecting human rights and freedoms;

WHEREAS the Abenaki, Algonquin, Attikamek, Cree, Huron, Innu, Malecite, Micmac, Mohawk, Naskapi and Inuit Nations exist within Québec, and whereas the principles associated with that recognition were set out in the resolution adopted by the National Assembly on 20 March 1985, in particular their right to autonomy within Québec;

WHEREAS there exists a Québec English-speaking community that enjoys long-established rights;

WHEREAS Québec recognizes the contribution made by Quebecers of all origins to its development;

WHEREAS the National Assembly is composed of Members elected by universal suffrage by the Québec people and derives its legitimacy from the Québec people in that it is the only legislative body exclusively representing the Québec people;

Source: Excerpted from Government of Quebec, Bill 99. Adopted by the National Assembly of Quebec on December 7, 2000.

WHEREAS it is incumbent upon the National Assembly, as the guardian of the historical and inalienable rights and powers of the Québec people, to defend the Québec people against any attempt to despoil it of those rights or powers or to undermine them;

WHEREAS the National Assembly has never adhered to the Constitution Act, 1982, which was enacted despite its opposition;

WHEREAS Québec is facing a policy of the federal government designed to call into question the legitimacy, integrity and efficient operation of its national democratic institutions, notably by the passage and proclamation of the Act to give effect to the requirement for clarity as set out in the opinion of the Supreme Court of Canada in the Quebec Secession Reference (Statutes of Canada, 2000, chapter 26);

WHEREAS it is necessary to reaffirm the fundamental principle that the Québec people is free to take charge of its own destiny, determine its political status and pursue its economic, social and cultural development;

WHEREAS this principle has applied on several occasions in the past, notably in the referendums held in 1980, 1992 and 1995;

WHEREAS the Supreme Court of Canada rendered an advisory opinion on 20 August 1998, and considering the recognition by the Government of Québec of its political importance;

WHEREAS it is necessary to reaffirm the collective attainments of the Québec people, the responsibilities of the Québec State and the rights and prerogatives of the National Assembly with respect to all matters affecting the future of the Québec people;

THE PARLIAMENT OF QUÉBEC ENACTS AS FOLLOWS:

Chapter I

THE QUÉBEC PEOPLE

1. The right of the Québec people to self-determination is founded in fact and in law. The Québec people is the holder of rights that are universally recognized under the principle of equal rights and self-determination of peoples.

2. The Québec people has the inalienable right to freely decide the political regime and legal status of Québec.

3. The Québec people, acting through its own political institutions, shall determine alone the mode of exercise of its right to choose the political regime and legal status of Québec.

No condition or mode of exercise of that right, in particular the consultation of the Québec people by way of a referendum, shall have effect unless determined in accordance with the first paragraph.

4. When the Québec people is consulted by way of a referendum under the Referendum Act, the winning option is the option that obtains a majority of the valid votes cast, namely fifty percent of the valid votes cast plus one.

Chapter II

THE QUÉBEC NATIONAL STATE

5. The Québec State derives its legitimacy from the will of the people inhabiting its territory.

The will of the people is expressed through the election of Members to the National Assembly by universal suffrage, by secret ballot under the one person, one vote system pursuant to the Election Act, and through referendums held pursuant to the Referendum Act.

Qualification as an elector is governed by the provisions of the Election Act.

6. The Québec State is sovereign in the areas assigned to its jurisdiction within the scope of constitutional laws and conventions.

The Québec State also holds, on behalf of the Québec people, any right established to its advantage pursuant to a constitutional convention or obligation.

It is the duty of the Government to uphold the exercise and defend the integrity of those prerogatives, at all times and in all places, including on the international scene.

7. The Québec State is free to consent to be bound by any treaty, convention or international agreement in matters under its constitutional jurisdiction.

No treaty, convention or agreement in the areas under its jurisdiction may be binding on the Québec State unless the consent of the Québec State to be bound has been formally expressed by the National Assembly or the Government, subject to the applicable legislative provisions.

The Québec State may, in the areas under its jurisdiction, establish and maintain relations with foreign States and international organizations and ensure its representation outside Québec.

8. The French language is the official language of Québec.

The duties and obligations relating to or arising from the status of the French language are established by the Charter of the French language.

The Québec State must promote the quality and influence of the French language. It shall pursue those objectives in a spirit of fairness and open-mindedness, respectful of the long-established rights of Québec's English-speaking community.

Chapter III

THE TERRITORY OF QUÉBEC

9. The territory of Québec and its boundaries cannot be altered except with the consent of the National Assembly.

The Government must ensure that the territorial integrity of Québec is maintained and respected.

10. The Québec State exercises, throughout the territory of Québec and on behalf of the Québec people, all the powers relating to its jurisdiction and to the Québec public domain.

The State may develop and administer the territory of Québec and, more specifically, delegate authority to administer the territory to local or regional mandated entities, as provided by law. The State shall encourage local and regional communities to take responsibility for their development.

Chapter IV

THE ABORIGINAL NATIONS OF QUÉBEC

11. In exercising its constitutional jurisdiction, the Québec State recognizes the existing aboriginal and treaty rights of the aboriginal nations of Québec.

12. The Government undertakes to promote the establishment and maintenance of harmonious relations with the aboriginal nations, and to foster their development and an improvement in their economic, social and cultural conditions.

Chapter V

FINAL PROVISIONS

13. No other parliament or government may reduce the powers, authority, sovereignty or legitimacy of the National Assembly, or impose constraint on the democratic will of the Québec people to determine its own future.

14. The provisions of this Act come into force on the dates to be fixed by the Government.

52 Canada: Love It or Don't Leave It!

Alain Noël (2000)

EDITORS' INTRODUCTION

Alain Noël teaches in the Department of Political Science at the Université de Montréal. He has published extensively on social policy and federalism from a comparative perspective. He was also a member of the Quebec Commission on Fiscal Imbalance. He is a regular contributor to Policy Options, *the magazine of the Institute for Research on Public Policy (IRPP).*

When I was a graduate student in the United States, in the mid-1980s, I first came across an instance of bumper-sticker philosophy that is very well-known but was then new to me. It said "America, love it or leave it!" At the time, I had no more than a bumper-sticker reaction to this exhortation. I felt ill at ease with the idea but did not give it much thought. I was uncomfortable, of course, because the message was aimed to some extent at immigrants and foreigners. More broadly, however, it concerned all Americans because it applied to politics a logic that belongs to the market, to counter the very possibility of democratic deliberation. "Voice," as Albert Hirschman so aptly put it, was denied in the name of an unlikely and necessarily painful possibility of "exit."

It dawned on me as I listened to the debate on clarifying the terms of a future referendum, that, in recent years, Canada has been busy reinventing this bumper-sticker philosophy. Canadianized, the exhortation becomes "Canada, love it or don't leave it!" It may take a few months before you see the sticker on a bumper near you, but it does not take much effort to recognize, here, the dual logic of Plan A and Plan B as it applies to Quebec.

In a remarkable article published in the last issue of *Globe, revue internationale d'études québécoises,* James Tully argues that Canada is not a free multinational society because it does not allow its members to seek changes to the constitutional rules of mutual recognition. The key, for Tully, is not to reach a definitive arrangement that would solve all problems, but rather to create a framework that allows a deliberation about rules and recognition that can never be completed or ended. The issue is not recognition as such, but rather freedom. Quebec, in this perspective, is not free in Canada because constitutional amendments can be adopted without its consent, because it cannot in practice seek constitutional recognition, and because it would be bound, following a referendum, by constitutional rules it has not approved. Native peoples share a similar, perhaps even more difficult, situation. The choices are stark: You take Canada as it is and learn to love it (Plan A) or you accept that you cannot leave it (Plan B).

Source: *Policy Options* (Institute for Research on Public Policy), vol. 21, no. 1 (January–February 2000). Reprinted by permission.

This is not simply a symbolic or abstract constitutional question. As Tully notes, debates about recognition also define power relations in a society. On a series of concrete questions, Canada now marches on as if Quebec did not exist or did not matter. The social union is a case in point.

I have written elsewhere on the Feb. 4, 1999, agreement on the social union and do not wish to dwell on specific aspects of the framework or on its implications for social policy. Three points must be emphasized, however. First, even though the agreement did not produce a constitutional or even a legal document, it was nevertheless a major departure because it brought the federal government and all the provinces except Quebec to accept a new set of intergovernmental rules in social policy. For the first time, the provinces recognized, indeed celebrated, the legitimacy of the federal spending power in social policy. This recognition, which strengthened federal leadership in social policy, was granted in exchange for a weak and limited constraint on the future use of the spending power, and it was accompanied by an affirmation of mobility and equality that tended to displace diversity and federalism as central values of Canadian federalism. Second, this agreement was perfectly in line with the priorities of post-1982 Canada. It further entrenched the majoritarian impulse to define a single, monochrome, Canadian identity, unencumbered by the difficulties of multiplicity and federalism. Third, the Feb. 4 agreement was, once again, obtained without the consent of the Quebec government. As with the constitution, Quebec will be bound by an agreement it did not demand and did not approve. More needs to be said on this last point.

In Saskatoon, in August 1998, the Quebec government joined a modified inter-provincial consensus, to participate fully in the ongoing federal–provincial discussion on the social union. To do so, the government made three important concessions: It left aside unsolved constitutional difficulties to join an ambitious inter-provincial bargaining process; it accepted much of the inter-provincial discourse on the social union; and it recognized implicitly a legitimate role for the federal government in social policy. In exchange, the other provinces agreed to include a strong opting-out formula in their common position.

The importance of Quebec's concessions has been underestimated by commentators, both in Quebec and in English-Canada. When the provinces turned around to accept, just a few days later, a framework that represented even less than their long-held pre-Saskatoon position, most concluded the Quebec government was responsible, because it never intended to reach an agreement. The fact that real concessions had already been made was not recognized. The fact, as well, that the provinces did not even come close to their own demands did not seem important. Is it worth adding that nothing was heard from all those "ordinary Canadians" who clamored, in the recent past, against 11 men bargaining the fate of the country in the secrecy of a closed room?

The domination described by James Tully extends well beyond constitutional politics. In the 1960s, the necessity of acknowledging and taking into account the demands of the Quebec government played a critical role in all federal–provincial negotiations. This imperative does not exist any more. Concessions made by the Quebec government are automatically deemed insincere and irrelevant. Even the views of Quebec's federalist official opposition are not worth a worry. The rules, all rules, can be changed and applied to Quebec without its consent. In fact, it is not even necessary to acknowledge dissent. Quebecers, in any case, have nowhere to go. "Canada, love it or don't leave it!"

This approach is not simply federal or federal–provincial policy. The organization of the Mont-Tremblant conference on federalism demonstrated how respected Canadian scholars could happily contribute to setting up, in Quebec, a meeting so obviously and so intentionally beside the point. I was struck, also, by how enthusiastic, even cheerful, these colleagues and experts of Canadian federalism were to see an American president come to Quebec, and to Canada, to downgrade to a tribal impulse more than a hundred years of collective efforts to build a democratic and pluralist francophone society that could be recognized as distinct and legitimate by other Canadians. President Clinton overlooked what Samuel La Selva has called the moral foundations of Canadian federalism, the always difficult attempt to have "both a common way of life and different ways of life," to see only "the most primitive human failing—the fear of the other," and Canadians, experts in Canadian federalism, approved and applauded.

For Quebec society, and eventually for Canada, this situation is corrosive. Federalists, inside and outside Quebec, are still fighting the fight and they are tempted by the possibility of crushing the opponent, even if it means attacking Quebec society and Quebecers at the same time. In the last issue of *Politique et sociétés*, Maryse Potvin documents convincingly the rise of anti-Quebec racism in Canadian political discourse.

Quebecers and their institutions are routinely denigrated, and it is now good political science to associate the search for recognition of Quebecers and of native peoples to the demands of all conceivable groups down to the "collectivity of socially malcontent anarchist poets" (as does Michael Lusztig in the September 1999 issue of the *Canadian Journal of Political Science*). Quebecers unhappy with the status quo, on the other hand, are tempted by a retreat from politics and from social responsibility, and by the same inclination to denigrate their own society. This dual tendency to reject Quebec society has concrete consequences. "National pride," writes American philosopher Richard Rorty, "is to countries what self-respect is to individuals: a necessary condition for self-improvement ... [J]ust as too little self-respect makes it difficult for a person to display moral courage, so insufficient national pride makes energetic and effective debate about national policy unlikely." Unable to "achieve their country," as Rorty puts it, Quebecers are not likely to engage in "imaginative and productive" political deliberation. As for Canadians, they are not much better off, with a large proportion of the country's population effectively disengaged from policy debates and with only one political party able to govern. Then again, this may be what many Canadians want.

Meanwhile, the world is changing. In the postwar years, the social and political institutions that emerged to define citizenship emphasized formal rights and redistribution. These institutions were not always conceived and produced by governments and were often decentralized or multi-layered. In Canada, for instance, numerous compromises were necessary, between the encompassing objectives of many and the reality of federalism. Still, universal patterns and "national" standards were privileged, often at the expense of diversity, difference and the federal principle. In recent years, changes associated with what German sociologist Ulrich Beck has called the second modernity, and the rise of new, more demanding, expectations have been calling into question the achievements of this period. In different ways, both the left and the right now pay more attention to difference and democracy, to the possibility for citizens to control the production as well as the distribution of social services. The issue, as Tully explains on a different level, is not simply rights and redistribution but also freedom. Obsessed by its unachieved, traditionally modern dream of sameness and universality, Canada is not up to this contemporary challenge. For now, authoritarianism seems to have more appeal than social and political renewal.

Quebecers have few options and limited means. Because much depends on innovations defined from below, by persons and social movements, there are still many possibilities. But the local cannot solve the national. And for this, there is no use counting on Canada. The response belongs to Quebecers alone. Together, they must reaffirm positive projects Quebec can pursue on its own, and work on a collective moral identity that is worth achieving.

Questioning Constitutional Democracy in Canada

François Rocher and Nadia Verrelli (2003)

EDITORS' INTRODUCTION

François Rocher is a professor of political science at the University of Ottawa who specializes in Canadian and Quebec politics, federalism, citizenship and identity politics, and nationalism. He has served as president of the Société québécoise de science politique (2001–2) and co-director of the Canadian Journal of Political Science *(1996–99).*

Nadia Verrelli received her doctorate in political science from Carleton University. She is a research associate at the Institute for Intergovernmental Relations, Queen's University.

Accommodating diversity at a political level implies that the state, first, formally recognizes the diversity and, second and arguably more importantly, secures political avenues for the expression of this diversity. Does the federal government's latest quest to deal with the demands of the Quebec people to have its diversity accommodated both politically and constitutionally embody these two ideals? This is the question we attempt to address in this paper by examining the political significance of the *Bill to Give Effect to the Requirement for Clarity as Set Out in the Opinion of the Supreme Court of Canada in the Secession Reference*, also referred to as the *Clarity Act* or Bill C-20. More specifically, we focus on the degree to which C-20 embodies the redefinition of constitutional democracy that was pronounced in the 1998 *Reference re Secession of Quebec*, or the *Secession Reference*. In its opinion, the Supreme Court conceptualized constitutional democracy as "a complex set of practices in which the irreducible conflicts over the recognition of diversity and the requirements of unity are conciliated over time." Implicit in this re-conceptualization are the principles of freedom and justice—two fundamental principles on which the Canadian political order was founded. Does the *Clarity Act* reflect this re-conceptualization? That is, to what extent does C-20 reinforce the legitimacy of the Canadian political order?

In the first section of this paper, we examine the Supreme Court's opinion in the *Secession Reference*, exploring the theoretical questions raised by the Court. We then analyze the *Clarity Act* and the issues raised by this federal initiative. Both the *Secession Reference* and the federal government's response to it in the form of C-20 are examined in terms of the principles of constitutional democracy. In the last section, we look at the debates the *Secession Reference*

Source: Excerpted from "Questioning Constitutional Democracy in Canada: From the Canadian Supreme Court Reference on Quebec Secession to the Clarity Act" by François Rocher and Nadia Verrelli. In *The Conditions of Diversity in Multinational Democracies*, edited by Alain-G. Gagnon, Montserat Guibernau, and François Rocher. Montréal: Institute for Research on Public Policy, 2003. Notes omitted. Reprinted by permission.

and C-20 precipitated within the media and amongst academics. More specifically, we examine which issues, and what aspects of these issues, were prioritized in Quebec and in the rest of Canada. The *Clarity Act*, part of the federal government's "Plan B" in dealing with the Quebec crisis, was supposed to, first and foremost, clarify the issues regarding the possible secession of Quebec and, second, enable the political accommodation of diversity. It accomplished neither objective; in fact, it further blurred the issues and, in a very real sense, has the potential to silence the democratic will of the Quebec people.

The Concept of Constitutional Democracy

In 1995, the government of Quebec held a referendum offering Quebecers the option of sovereignty while maintaining a partnership with the rest of Canada. The referendum question was the following: "Do you agree that Quebec should become sovereign, after having made a formal offer to Canada for a new economic and political partnership, within the scope of the bill respecting the future of Quebec and of the agreement signed on June 12, 1995?" A narrow majority of 50.6 per cent voted against this option. In September 1996 the federal government, responding to the plethora of criticisms vis-à-vis the strategy it undertook during the referendum campaign, referred three questions to the Supreme Court of Canada regarding the constitutional ability of the province of Quebec to unilaterally secede from Canada: 1) Does the Quebec government, under the Constitution, have the right to secede unilaterally? 2) Under international law, does it have this right? Further, does Quebec have the right to self-determination that will enable it to proceed with a unilateral secession? 3) If there is a conflict between domestic and international law, which of the two takes precedence?

On August 28, 1998, the Supreme Court rendered its opinion. On the first question, that of whether or not Quebec could, under the Canadian Constitution, proceed with a unilateral secession, the Court responded that it could not. On the second question, the Court answered that since Quebec cannot be regarded as "being oppressed" within the Canadian political framework, the government of Quebec does not have the right, under international law, to proceed with a unilateral secession. Since domestic law and internal law do not conflict, there was no need to answer the third question.

Within the Court's detailed opinion, which surpassed simple and straightforward answers, three points, fraught with consequences, must be singled out. First, the Court indicated that the secession project is legitimate if it is supported by the people through a "clear" referendum. According to the judges, "the referendum result, if it is to be taken as an expression of the democratic will, must be free of ambiguity both in terms of the question asked and in terms of the support it achieves." The Court went on to add that the democratic legitimacy of the secessionist project denoted a constitutional obligation to negotiate on the rest of the country insofar as "the continued existence and operation of the Canadian constitutional order cannot remain indifferent to the clear expression of a clear majority of Quebecers that they no longer wish to remain in Canada." These negotiations, which would inevitably be difficult and whose results would obviously be uncertain, should take into account the interests of all the parties concerned (the governments of Canada and of Quebec and the other provinces, and other participants). Further, they should touch upon complex questions, which according to the Court may include economic interests, national debt, rights of linguistic minorities and the rights of Aboriginal peoples. However, the Court did not come to any conclusion concerning the substance of these negotiations. Finally, the Court, not wanting to decide the substantive issues, left the intricacies of the debate in the hands of the political players. In the Court's view, the process should be evaluated by the political actors who "would have the information and expertise to make the appropriate judgment as to the point at which, and circumstances in which, those ambiguities are resolved one way or the other." It is the voters who, in the final analysis, are best able to evaluate the different positions of those who partake in the negotiation process.

Overall, the opinion rendered in the *Secession Reference*, particularly the obligation to negotiate, is based on four fundamental principles: federalism, democracy, constitutionalism and the rule of law, and the protection of minorities; all four are equally important, as no one principle takes precedence over another. According to the Court, these principles must clarify the comprehension of the constitutional text. Although they are not explicitly written in the constitution, "the principles dictate major elements of the architecture of the Constitution itself and are as such its lifeblood."

Underpinning these fundamental principles is the notion of constitutional democracy, which the Court conceptualized in both a procedural and a substantive manner. Referring to the decision in the *OPSEU v. Ontario* case, it defined the concept as "the basic structure of our Constitution, as established by the Constitution Act, 1867, [which] contemplates the existence of certain political institutions, including freely elected legislative bodies at the federal and provincial levels." Representative democracy is therefore stressed. In this view, a political system is contingent upon the principle of majority rule. It is linked to, among other things, the objective of governmental autonomy so that a sovereign people can exert their right of autonomy via the democratic process. It is in these relatively simple and traditional terms that the Court understands the democratic principle: "Historically, this Court has interpreted democracy to mean the process of representative and responsible government and the right of citizens to participate in the political process as voters."

The Court's understanding of the democratic principle, however, surpasses the formal framework of representative and responsible government. It broadened its initial definition to include a less tangible dimension: democracy is also perceived as a process of deliberation, discussion, debate, expression of opinions, compromises and negotiations. In this sense, which is particularly important in the context of the *Secession Reference*, "no one has a monopoly on truth, and our system is predicated on the faith that in the marketplace of ideas, the best solutions to public problems will rise to the top. Inevitably, there will be dissenting voices. A democratic system of government is committed to considering those dissenting voices, and seeking to acknowledge and address those voices in laws by which all in the community must live." It is the integrity of this approach of substantive democracy that gives rise to the obligation to engage in constitutional negotiations in order to take into account the democratic expression of a province seeking a constitutional change.

This definition of constitutional democracy is supplemented by the principles of constitutionalism and the rule of law. The former requires that all government actions conform to the constitution of Canada. The latter, "vouchsafes to the citizens and residents of a country a stable, predictable and ordered society in which to conduct their affairs. It provides a shield for individuals from arbitrary state action." In short, the principle of popular sovereignty alone cannot be invoked to justify changes that are inherently constitutional; secession is one example of such a change. Political representatives must act within the constitutional framework. However, this is not a limitation; changes can be made to the constitution if they are so desired by an enhanced majority.

The Court's conceptualization of constitutional democracy conforms to the tradition that it itself established. Post-Charter court decisions have rested on an interpretation of democracy that emphasizes the primacy of individual rights, free from encroachment by the state. However, these individual freedoms, fundamental to democracy, may be limited in the name of defending underprivileged groups and more particularly in the name of multiculturalism and tolerance values. This dimension underpins the Court's assertion that parliamentary supremacy has been replaced by constitutional supremacy.

In the end, however, democracy, which is expressed through the will of the people (particularly via a referendum) and more generally through the election of representatives, cannot trump the rule of law. Justly, the Court stated that a system of government cannot be based solely on popular sovereignty and must also have democratic legitimacy. However, the interaction between the rule of law and the democratic principle is treated on a hierarchical basis in which the first is privileged. This is hardly surprising when considering the subject matter of the *Reference*, the constitutionality of a *unilateral* secession, which would bring into question the integrity of the state and the viability of the constitution. However, the mandate of the Court is to protect both and by doing this, it ensures its raison d'être. In short, the support of the principle of the rule of law is hardly surprising if one understands that the reasoning of the Court aims at reinforcing the old machinery of which it is one of the significant wheels.

The Supreme Court's views on the principle of constitutional democracy enable us to consider the ways in which the Canadian political system guarantees the full autonomy and the full liberty of its various components. For James Tully:

> The answer is that a multinational society will be free and self-determining just insofar as the constitutional rules or recognition and association are open to challenge and amendment by the members. If they are not opened, they constitute a structure of domination, the members are not self-determining, and the society is un-free. Freedom *versus* domination is thus the emerging focus of politics in multinational societies at the dawn of the new millennium.

According to Tully, the *Reference*, which stresses that the members of a constitutional democracy have the right to initiate political and constitutional changes and that the other parties have the constitutional obligation to negotiate these changes, recognizes that the Canadian constitution is not a straitjacket. In other words, Quebec's right of self-determination is entirely recognized. However, political reality requires that the general principles translate into a real capacity for change. The right of self-determination and the obligation to negotiate need to be exercised through institutional mechanisms and, particularly, through the procedures giving them effect. Tully specifies that "if a constitutional democracy does not embody this right and duty in its political and constitutional practices, and so allow struggles for and against recognition to be played freely, it is a closed structure of domination and confined with regard to self-determination."

For Tully, the *Reference* is revolutionary in that it reorients the traditional understanding of constitutional democracy from an "end-state" perspective to an "activity-oriented" one. The articulation of the four fundamental principles identified by the Court would constitute a response to the justification of the sovereignty of Quebec, being that the federal regime is blocked. Further, it would give a new justification for continuing democratic activity permitting the reconciliation of diversity and unity within Canada.

This enthusiastic reading of the *Reference*, however, must be put into perspective in light of the multiple inaccuracies, silences and ambiguities evident in the Court's opinion. After the publication of the *Reference*, commentators and politicians focused mainly on two dimensions of the opinion: one, the requirement for "clarity" imposed by the Court on both the referendum question put to the people and the majority obtained ("a clear majority on a clear question," to reiterate the expression of the Court) and, two, the constitutional obligation to negotiate.

Common sense cannot oppose the requirement of clarity. The Court, however, did not specify what it meant by "clarity" other than to indicate that "the referendum result, if it is to be taken as an expression of the democratic will, must be free of ambiguity both in terms of the question asked and in terms of the support it achieves." Rendering the matter even less precise, the Court stated that it was up to the political actors to judge the clarity of the question and of the majority, and in essence, to judge the legitimacy of both. The reasoning of the Court thus presents two conflicting concepts, clarity on the one hand and confusion or ambiguity on the other. It is not surprising that the Court failed to define what constitutes a clear question or even the conditions to meet or establish this "clarity," as it is impossible to do so. To call into question the notion of "clarity," the cornerstone of the prescriptive dimension of the *Reference*, does not mean that we are in favour of ambiguity, nor are we calling for its elimination.

Ambiguity can be important and, to a certain extent, desirable. Can Erk and Alain-G. Gagnon accurately point out that "in federal systems with deep disagreements over the nature of the political community, there might be no common ground to establish a consensus. Consequently, quests for legalistic precision can only aggravate the conflict. Efforts to clarify legally the federal arrangement are therefore unlikely to ensure the stability of multinational federations." Constitutional ambiguity therefore may be "a way to keep the federation going." The nature of a complex society like Canada is ambiguity; to remove it by demanding clarity is to undermine the Canadian federation.

Our support for both the notions of ambiguity and clarity may seem schizophrenic. Such is not the case. We do not aim to make a case for either; our point is simply that the Court put forth a false dichotomy. Moreover, it implicitly made a political judgment about past referenda and disputed the legitimacy of the past and present strategies of the Quebec government, an opening that the federal government was quick to exploit.

Democracy implies a continuous process of deliberation, dialogue, discussion, and debate. Terms are not defined with unequivocal certainty, as the comprehension of these terms functions in the context in which they are used. Moreover, is "clear" that which is easy to understand or clarify? Is it apparent or obvious? In addition, political resolutions invariably bring forth multiple ramifications when dealing with complex questions. Effort is required not only on the part of the political actors to ensure that their point of view is well understood, but also on the part of citizens to understand what is involved in these proposed resolutions. In this sense, a situation may be simultaneously complex and intelligible, provided that effort is made in that direction. To impose an obligation of clarity is to say that all members of a political community share the same point of view; this is both unrealistic and impossible, not to mention undesirable. Essentially, the Court, by requiring that the political actors determine if the conditions of clarity are respected, granted one party *un droit de regard* over the other (in this circumstance, the rest of Canada over the Quebec approach); one can also argue that a veto over the citizen's interpretation or perception of the resolution was also granted. Seeing that the political debate imposes, by its very nature, continuous discussion, it involves tensions while emanating the sense that the terms used act in everyone's interests; one cannot expect that there exists only one understanding of the words, notions and terms.

This is not to say that the political arena is full of confusion, but as the Court emphasizes "no one has a monopoly on truth, and our system is predicated on the faith that in the marketplace of ideas, the best solutions to public problems will rise to the top." The obligation of clarity seems to contradict this statement.

It can also be argued that this obligation defines democracy in apolitical terms. On the one hand, democracy ought to be considered as a marketplace of open deliberations, where ideas and notions are not necessarily perceived in a uniform manner. Political debates are essentially ambiguous; the meaning of the terms used may be interpreted differently depending on the audience, places, context, and the moment of their use. On the other hand, the imposition of this obligation of clarity, good in and of itself as no one favours confusion or ambiguity, is inspired by a Manichean vision of politics. The political approach essentially involves actors who put forth objectives and orientations that contain some form of ambiguity, thus allowing for several interpretations. The events surrounding the renewed Constitution eloquently show that contradictory interpretations of the government's intentions were made. From 1987 to 1992, the notion of "distinct society," for example, however clear for some, seemed vague to others. Nonetheless, this did not prevent the federal government of the time from holding a referendum on this very complex constitutional proposal in the Charlottetown Accord. It would have been very difficult to meet the obligation of clarity as set out by the Court if the political actors had had to agree on the meaning of the term.

Furthermore, the Court is far from being clear on what it means by a "clear majority." Without being explicit, it called into question the principle universally accepted (by all constitutional democracies) of 50 per cent plus one; this principle ensures that a majority is obtained if the 50 per cent plus one threshold is crossed. The Court indicated that it used "clear majority" in the qualitative sense, without clarifying what it meant by that.

Without a doubt, the most astonishing element of the *Secession Reference* is the obligation to negotiate. All parties concerned must take this seriously. Moreover, they must proceed to negotiate in good faith. However, beyond this general injunction, many elements remain particularly vague. First, the good faith of the political actors is subjected to the recognition of all parties involved. Further, this good faith does not necessarily lead to the realization of an agreement if the interests of both parties are irreducible. One could be tempted to judge good faith according to the accepted compromises; however, it is not always possible to obtain the latter even if the negotiations are being conducted in good faith. In the event that negotiations break down, it would be up to the international community to judge the legitimacy of a unilateral secession insofar as there exists, ultimately, no legal recourse to prevent it.

If, on the other hand, the Government of Quebec succeeds in asking an "acceptable" referendum question and obtaining an "acceptable" majority (judged by the rest of Canada), the question of which formal constitutional amending formula ought to be used to ensure its legal secession must still be answered. Nowhere in the *Reference* is there the question of which rules ought to preside over the negotiations. The Court was satisfied with re-emphasizing that "the negotiation process ... would require the reconciliation of various rights and obligations by the representatives of two legitimate majorities, namely, the clear majority of the population of Quebec, and the clear majority of Canada as a whole, whatever that may be. There can be no suggestion that either of these majorities 'trumps' the other." Beyond this, the Court was silent. Consequently, there is no doubt that the results of the negotiations would be subject to the current constitutional amending formula. Taking into account the nature of the sovereignty issue, the unanimous consent of the provinces and the consent of the federal government would have to be obtained. If, for one reason or another, a province refused to ratify the proposed amendments, we could ask ourselves how a majority—in this case, Canada outside Quebec—could avoid not only having the upper hand but also using that upper hand to the detriment of Quebec's constitutional agenda.

One could think, like the constitutionalist Peter Hogg, that "the vague principles of democracy and federalism, which were relied upon by the Court, hardly seem sufficient to require a federal government to negotiate the dismemberment of the country that it was elected to protect." Furthermore, the multiple shady and inaccurate areas of the Secession *Reference* left a margin of interpretation sufficiently large enough to enable the negation of the very principles the Court identified as the heart of the Canadian constitutional regime. Jacques-Yvan Morin draws upon this point:

> The Supreme Court, with an eye on international law and opinion, has legitimized the *objectives* pursued by a substantial part of the Quebec people, but has failed to set out the *means* by which the principles upon which it has based its arguments can be carried out peaceably and with the greatest chance of mutual success. Can one speak of a "balanced" judgment? For Quebec, there is the satisfaction of being right in the field of principles; for Ottawa, a victory in the decisive elements that are the instruments of *realpolitik*.

In this context, it is not surprising, as Tully points out, that political observers have focused on the second part of the *Reference*, which concentrates on the political dimensions of the document, rather than on the principles that informed the Court's opinion. It *is* surprising that political observers did not underline the contradictions between the broad and generous principles of the first half of the *Reference* in light of its real implications. Instead, the federal government, acting rather quickly, adopted in June 2000 Bill C-20, the *Clarity Act*, in order to give effect to the requirements of clarity as set out in the *Secession Reference*. ...

Conclusion

The problem with the *Clarity Act* and the analysis that followed is our relentless focus on the wording of the question in future referenda. This ignores the root of the problem, that of linguistic duality and the diversity of Canada. As Ryan argued, since the *Secession Reference*, the public has been concerned with two issues, clarity of the question and the meaning of "clear majority"; the *Clarity Act* reinforces these two issues. This narrow focus allows us to miss and, more importantly, ignore (which of course is harmful in itself) the crux of the conflict between Quebec and the rest of Canada. Instead, we should focus on more important questions: Why does a sovereigntist movement exist in Quebec? Why has this movement been so significant over the past quarter-century? What is the best strategy to counter the idea of Quebec sovereignty? Rather than forcing Canadians, especially Quebecers, to choose between federalists or sovereigntists, the federal government, with the rest of the country, ought to engage in the endeavour of combining the two and not kill the possibility of reconciling unity through diversity.

Furthermore, the media, political observers and the federal government have focused on the second part of the *Secession Reference* and have failed to recognize the inherent contradictions of the Court's opinion—the conflict between constitutional democracy and the requirement of clarity. The former entails open and continuous debate, whereas the latter enforces one fixed definition of clarity. In the case of the *Clarity Act*, that one definition is the federal government's. The *Clarity Act*, in limiting what can be asked in a referendum on sovereignty, displaced the decision of defining clarity not only from the people of Quebec, but also from the people of Canada as a whole. Under the act, the federal government alone has the power to define clarity. The Court, by presenting a very formalized definition of constitutional democracy through its demand for clarity, which is in and of itself ambiguous, enabled the subsequent action of the federal government. Democracy implies the existence of many debates, the purpose of which are to convince both the opposing party and the rest of the polis of one's point of view. This is the soul of democracy. By the Court's requiring one notion of clarity and by the federal government's assigning itself as the spokesperson for defining or, better yet, setting the parameters of this notion, debate is ended and democracy, even as the Court defined it, is stifled.

References

Gagnon, A.-G. and C. Erk. "Legitimacy, Effectiveness, and Federalism: On the Benefits of Ambiguity," in *Canadian Federalism: Performance, Effectiveness, and Legitimacy*, ed. Bakvis, H. and G. Skogstad. Don Mills, ON: Oxford University Press, 2002.

Hogg, P. W. "The Duty to Negotiate." *Canada Watch*, Vol. 7, nos. 1–2 (January–February 1999): 1, 33–34.

Lajoie, A. "La primauté du droit et la légitimité démocratique comme enjeux du Renvoi sur la sécession du Québec." *Politique et Sociétés*, Vol. 19, nos. 2–3 (2000): 31–42.

Lajoie, A., R. Robin, S. Grammond, H. Quillinan, L. Rolland, S. Perrault and A. Chitrit. "Les représentations de 'société libre et démocratique' à la Cour Dickson, la rhétorique dans le discours judiciaire canadien." *Osgoode Hall Journal*, Vol. 32, no. 2 (1994): 295–391.

Morin, J.-Y., "A Balanced Judgment?" *Canada Watch*, Vol. 7, nos. 1–2 (January–February 1999): 3–5.

Ryan, Claude. "Consequences of the Quebec Secession Reference: The Clarity Bill and Beyond." *C.D. Howe Institute Commentary*, no. 139, April 2000. http://www.cdhowe.org/pdf/ryan.pdf (accessed June 19, 2001).

Tully, James. *The Unattained Yet Attainable Democracy: Canada and Quebec Face the New Century*. Montréal: Programme d'études sur le Québec de l'Université McGill, 2000.

——. "Introduction," in *Multinational Democracy*, ed. Alain-G. Gagnon and James Tully. Cambridge: Cambridge University Press, 2001.

54 Constitutional Politics: In a New Era Canada Returns to Old Methods

Peter H. Russell (2006)

EDITORS' INTRODUCTION

Peter Russell, Professor Emeritus at the University of Toronto, is one of Canada's most eminent writers and commentators on the Constitution. His books include Constitutional Odyssey: Can Canadians Become a Sovereign People?, *now in its third edition. He is an Officer of the Order of Canada and a Fellow of the Royal Society of Canada.*

Quietly, almost silently, Canada's constitutional politics has entered a new era. The days when the national unity issue and attempts to resolve it dominated political life are behind us, at least for the time being. The last time we Canadians attempted a grand restructuring of our constitution was when a majority of us rejected the Charlottetown Accord in October 1992. After that, for another three years, a pending referendum on Quebec sovereignty kept the national unity issue at the top of our political agenda. Then, by the narrowest of margins, on 30 October 1995, the citizens of Quebec said no to the sovereignty option. Had a few thousand of them voted the other way we would surely have been plunged back into as deep a constitutional crisis as the country has ever known—with a Quebec premier claiming a mandate to unilaterally make Quebec an independent state, and a Canadian prime minister denying Quebec's right to do that (Russell, 2004).

As things turned out, the era of what I refer to as mega-constitutional politics came to an end with a whimper rather than a bang. The federal prime minister did a little bit of constitutional tinkering to honour his eleventh-hour promise in the referendum campaign. The Supreme Court laid down the constitutional rules governing secession, after which the federal parliament and Quebec's National Assembly enacted legislation staking out somewhat conflicting versions of their respective rights and roles in a secession crisis. Fortunately, after all that, the crisis didn't come. The sovereignist government in Quebec first lost its nerve, then, in April 2003, lost the provincial election.

Now some would say—and I fear this might include all too many political scientists—that with a federalist government in power in Quebec and national unity no longer a pressing matter, constitutional politics are behind us. One often hears the view expressed that since the Charlottetown Accord débâcle, Canada has fallen into "a constitutional deep-freeze." The contributors to a symposium convened by the Royal Society of Canada a year

Source: Excerpted from *Continuity and Change in Canadian Politics: Essays in Honour of David E. Smith*, edited by Hans J. Michelmann and Cristine de Clercy. Toronto: University of Toronto Press, 2006. Reprinted by permission.

after the Quebec referendum were almost all of the view that Canada was unlikely to survive without major constitutional change, but that constitutional reform was just about impossible. In the words of Alan Cairns, "constitutional reform is a god that failed" (Cairns, 1977). At one level this view is surely correct. Constitutional reform of the mega-constitutional variety—that is, through popular agreement on a set of formal constitutional amendments on the big issues that divide us—is a god that has failed. But that doesn't mean that constitutional politics and constitutional change are dead. Quite to the contrary, it means we are now in a new era of constitutional politics when a lot is taking place, not through the stormy, crisis-ridden processes of mega-constitutional politics, but through the quieter, incremental and much sunnier ways of organic constitutionalism—the very ways in which our constitutional system evolved through its first century.

It is appropriate to write about Canada's return to this older style of constitutional politics in a contribution to a *festschrift* honouring David Smith. Though David Smith kept company with those of us who became wrapped up in the mega-constitutional game, he never made it the centre of his work. The genius of his contribution to our discipline and our country has been to teach us about the evolution and implications of the institutions and political system we have rather than engaging in efforts to radically transform them. Now that we are getting back to a more modest approach to constitutional change, his work should be more relevant than ever. This can be seen in his recently published book, *The Canadian Senate in Bicameral Perspective* (Smith, 2003). Here, instead of treating Senate reform as cure for national unity ills or a fulfillment of our democratic dreams, he invites us to think carefully about the purpose of a second legislative chamber in our federal parliament. From this perspective, we learn that there is much that could be done through the traditional methods of small "c" constitutional change to enable the Senate to better fulfil its historic purpose. I will return to David's thoughts on doable Senate reform later in this essay.

Burke to Locke and Back Again to Burke

In *Constitutional Odyssey*, I juxtaposed two constitutional styles. One is the older English view that, instead of thinking of the constitution as a single document drawn up and agreed to at a particular point of time and containing all of a society's rules and principles of government, a constitution is the collection of laws, institutions, and political practices that have survived the test of time and are found to serve the society's interests tolerably well. Daniel Elazar referred to countries practicing this type of constitutionalism as organic polities and observed that in such societies "constitution-making and constitutional change come in bits and pieces" (Elazar, 1985: 244). In constitutional systems understood in this organic way, change is incremental and pragmatic, consent is implicit and informal. When one of the "bits and pieces" is not working satisfactorily, there is an effort to fix it. Whether the repair job is satisfactory, only time can tell. The political philosopher par excellence of organic constitutionalism was Edmund Burke. Burke was sceptical about the capacity of individuals through abstract reasoning to discern fundamental political truths. "The individual is foolish, but the species is wise" (Kirk, 1953). For Burke, the social contract that forms the foundation of a society is not between individuals here and now but between generations, each handing on to the next the product of its collective wisdom.

The constitutionalism I contrasted with the Burkean is that based on the political philosophy of John Locke. This is the idea that the constitution is a covenant among a sovereign people on how they are to be governed. The constitution so conceived is indeed the Constitution, with a great big capital "C"—a supreme law representing the enduring will of a single sovereign people containing a complete statement of its fundamental principles and institutions of governance. It is Lockean constitutionalism that underlies the foundational myth of the American Constitution, which is enacted by "We the people" as an expression of their enduring will as to how they are to be governed. The reality of how the American constitution was drawn up and ratified and has evolved over time was considerably different from the Lockean ideal. Nonetheless, in the age of democracy, the ideal of the Constitution, embodying the will of a sovereign people and serving as its highest law, stands as a compelling model for societies making new beginnings after world war, the withdrawal of empire, the overthrow of tyrannies—or, in the Canadian case, responding to a crisis of national unity. In these circumstances, constitution makers are driven to work at fashioning a new Constitution that can win the consent of the people through democratic means.[1]

Canadian constitutionalism certainly did not begin on a Lockean note. At the founding of the Canadian federation and through its first century, Canadian constitutionalism was essentially organic and Burkean. The British North America Act was not regarded as containing a comprehensive statement of the country's constitutional system. Many of the most important rules and principles of government—above all, the key practices of parliamentary government—were part of the country's constitutional inheritance from Great Britain and took the form of informal constitutional conventions. Over the next century, Canada's constitutional system changed and adapted, notably becoming far more thoroughly federal than many of the Founding Fathers intended. The changes occurred incrementally and through a variety of means, including political agreements and practices, legislation establishing new institutions (like the Supreme Court), judicial decisions, and the occasional amendment of the BNA Act. There was plenty of politics in all of this, they were relatively low key and never of crisis proportions.

We began to move towards a different kind of constitutionalism when the country—or at least its leaders—became serious about ending the written Constitution's formal legal tie to the imperial Parliament. Bringing the Constitution home to Canada raised the question of who in Canada should have custody of it—that is, which governments or people should have the power to amend the Constitution? Now if the formal capital "C" Constitution is to be treated as Canada's supreme law, this question comes down to agreeing on nothing less than who or what should be the supreme Canadian law-maker or sovereign. Should it be the Parliament of Canada? Or Parliament plus all or some of the provincial legislatures? Should Quebec, as the homeland of a founding people, be given a special role? Or should it be a simple majority of the Canadian people, or some kind of special majority? There were supporters for all of these answers, each reflecting a fundamentally different vision of what kind of political society Canada is or should become. As Canadians wrestled with this difficult question, some of the participants, beginning with a now secular but very nationalist Quebec, began to insist that it wasn't enough simply to "bring the Constitution home" but while we are at it we should redo the Constitution—in effect we should make a new beginning. Of course, the dualistic vision of Canada which Quebec nationalists wanted to write into a rewritten constitution was very different from other Canadians' vision of the country.

And so for a generation, from the late 1960s to the early 1990s, Canadians tied themselves in knots trying to reach agreement on their constitution.

Increasingly, the endeavour took on a Lockean hue: the Canadian people should be sovereign and the constitution should express their will, with the crisis-laden corollary that if they couldn't agree, their federation might break up. The climax came with the Charlotte-town Accord—a kitchen-sink-full of constitutional reforms designed to placate every possible source of constitutional discontent in the land but rejected for a host of conflicting reasons by a majority of Canadian people in a majority of provinces.

Though Charlottetown had a negative result, it was, as they used to say, quite a learning experience. Canadians learned that if they are a sovereign people they are capable of exercising their sovereignty only in a negative way. They can use their constitutional power to reject but not approve changes in anything fundamental. What is more, Canadians learned that the very effort of trying to reach a popular accord on restructuring fundamental parts of the formal, capital "C" part of their constitutional system would likely deepen their discord. The people of Quebec must surely have learned the same lesson from the 1995 referendum. They were no more able than Canadians to act positively as a sovereign people and reach a broad consensus on that jurisdiction's constitutional future. And so the Lockean constitutional god was dead—both for Canada as a whole and for Quebec. Which brings us back to Burke. ...

Note

1. I have developed this theme more fully in "Can the Canadians Be a Sovereign People?" in *Constitutional Politics in Canada and the United States*, ed. Stephen Newman (Albany: State University of New York, 2004).

Constitutional Change in the 21st Century

Sujit Choudhry (2008)

EDITORS' INTRODUCTION

Sujit Choudhry teaches at the Faculty of Law, University of Toronto, where he holds the Scholl Chair. His research and teaching interests are in constitutional law and theory, and health law and policy. He has served as a constitutional adviser to a broad range of public sector and private sector organizations, and is actively involved in public policy development.

Introduction

The contemporary debate over the federal spending power fills me with both a sense of déjà vu and nostalgia—déjà vu because it has gone on for so long, and nostalgia because of my own involvement in it.

As a country, we have been debating the questions of whether there are justiciable limits on the federal spending power, and whether we should amend the constitution to include such limits, ever since the Privy Council announced the existence of that power *in the Unemployment Insurance Reference*. Indeed, controversies over the federal spending power have been at the heart of the politics of social policy, which in turn have been at the very centre of federal–provincial relations since the rise of the Canadian social union after the Second World War. Throughout, debates about the federal role in social policy have not merely been debates over the design of social programs, or even about the appropriate division of labour between the federal and provincial governments. Rather, the politics of social policy have been a terrain for competing nationalisms. In the post-war period, the construction of the welfare state has been central to a pan-Canadian nationalism, centred on the federal government. Though the origin of modern Quebec nationalism is a complex story, to a considerable extent it was a defensive response to this federally-led nation-building project. Federal social policy activism meant an increase in the importance of federal institutions, especially the federal bureaucracy, which worked in English and in which francophone Quebecers were a small minority.

For over a decade, I have contributed to these debates myself. There are three strands to my work. First, I have devoted considerable attention to the legal framework governing shared-cost programs, in particular the design and enforcement of federal statutes authorizing transfers to the provinces and territories conditioned on compliance with national standards for medicare. In short, I have argued that national standards have rarely been enforced by

Source: Excerpted from *Queen's Law Journal*, vol. 34, no. 1 (Fall 2008). Notes omitted. Reprinted by permission.

the federal government. In addition, I have suggested that they be fundamentally rethought. They should be converted into self-imposed provincial benchmarks, with provincial performance assessed and publicly reported on by an independent third party agency (such as the Health Council of Canada), and with enforcement being left to the provincial political process.

Second, I have turned my mind to the constitutional architecture within which these arrangements have developed. Two constitutional assumptions underlie the development of the social union: the federal government lacks direct jurisdiction over the design and delivery of social programs, and intergovernmental agreements are judicially unenforceable. I have tried to suggest that these should now be reconsidered. In particular, I have argued that the strongest criticism of the federal spending power—the incoherence of granting the federal government fiscal jurisdiction in areas where it lacks regulatory jurisdiction—does not necessarily lead to the conclusion that it should not be able to make conditional transfers to underwrite provincial social programs. Rather, in light of the modern Supreme Court of Canada's expansive conception of federal jurisdiction, an argument could be crafted under the Peace, Order and Good Government (POGG) power for federal jurisdiction over social policy. ...

The point I want to make is that the constitutional politics of social policy are part of this much larger story of constitutional change. From the standpoint of the 20th century, the failure to provide for the welfare state was one of the most conspicuous gaps in our 19th century constitution. To be sure, section 92(7) grants the provinces jurisdiction over hospitals, asylums, charities and "eleemosynary institutions." But these are arguably references to private forms of social provision, and they fall far short of giving clear jurisdiction over the welfare state which, as the Rowell-Sirois Commission accurately observed, was no doubt beyond the contemplation of the framers of the 1867 constitution. Notwithstanding the lack of clear constitutional guidance on jurisdiction over social policy, Canadians have managed, by a variety of means, to change the constitution to create a uniquely Canadian version of the welfare state, and one which was adapted to the reality of federalism.

The courts have played an unusual role in this constitutional story. On the one hand, their place in it has been central. It was the courts that created the constitutional space for the social union, through the Privy Council's pivotal judgment in the *Reference Re The Employment and Social Insurance Act.* While finding that the federal scheme of mandatory, contributory unemployment insurance was unconstitutional, the Privy Council affirmed the constitutionality of conditional federal grants to individuals, institutions and other levels of government—a power that is nowhere referred to in the constitutional text. This judgment raised a number of important questions about the contours of the spending power, such as when a federal condition shades into a colourable intrusion into provincial jurisdiction, questions one would have expected to give rise to subsequent litigation. But although these contours have been the subject of intense political dispute, the spending power has never been brought back to the courts by governments, largely because governments have found that the risks of constitutional litigation would outweigh its potential benefits.

Political institutions have taken the lead in crafting the constitutional instruments that constitute and regulate the social union. Intergovernmental agreements, such as those entered into under the former Canada Assistance Plan, were one way to codify the results of federal–provincial negotiations. The Social Union Framework Agreement, although of questionable practical importance, is also in this tradition. But of far greater importance are the various statutes creating shared cost programs. In their current form, these statutes have a complicated genealogy, deriving from those creating Medicare, creating shared cost programs in the social assistance area and providing for financial transfers. The genealogy is tied not only to health insurance and social assistance, but also to the unconditional transfers that are part of equalization.

So, layered on top of our 19th century political constitution is a 20th century fiscal constitution consisting of constitutional doctrine, intergovernmental agreements, and federal statutes creating shared cost programs and equalization. But the fit between our 19th and 20th century constitutions is far from perfect. At its root, the problem is one of competing constitutional logics. The logic of the 19th century constitution is to align jurisdiction over policy areas with policy instruments. A powerful illustration is provided by the *Labour Conventions* case, which established the important point that jurisdiction over treaty implementation tracks ss. 91 and 92—*i.e.*, the mere fact that a treaty was on the table did not serve to modify the division of powers. Extended to the federal spending power, this reasoning would render unconstitutional *any* condition attached to federal monies in areas of provincial jurisdiction. However, that has not occurred because our 20th century fiscal constitution clearly divorces the federal government's regulatory jurisdiction from its fiscal jurisdiction. Similarly, the 20th century constitution distinguishes between treaty negotiation, which by constitutional practice vests with the federal crown, and treaty implementation, which tracks the division of powers. It is the friction between the 19th and 20th century constitutions, and more fundamentally, the clash between their underlying logics, which more than anything else has generated over five decades of conflict over the federal spending power.

The 21st Century

Viewed in broader historical perspective, the constitutional politics of the spending power are the product of a larger process of constitutional adaptation. This raises the following question. Suppose our constitution comes under pressure to change again. What will the constitutional politics of the spending power look like in the 21st century? To answer this specific question, I want to identify an emerging set of pressures on our broader constitutional arrangements, and then come back to the issue of the spending power. In short, I want to suggest that our constitution is increasingly out of sync with some key demographic facts.

First, although Canada's population grew considerably over the 20th century, that growth is increasingly and disproportionately concentrated in certain provinces. For example, between 1981 and 2006, the country's population grew from 24.3 million to 31.6 million. Of this growth, 82 per cent occurred in Ontario, Alberta and British Columbia, whose share of total population continues to rise. Every other province has seen its relative share decline over the same period. In absolute terms, Saskatchewan experienced no growth, and Newfoundland and Labrador's population actually declined. Moreover, a variety of scenarios project that population growth will continue to be concentrated in Ontario, Alberta and British Columbia, both in absolute and relative terms.

Second, Canada has become an urban nation. In 1901, 37 per cent of Canadians lived in urban regions. By 2006, that figure had risen to 80 per cent. Within urban Canada, population is increasingly concentrated in our largest urban centres, known as Census Metropolitan Areas (CMAs), which are now home to 68 per cent of Canadians. Even more dramatically, 10 million people now live in metropolitan Toronto, Montreal and Vancouver, although those cities account for only 0.1 per cent of Canada's total territory. The rise of urban Canada has been fuelled by two kinds of migration, international and internal. Over time, immigrants have increasingly tended to settle in Toronto, Montréal and Vancouver. Nearly three-quarters of the immigrants who arrived in Canada between 1991 and 2001 settled in those three cities, 43 per cent in Toronto alone. Migration of persons born within Canada has been an equally dramatic trend. This migration has mostly been to CMAs around Toronto, Montreal and Vancouver, and away from rural Canada.

Third, Canada's population is aging. In 1946, its median age was 28. By 2006, it had risen to 39. Even assuming immigration at present or higher levels, the median age is projected to continue to rise to between 45 and 50 by 2056. As a consequence, Canada's dependency ratio —the number of persons not of working age for every 100 of working age—will increase rapidly. In 2005, this was 44. In 2031, it is projected to be as high as 61. Moreover, the aging of Canada's population intersects with the other two demographic trends mentioned above. The youngest parts of Canada will overlap considerably with those where population is increasingly concentrated: urban Canada, Ontario and Alberta. Rural Canada and the Maritime provinces are, and will remain, the oldest. The fact that persons between 15 and 29 are the most likely to migrate from rural to urban areas has played a key role in the aging of rural Canada.

A new issue for constitutional politics in the 21st century is how our institutions will respond to these profound demographic changes. At the most fundamental level, the question is this: will votes, political power and public expenditure follow people as they make choices about where to work and live, and in the process, fundamentally alter the geographic distribution of Canada's population? This basic question is already forcing itself onto the constitutional agenda, and will continue to play out in three interrelated arenas: political representation, economic policy and social policy. ...

Conclusion

Let me conclude with this point. Debates over the conditions to be attached to the exercise of the federal spending power—prior provincial consent, opt-outs with compensation, and so on—are debates of the 20th century. We are now in a new century, and new issues are already upon us. How we talk about the spending power will necessarily change as part of a larger reconfiguration of political and economic power.

PART 5

The Courts and the Charter

Introduction

It is only since adopting a constitutional charter of rights that the study of judges and the courts has been broadly accepted as an important branch of Canadian political science. But the judiciary did play a significant role in Canadian political life well before the arrival of the Charter. Canada's highest court up to 1949 was a British court, the Judicial Committee of the Privy Council. The JCPC's decisions interpreting the federal division of powers in the Canadian Constitution had an important influence on the functioning of the Canadian federation.

The British judges who staffed the Judicial Committee of the Privy Council had their fans and their critics in Canada. Their vigorous protection of provincial rights found strong support in Quebec and among provincial premiers. But politicians and legal scholars in English Canada who favoured a strong central government were critical of the JCPC. Alan Cairns's classic overview of the decisions of the Judicial Committee as the judicial arbiter of Canada's federal system opens Part 5. Cairns's analysis of the JCPC's critics shows that, while the critics shared a common view about the need for a more centralist approach to constitutional interpretation, they lacked a coherent theory of how judges ought to interpret a constitution.

Though opinion in Canada was divided on the constitutional jurisprudence of the Judicial Committee, the debate had the effect of strengthening judicial nationalism in the country and lent support for abolishing appeals to the Judicial Committee and making the Supreme Court of Canada the country's highest court. In 1949, the Supreme Court of Canada became supreme in fact as well as in name.

The addition of the *Canadian Charter of Rights and Freedoms* to Canada's Constitution in 1982 (included as an addendum to this introduction) resulted in a quantum leap in the political prominence of the Supreme Court of Canada. As Peter Russell's essay "The Political Purposes of the Canadian Charter of Rights and Freedoms" points out, this was not one of the intended purposes of the Charter's political sponsors. A constitutional charter of rights and freedoms was Pierre Elliott Trudeau's top priority for constitutional reform. He saw the Charter as a necessary antidote to the centrifugal forces of Quebec nationalism and provincial government demands for more powers. By giving expression to the shared values of Canadians it would help to unify the country. But Russell argues that, while the Charter's capacity for unifying the country was dubious, its tendency to increase judicial power was much more certain. The chapters that follow in this section bear out Russell's prediction.

As the power of courts to make decisions on controversial and politically salient matters became apparent in the Charter era, a lively political debate arose on the democratic legitimacy of this expansion of judicial power. The article by Peter Hogg and A.A. Bushell entitled "The Charter Dialogue Between Courts and Legislatures" was a seminal contribution to this debate. Hogg and Bushell systematically examine the various ways in which the Charter provides for interaction between the courts and legislatures. They argue that the frequency of these interactions amounts to a continuing "dialogue" in which courts rarely have the final word in accommodating legislation to the requirements of the Charter.

In a later selection, Howard Leeson examines the background and operation of the Canadian Charter's most distinctive feature, the notwithstanding clause, which permits legislatures to immunize legislation from Charter-based judicial review. Leeson explains how crucial this clause was in gaining support for the Charter from provincial premiers who were concerned about a constitutional charter empowering the courts to overturn the decisions of elected legislatures. Leeson also shows how infrequently the override clause is used. He suggests that one reason for this is politicians' fear of the political consequences of reversing court decisions on rights and freedoms. If that fear is well-founded it may also mean that judicial decisions upholding Charter rights have generally not gone strongly against public opinion.

Even if there has been a considerable measure of public support for court decisions on the Charter, this has not blunted attacks on the Supreme Court of Canada by academics, journalists and right-of-centre politicians for the Court's allegedly "activist" approach to the Charter. The intensity of these attacks is evident in Chief Justice Beverly McLachlin's discussion of the role of courts, legislatures, and executives in the Charter era. The chief justice emphasizes the democratic process that produced the Charter and rejects the suggestion that in giving force and effect to it the judiciary are usurping power. The chief justice's words would not persuade F.L. Morton and Rainer Knopff, the authors of a much-discussed book, *The Charter Revolution and the Court Party*. "Judges and the Charter Revolution," the excerpted chapter from their book, addresses the many ways in which the Supreme Court has chosen approaches that give greater scope to the Charter's impact. Morton and Knopff view the Supreme Court justices, together with Charter enthusiasts in the academic and legal community and organizations that support Charter litigation, as forming a "court party" which uses the Charter to promote an agenda of social reform.

In contrast to Knopff and Morton, Gregory Hein, the author of the final entry in Part 5, sees use of Charter litigation by marginalized groups who have relatively little influence on the institutions of democratic politics as enhancing democracy. Hein's data show that interest group litigation is by no means the monopoly of groups with little economic or political power. Powerful corporate and economic groups will use Charter litigation if they see it as an effective way of protecting or advancing their interests. But for marginalized groups such as gays and the handicapped, Charter litigation provides exceptional opportunities for ensuring that their voice is heard in the formation of public policy.

Whether one sides with Knopff and Morton or with Hein, students of Canadian government and politics must recognize the validity of the old adage that going to court to vindicate rights, be they provincial rights, Aboriginal rights, or individual rights and freedoms, is "politics by other means."

Further Suggested Reading

Thomas M.J. Bateman, Janet L. Hiebert, Rainer Knopff, and Peter H. Russell, *The Court and the Charter: Leading Cases.* Toronto: Emond Montgomery Publications, 2008.

Government of Canada, *The Constitution Act, 1867.* http://laws.justice.gc.ca/en/const/index.html.

Janet L. Hiebert, *Charter Conflicts: What Is Parliament's Role?* Montreal and Kingston: McGill-Queen's University Press, 2002.

James B. Kelly, *Governing with the Charter: Legislative and Judicial Activism and Framers' Intent.* Vancouver: UBC Press, 2005.

Guy Laforest, "The Internal Exile of Quebecers in the Canada of the Charter." In James B. Kelly and Christopher P. Manfredi, eds., *Contested Constitutionalism: Reflections on the Canadian Charter of Rights and Freedoms.* Vancouver: UBC Press, 2009.

Christopher P. Manfredi, *Judicial Power and the Charter: Canada and the Paradox of Liberal Constitutionalism*, 2nd edition. Toronto: Oxford University Press, 2001.

Peter H. Russell, Rainer Knopff, Thomas M.J. Bateman, and Janet L. Hiebert, *The Court and the Constitution: Leading Cases.* Toronto: Emond Montgomery Publications, 2008.

John Saywell, *The Lawmakers: Judicial Power and the Shaping of Canadian Federalism.* Toronto: University of Toronto Press, 2002.

Richard Sigurdson, "Left- and Right-Wing Charterphobia in Canada: A Critique of the Critics." *International Journal of Canadian Studies* 7-8, Spring-Fall 1993.

James Snell and Frederick Vaughan, *The Supreme Court of Canada: History of the Institution.* Toronto: University of Toronto Press, 1985.

Donald A. Songer, *The Transformation of the Supreme Court of Canada.* Toronto: University of Toronto Press, 2008.

Various contributors, "Charter Dialogue: Ten Years Later." Special issue of *Osgoode Hall Law Journal* 45(1), Spring 2007.

José Woehrling, "The Canadian Charter of Rights and Freedoms and Its Consequences for Political and Democratic Life and the Federal System." In Alain-G. Gagnon, ed., *Contemporary Canadian Federalism: Foundations, Traditions, Institutions.* Toronto, University of Toronto Press, 2009.

Canadian Charter of Rights and Freedoms

Part I of the Constitution Act, 1982

Whereas Canada is founded upon principles that recognize the supremacy of God and the rule of law:

Guarantee of Rights and Freedoms

1. The *Canadian Charter of Rights and Freedoms* guarantees the rights and freedoms set out in it subject only to such reasonable limits prescribed by law as can be demonstrably justified in a free and democratic society.

Fundamental Freedoms

2. Everyone has the following fundamental freedoms:

(*a*) freedom of conscience and religion;

(*b*) freedom of thought, belief, opinion and expression, including freedom of the press and other media of communication;

(*c*) freedom of peaceful assembly; and

(*d*) freedom of association.

Democratic Rights

3. Every citizen of Canada has the right to vote in an election of members of the House of Commons or of a legislative assembly and to be qualified for membership therein.

4. (1) No House of Commons and no legislative assembly shall continue for longer than five years from the date fixed for the return of the writs of a general election of its members.

(2) In time of real or apprehended war, invasion or insurrection, a House of Commons may be continued by Parliament and a legislative assembly may be continued by the legislature beyond five years if such continuation is not opposed by the votes of more than one-third of the members of the House of Commons or the legislative assembly, as the case may be.

5. There shall be a sitting of Parliament and of each legislature at least once every twelve months.

Mobility Rights

6. (1) Every citizen of Canada has the right to enter, remain in and leave Canada.

(2) Every citizen of Canada and every person who has the status of a permanent resident of Canada has the right

(*a*) to move to and take up residence in any province; and

(*b*) to pursue the gaining of a livelihood in any province.

(3) The rights specified in subsection (2) are subject to

(*a*) any laws or practices of general application in force in a province other than those that discriminate among persons primarily on the basis of province of present or previous residence; and

(*b*) any laws providing for reasonable residency requirements as a qualification for the receipt of publicly provided social services.

(4) Subsections (2) and (3) do not preclude any law, program or activity that has as its object the amelioration in a province of conditions of individuals in that province who are socially or economically disadvantaged if the rate of employment in that province is below the rate of employment in Canada.

Legal Rights

7. Everyone has the right to life, liberty and security of the person and the right not to be deprived thereof except in accordance with the principles of fundamental justice.

8. Everyone has the right to be secure against unreasonable search or seizure.

9. Everyone has the right not to be arbitrarily detained or imprisoned.

10. Everyone has the right on arrest or detention

(*a*) to be informed promptly of the reasons therefor;

(*b*) to retain and instruct counsel without delay and to be informed of that right; and

(*c*) to have the validity of the detention determined by way of *habeas corpus* and to be released if the detention is not lawful.

11. Any person charged with an offence has the right

(*a*) to be informed without unreasonable delay of the specific offence;

(*b*) to be tried within a reasonable time;

(*c*) not to be compelled to be a witness in proceedings against that person in respect of the offence;

(*d*) to be presumed innocent until proven guilty according to law in a fair and public hearing by an independent and impartial tribunal;

(*e*) not to be denied reasonable bail without just cause;

(*f*) except in the case of an offence under military law tried before a military tribunal, to the benefit of trial by jury where the maximum punishment for the offence is imprisonment for five years or a more severe punishment;

(*g*) not to be found guilty on account of any act or omission unless, at the time of the act or omission, it constituted an offence under Canadian or international law or was criminal according to the general principles of law recognized by the community of nations;

(*h*) if finally acquitted of the offence, not to be tried for it again and, if finally found guilty and punished for the offence, not to be tried or punished for it again; and

(*i*) if found guilty of the offence and if the punishment for the offence has been varied between the time of commission and the time of sentencing, to the benefit of the lesser punishment.

12. Everyone has the right not to be subjected to any cruel and unusual treatment or punishment.

13. A witness who testifies in any proceedings has the right not to have any incriminating evidence so given used to incriminate that witness in any other proceedings, except in a prosecution for perjury or for the giving of contradictory evidence.

14. A party or witness in any proceedings who does not understand or speak the language in which the proceedings are conducted or who is deaf has the right to the assistance of an interpreter.

Equality Rights

15. (1) Every individual is equal before and under the law and has the right to the equal protection and equal benefit of the law without discrimination and, in particular, without discrimination based on race, national or ethnic origin, colour, religion, sex, age or mental or physical disability.

(2) Subsection (1) does not preclude any law, program or activity that has as its object the amelioration of conditions of disadvantaged individuals or groups including those that are disadvantaged because of race, national or ethnic origin, colour, religion, sex, age or mental or physical disability.

Official Languages of Canada

16. (1) English and French are the official languages of Canada and have equality of status and equal rights and privileges as to their use in all institutions of the Parliament and government of Canada.

(2) English and French are the official languages of New Brunswick and have equality of status and equal rights and privileges as to their use in all institutions of the legislature and government of New Brunswick.

(3) Nothing in this Charter limits the authority of Parliament or a legislature to advance the equality of status or use of English and French.

16.1. (1) The English linguistic community and the French linguistic community in New Brunswick have equality of status and equal rights and privileges, including the right to distinct educational institutions and such distinct cultural institutions as are necessary for the preservation and promotion of those communities.

(2) The role of the legislature and government of New Brunswick to preserve and promote the status, rights and privileges referred to in subsection (1) is affirmed.

17. (1) Everyone has the right to use English or French in any debates and other proceedings of Parliament.

(2) Everyone has the right to use English or French in any debates and other proceedings of the legislature of New Brunswick.

18. (1) The statutes, records and journals of Parliament shall be printed and published in English and French and both language versions are equally authoritative.

(2) The statutes, records and journals of the legislature of New Brunswick shall be printed and published in English and French and both language versions are equally authoritative.

19. (1) Either English or French may be used by any person in, or in any pleading in or process issuing from, any court established by Parliament.

(2) Either English or French may be used by any person in, or in any pleading in or process issuing from, any court of New Brunswick.

20. (1) Any member of the public in Canada has the right to communicate with, and to receive available services from, any head or central office of an institution of the Parliament or government of Canada in English or French, and has the same right with respect to any other office of any such institution where

(*a*) there is a significant demand for communications with and services from that office in such language; or

(*b*) due to the nature of the office, it is reasonable that communications with and services from that office be available in both English and French.

(2) Any member of the public in New Brunswick has the right to communicate with, and to receive available services from, any office of an institution of the legislature or government of New Brunswick in English or French.

21. Nothing in sections 16 to 20 abrogates or derogates from any right, privilege or obligation with respect to the English and French languages, or either of them, that exists or is continued by virtue of any other provision of the Constitution of Canada.

22. Nothing in sections 16 to 20 abrogates or derogates from any legal or customary right or privilege acquired or enjoyed either before or after the coming into force of this Charter with respect to any language that is not English or French.

Minority Language Educational Rights

23. (1) Citizens of Canada

(*a*) whose first language learned and still understood is that of the English or French linguistic minority population of the province in which they reside, or

(*b*) who have received their primary school instruction in Canada in English or French and reside in a province where the language in which they received that instruction is the language of the English or French linguistic minority population of the province,

have the right to have their children receive primary and secondary school instruction in that language in that province.

(2) Citizens of Canada of whom any child has received or is receiving primary or secondary school instruction in English or French in Canada, have the right to have all their children receive primary and secondary school instruction in the same language.

(3) The right of citizens of Canada under subsections (1) and (2) to have their children receive primary and secondary school instruction in the language of the English or French linguistic minority population of a province

(*a*) applies wherever in the province the number of children of citizens who have such a right is sufficient to warrant the provision to them out of public funds of minority language instruction; and

(*b*) includes, where the number of those children so warrants, the right to have them receive that instruction in minority language educational facilities provided out of public funds.

Enforcement

24. (1) Anyone whose rights or freedoms, as guaranteed by this Charter, have been infringed or denied may apply to a court of competent jurisdiction to obtain such remedy as the court considers appropriate and just in the circumstances.

(2) Where, in proceedings under subsection (1), a court concludes that evidence was obtained in a manner that infringed or denied any rights or freedoms guaranteed by this Charter, the evidence shall be excluded if it is established that, having regard to all the circumstances, the admission of it in the proceedings would bring the administration of justice into disrepute.

General

25 . The guarantee in this Charter of certain rights and freedoms shall not be construed so as to abrogate or derogate from any aboriginal, treaty or other rights or freedoms that pertain to the aboriginal peoples of Canada including

(*a*) any rights or freedoms that have been recognized by the Royal Proclamation of October 7, 1763; and

(*b*) any rights or freedoms that now exist by way of land claims agreements or may be so acquired.

26. The guarantee in this Charter of certain rights and freedoms shall not be construed as denying the existence of any other rights or freedoms that exist in Canada.

27. This Charter shall be interpreted in a manner consistent with the preservation and enhancement of the multicultural heritage of Canadians.

28. Notwithstanding anything in this Charter, the rights and freedoms referred to in it are guaranteed equally to male and female persons.

29. Nothing in this Charter abrogates or derogates from any rights or privileges guaranteed by or under the Constitution of Canada in respect of denominational, separate or dissentient schools.

30. A reference in this Charter to a Province or to the legislative assembly or legislature of a province shall be deemed to include a reference to the Yukon Territory and the Northwest Territories, or to the appropriate legislative authority thereof, as the case may be.

31. Nothing in this Charter extends the legislative powers of any body or authority.

Application of Charter

32. (1) This Charter applies

(*a*) to the Parliament and government of Canada in respect of all matters within the authority of Parliament including all matters relating to the Yukon Territory and Northwest Territories; and

(*b*) to the legislature and government of each province in respect of all matters within the authority of the legislature of each province.

(2) Notwithstanding subsection (1), section 15 shall not have effect until three years after this section comes into force.

33. (1) Parliament or the legislature of a province may expressly declare in an Act of Parliament or of the legislature, as the case may be, that the Act or a provision thereof shall operate notwithstanding a provision included in section 2 or sections 7 to 15 of this Charter.

(2) An Act or a provision of an Act in respect of which a declaration made under this section is in effect shall have such operation as it would have but for the provision of this Charter referred to in the declaration.

(3) A declaration made under subsection (1) shall cease to have effect five years after it comes into force or on such earlier date as may be specified in the declaration.

(4) Parliament or the legislature of a province may re-enact a declaration made under subsection (1).

(5) Subsection (3) applies in respect of a re-enactment made under subsection (4).

Citation

34. This Part may be cited as the *Canadian Charter of Rights and Freedoms.*

56 The Judicial Committee and Its Critics

Alan C. Cairns (1971)

EDITORS' INTRODUCTION

In 1971, Alan Cairns, one of Canada's leading political scientists, wrote this analysis of the work of the Judicial Committee in interpreting the Canadian Constitution. Although Privy Council appeals had been terminated in 1949 and the Supreme Court of Canada was now truly supreme, there remained a good deal of interest in assessing its performance as the judicial umpire of the Canadian federation. Cairns' penetrating analysis of the JCPC's critics both in politics and in law shows that they lacked a clear and coherent understanding of how judges should carry out the responsibilities of constitutional interpretation.

The interpretation of the British North America Act by the Judicial Committee of the Privy Council is one of the most contentious aspects of the constitutional evolution of Canada. As an imperial body the Privy Council was unavoidably embroiled in the struggles between imperialism and nationalism which accompanied the transformation of Empire into Commonwealth. As the final judicial authority for constitutional interpretation its decisions became material for debate in the recurrent Canadian controversy over the future of federalism. The failure of Canadians to agree on a specific formula for constitutional amendment led many critics to place a special responsibility for adjusting the BNA Act on the Privy Council, and then to castigate it for not presiding wisely over the adaptation of Canadian federalism to conditions unforeseen in 1867.

Given the context in which it operated it is not surprising that much of the literature of judicial review, especially since the depression of the thirties, transformed the Privy Council into a scapegoat for a variety of ills which afflicted the Canadian polity. In language ranging from measured criticism to vehement denunciation, from mild disagreement to bitter sarcasm, a host of critics indicated their fundamental disagreement with the Privy Council's handling of its task. Lords Watson and Haldane have been caricatured as bungling intruders who, either through malevolence, stupidity, or inefficiency channelled Canadian development away from the centralized federal system wisely intended by the Fathers.

This article will survey the controversy over the performance of the Privy Council. Several purposes will be served. One purpose, the provision of a more favourable evaluation of the Privy Council's conduct, will emerge in the following discussion. This, however, is a by-product of the main purpose of this article: an assessment of the quality of Canadian jurisprudence

Source: Excerpted from *Canadian Journal of Political Science*, vol. IV, no. 3 (September 1971). Notes omitted. Reprinted by permission.

through an examination of the most significant, continuing constitutional controversy in Canadian history. The performance of the Privy Council raised critical questions concerning the locus, style, and role of a final appeal court. An analysis of the way in which these and related questions were discussed provides important insights into Canadian jurisprudence.

Varieties of Criticism

Criticisms of the Privy Council can be roughly separated into two opposed prescriptions for the judicial role. One camp, called the constitutionalists in this essay, contained those critics who advocated a flexible, pragmatic approach so that judges could help to keep the BNA Act up to date. Another camp, called the fundamentalists, contained those who criticized the courts for not providing a technically correct, logical interpretation of a clearly worded document.

According to the fundamentalists the basic shortcoming of the Privy Council was its elementary misunderstanding of the act. The devotees of this criticism, who combined a stress on the literal meaning of the act with a widespread resort to historical materials surrounding Confederation, had four main stages in their argument. Naturally, not all critics employed the full battery of arguments possible.

1. The initial requirement was the provision of documented proof that the Fathers of Confederation intended to create a highly centralized federal system. This was done by ransacking the statements of the Fathers, particularly John A. Macdonald, and of British officials, for proof of centralist intent. Given the known desire of some Fathers for a "legislative union," or the closest approximation possible in 1867, a plethora of proof was readily assembled.

2. The next logical step was to prove that the centralization intended was clearly embodied in the act. This was done by combing the act for every indication of the exalted role assigned to Ottawa and the paltry municipal role assigned to the provinces. This task required little skill. Even the least adept could assert, with convincing examples, that the division of powers heavily favoured Ottawa. If additional proof seemed necessary the dominance of the central government could also be illustrated by referring to the provisions of the act dealing with the disallowance and reservation of provincial legislation, and with the special position of the lieutenant governor as a federal officer.

   Once concordance was proved between what the Fathers intended and what they achieved in the act the critics could then delve into a vast grab bag of pre-Confederation sources for their arguments. This greatly increased the amount of material at their disposal, and strengthened their claim that a prime reason for Privy Council failure was its unwillingness to use similar materials.

3. The third feature of this fundamentalist approach was a definition of the judicial role which required of judges no more and no less than the technically correct interpretation of the act to bring out the meaning deliberately and clearly embodied in it by the Fathers. Where necessary the judges were to employ the methods of historical research in performing this task. ...

4. Proof that the Fathers had intended and had created a centralized federal system in the terms of the BNA Act, coupled with the transformation of the judge into a historian, provided conclusive evidence of the failure of the Judicial Committee. This was done by contrasting the centralization intended and statutorily enacted with the actual evolution of the Canadian polity towards a more classical decentralized federalism, an evolution to which the courts contributed. Since the judges were explicitly directed to apply the act literally it was obvious that they had bungled their task. As W.P.M. Kennedy phrased it, their "interpretations cannot be supported on any reasonable grounds. They are simply due to inexplicable misreadings of the *terms* of the Act." The same point was made in more polemical fashion by J.T. Thorson in a parliamentary debate on the Privy Council's treatment of the Bennett New Deal legislation:

> ... they have mutilated the constitution. They have changed it from a centralized federalism, with the residue of legislative power in the dominion parliament, to a decentralized federalism with the residue of legislative power in the provinces—contrary to the Quebec resolutions, contrary to the ideas that were in the minds of the fathers of confederation, contrary to the spirit of confederation itself, and contrary to the earlier decisions of the courts. We have Lord Haldane largely to blame for the damage that has been done to our constitution.

In summary, the fundamentalists simply asserted that the Privy Council had done a bad job in failing to follow the clearly laid out understandings of the Fathers embodied in the BNA Act. O'Connor, the author of the most influential criticism of the Privy Council, viewed their decisions as indefensible interpretations of a lucidly worded constitutional document. He felt that the act was a marvellous instrument of government, the literal interpretation of which would have been perfectly consonant with the needs of a changing society. ...

Underlying the specific criticisms of the Privy Council there was the overriding assumption that a powerful central government endowed with broad ranging legislative authority and generous financial resources was an essential requirement of modern conditions. "The complications of modern industry and of modern business," asserted W.P.M. Kennedy in 1932, "will sooner or later demand national treatment and national action in the national legislature." ...

Thus the critics, particularly the constitutionalists, were convinced that both domestic and foreign policy requirements necessitated the dominance of the central government in the federal system. Their opposition to the Privy Council on grounds of policy was backed by a growing Canadian nationalism. Even some of the early supporters of the Privy Council had recognized that in the fullness of time the elimination of appeals was inevitable. Nationalist arguments had been used by Edward Blake when the Supreme Court was established in 1875. They were later to form a staple part of John S. Ewart's long campaign for Canadian independence in the first three decades of this century. To Ewart the appeal was "one of the few remaining badges of colonialism, of subordination, of lack of self-government." A later generation of critics reiterated Ewart's thesis. In 1947 F.R. Scott stated that the continuation of appeals "perpetuates in Canada that refusal to shoulder responsibility, that willingness to let some one else make our important decisions, which is a mark of immaturity and colonialism." The nationalist argument was incorporated in the official justifications of the Liberal government when appeals were finally abolished in 1949. ...

The nationalist attack on the Privy Council was fed by the special pride with which many Canadian writers asserted the superiority of Canadian over American federalism. The centralized variant of federalism established north of the "unguarded frontier," in reaction to the destructive effects of a decentralized federalism which the American civil war allegedly displayed, was for many critics part of the political distinctiveness of Canada which they prized. In these circumstances for a British court to reverse the intentions of the farsighted Fathers was doubly galling. This helps to explain the bitterness with which Canadian writers frequently contrasted the divergent evolutions of the American and Canadian federal systems away from their respective points of origin.

Explanations of the Judicial Committee

Critics of the Privy Council attempted to explain, as well as condemn, the results they deplored. In addition to explanations in terms of incompetence critics offered specific interpretations of the Privy Council's conduct. ... A legal explanation of the Privy Council's conduct has been given recent support by Professor Browne's attempted justification of the claim that the act was in fact properly interpreted in the light of its evident meaning.

Occasionally critics suggested that Privy Council decisions were influenced by political considerations inappropriate to a court. While the nature of these considerations was seldom made clear, the most frequent accusation was that imperial interests were best served by a weak central government. This explanation was consistent with the political bias most frequently attributed to the court, the protection and enhancement of the position of the provinces in Canadian federalism. Proof of this was found in cases favouring the provinces, or restricting federal legislation, and in the provincialist statements which these cases frequently contained. Critics also pointed to the several occasions on which the Privy Council referred to the BNA Act as a compact or a treaty. Further proof could be found in the speeches by Lord Haldane explicitly noting a protective attitude to the provinces, especially by his predecessor Lord Watson. Haldane's candid admissions are of special significance because of the propensity of Canadian critics to single out these two judges for particularly hostile treatment. Haldane stated of Watson:

> ... as the result of a long series of decisions, Lord Watson put clothing upon the bones of the Constitution, and so covered them over with living flesh that the Constitution of Canada took a new form. The provinces were recognized as of equal authority co-ordinate with the Dominion, and a long series of decisions were given by him which solved many problems and produced a new contentment in Canada with the Constitution they had got in 1867. It is difficult to say what the extent of the debt was that Canada owes to Lord Watson ...

Haldane was also explicit that a judge on the Privy Council had "to be a statesman as well as a jurist to fill in the gaps which Parliament has deliberately left in the skeleton constitutions and laws that it has provided for the British colonies." In view of these overt indications of a policy role favouring the provinces there can be no doubt that Watson and Haldane consciously fostered the provinces in Canadian federalism, and by so doing helped to transform the highly centralist structure originally created in 1867.

An alternative policy explanation deserves more extensive commentary. This was to identify the court with more or less subtlety as defenders of free enterprise against government encroachments. Spokesmen for the Canadian left, such as Woodsworth and Coldwell, were convinced that "reactionary interests have sought to shelter and to hide" behind the BNA Act. F.R. Scott asserted that the "large economic interests" who were opposed to regulation sided with the provinces who would be less capable of their effective regulation than would the federal government. The courts, as both Scott and Professor Mallory noted, responded favourably to the protection from control which business sought.

Mallory's description is apt: "The force that starts our interpretative machinery in motion is the reaction of a free economy against regulation ... In short the plea of *ultra vires* has been the defence impartially applied to both legislatures by a system of free enterprise concerned with preventing the government from regulating it in the public interest." ... The tactics of business and labour were pragmatic reflections of self-interest. A necessary consequence of a federal system is that each organized interest will seek to transform the most sympathetic level of government into the main decision-maker in matters which concern it. The evaluation to be put on these tactics, and the responses of the courts to them, however, is another matter. Regardless of the groups which align themselves with different levels of government at different times, it is far from clear that support for provincial authority is necessarily reactionary and support for federal authority necessarily progressive. ...

In brief, collectivism, in Canada as elsewhere, had to be fought out in a variety of arenas, before mass electorates, in parliaments, and in courts. In each arena there were supporters and opponents of the emerging transformation in the role of public authority. The real question is not whether courts were embroiled in the controversy, or whether some judges sided with "reactionary" forces. It would be astonishing if such were not the case.

The important questions are more difficult and/or more precise. Were the courts more or less receptive than other elite groups to collectivism? Where did they stand in the general trend to the welfare, regulatory state? What were the links between judges and courts and the various influential groups that appeared before them? How did the Privy Council compare with other final appeal courts, or with lower Canadian courts, in its response to collectivism? Research on these questions would be extremely informative in pinning down the role of courts in the transition from the night watchman state to the era of big government.

Supporters of the Judicial Committee

Depression criticism, followed in the next decade by the elimination of appeals, had the effect that the period in which the Privy Council was under strongest attack has probably had the greatest effect on contemporary attitudes to it. Some of the most influential academic literature dealing with judicial review comes from that period and its passions. As a consequence the Privy Council has typically received a very bad press in numerous influential writings by historians, political scientists, and lawyers in the past forty years.

In these circumstances, it is salutary to remember that if its critics reviled it, and turned Watson and Haldane into almost stock figures of fun, the Privy Council nevertheless did have a very broad body of support. Many highly qualified and well-informed analysts gave it almost unstinting praise. Indeed, if its critics reviled it too bitterly, its supporters praised it too generously. Often they wrote in fulsome terms, replete with awe and reverence for this most distinguished court.

It was described as "this splendid body of experts," as "one of the most unique tribunals in the world," as a body of judges which "possesses a weight and efficiency as a supreme

Judicial tribunal unequalled in the history of judicial institutions ... a tribunal supremely equipped for the task—equipped for it in unexampled degree." In 1914 Sir Charles Fitzpatrick, the chief justice of Canada, claimed that "amongst lawyers and Judges competent to speak on the subject, there is but one voice, that where constitutional questions are concerned, an appeal to the Judicial Committee must be retained." ...

The defenders and supporters of the Judicial Committee typically intermingled judicial and imperial arguments. The alleged contribution of the board to uniformity of law between Britain and her colonies and dominions straddled both arguments while the general assertion that the court was a link of empire was explicitly imperial. It was also from this vantage point—that of a British citizen across the seas—that appeals were viewed and defended as a birthright, and much sentiment was employed over the right to carry one's appeals to the foot of the throne.

A reading of the eulogies of the Privy Council prior to 1930 makes it clear that its most important source of Canadian support was imperial, and only secondarily judicial. The bulk of its supporters regarded it as an instrument of empire. Rather than viewing its dominant position in the judicial structure as a symbol of Canadian inferiority, they derived pride and dignity from the empire of which it was a part. ...

Sociological Justification of the Judicial Committee

The defence of the Privy Council on grounds of its impartiality and neutrality is, however, difficult to sustain in view of the general provincial bias which ran through their decisions from the 1880s. This was the most consistent basis of criticism which the Judicial Committee encountered. A defence, therefore, must find some support for the general provincialist trend of its decisions.

It is impossible to believe that a few elderly men in London deciding two or three constitutional cases a year precipitated, sustained, and caused the development of Canada in a federalist direction the country would otherwise not have taken. It is evident that on occasion the provinces found an ally in the Privy Council, and that on balance they were aided in their struggles with the federal government. To attribute more than this to the Privy Council strains credulity. Courts are not self-starting institutions. They are called into play by groups and individuals seeking objectives which can be furthered by judicial support. A comprehensive explanation of judicial decisions, therefore, must include the actors who employed the courts for their own purposes.

The most elementary justification of the Privy Council rests on the broad sociological ground that the provincial bias which pervaded so many of its decisions was in fundamental harmony with the regional pluralism of Canada. The successful assertion of this argument requires a rebuttal of the claim of many writers that the Privy Council caused the evolution of Canadian federalism away from the centralization of 1867.

From the vantage point of a century of constitutional evolution the centralist emphasis of the Confederation settlement appears increasingly unrealistic. In 1867 it seemed desirable and necessary to many of the leading Fathers. "The colonial life had been petty and bitter and frictional, and, outside, the civil war seemed to point to the need of binding up, as closely as it was at all possible, the political aspirations of the colonies." Further, it can be argued that what appeared as overcentralization in the light of regional pluralism was necessary to establish the new polity and to allow the central government to undertake those nation-building tasks which constituted the prime reasons for union.

It is, however, far too easily overlooked, because of the idolatry with which the Fathers and their creation are often treated, that in the long run centralization was inappropriate for the regional diversities of a land of vast extent and a large, geographically concentrated, minority culture. The political leaders of Quebec, employing varying strategies, have consistently fought for provincial autonomy. The existence of Quebec alone has been sufficient to prevent Canada from following the centralist route of some other federal systems. In retrospect it is evident that only a peculiar conjuncture of circumstances, many of them to prove ephemeral, allowed the degree of central government dominance temporarily attained in 1867. ...

It would be tedious and unnecessary to provide detailed documentation of the relative appropriateness of the decisions of the Judicial Committee to subsequent centrifugal and centripetal trends in Canadian society. It can be generally said that their decisions were harmonious with those trends. Their great contribution, the injection of a decentralizing impulse into a constitutional structure too centralist for the diversity it had to contain, and the placating of Quebec which was a consequence, was a positive influence in the evolution of Canadian federalism. Had the Privy Council not leaned in that direction, argued P.E. Trudeau, "Quebec separatism might not be a threat today: it might be an accomplished fact." The courts not only responded to provincialism. The discovery and amplification of an emergency power in section 91 may have done an injustice to the intentions of Macdonald for the residuary power, but it did allow Canada to conduct herself virtually as a unitary state in the two world wars in which centralized government authority was both required and supported.

The general congruence of Privy Council decisions with the cyclical trends in Canadian federalism not only provides a qualified sociological defence of the committee but also makes it clear that the accusation of literalism so frequently levelled at its decisions is absurd. Watson and Haldane in particular overtly and deliberately enhanced provincial powers in partial defiance of the BNA Act itself. The Privy Council's solicitous regard for the provinces constituted a defensible response to trends in Canadian society. ...

The Weakness of the Judicial Committee

The Judicial Committee laboured under two fundamental weaknesses, the legal doctrine which ostensibly guided its deliberations, and its isolation from the setting to which those deliberations referred.

The basic overt doctrine of the court was to eschew considerations of policy and to analyse the BNA Act by the standard canons for the technical construction of ordinary statutes. The objection to this approach is manifold. Numerous legal writers have pointed out that the rules of statutory construction are little more than a grab bag of contradictions. It is also questionable whether a constitution should be treated as an ordinary statute, for clearly it is not. In the British political system, with which judges on the Privy Council were most acquainted, it is at least plausible to argue that the doctrine of parliamentary supremacy, and the consequent flexibility of the legislative process, provides some justification for the courts limiting their policy role and assigning to parliament the task of keeping the legislation of the state appropriate to constantly changing circumstances. The BNA Act, however, as a written constitutional document, was not subject to easy formal change by the amending process. Consequently, the premise that the transformation of the act could be left to law-making bodies in Canada, as in the United Kingdom, was invalid. A candid policy role for a final appeal court seems to be imperatively required in such conditions.

Even in the absence of this consideration it is self evident that no technical analysis of an increasingly ancient constitutional document can find answers to questions undreamt of by the Fathers. The Privy Council's basic legal doctrine was not only undesirable, therefore, it was also impossible. In reality, as already indicated, the Privy Council obliquely pursued a policy of protecting the provinces. The clear divergence between the act as written and the act as interpreted makes it impossible to believe that in practice the Privy Council viewed its role in the narrow, technical perspective of ordinary statutory construction. The problem of the court was that it was caught in an inappropriate legal tradition for its task of consti-tutional adjudication. It partially escaped from this dilemma by occasionally giving overt recognition to the need for a more flexible, pragmatic approach, and by covertly masking its actual policy choices behind the obfuscating language and precedents of statutory interpretations.

The covert pursuit of policy meant that the reasoning process in their decisions was often inadequate to sustain the decision reached. This also helps to explain the hypocritical and forced distinguishing of previous cases which was criticized by several authors. Further, the impossibility of overt policy discussion in decisions implied the impossibility of open policy arguments in proceedings before the court. Inevitably, the court experienced severe handi-caps in its role as policy-maker. ...

The second main weakness of the Privy Council was its isolation from the scene to which its judgments applied. Its supporters argued otherwise by equating its distance from Canada with impartiality. Judges on the spot, it was implied, would be governed or influenced by the passions and emotions surrounding the controversy before them. British judges, by contrast, aloof and distant, would not be subject to the bias flowing from intimate acquaintance.

The logic of this frequently espoused position was curious. The same logic, as J.S. Ewart satirically observed, implied the desirability of sending British cases to the Supreme Court at Ottawa, but no such proposals were forthcoming. "Local information and local methods," he continued, "are very frequently essential to the understanding of a dispute. They are not disqualifications for judicial action."

The critics were surely right in their assertions that absence of local prepossessions simply meant relative ignorance, insensitivity, and misunderstanding of the Canadian scene, defi-ciencies which would be absent in Canadian judges. "The British North America Act," Ed-ward Blake had asserted in 1880, "is a skeleton. The true form and proportions, the true spirit of our Constitution, can be made manifest only to the men of the soil. I deny that it can be well expounded by men whose lives have been passed, not merely in another, but in an op-posite sphere of practice ..." The same argument was reiterated by succeeding generations of critics until the final elimination of appeals.

The weakness flowing from isolation was exacerbated by the shifting composition of the committee which deprived its members of those benefits of experience derived from con-stant application to the same task. "The personnel of that Court," stated a critic in 1894, "is as shifting as the Goodwin Sands. At one sitting it may be composed of the ablest judges in the land, and at the next sitting its chief characteristic may be senility and general weakness." This instability of membership contributed to discontinuities in interpretation as membership changed. It also allowed those who sat for long periods of time, as did Watson and Haldane, to acquire disproportionate influence on Privy Council decisions. ...

The single opinion of the court, while it possibly helped to sustain its authority and weaken the position of its critics, had serious negative effects. Jennings pointed out that "the absence of a minority opinion sometimes makes the opinion of the Board look more logical and more obvious than it really is. The case is stated so as to come to the conclusion already reached by the majority in private consultation. It is often only by starting again and deliberately striving to reach the opposite conclusion that we realize that ... there were two ways of looking at it." The absence of dissents hindered the development of a dialogue over the quality of its judgments. Dissents provide a lever for the critic by their indication of a lack of judicial unanimity, and by their provision of specific alternatives to the decisions reached. ...

The Confusion of the Critics

For the better part of a century the performance of the Judicial Committee has been a continuing subject of academic and political controversy in Canada. Even the elementary question of whether its work was basically good or fundamentally bad has elicited contrary opinions. The distribution of favourable and critical attitudes has shifted over time. From the turn of the century until the onset of the depression of the thirties informed opinion was generally favourable. Subsequently, English-Canadian appraisals became overwhelmingly critical. ...

In the period up to and subsequent to the final abolition of appeals in 1949 there was a consistent tendency for opposed evaluations of the Judicial Committee to follow the French-English cleavage in Canada. This divergence of opinion was manifest in French-Canadian support for the Judicial Committee, with opposition on grounds of nationalism and its provincial bias largely found in English Canada. Many English-Canadian writers hoped that the Supreme Court, as a final appeal court, would adopt a liberal, flexible interpretation, eroding at least in part the debilitating influence of *stare decisis*. In practical terms, their pleas for a living tree approach presupposed a larger role for the central government than had developed under the interpretations of the Judicial Committee. In essence, one of the key attitudes of the predominantly English-Canadian abolitionists was to view a newly independent Supreme Court as an agent of centralization. The very reasons and justifications which tumble forth in English-Canadian writings caused insecurity and apprehension in French Canada which feared, simply, that if English-Canadian desires were translated into judicial fact the status and influence of the provinces which had been fostered by British judges would be eroded. The American-style supreme court sought by the constitutionalist critics of the Privy Council was justifiably viewed with apprehension by French-Canadian observers. They assumed, not unfairly, that if such a court heeded the bias of its proponents it would degenerate into an instrument for the enhancement of national authority. These contrary English and French hopes and fears are closely related to the present crisis of legitimacy of the Supreme Court.

An additional significant cleavage in Canadian opinion was between those fundamentalist critics who opposed the Judicial Committee for its failure to provide a technically correct interpretation of a clearly worded document, and the constitutionalists who castigated it for its failure to take a broad, flexible approach to its task.

The fundamentalist approach, already discussed, imposed on the courts the task of faithfully interpreting a document in terms of the meanings deliberately embodied in it by the Fathers of Confederation. This approach was replete with insuperable difficulties. ...

In brief, if the performance of the Privy Council was, as its critics suggested, replete with inconsistencies and insensitivity, the confused outpourings of the critics displayed an incoherence completely inadequate to guide judges in decision-making. To contrast the performance of the Judicial Committee with the performance of its opponents is to ignore the dissimilarity of function between artist and critic. It is however clear that the Judicial Committee was much more sensitive to the federal nature of Canadian society than were the critics. From this perspective at least the policy output of British judges was far more harmonious with the underlying pluralism of Canada than were the confused prescriptive statements of her opponents. For those critics, particularly on the left, who wished to transform society, this qualified defence of the Judicial Committee will lack conviction. However, such critics have an obligation not only to justify their objectives but also the role they advocated for a non-elected court in helping to attain them.

Whether the decline in the problem-solving capacity of governments in the federal system was real or serious enough to support the criticism which the Privy Council encountered involves a range of value judgments and empirical observations of a very complex nature. The purpose of this paper has been only to provide documentation for the minimum statement that a strong case can be made for the Judicial Committee, and to act as a reminder that the basic question was jurisprudential, a realm of discussion in which neither the Privy Council, its critics, nor its supporters proved particularly illuminating.

The Abolition of Appeals and an Inadequate Jurisprudence

It is valid, if somewhat perverse, to argue that the weakness and confusion of Canadian jurisprudence constituted one of the main justifications for ending appeals to the Privy Council. The attainment of judicial autonomy was a prerequisite for a first class Canadian jurisprudence. Throughout most of the period of judicial subordination the weaknesses in Canadian legal education produced a lack of self-confidence and a reluctance to abolish appeals. As long as the final court of appeal was an alien body the jurisprudence which did exist was entangled with the emotional contest of nationalism and imperialism, a mixture which deflected legal criticism into side issues. In these circumstances the victory of nationalism was a necessary preliminary to the development of an indigenous jurisprudence which has gathered momentum in the past two decades.

It is also likely that the quality of judicial performance by Canadian courts was hampered by subordination to the Privy Council. The existence of the Privy Council undermined the credibility of the Supreme Court and inhibited the development of its status and prestige. The Supreme Court could be overruled by a superior, external court. In many cases it was bypassed as litigants appealed directly from a provincial court to the Privy Council. Finally, the doctrine of *stare decisis* bound the Supreme Court to the decisions of its superior, the

Privy Council. The subject status of the Supreme Court and other Canadian courts was further exacerbated by the absence of dissents which reduced the potential for flexibility of lower courts in subsequent cases. In spite of the quality of its performance the dominant position of the Privy Council in the Canadian judicial hierarchy was an anomaly, incompatible with the evolving independence of Canada in other spheres, and fraught with too many damaging consequences for its elimination to be regretted.

The inadequate jurisprudence, the legacy of nearly a century of judicial subordination, which accompanied the attainment of judicial autonomy in 1949, has harmfully affected the Supreme Court in the last two decades. The Supreme Court, the law schools, the legal profession, and the political élites have been unable to devise an acceptable role for the court in Canadian federalism. Shortly after the court attained autonomy the institutional fabric of the Canadian polity, the court included, began to experience serious questioning and challenges to its existence. The Diefenbaker Bill of Rights was succeeded by the Quiet Revolution with its confrontation between rival conceptions of federalism and coexistence. Additional uncertainty has been generated by the proposed Trudeau Charter which, if implemented, will drastically change the significance of the judiciary in our constitutional system. In the unlikely event that a significantly different BNA Act emerges from the present constitutional discussions the court will face the task of imparting meaning to a new constitutional document delineating a division of powers different from the existing division. To these factors, as indications of the shifting world of judicial review, can be added the possibility that the court may be reconstituted with a new appointment procedure, with a specific entrenched status, and perhaps even as a special court confined to constitutional questions.

It would be folly to suggest that the above problems would not exist if Canadian jurisprudence had been more highly developed. Their source largely lies beyond the confines of the legal system. On the other hand, the confused state of Canadian jurisprudence documented in this article adds an additional element of difficulty to their solution.

57 The Political Purposes of the Canadian Charter of Rights and Freedoms

Peter H. Russell (1983)

EDITORS' INTRODUCTION

Peter Russell, a political scientist with a long-standing interest in the judiciary, was invited by the editors of the Canadian Bar Review *(CBR) to write this article on the political purposes of the Charter for a special issue of the CBR on the* Charter of Rights, *published shortly after the Charter came into force. Russell's article aimed at preparing Canadians for the main political consequence of adopting a constitutional bill of rights. Although the Charter's principal political sponsors thought that the Charter's main purpose was to serve as an instrument of national unity, Russell predicted that its main effect would be to increase the role of the judiciary in making decisions on the metes and bounds of Canadians' rights and freedoms.*

Discussion of Canada's new constitutional Charter of Rights and Freedoms should not overlook the broad political purposes which inspired Canadian politicians to propose it and induced so many Canadian citizens to support it. In the long run, it is in terms of these broad political purposes that the Charter should be, and probably will be, judged.

The political purposes of the Charter can be thought of as falling into two general categories. These two kinds of purposes are, as I shall show, closely related, although analytically distinct. The first has to do with national unity and the Charter's capacity to offset, if not reverse, the centrifugal forces which some believe threaten the survival of Canada as a unified country. This national unity function of the Charter is most relevant to explaining why politicians, especially those who led the federal government, pushed so hard for a charter. The second kind of purpose is the conviction that a charter will better protect, indeed will even "guarantee," fundamental rights and freedoms. Belief in this purpose is most relevant to explaining the widespread public support for the Charter. In this article I will examine each of these purposes in turn and the prospects of their being fulfilled by the Charter.

I. National Unity

To understand the national unity rationale of the Charter, it is necessary to recall the context in which the federal government made a charter its number one priority for constitutional reform.

In the mid-1960s right up to the Confederation of Tomorrow Conference organized by the Premier of Ontario, John Robarts, in the fall of 1967, the Liberal Government in Ottawa

Source: *Canadian Bar Review*, vol. 61 (1983). Notes omitted. Reprinted by permission.

was not interested in constitutional reform of any kind. Patriation with an amending formula had been very nearly achieved in 1964. Since then only Quebec had been pushing for constitutional change. But Quebec had drastically raised the stakes. The Lesage Liberals followed by Daniel Johnson's Union Nationale administration insisted that the price of Quebec's support for patriation of the Canadian Constitution would be agreement on substantive constitutional reform giving Quebec more recognition and power as the French Canadian homeland. This demand of Quebec provincial leaders for major constitutional change reflected a wholly new phase in Quebec nationalism. Historically the constitutional position of Quebec leaders had been profoundly conservative. Their prime concern had been to preserve the rights they believed had been acquired for Quebec and French Canada in the constitution of 1867. But now, under the impetus of Quebec's "quiet revolution," the province's leading politicians had become constitutional radicals. So long as these Quebec demands for radical change were the central preoccupation of constitutional debate, it was not in the federal government's interest to encourage the process of constitutional reform. The proposals likely to dominate such a debate, if they went far enough to placate Quebec nationalism, would either go too far in weakening the involvement of the federal government in the life of Quebec or else give Quebec representatives in federal institutions such a privileged place as to alienate opinion in the rest of the country. So the Pearson government at first tried to respond to Quebec through pragmatic adjustments in fiscal and administrative arrangements and took a dim view of Premier Robarts' constitutional initiative.

However, the very success of the Confederation of Tomorrow Conference in raising national expectations about both the necessity and the possibility of responding creatively to Quebec's constitutional discontents seemed to convince the Prime Minister and his Justice Minister, Pierre Trudeau, who was soon to succeed him, that a different strategy was needed. The constitutional issue could no longer be kept on the back burner. But if constitutional reform was to be seriously pursued, it was essential that Quebec's demands be countered by proposals designed to have a unifying effect on Canada. It was at this point that the federal government urged that a charter of rights be at the top of the constitutional reform agenda.

After the Confederation of Tomorrow Conference, Prime Minister Pearson suggested to the provincial governments "that first priority should be given to that part of the Constitution which should deal with the rights of the individual—both his rights as a citizen of a democratic federal state and his rights as a member of the linguistic community in which he has chosen to live." This was the position his government took at the Constitutional Conference in February 1968. Prime Minister Trudeau took exactly the same position. His government's paper prepared for the February 1969 Constitutional Conference repeated the commitment to a charter of rights as the first priority in constitutional change. "To reach agreement on common values," Trudeau argued, was "an essential first step" in any process of constitutional renewal. From this point until the final enactment of the Constitution Act, 1982, giving constitutional expression to fundamental rights including language rights was the Trudeau government's first constitutional priority. ...

The Charter's attractiveness to the leaders of the federal Liberal Party as the centrepiece of their constitutional strategy was decisive in improving the political fortunes of the project of entrenching rights and freedoms in the Canadian constitution. Since World War II there had been a great deal of discussion of the Bill of Rights idea both within and outside Parliament. The prime stimulus of this discussion was international—the concern for human rights arising from the war against fascism and Canada's obligations under the United Nations Declaration of Human Rights. Domestic events also stimulated interest in a Bill of Rights. At the federal level, there was regret concerning the treatment of Japanese Canadians during the war and the denial of traditional legal rights in the investigation of a spy ring following the Gouzenko disclosures in 1946. At the provincial level the persecution of Jehovah's Witnesses by the Duplessis administration in Quebec, the treatment of Doukhabors and other religious minorities in the west and the repression of trade unionism in Newfoundland were major *causes célèbres*. There was also a touch of the national unity theme in the submissions made on a number of occasions to parliamentary committees on the implications of post-war immigration. The addition of such large numbers of new Canadians with no education or experience in liberal democratic values, it was argued, meant that Canada could no longer rely on the British method of protecting civil liberties. For such a heterogeneous population a written code was needed. Liberal leaders were not moved by these arguments for a Canadian Bill of Rights. The C.C.F. was the only national party to commit itself to establishing a Bill of Rights. And it was under a Progressive Conservative government led by John Diefenbaker that a statutory Bill of Rights affecting only the federal level of government was enacted in 1960.

Pierre Trudeau, before he entered politics and joined the Liberal Party, expressed interest in a constitutional Bill of Rights. In 1965, as a legal academic writing a background paper on how to deal with the Quebec agitation for constitutional change, he placed a Bill of Rights in first place on his list of constitutional reform proposals. But the main thrust of his paper was to dissuade Quebecers from relying on constitutional reform to solve their problems of political and social modernization. His constitutional reform proposals were for "some day" in the future. ... In any event, by 1967 that distant day when constitutional reforms should be undertaken had suddenly arrived. Speaking to the Canadian Bar Association as Justice Minister in 1967 Trudeau announced his government's conclusion that a constitutional Bill of Rights proposal was "the best basis on which to begin a dialogue on constitution reform between the federal government and provincial governments," and he emphasized that in taking this approach: "Essentially we will be testing—and, hopefully, establishing—the unity of Canada." ...

Aside from the political and strategic advantages of the Charter, it may also have had some purely intellectual or even aesthetic attractions for Mr. Trudeau and some of his colleagues. Federal government position papers put forward the view that the rational approach to the constitution was to begin with a statement of the fundamental values of the Canadian political community. This notion of constitutional rationality, of the constitution as a logical construct built on an explicit formulation of first principles, may be a manifestation of French rationalism and the civil law tradition with its penchant for deduction from codified principles in contrast with English empiricism and the inductive nature of common law. Even if there is some validity in this kind of ethnic stereotyping, it surely cannot account for the strength of the Trudeau government's political commitment to the Charter.

That commitment proved to be very strong indeed. A version of a constitutional Bill of Rights took pride of place in the Victoria Charter which Mr. Trudeau came so close to negotiating successfully with the provincial Premiers in 1971. Again in 1978 when, in response to the electoral victory of the separatists in Quebec, the federal government embarked on another serious programme of constitutional reform, a constitutional charter, albeit one which at first would not bind the provinces, was given a prominent position. But it was the inclusion of a constitutional Charter of Rights binding on the provinces in the package of constitutional change which Mr. Trudeau threatened to achieve, if necessary, unilaterally without provincial support that demonstrates how deeply he and his government believed in its benefits. At this point, when federal-provincial negotiations on the constitution were at an impasse, it would have been ever so much easier, from a political point of view, for the federal government to have proceeded simply with patriation and an amending formula. The insistence on coupling a constitutional charter with patriation shows how strongly the Trudeau government believed in the nation-building potential of a constitutional charter. They would risk dividing the country in order that it might become more united. This nation-building aspect of the Charter was the central thesis of Mr. Trudeau's final parliamentary speech on the Charter:

> Lest the forces of self-interest tear us apart, we must now define the common thread that binds us together.

Will the Charter fulfill the expectations of its political sponsors in promoting national unity? In the context of the immediate exigencies of Canada's constitutional debate the Charter did provide a useful counterpoise to demands for greater provincial powers. But the national unity benefits of such a manoeuvre were discounted, if not eliminated by Mr. Trudeau's unilateralism and by the failure, in the end, to secure the Quebec government's assent to the constitutional package. The thirst for more provincial power or more effective representation in national institutions evident in Quebec and western Canada has not been quenched by "the people's package." In the long run, the Charter's efficacy in contributing to national unity will depend not on its utility to federal politicians at a particular stage in the constitutional debate but on its real potential for strengthening the Canadian political community.

The most frequently and widely acclaimed unifying effect of a charter is its capacity to serve as a unifying symbol. The symbolic function of a constitutional charter was, for instance, emphasized by the Canadian Bar Association's Committee on the Constitution:

> A clear statement in the Constitution of the fundamental values all Canadians share would, we think, have an important unifying effect. It would inculcate in all citizens, young and old, a consciousness of the importance of civil liberties and an authoritative expression of the particular rights and liberties our society considers fundamental.

Lawyers and politicians seem very confident about the Charter's symbolic impact. And they may be right! Social scientists have stressed the important role that symbols play in shaping political attitudes and beliefs. Murray Edelman, for example, in his classic study of *The Symbolic Uses of Politics* goes so far as to suggest that all political constitutions are "largely irrational, in genesis and in impact." But exactly how the emotional chemistry of laws as political symbols operates, in precisely what kind of circumstances a particular set of symbols (for instance a constitutional charter of rights) will have a particular effect (for instance strengthening national unity), has not been established. ...

There are certain parts of the Charter which are clearly intended to be unifying not only symbolically but also in terms of their real effects on government policy and citizens' rights.

These are the sections dealing with mobility and language rights. The mobility rights in section 6 aim at overcoming the "balkanization" of Canada by giving citizens the right "to take up residence and to pursue a livelihood anywhere in Canada without discrimination based on the previous province of residence." The language clauses, by giving formal constitutional recognition, for the first time, to English and French as Canada's Official Languages, by extending the constitutional right to use these languages to dealings with the executive branch of the federal government and with all branches of government in New Brunswick and, most importantly, by establishing minority language education rights for the English in Quebec and the French outside of Quebec, aim at giving greater reality to the ideal of the whole of Canada being a homeland for French-speaking as well as English-speaking Canadians.

For the Liberal government these sections were the heart of the Charter. Their importance is underlined by the fact that section 33 which permits the federal and provincial legislatures to override sections of the Charter does not apply to these rights. In his speech introducing the Charter to the House of Commons, Mr. Chretien, the Minister of Justice, referred to these rights as "fundamental to what Canada is all about." They express the pan-Canadian nationalism which, at the level of ideology, is the counter to the nationalism of Quebec separatism. Since entering politics in the 1960's Mr. Trudeau had, in a sense, been engaged in a rival programme of nation-building to that of Quebec independentistes. At the centre of this programme was the task of persuading the Québécois that they could best fulfill themselves by enjoying the opportunities flowing from membership in a Canadian community wider than Quebec. It was for this reason that these nationalist provisions of the Charter, especially the language rights, were of such great importance to Mr. Trudeau and his Quebec colleagues. They were also the only part of the whole constitutional package which, by any stretch of the imagination, Mr. Trudeau and his federalist allies could point to as fulfilling the commitment they had made during the Quebec Referendum campaign to "constitutional renewal."

What is the potential of these sections for realizing their nationalist objectives? So far as mobility rights are concerned, section 6 is not likely to make any great inroads on the economic balkanization of Canada. To begin with it deals only with labour mobility and not with other major obstacles to a Canadian common market such as discriminatory tax and government purchasing policies. Moreover, section 6's impact on labour mobility was severely curtailed by the qualification introduced as part of the November Accord between the federal government and nine provinces. This proviso will shield from the Charter the protective employment policies of provinces experiencing above average unemployment. Still, section 6 may turn out to be an important check on provinces like Alberta endeavouring to preserve their relative prosperity by denying provincial services to Canadians from other provinces.

The language rights relate to a more intractable dimension of the national problem—the question of identity. Here, section 23, the language of education clause, makes a more significant contribution than sections 16 to 20 which deal with the language of government. The latter do little more than elevate statutory rights into constitutional rights. Any symbolic gains for national unity that may flow from such a change are largely offset by the persistence of the government of Ontario, the province with the largest Francophone minority, in refusing to give constitutional status to bilingualism in the public life of that province. The language of education section is bound to spark controversy in the short run. In Quebec it collides directly with educational policies emanating from Franco-Quebec nationalism that deny English Canadians who move to Quebec access to the province's English schools. This collision was softened by a last minute concession that makes the rights of new Canadian citizens whose English education was obtained outside of Canada to send their children to Quebec's English schools conditional on the agreement of the Quebec legislature. The rights which section 23 extends to the small francophone minorities in the western provinces will do nothing to reduce alienation in the west where there is little respect for the fundamental nature of French-English dualism in the Canadian experience.

Nevertheless it could turn out that these divisive effects were only short term and that in the longer run were worth risking if the Charter's recognition of bilingualism makes it more likely that Canada will survive as a common homeland for English and French-speaking North Americans. But the rights contained in the Charter, even when added to all that has been done to promote bilingualism outside of the Constitution, may be too little too late to overcome the legacy of political and judicial policies which in the late 1800's and early 1900's gave priority to provincial rights over minority cultural rights and thereby prevented the building of a dualistic society on the new Canadian frontier. I suspect that if Canada overcomes Quebec separatism, it will be not so much because recognition of bilingualism in the "new" Canadian Constitution is decisive in the battle for the hearts and minds of the Québécois but because of the exhaustion of nationalist politics brought on by more compelling economic concerns.

But it is neither through the Charter's nationalist provisions nor its symbolic force that the Charter is likely to have its strongest centripetal effect on the Canadian polity. I think the Charter's nationalizing influence will be felt most through a process scarcely mentioned by its political sponsors—the process of judicial review. It is primarily through judicial decisions interpreting the Charter—applying its general terms to particular laws and government activities—that the Charter will come to play an important part in the on-going political life of Canada.

Now it may seem rather perverse to think of judicial interpretation of the Charter as a unifying process. Judicial decisions based on the Charter will frequently be concerned with sensitive political issues and are therefore bound to be controversial. Consider, for instance, the sharp divisions of opinion within Canadian society on such issues as censoring pornography, school prayers, abortion, police powers, compulsory retirement and affirmative action. Judicial decisions on claims made under the Charter will touch on all of these issues. American experience demonstrates that judicial decisions in these areas are bound to anger the losers as much as they please the winners. Given the political sparks that judicial interpretation of the Charter will set off, why do I ascribe unifying consequences to the process of judicial review?

Judicial decisions on the Charter will be unifying in that the very debates and controversies they produce will be national and on issues that transcend the regional cleavages which are usually a feature of national political controversy in Canada. Court cases on the Charter normally will not pit region against region or the provinces against the "feds." Instead the principal protagonists will be interest groups and aggregations of individuals from all parts of Canada. For instance, litigation dealing with police powers (the first major policy field in which judicial interpretation of the Charter is likely to be of political importance) will find small "c" conservatives aligned against small "l" liberals all across the country. Although the controversy will be intense, it will be waged on a national level in the arena of national politics and on grounds that do not call into question the legitimacy of Canada as a national political community. It is in this sense that the Charter may well turn out to be a nation-building instrument.

There is an even more direct sense in which judicial interpretation of the Charter will be a nationalizing process. In interpreting the Charter, the Supreme Court of Canada, at the top of the judicial structure, will set uniform national standards—often in policy areas which otherwise would be subject to diverse provincial standards. Film censorship, school prayers and discrimination in employment practices are all clear examples. In contrast to the executive and legislative power, the judicial power in Canada is essentially unified. Policy directives flowing from Supreme Court decisions on the Charter are transmitted through a single hierarchy of appeals that binds all the courts in the land, and shapes the rights of all Canadians and the powers of all who govern.

It is true that section 33 by permitting legislatures to override certain sections of the Charter—for five years at a time—modifies judicial supremacy. However, because of the adverse political consequences that a government would usually risk in using this power, I very much doubt that it will be frequently used. In the case of Quebec, where the P.Q Government has already purported to have used the section on a blanket basis, it has been invoked not to protect provincial policies from the impact of judicially established standards but as part of a campaign challenging the legitimacy of changes in the constitution made without the consent of Quebec's provincial government. ...

In selling the Charter, the federal government tended to ignore this dimension of the Charter. Federal representatives were at pains to point out that the Charter involves "no transfer of powers from the provinces to the federal government." These disavowals of any centralizing implications of the Charter are entirely valid providing one interprets "government" narrowly to exclude the judicial branch. However, in this day and age, it is only on the basis of a blind, and most anachronistic view of the judicial process that the policy making role of the judiciary, above all in interpreting the broad language of a constitutional Bill of Rights, could be denied. Once the discretion and choice necessarily involved in interpreting that language is recognized, the centralizing tendencies of judicial review must be acknowledged. As the Supreme Court's capacity to function as a kind of national Senate reviewing the reasonableness of provincial laws and policies becomes evident, the reality of judicial power will overtake the rhetoric of federal politicians. Among other things, this will mean that the federal government's monopoly of the power to appoint judges, not only to the Supreme Court of Canada but to all of the higher provincial courts, will be increasingly questioned. ...

Such a development assumes a widening recognition of the importance of judicial power in determining the actual policy consequences of a constitutional charter. Public awareness of that power is still in the making. The popularity of the Charter was based primarily on a belief that one basic policy would flow automatically from the Charter—the better protection of fundamental rights and freedoms. It is to the analysis of that belief and the likelihood of the Charter's fulfilling it that I now turn.

II. Protecting Rights and Freedoms

"Protecting rights and freedoms" is a deceptively simple idea. Those who accept such a slogan as a fair summary of what a constitutional Bill of Rights is all about could hardly be expected to be anything other than enthusiastic about adding a charter to the Canadian Constitution. As Yvon Pinard, the government's House Leader, echoing so many of his colleagues, put it, "what is wrong with the fundamental freedoms of Canadian citizens being protected forever by the Canadian constitution?" What indeed could possibly be wrong with such a project if that was basically all there was to it? Surely all of us would be mad to reject or even to question a proposal that is guaranteed to protect our individual rights and freedoms forever.

While this simplistic language undoubtedly assisted in winning public support for the Charter, it is not very helpful in understanding the real political consequences of such an instrument. The trouble with this language is that it tends to reify fundamental rights and freedoms, by treating them as things which people either possess in their entirety or not at all. But in our actual civic experience we do not encounter these rights and freedoms in such a zero-sum fashion. We enjoy more or less of them. What we have to settle about these rights and freedoms is not whether or not we will "have" them but what limits it is reasonable to attach to them and how decisions about these limits should be made.

Those parts of the Charter which deal with what might be termed universal rights and freedoms (as opposed to rights and freedoms based on the particular circumstances of Canadian history) are related to core values or ideals of all contemporary liberal democracies: political freedom, religious toleration, due process of law and social equality. In Canada for some time now there has been no serious debate about the *minimum* extent to which each of these values should be realized in the laws and practices of our state. The right to criticize the government and to organize non-violent opposition to it has been basically unquestioned since the middle of the last century. Since the Quebec Act of 1774, it has been accepted that individuals should not suffer civil disabilities because of their religious beliefs nor be forced to subscribe to the tenets of any religion. At least since the advent of legal aid, Canadians charged with a criminal offence have had access to a fair trial. As in other liberal democracies, social equality has been the last of the core values to gain effective recognition. But now there is wide-spread acceptance of the ideal that each person should be treated as an individual on his or her merits and not penalized or denied opportunities by the state because of gender, skin colour, ethnic background or other distinguishing characteristics of birth.

As we move out from the central core of these values, we encounter restrictions and limits on each, and considerable controversy about the right limits. Have we gone far enough in removing restrictions on political speech or should we go further and narrow the civil wrong of defamation when politicians are the targets of criticism, or perhaps eliminate the crime of inciting race hatred? Should the protection of political speech extend to the public exhibition of all kinds of sexual activities? Is it right to limit the freedom of broadcasters in order to nurture our national culture? Should religious freedom be extended to the point where no one should suffer an economic penalty (like closing a business on Sundays) in order to comply with a law originally introduced for religious reasons, or to the point where no one is obliged to obey a law that offends his religious or philosophic beliefs—no matter how eccentric those beliefs? How far back in the pre-trial proceedings of our criminal justice system should we extend the right to counsel? Should it apply (and in the case of indigent persons, be paid for by the state) to all offences however minor—even to infractions of parking by-laws? Should the police be able to use evidence from private premises only when they have obtained it through a judicially authorized search warrant? What about evidence they come upon by chance in effecting an arrest or responding to a citizen's complaint? Should we begin to make amends for inequalities suffered in the past by adopting laws that discriminate against males and Caucasians? Should the premises of private clubs that practice racial dis-crimination receive police protection? Should our courts enforce wills that discriminate on the basis of religion or race or gender? How far should we go in ensuring that all of our public facilities are fully accessible to the physically handicapped?

It is in the way we deal with these questions that the Charter will have its main effect. A constitutional charter guarantees not that there will be no limits to rights and freedoms but that a change will be made in the way our society makes decisions about these limits. At the initial level, decisions on these limits will still be made, for the most part, by the legislature and executive, although where common law remains important—for instance, contempt of court, the law of libel and the law of evidence—even the initial decisions will be judge-made rules of law. A charter introduces a second level of decision making in which decisions made at the first level are subjected to a process of judicial review triggered by litigants who claim that a particular limit is excessive or unreasonable. Not only that, but what is most dramatic about this process when it is based on a constitutional as opposed to a statutory charter—and accounts, of course, for the language of "entrenchment" and "guarantees"—is that the results of this second level of decision-making, especially when they issue from the highest court, are very difficult to change. These judicial decisions can only be altered by the difficult process of constitutional amendment, by a change in judicial outlook (resulting, perhaps, from a change in the composition of the bench) or through the exercise of that unique Can-adian option—the legislative override power.

Considered from this point of view, the legislative override is not as contradictory a fea-ture of the new Canadian Charter as some of its detractors have claimed. Section 33 has been denounced as incompatible with the Charter's basic purpose:

> The whole object of a charter is to say, you never opt out, they're inalienable rights. If you believe in liberty, if you believe in rights, the rights are not inalienable. (Edward Greenspan)

But note how this objection assumes the zero-sum, absolute nature of rights and free-doms. Once the fallaciousness of that assumption is recognized, and the hard issues concern-ing the proper limits of rights are acknowledged, the legislative override appears in a more acceptable light. The legislative override simply enables a legislature to put off for five years judicial review of its decision to accept a particular limit on a right or freedom.

In treating the Charter as primarily affecting the way we make decisions about the limits on fundamental rights and freedoms, I do not mean to call into question beliefs about the fundamental nature of certain rights or principles of government. I believe that the right to government based on the consent of the governed rather than on coercion, freedom from the theocratic enforcement of a particular religious creed, the right to be secure from arbi-trary and unlawful deprivations of one's personal liberty or property, and recognition of the essential dignity of every human being regardless of race, colour, creed or gender are basic requirements of good government that derive from man's nature. For countries in the liberal democratic tradition these principles constitute fundamental purposes of government. As general principles, I cannot see that they are any less fundamental to liberal democracies without constitutional charters—for example, Australia, pre-charter Canada, and the United Kingdom—than they are in countries with constitutional charters—for example, Ireland, Japan, the United States and West Germany. What I am insisting upon is the difference between a right stated as a general principle and operative rules of law affecting that principle. ...

The expectation of those who supported a constitutional charter on the grounds that it would guarantee rights and freedoms might be more realistically phrased as a belief that a charter will at least work against tightening existing limits on rights and freedoms and might even lead to the reduction of some restrictions. In this way, it might be argued, a constitutional charter will preserve and possibly expand fundamental rights and freedoms.

There can be no doubt that the Charter will promote a more systematic review of public policies in terms of the rights and freedoms included in the Charter. At least initially, this review will involve more than the judiciary. Already police officials have been taking steps to bring police practices into line with the standards of due process set out in the Charter. Ministries of the Attorney General have been scouring statute books for possible breaches of the Charter. The three-year postponement of the coming into force of the equality rights in section 15 is designed to facilitate an intensive review of discriminatory aspects of law and policy so that potential conflicts with the Charter can be minimized. Even though the Charter does not contain an equivalent of section 3 of the Canadian Bill of Rights which required the Minister of Justice to scrutinize draft regulations and Bills for inconsistencies with the Bill of Rights, still it is likely that at both the federal and provincial levels legal advisers to the government will examine legislative proposals in the light of the new Charter's provisions.

But the judicial branch will be the most important forum for the systematic application of Charter standards. Judicial opinions will be authoritative on the specific meanings to be given to the Charter's general principles. In most instances judicial decisions will be final and definitive on the proper limits of rights and freedoms. Moreover, initiation of the judicial review process is essentially independent of the executive and legislative branches of government. Where constitutional rights and freedoms rather than the division of powers are at issue, the process of judicial review will normally be "turned on," so to speak, by individuals and groups, not by governments. As a result the spectrum of interests that can influence the agenda of law reform is considerably widened. ...

This opening up of the law reform process may be the major democratizing consequence of a constitutional charter. But what are the substantive results of this process likely to be? There can be no doubt that old and new restrictions on rights and freedoms are more apt to be challenged under a charter. But will the results of these challenges necessarily expand rights or freedoms or prevent their contraction? Here we must acknowledge a great deal of uncertainty. The political orientations and legal philosophies of the judiciary are not static. If American experience with constitutional "guarantees" teaches us anything it is that over the decades or even centuries of judicial interpretation we should expect periods of both judicial conservatism and judicial liberalism. Because politicians play the crucial role in the selection of judges it is unlikely that the ideological profile of the judiciary will differ dramatically from that of the countries' dominant political elite. Changes in judicial attitudes may lag behind changes in the political culture, but in the long run these attitudes will reflect major shifts in popular political orientations.

Even if Canada does experience a relatively liberal period of judicial review under the Charter, it does not follow that all of the consequences for fundamental rights and freedoms will be positive. To begin with rights and freedoms conflict with one another. A freedom may be expanded at the expense of another right. It is not difficult to think of possibilities: review of our laws concerning contempt of court may expand free speech while adversely affecting the right to a fair trial; contraction of police powers through interpretation of legal rights may better protect the rights of criminally accused while diminishing the effective protection to the right to life and personal security of the victims of crime. Nor can it be said that the rights of minorities are bound to be beneficiaries of a liberally interpreted charter. Leaving aside the question of why in a democratic society the views of minorities should be systematically favoured on basic policy questions over the view of the majority, there is the difficulty of identifying the relevant minority on the legislative issues which will be the subject of judicial review. On the pornography issue, for instance, which is the preferred minority —the conservatives who believe present restrictions provide insufficient protection of human dignity or radicals who regard these same restrictions as an illegitimate encroachment on free expression? On many of the issues to be decided under the Charter the interested public consists not of a majority and *the* minority but of a number of minorities some of which will feel benefited by and others which will feel offended by the outcome of judicial review.

Lawyers are too prone to think of rights and liberties entirely in legal terms. They are apt to ignore the possibility that judicial decisions which remove or narrow legislative restrictions on rights and freedoms can have the effect of expanding social or economic constraints. The issues raised by the Kent Commission on corporate concentration of the press provide a good illustration. It is possible that the courts will find legislation enacted in response to the Kent Commission to be an unconstitutional violation of "freedom of the press and other media of communication." If this occurs, it would mean the continuation of restrictions on the expression of political opinion stemming from the concentration of ownership of the means of mass communication. Harold Innis warned Canadians some years ago of the bias which results from viewing freedom of speech through the prism of an excessive legalism. It would be a pity if adoption of a constitutional charter of rights blunted our capacity to recognize that the state is not the only centre of power in our society capable of restricting freedom or equality or of abusing rights.

Here again we encounter the complexity of rights and freedom issues. Rights and freedoms do not form a simple piece of whole cloth which by some new constitutional mechanism can be made to expand in a single direction. Around any civil liberties issue there will likely be a cluster of rights and social interests some of which will be affected positively and others of which will be affected negatively by contracting a legal restriction on a particular right or freedom. This does not mean that we must be agnostic about what is the right way to treat an issue or that there is no better way than that embodied in the existing legislative arrangements. But it does suggest how facile it is to regard a broad liberal construction of a guarantee as always yielding the most reasonable balance—the result which provides the fairest treatment of rights and freedoms.

There is also the possibility that the courts will render conservative decisions—that is decisions that uphold existing laws and practices as not violating rights and freedoms or at least as not constituting unreasonable limitations on these rights and freedoms. The libertarian enthusiast of a charter of rights may think that while such decisions will be disappointing in that they represent missed opportunities for expanding rights and freedoms, still such decisions cannot reduce rights and freedoms. Conservative decisions, it might be contended, may not push out the limits on rights and freedoms but neither will they push those limits in. But this argument overlooks the way in which a decision upholding existing arrangements as constitutional can legitimize the status quo. There may be a tendency under a constitutional charter of rights and freedoms to accept as a corollary of the proposition that "if it is unconstitutional it must be wrong" the proposition that "if it is constitutional it must be right." There is an element of this in American constitutional history. The Supreme Court decision in *Plessy v. Ferguson* did not establish racial segregation in American schools, but by putting the constitutional seal of approval on separate but equal facilities it created an additional obstacle for proponents of integration. ...

The point in questioning libertarian expectations of the constitutional Charter is not to renew the debate on whether Canada should "entrench" rights. For all practical purposes that debate is over. Canada has a constitutional charter and all of us, its former opponents and supporters alike, must learn to live with it intelligently. To do this it is necessary to discard the rhetoric of the Charter's political salesmen and adopt a more realistic appraisal of the Charter's potentialities. Such an understanding requires that we bear in mind the Charter's consequences not only for policy results but also for the policy process.

The principal impact of a charter on the process of government can be neatly summarized as a tendency to judicialize politics and politicize the judiciary. The political leaders who led the campaign for the Charter gave little attention to this consequence of a charter. When they did refer to it, they did so in a very optimistic vein. Mr. Chrétien, for instance, in acknowledging the important policy questions which judges will have to decide in interpreting the language of education section of the Charter, said:

> I think we are rendering a great service to Canada by taking some of these problems away from the political debate and allowing the matter to be debated, argued, coolly before the courts with precedents and so on.

Unquestionably Canada can benefit from the rationality which a thoroughly researched, well reasoned judicial decision can bring to the resolution of a difficult question of social or political justice. Such benefits will contribute to national unity if cogent judicial decisions help build a stronger national consensus on such historically divisive issues as language rights. But, while acknowledging these possible benefits, we should not lose sight of the possibility that excessive reliance on litigation and the judicial process for settling contentious policy issues can weaken the sinews of our democracy. The danger here is not so much that non-elected judges will impose their will on a democratic majority, but that questions of social and political justice will be transformed into technical legal questions and the great bulk of the citizenry who are not judges and lawyers will abdicate their responsibility for working out reasonable and mutually acceptable resolutions of the issues which divide them.

Mitigation of this danger to Canadian democracy will require, on the part of both judges and the public, a sensitivity to the hazards of a judicial imperium. It would be a tragic self-delusion for judges to believe that they can escape the dilemmas of the new power which the

Charter has thrust upon them by resorting to a kind of knee-jerk conservatism. An automatic upholding of virtually everything challenged under the Charter would bestow the mantle of constitutionality on all manner of legislation, government practice and police activity. It would be equally unfortunate if Canadian judges were to go to the other extreme of "government by judiciary" and become guilty of what an American critic of the United States judiciary refers to as "a kind of moral arrogance and judicial imperialism in undertaking to solve social problems for which they lack the competence, wisdom, or, for that matter, charter to undertake."

No simple recipe for avoiding these extremes can be written. But there is one change in the methodology of judicial decision making that Canadian judges should consider. That is softening, if not discarding, the taboo against the use of legislative history in interpreting the general language of the Charter. There was an extensive parliamentary discussion of the Charter. If counsel and judges mine the record of this discussion, I think there is less danger of the Canadian judiciary constituting itself a constituent assembly fabricating constitutional law without reference to the expectations of the original framers. No doubt the light which the historical record casts on some points will be scant and uncertain. The trouble with such a massive constitutionalization of rights as was undertaken in the new Canadian Charter is that, despite many days of discussion in the Joint Parliamentary Committee on the Constitution and debate in the House of Commons and the Senate, some difficult points were glossed over lightly or settled in last minute, private negotiations. Still there are sections which were extensively discussed in Parliament. The concepts and purposes embodied in some of these sections evolved through well reported political negotiations outside of Parliament. A good example is section 23 on the language of education. Examination of this legislative and political background material may rarely, if ever, uncover the full range of meaning which it was intended should attach to a constitutional guarantee, but it may often be a reliable guide to what was *not* included in the intentions of the constitution makers.

A new discipline will also be required by the public that evaluates the work of judges. If Canadians are to enjoy the cool rationality which Mr. Chrétien and others believe should result from the adjudication of disputes about constitutional rights, there must be a wider public capacity for giving consideration to judicial reasons. If for the public it is only the judicial outcome—"the bottom line"—that counts, our judges will tend to become simply another group of politicians and we will realize little of the distinctive benefits to be derived from expanding the judiciary's policy-making responsibilities. On the other hand, public debate and discussion of judicial decisions must not be muted by awe of the judicial office. It must be remembered that what is at stake in applying the norms of a constitutional charter of rights to the ever-changing details of our public life is the balance to be struck among our fundamental political values. In a democracy the public should not be disenfranchised from this area of decision-making. Unfortunately, the political rhetoric of "guarantees," "entrenchment" and "inalienable rights" used to promote the Charter has left the Canadian public ill-prepared for life under the Charter.

58 The Charter Dialogue Between Courts and Legislatures
or Perhaps the Charter of Rights Isn't Such a Bad Thing After All

Peter W. Hogg and Allison A. Bushell (1997)

EDITORS' INTRODUCTION

This 1997 article on Charter dialogue by Peter Hogg, one of Canada's leading constitutional law scholars, and his Osgoode Hall colleague A.A. Bushell has become a centrepiece in debates about the Charter. Hogg and Bushnell mapped the various ways that courts and legislatures can interact in applying the Charter to legislation. These modes of interaction they call a "dialogue" between courts and legislatures. In their view, recognizing that judicial decisions on the Charter may trigger legislative responses shows that courts often do not have the last word on how the Charter should apply to legislation. This dynamic, they argued, should help meet concerns that, under the Charter, courts have usurped the role of elected legislators.

I. Introduction: The Charter of Rights as a "Bad Thing"?

A. *The Legitimacy of Judicial Review*

The subtitle of this article is "Perhaps the Charter of Rights Isn't Such a Bad Thing After All." The view that the Charter is a "bad thing" is commonly based on an objection to the legitimacy of judicial review in a democratic society. Under the Charter, judges, who are neither elected to their offices nor accountable for their actions, are vested with the power to strike down laws that have been made by the duly elected representatives of the people.

The conventional answer to this objection is that all of the institutions of our society must abide by the rule of law, and judicial review simply requires obedience by legislative bodies to the law of the constitution. However, there is something a bit hollow and unsatisfactory in that answer. The fact is that the law of the constitution is for the most part couched in broad, vague language that rarely speaks definitively to the cases that come before the courts. Accordingly, judges have a great deal of discretion in "interpreting" the law of the constitution, and the process of interpretation inevitably remakes the constitution into the likeness favoured by the judges. This problem has been captured in a famous American aphorism: "We are under a Constitution, but the Constitution is what the judges say it is."

Source: Excerpted from *Osgoode Hall Law Journal*, vol. 35, no. 1 (1997). Notes omitted. Reprinted with permission.

B. *The American Experience*

In the United States, the anti-majoritarian objection to judicial review could not be ignored. The long history of the American Bill of Rights revealed massive shifts in the judicial view of the meaning of the Bill—shifts that could not be explained except as changes in the attitudes of the judges to social and economic policies. The decisions of the Warren Court (1953–1969), starting in 1954 with *Brown v. Board of Education* and ending in 1973 with *Roe v. Wade* (a case that was actually decided after Warren C.J.'s retirement), wrote a whole new chapter of American constitutional law, and one that was openly a departure from earlier jurisprudence. There had been similar shifts in judicial interpretation before, especially the overruling of *Lochner v. New York* in 1937, but the decisions of the Warren Court coincided with the existence of a large class of full-time law professors whose academic duties required that they provide thoughtful analysis of new developments in the Supreme Court of the United States. Most law professors shared the civil libertarian values of the Warren Court and approved of the outcomes, but they could not ignore the widespread unpopularity of the decisions, and they had to face up to the anti-majoritarian objection to judicial review.

A small beleaguered minority of professors simply said that the Warren Court had departed from the original meaning of the constitutional text, and that the Court was wrong to do so. This was a courageous solution to the theoretical problem, but it was not particularly helpful, since it did not make the decisions go away. The great bulk of the academic commentary was devoted to advancing ingenious theories to justify judicial review, and each new theory provoked a further round of criticism and new theories until the literature reached avalanche proportions. Most of the ideas are somewhat relevant to Canada as well as the United States, and some Canadian law professors joined the debate and attempted to apply the ideas to judicial review in Canada.

II. Dialogue: Why the Charter May Not Be Such a "Bad Thing"

A. *The Concept of Dialogue*

The uninitiated might be excused for believing that, given the deluge of writing on the topic, everything useful that could possibly be said about the legitimacy of judicial review has now been said. However, one intriguing idea that has been raised in the literature seems to have been left largely unexplored. That is the notion that judicial review is part of a "dialogue" between the judges and the legislatures.

At first blush the word "dialogue" may not seem particularly apt to describe the relationship between the Supreme Court of Canada and the legislative bodies. After all, when the Court says what the Constitution requires, legislative bodies have to obey. Is it possible to have a dialogue between two institutions when one is so clearly subordinate to the other? Does dialogue not require a relationship between equals?

The answer, we suggest, is this. Where a judicial decision is open to legislative reversal, modification, or avoidance, then it is meaningful to regard the relationship between the Court and the competent legislative body as a dialogue. In that case, the judicial decision causes a public debate in which Charter values play a more prominent role than they would if there had been no judicial decision. The legislative body is in a position to devise a response that is properly respectful of the Charter values that have been identified by the Court, but which accomplishes the social or economic objectives that the judicial decision has impeded. Examples of this will be given later in this article.

B. How Dialogue Works

Where a judicial decision striking down a law on Charter grounds can be reversed, modified, or avoided by a new law, any concern about the legitimacy of judicial review is greatly diminished. To be sure, the Court may have forced a topic onto the legislative agenda that the legislative body would have preferred not to have to deal with. And, of course, the precise terms of any new law would have been powerfully influenced by the Court's decision. The legislative body would have been forced to give greater weight to the Charter values identified by the Court in devising the means of carrying out the objectives, or the legislative body might have been forced to modify its objectives to some extent to accommodate the Court's concerns. These are constraints on the democratic process, no doubt, but the final decision is the democratic one.

The dialogue that culminates in a democratic decision can only take place if the judicial decision to strike down a law can be reversed, modified, or avoided by the ordinary legislative process. Later in this article we will show that this is the normal situation. There is usually an alternative law that is available to the legislative body and that enables the legislative purpose to be substantially carried out, albeit by somewhat different means. Moreover, when the Court strikes down a law, it frequently offers a suggestion as to how the law could be modified to solve the constitutional problems. The legislative body often follows that suggestion, or devises a different law that also skirts the constitutional barriers. Indeed, our research, which surveyed sixty-five cases where legislation was invalidated for a breach of the Charter, found that in forty-four cases (two-thirds), the competent legislative body amended the impugned law. In most cases, relatively minor amendments were all that was required in order to respect the Charter, without compromising the objective of the original legislation.

Sometimes an invalid law is more restrictive of individual liberty than it needs to be to accomplish its purpose, and what is required is a narrower law. Sometimes a broader law is needed, because an invalid law confers a benefit, but excludes people who have a constitutional equality right to be included. Sometimes what is needed is a fairer procedure. But it is rare indeed that the constitutional defect cannot be remedied. Hence, as the subtitle of this article suggests, "perhaps the Charter of Rights isn't such a bad thing after all." ...

C. Our Definition of Dialogue

In order to examine how the dialogue between Canadian courts and legislatures has unfolded, we surveyed a total of sixty-five cases in which a law was struck down for a breach of the Charter. These include all of the decisions of the Supreme Court of Canada in which a law was struck down, as well as several important decisions of trial courts and courts of appeal which were never appealed to the Supreme Court of Canada. The breakdown of the cases we looked at is depicted below.

For each case, we searched the regulations and statute books for evidence of a response to the declaration by a court that a law was of no force or effect. These "legislative sequels" are the basis for the discussion of dialogue which follows.

Accordingly, the "dialogue" to which this article refers consists of those cases in which a judicial decision striking down a law on Charter grounds is followed by some action by the competent legislative body. In all of these cases, there must have been consideration of the judicial decision by government, and a decision must have been made as to how to react to it. This may also have occurred in cases where a decision was not followed by any action by the competent legislative body. However, we have not essayed the difficult task of documenting all of the occasions when Charter cases were discussed within government but were not followed by legislative action.

III. Features of the Charter That Facilitate Dialogue

A. *The Four Features That Facilitate Dialogue*

Why is it usually possible for a legislature to overcome a judicial decision striking down a law for breach of the Charter? The answer lies in four features of the Charter: (1) section 33, which is the power of legislative override; (2) section 1, which allows for "reasonable limits" on guaranteed Charter rights; (3) the "qualified rights," in sections 7, 8, 9 and 12, which allow for action that satisfies standards of fairness and reasonableness; and (4) the guarantee of equality rights under section 15(1), which can be satisfied through a variety of remedial measures. Each of these features usually offers the competent legislative body room to advance its objectives, while at the same time respecting the requirements of the Charter as articulated by the courts.

1. SECTION 33 OF THE CHARTER

Section 33 of the Charter is commonly referred to as the power of legislative override. Under section 33, Parliament or a legislature need only insert an express notwithstanding clause into a statute and this will liberate the statute from the provisions of section 2 and sections 7–15 of the Charter. The legislative override is the most obvious and direct way of overcoming a judicial decision striking down a law for an infringement of Charter rights. Section 33 allows the competent legislative body to re-enact the original law without interference from the courts.

In practice, section 33 has become relatively unimportant, because of the development of a political climate of resistance to its use. Only in Quebec does the use of section 33 seem to be politically acceptable. And even in Quebec there is only one example of the use of section 33 to overcome the effect of a judicial decision. This was a response to the decision of the Supreme Court of Canada in 1988 in *Ford v. Quebec (A.G.)*, which struck down Quebec's law banning the use of languages other than French in commercial signs. After that decision, Quebec enacted a new law that continued to ban the use of any language but French in all outdoor signs (while allowing bilingual indoor signs), and the province protected the new law with a section 33 notwithstanding clause. ...

2. SECTION 1 OF THE CHARTER

Section 130 of the Charter subjects the rights guaranteed by the Charter to "such reasonable limits prescribed by law as can be demonstrably justified in a free and democratic society." In principle, all the guaranteed rights, and certainly all those couched in unqualified terms, can be limited by a law that meets the standards judicially prescribed for section 1 justification. Those standards, which were laid down in 1986 in *R. v. Oakes*, are as follows: (1) the law must pursue an important objective; (2) the law must be rationally connected with the objective; (3) the law must impair the objective no more than necessary to accomplish the objective; and (4) the law must not have a disproportionately severe effect on the persons to whom it applies. Experience with section 1 indicates that nearly all laws meet standards (1), (2), and (4). The dispute nearly always centres on standard (3)—the minimal impairment or least restrictive means requirement. Therefore, when a law is struck down for breach of the Charter, it nearly always means only that the law did not pursue its objective by the means that would be the least restrictive of a Charter right. If it had done so, then the breach of the Charter right would have been justified under section 1.

When a law that impairs a Charter right fails to satisfy the least restrictive means standard of section 1 justification, the law is, of course, struck down. But the reviewing court will explain why the section 1 standard was not met, which will involve explaining the less restrictive alternative law that would have satisfied the section 1 standard. That alternative law is available to the enacting body and will generally be upheld. Even if the court has a weak grasp of the practicalities of the particular field of regulation, so that the court's alternative is not really workable, it will usually be possible for the policymakers to devise a less restrictive alternative that is practicable. With appropriate recitals in the legislation, and with appropriate evidence available if necessary to support the legislative choice, one can usually be confident that a carefully drafted "second attempt" will be upheld against any future Charter challenges. ...

In *RJR-MacDonald Inc. v. Canada (A.G.)* (1995), the Supreme Court of Canada struck down a federal law that prohibited the advertising of tobacco products. In its discussion of the least restrictive means standard, the Court made clear that it would have upheld restrictions that were limited to "lifestyle advertising" or advertising directed at children. Within two years of the decision, Parliament enacted a comprehensive new Tobacco Act. The new Act prohibits lifestyle advertising and restricts advertising to media which is targeted at adults, but allows tobacco manufacturers to use informational and brand-preference advertising in order to promote their products to adult smokers. ...

3. QUALIFIED CHARTER RIGHTS

Several of the guaranteed rights under the Charter are framed in qualified terms. Section 7 guarantees the right to life, liberty, and security of the person, but only if a deprivation violates "the principles of fundamental justice." Section 8 guarantees the right to be secure against "unreasonable" search or seizure. Section 9 guarantees the right not to be "arbitrarily" detained or imprisoned. Section 12 guarantees against "cruel and unusual" punishment. There is some uncertainty in the case law as to whether the qualified rights are subject to section 1, although the dominant view is that they are. But, even if section 1 has no application to the qualified rights, by their own terms they admit of the possibility of corrective legislative action after a judicial decision has struck down a law for breach of one of the rights.

For example, section 8 does not prohibit search and seizure, but only "unreasonable" search and seizure. ...

4. EQUALITY RIGHTS

Section 15(1) of the Charter prohibits laws which discriminate on the basis of nine listed grounds, namely race, national or ethnic origin, colour, religion, sex, age or "mental or physical disability," or laws which discriminate on the basis of any ground that is analogous to the listed grounds. Typically, where a law is declared to be unconstitutional for a violation of section 15(1), the problem is that the law is underinclusive, such that persons in the applicant's position, who have a constitutional right to be included, suffer the disadvantage of being excluded. A judicial decision under section 15(1) does force the legislature to accommodate the individual or group that has been excluded. Nevertheless, there are a number of different ways of complying with section 15(1) that allow the competent legislative bodies to set their own priorities.

The most obvious solution is to extend the benefit of the underinclusive law to the excluded group. For example, when the Nova Scotia Court of Appeal held that a law extending family benefits to single mothers, but not to single fathers, was unconstitutional, the Family Benefits regulations of that province were promptly modified to allow equal access to family benefits for single parents of both genders. The Nova Scotia legislature obviously considered that the provision of family benefits was of sufficient importance that the program should be extended rather than eliminated. However eliminating (or reducing) a government benefit is another option which is open to a legislature where a law has been held to be underinclusive. After all, it is not the applicant's right to a government cheque, but rather his or her right to equality, that the Court has affirmed. ...

IV. Barriers to Dialogue: Some Charter Decisions May Not Be "Open for Discussion"

A. Three Situations Where Dialogue Is Precluded

While it is generally the case that Charter decisions leave some options open to the competent legislative body, and allow a dialogue to take place between the courts and legislatures, we must acknowledge that there may be some circumstances where the court will, by necessity, have the last word. There appear to be three situations where this will be the case: (1) where section 1 of the Charter does not apply; (2) where a court declares that the *objective* of the impugned legislation is unconstitutional; and (3) where political forces make it impossible for the legislature to fashion a response to the court's Charter decision.

1. WHERE SECTION 1 DOES NOT APPLY

It is possible that some of the rights protected under the Charter are framed in such specific terms that there is no room for Parliament or a provincial legislature to impose "reasonable limits" on those rights. This was the position taken by the Supreme Court of Canada, with respect to minority language education rights, in the very first Charter case considered by the Court. That case was *Quebec (A.G.) v. Quebec Protestant School Boards* (1984). It concerned provisions in Quebec's Charter of the French Language, which restricted admission to English-language schools in Quebec to those children whose parents had been educated in the English language *in Quebec.* ...

2. WHERE THE OBJECTIVE OF THE LAW IS UNCONSTITUTIONAL

Even where a court has been willing to entertain arguments under section 1 of the Charter, a decision striking down a law for a breach of the Charter will be virtually impossible to overcome if the court determines that the law fails the first test of section 1 justification: the requirement that the law have a "pressing and substantial purpose" that justifies limiting a Charter right. In practice, the courts have rarely declared that a law does not meet this initial threshold. However, there are a few exceptions in the case law, particularly for laws in which the purpose of the law, as opposed to the law's *effects*, are found to violate the Charter.

The first example is *R. v. Big M Drug Mart Ltd.* (1985), in which the Supreme Court of Canada struck down the federal Lord's Day Act. In that case, the Court determined that the purpose of the Act was "to compel the observance of the Christian Sabbath." This was a violation of the guarantee of freedom of religion under section 2(a) of the Charter. Moreover, because the Court held that the Lord's Day Act's primary objective was contrary to the Charter, there was no possibility of advancing the same objective through a subsequent amendment of the Act. Accordingly, the Court had the last word when it struck down the Lord's Day Act. The Act was never repealed, but was simply dropped from the next consolidation of federal statutes. ...

3. WHERE POLITICAL FORCES PRECLUDE LEGISLATIVE ACTION

A third situation that may obstruct dialogue between courts and legislatures is where an issue is so controversial that it seems to preclude a legislative response to a judicial decision striking down a law for a breach of the Charter. An example of this is the situation which arose after the decision in *R. v. Morgentaler* (1988). In *Morgentaler*, the restrictions on abortion in the Criminal Code were struck down as unduly depriving pregnant women of liberty or security of the person, contrary to section 7 of the Charter. In *obiter*, the Court added that a less restrictive abortion law could possibly be upheld. In 1990, a bill which would have implemented a less restrictive abortion law was introduced into Parliament. However that law was defeated on a tied vote in the Senate, and the divisive issue of abortion has never been revisited, either in terms of a new law, or even in terms of the formal repeal of the law that was declared unconstitutional in 1988. While neither the Charter nor the Court precluded a legislative response to the *Morgentaler* decision, the abortion issue is so politically explosive that it eludes democratic consensus. Accordingly, the Court's decision, striking down Canada's old abortion law, remains the last word on this issue.

Where political forces, as opposed to the judicial decision itself, are the reason for a lack of response from the competent legislative body after a law is struck down on Charter grounds, it can hardly be said that unelected judges are stifling the democratic process. Quite the opposite is true, in fact; the Charter decision forces a difficult issue into the public arena that might otherwise have remained dormant, and compels Parliament or a legislature to address old laws that had probably lost much of their original public support. If a new law is slow to materialize, that is just one of the consequences of a democratic system of government, not a failing of judicial review under the Charter.

V. The Nature of Dialogue Between Canadian Courts and Legislatures

A. *Most Decisions Have Legislative Sequels*

The decisions which have just been discussed, in which a dialogue between the court and the competent legislative body has not been possible, are truly exceptional. As we alluded to earlier in this article, we have found that the majority of cases in which laws have been struck down on Charter grounds have given rise to a dialogue between the court and Parliament or the provincial legislature. This trend is reflected in the accompanying table.

Table I
Type of Legislative Sequel

	Fed.	BC	AL	SK	ON	QUE	NS	‡Oth.	Tot.
†Mod. Before	9	1	0	0	1	0	0	0	11
Repeal	3	1	1	0	1	0	0	1	7
Mod. After	21	2	0	0	4	3*	2	1	33
Used s. 33	0	0	0	1	0	1	0	0	2
Did Nothing	10	0	0	0	1	0	1	1	13

* There were two sequels to the case of *Ford v. Quebec (A.G.)*, [1988] 2 S.C.R. 712: (1) use of legislative override; and (2) modification of the original law. Both of these are reflected in this table. Thus, the total number of cases is 66.

† Denotes a law that was modified before a final decision was rendered by the highest reviewing court.

‡ Other denotes delegated legislation, specifically municipal by-laws and Rules of the Alberta Law Society.

Legislative action of some kind has followed all but thirteen of the sixty-five cases we surveyed; fully 80 per cent of the decisions in this survey have generated a legislative response. Of the thirteen cases without sequels, at least two have been the subject of proposed legislation, and another three have only been decided within the last two years, making it premature to discount the possibility of a legislative sequel in the future.

Are all legislative sequels examples of dialogue? We have taken the position that any legislation is dialogue, because legislative action is a conscious response from the competent legislative body to the words spoken by the courts. However, there may be room for debate about exactly what counts as dialogue. For example, in seven of the cases we surveyed, Parliament or a provincial legislature simply repealed the provision that was found to violate the Charter. In those cases, the competent legislative body simply acquiesced in the decision of the court, and it might be argued that no true "dialogue" took place. Similarly, in several cases where competent legislative bodies amended their laws, the remedial legislation merely implemented the changes the reviewing court had suggested. No effort was made to avoid the result reached by the court, and in at least one case there was no possibility of doing so. Consequently, those cases, too, might be excluded from the meaning of dialogue.

But it is probably casting the notion of dialogue too narrowly to discount those remedial measures that have merely followed the directions of the Court, either by repealing or amending an unconstitutional law. After all, it is always possible that the outcome of a dialogue will be an agreement between the participants! ...

B. Legislative Response to Decisions Is Generally Prompt

Another finding that emerged from our survey is that Canadian legislators typically respond promptly to decisions in which a law has been struck down on Charter grounds. The accompanying table displays the response time for the cases we considered.

Table II
Timing of Legislative Response

	Fed.	BC	AL	SK	ON	QUE	NS	Oth.	Tot.
Before Final Dec'n	9	1	0	0	1	0	0	0	11
<2 yrs	13	3	1	1	4	2	2	2	28
3–5 yrs	8	0	0	0	1	0	0	0	9
>5 yrs	3	0	0	0	0	1	0	0	4

Out of the fifty-two cases in which Parliament or a provincial legislature has implemented corrective legislation, in thirty-nine cases (or 75 per cent), the legislative response came within two years. In nine cases, the legislative response took more than two years, but less than five. In only four cases did a legislative response take more than five years to be enacted. ...

C. Legislators Are Engaging in "Charter Speak"

The nature of the Charter dialogue between Canadian courts and legislatures is not reflected in numbers alone. The language of post-Charter laws themselves, particularly in statutory preambles and purpose clauses, suggests that Canadian legislators are engaging in a self-conscious dialogue with the judiciary. Where laws closely skirt the boundaries of the Charter, and particularly where new laws are enacted to replace those that have been struck down on Charter grounds, it is not uncommon for the preamble to a statute to explain how the measures taken in the legislation are directed at a "pressing and substantial" objective, and are intended to "reasonably limit" rights and freedoms. ...

D. *Dialogue May Occur Even When Laws Are Upheld*

This article has focussed primarily on the legislative changes that have followed decisions striking down laws for a breach of the Charter. However, it should be noted that judicial decisions can occasionally have an impact on legislation even when the court does not actually strike down any law.

An example of this is the aftermath of the 1995 judgment in *Thibaudeau v. Canada*. The case concerned provisions in the Income Tax Act which allowed a non-custodial parent to deduct child-support payments from (generally his) income, and which required a custodial parent to include child support payments in (generally her) income. The applicant, a custodial parent, claimed that her obligation to pay income tax on the child-support payments she received from the non-custodial parent infringed section 15(1) (the equality guarantee) of the Charter. However, a majority in the Supreme Court of Canada rejected her claim, holding that there was no breach of section 15(1). Ms. Thibaudeau's case attracted a great deal of media attention, and exposed the fact that the Income Tax Act could sometimes lead to hardship for custodial parents. Consequently, even though the Attorney General of Canada had prevailed in the courts, he announced shortly after the *Thibaudeau* decision that Parliament would change the inclusion-deduction scheme for child support payments in the Income Tax Act. Amendments to the Act were enacted in 1997, under which child support payments are no longer deductible by the non-custodial parent, and are no longer taxable as income of the custodial parent.

Parliament's response to the *Thibaudeau* decision emphasizes that it is a mistake to view the Charter as giving non-elected judges a veto over the democratic will of competent legislative bodies. Canada's legislators are not indifferent to the equality and civil liberties concerns which are raised in Charter cases, and do not always wait for a court to "force" them to amend their laws before they are willing to consider fairer, less restrictive, or more inclusive laws. The influence of the Charter extends much further than the boundaries of what judges define as compulsory. Charter dialogue may continue outside the courts even when the courts hold that there is no Charter issue to talk about.

VI. Conclusion

Our conclusion is that the critique of the Charter based on democratic legitimacy cannot be sustained. To be sure, the Supreme Court of Canada is a non-elected, unaccountable body of middle-aged lawyers. To be sure, it does from time to time strike down statutes enacted by the elected, accountable, representative legislative bodies. But, the decisions of the Court almost always leave room for a legislative response, and they usually get a legislative response. In the end, if the democratic will is there, the legislative objective will still be able to be accomplished, albeit with some new safeguards to protect individual rights and liberty. Judicial review is not "a veto over the politics of the nation," but rather the beginning of a dialogue as to how best to reconcile the individualistic values of the Charter with the accomplishment of social and economic policies for the benefit of the community as a whole.

Courts, Legislatures and Executives in the Post-Charter Era

Beverley McLachlin (1999)

EDITORS' INTRODUCTION

In the Charter era, chief justices of the Supreme Court of Canada have felt compelled to speak out and explain the Court's role, especially in interpreting the Charter of Rights. *This essay by Beverley McLachlin, the first woman jurist to head Canada's highest court, is a good example. When chief justices engage in this kind of public discourse they must avoid defending or explaining any particular decision. Were they to break this rule, their words might be taken by lawyers as additional reasons for the court's decision. Here we can see that the chief justice, in responding to criticisms that the court has been made itself a self-appointed legislature, emphasizes the courts' responsibility to take seriously constitutional laws made by democratically accountable political leaders.*

> *Courts striking down laws is nothing new in Canada, as a review of both the* Persons Case *in the 1920s and the* Alberta Press Case *in the 1930s makes clear. The* Charter of Rights and Freedoms *has clearly given impetus to the assertion of rights and to the pursuit of equality. But the courts have not shown undue "activism" or radically re-made law, and have not generally taken it upon themselves to find the social compromises that remain the appropriate domain of legislatures.*

In 1982, on a cold, windy day on Parliament Hill, the Queen signed the *Canadian Charter of Rights and Freedoms* into law. It marked a momentous step in Canadian constitutional history. Some, including many in England, viewed the step with grave apprehension. Today, it seems much less singular. Now the British have passed their own written Bill of Rights. In Africa, in Asia, in Europe—everywhere—people seem to have or to be getting constitutional bills of rights. New Zealand has a charter. Australia does not, but its High Court is nevertheless prepared to strike down laws on the basis of unwritten constitutional conventions. People vehemently defend their own particular charter versions. The British, for example, make much of the fact that their Bill of Rights does not automatically invalidate offending legislation, instead giving Parliament one year to amend the law. But whatever the mechanism for ensuring compliance of the law with the basic charter principles, in the end it is a safe guess that substantial compliance there will be.

Source: *Policy Options* (Institute for Research on Public Policy), vol. 20, no. 5 (June 1999). This is the text of a speech she delivered in Ottawa in April 1999 at a conference entitled "Guiding the Rule of Law in the 21st Century." Reprinted by permission.

All over the world, people are subjecting their parliaments to a higher constraint, that of the written constitution. This may be the short answer to the debate that fills so many Canadian newspaper columns about whether we should or should not have a charter. It is increasingly difficult to imagine any modern democracy without a charter that sets out agreed-upon principles governing the conduct of parliament. Constitutional, rights-based democracy is swiftly becoming the international norm, if it has not already so become. It seems fair to suppose that sooner or later Canada, whose Parliament and legislatures were from their inception subject to the constraints of the *British North America Act*, would have entrenched in a constitutional form the fundamental principles upon which our democracy and legal order are based, just as so many other countries have done or are poised to do.

This is the background against which we must set the Canadian Charter—a world that increasingly accepts that legislatures may properly be limited by the need to conform to certain basic norms—norms of democracy, norms of individual liberties like free expression and association, norms governing the legal process by which the state can deprive people of their liberty and security, and norms of equal treatment. No longer is democracy synonymous with naked populism. The world increasingly accepts that while the will of the people as expressed through their elected representatives must be paramount, that will should always respect the fundamental norms upon which the very notion of democracy and a civil society repose, and upon which the legitimacy of the legislative assemblies themselves is founded.

In one sense, the reordering of democracy necessitated by the entrenchment of constitutional rights norms is merely an evolutionary adjustment of the Canadian democratic landscape. Anyone who supposes that, prior to the Charter, Parliament and the legislatures were not constrained by basic constitutional principles, including fundamental democratic rights, has not studied our history closely enough. And anyone who supposes that the courts pre-Charter did not hear and decide on challenges to legislative powers is equally mistaken. From the beginning of Canadian democracy, courts have had the task of deciding whether laws challenged as going beyond the powers of the legislature that enacted them were valid or not. Moreover, even without a written bill of rights, courts required legislatures to conform to the basic principles of democratic government and equality. They did this through interpretation and in some cases—and this surprises some people—through striking laws down. Let me cite an example of each.

The first example is interpretative. It shows how, 50 years ago, the courts used the process of interpretation to recognize equality rights in Canada. Canada, of course, was founded amid the patriarchal notions prevalent in the mid-nineteenth century. Professions, governance—indeed, everything outside domestic work and a little teaching and nursing—was strictly reserved for men. When Emily Murphy was sworn in as a police magistrate in 1916 in Alberta, she was met on her second case with a challenge to her jurisdiction. The challenge went this way: Only "persons" are entitled to sit as judges. "Persons" means men. You are not a man. Therefore you cannot sit as a judge. Or to put it in the quaint but precise terms of Edwardian legalese: "Women are persons for pains and punishments, but not for privileges. Sitting as a judge is a privilege. Therefore, you, a woman, cannot sit as a judge."

To us this argument sounds ridiculous. But in the early 1900s it was not. Courts in England and in various parts of Canada had repeatedly ruled that laws enabling persons to do certain things—be they to practice law or medicine or sit as judges—applied only to men.

Outside the criminal law, which applied regardless of sex, the word "persons," interpreted legally, meant "men." So the lawyer who challenged Emily Murphy's jurisdiction to sit as a police magistrate was on sound legal ground. But Emily Murphy refused to accept the legal status quo. She believed the law to be fundamentally unjust and decided to seek its change. She brought a case before the Supreme Court of Alberta and obtained a ruling, revolutionary at the time, that "persons" in the Judges' Act included women.

But that was not the end of the story. The federal government did not accept the view of the Supreme Court of Alberta that "persons" included women. It continued to deny women the right to sit in the Senate of Canada on the ground that women were not "persons" within the meaning of those provisions of the *British North America Act* dealing with the constitution of the Senate. Emily Murphy and four cohorts in Alberta sued again, this time for an order that "persons" included women. The government fought them all the way. They pursued their claim to the Supreme Court of Canada, which ruled against them. So they raised more money and took their case all the way to the Judicial Committee of the Privy Council in London, which was then Canada's court of last resort. There, finally, in a decision that has come to be known as the "Persons Case," they prevailed.

The Privy Council, in a landmark ruling that affected the law not only in Canada but in Britain and throughout the Commonwealth, held that contrary to previous law, "persons" should be read to include women. Viscount Sankey proclaimed that the Constitution of Canada was "a living tree, capable of growth and expansion within its natural limits. The object of the Act was to grant a Constitution to Canada … Their Lordships do not conceive it to be the duty of this Board—it is certainly not their desire—to cut down the provisions of the Act by a narrow and technical construction, but rather to give it a large and liberal interpretation …"

In the course of interpreting the Constitution this way, two important things occurred: The law was altered, indeed fundamentally reversed; and women were accorded vast new rights they had not enjoyed before. Many people didn't like the ruling, and many people, we can safely speculate, muttered darkly about judicial activism. Sound like the Charter? Indeed, yes. Of course, at the time, it would have been open to Parliament to pass a new law saying expressly that women could not sit as senators. But reading the history books, one gets the sense that parliamentarians were not keen to remove from women what the Privy Council had found to be a fundamental right: the right to participate in the governance of the nation.

The second example illustrates how pre-Charter courts could and did require legislatures to conform to the fundamental principles of justice by striking down offending legislation. I refer to the 1938 *Alberta Reference*. The times were hard, people were desperate, and extreme ideas held great appeal. One of the strongest majoritarian governments Canada had ever known, the Aberhart government in Alberta, determined that for the good of the people, it must restrict the press' criticism of the government's economic policies. So it passed an act, modestly entitled "An Act to Ensure the Publication of Accurate News and Information," requiring critical comment to be submitted to the government for advance inspection.

Canada then possessed no bill of rights or Charter. It had only the *British North America Act*, setting forth the division of powers between the federal and provincial governments. Nowhere did that Act mention free speech. Yet the Supreme Court of Canada struck the bill down. Although the result was ultimately based on the fact that the entire scheme was beyond the legislative competence of the provinces, the Court commented on the impact of this particular Act. It held that there was an implied guarantee in the Canadian Constitution that protected free expression about the conduct of government. Free speech was one of the pillars upon which the very notion of democracy itself existed. Free speech, said Chief Justice Duff, was "the breath of life for parliamentary institutions." As such, the legislature of Alberta was bound by it, even though it did not formally appear in the *British North America Act.*

These are but two examples. There are many others. In the area of criminal law and evidence, for example, pre-Charter courts modified and adapted the common law and interpreted legislation in a way that ensured that the fundamental liberties of the individual were maintained. Thus, Charter rights did not spring, full-grown from the head of Zeus. Canadians had rights long before the Charter and the courts served as the guardians of those rights. The Charter accepted this tradition and entrenched the role of judges as interpreters and guardians of the rights it guaranteed. Once we came to realize as a community that some rights were fundamental, there was really no alternative. As former Supreme Court Justice Bertha Wilson wrote in the April 1999 issue of *Policy Options*, "You cannot entrench rights in the Constitution without some agency to monitor compliance. The judiciary was the obvious choice."

So in one sense, the Charter is old news. Yet in another, it has changed things, indeed, changed them profoundly. On a micro level, it has forced us to update our laws of criminal evidence and procedure. It has given impetus to the move to require governments to treat their citizens equally, without discrimination, regardless of factors like race, religion, sex or age. It has forced examination of electoral practices, like manipulative riding boundaries and bans on polling. And it has required us to consider again precisely where we should draw the line between the individual's right of free expression and the need to protect the community from harmful expression.

On the macro level, change has been equally important. I accept the frequently-made charge that the Charter has changed the way Canadians think and act about their rights. The Charter has made Canadians realize on a profoundly personal level what perhaps they had formally recognized only in a detached, intellectual sense: that their rights belong to them, that these rights are a precious part of their personal inheritance, and that they must exercise them and vigilantly protect them if they are to keep them healthy and strong.

If this is a culture of rights, then I welcome it. The debate we see every day on the editorial pages of our newspapers about the ambit of our rights and where lines should be drawn between conflicting rights and between the rights of the individual and the interest of the community, can only strengthen our society and our sense of being partners in this Canadian venture. It is the mark of a civil society, of a healthy mature democracy, that such things are debated in the newspapers and on the talk shows of our country, and not swept under the rug or, worse yet, fought out in back alleys and trenches.

The second general way the Charter has changed Canadian society is that it has increased the profile of the judicial branch of government. Before we had a Charter, judges were marking boundaries between rights, changing the law to reflect settled and emergent conceptions of rights, and occasionally even striking down laws that violated fundamental rights. However, the Charter, by putting the people's rights up front and centre, has accelerated the process. It is easier to challenge a law on the ground that it violates a fundamental right when you have in your hand a document that specifically proclaims your entitlement to that right. Compared to the task faced by Emily Murphy and her cohorts, for example, it is easier to change a legal interpretation that produces inequality, like the traditional interpretations of the word "persons," when you possess a document that commits the government to equal treatment. Moreover, people's new awareness of their rights has led individuals and interest groups—and they are to be found on both sides of virtually every issue—to come together and mobilize to protect their conception of a particular right. So the Charter has increased the challenges to laws on the basis of rights and thus incidentally increased the profile of courts called upon to resolve these issues.

This brings us to the current debate over whether the formal realignment in powers that the Charter has brought about has left too much power in the hands of judges. Depending on how the commentator views the issue, it is put in different terms. Some common variants include:

- "Judges have used the Charter to effect a giant power-grab."
- "Unelected judges are running the country."
- And simply, "Judges are too activist."

The idea of an overt power grab is easily dismissed. There is no evidence that judges, individually or collectively, particularly wanted the Charter or that, once it arrived, they decided to use it to entrench their power at the expense of Parliament and the elected legislatures. Equally easily dismissed is the idea that unelected judges are running the country. True, judges are unelected, and I believe should remain unelected, having considered the conflicts of interest and related problems an elected judge system presents. But that does not mean they cannot properly act as referees between conflicting rights and interests and as interpreters of the Constitution and the law. Nor does it mean that they are running the country.

Anyone seriously putting forth such a charge must confront the existence of Section 1 of the Charter, which permits the legislatures to trench on guaranteed rights to the extent that such a course can be shown to be justified in a free and democratic society.

Should s. 1 fail to confirm a law, Section 33 is also available to permit the elected representatives of the community to override the courts' assessment of what the rights of the individual require.

At this point the proponents of the theory that the judges are running the country shift to pragmatic arguments. It's too hard to justify infringements under s. 1 or to use s. 33 to override judicial decisions, they argue. There is something in this. It is true that, as a practical matter, it is not easy for legislatures to say to the people, or even a small unpopular subgroup of the people, "Notwithstanding your rights, we are going to violate them." But that, I believe, is as it should be. Individual rights have substance and they should not lightly be cast aside. But the fact remains that, in some circumstances, Parliament and the legislatures can override judicial decisions on the Charter if the considered sentiments of the community make it politically feasible to do so. We must therefore reject the arguments that the judges of Canada have used the Charter to effect a power grab and are running the country.

This leaves the charge of judicial activism. Judges, it is said, are too eager to overturn laws, too ready to strike statutes down, too apt to "rewrite" laws enacted by Parliament and the legislatures. I note at the outset that there is not much hard evidence that judges are inappropriately activist, whatever that may mean. A recent study by Professor Patrick Monahan of Osgoode Hall Law School concludes on the basis of considerable statistical analysis that the Supreme Court of Canada, far from being activist, as many have charged, is rather inclined to be judicially conservative and deferential to the elected arms of government. The same study suggests that it is very hard to find instances of the Court "rewriting" laws. Given the absence of any contrary studies of similar depth, this should at least give the critics pause.

Beyond this, it seems to me that if we are to talk sensibly about judicial activism, we must define our terms. Judicial activism means almost as many things to its critics as did the parts of the elephant to the blind men in the old parable.

Some people equate judicial activism with any judicial decision that changes the law. The theory here is that it is the job of judges to apply the law as it is found to exist, never to change or update it. This theory betrays a misapprehension of what judges have always done under both the common law and the civil law of this country. The venerable tradition of developing the law through an accumulation of precedent lies at the heart of our legal system, and is the lifeblood of a socially responsive body of law. New circumstances are brought before the courts. In applying the law, be it a previous case or a provision of the Charter, judges examine the law and the circumstances to see whether the old law should apply or whether it now seems unjust to do so. If a careful analysis reveals that the old law no longer reflects what is considered to be fair and appropriate, it is modified. This involves changing the law. But if changing the law is judicial activism, then judicial activism is neither new nor undesirable.

Ah, the critic says, but judicial activism is not merely changing the law, but changing the law too much. There is some truth in this. Radical changes of the law can be considered "activist" by definition. However, this does not get us any closer to answering the question of whether the Charter has made judges activist. We are left with many difficulties. The first problem is whether the fact that a change is radical necessarily means it is bad. Was it necessarily bad that the Privy Council in 1929 ruled that the word "persons" included women, thereby opening public life and the professions to women? The change was radical, but most would argue, desirable and long overdue.

The second difficulty lies in defining "radical." One person's "sensible incremental development" is another's "radical alteration of the law." Judicial activism in this sense thus often reduces itself to a debate about whether one likes or does not like a particular judicial decision. This does not bring us much closer to answering the question of whether the Charter has made judges inappropriately activist.

This concept of judicial activism is closely related to what I call the "political mirror" model of judicial activism. On this view, a decision is "activist" if it does not accord with one's political or legal viewpoint. This has led to the situation where both conservatives and liberals accuse the courts under the Charter of being too activist. Conservatives assail liberal, rights-affirming decisions as "activist." Liberals, on the other hand, assail as "activist" those decisions in which, rather than setting aside the law, the courts ignore or read down Charter provisions. Thus, as Professor Lorraine Eisenstat Weinrib wrote in the April 1999 issue of *Policy Options*, "It is the deferential, conservative justices who have been impermissibly activist. They have consistently ignored the values of the Charter text, its political history and its stated institutional roles." With the fire coming from both quarters, what, one might be forgiven for asking, is a judge to do?

Another version of judicial activism equates it with result-oriented, agenda-driven judging. I am the first to say that if it could be shown that Canadian judges were engaging in this kind of judging it would be bad. Judges must be impartial. They must not be biased. Their job is to study the law and the facts, listen to all the arguments pro and con, and after due deliberation, rule as their intellect, informed conscience, and training dictate. The spectre of agenda-driven judging is, to the best of my knowledge, just that—a spectre. If established, it would be a terrible thing and could not be tolerated. But it is not established.

It seems to me that people too often confuse agenda-driven judging, which would be bad, with judicial consistency, which is good. In the course of their work, judges may have developed fairly firm views about what a particular Charter provision means or where lines should be drawn between conflicting rights and interests. It is the task of the judge, at the beginning of each new case, to suspend those views and reconsider them in light of the submissions of the parties in that particular case. Yet if the judge, after considering all the submissions, arrives at a conclusion similar to that which he or she arrived at before, that is no cause for alarm. Indeed, it suggests a rational, carefully considered approach to the task of judging.

I am left with the feeling that the vague term "judicial activism," to the extent that it is used as more than merely a proxy for decisions the critic does not like, has to do with the fear that judges will depart from the settled law—that they will take advantage of the fact that no one, except for Parliament or the legislatures under s. 33, can override them, to foist unwarranted and unjustified laws on the people. The fear is well-known to jurists and not confined to rights litigation. Long before charters of rights were dreamed of, the English spoke ominously of "palm tree" justice, evoking the image of a colonial magistrate, seated under his judicial palm tree, meting out whatever decisions happened to seem right to him in the particular cases at hand.

The opposite of palm tree justice, or what we may call judicial activism in the Charter era, is justice rooted in legal principle and appropriate respect for the constitutional role of Parliament and the legislatures. The law has developed rules and ways of proceeding to assist judges in avoiding the evils of unprincipled, inappropriately interventionist judging. The first rule is that judges must ensure that their decisions are grounded in a thorough understanding of the Charter provisions at issue and the jurisprudence interpreting it. Where previous authority exists, changes should follow incrementally—absent the rare case of where manifest error is demonstrated, such as, for example, in the *Persons Case*. While the language of the Charter is open-textured and leaves room for judicial discretion in certain areas, it provides more guidance to those who study its language and values than is often realized. To quote Professor Weinrib again: "The Charter itself provides significant guidance for judicial interpretation."

It is still very early days for the Canadian Charter. But already we have a significant body of jurisprudence fleshing out its guarantees. Future decisions will build on this. The first time a Charter pronouncement is made that seems to change the law, it may strike many as "activist." But as a body of principle develops, the foundation of court decisions on the words of the Charter and the stable nature of the jurisprudence will become more apparent.

The second rule judges should follow is that they should be appropriately respectful of the role of Parliament and the legislatures and the difficulty of their task. While always important, this rule assumes particular significance in cases where the Charter or law at issue permits two or more interpretations or authorizes the judge to exercise discretion. "Appropriate respect" presupposes an understanding of the role of the legislative branch of government as the elected representative of the people to enact laws that reflect the will and interests of all the people.

To state this role is to acknowledge the difficulty of its execution. In a society as diverse and complex as ours, enacting laws is rarely a simple process of codifying the will of the people. It is rather a delicate task of accommodating conflicting interests and rights. Compromise is the watchword of modern governance. Judicial decision-making, on the other hand, is necessarily a blunt instrument, incapable of achieving the balances necessary for a workable law acceptable to society as a whole (on this point see Professor Rainer Knopff's paper in the April 1999 issue of *Policy Options*).

This is not to say that, where an individual's constitutional rights are at stake, the courts must always accept the compromises the legislators work out. Where laws unjustifiably violate constitutional rights, it is the clear duty of the courts to so declare, with the result that the offending law is to that extent null and void under Section 52 of the Charter. Slavish deference would reduce Charter rights to meaningless words on a scrap of paper. It is to say, however, that judging should be grounded in principle and an appropriate respect for the different roles of the elected representatives of the people and the courts.

Thus far in our Charter's short history, the courts have repeatedly countenanced respect for the choices of Parliament and the legislatures. They have repeatedly affirmed that it is not the court's role to strike the policy compromises that are essential to effective modern legislation. The role of the courts is the much more modest but nevertheless vital task of hearing constitutional claims brought by individuals, identifying unconstitutional legislative acts where such can be demonstrated, and applying the Charter we have all agreed upon.

60 The Notwithstanding Clause: A Paper Tiger?

Howard Leeson (2000)

EDITORS' INTRODUCTION

Section 33 of the Charter, the so-called notwithstanding clause, permits legislatures to immunize legislation from Charter review for five years. At the time the Charter was adopted, the clause was regarded as a democratic safety device that would enable elected legislatures to override courts. University of Regina political scientist Howard Leeson draws on his experience as a member of the Saskatchewan government team that played a key role in the 1980–82 constitutional negotiations to explain the genesis of the notwithstanding clause. Important as the clause was in securing provincial support for the Charter, Leeson's article shows how infrequently it has been invoked. His analysis suggests various reasons why political leaders have been reluctant to override the courts on Charter issues.

Introduction

Any discussion about section 33 of the *Constitution Act 1982*, the so-called notwithstanding clause, involves notions about how power ought to be shared in a society, about sovereignty and the role of the individual, and about how these arrangements should be set out in written or conventional constitutional arrangements. As Peter Russell said in his book, *Constitutional Odyssey*:

> As people on other continents at other times have learned before us, the ideal of self-determination is as challenging as it is alluring ... When constitutional legitimacy comes to rest on the sovereignty of the people, the threshold question becomes just who these people are who are capable of sharing a common constitution based on their mutual consent.

In particular, in an era when individual rights have been expanded and safeguarded in law and the ability of governments to interfere with them has been circumscribed in constitutions, the question of who should safeguard rights is far from trivial. The approach of Britain, until its increasing entanglement with the European Union, was to locate ultimate power in Parliament. The American response, albeit appropriated by the courts themselves after 1803, has been to give ultimate power to the courts. Increasingly in liberal democratic societies, the American model, that the courts should be entrusted with this responsibility, has been adopted. For a number of reasons, they are perceived as best able to arbitrate questions of rights, especially when it involves the state or its agents. Usually, however, judges are

Source: Excerpted from *Choices* (Institute for Research on Public Policy), vol. 6, no. 4 (June 2000). Notes omitted. Reprinted by permission.

not democratically chosen and lack the legitimacy of having been elected. As well, they most often come from privileged academic or social backgrounds, rendering the courts unrepresentative of the general population. For these and other reasons, there is a reluctance on the part of many to give the courts the final say in questions that may be fundamental to the functioning of society.

In Canada, with the adoption of the *Charter of Rights and Freedoms* in 1982, an attempt was made to balance the two approaches. This was done through the insertion of a *nonobstante* clause, section 33, which allows the legislatures and Parliament of Canada, in certain instances, to override the provisions of the Charter. As might be expected, this attempt at compromise has drawn criticism from both sides of the debate about how best to protect rights. Supporters of the judicial approach are outraged that legislatures may still apply majoritarian standards to questions of fundamental rights, while supporters of parliamentary sovereignty consider any devolution of sovereignty to non-elected judges to be a violation of democratic principles. ...

The story of how we came to adopt this provision is an interesting one. The conceptual origins of section 33(1) are found in earlier arrangements of the role of governments and bills of rights. However, the particular version that emerged in November 1981 and was ultimately enacted in 1982 had more to do with the raw politics of bargaining and chance phone calls late at night than with reasoned debate about what might constitute a rational compromise between democracy and constitutional law. Some may see this as an unacceptable way to write the most fundamental document of Canadian society. It was, as is often the case, the best that could be done at the time. ...

The Philosophical Roots of Section 33

Given the controversial nature of section 33, one might expect its origins to be clothed in anonymity. However, there is no shortage of people claiming authorship of both the idea and the specific form of this clause in the existing constitution. Such attention may reflect only the number and zeal of those who seek social prestige and attention in claiming credit for obscure causes. More likely, it reflects the firm and widely held belief that this particular section is not only a good addition to our constitution, but absolutely necessary to the health of Canada's democracy. ...

The debate about who should make the final decision on any issue on behalf of the group or society has a long history. The exercise of this power has most often been associated with religious agencies, but secular authorities have often contested the right of churches to arrange "earthly" affairs. This clash continues in many societies in the 21st century, modern Iran being a good example of a state where the religious and secular authorities continue to debate their respective roles.

For countries like Canada with a parliamentary system, the contest between the monarchy and parliament has long been settled. Indeed, the contest between the executive and parliament seems to have shifted to become a contest between the cabinet and the House of Commons, which many believe has been won not only by the cabinet but, even more important, by the prime minister. Thus, in most parliamentary systems the judiciary has come late to the struggle, and has only recently been armed with written bills of individual rights that give it immense constitutional power.

Although this dimension of the struggle is quite recent in Canada, it is now fully engaged. It rests on the principle that no agency of the state, whether religious or secular, ought to be able to interfere with the individual's right to conduct his or her affairs in certain matters. This kind of prohibition has some parallel in human history, but the force with which it is asserted in modern society can be traced to two principles inherent in the notions of classical liberalism: the rule of law and democracy. The latter ensures that only elected bodies pass constitutional amendments that set the parameters of individual rights. The former restrains the zeal of elected bodies. Together they underwrite the powers inherent in modern constitutions. Patrick Monahan puts it this way:

> A country's constitution is the set of fundamental principles that together describe the organizational framework of the state and the nature, the scope of, and the limitations on the exercise of state authority. ...

The Patriation of the Constitution

The turbulent political events of 1980 and 1981 mark a significant watershed in the history of Canada. It was an extraordinary time. In Quebec, the federal Liberals were returned with almost every seat, the first referendum on sovereignty was held and defeated, the Parti québécois was re-elected in 1981, and patriation of the constitution was agreed to over the objections of the Quebec legislature. ...

It is difficult to overestimate the impact of the conjunction of these events. By the summer of 1980 the political situation of 1979 had effectively been reversed, and this was crucial to the patriation efforts. It was now the Trudeau Liberals who had successfully defeated the Parti québécois in a referendum in Quebec and who had a new majority mandate, while the Parti québécois had lost the referendum and were clinging to power in their fifth year. To use sports parlance, momentum was on the Liberal side. As we now know, the Prime Minister had decided to proceed with patriation and a charter, even if it meant acting unilaterally. ...

There was discussion of the *nonobstante* clause, initiated mainly by Saskatchewan, but the federal officials and ministers did not even agree to consider it. This was quite different from the negotiations in 1979, when the federal government agreed to its inclusion and use in regard to judicial and nondiscrimination rights. As they were fond of saying that summer, "That was then and this is now." ...

As we know, the First Ministers' Conference of September 1981 failed to produce an agreement and the federal government proceeded unilaterally with a package of proposals that included a charter of rights but no *nonobstante* clause. It did not surface again until November 1981, when, after the Supreme Court decision in September declaring the federal action unconstitutional in the conventional sense, the first ministers assembled in Ottawa for one last attempt to secure agreement on a package.

In the raw bargaining of the First Ministers' Conference between November 2 and 5, 1981, it became apparent that if there was to be an agreement there would have to be a charter with language rights that was acceptable to the federal government, an amending formula that was acceptable to the provinces, and "something" on natural resources. ...

Most of the conference was *in camera* with no minutes. Our knowledge of what went on is limited to the personal notes of those of us who were there. It is fair to say that most of the discussion surrounded the amending formula, but there was a fair amount on the charter.

Generally, everyone knew that one part of an agreement depended on progress in another area. Real bargaining began on the second day and was most intense on the Wednesday afternoon. At that point, the Prime Minister and the Premiers of Alberta and Saskatchewan had an exchange on the integration of the amending formula with a charter that had a notwithstanding clause. Trudeau attempted to point out what he considered a logical inconsistency in [Saskatchewan Premier Allan] Blakeney's position, that is between his argument to make the charter more flexible with a notwithstanding formula and his support for a fairly rigid amending formula. ...

As we know, during the night a series of negotiations took place that eventually resulted in the package of proposals that became the patriation package. These negotiations on the night of November 4, 1981 did not include the Premiers of Quebec and Manitoba. Both were considered unlikely to agree to a package, the former because of Quebec's stand on sovereignty and the latter because of his inflexibility on an entrenched charter of rights. In anticipation of a conference failure, the Premier of Manitoba had already returned the previous day to campaign in the provincial election. Officials, ministers and some of the other Premiers met and spoke on the phone during the night. They managed to put together a compromise package.

In effect, the provinces traded the amending formula for the charter. There were already some changes to the charter that had been accepted in Parliament in the unilateral action period in 1981; the major change of the November 1981 First Ministers' Conference was the inclusion of a notwithstanding clause, section 33. This was a *sine qua non* for most of the provinces that had opposed Trudeau. The matter of its ambit was undetermined, however. In the original draft of a compromise document, both Saskatchewan and Newfoundland restricted its application to sections 7–15, legal and nondiscrimination rights. This was consistent with the proposals of the previous three years. Alberta insisted, however, that it apply as well to section 2 pertaining to fundamental rights and freedoms. The others agreed. This proposal was communicated to Ontario, and through them to the federal government. At 3:00 a.m. on November 5, 1981, members of the Ontario delegation contacted the author to determine whether or not Alberta was firm in the application of the notwithstanding clause to fundamental rights and freedoms. I indicated that I thought that they were and that it would have to stay. Jean Chrétien and the federal delegation were furious at this.

At the private meeting of first ministers the next day, the subject of the *nonobstante* clause was one of three important issues. Trudeau tried to raise the legislative majority required to opt out, a time limit on the *nonobstante* clause and a First Ministers' Conference on aboriginal rights:

> Trudeau: I'll tell you my opinion. I deeply feel that it is a mistake not to be able to go to the people. But I'm prepared to swallow too. [On the opting out] I put a suggestion to you. When it was considered by you, [earlier in 1981] you considered a 2/3 vote [in the legislature] but it's a bit late in the day. [On notwithstanding] Let's give it the test of time. A compromise came to me. I propose a compromise to you. That the *nonobstante* have a five-year sunset clause. I don't think that we can drop aboriginal rights out completely. My suggestion. Put in a First Ministers' Conference for the future.

All these suggestions were accepted by the nine provinces that had agreed to the morning's proposals. Quebec refused to agree to the package. The inclusion of a notwithstanding clause in the charter of rights had become a reality.

Reaction and Further Changes

The first ministers knew that the original accord was a fragile deal. Indeed, at the end of the private session Trudeau held up the copy signed by the nine premiers and said, "I better take this and run." They had agreed on two key issues: first, that the legal drafting should take place immediately, and second, that no substantive changes would be made to the accord without the agreement of all. ...

Use of Section 33 After 1982

Given the ferocity of the debate about the inclusion of a *nonobstante* clause, one might have expected its use to be frequent and controversial after the proclamation of the *Charter of Rights and Freedoms* in 1982. Such has not been the case. It has only been used by two legislatures, Quebec and Saskatchewan. Not unexpectedly, the use of section 33 by the Quebec legislature was controversial. In 1982 the Parti Québécois government secured passage of Bill 62 in the legislature, which added a standard notwithstanding clause to each of the statutes in force in the province. As well, it became standard practice to add the clause to each new bill. This use of section 33 was in protest against the fact that Quebec had not agreed to the constitution in 1981. The practice continued until 1985, when the new Quebec Liberal government discontinued it. This blanket use was challenged in court on several grounds. The Quebec Court of Appeal struck down this use of section 33, but its decision was reversed by the Supreme Court of Canada.

The Liberal government of Quebec used section 33 on five different occasions. Four appear to have been uncontroversial. The fifth, in 1988, was extremely controversial. In that year the Supreme Court of Canada struck down a portion of Bill 101, Quebec's language law, which dealt with the use of languages other than French on commercial signs. In effect, the court said that the law in question was an infringement of the Charter right to freedom of expression. A majority of francophone Quebecers still felt that this portion of Bill 101 was necessary to protect the French language in the province. The Liberal government was forced to respond by reinstating the portion of the law dealing with exterior signs, using section 33 to exempt it from the Charter.

While this action was popular in Quebec, the use of the notwithstanding clause in this manner provoked a negative reaction in the rest of Canada. Many believe that this action was mainly responsible for the defeat of the Meech Lake Accord, because it allowed some provincial governments (Manitoba in particular) to procrastinate and build opposition to the agreement.

The Prime Minister at the time, Brian Mulroney, made it quite clear that he believed section 33 was both unacceptable and a mistake. In a speech to the House of Commons in 1989 he said:

> The framers of the flawed Constitution Act of 1982 inserted the notwithstanding clause which limits our most fundamental freedoms ... never before nor since in our history has a Prime Minister of Canada made a concession of such magnitude and importance. Never before has the surrender of rights been so total and abject.

After the defeat of Meech Lake, the Mulroney government made some half-hearted efforts at seeking the repeal or modification of the clause, but they came to nothing.

The use of section 33 in Saskatchewan was less spectacular, but equally controversial in the province. The specific case involved a labour dispute between the government of Saskatchewan and its workers, represented by the Saskatchewan Government Employees' Union (SGEU). In the fall of 1985, in an attempt to put pressure on the government, the SGEU had commenced rotating strikes. In January a mediator released a report, which the union rejected. The government of Premier Grant Devine decided to end the dispute by legislation. On January 30, 1986, it recalled the legislature and introduced Bill 144, an act that forced the union back to work and provided the terms of a new collective agreement. The act was remarkable in one respect: it contained a clause exempting it from the *Charter of Rights and Freedoms*.

The reason for doing so was rooted in a 1984 court decision, in which another piece of labour legislation had been struck down. That legislation had ordered the dairy workers in the province back to work, but had been struck down by the Saskatchewan Court of Appeal on the basis that it infringed on freedom of association as guaranteed in the Charter. (Eventually the Supreme Court reversed this decision.)

The addition of the notwithstanding clause was challenged on several bases, but one in particular was novel. It was the first time outside Quebec that the notwithstanding clause had been used prospectively, that is, not in response to a court decision, but in anticipation of it. Interestingly, many who had agreed with the insertion of a *nonobstante* clause in 1981 had not anticipated that it would be used to "bullet-proof" legislation. As we know, the use of the clause in this way is not prohibited, and one can anticipate that it might be used this way again in the future.

These are the only actual uses of the notwithstanding clause since 1982. It has been 12 years since Quebec used it. As we will see in the following discussion, its use has been urged many times and has even been publicly contemplated by the Premier of Alberta, but to no avail.

Post-Patriation Arguments About Section 33

Arguments about section 33 inevitably involve rights and the best way to protect them. That is, everyone is in favour of rights, no one is against them. Thus, when reduced to its essence, the debate raises two basic questions: what should be considered a right, and which institution can best protect those rights, the courts or the legislatures? …

Most of the arguments about section 33 are set out in two articles, one by John Whyte and the other by Peter Russell, both published by the *Alberta Law Review*, in 1990 and 1991, respectively. Whyte vigorously attacks the insertion of the clause, despite the ironic fact that he was the chief constitutional advisor to Premier Allan Blakeney at the time of the adoption of the clause in 1981. …

In dealing with the argument that charters erode majoritarian control, he expresses the view, albeit somewhat weakly, that democracy is not solely about majorities. Indeed, he proposes a more profound concept of democracy that includes political participation, equality, autonomy and personal liberty. He goes on to say that "the point that needs to be made is that the democratic principle provides a powerful pedigree for judicial control over political choices that erode some fundamental human rights." He also dismisses arguments based on federalism, largely because of the idea that the courts have been heavily involved in making final decisions that bind parliaments.

Whyte's argument rests primarily on the assumption that the judiciary is not as subject as Parliament or a legislature to political whim, that it is a more trustworthy agency when dealing with individual rights:

> The primary reason for wishing to do away with the override clause is that the anxiety that produced the political demand for entrenched rights cannot be rationally calmed in the face of the legislative power granted by section 33. That anxiety is simply this: political authority will, at some point, be exercised oppressively; that is, it will be exercised to impose very serious burdens on groups of people when there is no rational justification for doing so.

He goes on to list examples of this oppression, many of which are familiar.

In answering the challenge, Peter Russell avoids wholehearted support for the *nonobstante* clause. Indeed, he has been criticized by some for being so lukewarm that he does more damage than detractors do. However, in examining the substance of the arguments, while rejecting what he calls Whyte's "disdain for democracy," he correctly defines the main issue as the choice between judicial and legislative supremacy, and concludes that Whyte is wrong. Russell argues strongly that legislative and judicial supremacy are both wrong. In effect, he seeks the middle ground between those who see no role for the legislature in defining and enforcing rights and those who abhor entrenched charters for detracting from parliamentary sovereignty:

> In a nutshell, the argument about the substance of decision-making is as follows. Judges are not infallible. They make decisions about the limits and nature of rights and freedoms which are extremely questionable. There should be some process, more reasoned than court packing and more accessible than constitutional amendment, through which the justice and wisdom of these decisions can be publicly discussed and possibly rejected. A legislative override clause provides such a process.

He goes on to enlarge on this argument and provide examples. Finally, he concludes:

> Are the judiciary and the judicial process so inherently superior to the legislature and the processes of ordinary politics that we are justified in running these risks? Professor Whyte apparently thinks they are. ... I would submit that judicial review of legislation under the Charter, in turn, has its own limitations and blind spots. Judges often fail to take into account, and indeed sometimes are exposed to the scantiest submissions on, the relationship of challenged law to its total social or political context.

In effect, Russell is arguing for a "common sense" policy of sober second thought, allowing each branch of government to correct the deficiencies in the work of the other. ...

Section 33—A Paper Tiger?

Whatever the expectations of those who supported or opposed the inclusion of section 33 in the Constitution Act, it is probably fair to say that no one could have predicted the lack of enthusiasm shown by Parliament and the provincial legislatures for its use. As noted above, it has only been used in two provinces, and it has never been used by Parliament. This is not because of a lack of controversy surrounding some of the decisions by the Supreme Court.

How can we explain what has not happened? One way would be to say that legislatures are being deferential to the courts in their new role, that they understand and accept the new relationship between the two institutions, a relationship in which the courts have the lead in matters relating to rights. This is unlikely. As Peter Russell points out, legislatures have not exactly been deferential in the past, and there is no evidence to suggest that this attitude has changed. That is, one cannot point to a series of debates in Parliament or the legislatures centred on this issue in which the houses came to the conclusion that they needed to accept a new role.

However, it is possible that attitudes toward the courts are being shaped in a more subtle way. In most matters, legislatures are subject to tight party discipline. This restricts the ability of members to express a legislative view on judicial decisions, apart from the view expressed by the executive branch of government. Recommendations on how to respond to court decisions come from ministers of justice on the advice of government lawyers. It is part of the system and culture that these officials are used to being deferential to courts and inclined to see their own future career options in that field. It is quite possible that this has an impact on decisions about the use of section 33.

Another explanation might lie in public perceptions. That is, judges are held in much higher esteem than legislators, who are viewed as "politicians." Recent polls indicate that the public not only rejects the idea that judges have too much power, they actually believe that judges should have more power. Thus, in any fight between the two branches the legislators are unlikely to win. While this may seem plausible and have some impact on a decision about the use of section 33, it is probably not the major variable involved. Any fight between the two branches would involve a specific case or issue, which usually focuses the dispute away from the legitimacy of the protagonists. Put another way, being on the "right side" of the issue is more important than who you are in most cases.

A third explanation is that the use of section 33 might cause such a public outcry that legislators are afraid to use it. Again, this seems like an attractive explanation. Amongst the "chattering classes" there is substantial opposition to the very existence of section 33. Surely legislators would be reluctant to incur public wrath for its use.

Again, however, the evidence is at best mixed in this regard. When section 33 was used in Quebec, public opinion was either favourable or neutral. Most of the informed public inside Quebec was also supportive. Outside the province opinion was generally opposed, but it made little difference. By contrast, in Saskatchewan in 1986 most of the informed opinion was fiercely opposed to the way that section 33 was used. The general public seemed apathetic. The government proceeded in spite of the opposition of the "chattering classes."

In Alberta section 33 was not actually used, but it was contemplated. In the *Vriend* case [*Vriend v. Alberta*, 1998], the Supreme Court "read in" a new section to Alberta human rights legislation protecting individuals from discrimination based on sexual orientation. The government of Alberta briefly considered using section 33 to exempt the legislation from the court decision, but decided not to do so. This was not because the legislature would have demurred. There was some political pressure not to use the clause, both from inside and outside the province, but there was also pressure in favour of its use. The consensus in the media seems to be that negative pressure caused the government to back down, but we have no way of really knowing this.

A better case for the use of section 33, one where public opinion seemed to be strongly behind government policy, involved the Supreme Court decision on tobacco advertising. In 1995 the Supreme Court held that the Tobacco Products Control Act violated section 2 of the Charter, because it forbade the advertising of tobacco products. The court held that a total ban was too drastic, and indicated that a "targeted" ban might be acceptable. The decision caused a political furor because there was considerable social support for the control of this deadly product. The government responded by deferring to the court and redrafting legislation. ...

This was hardly a case of an embattled minority needing court protection for its right to free speech. These were wealthy and powerful corporations using the courts to accomplish a commercial objective that they could not accomplish through the political process. The Parliament of Canada ought to have used the notwithstanding clause, if for no other reason than to buy time to sort out its legal situation. But despite many calls for its use, and powerful public support, the government decided to defer to the court.

It is not clear that public opinion was a determining factor in the cases we have studied.

Three other explanations for the reluctance to invoke the notwithstanding clause need to be considered. The first is the "nuclear bomb" theory. That is, that the use of section 33 would be considered in most cases to be radical overkill, the equivalent of dropping the nuclear bomb in a war. There are other, less costly ways for legislatures to achieve their objectives. This may be a consideration, but only in marginal cases. Another explanation is that the use of section 33 is not a long-term solution to a problem involving a court decision on a Charter right, since the problem will return again in five years. This might be a small consideration, but it would not explain the federal government's reluctance in the case of the tobacco advertising decision. Finally, it could also be argued that in most cases the courts have been on the right track and that there has been no need for greater use of section 33. This is an interesting argument, which may in general be true. However, there are far too many specific cases where it could have been used for us to conclude that courts have been near perfect.

Since no single explanation seems powerful enough to fit each case, we are left with the rather weak conclusion that it is a combination of all of the above (and perhaps others not mentioned here), and that further study is needed to refine possible explanations.

If the legislatures have been reluctant to use section 33, the courts have not been reluctant to expand their role. Indeed, in the last decade they have been aggressive in enlarging their role and increasing their power in many respects. ...The most flagrant example of judicial expansion came in the so-called "Judges' Pay" decision. In this judgement the Supreme Court rendered a decision involving remuneration schemes for provincial court judges in four provinces. The provincial judges had asked that various statutes freezing or reducing their remuneration be declared unconstitutional on the basis that they violated the independence of the judiciary.

In summary, the Supreme Court ruled, Justice La Forest G. dissenting, that the actions and statutes involved were unconstitutional. Some of the pronouncements in the judgement are breathtaking in their ambit. Not only did the Court strike down pay decisions, it went on to prescribe how such matters must be handled in the future:

> However, to avoid the possibility of, or the appearance of, political interference through economic manipulation, a body, such as a commission, must be interposed between the judiciary and other branches of government. The constitutional function of this body would be to depoliticize [sic] the process of determining changes to or freezes in judicial remuneration.

There is no constitutional basis for this type of body, nor any authority for the court to create it. The Court simply "read in" a constitutional amendment creating commissions. The decision goes on to say, "*Any changes to or freezes in judicial remuneration made without prior recourse to the body are unconstitutional* [emphasis added]."

The Court based its judgement on the Preamble to the *Constitution Act of 1867*, and section 11(d) of the Charter. ...

Several things are noteworthy about this case. First, there is no apparent recognition by the court that it was in a conflict of interest. In the case of members of the legislatures, although they are allowed to set their own remuneration levels, members are subject to election within five years. Nor are there constitutional provisions that ensure that pay levels for members will not be reduced. That the court decided this matter as it did, without recognizing a conflict, is unacceptable. Second, the judicial scholarship involved in asserting that the Preamble to the *Constitution Act of 1867* contemplates judicial independence of the type asserted in this judgement is questionable, to say the least. Finally, while judges may incidentally "fill in the gaps" in the constitution through the extension of principles, this decision does much more. It actually creates new institutions. The issue here, however, is that none of the legislatures involved contemplated using the notwithstanding clause in this case. It should have at least been discussed, since the case turned in part on section 11(d).

Conclusions

Three important conclusions can be drawn from this discussion. The first is that section 33 now appears to be a paper tiger. It may become the equivalent of the powers of reservation and disallowance, available in theory, but not used in practice. This is, in part, due to the reasons argued above. It is also true that the less it is used, the less likely that it will be used.

Second, as anticipated ... the courts have wandered deeply into social decisions that they are ill-equipped to address. Although they did not ask for this power, they must be restrained in their use of it.

Section 33 is not the instrument to correct this problem in the long run. It is at best a temporary stopgap to enable more dialogue. But it should not be abandoned.

Finally, given the power of the courts, we must think more about reform of the judiciary. This has to include appointment procedures, tenure, and the relationship between the courts and legislatures. If nothing is done, the observation by American jurist Charles Evan Hughes that "we are under a constitution, but the constitution is what the judges say it is" will be true.

61 Judges and the Charter Revolution

F.L. Morton and Rainer Knopff (2000)

EDITORS' INTRODUCTION

Rainer Knopff and F.L. ("Ted") Morton have been two of the Supreme Court's sternest critics. Their central argument is captured in the title of the book from which this chapter is taken, The Charter Revolution and the Court Party. *They see the Charter as amounting to a revolutionary change in Canada's system of government, a change brought about by a coalition of like-minded social reformers on the bench, in the legal profession, the law schools, and special interest groups. Together these groups constitute the Court Party. It is not so much the policy agenda of the Court Party that they object to but the undemocratic means it uses to achieve its objectives. In the chapter we have excerpted from their book, Morton and Knopff identify the procedural and interpretative moves whereby the Supreme Court has advanced the Court Party's agenda.*

People have been taught to believe that when the Supreme Court speaks it is not they who speak but the Constitution, whereas, of course, in so many vital cases, it is they who speak and not the Constitution.

> US Supreme Court Justice Felix Frankfurter in a letter to President Franklin D. Roosevelt.

The Charter does not so much guarantee rights as give judges the power to make policy by choosing among competing interpretations of broadly worded provisions. Judges often deny that they make policy, insisting that they are simply applying the Charter, and thus implementing established legal policy. In *Vriend*, for example, the Supreme Court spoke of judges as "trustees" of the Charter whose job it was to scrutinize the work of the other branches of government in the name of the "new social contract" it represented. The hollowness of these denials is evident whenever some of the trustees disagree with others about how to interpret the Charter, as members of appeal court panels regularly do. During the Charter's first decade, for example, fewer than 60 per cent of the Supreme Court's Charter decisions were unanimous, compared with an average of over 80 per cent for its non-Charter rulings. From 1991 to 1998 the rate of unanimous Supreme Court Charter decisions dropped further, to less than 50 per cent—to the dismay of lower court judges, who are supposed to follow Supreme Court precedents.

When judges disagree, each one indulges in the legal fiction that his understanding of the Charter is correct and that his colleagues are mistaken. In fact, there are usually several plausible interpretations and no obviously correct answer. The Charter, in short, is largely indeterminate with respect to the questions that arise under it. Does the section 2 guarantee

Source: Excerpted from *The Charter Revolution and the Court Party* by F.L. Morton and Rainer Knopff. Peterborough, ON: Broadview Press, 2000. Notes omitted. Reprinted by permission.

of freedom of expression prevent the censorship of pornography or hate literature, or do the section 15 equality rights justify—perhaps even require—such censorship? Does section 7, which guarantees "everyone's" right to "life, liberty, and security of the person," protect the life of a fetus or the liberty of a woman to have an abortion? No clear answer to these questions can be found in the broadly worded text of the Charter, and judges are thus free to choose.

Judicial policymaking requires more than interpretive discretion, however. The traditional barriers that restrict access to the courts, and thus limit the scope of the courts' policy review powers, must also be removed. The classic adjudication-of-disputes function of courts places many such restrictions on both litigants and courts: the rules of standing, mootness, intervener (third-party) participation, and others. Step by step, these have been removed by the Supreme Court. The result is that many policy decisions that offend well organized interest groups can now be directly challenged. In a dazzling exercise of self-empowerment, the Supreme Court has transformed itself from an adjudicator of disputes to a constitutional oracle that is able and willing to pronounce on the validity of a broad range of public policies. ...

Judicial Discretion

Judicial discretion tends to be most vigorously denied when it is most flagrantly employed. In a democratic age, those who use or benefit from the power of appointed and unaccountable offices typically deny the reality of that power lest they undermine its legitimacy. In the case of judges, the denials will not withstand scrutiny.

There are three main ways in which judges might deny the claim that the Charter revolution is caused chiefly by judicial discretion: (1) that the Charter gives effect to certain obvious or core values that are beyond the discretion of judges to transform; (2) that some parts of the Charter revolution are clearly required by the Charter's text; and (3) that where the text is unclear, judges can find objective guidance for their decisions in such non-textual sources as the original intent, traditional understanding, or essential purpose of Charter rights.

Upon inspection, none of these constraints on judicial discretion turns out to be significant. Some of them, especially the claims of original intent or traditional understanding, might indeed tie judicial hands. However, they have been rejected by the interpretive community of judges and Charter experts. The other constraints either impose no limits of practical significance or actually enhance judicial discretion.

Core Values Do Not Constrain Judicial Discretion

The Charter is not completely malleable; it is not a blank cheque made out to judicial power. On the contrary, its provisions clearly give effect to a number of unchallenged and uncontested core values. Virtually everyone in contemporary Canada would agree, for example, that a theocratic religious establishment would violate freedom of religion; that prohibiting the political participation of women or racial minorities would infringe equality and democratic rights; and that hanging pickpockets would constitute cruel and unusual punishment.

The Charter is perfectly clear about such questions. And perfectly useless. The core values guaranteed by the Charter were already legally established in common law and statutory form well before its entrenchment in 1982. More importantly, they were solidly embedded in the beliefs and habits of Canadian citizens. Precisely because there *is* a consensus about the core values of the Charter, however, they will not arise as questions for judicial determination.

There are, of course, plenty of questions that do arise for judicial determination, which is to say that there is widespread, and often passionate, disagreement about the meaning of the Charter. But do these disagreements really go to the core of Charter values? How could it be that "we find ourselves arguing, so vehemently and so often, about the very core of what we have, as participants in a democratic polity, long since presumably agreed upon?" How can a society simultaneously agree upon and endlessly dispute its foundational norms?

The answer is that our disagreements about the Charter—the questions we actually litigate—involve not the well established core but the indeterminate peripheral meaning of Charter rights. While the core meaning of a right may be widely agreed upon, its outer-limits are inherently contestable. Religious freedom is certainly infringed by theocratic establishments, but what about laws that criminalize the use of certain drugs? Do religions that make sacramental use of those drugs have a fundamental right to an exemption not available to others? Some claim such a right to be exempted on religious grounds from otherwise valid laws, but John Locke, universally recognized as a friend of religious freedom, argued against it. This is not a disagreement that pits tyrants against the true friends of liberty; it is a disagreement that divides liberal democrats of good standing. ...

Canada in short, would remain a member in good standing of the liberal democracies of the world regardless of the outcome of such Charter issues as whether Sikhs in the RCMP are allowed to wear turbans or the legal definition of spouse is read to include homosexuals. The "wrong" answer to such questions does not turn the country into a tyranny, though that is precisely what rights claimants tend to argue. Rights claiming under the Charter, in other words, often represents the attempt to enhance the normative appeal of a debatable policy claim by casting the other side in the debate as evil and tyrannical. Exaggerating policy claims is, of course, a natural and ineradicable feature of political life, but healthy polities seek ways of moderating the bellicose tendency to exaggerate. Charter-based rights talk fuels this dangerous tendency rather than checking it. ...

To summarize, legal indeterminacy and judicial discretion emerge not with respect to core values, about which consensus exists, but with respect to second-order questions, about which dissensus prevails. Canadians may agree that the Charter prohibits theocracy or grossly discriminatory laws, but they certainly do not agree about what it implies for mandatory retirement or the public funding of religious schools. No one nowadays advocates the hanging of pickpockets, but many people support capital punishment for the most heinous crimes. The Charter supplies few obvious answers to the second order questions that actually come before the courts. The text rarely settles such issues of reasonable disagreement; judges do. The Charter's core values—those matters that the text *does* settle—are not responsible for the Charter revolution.

Textual Innovation Has Not Constrained Judicial Discretion

While the text of the Charter rarely mandates significant policy change in areas of reasonable disagreement, it does so in a few instances. A second line of defense against the charge of unbridled judicial law-reform is thus to point to those sections of the Charter which clearly do effect legal change. For example, section 24(2) of the Charter creates an exclusionary rule where none had existed before. Whether or not to exclude perfectly reliable evidence because of improprieties in the way it was collected remains much more controversial than the hanging of pickpockets, yet the Charter unmistakably mandates such exclusion in certain circumstances.

Similarly, whereas the equality provision in the 1960 Bill of Rights guaranteed only "equality before the law," section 15 of the Charter contains the additional guarantees of "equality under the law" and "equal benefit of the law." The history of section 15 shows that these phrases were added, at the behest of feminist lobbying, to overrule the *Lavell* and *Bliss* decisions, two Bill of Rights decisions from the 1970s. In *Lavell*, the Supreme Court held that "equality before the law" required only equal application of the laws, not equal laws; it thus upheld a provision of the Indian Act that blatantly discriminated against Native women because it discriminated against all of them in the same way. In *Bliss*, the Court suggested that government benefit programs, such as unemployment insurance, were exempt from equality requirements. The new wording of section 15 directed the courts to give a more substantive meaning to equality under the Charter.

Another example is section 10(b) of the Charter, which not only replicates the Bill-of-Rights guarantee of a right to counsel upon detention or arrest, but adds an American-style requirement for police to inform detainees of this right. In its 1964 *Miranda* decision, the American Supreme Court added such a requirement to the pre-existing right to counsel in the US Constitution. The Canadian Supreme Court refused to add a similar requirement to the 1960 Bill of Rights in the 1978 case, *Hogan v. The Queen*. In effect, section 10(b) of the Charter overrules *Hogan*.

Section 23 of the Charter provides yet another example. It imposes on provincial governments new obligations to provide primary and secondary education to official language minorities in their own language.

Such exceptions notwithstanding, relatively little of the Charter revolution can be explained by textually mandated change. Despite a few textual innovations in the Charter, Canadians did not go to bed on April 17, 1982 with a substantially new set of rights and freedoms. For the most part, the Charter simply constitutionalized concepts—religious freedom, freedom of expression, fair trial, the right against self-incrimination, etc.—that had a long history of legal protection in this country. Common law and statute, including the 1960 statutory Bill of Rights, had protected them. Although the legal *status* of many of these concepts changed through constitutional entrenchment in 1982, there was generally no textual indication that their *content* was also to change. The fact that the Charter revolution is more a judicial than a legal revolution is evident in the many cases that brought about dramatic legal change without any textual warrant for such change.

For example, nowhere does the Charter explicitly give suspects the right to remain silent during pre-trial investigation. Indeed, civil libertarians' requests to place this right in the Charter were rejected by the framers. This did not stop the Supreme Court from reading in

such a right as a necessary corollary of both the Charter's right to counsel and its requirement of "fundamental justice." Nor did it stop the Court from extending the Canadian version of this right to blood-sample and lineup evidence gathered in the absence of counsel,
something that not even the American version requires. ...

Even where clear textual changes exist, the legal transformations undertaken in their
name are often anything but obvious. As noted earlier, the Charter does explicitly provide
for the exclusion of evidence if it has been "obtained in a manner that infringed or denied"
Charter rights. However, unlike the American rule, which tended toward automatic exclusion, the new Canadian exclusionary rule was explicitly conditional. Only if a judge deemed
that "its admission would bring the administration of justice into disrepute" was evidence
to be excluded. During the framing process, the government defended this new wording on
the grounds that it would allow exclusion only in extreme, and therefore rare, circumstances.

In the hands of the Supreme Court, however, exclusion has become anything but rare. In
a series of rulings, the most important of which is *R. v. Collins*, the Supreme Court has progressively lowered the threshold for exclusion of evidence. Given this low threshold, the
Court has chosen to exclude evidence 45 per cent of the time; when the evidence takes the
form of confessions or other incriminating statements, the exclusion rate jumps to 60
percent.

Critics claim that the Court has "produced [an exclusionary] rule which bears little resemblance to the text of the section." Even those who applaud this development concede
that "neither the rigour of the exclusionary rule nor its extension ... were anticipated by the
framers of the Charter. Both are due to the Court's willingness to give its provisions a purposive interpretation." By 1996 Crown prosecutors had become so frustrated with the judges'
frequent exclusion of reliable evidence, including involuntary police line-up identification
and blood samples, that the attorney-general of Canada asked the Supreme Court to formally overrule the *Collins* precedent. The Court not only refused, but extended the list of
prohibited forms of self-incrimination to include involuntary DNA samples.

The equality rights provision of the Charter—section 15—provides a second example of
how judicial innovations have gone well beyond those mandated by the text. As noted above,
the framers expanded the traditional wording of the right to force judges to scrutinize the
substance of laws as well as their application and administration. However, the opening
words of section 15 refer to these expanded rights as belonging to "every individual." Despite
such textual clarity, the Supreme Court has interpreted equality rights in a manner that extends them mainly to members of so-called disadvantaged groups. ...

In sum, while the Charter does include some textual innovation, this innovation explains
relatively little of the Charter revolution. Most of the important questions arising under the
Charter have been settled by judges exercising policymaking discretion, not by its text.

Original Intent, Traditional Understanding, and Purposive Analysis Do Not Constrain Judicial Discretion

Does the inability of the naked text to settle the kinds of questions typically raised under the
Charter necessarily mean that they are settled by judicial discretion? When laws fail to settle
questions arising under them, it used to be common to look behind the unclear text and

consult the intention of the law's framers. And when the original intent was unclear or ambiguous, judges often fell back on the well-established or traditional understanding of the relevant legal language. Reliance on either original intent or traditional understanding provides a strong *prima facie* answer to the charge of judicial policymaking. Judges who can plausibly claim to be giving effect to the framers' intent or to longstanding understandings are indeed applying the law, not their personal policy predilections. A currently popular alternative to original intent and traditional understanding is "purposive analysis," which seeks to deduce answers to interpretive questions from the broader purposes of the legal provision. Can Canada's judges rely on original intent, traditional understanding, or purposive analysis to avoid the charge that they, more than the Charter itself, are responsible for the Charter revolution?

They certainly can't rely on the concept of traditional understanding, which can act only as a brake on policy innovation. ... But, while the courts have occasionally used the Charter to protect existing practice against legislative innovation, they have often used it to initiate new policy themselves. In effect, the Supreme Court, inspired by its academic chroniclers, has inverted the traditional understanding of constitutionalism and judicial review as conserving forces, and transformed them into instruments of social reform. Rather than serving as a prudent brake on political change, the judiciary has become a catalyst for change.

If traditional understanding cannot explain the Charter revolution, can original intent do so? Where the text does not clearly require a policy innovation, in other words, might the framers nevertheless have intended that innovation? It seems improbable. Because the questions that arise under the Charter are contentious, second-level questions, about which no consensus exists, it is unlikely that the framers would have come down clearly on one side or the other. To have done so, moreover, would arguably have been inappropriate. The relative permanence and loftiness of constitutional law, one might think, should be used to enshrine principles of deep consensus, not to settle ongoing matters of reasonable disagreement. If the framers had nevertheless intended to settle a highly contested issue, wouldn't they have been absolutely clear about it in the text, rather than leaving it to the discretion of judges? One cannot escape the conclusion that when the text is unclear, judicial policy innovation undertaken in its name cannot be justified in terms of the original intent of the framers.

This conclusion is borne out when one actually looks for evidence of original intent on some of the more contentious questions that have been answered by the courts. Original intent is admittedly a slippery concept. For instance, different framers might intend to achieve very different things with precisely the same legal wording. Still, the evidence we do have makes it difficult for the Supreme Court to claim that its substantive policy innovations are grounded in original intention rather than judicial discretion.

We have already noted, for example, that the Court ran counter to the expectations of many of the framers when it created a pre-trial right to silence for criminal suspects and operated the exclusionary rule in a manner that makes exclusion of evidence the rule rather than the exception. The same is true of Henry Morgentaler's successful Charter challenge to the abortion provisions of the Criminal Code. During the framing process, the Trudeau government rejected numerous petitions from both pro-choice and pro-life groups to entrench their respective positions in the Charter. There was strong evidence that influential framers intended to leave abortion entirely to the regular political process, beyond the scope of judicial review. This evidence was cited by the two dissenting judges in *Morgentaler*, who argued vigorously in favour of a hands-off approach by the Court. Not surprisingly, the five-judge majority in *Morgentaler* did not appeal to original intent to justify their activism; indeed, they ignored the issue of original intent altogether. ...

The issue of gay rights provides another example of the disjunction between framers' intent and judicial policymaking. During the period of Chartermaking, the Trudeau government and the Parliamentary Committee on the Constitution rejected repeated requests by gay rights activists to insert protection for sexual orientation in the Charter. As with the abortion issue, the lack of any societal consensus on these issues counselled against addressing them in the Charter. Trudeau's advisors feared that anticipated public controversy might swamp their entire package of constitutional reform. As recently as 1992, sexual orientation was not included in the Charlottetown Accord, despite symbolic mention of all the other Charter groups. Nevertheless, in its 1995 *Egan* ruling the Supreme Court added sexual orientation to the list of prohibited grounds of discrimination in section 15.

True, there is evidence that some framers, such as Jean Chrétien (then the justice minister), were prepared to leave the matter of gay rights to future judicial discretion. Indeed, Patrick Monahan contends that Chrétien's view was common among the framers. "They had," says Monahan, "a relatively sophisticated and realistic view of the nature of the adjudication process," one that recognized "the significant degree of discretion available to courts interpreting constitutional texts." The framers, in this view, undoubtedly had "substantive intent" about particular policy issues, but they did not necessarily regard "those substantive views as conclusive." If one wants to be "really serious about fidelity to the intention of the drafters," argues Monahan, one must acknowledge their intent to hand over considerable policymaking discretion to the judiciary. The drafters, he contends, "saw their task as making educated guesses as to how the courts might interpret particular constitutional language, and choosing the language which was most likely to secure for them the results they desired," while accepting that their expectations might be upset by "inevitable" judicial originality. In other words, what might be called the framers' general intent to confer broad policy discretion on the courts takes precedence over their specific or substantive intent about particular policy questions that might arise for judicial determination.

This kind of claim has become a regular feature in judicial defences of the Charter revolution. In the 1985 *British Columbia Motor Vehicle Reference*, for example, Justice Lamer confronted the charge that the Charter had created a "judicial 'super-legislature' beyond the reach of parliament, the provincial legislatures and the electorate." To the extent that this is true, Lamer reminded his readers, critics should blame not the courts but "the elected representatives of the people of Canada. It was those representatives who extended the scope of constitutional adjudication and entrusted the courts with this new and onerous responsibility." ...

Surely a general intent to permit judicial discretion cannot be used to escape the charge that it is precisely this discretion, not the intent of the framers, that accounts for particular, substantive policy innovations undertaken in the name of the Charter. Framers who intend judicial *discretion* necessarily leave judges free to take different paths on controversial policy questions. If the general intent underlying the Charter truly gives judges policy discretion, then they can just as plausibly defer to the other branches of government as oppose them. Commentators who claim that deferential judgments themselves violate the Charter by ignoring "the values of the Charter text, its political history and its stated institutional roles" cannot simultaneously embrace a general intent of judicial *discretion*; they must be claiming an activist substantive intent to transform particular policies. One cannot have it both ways.

In fact, as we have seen, it is exceedingly difficult to explain judicial policy innovations in terms of the substantive intent of the framers. Understanding this difficulty, the Supreme Court itself rejected substantive intent as a significant standard of interpretation early in its Charter jurisprudence in the *British Columbia Motor Vehicle Reference*, the very case in which Justice Lamer embraced the general intent to confer policymaking power on the courts. *BC Motor Vehicles* confronted the Court with the question of whether section 7 of the Charter—the right not to be deprived of life, liberty or security of the person except in accordance with the principles of fundamental justice—was to be given a substantive or procedural meaning. On a procedural reading, governments could infringe the rights to life, liberty, and security of the person, as long as they did so in a manner that was procedurally fair. On a substantive reading, even procedural fairness could not justify some violations of the section 7 rights. There was ample documentary evidence that many of the most influential framers intended the narrower, procedural reading.

Such evidence did not deter Justice Lamer. Characterizing indications of substantive intent as "inherently unreliable" and "nearly impossible of proof," Lamer declared that, "it would be erroneous to give these materials anything but minimal weight." If the Court bound itself to substantive intent, he warned, the Charter's rights and freedoms would "in effect become frozen in time to the moment of adoption, with little or no possibility of growth and adjustment to changing societal needs." The preferred alternative, Lamer concluded, is to approach the Charter as "a living tree ... [capable] of growth and adjustment over time." ...

If neither original intent nor traditional understanding provide objective support for the judicial policy innovations undertaken in the name of the Charter, can such support be found in purposive analysis? Can Charter decisions be more objectively rooted in the broader purposes of the Charter's language than in the original intent of its framers? Our judges certainly think so. As the Supreme Court downplayed substantive original intent in its early Charter jurisprudence, it enthusiastically embraced purposive analysis as a way of justifying its policy innovations.

According to purposive analysis, judges should be guided by the essential purpose of a Charter right, or by the set of interests that the right is designed to protect. To discern the relevant purpose, judges are to look not to the intentions (or purposes) of the framers but to the evolving traditions of our society. The emphasis here is not on tradition simply, but on *evolving* tradition. Purposive analysis is forward looking. It draws on the past, but does so selectively, and only to discern a trend whose perfection or end point can be achieved by judicial policymaking. The point is not to maintain tradition against legislative policy innovation, but to justify judicial policy innovation. As we have argued elsewhere, "purposive analysis generally means the selective abstraction of highly general concepts from the tradition of liberal democracy in order to transform actual practice." The problem is that almost anything can be abstracted from the past in this way. In Peter Russell's words, "The history and philosophy of liberal democracy do not exactly form an open book containing clear definitions of the activities and interests" to be protected by the Charter. Russell concludes that purposive analysis "is an approach which may not yield the same results for all who apply it." In purposive analysis we confront yet another recipe for judicial discretion rather than a source of objectivity. Combined with the living tree approach, purposive analysis of rights enhances the ability of courts to act as agents of policy reform. It gives them free rein to discover new meaning in broadly conceived constitutional principles and to establish new rights if societal need, as appointed judges understand it, calls for them.

In sum, none of the defences against the charge of judicial discretion and policymaking work. ...

The attempt to deny or hide this truth can lead to a certain mendacity in judicial decision-making. In other words, to the extent that judges labour to camouflage their discretionary choices as the inescapable commands of the Charter, their overt reasons for deciding as they do may not be their real reasons. Consider the revelations provided in an interview given by Chief Justice Lamer on the fifteenth anniversary of the Charter in 1997. Lamer sought to defend what he admitted was one of the Supreme Court's most controversial Charter decisions, the *Morgentaler* abortion ruling. While claiming that he was "personally" against abortion, he added that he also believed that, "I should not impose upon others my personal beliefs." What then was the basis for his decision? Instead of pointing to a section of the Charter or some other conventional source of legal authority, Lamer invoked public opinion. Arguing that Canadians were split about 50–50 on the issue of abortion, he said "you should not make a crime out of something that does not have the large support of the community ... Who am I to tell 50 per cent of the population that they are criminals?'

For all the talk of living trees and purposive analysis, what Justice Lamer is really up to, it appears, is surveying public opinion and ensuring that public policy has "the large support of the community." Presumably, this is the kind of thing he had in mind when he said in a 1999 interview that in some of its controversial rulings, the Court was "just keeping in sync with society." Even if we accepted this as a legitimate judicial role, we might wish that Lamer would get his facts straight. Canadian public opinion toward abortion had not changed significantly since Parliament's 1969 abortion reform law and a plurality of Canadians have always supported the kind of policy compromise the 1969 law represented. ...

It is certainly true that policymaking discretion is inherent in the interpretive enterprise. Judicial policymaking, as we have ourselves argued many times, is quite unavoidable. But legislatures can overrule judicial interpretations of the common law or legislation much more easily than they can overrule Charter rulings, the section 33 override clause to the contrary notwithstanding. Although legislative majorities also cannot overrule the jurisprudence of federalism, it is more limited in scope. Deciding under the Charter *whether* government as such may (or must) do something, goes far beyond deciding *which* government may do it. As Ian Hunter has aptly put it, "It may be true that elephants and chipmunks are both mammals, but to fail to acknowledge the difference between them is wilful deception."

While it is true, in other words, that judicial discretion under the Charter is just one example of unavoidable judicial discretion, it is disingenuous to say that there is nothing new or different about it. Recall Chief Justice Lamer's comment that, with the advent of the Charter, the courts have been "drawn into the political arena to a degree unknown prior to 1982." Surely this would not have been the case if there was really nothing new going on. In fact, not only does the Charter provide broader scope for judicial policymaking, but the judges' embrace of the living tree and purposive analysis has significantly enhanced their policymaking potential. The sheer scope of judicial policy involvement under the Charter is certainly new, as are such innovations as judges rewriting legislation themselves rather than simply striking it down and allowing legislatures to decide how (or whether) to rewrite it. Indeed, as the next section shows, the innovations discussed thus far do not exhaust the institutional retooling undertaken by judges in the service of greater policy influence.

Oracularism

If newly created judicial standards are to have widespread effect on public policies, they must apply well beyond the confines of the particular case before the court. Thus, encouraged and applauded by the advocacy scholarship of Court Party academics, the Supreme Court has transformed the judiciary from an adjudicative institution, whose primary purpose is to settle concrete disputes between individuals or between individuals and the state, into an oracle of the constitution, whose primary purpose is to solve social problems by issuing broad declarations of constitutional policy. Accompanying the substantive revolution described above, in other words, has been an equally important procedural revolution. The Court has swept aside traditional common law rules that restricted access to the courts and limited the scope of judicial influence.

Traditionally, the defining characteristic of courts was their dispute adjudication function. Yes, judges also interpret, and thus add to, the law, but such judicial law making was strictly confined by the adjudicative context. This meant that constitutional rights were understood to be not just "for" but also "by" individuals. Individual litigants raised rights claims in the course of settling legal disputes with the state. Among other things, this meant that the dispute came first, the constitutional issue second. The corollary to this was that the courts might never address many important constitutional questions. This was perfectly acceptable because constitutional interpretation and enforcement was not a monopoly of judges.

The Supreme Court of Canada has abandoned this view. It now sees itself as the authoritative oracle of the constitution, whose main job is to develop constitutional standards for society as a whole, rather than just for the litigants before it. The establishment of constitutional policy now comes first, the concrete dispute second. Indeed, with the important exception of criminal cases involving legal rights, the individual litigant is vanishing in Charter litigation. Corporations bring cases, and for policy charged cases, interest groups are increasingly prominent carriers of Charter litigation, if not as litigants, then as financial backers or interveners.

The Supreme Court has expedited interest group use of litigation, and thus its own policy-review role, by eliminating two of the three most significant barriers to access to the courts: standing and mootness. (The third barrier, costs, has been removed by government subsidies of Charter litigation through the federal Court Challenges Program and provincial legal aid programs.)

The doctrine of standing required the existence of a real-world legal dispute before a court could take jurisdiction. This prevented lawsuits by individuals who objected to a law for policy reasons but were not directly affected by it. As recently as 1981, Chief Justice Laskin articulated the rationale for standing in the first *Borowski* appeal when he wrote that "mere distaste [for a policy] has never been a ground upon which to seek the assistance of a Court." This restriction on citizen access limited the opportunities for judges to review legislation, but protected the courts from constantly being forced into confrontations with Parliament by disgruntled losers in the political arena. But Laskin spoke in dissent. A majority of the Supreme Court voted to grant Joe Borowski standing to challenge Canada's abortion law despite the fact that he was not directly affected by it.

Similarly, the doctrine of mootness restricted access to the courts by requiring that a legal dispute still be a "live" dispute. If the original parties had resolved their differences, gone away or died, judges were barred from pronouncing on the legal questions raised. The Supreme Court began chipping away at this restriction in its very first Charter ruling: it ruled on the validity of Ontario's restriction on non-citizens becoming lawyers even though the original plaintiff had long since become a Canadian citizen and a member of the bar. In 1988, the Court ruled on the validity of Saskatchewan's English-only parking-tickets, even though the offender/challenger, an activist French-Catholic priest, had died. Most recently, the Court ruled that homosexual couples were entitled to spousal-support protections upon the breakup of their relationships despite the fact that the couple who brought the case— known to the public as M. and H.—had reconciled. ...

The Supreme Court has further facilitated interest group litigation by adopting a new, open-door policy for non-government interveners. Interveners are not parties to the dispute, but may be affected by or have an interest in the resolution of the legal questions raised. They thus seek to intervene in the appeal to signal their interest and present their opinions on the issue to the court. Historically, the Supreme Court had been stingy in granting intervener status to citizens or interest groups, precisely because the latter were not parties to the actual dispute, the Court's primary focus.

Initially the Court was wary about allowing interest groups to intervene in Charter decisions. Groups such as LEAF and the CCLA quickly realized that without access as interveners, they would be deprived of direct participation in the interpretive development of Charter law in the critical early cases. Beginning in 1984, they mounted a furious public relations campaign in law journals, at academic conferences, and by private and public letters to persuade the Court to loosen the rules on intervention. In 1986, the Court relented and adopted what amounts to an open-door policy on interveners. In 1987, it accepted 95 per cent of the intervener applications it received, up from 20 per cent in 1985. The acceptance rate has remained in the 80 to 90 per cent range.

Drawing on the American experience of systematic litigation strategies, a new breed of Canadian interest groups seized the opportunity offered by the Court's change of heart. Applications from non-government interveners tripled from 1986 to 1987. In the first three years of Supreme Court Charter decisions there were only 17 non-government interveners. By 1990, more than 100 interest-group interveners participated in over half of all the Supreme Court's Charter cases. By the end of 1993, the number had risen to 229. ...

Interest groups intervene out of policy concerns that may be quite different from the more practical concerns of the immediate parties. In such cases, they have benefited from the Court's willingness to address issues not actually raised by the factual situations of the parties. In *Big M Drug Mart*, the Court struck down the Lord's Day Act as a violation of freedom of conscience despite the fact that the litigant challenging the law, a corporation, could not have a religious conscience. ...

The Court has further empowered itself by changing the status of its own *obiter dicta*. Literally, "words spoken in passing," *obiter dicta* are those portions of a judgment that are outside the reasons—the *ratio decidendi*—that actually determine the outcome of a case. They are asides, or digressions. In common law jurisdictions, the *obiter dicta* of appeal courts have never been considered binding on lower courts. In Canada, the Supreme Court changed this in a 1980 decision in which it ruled that its own judicially considered *obiter* have the force of law. Baar points out that this is what bound lower courts to apply the Supreme Court's "6 to 8 month *Askov* rule" to all cases. In *Askov*, the Supreme Court had found that nearly two years of delay between committal and trial amounted to a Charter violation, and then, in obiter, opined that anything over six to eight months was similarly unreasonable. When lower courts began applying this standard, over 40,000 cases were stayed, dismissed or withdrawn in Ontario alone, prompting the Supreme Court later to complain that it had been misunderstood. As Baar notes, "The binding force of judicially considered *dicta* in Canada gives its Supreme Court much more leverage than its American counterpart."

Although the Canadian Supreme Court occasionally surpasses its American counterpart, in many respects the high courts of both countries have undertaken the same kind of institutional retooling. Prodded and encouraged by the new generation of Canadian legal academics who had studied American constitutional law—many of them at US law schools—the Canadian Court has gone down much the same path taken by its American counterpart a generation earlier. As a prelude to its own rights revolution of the 1960s, the Warren Court (named after its Chief Justice, Earl Warren) began by sweeping aside the traditional restrictions on access such as mootness and standing. ... If, as Laurence Tribe observes, the approach to such issues as standing and mootness describes "an institutional psychology: an account of how ... the Justices of the Supreme Court view their own role," then the Warren Court clearly viewed its role as "that of an active partner with the executive branch in the transformation of American politics." Our own Supreme Court's institutional retooling under the Charter indicates that it aspires to a similar role.

Conclusion

The Charter provides the occasion for judicial policymaking, but the document itself is not the most important explanation for that policymaking. Judges themselves have chosen to treat the Charter as granting them open-ended policymaking discretion. They do not always admit their discretion; indeed, they often try to camouflage it. But their attempts to do so cannot withstand close inspection and are contradicted by the judges' own, more frank off-the-bench observations.

In addition, the Supreme Court has multiplied the opportunities for judicial policymaking by substantially redesigning itself—changing its rules of evidence, relevance, standing, mootness, and intervener status—from a constitutional adjudicator to a constitutional oracle. This institutional retooling, combined with the new sophistication of Canadian interest groups in using litigation, means that few major government policy initiatives are likely to escape a Charter challenge. Judicial intervention in the policymaking process is no longer *ad hoc* and sporadic, dependent upon the fortuitous collision of individual interests and government policy; it has become systematic and continuous. The Supreme Court now functions more like a *de facto* third chamber of the legislature than a court. The nine Supreme Court justices are now positioned to have more influence on how Canada is governed than are all of the parliamentarians who sit outside of cabinet.

62 Interest Group Litigation and Canadian Democracy

Gregory Hein (2000)

EDITORS' INTRODUCTION

This article by Gregory Hein provides a counterargument to Knopff and Morton. Hein shows how Charter litigation enables marginalized groups who have little leverage on the processes of majoritarian democracy to have their interests given serious consideration. The data Hein draws upon here were assembled in preparing his doctoral dissertation, which is the most comprehensive empirical study of interest group use of the courts ever carried out in Canada. Hein's research shows that powerful corporate and economic interests also use the courts to defend and advance their interests. But Charter litigation provides groups with less access to centres of power in the democratic state, and less to offer by way of votes or money, exceptional opportunities to influence public policy. In this way, he argues, the Charter should be seen as widening Canadian democracy.

Interest Groups in Court

The Debate

Anyone who wants to understand judicial politics in Canada has to consider the efforts of organized interests. Groups are at the centre of most policy debates, trying to persuade an audience of elected officials, bureaucrats, editorialists and ordinary citizens to accept rival positions. The stakes are higher when they enter the courtroom. Organizations shoulder the burden of representing thousands of individuals, hundreds of unions scattered across the country, or entire industries. Some use impressive resources to mobilize the law, deploying teams of lawyers and expert witnesses. Advocates who want to reform society urge courts to make the bold decisions that infuriate critics of judicial activism.

Instead of asking conventional legal questions, they often present novel arguments that stretch the boundaries of law.

Canadians can no longer ignore interest group litigation because it affects the style and substance of our political life. Though a specialized activity practiced by lawyers and discussed by legal scholars, it has become an important strategy for interests trying to shape public policy. Stories about court challenges are reported in the media every week and interest groups participate in most of the cases: civil libertarians guard free expression with vigilance, even if their efforts help men who produce and consume child pornography; disabled

Source: Excerpted from *Choices* (Institute for Research on Public Policy), vol. 6, no. 2 (March 2000). Notes omitted. Reprinted by permission.

people refuse to accept laws that ignore their needs; feminists take on defence lawyers who attack Criminal Code measures designed to counter sexual assault; pro-choice activists and pro-life groups return to court to argue about the presence or absence of fetal rights; gays and lesbians pursue an ambitious campaign to stop discrimination based on sexual orientation; First Nations assert Aboriginal treaty rights; hunters enter the courtroom to oppose measures that restrict the use of guns; groups that promote law and order denounce judges for paying too much attention to the rights of the criminally accused and too little attention to the victims of violent crimes. Unions enter the judicial system to help workers and corporations challenge regulations that frustrate their ability to maximize profits. Their adversaries also litigate. Environmentalists and economic nationalists try to enforce laws that discipline the free market.

Canadians who find these efforts unsettling identify several concerns. Organizations raise difficult moral, economic and political questions, but courts are not designed to sustain public discussions on complex issues. The most controversial claims pit courts against legislatures by asking judges to reject choices made by elected officials. Political life is pulled into our judicial system by groups that generate a steady stream of cases, but without confirmation hearings we know little about the men and women elevated to the Supreme Court. We know even less about superior court judges who also exercise broad powers. These fears are expressed by those who think that litigation can undermine the struggle for a better society and by those who insist that democracy is threatened by organizations that encourage judicial activism.

The debate in the 1980s was initiated by critical legal scholars and neo-Marxists who refused to believe that courts would be transformed into brash agencies of social change. Their assessment was scathing. The Charter cannot create a forum of principle elevated above the fray of politics, they argued, because courts are not immune from the public pressures, economic realities and ideological contests that affect legislatures. Citizens have new guarantees, but they are grandiose declarations that will not alter the allocation of power and the distribution of wealth. What did these skeptics predict? The barriers impeding access to legal remedies would not wither away. Working people would fail to win dramatic victories because too many judges are guided by values that favour corporate interests. Feminists so determined to win in court would soon discover grave dangers—their resources would be depleted and their adversaries would use the Constitution to attack the welfare state. After discovering the limits of litigation, activists trying to build a just society would see that Parliament is the real engine of reform.

The debate in the 1990s has been dominated by scholars and politicians on the right. According to their account, activists on the left have been wildly successful because so many judges are "removed from reality." These interests flood the courts because they cannot win the support of legislative majorities: most voters find their demands radical and dogmatic. We are told that gays and lesbians want to impose values that will undermine the traditional family. Aboriginal peoples are determined to establish title over huge tracts of land and secure access to lucrative resources just by presenting flimsy oral histories. Feminists promote an interpretation of equality that leads to "reverse discrimination." Civil libertarians, by guarding the rights of alleged criminals, make it more difficult for police and prosecutors to secure law and order. For critics on the right, these "special interests" belong to a coalition which could be called the "court party." They bring the claims that fuel the growth of judicial power. Instead of trying to build public support for their ideas, these activists urge the Supreme Court to expand social services and benefits, alter the meaning of Aboriginal treaties written centuries ago, bolster regulatory regimes or repair legislative omissions. This use of litigation diminishes Canadian democracy, we are told, because it allows members of the court party to circumvent the legislative process.

This study offers an alternative argument by marshalling a large body of empirical data. The account advanced by conservative critics is incomplete and misleading. While warning us about "zealous" activists who invite judicial activism, they never tell us that courts are filled with a broad range of interests that express a wide array of values. Litigants talk to judges about child custody, labour disputes, income tax policy, advertising laws, medical procedures that cause harm, and the dangers of hazardous substances. This diversity exists because successive generations of Canadians have asked courts and governments to create new opportunities to participate in the judicial system and the legislative arena. We will see that critics on the right are correct when they argue that social activists are eager to pursue legal strategies. However, their interpretation ignores the economic interests that also appreciate the benefits of litigation. Corporations exert a surprising degree of pressure by asking judges to scrutinize the work of elected officials.

At the heart of this argument is an important analytical distinction designed to help us understand the strategic choices that groups make. The propensity to litigate is elevated by *stable characteristics*. Interests will be more inclined to mount court challenges when they have impressive legal resources, collective identities energized by rights, and normative visions that demand judicial activism. Strategic choices are also affected by *changing circumstances* that can make litigation seem attractive or even essential. Interests take advantage of interpretive opportunities, counter immediate threats that can be addressed by judges, and move policy battles into the courtroom when their political resources have been eroded.

The evidence below suggests that Aboriginal peoples, Charter Canadians, civil libertarians, and new left activists have the greatest potential to influence public policy through litigation because they are pulled and pushed into the courtroom by both stable characteristics and changing circumstances. These interests can be called *judicial democrats* because a provocative idea is embedded in their legal arguments and political appeals—judicial review can enhance democracy. Finding deficiencies that weaken our system of government, they believe that the courts should listen to groups that lack political power, protect vulnerable minorities and guard fundamental values, from basic civil liberties forged by the common law tradition to ecological principles that have emerged in the past century.

This study also reveals that corporations do not have the stable characteristics that elevate the propensity to litigate. However, they do confront the changing circumstances that make legal action a compelling strategic manoeuvre. Businesses enter the courtroom to counter hostile actions, to block investigating government agencies and when their political resources have been depleted.

The Study

In vibrant liberal democracies, we find a dizzying array of interests that take different shapes: incorporated companies, unions with compulsory membership, unconventional organizations that belong to social movements, associations that represent entire industrial sectors, societies of professionals, and legal advocacy groups that have been designed to fight court battles. Theoretical perspectives devise classifications to order this universe of activity, often by emphasizing a single variable. We also find shifting boundaries in our discourse because political players define their aspirations and rename their opponents. After considering the academic literature and the current debate over judicial activism, nine categories were identified that are both coherent and salient. Examples appear in Table 1.

- Aboriginal peoples have a unique claim to land and resources as the first inhabitants of the continent now called North America. They are nations struggling to win recognition of land, treaty and self-government rights.
- Civil libertarians are determined to stop the state from undermining traditional guarantees that many individuals prize. Students, journalists, writers, church activists and defence lawyers challenge laws that violate freedom of expression, freedom of religion and rights that protect the criminally accused.
- Corporate interests are businesses that compete in a range of sectors: financial, retail, manufacturing, construction, pharmaceutical, agricultural, communications and natural resources. Their advocacy groups demand low levels of taxation, flexible regulatory regimes and trade liberalization.
- Labour interests are organized into unions and advocacy groups that represent miners, loggers, civil servants, teachers, nurses, police officers, auto-makers and technicians. Eager to improve the lives of workers, they defend the welfare state and oppose trade policies that produce unemployment.
- Professionals have the credentials to practice as lawyers, judges, accountants, academics, pharmacists, doctors, architects and engineers. Most work in the private sector as entrepreneurs, but some are employed by large public institutions. They pursue collective action to promote their interests and to protect the integrity of their respective professions.
- Social conservatives want to preserve traditional values sustained for centuries by church and family. They oppose open access to abortion services, homosexuals who demand "special rights," gun regulations that punish citizens without reducing crime, feminists who want to marginalize fathers, and a popular culture that encourages promiscuity.
- Groups that represent victims want to help individuals hurt by cancer, AIDS, drug addiction, smoking, intoxicated drivers, violent crimes, mining tragedies, silicone breast implants, the transmission of infected blood and sexual abuse in schools.
- Charter Canadians believe that state intervention is required to solve pressing social problems. They derive inspiration and impressive legal resources from the 1982 Constitution. Groups representing ethnic, religious and linguistic minorities, women and the disabled can base their claims on guarantees designed to protect their interests.
- New left activists also believe that state intervention is needed to address grave social problems, but they do not enjoy constitutional rights that were explicitly designed to protect their interests. Environmentalists, gays and lesbians, anti-poverty advocates and economic nationalists can invoke the Charter to stop military tests, fight discrimination, preserve wild spaces and stop governments from dismantling the welfare state, but they have to hope that judges will use their discretion to extend the scope of existing guarantees.

Table 1: Categories of Organized Interests

Aboriginal Peoples	Assembly of First Nations
	Assembly of Manitoba Chiefs
	Congress of Aboriginal Peoples
	Dene Nation
	Native Council of Canada
	Union of New Brunswick Indians
Civil Libertarians	Amnesty International
	Canadian Civil Liberties Association
	Canadian Council of Churches
	Canadian Federation of Students
	Centre for Investigative Journalism
	Criminal Lawyers' Association
Corporate Interests	Canadian Bankers' Association
	Canadian Manufacturers' Association
	Canadian Telecommunications Alliance
	Merck Frosst Canada
	Thomson Newspapers
	R.J.R. MacDonald
Labour Interests	Canadian Labour Congress
	International Longshoremen's and Warehousemen's Union
	National Federation of Nurses' Unions
	Public Service Alliance of Canada
	Union des employés de service
	United Fishermen and Allied Workers' Union
Professionals	Association provinciale des assureurs-vie du Québec
	Association québécoise des pharmaciens propriétaires
	Canadian Association of University Teachers
	Canadian Bar Association
	Canadian Institute of Chartered Accountants
	Canadian Medical Association
Social Conservatives	Alliance for Life
	Evangelical Fellowship of Canada
	Human Life International
	Inter-Faith Coalition on Marriage and the Family
	National Firearms Association
	REAL Women
Victims	Canadian Cancer Society
	Canadian Council on Smoking and Health
	Canadian HIV/AIDS Legal Network
	Canadian Resource Centre for Victims of Crime
	Central Ontario Hemophilia Society
	Westray Families
Charter Canadians	Canadian Council of Refugees
	Canadian Disability Rights Council
	Canadian Jewish Congress

> Fédération des francophones hors Québec
> Native Women's Association of Canada
> Women's Legal Education and Action Fund

New Left Activists Canadian Peace Alliance
Council of Canadians
Equality for Gays and Lesbians Everywhere
National Anti-Poverty Association
Sierra Legal Defence Fund
Société pour vaincre la pollution

To understand the legal strategies that these groups pursue, every decision appearing in the Federal Court Reports (1,259) and the Supreme Court Reports (1,329) from 1988 to 1998 was reviewed. My Court Challenges Database records relevant facts about each case, including the legal status of litigants. Organizations appear as *parties* when they have a direct stake in a case. If groups are allowed to participate as *intervenors*, they can present oral arguments and written submissions to address issues raised in a dispute. To understand the purpose of litigation, six possible targets were identified.

- Groups can achieve their objectives by confronting *private parties*. They counter individuals, unions, professional associations and corporations.
- Litigants also take aim at *bureaucratic officials* who exercise limited statutory powers. Some work for line departments, but most have positions on boards, tribunals, commissions and inquiries.
- Organizations can bring claims against *cabinet ministers* to block unfavourable decisions or to make governments act. By seeking writs of mandamus, they can ask courts to enforce mandatory duties.
- The stakes are higher when groups mobilize the law to overturn the *statutes and regulations* that are introduced by governments.
- To improve their chances of winning future contests, litigants can try to shape *judicial interpretations*. The primary goal of this strategy is to direct judges when they define the meaning, purpose and scope of common law rules, ordinary statutes and constitutional guarantees.
- Groups also enter the courtroom to defend favourable policies when their adversaries launch *hostile actions*. ...

Interest Group Litigation Before the Charter

Courts played an important role before the Charter was entrenched by protecting property, hearing administrative actions, enforcing the criminal law and resolving disputes between both levels of government. Certain interests appreciated the potential value of litigation. Businesses filled the judicial system to advance pecuniary and proprietary claims. They also attempted to influence public policy. This became very apparent during the 1930s, when corporations invoked the division of powers to obstruct the growth of the welfare state.

They succeeded when the Judicial Committee of the Privy Council promoted provincial autonomy and economic liberties by invalidating federal laws.

Courts were also asked to defend civil liberties, even in the nineteenth century. Most cases were initiated by individuals facing charges or governments fighting jurisdictional battles, but organizations supported some challenges at a distance. Francophones and Roman Catholics in Manitoba asserted constitutional rights that guarantee the use of French in public institutions and funding for denominational schools. After winning the right to vote, suffragettes turned their attention to a provision in the Constitution that was interpreted to exclude women from the Senate. In a case that is still celebrated by feminists, they persuaded the Judicial Committee of the Privy Council that the term "qualified persons" encompassed both sexes. This campaign was backed by the National Council of Women and a number of smaller groups. In the 1950s, prominent members of the legal community began helping religious minorities and communists who were deemed to be "subversives." By the 1970s, feminists were hoping that courts would use the Canadian Bill of Rights to eliminate discrimination. At the same time, environmentalists were exploring various claims to punish corporations and governments for failing to respect new pollution laws.

These efforts were exceptional. For more than a century, few organizations entered the courtroom to affect public policy. It was possible to have a complete understanding of Canadian politics without ever thinking about interest group litigation. The labour movement concentrated on the party system because courts did little to help workers; relying on the assumptions of classical liberalism, judges allowed market forces to settle most issues. Activists who wanted to solve social problems pressured legislators and devised novel strategies in order to change public attitudes, but few imagined that litigation could be turned into an instrument of reform. While achieving some of their objectives in court, corporations lobbied cabinet ministers and senior officials because they appreciated the importance of elite accommodation and the power of bureaucracies.

Interest Group Litigation After the Charter

This study reveals that a transformation has occurred. Interest group litigation is now an established form of collective action. Organizations present 819 claims between 1988 and 1998. They appear as parties or intervenors in 30 percent of the disputes considered by the Federal Court and the Supreme Court. Figure 1 records the frequency of participation.

Figure 1
Organized Interests in Court, 1988–1998

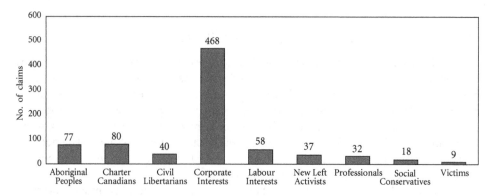

Source: Court Challenges Database.

Groups from every category pursue legal strategies. This single finding is remarkable—we now find the same mix of political players trying to influence courts and governments. But if there has been an important change, we also find elements of continuity. Court dockets are still laden with corporations. They bring 468 legal actions, far more than the other interests. Companies engage in civil litigation against private parties, and challenge regulations governing banking, federal elections, international trade, environmental protection and the pharmaceutical industry. Groups representing professionals participate in 32 cases. They try to win higher salaries as employees and as experts they talk to judges about a range of issues, including the principles that guide child custody disputes and criminal investigations. Very few of their challenges try to alter major public policies. The unions and advocacy groups that represent labour interests bring 58 claims. They back members alleging gender discrimination, fight for higher salaries, counter measures that undermine collective bargaining, try to escape criminal contempt charges and assert the right to strike.

The big change is that courts now hear from interests that struggled for decades to win access. For more than a century, courts and governments in Canada maintained barriers that discouraged or even prevented litigation. The Indian Act was amended in 1927 to stop Aboriginal peoples from bringing legal claims. Although this restriction was lifted in 1951, the Supreme Court did not begin to recognize and protect Aboriginal rights until 1973, when it considered a case brought by the Nisga'a. ...

Some interests were also hampered by weak legal resources. Environmentalists discovered that few regulatory laws established the causes of action and the precise mandatory duties that make litigation more effective. Governments resisted these measures because they believed that legal campaigns would diminish their autonomy and disrupt political life. Groups could base their claims on the *Canadian Bill of Rights* after 1960. A minor provision in the Indian Act was found to be inconsistent with the guarantee of equality a decade later. This ruling encouraged feminists and civil libertarians who were eager to help victims of discrimination, but it turned out to be an aberration. Subsequent decisions returned to a narrow interpretation of equality. Litigants also confronted a wall of judicial deference. In the end, most members of the Supreme Court refused to believe that the doctrine of legislative supremacy could be constrained by an ordinary federal statute that lacked constitutional status.

Figure 1 reveals that litigation is now an important strategy for groups that once confronted these obstacles:

- Aboriginal peoples launch 77 claims between 1988–98. First Nations take on the federal government when it fails to act in their best interests; they secure title to land by asserting Aboriginal rights and challenge laws that fail to respect treaty rights.
- Charter Canadians are just as active: 80 legal arguments are presented to oppose measures restricting abortion services, to chastise provincial governments for breaching language rights, to reveal racism in the criminal justice system, and to overturn election laws that discriminate against the mentally ill.
- Civil libertarians participate in 40 cases that attack policies impairing democratic rights, fundamental freedoms and guarantees that protect the criminally accused.
- New left activists bring 37 claims. They enter the courtroom in order to protect delicate ecosystems, help poor people facing arrest, overturn policies that exclude homosexuals, and counter measures that limit demonstrations.

- Social conservatives bring fewer claims, only 18. The most controversial claims try to persuade courts to recognize fetal rights. Unlike their American allies and their Canadian adversaries, social conservatives have not formed any legal advocacy groups; these are specialized organizations designed to fight legal campaigns. In the early 1990s, the Canadian Rights Coalition was established to take on doctors who dared to perform abortions, but it soon disappeared.
- Organizations that represent victims bring even fewer court challenges, only nine. They usually participate outside the courtroom. Most legal claims are brought by individuals who allege negligence or breach of trust to win compensation. Class actions are also orchestrated to counter threats that harm hundreds of victims.

We find this diverse range of interests pursuing litigation because governments and courts have created new opportunities to participate. The Charter was entrenched by federal politicians who wanted to strengthen the national community and weaken regional identities. Though guided by this strategic calculation, they also sensed that a shift was occurring. A growing number of citizens were willing to accept or even embrace the idea of constitutional guarantees because their attitudes and expectations had been affected by the international rights movement and the work of the United Nations and by social movements in Canada and the United States that were mobilizing to promote free expression, equality, and reproductive rights. Since the patriation round in 1982, governments have introduced funding programs and statutory rights to make administrative regimes, the regulatory process and the judicial system more accessible.

The Supreme Court has also introduced changes that have encouraged interest group litigation. The law of standing has been liberalized in stages. The old common law rule favoured property owners and corporations trying to protect private rights and filtered out citizens who wanted to address public problems. Under the new rule, applicants who ask a serious legal question and demonstrate a "genuine interest" can win access if certain conditions are satisfied. The Supreme Court has also relaxed the requirements for intervening. Groups with a record of advocacy displaying expertise in a particular area usually receive permission to appear as friends of the court. ...

Challenging Elected Officials

Claims that challenge elected officials are more captivating because the stakes are higher. When litigants target Cabinet decisions and public policies they ask appointed judges to reject choices made by politicians who have won the support of citizens in general elections. The consequences can be unsettling, even for Canadians who admire the Charter and recognize the legitimacy of judicial review. Decisions can rearrange legislative agendas that reflect public concerns, strain regulatory regimes already burdened by onerous responsibilities, alter spending priorities when governments are striving to trim deficits and spark violent reactions that divide communities. The evidence presented in Table 2 cuts to the very heart of the debate over judicial activism. It demonstrates which interests exert pressure on the federal state by challenging laws and political executives.

Professionals oppose mandatory retirement, social conservatives attack laws that fail to protect the fetus, and unions question measures that restrict collective bargaining and the right to strike, but these are the exceptions. They bring only 10 percent of the claims that target elected officials and most cases try to knock down minor provisions. Groups supporting victims never pursue this strategy.

Far more pressure is generated by the interests that worry critics on the right. Aboriginal peoples, Charter Canadians, civil libertarians and new left activists bring 52 percent of the claims that attack Cabinet decisions and public policies. To win, these litigants have to persuade judges to accept a controversial role—to be full partners in the legislative process who use their skills to solve pressing problems and exercise their authority to improve society. Aboriginal peoples and new left activists question laws passed by both levels of government, but they often target cabinet ministers. First Nations, alleging a breach of trust, demand the enforcement of a broad fiduciary duty that requires the federal government to act in their best interests. Invoking Aboriginal rights, they hope to establish title to huge tracts of land worth billions of dollars and try to expand existing treaties to secure better access to natural resources. Environmentalists try to stop massive projects that are championed by provinces hungry for new sources of revenue. Cabinet ministers responsible for telecommunications and social assistance are confronted by anti-poverty activists.

Charter Canadians and civil libertarians also pursue this strategy, but they tend to target statutes and regulations. Feminists try to remove measures restricting access to abortion services. Religious minorities oppose immigration procedures that violate the right to counsel and military policies that discriminate against Jewish officers. Groups representing the disabled try to knock down *Criminal Code* provisions that discriminate against the mentally ill. ...

Table 2: Targeting Elected Officials 1988–1998

Organized Interests	Cabinet Ministers		Statutes and Regulations		Total	
	No. of claims	(%)	No. of claims	(%)	No. of claims	(%)
Corporate Interests	48	42	45	34	93	38
Aboriginal Peoples	33	29	18	14	51	21
Charter Canadians	10	9	19	14	29	12
New Left Activists	15	13	9	7	24	10
Civil Libertarians	2	2	20	15	22	9
Labour Interests	3	3	9	7	12	5
Social Conservatives	1	1	6	5	7	3
Professionals	1	1	5	4	6	2
Victims	0	0	0	0	0	0
Totals	113	100	131	100	244	100

Source: Court Challenges Database.

The big surprise is that corporate interests are so active in targeting elected officials. Table 2 reveals that they present 38 percent of the claims that challenge laws and Cabinet decisions. Requesting writs of mandamus, businesses try to enforce rules governing international trade. Invoking the federal division of powers, they attack laws that address competition, new drugs, environmental protection and tax policy. The Charter is also mobilized by corporate litigants. Companies insist that marketing regimes controlling interprovincial trade violate mobility rights and the guarantee of equality. Media corporations challenge laws that restrict their ability to collect and disseminate information. The owners of Thomson Newspapers, for example, won a dramatic victory in 1998, when they persuaded the Supreme Court to nullify a measure that barred the publication of opinion polls at the end of election campaigns. Some of the most controversial cases seek to protect commercial expression by knocking down social policies. Corporations, for instance, have challenged provisions that prevent advertising aimed at children and the advertising of tobacco products and liquor. ...

Interest Group Litigation and Canadian Democracy

This study tells us what we need to know to contemplate the effects and implications of interest group litigation.

- The central insight is that Aboriginal peoples, Charter Canadians, civil libertarians, and new left activists are drawn into court by the stable characteristics that elevate the propensity to litigate and by the changing circumstances that make legal strategies seem compelling. These are the judicial democrats. They will continue to generate a steady stream of controversial claims because they believe that democracy can be enhanced by judicial review.
- Judicial democrats are not in court alone. The judicial system is filled with a wide array of groups that express a broad range of values. This diversity is a triumph for citizens who struggled for decades to win new opportunities to participate in our public institutions.
- Some organized interests are reluctant litigants. Professionals, social conservatives and victims mobilize the law sporadically. Although groups that represent workers are more willing to bring legal claims, they usually attack bureaucratic officials, leaving major public policies unscathed.
- Corporations do not display a propensity to litigate, but they do encounter the changing circumstances that push interests into the courtroom. They ask judges to overturn cabinet decisions and laws passed by both levels of government, often to resist state intervention.

The purpose of this study is to understand a controversial form of collective action, but it can also help us assess the current relationship between citizens, legislators, and judges. In the debate over judicial activism, most commentators exaggerate the hazards and underestimate the rewards. Courts interpreting cryptic constitutional declarations and treaties signed centuries ago do make decisions that cause turmoil. They can disrupt legislative agendas, strain regulatory regimes already burdened by arduous responsibilities and force governments to adjust the allocation of resources. Our political life, as a consequence, is probably less tranquil and more uncertain today. However, we now have a judicial system that responds to a diverse range of interests. Judges hear from professionals advancing pecuniary claims, Aboriginal peoples who want their treaty rights respected, and environmentalists who monitor the erosion of important ecosystems. Courts enforcing the Charter help businesses trying to protect commercial expression, homosexuals who want the family law remedies that heterosexuals expect and linguistic minorities struggling to preserve their culture. That so many groups are able to advance their claims through the courts is an accomplishment that Canadians should celebrate.

Critics troubled by active courts want to restore the relative calm we once enjoyed by resurrecting "traditional judicial review." What do they propose? The Supreme Court has to bring back the old standing requirements, discourage interests from intervening, consider only narrow legal questions raised by live controversies and question the value of extrinsic evidence. They resent judges who allow political adversaries to clutter the courtroom, evaluate policy alternatives with misplaced confidence and try to settle future disputes in a single decision. Conservative critics believe that prudence should replace arrogance. It is too easy for judges to advance their personal preferences, they insist, if the "living tree metaphor" can be invoked as a license to alter the meaning and scope of enumerated guarantees. The Supreme Court has to remember the primary purpose of a liberal democratic constitution: to protect individuals by placing limits on the state. Legal remedies should not increase the presence of the state. Judges should never punish governments for failing to act by filling perceived omissions. They should also resist the temptation to expand services, benefits, regulatory regimes and Aboriginal treaties.

This argument can sound appealing, especially when the Supreme Court delivers a decision that divides the country. Still, the measures that conservative critics propose have a distinct bias that Canadians should know about. Resurrecting traditional judicial review would filter out certain interests and values. Returning to the old rules governing standing and intervenor status would hurt public interests unable to demonstrate a direct stake in a dispute. Excluding extrinsic evidence would make it more difficult for litigants who want to trace the adverse effects of a law. Freezing the meaning and scope of constitutional guarantees would leave judges unable to address new social problems that create discrimination. If courts only placed limits on the state, litigation would be a poor strategy for citizens who want to bolster regulatory regimes or expand social services. Taken together, these obstacles would hinder interests concerned about racism, homophobia, gender inequality, environmental degradation, poverty, the lives of the disabled and the plight of Aboriginal peoples. Traditional judicial review would not, however, frustrate litigants advancing conventional pecuniary claims and legal action would still be an effective strategy for interests that want to resist state intervention.

Although constrained courts would cause fewer disruptions, we would pay a price. Litigation would help corporations but not groups trying to address public problems. Critics of judicial activism stumble here. They want to stop social reformers from seeking the legal remedies that businesses have always requested. Seen from this perspective, the current relationship between citizens, legislators, and judges is attractive because it meets a basic requirement of democracy that many Canadians embrace. Nations composed of diverse interests should not have institutions that respond to some and ignore others.

PART 6

Ideologies and Identities

Introduction

Understanding Canada requires understanding the political ideas and ideologies that underpin its regional and national parties, and that are manifested in its electoral politics. The writings included in this part reveal that conflict over political ideas in Canada rests in some part on left–right cleavages but on many others as well, including a struggle over Canadian identity vis-à-vis its neighbours to the south and the importance of place and the value of regional identities and loyalties in the overall makeup of the country, and extends to how one perceives Canada's role, and the projection of its values, in an increasingly complex world beyond its borders.

Sir Wilfrid Laurier's essay is as much an articulation of what it means to be a francophone liberal in post-Confederation Quebec as it is an essay on the ideological differences between the Conservative and Liberal parties. Those differences he characterizes as between those who cling "with fondness to whatever is ancient" (quoting Macaulay) and those who discern the imperfections that exist and seek to improve them. That articulation of the left–right divide is a theme of much of the political writing represented here, including the CCF's explicitly socialist program in the 1930s, Leo Panitch's analysis of class and power in Canadian politics and political culture, and George Grant's nationalistic defence of more conservative and communitarian Canadian values in the face of American capitalism and cultural imperialism in *Lament for a Nation*.

Gad Horowitz's task is to account for that left–right divide in Canadian politics and political culture and to argue that Canada is not simply a political cultural mirror of the United States, as political scientists Louis Hartz and Kenneth McRae had claimed in their analyses of North American political culture. Hartz and McRae argue that political cultures in "settler" societies reflect those of the societies from which new immigrants come, cultures that then "congeal" and influence subsequent generations. Hartz and McRae maintain that English Canada and the United States are both essentially liberal "fragments" in the tradition of Lockean Britain, whereas Quebec and Latin America are "feudal fragments" founded by emigrants from pre-liberal France, Portugal, and Spain. That political cultural congealment of a single tradition explains the lack of extreme ideological politics in the United States and the political contestation of two parties around essentially liberal ideas. As Horowitz points out, however, party politics in English Canada is much different from that in the United States because of the presence of an organized socialist tradition in Canada at the partisan level in the CCF/NDP. That socialist tradition in Canada was made possible by the mixing of a liberal tradition with a "tory touch" brought by the Loyalists to Canada around the time of the American Revolution.

Nelson Wiseman's 1981 essay and Donald Forbes's 1987 essay offer both a challenge to and a refinement of Horowitz's initial thesis—with Wiseman urging scholars to pay attention to regional political cultures manifest at the provincial party level, and Forbes arguing that a better label for the Quebec "feudal fragment" is actually *nationalism*—but both remain solidly with the more historical, intuitive Canadian political cultural tradition, observing the influence of both settlement patterns and principal ideological traditions in provincial politics. Their methods stand in contrast to Leo Panitch's more Marxian analysis of class politics in Canada, and Neil Nevitte's and Michael Adams's more public opinion survey–driven analyses of current Canadian cultural values.

They all agree, however, that the struggle to understand Canadian political thought rests as much on understanding Canadian identities as on understanding left–right politics in Canada. William Christian's essay on Harold Innis unveils the work this seminal historian has done to unpack the impact of the land and its exploitation on the Canadian economy and Canadian identity. René Lévesque and Pierre Vallières reflect on Quebec's place within an anglophone North American culture and their writings are striking statements of sovereigntist thinking. Preston Manning's speech at the founding of the Western Canadian populist Reform Party in 1987 similarly unveils Western Canadians' feeling of alienation from central Canadian culture and values, although Roger Gibbins's piece from the fall of 2009 illustrates the extent to which influence has shifted westward in the intervening years. Robert Finbow explores the many variations in political identity within Atlantic Canada, offering a much more heterogeneous portrait of the region than is commonly understood.

In many of the writings represented here, what it means to be a Canadian or Québécois is often juxtaposed with being a North American or a Brit, and one's loyalties to the Canadian or Québécois state are often declared undermined by one's love of things American or British. This is as visible in Adams's current analysis of English Canadian and American public opinion surveys, as it is in Campbell's historic speech to the Empire Club of Canada. In this speech, Campbell declares that one can best remain a Canadian only as a member of the British empire rather than as a member of the growing American empire. It is a similar fear of loss of Canadian constitutional sovereignty to American imperialism that inspires George Grant to write *Lament for a Nation*. Grant states that "The central problem for nationalism in English-speaking Canada has always been: in what ways and for what reasons do we have the power and the desire to maintain some independence of the American empire?"

Campbell's triumphalism about the superiority of British imperialism, read today, comes across as insensitive to those who experienced British imperialism as colonialism, as many immigrants to Canada did in their home countries, and insensitive to the aspirations of multinational groups within Canada: that is, francophones in Quebec, and First Nations peoples. Indeed, Pierre Vallières articulates the plight of the Québécois as akin to African Americans in the United States: "exploited men, second class citizens." He queries, "Have they not been, ever since the establishment of New France in the seventeenth century, the servants of the imperialists … ? Were they not imported, like the American blacks, to serve as cheap labor in the New World?" Lévesque's statement, meanwhile, establishes the principles to justify the formation of a politically sovereign Quebec as a bulwark against Anglophone North American hegemony.

In contrast, Campbell's confidence in the ability of Canadians "to keep themselves apart, as an individual people, as the Scotland of North America, for a thousand years to come" under the protection of British constitutional principles, parallels Laurier's arguments regarding the value of constitutional democracy as a means to preserve and promote regional and national identities and especially as the best means of protecting the francophone minority defeated on the Plains of Abraham. Laurier's speech counters the criticisms of religious critics of the time who claimed that the faithful ought to demonstrate greater allegiance to the Church than to the state, but it can also be read, in contemporary terms, as a powerful affirmation of the institutions of Canadian constitutional democracy. Other commentators in this section, such as René Lévesque, Pierre Vallières, and Preston Manning, express far less confidence in the representative quality of those institutions.

This brings us to the final theme, that of Canada's role in the world at large. Prime Minister Paul Martin's 2004 speech to a Washington audience during the height of the war on terror and the Iraq War illustrates the delicate dance Canada must often do as it promotes its own values in the world while working to maintain cordial relations with US administrations. But Andrew Cohen's *While Canada Slept* punctures many of the myths Canadians cling to, arguing that any influence we may have enjoyed in the past has declined markedly in recent decades. However, both Martin and Cohen would agree that Canada still has the potential to achieve great things on the international stage.

Further Suggested Reading

Janet Ajzenstat and Peter J. Smith, *Canada's Origins: Liberal, Tory, or Republican?* Ottawa: Carleton University Press, 1995.

Henri Bourassa, *The French-Canadian in the British Empire.* London: John Murray, 1902.

Henri Bourassa, "The Program of the Nationalist League," 1903. In H.D. Forbes, ed., *Canadian Political Thought.* Toronto: Oxford University Press, 1985.

Alan Cairns, "Political Science in Canada and the Americanization Issue." *Canadian Journal of Political Science* 8(2), 1975.

William Christian and Colin Campbell, *Political Parties and Ideologies in Canada*, 3rd edition. Toronto: McGraw-Hill Ryerson, 1990.

George Grant, "An Ethic of Community." In Michael Oliver, ed., *Social Purpose for Canada.* Toronto: University of Toronto Press, 1961.

Harold Innis, *Empire and Communication.* Toronto: Oxford University Press, 1950.

Harold Innis, *The Bias of Communication.* Toronto: University of Toronto Press, 1951.

Sir John A. Macdonald, Speech on the Quebec Resolutions, 1865.

C.B. MacPherson, *Democracy in Alberta: Social Credit and the Party System.* Toronto: University of Toronto Press, 1962.

Pierre Elliott Trudeau, "New Treason of the Intellectuals." In *Federalism and the French Canadians.* Toronto: MacMillan, 1968.

John Wilson, "Towards a Society of Friends: Some Reflections on the Meaning of Democratic Socialism." *Canadian Journal of Political Science* 3, 1970.

Nelson Wiseman, *In Search of Canadian Political Culture.* Vancouver: UBC Press, 2007.

63 Lecture on Political Liberalism

Wilfrid Laurier (1877)

EDITORS' INTRODUCTION

Sir Wilfrid Laurier served as member of Parliament for the Liberal Party first for the riding of Drummond and Arthabaska in Quebec (1874–77), and then for Quebec East (1877–1919). He served as prime minister of Canada between 1896 and 1911 and then leader of the opposition until his death in 1919. His tenure as prime minister marked the first time the Liberal Party dominated federal politics in Canada's young history; he was also the country's first francophone prime minister. This speech, a "Lecture on Political Liberalism," was delivered in Quebec City to a group called "Le Club Canadien de Québec" in 1877, when Laurier was still an MP.

Lecture on Political Liberalism

Delivered by Wilfrid Laurier, Esq., M.P., on the 26th of June, 1877, in the Music Hall, Quebec, Under the Auspices of "Le Club Canadien."

Mr. Chairman, Ladies and Gentlemen,

I cannot conceal that it is with a certain feeling of pleasure I have accepted the invitation to come here to explain the doctrines of the liberal party, and what is the exact meaning of the word "Liberalism," as understood by the Liberals of Quebec. ...

I know that Catholic Liberalism is condemned by the head of the church; and I may be asked what is Catholic Liberalism. At the threshold of the question I refrain. The question is not included in my subject, and moreover is beyond my power to elucidate. But I may also say that Catholic Liberalism is not Political Liberalism. If it were true that ecclesiastical censure against Catholic Liberalism should apply to Political Liberalism, this fact would constitute for us, French in origin and Catholic in religion, a state of things the consequence of which would be as strange as sad. The fact is, we French Canadians are a conquered race. This is a sad truth to tell, but it is nevertheless the truth. But if we are a conquered race, we have also made a conquest, the conquest of Liberty. We are a free people. We are in the minority; but we have preserved all our rights and privileges. But what is it that guarantees us this liberty? It is the constitution that was won for us by our fathers and which we, today, enjoy. We have a constitution that has been granted to us for our own defence. We have no more rights nor greater privileges, but we have as many rights and privileges as the other races which, with us, constitute the Canadian family. Again, it must not be forgotten that the other members of the Canadian family are divided into two parties, the Liberal and the Conservative.

Now, if we who are Catholics had no right of choice, if we had not the right of belonging to the liberal party, one of two things must occur: either we would be obliged to completely abstain from taking part in the direction of public affairs, and then the constitution, which was granted to us for our protection, would be but a dead letter, or we should have to take part in the administration of state affairs under the direction and for the benefit of the conservative party; thus, our action being no longer free, the constitution would be a dead letter in our hands, and we would moreover, have to suffer the disgrace of being, for the other members of the Canadian family who make up the conservative party, mere tools or supernumeraries. Do not these absurd consequences, but of which no one can deny the strict correctness, show, in the most undoubted manner, how utterly false the assertion is that a Catholic cannot belong to the liberal party?

Since providence has united in this part of the world, populations of different origins and creeds, is it not manifest that these different people should have interest identical and in common; and in regard of anything relating to its interest, each is free to belong to the liberal party or to the conservative party, according as conscience directs them to follow one or the other.

As for myself I belong to the liberal party. If to be a liberal is a term of reproach, that reproach I accept. If it is a crime to be a liberal, then I am guilty. One thing only I claim, that is, that we be judged according to our principles. I would be ashamed of our principles if we did not dare to avow them. Our cause would not be worth the efforts to secure victory, if the best means of doing so were to conceal its nature. The liberal party have been for twenty-five years in opposition, let it be twenty-five years more if the people be not ready to accept its ideas, but let it march with fearless brow, with its banners unfurled in the face of the country. It behoves, however, before all things to understand the meaning, the values and the bearing of the word "Liberal," and of the term "Conservative."

I affirm that there is nothing so little understood in this country, by those who attack it, as Liberalism. There are several reasons for this.

We were but yesterday initiated into representative institutions—the English population understood the working of these institutions by a sort of intuition, strengthened further by a century's experience. Our population, as yet, scarcely know them. Education has but begun to be spread amongst us; and for those who are educated, our French training naturally leads us to the study of modern liberty, not in the classic land of liberty, not in the History of old England, but amongst the nations of continental Europe, amongst the nations that are allied to us in blood or in religion. And, unfortunately, the history of liberty is written there in characters of blood, in the most heartrending pages of the history of the human race. Terrified by these mournful records, you will find amongst all classes of educated people loyal souls, who look with horror upon the spirit of liberty, imagining that that spirit of liberty must, here, result in the same disasters and crimes as in the countries of which I speak. For these well meaning minds, the very name of Liberalism is fraught with national calamity.

Without entirely censuring these fears but without allowing ourselves to be terrified by them, let us ascend to the very source and examine calmly what is, at bottom, the meaning of these two words, *Liberal* and *Conservative*. What idea is concealed beneath the word "Liberal" which has been subjected to so many anathemas? What does the word "Conservative" mean which seems so sacred, that it is modestly applied to all that is good? Is the one, as it is pretended, as in fact it is affirmed every day to be, a new form of error? Is the other, as it is constantly insinuated, synonymous of good, in all its phases? Is the one, revolution, anarchy, disorder? Is the other the sole safe principle of society? Such are the questions which are asked every day in this country. These subtle distinctions, which are continually brought forward in our press, are nevertheless old. They are but the repetition of the dreams of certain French publicists who, shut up in their studies, look only upon the past, and who bitterly criticise everything that now exists because existing things do not resemble those of old. Such people say that the Liberal idea as well as its opposite is not new. It is as old as the world, and it is to be found in every page of its history. But it is only today that we understand its forces and its laws and know how to utilize them. Steam existed before Fulton; but it is only since Fulton that we know the scope of its power and how to make it produce its marvellous results. It is the combination of the tube and piston that serves to utilize the steam. It is the form of representative government that has revealed to the world the principles—Liberalism and Conservatism; and it is that form of government that draws from each its full powers.

On no subject in human affairs, does truth manifest itself in an equal degree to each intelligence. Some dive deeper into the unknown but grasp less at a time. With others the contemplation, although it be less penetrating, yet as far as that vision extends, they see more clearly. This primordial distinction explains at once to a certain degree the Liberal idea and that of Conservatism. For this reason alone, the same object will not be viewed in the same manner by different persons. For this sole reason some will take a route which others will avoid, when, however, both intend to reach the same end. But there is one conclusive reason that explains the nature, the reason, the why and the wherefore of the two different ideas. Macaulay in the history of England defines this in a remarkably clear manner. Speaking of the assembling of the British Houses of Parliament, in the second session of the Long Parliament, in the reign of Charles the First, the celebrated historian uses the following words:

> From that day dates the corporate existence of the two great parties, which ever since have alternately governed the country. In one sense indeed the distinction which then became obvious had always existed and always must exist. For it has its origin in diversities of temper, of understanding and of interest, which are found in all societies and which will be found till the human mind ceases to be drawn in opposite directions by the charm of habit and by the charm of novelty; not only in politics but in literature, in arts, in science, in surgery and in mechanics, in navigation and agriculture, nay even in mathematics we find this distinction. Everywhere there is a class of men who cling with fondness to whatever is ancient, and who, even when convinced by overpowering reason that innovation would be beneficial, consent to it with many misgivings and forebodings. We find also, everywhere, another class of men, sanguine in hope, bold in speculation, always pressing forward, quick to discern the imperfections of whatever exists, disposed to think lightly of the risks and inconveniences attending improvements, and disposed to give every change credit for being an improvement.

The first are the conservative; the second are the liberal. Such is the real sense, the true explanation of both principles liberal and conservative. They are two attributes of our nature. As Macaulay admirably says, they are to be found everywhere, in the arts, sciences, in all branches of speculative knowledge; but it is in politics they are most apparent. Thus, those who condemn liberalism as a new idea, have not reflected upon what is happening every day before our eyes. Those who condemn liberalism as an error, have not considered that they thereby condemn an attribute of human nature. Now it must not be forgotten that the form of our government is a constitutional monarchy. It is this instrument which brings out in relief, and places in action the two principles of liberalism and conservatism.

We, liberals, are frequently accused of being republicans. I do not point out this reproach to refute it. It is not necessary to reply to such a reproach. I simply say that the form of government means little; let it be monarchical or republican, from the moment the people have the right to vote and possess a responsible government, they have the full measure of their liberty. However, liberty would soon be an empty word if she did not restrain those in power. A man whose astonishing wisdom has laid down the axioms of the science of government with unerring exactitude, Junius says: *Eternal vigilance is the price of liberty*.

Yes, if a people wish to remain free, they must, like Argus, have a hundred eyes and ever be on the watch. If they sleep, if they become weak, each moment of indolence involves the loss of some portion of their rights. An eternal, unceasing vigilance is the price which must be paid for the inestimable boon of liberty. Now, constitutional government is adapted even to a greater extent than a republic to the exercise of this necessary vigilance.

On one side you have those who govern, on the other, those who watch. On one side are those who are in power, and are interested in retaining it; on the other are those who are interested in attaining it themselves.

What shall be the means of cohesion which will unite these different parties? What shall be the principle, the sentiment that will array the different elements of the population either on the side of those who govern or of those who watch? It will be either the liberal or the conservative principle. You will see together those who are attracted by the charm of novelty, and you will see together those who are attracted by the charm of habit. You will see on one side those who attach themselves to everything that is ancient, and on the other side those who are always ready to reform.

I now ask whether between these two ideas which form the basis of these parties there can exist a moral difference; is one radically good and the other radically bad? Is it not manifest that both are, what are called in morals *indifferent*? That is to say, that both are susceptible to appreciation, of thought and choice. Would it not be as unjust as it is absurd to condemn or approve either one or the other, absolutely good or bad?

Both are susceptible of great good and great evil. The Conservative, who defends the old institutions of his country can do much good, while he may perpetrate a great evil if he persists in perpetuating intolerable abuses. The Liberal who fights against those abuses, and who after unceasing efforts eradicates them, may be a public benefactor, while the Liberal who would raise a profane hand against its sacred institutions, would prove a scourge not only of his country, but of humanity.

Therefore, I am far from making the convictions of our adversaries an object of reproach, but as for myself I am, as I have already said, a Liberal. I am one of those who believe that in all human affairs there are abuses to reform, new horizons to discover, and new forces to develop.

In fact Liberalism appears to me on all points to be superior to the other principle. The Liberal principle is in the very essence of our nature, in that thirst for happiness which we all feel in this life, which follows us everywhere, to be, however, never completely satisfied on this side of the grave. Our souls are immortal, but our means are limited. We unceasingly approach toward an ideal which we never reach. We dream of the highest good, but secure only the better. Hardly have we reached the limits we have yearned after, when we discover new horizons, which we have never dreamed of. We rush towards them, and when they have been reached in their turn, we find others which lead us on further and further.

Thus shall it be as long as man is what he is, as long as the immortal soul dwells in the mortal body, so long shall its desire be beyond its means, its actions can never equal its conceptions. He is the true Sysiphus of the fable, its completed work has ever to be recommenced.

This condition of our nature is exactly what constitutes the greatness of man; for it urges him ceaselessly to push forward to progress; our means are finite but our nature can be improved, and we have the infinite as our field of labor. There is then always room to improve our condition, to perfect our nature, and to render life more easy to a greater number. This it is which, in my opinion, constitutes the superiority of Liberalism. ...

It is true that there exists, in Europe, in France, in Italy and in Germany, a class of men who call themselves liberals, but who are liberal but in name, and who are the most dangerous of men. They are not Liberals, they are Revolutionists. Their principles carry them so far that they aspire to nothing less than the destruction of modern society. With these men we have no connection, but it is the tactics of our adversaries incessantly to compare us to them. Those accusations are beneath us, and the only reply worthy of us is to state our true principles and to always act in a manner conformable to them. ...

[L]ike the greater part of the young men of the country, I was educated by priests, and amongst young men who have become priests. I flatter myself that I have sincere friends amongst them, and to them at least I can and do say: "Can you find under the sun a happier country than ours, where the Catholic church is freer, and enjoys greater privileges"? Why then do you try to claim rights incompatible with our state of society, to expose the country to agitation, the consequences of which it is impossible to foresee.

But, I address myself generally to my countrymen and tell them: "We are a happy and free people; we owe this freedom to the Liberal institutions which govern us, which we owe to our forefathers and to the wisdom of the mother country.

"The policy of the Liberal party is to guard these institutions, to defend and propagate them, and under the rule of these institutions to develop the latent resources of our country. Such is the policy of the Liberal party, and it has none other."

Now to fully appreciate the value of our present institutions, let us compare our condition with what it was before they were granted to us.

Forty years ago the country was in a state of feverish excitement, and agitation which in a few months later, culminated in rebellion. The British Crown was upheld in the country, but by powder and shot. And yet what did our forefathers demand? Nothing else than our present institutions; these institutions were granted and loyally applied and behold the consequences; the English flag floats from the ancient Citadel of Quebec; it floats this evening above our heads and yet there is not a single English soldier in the country to defend it; its sole defence is the consciousness that we owe to it the liberty and security we find under it.

What Canadian is there who, comparing his own with even the freest of other countries, but feels proud of its institutions?

What Canadian is there who in going through the streets of this old city, and seeing the monument a few feet from this place, erected to the memory of two brave men, who fell on the same field of battle in fighting for the possession of this country, but feels proud of his country? In what country under the sun could you find a similar monument erected to the memory of the conqueror and the conquered. In what country under the sun could you find the names of the victor and the vanquished honored in the same degree, occupying the same place in the sentiments of the population.

Gentlemen, when in this last battle, commemorated by the monument erected to Wolfe and Montcalm, the cannon spread death among the French ranks, when the old heroes, whom victory had so often followed, saw her at last deserting them, when reclining on the sod, feeling their heart's blood flowing and life departing, they saw, as a consequence of their defeat, Quebec in the hands of the enemy and their country forever lost; no doubt their last thoughts turned towards their children, towards those whom they left without protection and without defence; doubtless they saw them persecuted, enslaved, humiliated; and then we may imagine their last breath to have been a cry of despair.

But, if on the other hand, heaven had permitted the veil of the future to be raised before their expiring vision, if heaven permitted them, before their eyes closed forever, to penetrate the unknown, if they could have seen their children free and happy, walking proudly in every rank of society; if they could have seen in the ancient cathedral the seat of honor of the French governors occupied by a French Governor, if they could have seen the spires of churches piercing the azure in every valley from the waters of the Gaspé to the plains of the Red River; if they could have seen this old flag which reminds us of their greatest victory, triumphantly borne in all our public ceremonies; finally, if they could have seen our free institutions, may we not believe that their last breath was softened to a murmur of thanks to heaven, and that they found consolation as they died.

If the shades of those heroes yet move about this old city for which they died, and if they are on this evening in this hall, we liberals may believe, at least we have the dear illusion, that their sympathies are entirely with us!

Wilfrid Laurier

64 Imperialism in Canada

W. Wilfred Campbell (1904)

EDITORS' INTRODUCTION

W. Wilfred Campbell was a member of the Anglican clergy and, later in life, a civil servant. He is also the author of numerous poems and other writings about Canada. Campbell delivered this speech to the Empire Club of Canada on November 23, 1904, one year after that speakers' forum was established in Toronto. The club's historic mandate, as its website declares, was to have "a distinctive basis of British unity in its work and policy." Campbell's essay fits well with the Empire Club's mission to ward off anti-British sentiment in favour of American fealty. In the essay Campbell baldly declares, "We have but one choice between two different imperialisms, that of Britain and that of the Imperial commonwealth to the south." He goes on to state, "if we ever hope ultimately to be a nation, we must in self-defence stay within the British Imperial system; whereas to enter that of the American means sheer annihilation of all our personality as a people."

Mr. Chairman,

I will not deal with the patriotic side of Imperialism more than to say that I feel we are all loyal British subjects as well as Canadians. I must insist, however, at the start, that the true Imperialist is as good a Canadian as any. I protest against the local Independence man calling himself the only true Canadian. I would retort: "Little he knows of Canada, who only Canada knows." I claim to be an Imperialist not only from the heart, but also from the head, and one of my strongest claims for Imperialism is that I believe it the only means by which there will ever be a real Canadian nation.

If we have in a sense become Americanized, it is our own fault as a people. It is because we have failed to develop our inward and Imperial resources apart from the material. It is because we have failed to use those present-day mediums, the press, the platform, the school, the pulpit, the library, the Parliament, as organizations to educate, influence and inspire our people toward Imperial and Canadian ideals. It is necessary to educate through the mediums I have mentioned, or else we as a people will go to the wall. What we want more than anything else is an inter-imperial Press Bureau established in London, England, to control, influence and elevate the press of the Empire. I would have editorials and all sorts of reading matter, clipped wholly or in part from the press of the Empire and re-circulated throughout the Empire, so that the daily and weekly thought, news and opinion of the various parts should be circulated throughout the whole. I would replace with this the large amount of what is called American boilerplate in our many Canadian local papers. I would have it attractive as well as elevating and unifying in influence. Let a people in an Empire have their press literature common to all, and the ends of the earth will not separate them.

Then there are the churches; they should be practical influences in Imperial union. It is the duty of Christianity to keep such a great moral force as the British Empire solid and lasting. It is our duty, in short, to organize and use all the practical means possible, because without organization we can do nothing. There is today a great misconception as to the true meaning of Imperialism. Present-day Imperialism is more than a mere self-satisfied jingoism, and a desire to emulate the splendours of ancient Rome. What its opponents fail to see is that true Imperialism, as it stands today, is more than an opinion; it is a vital force, a sort of necessary phase of human progressiveness; that instead of being the foe to the individual national life, it is the greatest necessary means to that end. My belief is that it is the one wicket-gate through which any young people of today can ever hope to finally attain a true national entity. Imperialism is a force which has seized the civilized world, and not to understand and recognize the new Imperial element in the world's progress, is, for the individual, to stamp himself as behind the times; and for the people to acknowledge itself uncivilized.

This Imperial idea is largely a desire to pool interests. It has permeated Canada. The union of churches, the confederation of the Provinces, the departmental store, the trust, the forming of societies for mutual interest, the very trades unions; in short all movements by which the mottoes "union is strength" and "the good of the many," are illustrated and carried out, are a part of this mysterious wave of human interest toward a newer, larger future—that new Imperialism which is taking possession of the modern world. It is, after all, the constructive form which the democracy is taking after its destructive period has passed; and which men like Mr. Goldwin Smith have been looking for, but have not recognized. Just as Christianity was evolved out of Judaism, so the present Imperialistic movement is coming up as the constructive period of the democracy. There is nothing antagonistic to the democratic idea in this Imperialism. It is not merely a re-action. It is something more. Men and nations in the democratic period merely separated, emancipated themselves to come together again under better conditions and through freer relations. The democracy had not for its end the welfare of the mere individual, but rather the good of the many. ...

All our religion, our commerce, our culture, our thoughts, our education, our travel, our progress, our invention, our science, our literature, is a continual rebuke to the separatist. Yet, to the large mass of our people this truth is so little known. It is decidedly time to point out in no uncertain manner that Imperialism is not a mere desire of a portion of ours or any people; but that it is a great force in the modern world, swaying us all; that it is here to stay until it has performed its work of reconstructing the modern democracy.

Are not our churches, as missionary bodies, continually in danger of embroiling themselves in distant lands? If this is wrong, why allow them to do so? The most of our Canadian churches were mixed up in the Boxer troubles in China, troubles which nearly involved the whole world in war. Should they withdraw their interests and cease to be Imperial? Look at our commerce, it demands that we have world-wide relations. It daily exposes us to outside complications. Must it cease? What of our press? The most Imperial influence in the whole world today? Should we muzzle it, because it is hourly interesting us, as it has been for nearly a century, in outside affairs? Might not its very attitude in the present war irritate either nation? What of our reading matter, our literature, our science, our trade, the very ladies and their fashions? You may call it cosmopolitanism; but it is simply Imperialism in one form or another. It is interdependence, rather than independence. The men who went to South Africa were Imperialists, but so were the Papal Zouaves, who went to Italy to fight for the Pope; so have been all of our business men, scholars, students, politicians and men in whatever walk of life who have left our country to make their way in Britain, the States and other countries; or who, residing here, have obtained and accepted honours, titles and recognition from governments and learned societies outside of Canada. These, each and all, have by their action and desire, voiced the incompleteness of a mere narrow Canadianism, and its impotency to satisfy the ambition and ideal of any man who has ambitions and ideals. These are all in act and ideal Imperialist, and among them as remarkable examples are those Canadians whose ambitions have led them to the wider field of the Imperial Parliament, such as Messrs. Blake, Brown, Devlin and Parker. Some of these Canadians have, inconsistently, been among the bitterest separatists. They would keep the average Canadian narrow and isolated, while they themselves take advantage of the larger scope. Is this fair, is it just, to the people? Why should they take part in Imperial affairs and deny the right of the people to do so? This is only one among many of the inconsistencies of the opponents of present-day Imperialism, who, while openly fighting it, have shown by their very method of opposition the vital necessity of a greater centre of social, political and ideal unity, such as is found in the great capital of the British Empire and its central government.

The opponents of Imperialism are in a minority, but they are in their way active. They are the "Little Englander," the "Little Irelander" and the "Little Canadian." Sincere as they may be, they are behind the times. They still live in the destructive period of the democracy. It is quite possible that even great movements or parties may change places, and the one progressive party become in time the historical back number. By clinging to a mere political creed or idea long after it has performed its work, men can become as obsolete in idea as old words and old customs. Today the men who are little Englanders, little Irelanders and little Canadians are behind the times in their political ideals. Many of them are so far bemuddled in 18th century issues, 18th century bitterness, and 18th century ideals long accomplished, that they have forgotten that this is the 20th century. They have forgotten that much has taken place in the interval; that the world of today has outgrown the stage of mere expansion and individualistic antagonism; that life has become more self-controlled, that man's view, as a whole, is larger, saner and more centralized. They do not see that the foes to be fought today are not old-world tyrannies, but the evils of ignorance and materialism and their attending tyranny everywhere, especially on this continent.

"We bear with us the despot in our blood."

There is a law of mankind that the struggle for liberty must ever be against the ruling force in a people. The ruling power today and for a century past has been the people. The democracy has now become the tyrant. For this reason it is all-important that the people should be warned of the fact that the danger is now to be found in the democratic rather than the aristocratic element, which no longer rules. If the democracy were left to itself, it would soon bring its own destruction, but Imperialism, or the saner constructive period, has taken its place. Whereas the early democracy was necessarily separative, destructive, revolutionary, iconoclastic, negative, bitter, alienating, breaking down, despairing, so the newer democracy or Imperialism, is saner, wiser, calmer, tolerant, constructive, unifying, peaceful, practical and hopeful. ...

Mr. Goldwin Smith in his address before the Canadian Club, made the statement that, no matter what our outside affiliations and ties, our future as a Canadian people had to be worked out in connection with this continent. He instanced also the blending of the crosses on the Union Jack as an example of the power of geographical propinquity to triumph over all other influences. Though he did not say it in so many words, he meant us to understand that no effort on our part or no outside influence could prevent our ultimate absorption in the United States. Now this geographical axiom was cleverly put, and might seem true at a superficial glance. But I deny that it is proved either in history or in our own experience.

The map of Europe as a whole shows that the greatest antagonism and alienation exists between the countries bordering upon each other, such as France and Germany, Russia and Germany. Then the blending of the crosses on the Jack took, as Mr. Smith knows, a thousand years to accomplish; and its ultimate accomplishment then, under far different circumstances and conditions from those under which he would have Canada merge into the United States. The very blending of the crosses is even after all that time, a direct negative to Mr. Smith's philosophy, as it shows that it was no absorption, but a free union of three independent peoples, each maintaining its personality and ideals, under one flag, the blend of their several national banners. I am afraid Mr. Smith's argument is not worthy of his well-known historical outlook; and his illustration of the geographical propinquity idea is singularly unfortunate, as has been pointed out.

I am not such a fatalist, as he is, to believe that mere force of numbers and geographical considerations are the only forces left in the world. It is not only a challenge to the spirit of a free people, but an insult to their personality and worth to say that they are but the driftwood, the puppets of mere population and physical geography. I believe (and I think that I have studied the spirit and panorama of history as wisely as Mr. Smith, though not so long) that there are stronger forces in men than those of mere geographical considerations to unite them or keep them apart. And I believe that it is in the power of the Canadian people to keep themselves apart, as an individual people, as the Scotland of North America, for a thousand years to come, if God has a special work for them to perform. This is after all the secret of all true nationhood, aside from a strong conservative race individuality. I know all Canadians feel in their hearts that we have gone too far forward as a separate individual people on this continent to lightly surrender all our individuality as a people. Small as we may be, great as are our problems, our difficulties to solve, we would answer that, as a people, as a Canadian community, from the Citadel of Quebec to the Yukon, from Nova Scotia to British Columbia, two significant names, we are here to stay; and it will need a stronger argument than the geographical to convince the Canadian people otherwise; and a stronger force than mere territorial propinquity to destroy our hopes and spirit as an individual Canadian people.

We in Canada have to realize this world-force called Imperialism. We cannot, any more than could the Boer or the Mormon stand alone. We can no more get away from this world-influence as a people, than we can live without world-trade, world-news, and a myriad other world-influences which guide and fill our lives. If we are to be in the procession at all we must either choose for ourselves or be led as an inferior people. We have but one choice between two different imperialisms, that of Britain and that of the Imperial Commonwealth to the south. If we examine into the matter calmly, aside from other considerations, we cannot but see that if we ever hope ultimately to be a nation, we must in self-defence stay within the British Imperial system; whereas to enter that of the American means sheer annihilation of all our personality as a people. We will be merely a bundle of states added to the rest, and will lose everything we value, our laws, customs, political system; our whole identity as a people.

Whereas, if we stay in the British Imperial system as an integral part of it, we lose nothing, but keep all we have got, and have a chance, ultimately, of becoming a great individual community on the northern part of this continent. By remaining British, we do not cease to be Canadian. Our very remoteness from the great Imperial centre will in itself safeguard our own individuality as it has done in the past. The very ocean barrier which has been regarded as an obstacle will be a blessing rather than a curse to the Empire and to the sister states making up the Imperial whole. It is this very widespread condition of the British Empire which makes her the one possible ideal union of independent peoples.

On the other hand the American Imperialism has many attendant dangers, springing out of the country's very compactness. The imperial control of a vast continent such as this by one dominant force is not a very satisfactory thing to contemplate. It is absurd to think that the American Republic will always remain a bundle of separated States, as it now is, any more than it was to be expected that its original republican ideal could forever remain. We have seen that original ideal largely superseded; and we will also see in time the present State demarcations disappear. Even today many of the States count for little in the control of the whole. We have for years heard more of a Solid South, the West and the North, than we have of State individuality. There is a strong possibility of a gradual coming together of certain portions of the country in groups of States; and this would be a great improvement in the rule of the country and less costly to the people. As the Canadian population develops more and more in the West, this will be also necessary in some of our Eastern Provinces. There is nothing more absurd than many of these local Governments, and much of our political corruption arises out of their petty condition. This is especially true of the States. If, as Mr. Smith seems to feel, the ultimate fate of Canada is to become a part of the North American Federation; if, I repeat, such a fate is intended to be the destiny of this country in some distant period of the future, then how much better it would be to postpone that date until, under such a condition as I have described here, we might be able as a large and powerful community to dictate our terms, and like Scotland's relationship to England, still retain our personality, socially and politically, as a Canadian people. Our choice in short is Imperialism or Imperialism. The wise Canadian, aside from all other considerations, will choose that Imperialism which is the freest and best, namely the one which will advance and develop Canada as an independent country and our people into a great and important branch of the British peoples. Let us be true to our independence in the Empire, but let it be the independence of self-respect, of a mature, not a childish people. Let it be the independence of a responsibility to ourselves and the Empire. Let it be a sane, generous spirit of self-sacrifice, such as the relation that a well-regulated, well-to-do household would bear toward the immediate community which it helps to compose; not a false independence of suspicion, distrust and antagonism eternally, straining toward separation.

We must realize sooner or later that no true patriotism is ever built upon or fostered in hatred. A mere negative patriotism is none, and the greatest weakness of the destructive period of the democracy has been its element built upon hate. The sane, hopeful ideal of Imperialism is one that should permeate our people. It would raise us out of the narrow slough of mere localism, that political and social slayer of any people, and make of us finally, what we hope to be one day, a great nation. But we must work to create a common sentiment in a great Imperial ideal; for without a common sentiment of feeling, the Empire, as it stands today, cannot last.

65 The Regina Manifesto

CCF (Co-operative Commonwealth Federation) (1933)

EDITORS' INTRODUCTION

Led by Tommy Douglas, the CCF emerged as a national party in the midst of the Great Depression. In contrast to the federal Conservative and Liberal parties, the CCF was explicitly socialist in its ideology although democratic rather than revolutionary in its recommended means to achieve its policy goals. The Regina Manifesto is the CCF's policy program adopted at its first national convention in Regina, Saskatchewan in July 1933. It remained the official CCF program until 1956, at which time the CCF adopted the more rhetorically moderate and Keynesian Winnipeg Declaration. The CCF's Regina Manifesto articulates the party's aim "to replace the present capitalist system, with its inherent injustice and inhumanity, by a social order from which the domination and exploitation of one class by another will be eliminated." Ironically, many of the CCF's specific policy recommendations, such as publicly organized health, hospital and medical services, a national central bank "to control the flow of credit and the general price level," and a national labour code including "insurance covering illness, accident, old age, and unemployment" were adopted by other parties to became core national policies in subsequent decades.

Programme of the Co-operative Commonwealth Federation, Adopted at First National Convention (Regina, Saskatchewan, July 19–21, 1933)

The CCF is a federation of organizations whose purpose is the establishment in Canada of a Co-operative Commonwealth in which the principle regulating production, distribution and exchange will be the supplying of human needs and not the making of profits.

We aim to replace the present capitalist system, with its inherent injustice and inhumanity, by a social order from which the domination and exploitation of one class by another will be eliminated, in which economic planning will supersede unregulated private enterprise and competition, and in which genuine democratic self-government, based upon economic equality will be possible.

The present order is marked by glaring inequalities of wealth and opportunity, by chaotic waste and instability; and in an age of plenty it condemns the great mass of the people to poverty and insecurity. Power has become more and more concentrated into the hands of a small irresponsible minority of financiers and industrialists and to their predatory interests the majority are habitually sacrificed. When private profit is the main stimulus to economic

Source: Saskatchewan NDP Provincial Office.

effort, our society oscillates between periods of feverish prosperity in which the main benefits go to speculators and profiteers, and of catastrophic depression, in which the common man's normal state of insecurity and hardship is accentuated. We believe that these evils can be removed only in a planned and socialized economy in which our natural resources and principal means of production and distribution are owned, controlled and operated by the people.

The new social order at which we aim is not one in which individuality will be crushed out by a system of regimentation.

Nor shall we interfere with cultural rights of racial or religious minorities. What we seek is a proper collective organization of our economic resources such as will make possible a much greater degree of leisure and a much richer individual life for every citizen.

This social and economic transformation can be brought about by political action, through the election of a government inspired by the ideal of a Co-operative Commonwealth and supported by a majority of the people. We do not believe in change by violence.

We consider that both the old parties in Canada are the instruments of capitalist interests and cannot serve as agents of social reconstruction, and that whatever the superficial differences between them, they are bound to carry on government in accordance with the dictates of the big business interests who finance them.

The CCF aims at political power in order to put an end to this capitalist domination of our political life. It is a democratic movement, a federation of farmer, labour and socialist organizations, financed by its own members and seeking to achieve its ends solely by constitutional methods. It appeals for support from all who believe that the time has come for a far-reaching reconstruction of our economic and political institutions and who are willing to work together for the carrying out of the following policies:

1. Planning

The establishment of a planned, socialized economic order, in order to make possible the most efficient development of the national resources and the most equitable distribution of the national income.

The first step in this direction will be the setting up of a National Planning Commission consisting of a small body of economists, engineers and statisticians assisted by an appropriate technical staff. ...

The Commission will be responsible to the Cabinet and will work in co-operation with the Managing Boards of the Socialized Industries.

It is now certain that in every industrial country some form of planning will replace the disintegrating capitalist system. The CCF will provide that in Canada the planning shall be done, not by a small group of capitalist magnates in their own interests, but by public servants acting in the public interest and responsible to the people as a whole.

2. Socialization of Finance

Socialization of all financial machinery—banking, currency, credit, and insurance, to make possible the effective control of currency, credit and prices, and the supplying of new productive equipment for socially desirable purposes.

Planning by itself will be of little use if the public authority has not the power to carry its plans into effect. Such power will require the control of finance and of all those vital industries and services, which, if they remain in private hands, can be used to thwart or corrupt the will of the public authority. Control of finance is the first step in the control of the whole economy. The chartered banks must be socialized and removed from the control of private profit-seeking interests; and the national banking system thus established must have at its head a Central Bank to control the flow of credit and the general price level, and to regulate foreign exchange operations. A National Investment Board must also be set up, working in co-operation with the socialized banking system to mobilize and direct the unused surpluses of production for socially desired purposes as determined by the Planning Commission.

Insurance Companies, which provide one of the main channels for the investment of individual savings and which, under their present competitive organization, charge needlessly high premiums for the social services that they render, must also be socialized.

3. Social Ownership

Socialization (Dominion, Provincial or Municipal) of transportation, communications, electric power and all other industries and services essential to social planning, and their operation under the general direction of the Planning Commission by competent managements freed from day to day political interference.

Public utilities must be operated for the public benefit and not for the private profit of a small group of owners or financial manipulators. Our natural resources must be developed by the same methods. Such a programme means the continuance and extension of the public ownership enterprises in which most governments in Canada have already gone some distance. Only by such public ownership, operated on a planned economy, can our main industries be saved from the wasteful competition of the ruinous overdevelopment and over-capitalization which are the inevitable outcome of capitalism. Only in a regime of public ownership and operation will the full benefits accruing from centralized control and mass production be passed on to the consuming public.

Transportation, communications and electric power must come first in a list of industries to be socialized. Others, such as mining, pulp and paper and the distribution of milk, bread, coal and gasoline, in which exploitation, waste, or financial malpractices are particularly prominent must next be brought under social ownership and operation.

In restoring to the community its natural resources and in taking over industrial enterprises from private into public control we do not propose any policy of outright confiscation. What we desire is the most stable and equitable transition to the Cooperative Commonwealth. It is impossible to decide the policies to be followed in particular cases in an uncertain future, but we insist upon certain broad principles. The welfare of the community must take supremacy over the claims of private wealth. In times of war, human life has been conscripted. Should economic circumstances call for it, conscription of wealth would be more justifiable. We recognize the need for compensation in the case of individuals and institutions which must receive adequate maintenance during the transitional period before the planned economy becomes fully operative. But a CCF government will not play the role of rescuing bankrupt private concerns for the benefit of promoters and of stock and bond holders. It will not pile up a deadweight burden of unremunerative debt which represents claims upon the public treasury of a functionless owner class. ...

4. Agriculture

Security of tenure for the farmer upon his farm on conditions to be laid down by individual provinces; insurance against unavoidable crop failure; removal of the tariff burden from the operations of agriculture; encouragement of producers' and consumers' cooperatives; the restoration and maintenance of an equitable relationship between prices of agricultural products and those of other commodities and services; and improving the efficiency of export trade in farm products.

The security of tenure for the farmer upon his farm which is imperilled by the present disastrous situation of the whole industry, together with adequate social insurance, ought to be guaranteed under equitable conditions.

The prosperity of agriculture, the greatest Canadian industry, depends upon a rising volume of purchasing power of the masses in Canada for all farm goods consumed at home, and upon the maintenance of large scale exports of the stable commodities at satisfactory prices or equitable commodity exchange.

The intense depression in agriculture today is a consequence of the general world crisis caused by the normal workings of the capitalistic system resulting in: (1) Economic nationalism expressing itself in tariff barriers and other restrictions of world trade; (2) The decreased purchasing power of unemployed and under-employed workers and of the Canadian people in general; (3) The exploitation of both primary producers and consumers by monopolistic corporations who absorb a great proportion of the selling price of farm products. ...

5. External Trade

The regulation in accordance with the National plan of external trade through import and export boards.

Canada is dependent on external sources of supply for many of her essential requirements of raw materials and manufactured products.

These she can obtain only by large exports of the goods she is best fitted to produce. The strangling of our export trade by insane protectionist policies must be brought to an end. But the old controversies between free traders and protectionists are now largely obsolete. In a world of nationally organized economies Canada must organize the buying and selling of her main imports and exports under public boards, and take steps to regulate the flow of less important commodities by a system of licenses. By so doing she will be enabled to make the best trade agreements possible with foreign countries, put a stop to the exploitation of both primary producer and ultimate consumer, make possible the coordination of internal processing, transportation and marketing of farm products, and facilitate the establishment of stable prices for such export commodities.

6. Co-Operative Institutions

The encouragement by the public authority of both producers' and consumers' cooperative institutions.

In agriculture, as already mentioned, the primary producer can receive a larger net revenue through cooperative organization of purchases and marketing. Similarly in retail distribution of staple commodities such as milk, there is room for development both of public municipal operation and of consumers' cooperatives, and such cooperative organization can be extended into wholesale distribution and into manufacturing. Cooperative enterprises should be assisted by the state through appropriate legislation and through the provision of adequate credit facilities.

7. Labour Code

A National Labour Code to secure for the worker maximum income and leisure, insurance covering illness, accident, old age, and unemployment, freedom of association and effective participation in the management of his industry or profession.

The spectre of poverty and insecurity which still haunts every worker, though technological developments have made possible a high standard of living for everyone, is a disgrace which must be removed from our civilization. The community must organize its resources to effect progressive reduction of the hours of work in accordance with technological development and to provide a constantly rising standard of life to everyone who is willing to work. A labour code must be developed which will include state regulation of wages, equal reward and equal opportunity of advancement for equal services, irrespective of sex; measures to guarantee the right to work or the right to maintenance through stabilization of employment and through unemployment insurance; social insurance to protect workers and their families against the hazards of sickness, death, industrial accident and old age; limitation of hours of work and protection of health and safety in industry. Both wages and insurance benefits should be varied in accordance with family needs.

In addition workers must be guaranteed the undisputed right to freedom of association, and should be encouraged and assisted by the state to organize themselves in trade unions. By means of collective agreements and participation in works councils, the workers can achieve fair working rules and share in the control of industry and profession; and their organizations will be indispensable elements in a system of genuine industrial democracy.

The labour code should be uniform throughout the country. But the achievement of this end is difficult so long as jurisdiction over labour legislation under the B.N.A. Act is mainly in the hands of the provinces. It is urgently necessary, therefore, that the B.N.A. Act be amended to make such a national labour code possible.

8. Socialized Health Services

Publicly Organized Health, Hospital and Medical Services.

With the advance of medical science the maintenance of a healthy population has become a function for which every civilized community should undertake responsibility. Health services should be made at least as freely available as are educational services today. But under a system which is still mainly one of private enterprise the costs of proper medical care, such as the wealthier members of society can easily afford, are at present prohibitive for great masses of the people. A properly organized system of public health services including medical and dental care, which would stress the prevention rather than the cure of illness, should be extended to all our people in both rural and urban areas. This is an enterprise in which Dominion, Provincial and Municipal authorities, as well as the medical and dental professions, can cooperate.

9. B.N.A. Act

The amendment of the Canadian Constitution, without infringing upon racial or religious minority rights or upon legitimate provincial claims to autonomy, so as to give the Dominion Government adequate powers to deal effectively with urgent economic problems which are essentially national in scope; the abolition of the Canadian Senate.

We propose that the necessary amendments to the B.N.A. Act shall be obtained as speedily as required, safeguards being inserted to ensure that the existing rights of racial and religious minorities shall not be changed without their own consent. What is chiefly needed today is the placing in the hands of the national government of more power to control national economic development. In a rapidly changing economic environment our political constitution must be reasonably flexible. The present division of powers between Dominion and Provinces reflects the conditions of a pioneer, mainly agricultural, community in 1867. Our constitution must be brought into line with the increasing industrialization of the country and the consequent centralization of economic and financial power. ...

The Canadian Senate, which was originally created to protect provincial rights, but has failed even in this function, has developed into a bulwark of capitalist interests, as is illustrated by the large number of company directorships held by its aged members. In its peculiar composition of a fixed number of members appointed for life it is one of the most reactionary assemblies in the civilized world. It is a standing obstacle to all progressive legislation, and the only permanently satisfactory method of dealing with the constitutional difficulties it creates is to abolish it.

10. External Relations

A Foreign Policy designed to obtain international economic cooperation and to promote disarmament and world peace.

Canada has a vital interest in world peace. We propose, therefore, to do everything in our power to advance the idea of international cooperation as represented by the League of Nations and the International Labour Organization. We would extend our diplomatic machinery for keeping in touch with the main centres of world interest. But we believe that genuine international cooperation is incompatible with the capitalist regime which is in force in most countries, and that strenuous efforts are needed to rescue the League from its present condition of being mainly a League of capitalist Great Powers. We stand resolutely against all participation in imperialist wars. Within the British Commonwealth, Canada must maintain her autonomy as a completely self-governing nation. We must resist all attempts to build up a new economic British Empire in place of the old political one, since such attempts readily lend themselves to the purposes of capitalist exploitation and may easily lead to further world wars.

Canada must refuse to be entangled in any more wars fought to make the world safe for capitalism.

11. Taxation and Public Finance

A new taxation policy designed not only to raise public revenues but also to lessen the glaring inequalities of income and to provide funds for social services and the socialization of industry; the cessation of the debt-creating system of Public Finance.

In the type of economy that we envisage, the need for taxation, as we now understand it, will have largely disappeared. It will nevertheless be essential during the transition period, to use the taxing powers, along with the other methods proposed elsewhere, as a means of providing for the socialization of industry, and for extending the benefits of increased Social Services. ...

We propose that all Public Works, as directed by the Planning Commission, shall be financed by the issuance of credit, as suggested, based upon the National Wealth of Canada.

12. Freedom

Freedom of speech and assembly for all; repeal of Section 98 of the Criminal Code; amendment of the Immigration Act to prevent the present inhuman policy of deportation; equal treatment before the law of all residents of Canada irrespective of race, nationality or religious or political beliefs.

In recent years, Canada has seen an alarming growth of Fascist tendencies among all governmental authorities. The most elementary rights of freedom of speech and assembly have been arbitrarily denied to workers and to all whose political and social views do not meet with the approval of those in power. The lawless and brutal conduct of the police in certain centres in preventing public meetings and in dealing with political prisoners must cease.

Section 98 of the Criminal Code which has been used as a weapon of political oppression by a panic-stricken capitalist government, must be wiped off the statute book and those who have been imprisoned under it must be released. An end must be put to the inhuman practice of deporting immigrants who were brought to this country by immigration propaganda and now, through no fault of their own, find themselves victims of an executive department against whom there is no appeal to the courts of the land. We stand for full economic, political and religious liberty for all.

13. Social Justice

The establishment of a commission composed of psychiatrists, psychologists, socially minded jurists and social workers, to deal with all matters pertaining to crime and punishment and the general administration of law, in order to humanize the law and to bring it into harmony with the needs of the people.

While the removal of economic inequality will do much to overcome the most glaring injustices in the treatment of those who come into conflict with the law, our present archaic system must be changed and brought into accordance with a modern concept of human relationships. The new system must not be based as is the present one, upon vengeance and fear, but upon an understanding of human behaviour. For this reason its planning and control cannot be left in the hands of those steeped in the outworn legal tradition; and therefore it is proposed that there shall be established a national commission composed of psychiatrists, psychologists, socially minded jurists and social workers whose duty it shall be to devise a system of prevention and correction consistent with other features of the new social order.

14. An Emergency Programme

The assumption by the Dominion Government of direct responsibility for dealing with the present critical unemployment situation and for tendering suitable work or adequate maintenance; the adoption of measures to relieve the extremity of the crisis such as a programme of public spending on housing, and other enterprises that will increase the real wealth of Canada, to be financed by the issue of credit based on the national wealth.

The extent of unemployment and the widespread suffering which it has caused, creates a situation with which provincial and municipal governments have long been unable to cope and forces upon the Dominion government direct responsibility for dealing with the crisis as the only authority with financial resources adequate to meet the situation. Unemployed workers must be secured in the tenure of their homes, and the scale and methods of relief, at present altogether inadequate, must be such as to preserve decent human standards of living.

It is recognized that even after a Cooperative Commonwealth Federation Government has come into power, a certain period of time must elapse before the planned economy can be fully worked out.

During this brief transitional period, we propose to provide work and purchasing power for those now unemployed by a far-reaching programme of public expenditure on housing, slum clearance, hospitals, libraries, schools, community halls, parks, recreational projects, reforestation, rural electrification, the elimination of grade crossings, and other similar projects in both town and country. This programme, which would be financed by the issuance of credit based on the national wealth, would serve the double purpose of creating employment and meeting recognized social needs. ...

Emergency measures, however, are of only temporary value, for the present depression is a sign of the mortal sickness of the whole capitalist system, and this sickness cannot be cured by the application of salves. These leave untouched the cancer which is eating at the heart of our society, namely, the economic system in which our natural resources and our principal means of production and distribution are owned, controlled and operated for the private profit of a small proportion of our population.

No CCF Government will rest content until it has eradicated capitalism and put into operation the full programme of socialized planning which will lead to the establishment in Canada of the Cooperative Commonwealth.

66 Lament for a Nation

George Grant (1965)

EDITORS' INTRODUCTION

George P. Grant was a distinguished philosopher and essayist, whose writings have influenced political and philosophical debate from the 1960s to the present day. He was a professor of religion at McMaster University and professor of political science at Dalhousie University. Professor Grant wrote Lament for a Nation *specifically in response to the decision by the federal Liberal government to accept US nuclear arms on Canadian soil after it defeated the Conservative government under Prime Minister Diefenbaker. Grant feared that this signalled the eventual absorption of Canadian culture and identity into the United States. The essay is more than simply a concern about continental integration; it also reflects a concern about the loss of a community "which had a stronger sense of the common good and of public order than was possible under the individualism of the American capitalist dream." As does Campbell's essay on British imperialism, Grant expresses a belief that distinctive Canadian values, and protection of francophone and indigenous cultures, lie within the British conservative tradition of Burke rather than the American liberal tradition of Locke and Smith. But he is much more pessimistic than Campbell about those traditions' survival in the face of American imperialism; hence, the lament.*

The impossibility of conservatism in our era is the impossibility of Canada. As Canadians we attempted a ridiculous task in trying to build a conservative nation in the age of progress, on a continent we share with the most dynamic nation on earth. The current of modern history was against us.

A society only articulates itself as a nation through some common intention among its people. The constitutional arrangements of 1791, and the wider arrangements of the next century, were only possible because of a widespread determination not to become part of the great Republic. Among both the French and the British, this negative intention sprang from widely divergent traditions. What both peoples had in common was the fact they both recognized, that they could only be preserved outside the United States of America. The French were willing to co-operate with the English because they had no alternative but to go along with the endurable arrangements proposed by the ruling power. Both the French and the British had limited common ground in their sense of social order—belief that society required a high degree of law, and respect for a public conception of virtue. Both would grant the state much wider rights to control the individual than was recognized in the libertarian ideas of the American constitution. If their different conservatisms could have become

Source: Excerpted from *Lament for a Nation: The Defeat of Canadian Nationalism* by George Grant. Carleton Library Series, 1965. Notes omitted. Reprinted by permission.

a conscious bond, this nation might have preserved itself. An indigenous society might have continued to exist on the northern half of this continent.

To see why this intention failed in Canada, it is necessary to look more closely at the origins of both the French and the British traditions to see what has happened to them. To start with the British, it would be foolish to over-emphasize the niceties of theory among those who came to the St. John Valley or Upper Canada in the late eighteenth and early nineteenth centuries. It is difficult to put into words the conservatism of the English-speaking peoples in the Atlantic colonies or Upper Canada. The manifold waves of differing settlers must not be simplified into any common pattern. Much of English-speaking conservatism was simply a loyalty based on the flow of trade, and therefore destined to change when that flow changed. To repeat, Diefenbaker spoke with telling historical sense when he mentioned the Annexation Manifesto in his last speech to Parliament before the defeat of his government in 1963. He pointed out the similarity between the views of the Montreal merchants in 1849 and the wealthy of Toronto and Montreal in 1963. In neither case did they care about Canada. No small country can depend for its existence on the loyalty of its capitalists. International interests may require the sacrifice of the lesser loyalty of patriotism. Only in dominant nations is the loyalty of capitalists ensured. In such situations, their interests are tied to the strength and vigour of their empire.

This does not imply that the nationalism in English-speaking Canada was simply a front for interest. Many of its elements were shaped by that strange phenomenon, British conservatism, which led the settlers to try to build on the northern half of this continent an independent society. British conservatism is difficult to describe because it is less a clear view of existence than an appeal to an ill-defined past. The writings of Edmund Burke are evidence of this. Yet many of the British officials, many Loyalists, and later many immigrants felt this conservatism very strongly. It was an inchoate desire to build, in these cold and forbidding regions, a society with a greater sense of order and restraint than freedom-loving republicanism would allow. It was no better defined than a kind of suspicion that we in Canada could be less lawless and have a greater sense of propriety than the United States. The inherited determination not to be Americans allowed these British people to come to a *modus vivendi* with the more defined desires of the French. English-speaking Canadians have been called a dull, stodgy, and indeed costive lot. In these dynamic days, such qualities are particularly unattractive to the chic. Yet our stodginess has made us a society of greater simplicity, formality, and perhaps even innocence than the people to the south. Whatever differences there were between the Anglicans and the Presbyterians, and however differently their theologians might interpret the doctrine of original sin, both communities believed that the good life made strict demands on self-restraint. Nothing was more alien to them than the "emancipation of the passions" desired in American liberalism. An ethic of self-restraint naturally looks with suspicion on utopian movements, which proceed from an ethic of freedom. The early leaders of British North America identified lack of public and personal restraint with the democratic Republic. Their conservatism was essentially the social doctrine that public order and tradition, in contrast to freedom and experiment, were central to the good life. The British Crown was a symbol of a continuing loyalty to the state—less equivocal than was expected from republicans. In our early expansions, this conservative nationalism expressed itself in the use of public control in the political and economic spheres. Our opening of the West differed from that of the United States, in that the law of the central government was used more extensively, and less reliance was placed on the free settler. Until recently, Canadians have been much more willing than Americans to use governmental control over economic life to protect the public good against private freedom. To repeat, Ontario Hydro, the CNR, and the CBC were all established by Conservative governments. The early establishment of Ontario Hydro succeeded because of the efforts of an administrator, a politician, and a journalist, all of whom wrapped themselves in the Union Jack in their efforts to keep the development of electric power out of the hands of individual freedom.

English-speaking Canadians had never broken with their origins in Western Europe. Many of them had continuing connections with the British Isles, which in the nineteenth century still had ways of life from before the age of progress. That we never broke with Great Britain is often said to prove that we are not a nation but a colony. But the great politicians who believed in this connection—from Joseph Howe and Robert Baldwin to Sir John A. Macdonald and Sir Robert Borden, and indeed to John G. Diefenbaker himself—make a long list. They did not see it this way, but rather as a relation to the font of constitutional government in the British Crown. Many Canadians saw it as a means of preserving at every level of our life—religious, educational, political, social—certain forms of existence that distinguish us from the United States. ...

For all the fruitfulness of the British tradition in nineteenth-century Canada, it did not provide any radically different approach to the questions of industrial civilization. Canadians in particular felt the blessings of technology in an environment so hard that to master it needed courage. But conservatism must languish as technology increases. It was not conceivable that industrial society would be organized along essentially different principles from those to the south. Try to imagine whether Toronto could be a quite dissimilar community from Buffalo or Chicago, or Vancouver from Seattle, and this is to answer the question. What other kind of industrial civilization is likely to appear anywhere on earth, let alone on the northern frontier of Manifest Destiny?

Because of the British tradition, socialist movements have been stronger in Canada than in the United States. But socialism has been a weakening force in Canadian life since 1945. To repeat a previous generalization: democratic socialism is not, as it believed itself to be, the high crest of the wave of the future, but rather a phenomenon from the nineteenth century. Since 1945, the forces that will shape our future in the West show themselves to be bureaucratic state capitalism. The only time when democratic socialism was strong in Canadian industrial society was in Ontario during the utopian days at the end of the Second World War. But the Frost and Robarts régimes have shown what a feeble and transitory phenomenon that was. In Ontario, some form of planned economy was the only conceivable alternative to Americanization. But to have anticipated a socialist Ontario was to hope rather than to predict. Certainly its leadership could not have come from the good-natured Utopians who led our socialist parties. They had no understanding of the dependence of socialism and nationalism in the Canadian setting. Their confused optimism is seen in the fact that they have generally acted as if they were "left-wing" allies of the Liberal party. Socialist leadership in Canada has been largely a pleasant remnant of the British nineteenth century—the Protestant tabernacle turned liberal. Such a doctrine was too flaccid to provide any basis for independence. ...

[I]ndigenous cultures are dying everywhere in the modern world. French-Canadian nationalism is a last-ditch stand. The French on this continent will at least disappear from history with more than the smirks and whimpers of their English-speaking compatriots—with their flags flying and, indeed, with some guns blazing. The reality of their culture, and their desire not to be swamped, cannot save them from the inexorable facts in the continental case. Solutions vary to the problem of how an autonomous culture can be maintained in Québec. But all the answers face the same dilemma: Those who want to maintain separateness also want the advantages of the age of progress. These two ends are not compatible, for the pursuit of one negates the pursuit of the other. Nationalism can only be asserted successfully by an identification with technological advance; but technological advance entails the disappearance of those indigenous differences that give substance to nationalism. The solutions to this dilemma, which were attempted in the last few years, illustrate its nature. ...

René Lévesque's solution to the problem, unlike Duplessis's liaison with American capitalism, seems to attempt to build a semi-socialist society within the bounds of the province. The idea is to guarantee that the managerial élite be men of French culture, and that the control of the economy rest firmly in native hands. In such a scheme the continuance of Confederation is simply a question of convenience. If French civilization can be protected as a province within Confederation, then all well and good. If it cannot be, then separatism becomes a necessity. Levesque's brilliant description of Laurier as "a black king" shows the seriousness of his intention. ...

The financial pages of every newspaper are filled with announcements of French-speaking appointments to management. Continental capitalists have learnt that they are going to be in trouble if such appointments are not made. But when French nationalists derive satisfaction from these appointments, they would do well to remind themselves of the ancient adage: "I fear the Greeks, especially when they come with gifts." Corporations make concessions about management personnel for the sake of better relations with the alien community. These do not involve the basic control of the economy. Here the lines of battle will surely be drawn. How long will the people of Quebec be willing to pay the economic price of rejecting the terms laid down by big business for the development of power at Hamilton Falls? It is not likely that even such an unusual Liberal government as that of Prime Minister Lesage will be able to wrest control of the economy from the corporations and then keep it in the government's hands. ...

The new social sciences are dissolvents of the family, of Catholicism, of classical education. It is surely more than a language that Levesque wishes to preserve in his nation. New Orleans is a pleasant place for tourists. The dilemma remains. French Canadians must modernize their educational system if they are to have more than a peon's place in their own industrialization. Yet to modernize their education is to renounce their particularity. At the heart of modern liberal education lies the desire to homogenize the world. Today's natural and social sciences were consciously produced as instruments to this end.

In the immediate future, the wilder of the nationalist French-Canadian youths may hope to build some kind of Castro-like state in Quebec. As traditional Catholicism breaks up, there will be some exciting moments. A Catholic society cannot be modernized as easily as a Protestant one. When the dam breaks the flood will be furious. Nevertheless, the young intellectuals of the upper-middle class will gradually desert their existentialist nationalism and take the places made for them in the continental corporations. The enormity of the break from the past will arouse in the dispossessed youth intense forms of beatness. But after all, the United States supports a large beat fringe. Joan Baez and Pete Seeger titillate the *status quo* rather than threaten it. Dissent is built into the fabric of the modern system. We bureaucratize it as much as everything else. Is there any reason to believe that French Canada will be different? A majority of the young is gradually patterned for its place in the bureaucracies. Those who resist such shaping will retreat into a fringe world of pseudo-revolt.

What does Lévesque think is the place of Catholicism in the continuing French fact? The young French Canadians who desire a better society, because they grew up under Duplessis, believe in both nationalism and social freedom. Their liberalism is openly anti-Catholic and even existentialist or Marxist. Others accept Catholicism but are determined that the Church should be disestablished. But the old Church with its educational privileges has been the chief instrument by which an indigenous French culture has survived in North America. Liberalism is the ideological means whereby indigenous cultures are homogenized. How then can nationalism and liberalism merge together into a consistent political creed?

In 1918, Bourassa put the purposes of French-Canadian existence in clear words:

> *Notre tâche à nous, Canadiens-français, c'est de prolonger en Amérique l'effort de la France chrétienne; c'est de déjendre contre tout venant, le fallût-il contre la France elle-même, notre patrimoine religieux et national. Ce patrimoine, il n'est pas à nous seulement: il appartient à toute l'Amerique catholique, dont il est le foyer inspirateur et rayonnant; il appartient à toute l'Eglise, dont il est le principal point d'appui dans cette partie du monde; il appartient à toute la civilisation française, dont il est l'unique port de refuge et d'attache dans cette mer immense de l'américanisme saxonisant.*

Here is a national intention, beautifully expressed.

Bourassa's clarity about this intention was not matched by his understanding of what the twentieth century was going to be. He considered North America to be essentially *saxonisant* and dominated by an explicitly Protestant ethos—the "time is money" theology of a debased and secularized Calvinism. He lived in a world in which the British Empire still appeared a dominant force. Presumably he still thought of Latin America as in that twilight period of subservience to North America, which extended from the beginning of the nineteenth century. Above all, Bourassa does not seem to have been aware of the effect of homogenization—what industrial civilization would do to all countries and all religions. Industrial culture had arisen in Protestant societies and was the very form of *américanisme saxonisant* that surrounded his nation. Bourassa seems therefore to have identified the two, rather than to have recognized that technological culture was a dissolvent of all national and religious traditions, not simply an expression of one of them. There is little of Gandhi's rejection of industrialism in his writings, but rather the positive assumption that the culture of Quebec was French Christianity. Nationalism was for him something essentially conservative—the maintenance in his part of the world of the true way of life against the heresy of *americanisme saxonisant.* This was a wasting and tragic dream for our dynamic era. Nevertheless, despite his unawareness of the dynamism of the twentieth century, he was surely right when he said that Catholicism as well as Frenchness was necessary to make Quebec a nation.

Dynamic civilization has spread like oil over the surface of the world during the half-century since Bourassa wrote. The twentieth century is not something that belongs essentially to *l'américanisme saxonisant.* It is no longer potential but actual in Quebec. ...

The possibility of such a [liberalized] Catholicism in Quebec cannot be discussed apart from the relation of Catholicism to technology throughout the world. That intricate question cannot be discussed at length in this writing. Suffice it to say that, although the recent state-ments of the Papacy seem optimistic about the Church's ability to live with our age, it is still an open question whether Catholicism will be able to humanize mass Western society or be swept into the catacombs. What happens to the Catholic view of man, when Catholics are asked to shape society through the new sciences of biochemistry, physiological psychology, and sociology? These sciences arose from assumptions hostile to the Catholic view of man. Whatever the historical outcome, the ability of Catholicism to sustain a continuing Franco-American civilization appears dubious. ...

Lévesque, at least, appears to be aware how difficult it will be to preserve the French fact on this continent. The French-Canadian liberals who plead for the continuance of Confed-eration and the extension of co-operative federalism seem to be more naive. The confusion of these French-Canadian liberals is evident in a recent pronouncement by seven French-Canadian intellectuals under the title "An Appeal for Realism in Politics." This pronounce-ment is considered by its authors to be a Canadian—not a French-Canadian—manifesto. It is an appeal for the continuance of Confederation against the various parochialisms that threaten it. It puts forward the hope for a vital federalism that will accept the cultural diver-sity of Canada but will not be economically nationalist. It is not my purpose here to discuss its detailed proposals, but to quote its philosophical justification as an example of the present thought of French-Canadian liberal intellectuals. At the end of the manifesto, two reasons are given why the writers refuse to be "locked into a constitutional frame smaller than Can-ada." The second reason for this is described in the following language:

> The most valid trends today are toward more enlightened humanism, toward various forms of po-litical, social, and economic universalism. Canada is a reproduction on a smaller and simpler scale of this universal phenomenon. The challenge is for a number of ethnic groups to learn to live to-gether. It is a modern challenge, meaningful and indicative of what can be expected from man. If Canadians cannot make a success of a country such as theirs, how can they contribute in any way to the elaboration of humanism, to the formulation of the international structures of tomorrow? To confess one's inability to make Canadian Confederation work is, at this stage of history, to admit one's unworthiness to contribute to the universal order.

Leaving aside such questions as what makes a trend "valid" and what are the conditions of human enlightenment, the point at issue is that the authors assert their faith in universal-ism and in the continued existence of Canada at one and the same time. The faith in uni-versalism makes it accurate to call the authors liberal. But how can a faith in universalism go with a desire for the continuance of Canada? The belief in Canada's continued existence has always appealed against universalism. It appealed to particularity against the wider loy-alty to the continent. If universalism is the most "valid modern trend," then is it not right for Canadians to welcome our integration into the empire? Canadian nationalism is a more universal faith than French-Canadian nationalism. But if one is a universalist, why should one stop at that point of particularity?

Many French-Canadian liberals seem to espouse "enlightened humanism" and universal-ism as against the parochial Catholicism that inhibited them personally and politically when it ruled their society. They seem to expect liberalism to purge Catholicism, but to maintain within itself all that was best in the ancient faith. In this manifesto, for example, the authors espouse the continuance of indigenous cultures and regret the victimizing of the "Indians,

Métis, Orientals, Doukhobors, Hutterites, and dissidents of all kinds" in our past. They call for the democratic protection of such cultures. But do they not know that liberalism in its most unequivocal form (that is, untinged by memories of past traditions) includes not only the idea of universalism but also that of homogeneity? The high rhetoric of democracy was used when the Doukhobors were "victimized" under a French-Canadian Prime Minister. If the writers are to be truly liberal, they cannot escape the fact that the goal of their political philosophy is the universal and homogeneous state. If this is the noblest goal, then the idea of Canada was a temporary and misguided parochialism. Only those who reject that goal and claim that the universal state will be a tyranny, that is, a society destructive of human excellence, can assert consistently that parochial nationalisms are to be fought for. My purpose is not to debate at this point the question whether the "universal" values of liberalism lead to human excellence. What is indubitable is that those values go with internationalism rather than with nationalism. In this century, many men have known that the choice between internationalism and nationalism is the same choice as that between liberalism and conservatism. In a Canadian setting, internationalism means continentalism. French-Canadian liberalism does not seem to be the means whereby this nation could have been preserved.

All the preceding arguments point to the conclusion that Canada cannot survive as a sovereign nation. In the language of the new bureaucrats, our nation was not a viable entity. If one adds to this proposition the memory of the Liberals' policies, then one can truly say that the argument in their favour succeeds. They have been the best rulers for Canada because they have led the majority of us to accept necessity without much pain. *Fata volentem ducunt, nolentem trahunt.* Fate leads the willing, and drives the unwilling. The debt that we owe the Liberals is that they have been so willing to be led. The party has been made up of those who put only one condition on their willingness: that they should have personal charge of the government while our sovereignty disappears.

Canada has ceased to be a nation, but its formal political existence will not end quickly. Our social and economic blending into the empire will continue apace, but political union will probably be delayed. Some international catastrophe or great shift of power might speed up this process. Its slowness does not depend only on the fact that large numbers of Canadians do not want it, but also on sheer lethargy. Changes require decisions, and it is much easier for practising politicians to continue with traditional structures. The dominant forces in the Republic do not need to incorporate us. A branch-plant satellite, which has shown in the past that it will not insist on any difficulties in foreign or defence policy, is a pleasant arrangement for one's northern frontier. The pin-pricks of disagreement are a small price to pay. If the negotiations for union include Quebec, there will be strong elements in the United States that will dislike their admission. The kindest of all God's dispensations is that individuals cannot predict the future in detail. Nevertheless, the formal end of Canada may be prefaced by a period during which the government of the United States has to resist the strong desire of English-speaking Canadians to be annexed.

Conservatism, Liberalism,
and Socialism in Canada:
An Interpretation

Gad Horowitz (1966)

EDITORS' INTRODUCTION

Gad Horowitz is a distinguished political theorist and Professor Emeritus in the Department of Political Science at the University of Toronto. Although most of his writings focus on psychoanalytic theory, he is most famous for his keen observations concerning Canadian political culture and the importance of political ideology in explaining Canadian electoral and party politics. This essay, first published as an article in the Canadian Journal of Economics and Political Science *and then expanded upon in a book entitled* Canadian Labour in Politics *(1968), develops his central thesis on the relationship of Canadian socialism to Canadian toryism, and their distinctness from Canadian and American liberalism.*

Introduction: The Hartzian Approach

In the United States, organized socialism is dead; in Canada socialism, though far from national power, is a significant political force. Why this striking difference in the fortunes of socialism in two very similar societies?

Any attempt to account for the difference must be grounded in a general comparative study of the English-Canadian and American societies. It will be shown that the relative strength of socialism in Canada is related to the relative strength of toryism, and to the different position and character of liberalism in the two countries.

In North America, Canada is unique. Yet there is a tendency in Canadian historical and political studies to explain Canadian phenomena not by contrasting them with American phenomena but by identifying them as variations on a basic North American theme. I grant that Canada and the United States are similar, and that the similarities should be pointed out. But the pan-North American approach, since it searches out and concentrates on similarities, cannot help us to understand Canadian uniqueness. When this approach is applied to the study of English-Canadian socialism, it discovers, first, that like the American variety it is weak, and second, that it is weak for much the same reasons. These discoveries perhaps explain why Canadian socialism is weak in comparison to European socialism; they do not explain why Canadian socialism is so much stronger than American socialism.

Source: Excerpted from *Canadian Journal of Economics and Political Science*, vol. 32, no. 2 (May 1966). Some notes omitted. Reprinted by permission.

The explanatory technique used in this study is that developed by Louis Hartz in *The Liberal Tradition in America*[1] and *The Founding of New Societies.*[2] It is applied to Canada in a mildly pan-North American way by Kenneth McRae in "The Structure of Canadian History," a contribution to the latter book.

The Hartzian approach is to study the new societies founded by Europeans (the United States, English Canada, French Canada, Latin America, Dutch South Africa, Australia) as "fragments" thrown off from Europe. The key to the understanding of ideological development in a new society is its "point of departure" from Europe: the ideologies borne by the founders of the new society are not representative of the historic ideological spectrum of the mother country. The settlers represent only a fragment of that spectrum. The complete ideological spectrum ranges—in chronological order, and from right to left—from feudal or tory through liberal whig to liberal democrat to socialist. French Canada and Latin America are "feudal fragments." They were founded by bearers of the feudal or tory values of the organic, corporate, hierarchical community; their point of departure from Europe is before the liberal revolution. The United States, English Canada, and Dutch South Africa are "bourgeois fragments," founded by bearers of liberal individualism who have left the tory end of the spectrum behind them. Australia is the one "radical fragment," founded by bearers of the working class ideologies of mid-nineteenth-century Britain.

The significance of the fragmentation process is that the new society, having been thrown off from Europe, "loses the stimulus to change that the whole provides."[3] The full ideological spectrum of Europe develops only out of the continued confrontation and interaction of its four elements; they are related to one another, not only as enemies, but as parents and children. A new society which leaves part of the past behind it cannot develop the future ideologies which need the continued presence of the past in order to come into being. In escaping the past, the fragment escapes the future, for "the very seeds of the later ideas are contained in the parts of the old world that have been left behind."[4] The ideology of the founders is thus frozen, congealed at the point of origin.

Socialism is an ideology which combines the corporate-organic-collectivist ideas of toryism with the rationalist-egalitarian ideas of liberalism. Both the feudal and the bourgeois fragments escape socialism, but in different ways. A feudal fragment such as French Canada develops no whig (undemocratic) liberalism; therefore it does not develop the democratic liberalism which arises out of and as a reaction against whiggery; therefore it does not develop the socialism which arises out of and as a reaction against liberal democracy. The corporate-organic-collectivist component of socialism is present in the feudal fragment—it is part of the feudal ethos—but the radical rationalist-egalitarian component of socialism is missing. It can be provided only by whiggery and liberal democracy, and these have not come into being.

In the bourgeois fragment, the situation is the reverse: the radical rationalist-egalitarian component of socialism is present, but the corporate-organic-collectivist component is missing, because toryism has been left behind. In the bourgeois fragments "Marx dies because there is no sense of class, no yearning for the corporate past."[5] The absence of socialism is related to the absence of toryism.

It is *because* socialists have a conception of society as more than an agglomeration of competing individuals—a conception close to the tory view of society as an organic community—that they find the liberal idea of equality (equality of opportunity) inadequate.

Socialists disagree with liberals about the essential meaning of equality because socialists have a tory conception of society.

In a liberal bourgeois society which has never known toryism the demand for equality will express itself as left-wing or democratic liberalism as opposed to whiggery. The left will point out that all are not equal in the competitive pursuit of individual happiness. The government will be required to assure greater equality of opportunity—in the nineteenth century, by destroying monopolistic privileges; in the twentieth century by providing a welfare "floor" so that no one will fall out of the race for success, and by regulating the economy so that the race can continue without periodic crises.

In a society which thinks of itself as a community of classes rather than an aggregation of individuals, the demand for equality will take a socialist form: for equality of condition rather than mere equality of opportunity; for co-operation rather than competition; for a community that does more than provide a context within which individuals can pursue happiness in a purely self-regarding way. At its most "extreme," socialism is a demand for the *abolition* of classes so that the good of the community can truly be realized. This is a demand which cannot be made by people who can hardly see class and community: the individual fills their eyes.

The Application to Canada

It is a simple matter to apply the Hartzian approach to English Canada in a pan-North American way. English Canada can be viewed as a fragment of the American liberal society, lacking a feudal or tory heritage and therefore lacking the socialist ideology which grows out of it. Canadian domestic struggles, from this point of view, are a northern version of the American struggle between big-propertied liberals on the right and *petit bourgeois* and working-class liberals on the left; the struggle goes on within a broad liberal consensus, and the voice of the tory or the socialist is not heard in the land. This pan-North American approach, with important qualifications, is adopted by Hartz and McRae in *The Founding of New Societies*. English Canada, like the United States, is a bourgeois fragment. No toryism in the past; therefore no socialism in the present.

But Hartz notes that the liberal society of English Canada has a "tory touch," that it is "etched with a tory streak coming out of the American revolution."[6] The general process of bourgeois fragmentation is at work in both English Canada and the United States, but there are differences between the two fragments which Hartz describes as "delicate contrasts,"[7] McRae as "subtle" and "minor."[8] Put in the most general way, the difference is that while the United States is the perfect bourgeois fragment, the "archetype" of monolithic liberalism unsullied by tory or socialist deviations, English Canada is a bourgeois fragment marred by non-liberal "imperfections"—a tory "touch," and therefore a socialist "touch." The way Hartz and McRae would put it is that English Canada and the United States are "essentially" alike; differences are to be found but they are not "basic." Surely, however, whether one describes the differences as delicate, subtle, and minor or as basic, significant, and important depends on one's perspective, on what one is looking for, on what one wishes to stress. Hartz himself points out that "each of the fragment cultures … is 'unique,' a special blend of European national tradition, historical timing,"[9] and so on. He is "concerned with both general processes and the individuality of the settings in which they evolve."[10] Nevertheless, his main focus is on the uniformities, the parallel lines of development discovered in the comparative study of the United States and English Canada. This follows quite naturally from his *world* historical perspective, his emphasis on the three-way contrast of feudal, liberal, and radical fragments. From this perspective, the differences between English Canada and the United States are indeed "subtle" and "minor." But they are not absolutely minor: they are minor only in relation to the much larger differences among feudal, bourgeois, and radical fragments. If one shifts one's perspective, and considers English Canada from within the world of bourgeois fragments, the differences suddenly expand. If one's concern is to understand English-Canadian society in its uniqueness, that is, in contrast to American society, the differences become not "delicate" but of absolutely crucial importance. ...

The European nation has an "identity which transcends any ideologist and a mechanism in which each plays only a part."[32] Neither the tory, nor the liberal, nor the socialist, has a monopoly of the expression of the "spirit" of the nation. But the new societies, the fragments, contain only one of the ideologies of Europe; they are one-myth cultures. In the new setting, freed from its historic enemies past and future, ideology transforms itself into nationalism. It claims to be a moral absolute, "the great spirit of a nation."[33] In the United States, liberalism becomes "Americanism"; a political philosophy becomes a civil religion, a nationalist cult. The American attachment to Locke is "absolutist and irrational."[34] Democratic capitalism is the American way of life; to oppose it is to be un-American.

To be an American is to be a bourgeois liberal. To be a French Canadian is to be a pre-Enlightenment Catholic; to be an Australian is to be a prisoner of the radical myth of "mateship"; to be a Boer is to be a pre-Enlightenment bourgeois Calvinist. The fragments escape the need for philosophy, for thought about values, for "where perspectives shrink to a single value, and that value becomes the universe, how can value itself be considered?"[35] The fragment demands solidarity. Ideologies which diverge from the national myth make no impact; they are not understood, and their proponents are not granted legitimacy. They are denounced as aliens, and treated as aliens, because they *are* aliens. The fragments cannot understand or deal with the fact that *all* men are *not* bourgeois Americans, or radical Australians, or Catholic French Canadians, or Calvinist South Africans. They cannot make peace with the loss of ideological certainty.

The specific weakness of the United States is its "inability to understand the appeal of socialism" to the third world.[36] Because the United States has "buried" the memory of the organic medieval community "beneath new liberal absolutisms and nationalisms"[37] it cannot understand that the appeal of socialism to nations with a predominantly non-liberal past (including French Canada) consists precisely in the promise of "continuing the corporate ethos in the very process" of modernization.[38] The American reacts with isolationism, messianism, and hysteria.

English Canada, because it is the most "imperfect" of the fragments, is not a one-myth culture. In English Canada ideological diversity has not been buried beneath an absolutist liberal nationalism. Here Locke is not the one true god; he must tolerate lesser tory and socialist deities at his side. The result is that English Canada does not direct an uncomprehending intolerance at heterodoxy, either within its borders or beyond them. (What a "backlash" Parti-Pris or PSQ-type separatists would be getting if Quebec were in the United States!) In English Canada it has been possible to consider values without arousing the all-silencing cry of treason. Hartz observes that "if history had chosen English Canada for the American role" of directing the Western response to the world revolution, "the international scene would probably have witnessed less McCarthyite hysteria, less Wilsonian messianism."[39]

Americanizing liberals might consider that the Pearsonian rationality and calmness which Canada displays on the world stage—the "mediating" and "peace-keeping" role of which Canadians are so proud—is related to the un-American (tory and socialist) characteristics which they consider to be unnecessary imperfections in English-Canadian wholeness. The tolerance of English-Canadian domestic politics is also linked with the presence of these imperfections. If the price of Americanization is the surrender of legitimate ideological diversity, even the liberal might think twice before paying it.

Notes

1. New York: Harcourt, Brace (Toronto: Longmans), 1955; hereafter cited as *Liberal Tradition*.
2. New York: Harcourt, Brace and World (Toronto: Longmans), 1964); hereafter cited as *New Societies*.
3. Hartz, *New Societies*, 3.
4. *Ibid.*, 25.
5. *Ibid.*, 7.
6. *Ibid.*, 34.
7. *Ibid.*, 71.
8. Kenneth McRae, "The Structure of Canadian History," in *ibid.*, 239.
9. *Ibid.*, 72.
10. *Ibid.*, 34.
32. *Ibid.*, 15.
33. *Ibid.*, 10.
34. Hartz, *Liberal Tradition*, 11.
35. Hartz, *New Societies*, 23.
36. *Ibid.*, 119.
37. *Ibid.*, 35.
38. *Ibid.*, 119.
39. *Ibid.*, 120.

68 A Country That Must Be Made

René Lévesque (1968)

EDITORS' INTRODUCTION

René Lévesque was the founder of the Parti Québécois and Quebec premier from 1976 to 1985. He began his career as a journalist but in 1960 became a member of the Quebec Legislative Assembly as a member of the Liberal Party. He also served as a Liberal Party Cabinet minister under Premier Jean Lesage. He left the Liberal Party in 1967 after the party refused to discuss the issue of Quebec political sovereignty at its party convention. In 1968 he formed the Mouvement Souveraineté-Association, which then joined with other sovereignist parties to create the Parti Québécois in 1968. After the PQ formed the provincial government in 1976, it initiated a number of changes to promote Québécois language and culture. In 1980, the PQ launched a referendum on sovereignty-association that was defeated by a vote of 60 percent opposed and 40 percent in favour. As premier during the patriation of the Canadian constitution, Lévesque was one of the leaders of the "Gang of Eight" who refused to agree to a new constitution and became the sole hold-out after the federal government and other provincial premiers agreed to new terms, which Lévesque characterized as "the night of the long knives" (see reading 48). Lévesque remained premier of Quebec until his resignation in 1985. This essay was published in 1968 as part of a volume of writings, An Option for Quebec.

Vive le Québec Libre!

Charles de Gaulle

For my part, I believe in the quality of small nations:
here is where common values have a chance to sink deep roots.

Fernand Dumont

1 "Belonging"

We are *Québécois*.

What that means first and foremost—and if need be, all that it means—is that we are attached to this one corner of the earth where we can be completely ourselves: this Quebec, the only place where we have the unmistakable feeling that "here we can be really at home."

Being ourselves is essentially a matter of keeping and developing a personality that has survived for three and a half centuries.

Source: Excerpted from *An Option for Quebec* by René Lévesque. Montreal: Les Éditions de L'Homme, 1968; Les Éditions Typo, 1997.

At the core of this personality is the fact that we speak French. Everything else depends on this one essential element and follows from it or leads us infallibly back to it.

In our history, America began with a French look, briefly but gloriously given it by Champlain, Joliet, La Salle, La-Verendrye. ... We learn our first lessons in progress and perseverance from Maisonneuve, Jeanne Mance, Jean Talon; and in daring or heroism from Lambert Closse, Brébeuf, Frontenac, d'Iberville. ...

Then came the conquest. We were a conquered people, our hearts set on surviving in some small way on a continent that had become Anglo-Saxon.

Somehow or other, through countless changes and a variety of regimes, despite difficulties without number (our lack of awareness and even our ignorance serving all too often as our best protection), we succeeded.

Here again, when we recall the major historical landmarks, we come upon a profusion of names: Étienne Parent and Lafontaine and the Patriots of '37; Louis Riel and Honoré Mercier, Bourassa, Philippe Hamel; Garneau and Edouard Montpetit and Asselin and Lionel Groulx. ... For each of them, the main driving force behind every action was the will to continue, and the tenacious hope that they could make it worthwhile.

Until recently in this difficult process of survival we enjoyed the protection of a certain degree of isolation. We lived a relatively sheltered life in a rural society in which a great measure of unanimity reigned, and in which poverty set its limits on change and aspiration alike.

We are children of that society, in which the *habitant*, our father or grandfather, was still the key citizen. We also are heirs to that fantastic adventure—that early America that was almost entirely French. We are, even more intimately, heirs to the group obstinacy which has kept alive that portion of French America we call *Québec*.

All these things lie at the core of this personality of ours. Anyone who does not feel it, at least occasionally, is not—is no longer—one of us.

But *we* know and feel that these are the things that make us what we are. They enable us to recognize each other wherever we may be. This is our own special wave-length on which, despite all interference, we can tune each other in loud and clear, with no one else listening.

This is how we differ from other men and especially from other North Americans, with whom in all other areas we have so much in common. This basic "difference" we cannot surrender. That became impossible a long time ago.

More is involved here than simple intellectual certainty. This is a physical fact. To be unable to live as ourselves, as we should live, in our own language and according to our own ways, would be like living without an arm or a leg—or perhaps a heart.

Unless, of course, we agreed to give in little by little, in a decline which, as in cases of pernicious anaemia, would cause life to slip slowly away from the patient.

Again, in order not to perceive this, one has to be among the *déracinés*, the uprooted and cut-off.

2 The Acceleration of History

On the other hand, one would have to be blind not to see that the conditions under which this personality must assert itself have changed in our lifetime, at an extremely rapid and still accelerating rate.

Our traditional society, which gave our parents the security of an environment so ingrown as to be reassuring and in which many of us grew up in a way that we thought could, with care, be preserved indefinitely; that "quaint old" society has gone.

Today, most of us are city dwellers, wage-earners, tenants. The standards of parish, village, and farm have been splintered. The automobile and the airplane take us "outside" in a way we never could have imagined thirty years ago, or even less. Radio and films, and now television, have opened for us a window onto everything that goes on throughout the world: the events—and the ideas too—of all humanity invade our homes day after day.

The age of automatic unanimity thus has come to an end. The old protective barriers are less and less able to mark safe pathways for our lives. The patience and resignation that were preached to us in the old days with such efficiency now produce no other reactions than scepticism or indifference, or even rebellion.

At our own level, we are going through a universal experience. In this sudden acceleration of history, whose main features are the unprecedented development of science, technology, and economic activity, there are potential promises and dangers immeasurably greater than any the world ever has known.

The promises—if man so desires—are those of abundance, of liberty, of fraternity; in short, of a civilization that could attain heights undreamed of by the most unrestrained Utopians.

The dangers—unless man can hold them in check—are those of insecurity and servitude, of inhuman governments, of conflicts among nations that could lead to extermination.

In this little corner of ours, we already are having a small taste of the dangers as well as the promises of this age. ...

3 The Quiet Revolution

Now, in the last few years we have indeed made some progress along this difficult road of "catching up," the road which leads to the greater promise of our age.

At least enough progress to know that what comes next depends only on ourselves and on the choices that only we can make.

The enticements toward progress were phrases like "from now on," or "it's got to change," or "masters in our own house," etc.

The results can be seen on every side. Education, for us as for any people desirous of maintaining its place in the world, has finally become the top priority. With hospital insurance, family and school allowances, pension schemes, and the beginnings of medicare, our social welfare has made more progress in a few years than in the whole preceding century; and for the first time we find ourselves, in many of the most important areas, ahead of the rest of the country. In the economic field, by nationalizing electric power, by creating the S.G.F., *Soquem*, and the *Caisse de Dépôts* we have taken the first steps toward the kind of collective control of certain essential services without which no human community can feel secure. We also, at last, have begun to clean up our electoral practices, to modernize and strengthen our administrative structures, to give our land the roads that are indispensable to its future, and to study seriously the complex problems of our outmoded municipalities and underdeveloped regions.

To be sure, none of this has been brought to completion. What has been done is only a beginning, carried out in many cases without the co-ordination that should have been applied—and far too often in circumstances dictated by urgency or opportunity. All along the way there have been hesitations and, God knows, these still exist. In all these accomplishments mistakes have been made and gaps have been left—and whatever happens, even if we do a hundred times as much, this always will be so. ...

Yet another thing we have learned—and perhaps the most important: "The appetite comes with the eating." This is a phenomenon we can see everywhere as soon as a human group decides to move forward. It is called the "revolution of rising expectations." ...

4 The Basic Minimums

On this road where there can be no more stopping are a number of necessary tasks which must be attended to without delay. Neglecting them would endanger the impetus we have acquired, perhaps would slow it down irreparably.

And here we encounter a basic difficulty which has become more and more acute in recent years. It is created by the political regime under which we have lived for over a century.

We are a nation within a country where there are two nations. For all the things we mentioned earlier, using words like "individuality," "history," "society," and "people," are also the things one includes under the word "nation." It means nothing more than the collective will to live that belongs to any national entity likely to survive.

Two nations in a single country: this means, as well, that in fact there are *two majorities*, two "complete societies" quite distinct from each other trying to get along within a common framework. That this number puts us in a minority position makes no difference: just as a civilized society will never condemn a little man to feel inferior beside a bigger man, civilized relations among nations demand that they treat each other as equals in law and in fact.

Now we believe it to be evident that the hundred-year-old framework of Canada can hardly have any effect other than to create increasing difficulties between the two parties insofar as their mutual respect and understanding are concerned, as well as impeding the changes and progress so essential to both.

It is useless to go back over the balance sheet of the century just past, listing the advantages it undoubtedly has brought us and the obstacles and injustices it even more unquestionably has set in our way.

The important thing for today and for tomorrow is that both sides realize that this regime has had its day, and that it is a matter of urgency either to modify it profoundly or to build a new one.

As we are the ones who have put up with its main disadvantages, it is natural that we also should be in the greatest hurry to be rid of it; the more so because it is we who are menaced most dangerously by its current paralysis.

Primo Vivere

Almost all the essential tasks facing us risk being jeopardized, blocked, or quietly undone by the sclerosis of Canadian institutions and the open or camouflaged resistance of the men who manipulate them.

First, we must secure once and for all, in accordance with the complex and urgent necessities of our time, the safety of our collective "personality." This is the distinctive feature of the nation, of this majority that we constitute in Quebec—the only true fatherland left us by events, by our own possibilities, and by the incomprehension and frequent hostility of others.

The prerequisite to this is, among other things, the power for unfettered action (which does not exclude co-operation) in fields as varied as those of citizenship, immigration, and employment; the great instruments of "mass culture"—films, radio, and television; and the kind of international relations that alone permit a people to breathe the air of a changing and stimulating world, and to learn to see beyond itself. Such relations are especially imperative for a group whose cultural connections in the world are as evident and important as ours.

Our collective security requires also that we settle a host of questions made so thorny by the present regime that each is more impossible than the next. Let us only mention as examples the integrity of Quebec's territory, off-shore rights, the evident inacceptibility of an institution like the Supreme Court, and Quebec's need to be able to shape freely what we might term its internal constitution. ...

5 The Blind Alley

But we would be dreaming if we believed that for the rest of the country our minimum can be anything but a frightening maximum, completely unacceptable even in the form of bare modifications or, for that matter, under the guise of the constitutional reform with which certain people say they are willing to proceed with.

Not only the present attitude of the federal government, but also the painful efforts at understanding made by the opposition parties and reactions in the most influential circles in English Canada all give us reason to expect that our confrontation will grow more and more unpleasant.

From a purely revisionist point of view, our demands would seem to surpass both the best intentions displayed by the "other majority" and the very capacity of the regime to make concessions without an explosion.

If we are talking only of revision, they will tell us, our demands would lead to excessive weakening of that centralized state which English Canada needs for its own security and progress as much as we need our own State of Quebec. And they would be right.

And further, they could ask us—with understandable insistence—what in the world our political representatives would be doing in Ottawa taking part in debates and administrative acts whose authority and effectiveness we intend so largely to eliminate within Quebec.

If Quebec were to begin negotiations to revise the present frame of reference, and persisted in this course, it would not be out of the woods in the next hundred years. But by that time it is most likely that there would be nothing left worth talking about of the nation that is now trying to build a homeland in Quebec.

During the long wait we would soon fall back on the old defensive struggle, the enfeebling skirmishes that make one forget where the real battle is, the half-victories that are celebrated between two defeats, the relapse into divisive federal–provincial electoral folly, the sorry consolations of verbal nationalism, and, above all, ABOVE ALL ELSE—this must be said, and repeated, and shouted if need be—above all the incredible "split-level" squandering of energy, which certainly is for us the most disastrous aspect of the present regime.

And as for this waste of energy, English Canada suffers from it, too. And there, too, the best minds have begun to realize this fact, let there be no doubt of that. ...

6 The Way of The Future

We think it is possible for both parties to avoid this blind alley. We must have the calm courage to see that the problem can't be solved either by maintaining or somehow adapting the *status quo*. One is always somewhat scared at the thought of leaving a home in which one has lived for a long time. It becomes almost "consecrated," and all the more so in this case, because what we call "Confederation" is one of the last remnants of those age-old safeguards of which modern times have robbed us. It is therefore quite normal that some people cling to it with a kind of desperation that arises far more from fear than from reasoned attachment.

But there are moments—and this is one of them—when courage and calm daring become the only proper form of prudence that a people can exercise in a crucial period of its existence. If it fails at these times to accept the calculated risk of the great leap, it may miss its vocation forever, just as does a man who is afraid of life.

What should be concluded from a cool look at the crucial crossroads that we now have reached? Clearly that we must rid ourselves completely of a completely obsolete federal regime.

And begin anew.

Begin how?

The answer, it seems to us, is as clearly written as the question, in the two great trends of our age: that of the freedom of peoples, and that of the formation by common consent of economic and political groupings.

A Sovereign Quebec

For our own good, we must dare to seize for ourselves complete liberty in Quebec, the right to all the essential components of independence, *i.e.*, the complete mastery of every last area of basic collective decision-making.

This means that Quebec must become sovereign as soon as possible.

White Niggers of America

Pierre Vallières (1971)

EDITORS' INTRODUCTION

Pierre Vallières was a Montreal journalist and political activist. In 1965, he became a member of the nationalist revolutionary group, the Front de libération du Québec (FLQ). From 1963, the FLQ engaged in terrorist activities as a means to achieve Quebec independence, including several bombings, bank robberies, and kidnappings that resulted in a number of deaths. Vallières fled to New York and was arrested and held in detention until being deported to Canada in 1967, where he was convicted of manslaughter (he was subsequently acquitted). While imprisoned he wrote a number of works including, most famously, Nègres blancs d'Amérique, *translated as* White Niggers of America. *By the early 1970s, Vallières had renounced violence and he later became a member of the Parti Québécois.*

By Way of Introduction

In writing this book I claim to do no more than bear witness to the determination of the workers of Quebec to put an end to three centuries of exploitation, of injustices born in silence, of sacrifices accepted in vain, of insecurity endured with resignation; to bear witness to their new and increasingly energetic determination to take control of their economic, political, and social affairs and to transform into a more just and fraternal society this country, Quebec, which is theirs, this country where they have always been the overwhelming majority of citizens and producers of the "national" wealth, yet where they have never enjoyed the economic power and the political and social freedom to which their numbers and labor entitle them.

This book is the product both of day-to-day experiences in a given social milieu at a given time, and of a conscious political commitment which today seems to me irrevocable. My life experience has always been an integral part of a collective experience. Necessarily. And my political commitment also is an integral part of the awakening of the Québécois collectivity, more particularly of the working class. That is why this autobiographical account is also an account of the evolution of a whole social milieu. And that is why the ideas developed in this book reflect the evolution of the ideas of many men and many groups, an evolution that has in turn been brought about by the social transformations that have taken place in Quebec during these last years and which have been summed up in the expression "the quiet revolution."

Source: Excerpted from *White Niggers of America: The Precocious Autobiography of a Quebec "Terrorist"* by Pierre Vallières. Originally published in 1971 by Éditions Parti pris, Montreal.

This book is therefore not, strictly speaking, the product of an individual but of a milieu. The milieu is contemporary Quebec, but more especially Montreal and the metropolitan area. A man from the Gaspé would probably have written a quite different book.

This book is not perfect and does not pretend to be. Its observations are necessarily limited and incomplete. The ideas expressed lay no claim to the objectivity of a neutral person: they are biased and political. (It is often forgotten that in certain areas such as politics, "objectivity" too is an ideology—the ideology of the status quo.)

I mention men by name and I take sides concerning them. I denounce certain institutions highly respected in Quebec, and I have no pity or "understanding" for the Church and the ruling classes. But I do not seek controversy and I have not the slightest inclination to play the game of "impertinences," as the functionary Desbiens once did.[1] I describe the things I see, I note facts and draw simple conclusions from them, conclusions that are, so to speak, natural and that any unprejudiced man who is not compromised in the present system of exploitation can easily understand and remember if he observes the world around him, the world in which he moves and in which sooner or later he must determine his true place, take sides, and assume his responsibility.

Social responsibility is a virtue not often practiced in Quebec, even today. One does not hear much about it in sermons, lectures, and editorials. One hears only about order, social peace, and respect for laws. The social responsibility of the class presently in power is so missing from its order, its peace, and its laws that workers who demand the most elementary justice are forced to resort to physical violence to make themselves heard, merely *heard* (because of the noise they make) and not respected.

The ruling class has social responsibility only for its own interests. It doesn't give a damn about the 90 percent of the population who have nothing to say and no decisions to make in "their" democracy. The workers have already wasted too much time waiting for the "conversion" of those who have always robbed them and scoffed at them. The workers have already been deceived too many times by all the "pure" men of traditional politics, all the redeemers from the old parties, the René Lévesques, the Marcel Masses, and their kind.[2] The workers and all the clear-thinking people of Quebec must take *their* responsibilities in hand and stop relying on the Messiahs who are periodically thrown up by the system to fool the "ignorant."[3] Of course it isn't easy. There is a long and arduous road to travel. This book bears witness precisely to the efforts, the trials and errors we must be willing to go through in order to free ourselves from all the balls and chains that capitalist society attached to our feet as soon as we were born, chains which are sometimes so deeply embedded in our flesh that it is impossible to shake them off completely.

But determination can overcome anything at last, even the dictatorship of capitalism over the bodies and minds of the majority of Québécois. It is the responsibility of the workers of Quebec to learn to stand erect and to demand, to *take* what rightfully belongs to them. For it is abnormal, unjust, and inhuman that the economic and political power which governs the entire life of the workers should belong not to the workers themselves but to others, to parasites whose sole function, sole ambition, and sole interest is to accumulate unlimited profits out of the labor, the energy, the sweat, the life of the majority of citizens.

The true reason for the insecurity of the workers is not that their wages are inadequate, that jobs are scarce, or that they are ignorant; it is essentially that they have no control over economic and social policy. That is what the workers of Quebec have to get through their heads, as the saying goes. Because otherwise they will continue to remain for generations the "white niggers of America," the cheap labor that the predators of industry, commerce, and high finance are so fond of, the way wolves are fond of sheep.

Let us kill Saint John the Baptist![4] Let us burn the papier-mâché traditions with which they have tried to build a myth around our slavery. Let us learn the pride of being men. Let us vigorously declare our independence. And with our hardy freedom, let us crush the sympathetic or contemptuous paternalism of the politicians, the daddy-bosses and the preachers of defeat and submission.

It is no longer time for sterile recriminations but for action. There will be no miracles, but there will be war.

The White Niggers of America

To be a "nigger" in America is to be not a man but someone's slave. For the rich white man of Yankee America, the nigger is a sub-man. Even the poor whites consider the nigger their inferior. They say: "to work as hard as a nigger," "to smell like a nigger," "as dangerous as a nigger," "as ignorant as a nigger." Very often they do not even suspect that they too are niggers, slaves, "white niggers." White racism hides the reality from them by giving them the opportunity to despise an inferior, to crush him mentally or to pity him. But the poor whites who despise the black man are doubly niggers, for they are victims of one more form of alienation—racism—which far from liberating them, imprisons them in a net of hate or paralyzes them in fear of one day having to confront the black man in a civil war.

In Quebec the French Canadians are not subject to this irrational racism that has done so much wrong to the workers, white and black, of the United States. They can take no credit for that, since in Quebec there is no "black problem." The liberation struggle launched by the American blacks nevertheless arouses growing interest among the French-Canadian population, for the workers of Quebec are aware of their condition as niggers, exploited men, second-class citizens. Have they not been, ever since the establishment of New France in the seventeenth century, the servants of the imperialists, the white niggers of America? Were they not *imported*, like the American blacks, to serve as cheap labor in the New World? The only difference between them is the color of their skin and the continent they came from. After three centuries their condition remains the same. They still constitute a reservoir of cheap labor whom the capitalists are completely free to put to work or reduce to unemployment, as it suits their financial interests, whom they are completely free to underpay, mistreat and trample underfoot, whom they are completely free, according to law, to have clubbed down by the police and locked up by the judges "in the public interest," when their profits seem to be in danger.

Notes

1. This is an allusion to the great bestseller of the "quiet revolution," *Les Insolences du frère Untel* (*The Impertinences of Brother Anonymous*), by a teaching brother from north of Quebec. The author, who was later identified as Jean-Paul Desbiens, became an educational reformer in the civil service under the Liberal premier Jean Lesage.

2. René Lévesque is the leader of the centrist, pro-independence Parti québécois and a former minister in the Liberal Party government. Marcel Masse was Minister of Inter-Governmental Affairs in the National Union government.

3. This is an allusion to a remark by Jean Lesage, Quebec premier, who made the mistake of replying to a reporter who asked if he intended to hold a plebiscite on the Constitution: "How are you going to explain that to the ignorant?"

4. John the Baptist is the patron saint of French Canada, and in the folklore Jean-Baptiste is the old, traditional first name for a French Canadian. In many cities and villages there is a parade every year on his feast day, June 24. In the 1969 parade in Montreal, demonstrators tore the papier-mâché figure of St. John from its pedestal and hacked it up.

The Pattern of Prairie Politics

Nelson Wiseman (1981)

EDITORS' INTRODUCTION

Nelson Wiseman teaches political science at the University of Toronto and is an expert on Canadian politics and Canadian political culture. He deploys the tools of history and other qualitative methods to observe regional variation in Canada's political culture. His 2007 volume In Search of Canadian Political Culture *provides a comprehensive distillation of five regional political cultures in Canada (Atlantic Canada, Quebec, Ontario, the midwestern provinces of Manitoba and Saskatchewan, and the far Western provinces of Alberta and British Columbia). The article excerpted here, first published in* Queen's Quarterly, *provides a succinct statement of his thesis regarding the importance of studying regional political cultures in order to understand both federal and provincial elections and party politics, and is both a critique of and builds upon Gad Horowitz's famous essay.*

Canadian historians and social scientists have usually thought of the prairies as a more or less homogeneous unit whose politics have been essentially a response, a reaction, to externally imposed conditions: the tariff, the withholding of authority over natural resources by the federal government, discriminatory transportation policies, etc. This approach tells us substantially about east–west Canadian relations. By itself, however, it tells us little about diversity of political traditions *on* the prairies. What is needed is an interpretive analysis which comes to terms with intra-regional differences. Why, until quite recently, has Manitoba politics been so dominated by Liberal and Conservative regimes? Why has Saskatchewan been so receptive to the CCF–NDP? Why did Alberta spawn such a durable and unorthodox farmers' government (the UFA) and then, overnight, become the bastion of an equally unorthodox Social Credit regime?

Answers to these questions do not lie (although some clues do) in an analysis of the east–west relationship. Nor do the answers lie in analyses which focus strictly on party systems or economic conditions. An economic analysis may be used to explain why, in the landmark federal election of 1911, Saskatchewan and Alberta endorsed the Liberals and freer trade, but it will not explain why Manitoba endorsed the Conservatives and protection. An analysis of party systems may be used to explain why, at the provincial level, Saskatchewan and Alberta rejected the two older parties in favor of third parties. It will not explain, however, why those two third parties are at opposite poles of the Canadian political spectrum. Identifying and accounting for the differences among the three prairie provinces, therefore, is essential. But this too is insufficient because striking diversities are to be located not only

Source: Excerpted from "The Pattern of Prairie Politics" *Queen's Quarterly*, vol. 88, no. 2 (Summer 1981). Reprinted by permission.

among but also *within* the provinces. By the 1890s, for example, Manitoba had been remade in the image of western Ontario. Yet in 1919, Winnipeg exhibited a level of class consciousness and class conflict that was decidedly more reminiscent of the European than the North American scheme of things. In Saskatchewan, until 1945, the federal Liberal party was consistently stronger than in any other English Canadian province. But it was this same province that returned North America's first social democratic government, a CCF government whose ideology was rooted in the British Labour party. Inconsistent political patterns seem no less profound in Alberta where governing parties that are defeated at the polls have faded almost immediately.

The analysis employed here utilizes the concepts of ideology and ethnicity. Elements of Canadian toryism, liberalism and socialism have been present in varying proportions in each province. Political representatives of these ideological tendencies on the prairies include men as diverse as Rodmond Roblin, John Diefenbaker, Charles Dunning, J.W. Dafoe, J.S. Woodsworth, Tommy Douglas, Henry Wise Wood, and William Aberhart, none of whom were born on the prairies. Because the prairie provinces and their societies were moulded in the late nineteenth and early twentieth centuries this is not surprising. Ideas and ideologies first appeared on the prairies as importations.

It is very unlikely that a Rodmond Roblin or a Tommy Douglas, preaching what they did, could have become premiers of Alberta. William Aberhart would not likely have succeeded in Manitoba or Saskatchewan. Politicians are reflectors of their society, their environment, their times. They may be examined in terms which transcend quirks of personality. Their ideas and actions may be seen as reflections of the popular and ideological-cultural basis of their support.

The key to prairie politics is in the unravelling of the dynamic relationship between ideological-cultural heritage and party. In Manitoba, the imported nineteenth-century Ontario liberal party tradition (with "a tory touch") maintained political hegemony until 1969. In Saskatchewan, the dominant tone of politics has reflected a struggle between Ontario liberal and British socialist influences. In Alberta, American populist-liberal ideas gained widespread currency beginning in the very first decade of that province's existence. In all three provinces minorities of non-Anglo-American origins have, in their voting, helped make and break governments. These minorities, however, have not determined the ideological coloration of any major party.

Prairie political culture is best seen as the product of the interaction of four distinct waves of pioneering settlers. The first wave was a Canadian one. More precisely, it was largely rural Ontarian. This wave was a westward extension of English Canada's dominant charter group. Ontarians were a charter group in each prairie province but their impact was greatest in Manitoba. It seemed both fitting and telling, that one of Manitoba's premiers (Hugh John Macdonald) was the son of Canada's first prime minister. Tory-touched Canadian liberalism was the ideological core of nineteenth-century Ontario and its prairie offshoot.

A second distinct wave in prairie settlement was a new, modern, British group. Coming near the turn of this century, it was largely urban and working class. Transformed and battered by nineteenth-century industrialism, Britain's working class had begun to turn to socialism. Despite the cultural and ideological differences between the Ontario and new-British waves, their social status in the west was roughly equal, both groups being British subjects and Anglo-Saxon pioneers in British North America. The new-British wave had its greatest impact in the cities, most powerfully in the largest prairie city, Winnipeg. In Saskatchewan relatively large numbers of new British (and European-born) immigrants settled in rural areas and they produced Canada's most successful provincial social democratic party. It seemed both fitting and telling that Saskatchewan's premier in this labor-socialist tradition (Tommy Douglas) was British-born and grew up and was politically socialized in Winnipeg's new British labor-socialist environment.

The third wave in prairie settlement was American. More specifically it was midwest, great plains American. Like the Ontario wave, but unlike the new-British wave, it came out of an agrarian setting with deeply rooted agrarian values and settled, in overwhelming numbers, in rural areas. Because of their values and racial origin American Anglo-Saxons became the only non-Canadian, non-British charter group on the prairies. The dominant ideological strain carried by the American wave was similar but not identical to that carried by the Ontarians. It was, to be sure, liberal, but its liberalism was devoid of toryism. It was a radical "populist" liberalism that stressed the individual rather than the community or the state as a tory or socialist would. This wave's greatest impact was in rural Alberta, the continent's last agricultural frontier. Populist liberalism expressed itself in an unconventional farmers' movement/government known as the United Farmers of Alberta (UFA) and in the long tenure of Social Credit. It seemed both fitting and telling, that this wave's leading representative figure was a veteran Missouri populist (Henry Wise Wood).

The fourth and last wave of prairie settlement consisted of continental Europeans. Because of their numerous national origins, their roots and traditions were the most diverse of the four waves. They were, however, neither a charter group nor did they have a significant ideological impact (the eastern European and Finnish influences in the Communist Party being a minor exception). The non-Anglo-Saxons were "alien" and suspect in the eyes of the other three groups. At times their very presence was attacked and challenged; at best they were tolerated. The ideological and political role of the continental wave became largely one of deference. The continental wave had its greatest urban impact in Winnipeg and its greatest rural impact in Saskatchewan. These areas were also those in which the new-British wave had its greatest impact. The combined voting strength of these two waves was to lead to CCF-NDP victories in Manitoba and Saskatchewan in later years. The Old World ideological attributes of the continentals were dismissed as illegitimate on the prairies. Because of this continentals deferred to the parties based on the other three groups; but the continentals represented the largest swing factor in voting of the four waves. They helped elect and defeat parties anchored by the other waves; they neither anchored nor led a major party.

The foregoing description of the four distinct waves of prairie settlers is not intended to imply that all Ontarians were tory-touched liberals, that all new Britons were labor-socialists, that all Americans were populist-liberals, and that all continentals deferred ideologically and politically. Furthermore, it should be understood that not all Ontarians voted for the Liberals and Conservatives, not all new Britons voted CCF, and not all Americans voted UFA-Social Credit. The contention here, simply, is that without the new-British impact the CCF would never have attained the stature it did (indeed, it might not have been created at all); similarly, without the American impact the UFA-Social Credit phenomenon in Alberta would not have been anything like what it was; and without the Ontarians, prairie Liberal and Conservative parties would not have gained early hegemony. ...

American populist influences were greater in Saskatchewan than in Manitoba but they were secondary and not nearly as significant as in Alberta. In Alberta the American-style populist farmers association (the UFA) determined the complexion of successive provincial governments for years. Alberta populism, like American populism, attracted some socialists, but it rejected socialist ideology. CCF socialism, embraced in Saskatchewan, was rejected by Alberta farmers on the peculiarly American grounds that it represented a repudiation of their "rugged individualism."

Manitoba was the province most true to the values of rural Ontario. In the language rights debates it was more Orange than Ontario. Manitoba imported its early American-inspired farm organization—the Grange and the Patrons of Industry—only after they had become established in Ontario. Manitoba's Tory farmers rejected any suggestion of possible secession from Confederation and American annexation in the 1880s. ...

Although Manitoba Liberal and Conservative governments relied on rural support from continental-born immigrants, few Europeans, of either British or continental origins, were to be found in the higher echelons of either of these parties. Nor were many to be found in the United Farmers of Manitoba (UFM). "Canadian Ukrainians do not have any influence," declared one Ukrainian paper in 1932, the year of the CCF's birth. "We are poor and need political help. Ukrainian farmers and workers depend for their livelihood on the more powerful. This forces us to support a politically influential party. Affiliation with small radical parties brings us Ukrainians only discredit, and ruin." Such deference, however, did little for continental immigrants in the city. In the 1930s none of Winnipeg's banks, trust companies, or insurance firms would knowingly hire a Jew or anyone with a Ukrainian or Polish name. Nor would Anglo-Saxon premiers pick them for their cabinets.

Labor-socialist politics in Manitoba were as much determined by newly arrived Britons and Europeans as agrarian politics were determined by Ontarians. Winnipeg became the home of Canada's first independent Labour party (ILP), and by 1899, twenty-seven separate unions appeared at the May Day parade. A year later, the editor of Winnipeg's labor newspaper *The Voice* was elected to the House of Commons.

Within a decade the labor-socialist sectarianism of Europe was reproduced in Winnipeg. Two groups working outside of the dominant ILP influence were the Social Democratic party and the Socialist Party of Canada. By 1920–21 the two permanent parties that emerged were the British-led laborist ILP and the continental-based Communist party. Every imprisoned 1919 strike leader, except one, came from Britain to Winnipeg between 1896 and 1912. So too did most of the ILP leadership. The Communists, on the other hand, drew their inspiration from the Russian Revolution and scientific socialism. A small and insignificant British minority, including One Big Unionist and strike leader, R. B. Russell, stayed out of both camps. In Manitoba, as in Britain, laborism won over Marxism and syndicalism. By 1923, when the Ontario ILP was falling apart, the Manitoba ILP could boast that it held more than two dozen municipal and school board seats, the mayoralty of Winnipeg and representation in both federal and provincial parliaments. This modern, turn of the century British laborist tradition had its greatest Canadian urban impact in Winnipeg and Vancouver and, thus, the strength of the CCF-NDP in these cities. ...

Manitoba was ripe for an NDP victory in 1969 in a way that Ontario was not. In Ontario the impact of Anglo-Saxon voters, most of them long established in Canada, was more powerful than in Manitoba. This is another way of pointing out that Ontario is ideologically older than Manitoba in its liberalism and its conservatism, particularly in the rural areas, but in the cities too. There was a significant new British laborist impact in Ontario (e.g. Toronto mayor Jimmie Simpson in the 1930s) but, because of Ontario's relative oldness, it was not as profound as it was further west.

Manitoba had enough of Ontario in it to have sustained the only provincial Conservative party west of Ontario that has never collapsed. But it also had enough of modern Britain and continental Europe to provide CCFer J.S. Woodsworth and provincial Communist leader Bill Kardash with parliamentary seats between the 1920s and 1950s. Manitoba also had enough of the prairies in it to produce national and provincial Progressive parties in the 1920s. Their Ontario-born liberal leadership, however, led both of them back to the Liberal party.

As in Manitoba, provincial politics in Saskatchewan initially meant transplanting Ontarian politics. The provincial Liberal government operated at the pleasure of the Saskatchewan Grain Growers Association, the dominant political and economic organization in the province. Both the Liberals and the SGGA were led by the same figures and most of them had Ontario roots. The Progressive debacle in Ottawa, however, and the inability of the SGGA to break with the Liberals fuelled the formation of a rival agrarian organization: the Farmers Union of Canada. It was founded and first led by L. B. McNamee, a former British railway worker and trade unionist. This difference between the SGGA's Ontarian leadership and the Farmers Union British leadership broadly represented the difference between Ontario liberal and British socialist influences. The division became a central feature of Saskatchewan politics. ...

In Saskatchewan, however, unlike Manitoba and Alberta, there was a significant new-British *rural* presence. Although Saskatchewan attracted fewer Britons than either Manitoba or Alberta, it had almost as many British-born farm operators as the other two provinces combined. This British influence, coming later than the Ontario influx, took a longer time to assert itself. The farmer–labor connection in the Farmers Union was unique among prairie farm organizations of any significant size. Much of its support came from farmers in continental-based areas, areas that switched from the Liberals to the CCF between 1934 and 1944. The SGGA, like the neighboring UFM and UFA, had largely ignored the non-Anglo-Saxon farmers and had almost no following in areas settled by Europeans. All three organizations were rooted in the oldest and most established areas. ...

A contributing factor to the rise of socialism in Saskatchewan was that the cooperative movement was stronger there than in any other province. Moreover, Saskatchewan's cooperators were more socialist than their provincial neighbors. The cooperative movement became an integral part of the CCF's constituency in Saskatchewan and the movement's growth in the province was aided by a provincial government branch headed by a British immigrant experienced in the British cooperative movement. This "British" link reappears often in Saskatchewan history. ...

The CCF succeeded because it was British-led and ideologically British-based. The CCF's Britishness, its cultural acceptability, made it difficult to attack as alien. Its cultural legitimacy made it politically acceptable. It could therefore become an alternative to the Liberals for Saskatchewan's continental-origin citizens. Even more than in Manitoba, continental-origin citizens represented a large potential swing factor in voting. This helps explain why the CCF-NDP's success in Saskatchewan came twenty-five years before it did in Manitoba and why it was more profound in terms of votes and seats. The large rural British presence, combined with a large rural continental presence relative to Manitoba and Alberta, made it easier for continental-origin citizens in Saskatchewan to attach themselves to the CCF. This was exhibited in 1943 when another barrier to CCF aspirations was lowered: the Catholic Church declared its support for the cooperative movement, expressed concern respecting social welfare, and told its members they were free to vote for any party that was not communist. The CCF victory in 1944, therefore, was no surprise. ...

In the late 1950s Saskatchewan produced another political phenomenon, John Diefenbaker, who made it possible for the Conservatives to become a national party for the first time since 1935. In the 1940s, Manitoba preferred the Liberals, Saskatchewan the CCF, and Alberta Social Credit. Diefenbaker, unlike other national leaders, was neither an Anglo-Saxon nor was he identified with Central Canadian financiers. This made it possible for European-origin farmers to flock, for the first time, to the Conservative banner. Ethnic interaction and the passing of earlier prejudices no longer crippled the Conservatives in Saskatchewan's European-origin areas. At the same time, Diefenbaker's toryism and commitment to agricultural interests made him equally acceptable to rural, Anglo-Saxon, prairie farmers. They recognized him as an established, Ontario-born Canadian not as a European, naturalized one. Diefenbaker's populist image, another side of this phenomenon, helped him in Alberta where agrarian populism, as in the United States, eased its way into agribusiness. The prairies could therefore embrace the federal Conservative party after the 1950s because it was a qualitatively different party under Diefenbaker than it had been under Arthur Meighen, R. B. Bennett, John Bracken, and George Drew. ...

The politics of rural Alberta was as much influenced by the values of the American great plains as the politics of rural Manitoba by the standards of rural Ontario. In Alberta the various cultural waves, from Ontario, Britain, continental Europe, and the United States, came closest to arriving simultaneously. Early Ontario settlers in rural Alberta, as in Saskatchewan, encountered another ideological strain. It was not, however, a socialist challenge as it had been in Saskatchewan. It was, rather, a more militant, more radical, less tory form of petit-bourgeois liberalism than was the Canadian norm. It was not so much a challenge as a reinforcement, a radicalization, of the natural liberalism of transplanted Ontarians. There seemed little need, as there had been in Saskatchewan, for two rival agrarian organizations or for an ideologically distinct opposition party. The older parties simply re-oriented themselves. The Liberals and Conservatives became competitors vying for support from the American-influenced UFA. An MP remarked in the House of Commons that Alberta, "from the border northward to Edmonton, might be regarded as a typical American state." ...

American analogies are logical in Alberta. There is something to the argument that Aberhart comes closest among Canada's premiers to looking and sounding like a radical, populist, American governor. Many of his supporters referred to him as Alberta's Abraham Lincoln. But no one could compare prairie CCF leaders such as Douglas, Coldwell, Woodsworth, Queen, or even Irvine to American populists. One could identify them with a Norman Thomas but, to be more accurate, one would have to look to a Briton like Ramsay MacDonald, Labour's first prime minister.

An examination of Alberta's voting patterns reveals that they may be related directly to the patterns of settlement and to the ideological-cultural heritages of the settlers. Initial Ontario settlers in the south, particularly those who came before 1896 and settled along the

CPR line, voted for the party of the railroad, the federal Conservatives. The early twentieth-century American influx altered this. The American impact was most pronounced in southern and eastern Alberta, an area representing the key to political power in the province just as the southwest represented that key in Manitoba. The southern, American-settled parts of Alberta which were most favorable to prohibition in 1915 became the most favorable to the UFA from 1921 to 1935 and to Social Credit from 1935 to the early 1970s. Those areas in northern Alberta that tended toward the UFA were those whose population most closely resembled the American-anchored south. ...

The new British labor-socialist element in Alberta was largely isolated in the urban centres. Consequently, the CCF floundered. The British-anchored provincial CCF never managed to win more than two seats in Alberta. Significantly, both CCF MLAs in the 1950s were from the north and were second generation Ukrainians, as were large numbers of their constituents. These northeastern areas were among the very few where, in the 1920s, continental-born farmers outnumbered American-born ones. The CCF success here confirmed the shift, in a much less dramatic fashion than in Saskatchewan, from the Liberals to the CCF among non-Anglo-Saxons of continental, particularly eastern European, origin. In Saskatchewan, large numbers of rural continentals had swung their votes to support the party of large numbers of rural Britons, the CCF. In Alberta, however, there were both fewer continentals and fewer rural Britons. Thus, the CCF was a relatively minor force in Alberta's rural areas.

Manifestations of the American influence in Alberta abound. One example of a republican liberal tendency was the Alberta government's refusal to appear in 1938 before the Royal Commission on Dominion–Provincial Relations, addressing its comments instead to "the Sovereign People of Canada." Parliamentary government was described as a form of state dictatorship. Another example was the complaint of a Nebraska-born MLA who called the caucus form of government undemocratic and criticized the speech from the throne for making more of the 1937 coronation festivities than of Social Credit. Could such a sentiment respecting the coronation have been expressed at Queen's Park or in any other English Canadian provincial legislature?

In the 1970s prairie politics continued to be tied to prairie history. The hegemony of Ontario-anchored politics in Manitoba had succumbed temporarily to an alliance of an urbanized multi-ethnic working class and poorer non-Anglo-Saxon farmers led by the NDP. This alliance was unlike Saskatchewan's because it had little rural Anglo-Saxon support. In Saskatchewan, the CCF "formula" of 1944 has repeated itself with some consistency. Urbanization and ethnic assimilation in both provinces have generally aided the CCF-NDP, although this pattern may yet reverse itself as intermarriage and acceptance of ethnic leaders in the older parties increases. In Alberta, Social Credit gave way to the Conservatives; both are right-wing liberal parties which have, for half a century, offered policies that are either American in origin or in benefit. In part, Social Credit led to the Conservatives in the evolutionary, not radical, way that the UFA led to Social Credit. Although the conditions of the 1980s are different from those of the 1930s, Alberta Social Credit may yet disappear, just as the UFA did. The Conservatives have captured the ideological and popular base of Social Credit support just as Social Credit captured the ideological and popular base of UFA support.

Harold Innis: Communications and Civilization

William Christian (1985)

EDITORS' INTRODUCTION

William Christian, a former political science professor at the University of Guelph and a scholar of Canadian political thought and political ideologies, wrote this essay on Harold Innis in 1985. One of the best-known and original thinkers in Canadian academia, Innis was a professor of Canadian political economy at the University of Toronto. He is best known for his writing on media and communication theory, as well as economic history. He developed the "staples theory" of Canadian economic development, arguing that Canada's political economy rests on the development and export of raw materials such as fur, fish, forests, agricultural products, and fuel. Christian's commentary stands as a succinct exposition of Innis's intellectual contribution.

When Harold Innis delivered the 1948 Beit lectures on Imperial economic history at Oxford, his hosts must have been more than a little surprised when he began by discussing the rising of the star Sirius in Egypt in 4241 BC. Let us hope they were both patient and tolerant, since Innis devoted only four or five paragraphs to the British Empire, and little of that concerned its economic history. As he explained:

> I do not intend to concentrate on microscopic studies of small periods or regions in the history of the British Empire ... Nor shall I confine my interests to the British Empire as a unique phenomenon ... I shall attempt rather to focus attention on the other empires in the history of the West, with reference to empires of the East, in order to isolate factors which seem important for the purposes of comparison.

Innis was not unaware of the extent of his task. "Immediately one is daunted by the vastness of the subject. ..." Consequently, he offered to concentrate on "the subject of communication" because "it offers possibilities in that it occupies a crucial position in the organization and administration of government and in turn of empires and of western civilization."

Was this impertinence—a Baptist farmboy from Oxford County, Ontario, proposing to analyse the great civilizations of world history? Not at all. Innis, born in 1894, was at this time in his fifties, and probably stood as Canada's single most distinguished scholar. He had headed the University of Toronto's Political Economy Department since 1937 and more

Source: *The Round Table (Commonwealth Journal of International Affairs)*, vol. 74, issue 294 (April 1985). Reprinted by permission of Taylor & Francis Group.

recently had added the deanship of the graduate school to his administrative duties. The American Economic History Association had honoured him by choosing him as its second president, and he was the first foreign president of the American Economics Association at the time of his death in 1952.

His early work had established his creative brilliance as an economic historian. Two major books, *The Fur Trade in Canada* (1930) and *The Cod Fisheries* (1940), had attracted international attention both for their subject matter but also for their theoretical originality. Yet Innis's sweep and penetration and the philosophical character of his thought went largely unnoticed by his contemporaries, and it was not until Marshall McLuhan popularized communications studies that more than a handful recognized the lonely and heroic intellectual struggle Innis had been waging.

Comprehensive in scale, Innis's work from the outset was profoundly shaped by certain moral preoccupations. Pre-eminent among these was Innis's intense faith in a liberalism which celebrated the creative and free individual. He was keen throughout his writings to chronicle the successes of free human beings in escaping the forces, whether religious or secular, which sought to impose their control. Indeed he took no little pleasure in relating the difficulties and failures of monopolists in their attempts to impose their will. In the fur trade, for instance, "the individual trader became of more vital importance," and once he had paddled his canoe out of sight of Quebec City he behaved in ways about which "the colonial officers found occasion to complain." In the cod fishery the situation was even more favourable to individual initiative. Because little capital was required to enter the North Atlantic fishery small businessmen were able to defy the attempts of Parliament to regulate their activities on behalf of large vested interests. Again and again they eluded domination and did as they pleased in defiance of the authorities.

Innis's early works also tell a broader story about Canada. The *Fur Trade* deals with more than accounts and ledgers, or even unruly employees. As the merchants of Montreal and Quebec competed with the Hudson's Bay Company in the search for new sources of fur, they unwittingly created a transport and communication system that provided the infrastructure for the subsequent creation of the political entity called Canada. Against those of his contemporaries who contended that Canada was an economic absurdity which stood in the way of greater profits from closer ties with the USA, Innis replied in what was to become a famous epigram: "The present Dominion emerged not in spite of geography but because of it."

Although the *Fur Trade* explores a story that is apparently economic the heart of his concern transcended the narrow limits of any single discipline. He began his conclusion to this work with the observation that:

> Fundamentally the civilization of North America is the civilization of Europe and the interest of this volume is primarily in the effects of a vast new land area on European civilization. The opening of a new continent distant from Europe has been responsible for the stress placed by modern students on the dissimilar features of what has been regarded as two separate civilizations.

This grand theme of civilizations underlays Innis's earlier work in economic history, but his influence stemmed mostly from his more narrowly economic notions such as the staple thesis and the centre/margin theory. ...

The Depression had caused its share of human misery and intellectual danger, but worse was to come. In the Great War Innis had suffered physically; he was wounded and invalided out of the army. Hitler's war tore at his spirit and threatened the universities he so deeply loved. Philistine governments threatened the integrity and even the existence of their programmes, alleging that they contributed nothing of direct importance to winning the war. Innis faced a temptation as well. The University of Chicago wanted him and was apparently prepared to meet any conditions he might require. Why did he not yield? As George Grant explained: "He became a famous man in the western intellectual world and was offered big jobs in the powerful American academia and the cultivated British version. He stayed in Canada because it was his own and he ambiguously loved it." There was another reason too. He stayed because he remembered returning from the previous war, still walking with a cane as a result of his wound, to find universities pitifully unprepared to provide decent education for him and his comrades. He was determined not to betray this next generation.

He made his decision; he was to stay at Toronto. But during the summer, before the veterans would begin to return he was presented with an alluring opportunity—a trip to the Soviet Union. The occasion was an invitation from the Soviet Academy of Sciences to come to Moscow to celebrate its 220th anniversary. The Russians apparently shared Innis's belief that science had the capacity to bind together men from different nations.

Innis was away for slightly more than a month and during that time kept a diary which was published posthumously. The diary is typical of Innis's most interesting work. It shows his training as a social scientist, but more importantly it brings to the fore his abiding interest in and worry about the fundamental health of civilization.

Other than the sheer fun of his first trip on an airplane Innis had three important reasons for taking interest in this journey. First he saw a considerable number of similarities between Russia and Canada; Innis thought Canadians could learn from the way Russians had responded to a climate and geography which was in many ways similar to Canada's own. Second Innis believed that understanding the Soviet Union was essential if a decent world order was to be created out of the tragedy of war. Although he was clearly aware of the imperialist aspect of the Soviet regime, he believed that the West needed to understand Russia because it represented an offshoot of Greek culture which was complementary to and completed the more rationalist variant that was inherited by Western Europe and mediated to North America. Together the two strands combined the whole Greek legacy and each was incomplete without the other. To reject Russia was to refuse the chance of attaining wholeness in western civilization.

The third reason lay in a more methodological consideration; it could be said that Russia raised in a clear way many of the most important problems of bias. This idea was, as we have seen, present in his earlier work, and although protean, it was to become increasingly important. It is not easy to understand, and it is possible that Innis himself did not use it in a rigid or scientific manner. However, it is clear throughout the diary that Innis was fascinated by the difficulties of understanding the Soviet Union.

To do so, Innis thought, he had to overcome many differing biases. First, he had been trained as an economist and was therefore a specialist. His vision was therefore distorted and this distortion was all the more serious in the case of the Soviet Union because it was a country which had developed in defiance of the mainstream economic thinking of the West. Second, Innis was a Canadian; and Canada, as he pointed out, was a country which, unlike even the USA, and in sharp contrast to the Soviet Union, had a counter-revolutionary rather than revolutionary tradition. The presence in Canada of both French Canadian Catholics whose traditions stemmed from pre-revolutionary France and of United Empire Loyalists, whom Innis described as the counter-revolutionaries of the American revolution, created such powerful biases that it was even difficult for Canadians to understand Australia, let alone the Soviet Union.

Third, Innis came from a country in which the press was both free from state censorship and also commercial. The latter factor was especially significant as was the fact that the emphasis on consumer goods in western economies gave a particularly prominent place to advertising. Consequently, Innis suggested, an observer was likely to be misled by the kind of information available to him in a country with a controlled press and whose economy emphasized capital goods. Fourth, the Soviet Union was a great land power, both in military as well as economic terms. Western Europe by contrast and North America were dominated by international commerce and had a maritime military strategy.

Even were the observer able to neutralize these biases he would still not be free and clear. Russia had grown from the Byzantine version of the Roman Empire and had not been as influenced as Western Europe by the Roman Catholic Church and by Roman Law. Further it had a distinctive and difficult language which served as a barrier to the penetration of European ideas. To cap it all, when Russia had sought aid in creating an industrial revolution it had turned to a doctrinaire version of Marxism which had limited the possibilities of free creative thought.

For Innis the ultimate irony was that even worrying about the biases that impeded the understanding of other civilizations itself represented a bias that needed to be overcome. Innis's deep worry about the dangers that threatened his civilization came to preoccupy him from the mid-1940s until his death. He emerged from World War II with a deep and abiding dread, which he never lost, that his civilization was very likely to perish, and that it was already under attack from a new barbarism both internal and external. With such writers as Julien Benda and R.J. Collingwood he shared the worry that disaster was distressingly close; fanaticism and intolerance were corroding the foundations of his culture. They were becoming progressively more vicious in the new nationalistic forms which arose during the nineteenth century and now marched in ominous harmony with the development of new forms of communication. He feared that humanist culture in the West did not have the self-knowledge and self-confidence to withstand the onslaught of both Marxism and nationalism. It was his desire to obey the Delphic oracle's injunction to know thyself that led Innis to attempt to dispel the mystifying effects of the various biases.

On the plane home Innis reflected on these problems. These jottings provide a good summary of the central problems to which he was to devote himself for the remaining seven years of his life.

> Western civilization has much to learn from Russia and Russia much to learn from western civilization. Danger of each becoming fanatical and talking about the merits and demerits of the capitalist system in either case. System is a fanatical term. Of fundamental importance to the future of civilization that universities take the lead in adopting a neutral position. The search for truth offers a common ground to European civilization and the insistence on truth as dogma is an invitation to disaster.

The trip to Russia seemed to free his imagination. Appropriately he gave the title "Minerva's Owl" to his presidential address for the Royal Society of Canada. Hegel's bird takes its flight with the falling of the dusk, as a philosophy writes its grey on grey, we know that an age of the world has grown old. This thought—that his civilization had reached senescence and that only a determined act of meditation and reflection could save it from disaster—took hold of his soul and heart. As George Grant has noted, Innis was too much the social scientist to agree with Hegel that the world could only be understood and not revived by thought.

It was the enormous task of understanding and reviving western civilization to which Innis now set himself in earnest and with little hope of success. As an aid to his effort he began to keep a record of his reading, reflections and speculations in a document which has come to be known as his *Idea File*. Here his meditations knew no bounds and acknowledged no restrictions. To give some taste of the breathtaking sweep of Innis's imagination, consider the subjects with which he deals in a single, randomly chosen page.

- The fall of Constantinople, the consequent attempts of Rome to recapture its dominant position, and the ultimate religious developments in England and Germany as they rebelled against Rome's claims to pre-eminence.
- Arnold Toynbee's histories of civilization, which Innis characterized as the factory system applied to learning and scholarship.
- The conflict between landlords and manufacturers in English politics understood in terms of their different preoccupations, the latter more concerned with space and the former with time.
- The effect of advertising on the types of books published.
- The dangers of doing good, namely that it not only gives people a sense of power, but as well that there should be no limits on their power because they are using it for clearly desirable ends. Innis then points to the support that Christianity has lent to bureaucracy.
- A query whether the long novels of Dickens were the result of small type, which in turn had been used in England because of the stamp taxes on newspapers.
- The impact of American newspapers on the style of writers such as Hemingway and Crane.
- Finally, the question whether perhaps we venerated writing because it was necessary to appeal to supernatural forces in order to introduce it in the face of powerful prejudices favouring the oral tradition.

Were Innis merely a compiler of a universal fact-book, a man sitting down, as it were, to read the encyclopedia volume by volume, we might admire his energy and perseverance but we would scarcely take him seriously as a thinker. This brief list of topics is, after all, wildly diverse; but beneath it, and seen if at all only through a glass darkly, lies his deep abiding concern. For my part I am happy describing Innis in the last decade of his life as a moralist, a man preoccupied with questions of human excellence and the hindrances to its attainment in the world.

The kind of biases which impeded him in his attempt to come to terms with Soviet Russia were manifestations of a much broader difficulty. Again and again he turned his mind to try to probe the forces which prevented him and his contemporaries from seeing their own civilization objectively, understanding its problems and ministering to its ills. His answers were never dogmatic, only tentative; and his civilized reasonableness was entirely suitable in one who had noted that it was the search for truth, not truth, that made men free.

Outside Canada Innis is best known for what are called his communications studies, and I think that it is fair to suggest that it was he who created this field. It used to be suggested that Innis came upon this study as the logical consequence of his researches into the character of the Canadian economy. He had, as we have seen, written about the fur and fish trades, and he had also turned to an analysis of the staple products which had succeeded them in the development of the Canadian economy—timber, wheat, minerals, pulp and paper. The latter, exported mostly to the USA, provided the material basis for American publishing, especially popular journalism. Innis, this argument runs, simply shifted his attention from the supply of paper to an analysis of the reasons for which it was in demand.

It has been my concern in this paper to show that this view is at best only partly correct and that the contemporary world needs to attend to the writings of Harold Innis for more than insight into the nature of economic life. I have tried to show that from the very beginning of his career Innis was concerned with the problems of morality and saw his task as the analysis of civilizations on a scale that began as merely vast but eventually extended to incomparably epic. He certainly used his reputation as an economist and economic historian to gain a hearing for his views because he believed he was addressing matters essential to the maintenance of the integrity of civilization. Communication studies were a means to that end, and not merely one more deplorable specialization of academic life of the sort that threatened further to fragment the civilization of Europe.

No one should turn to Innis's later works, *Empire and Communications, Bias of Communication, Changing Concepts of Time*, in the hope of finding a neat and schematic answer to the effects of different media of communications on contemporary life. Part of the reason for this is tragically ordinary; Innis simply had not resolved the intellectual problems which he was investigating when death overtook him at the age of fifty-eight. However, there is more to it than that. If Marshall McLuhan was inclined to determinism in his analysis of the various media, Harold Innis was not. Innis, we know, talked about biases instead. What then was a bias of communication and why did we need to understand it?

In his reading about the various great empires or great civilizations—Egypt, Babylonia, Greece, Rome, Byzantium, and the various empires of later Europe —he was struck by the different materials which different societies used to record their thoughts. Some, such as the Babylonians, used oven baked clay tablets whereas others like the Romans after they had conquered Egypt had reliable and cheap access to papyrus and relied predominantly on it. Each of these different media of communication, he noted, had a bias of its own, a tendency to encourage the society to emphasize either space or time. Durable media of communication tended to encourage a structure which contributed to endurance, whereas lighter and more transitory materials made the administration of large areas more feasible, but tended to neglect problems related to temporal survival.

In civilizations, then, where a dominant medium of communication had arisen a general bias arose which permeated many aspects of that society's existence. The Babylonians, for example, attended to the problems of continuity through time, but it "has been suggested that the control of religion over writing and education entailed a neglect of technological change and military strength." On the other side Rome could control a vast empire because papyrus was readily transportable and the Romans had developed a language and a system of writing that could make full use of this medium. However, they were notoriously bad at dealing with the problems of survival through time, as their increasingly violent civil unrest and political assassinations indicated.

Each medium of communication, then, whatever its bias had weaknesses and what is worse encouraged the development of institutions which sought to secure a monopolistic control of the medium. Should this happen, it did not matter whether control fell to ecclesiastical or secular authorities; the consequences were comparable. The civilization would become more and more rigid and increasingly less able to adapt to changing circumstances. Creative thought, stifled at the centre, would take place increasingly at the periphery of the civilization, or even outside it altogether.

The development of monopolies of knowledge was undesirable for several reasons. First, they restricted imagination and individuality. These values, Innis believed, were necessary to any society's survival; they were also important for their own sake. Second, because the society had become biased in a particular direction, aspects of human development were eliminated or ignored and human beings were diminished in their diversity as a consequence. Finally the collapse of a civilization was never a particularly attractive event, since it involved enormous social costs. Looting, pillaging and the sacking of cities were the often unintended cost of the rigidification of a monopoly of knowledge and its successful challenge by another.

I have already suggested that Innis was not a determinist in his analysis of the impact of media of communication and it is important to understand this point. He had noted two civilizations which had to a considerable extent escaped the baneful consequences that had overtaken all the others. One of these was Byzantium, a culture remarkable for its achievements as well as for its longevity. Innis attributed its success to the fact that it had not fallen victim to a monopoly of knowledge. Rather, the Byzantine Empire, a state using papyrus and concerned with control over space, had been balanced by a church whose bibles were written on parchment and which emphasized control over time, or stability.

The other civilization which Innis admired was the Greece of classical antiquity. I mentioned earlier the influence of Cochrane on Innis as they discussed philosophy over lunch. For Innis it was the oral tradition that had given Greece its vitality and strength. "The power of the oral tradition was reflected in the institution of machinery [of government] designed to permit continuous adjustment." Homer and Plato, to name only the more obvious, held the western imagination because their writings captured the magical spell of the spoken word. However, even Greece was not safe from decline.

> The conquest of prose over poetry assumed a fundamental change in Greek civilization. The spread of writing destroyed a civilization based on the oral tradition, but the power of the oral tradition as reflected in the culture of Greece has continued throughout the history of the West, particularly at periods when the dead hand of the written tradition threatened to destroy the spirit of Western man.

The destruction of the spirit of Western man. This is the prospect which daunted Innis and which he devoted his prodigious intellectual efforts to arrest. His analysis is complex and I shall draw attention to only one factor. Innis thought that modern mass communications, particularly the British and American mass newspaper industries, had created an obsession with the present and with control over space that threatened to develop into a debilitating monopoly of knowledge. This medium had already heavily influenced the character of commercial radio broadcasting and there was every reason to fear even in Innis's own time that it would also mould the new medium of television.

However, none of these developments was inevitable. That was precisely the point of Innis's analysis. The previous civilizations that had, in part, escaped the control of a monopoly of knowledge had done so inadvertently. However, as creatures capable of conscious thought human beings were now in a position to understand the biases of the various media of communication. Our knowledge puts us in a privileged position since we are now able to escape from the influences of the dominant media if we so wish. We can in fact aim at the creation of a stable society in which different media of communication balance one another and allow human freedom and creativity to flourish.

However, if we were, as a civilization, to take the necessary steps it was essential to preserve the independence and the detachment of the universities, since they were of all modern institutions the ones most likely to promote the conditions necessary for balance. But the important fact was that it was now open to human beings to free themselves of the biases of their age because for the first time in history they were able to understand that these forces were acting on them.

None of this meant Innis was actually hopeful that his beleaguered civilization would survive. In fact I suspect that it was only the gravity of the problem and its consequences that kept him going at all. His beloved universities were more and more to lose their independence, and throughout the Western world in the 30 years since his death they have become increasingly dependent on political and social institutions who use them to resolve temporary political, economic and social problems. Scholars at the same time have shown themselves all too willing to grasp at fame, power and wealth and have allowed their research programmes to be decided by the industrialists and civil servants willing to fund them.

At the same time technological civilization continues to spawn new media of communication at an alarming rate. Considering the impact that printing in the vernacular had on the unity of Europe and the agony of the two great European civil wars of this century that arose in its wake, we must be alert in an era of mutual assured destruction to the unintended implications of changes in the media of communications.

> The average reader has been impressed by the miraculous, and the high priests of science, or perhaps it would be fair to say the pseudo-priests of science, have been extremely effective in developing all sorts of fantastic things, with great emphasis, of course, on the atomic bomb. I hoped to get through this paper without mentioning the atomic bomb, but I found it impossible.

72 "The West Wants In"

Preston Manning (1987)

EDITORS' INTRODUCTION

Preston Manning was the founding leader of the Reform Party of Canada and a member of Parliament from 1994 to 2002. He is the son of Ernest Manning, the Social Credit premier of Alberta (1943–1968). From 1965 until the forming of the Reform Party in 1987, Manning was a member of the federal Social Credit Party. In May 1987, in a speech delivered to the Western Assembly on Canada's Economic and Political Future, Manning declared that the new party's motto should be "The West Wants In." Manning went on to lead the party in the breakthrough elections of 1993 and 1997. The 1997 election marked a significant shift in federal electoral politics in that Manning became the Leader of the Official Opposition. After the 2000 federal election, where the Reform Party failed to make a significant breakthrough in Ontario and Quebec, party members sought an alliance with some Progressive Conservative party members to form the Canadian Reform Conservative Alliance. In that same year, Manning was unseated as the party head by Stockwell Day. The Alliance officially merged with the PC party in 2003 to become the Conservative Party of Canada, which went on to win the 2006 federal election under Stephen Harper. This speech represents many of the founding ideas of this Western-based and populist political party, including a desire for "Western Canadians to improve our economic and social condition, and our position within Canadian Confederation."

Introduction

As Delegates are aware, this Assembly was called to accomplish two purposes: 1. To develop an "Agenda for Change"—a list of basic reforms required by Western Canadians to improve our economic and social condition, and our position within Canadian Confederation. 2. To recommend an appropriate political vehicle for advancing the West's Agenda for Change over the next few years, including the next federal election.

Over the past few hours, we have been presented with various proposals for constitutional, economic, and social change. Tomorrow, Delegates will decide which of those should be included in the West's Agenda for Change.

Over the past few hours we have also heard an analysis of the existing federal political parties as potential vehicles for advancing the West's Agenda for Change.

My task is now to explore with you the advisability of creating a new, broadly-based federal political party with its roots in the West, as an appropriate vehicle for carrying forward the West's Agenda for Change.

Source: Preston Manning, "Choosing a Political Vehicle to Represent the West: A Presentation to the Western Assembly on Canada's Economic and Political Future." Vancouver, May 29–31, 1987. Reprinted by permission.

In doing so, I am assuming that while the West will continue to whole-heartedly support the promotional efforts of groups like the Triple E Senate Committee and Canada West Foundation, it is important to consider the necessity of a political vehicle which will carry the West's Agenda for Change directly into the political arena.

In discussing such a political vehicle, I am also assuming that the vast majority of Western Canadians want into, not out of, Confederation, and therefore reject a separatist party as an appropriate vehicle for political action.

A New Party in the Reform Tradition

Let me make clear from the outset that when we refer to the possibility of creating a new political party to represent the West, we are not talking about another splinter party or single-issue party, or yet another party of the strange and extreme. The West has produced too many of these in the past years, and there is no need for another.

Rather, if we think at all about the creation of a new federal political party to carry our concerns and contribution into the national political arena, we should be thinking about the creation of a new vehicle to represent the great political "reform tradition" which runs like a broad and undulating stream throughout the length and breadth of Canadian politics but which currently finds no suitable means of expression in any of the traditional federal parties.

The "reform tradition" to which I refer began in the mid-19th century when a group of reformers in the Canadian colonies—Joseph Howe in Nova Scotia, Robert Baldwin and Egerton Ryerson in Upper Canada, and Louis Lafontaine in Quebec—decided to fight against the vested political interests and inflexible colonial structures of their day to achieve responsible and responsive government.

In the 1860's, it was the Fathers of Confederation who embodied the reform tradition when Liberals like George Brown and Conservatives like Sir John A. Macdonald and Georges Cartier set aside old party structures and allegiances to create the great Liberal–Conservative coalition which brought into being the nation of Canada.

It would appear that the trauma of Confederation exhausted the spirit of radical political reform in Atlantic Canada and Ontario, for from that day to this those two regions of the country have been content to express themselves politically within the traditional framework of a two-party system dominated by the Liberal and Conservative parties.

There are, however, two great regions of this country where the spirit of political reform continues to manifest itself—usually in times of constitutional or economic stress—in the form of new political movements that seek to implement change by challenging and, on occasion, displacing, the traditional party structures.

One of those regions, of course, is the Province of Quebec; the other is the great Canadian Northwest.

If we could have afforded it, I would like to have lined the walls of this Assembly room with the portraits of the Western Reformers—the men and women who, since 1870, have sought to change Canada and advance Western Canadian interests through the creation of new political structures and programs.

Such a gallery of Western Reformers would include the following:

- Louis Riel, the first Western reformer, whose efforts resulted in the creation of the Province of Manitoba, and his Indian allies of later times, like Poundmaker, who fought the imposition of the federal welfare state on his proud people.
- F.W.G. Haultain and the Independent members of the old Territorial Legislature. Haultain was the man who resisted efforts to carve the Canadian Northwest into multiple provinces—who called himself a Big Westerner in favour of one big Western Province—and who negotiated the terms of the "Autonomy Bills" by which Alberta and Saskatchewan became Provinces.
- From 1905 into the 1920's it was the so-called "Farmers' Movement" which embodied the Western spirit of reform and which brought into being the Progressive Party—the first Western reform movement to break across the Canadian Shield and win substantial support in other parts of Canada. Its heroes included John Bracken, J.S. Woodsworth, and Thomas Crerar of Manitoba; Henry Wise Wood of Alberta; and Agnes Campbell McPhail, the first female Member of Parliament in Canada.
- In the 1921 federal election, the Progressives captured the second-largest number of seats in the Canadian House of Commons, and used their influence to secure the Crow's Nest freight rate reform and the Natural Resources Transfer Agreement.
- The Depression parties, the Canadian Commonwealth Federation or CCF in Saskatchewan under Tommy Douglas and M.J. Coldwell; the Social Credit movement in Alberta under William Aberhart and Ernest C. Manning, later expanded into British Columbia by W.A.C. Bennett; and the Reconstruction Party of H.H. Stevens with its base in the Province of British Columbia.

These are just some of the reformers of Western Canada—men and women who, when faced with unfair treatment by vested interests, or insensitive government controlled by Central Canadian parties, created new vehicles as instruments of change.

And if you are prepared to think of yourselves as Reformers—as people who want change in the conduct of our public affairs and who are prepared to create new structures to secure those changes—then the critics and the commentators who dismiss this Assembly as some isolated gathering of Western malcontents will be proven wrong.

If we talk about creating a new federal political party in this context, we are talking about reviving a tradition which is older than Confederation itself and as Western as Riel and the Farmers' Movement.

I would like to think that those reformers of by-gone days are looking down from some great Assembly in the sky and asking of our generation, "Do you have the courage and ability to lead on from where we left off?"

And tomorrow we will provide an answer to that question when we vote on whether to work within the existing party structures or to create a new structure to advance the West's Agenda.

Having, therefore, set our discussion of political vehicles in context, let me turn to the central question, "Is a new federal political party needed to advance the West's interests and concerns?"

Is a New Federal Party Needed? Four Reasons

Over the past three months, members of your Steering Committee and other Assembly committees have talked to a large number of Western Canadians, from Vancouver Island to the Manitoba–Ontario border. Not all of these are agreed that a new federal political party is required. But those who have been considering this option advance four main reasons for doing so. These reasons are:

1. Because the West is in deep trouble economically and structurally, yet no federal political party makes Western concerns and interests its top priority.
2. Because the Federal PC's are in decline all across the West, and this situation is creating a dangerous political vacuum.
3. Because the Federal Liberals and NDP as presently constituted are inappropriate vehicles for representing Western Canada.
4. Because the Federal Parliament, as dominated by the Central Canadian parties, is lacking in leaders and vision, and requires an influx of fresh blood and new ideas through a strong new competitor at the polls.

For the next few minutes, let us examine each of these reasons more carefully.

1. The West is in deep trouble economically and structurally, yet no federal political party makes Western concerns and interests its top priority.

In the words of my friend Ted Byfield, "People of every political stripe know that something is grievously wrong in Western Canada. Farmers can't afford to seed their crops, mines are closed, oil rigs lie derelict, shipyards are idle, food banks are besieged, the savings of many lifetimes have vanished, homes have lost their value, and a host of unemployed burst the welfare roils of every town and city."

Such economic conditions call for new directions, new proposals—for fundamental changes in national economic and social policy. Yet there is nothing really new for the West coming out of Ottawa from any of the traditional parties. Their top political priorities continue to be to hold or increase their support in Quebec and Ontario.

When something isn't working, you try to fix it. And if the old tools for fixing things don't work, you search for new tools.

2. The federal Progressive Conservatives are in decline all across the West, thereby creating a dangerous political vacuum.

If a federal election were to be held tomorrow, it is probably safe to say that about 50% of Western Canadians would not vote. This is exactly what happened in the recent Pembina by-election in Alberta. If this same voting pattern were to occur in a general election, some 80 Western seats would be up for grabs to whoever could organize 15–20% of the voters, an extremely unhealthy situation in a democratic state.

What are some of the reasons people advance for their lack of confidence in the federal Conservatives as a vehicle for advancing the West's interests? Let me cite just a few.

Some people mention their high expectations that the Mulroney government would introduce major changes in the scale and structure of the federal government during its first 18 months in office, and their profound disappointment when these changes didn't occur.

Others mention the government's slowness to remove the iniquitous Petroleum Gas Revenue Tax, its mishandling of the CF-18 contract, its slowness to enunciate a Western diversification policy, the continuation of patronage politics and appointments, and the failure to implement proposed reforms in the Unemployment Insurance program after spending years and millions of dollars on developing reform proposals.

As the popularity of the Mulroney Government declines across the country, there are many who have sadly concluded that the Progressive Conservative Party at the federal level has a congenital inability to govern. Certainly, its track record for most of the 20th century has been one of continuous disappointment: the periodic election of Conservative governments with enormous promise—Bennett in 1930, Diefenbaker in 1958, and Brian Mulroney in 1984 —only to see those mandates melt away in confusion and failure within five short years or less.

Whatever the reasons for the decline of the Federal PC's, if that Party is in fact headed for another 20 years in the political wilderness, they cannot be considered an appropriate vehicle for the implementation of the reform program required to raise the fortunes and influence of Western Canada within Confederation.

3. *The federal Liberals and NDP, as presently constituted, are also inappropriate vehicles for representing the interests of Western Canada.*

With respect to the Liberal Party of Canada, this is the party which said that it would reform itself after its defeat in the last general election. But this great reformation has not occurred, perhaps because the Liberals mistakenly believe that they can be returned to power as a result of the demise of the Conservatives, without undergoing any fundamental transformation.

On the Prairies, particularly in the rural areas, the professional Liberal politician is still defined as "a politician who puts party and patronage ahead of principles and province."

In Alberta, and throughout the petroleum sector, the federal Liberals are still referred to as "the gang of thieves that stole the 60 billion." The "60 billion" refers, of course, to the transfer of wealth from Western Canada to Central Canada which occurred under the infamous National Energy Program and federal petroleum pricing policies.

The National Energy Program provides perhaps the greatest reason why the resource-producing regions of this country should not entrust the conduct of the national government to the Liberal Party until at least another generation passes. The NEP constituted a deliberately planned and executed raid on the resource wealth of Western Canada for the short-term benefit of the federal Treasury and Eastern consumers. It was an unmitigated disaster for the producing provinces and the producing sector, the effects of which are felt to this day. Yet there has never been any apology from the Liberal Party of Canada; no formal inquiry as to how a national party with long government experience could ever have been induced to adopt such a policy; and no ironclad assurances announced to ensure that such a policy would not be instituted again if the price of petroleum were to rise once more. ...

Three Options

And so to summarize, the West is in deep trouble, but no existing federal political party makes our needs its number one priority. The West is in need of new instruments to advance new solutions, but the traditional political instruments at its disposal are flawed and unsympathetic. The present leaders of the federal parties offer no fresh vision for Canada and the West, and if a federal election were held today 50% of our people would not vote because they do not like any of the options.

The question arises, "What to do?" Only three options present themselves:

1. To continue to attempt to work within the existing structures, notwithstanding their past failures and bleak possibilities for the future. This is the position of those that support the status quo.
2. To pursue some extreme option—such as to threaten secession, and to actually take steps to bring that secession about. This is an option which is urged upon us by parties like the W.C.C.
3. Thirdly, there is the reform option—to seek constructively to change the structures and conditions which lie at the root of the West's difficulties and discontent through direct political action. ...

Directions to the Architects

If this Assembly were to support the concept of bringing into being a new federal political party to advance the West's Agenda, it is obvious that we should not be so foolish as to give the architects of that new party a "blank cheque" or a vague mandate. ...

As one who has studied all the previous Western reform movements in considerable detail, I would like to suggest that the following general specifications should be followed by those responsible for putting together any new federal political party to represent the West in the closing decade of the 20th century:

1. A new federal political party representing the West should have a positive orientation and vision.

A new federal party, born out of Western concerns and aspirations, should not be simply a negative reaction to the status quo. It should not simply be a party of protest with a litany of complaints and concerns, but rather a party of reform, with some positive alternatives to offer.

One of the problems of splinter parties and some interest groups in the West at the present time is that they are essentially reactionary and negative, rather than positive and pro-active. People want to hear what the West is FOR; they have heard enough about what the West is against. To quote the historian Thomas Lowery, "In every generation Canadians have had to rework the miracle of their political existence. ... Canada is a supreme act of faith." A federal political party which is incapable of inspiring that act of faith is unfit to govern Canada!

2. A new federal party representing the West should have standards of performance, policy, and people that exceed those of the existing federal political parties.

If you were to take a survey in most Western communities today and ask people what organizations render the greatest service to their communities, the name of a federal political party would not occur on a list of the top fifty. One of the reasons for this is that the standards of performance in federal politics have sunk to low levels.

The federal parties do virtually no screening of candidates or workers—as witnessed by the number of mediocre candidates and outright influence peddlers who managed to get themselves elected as Progressive Conservatives in the last federal election.

The federal parties do virtually no original or creative policy work any more—all this is left up to others. Federal political parties provide virtually no training or orientation for their own candidates or workers, other than media and public relations training. When these people get to Ottawa, many of them know little or nothing about the art of representation, or legislating, or public finance, or how to deal with the federal bureaucracy. They must "learn on the job," under a crushing workload, and the results are less than satisfactory.

Any business organization or social agency or union which invested as little money and effort in establishing standards and developing people as do our federal political parties, would be out of business in a year.

A new federal political party has a chance to establish higher standards and appropriate support services for people entering public life through that vehicle, and these standards and support levels should be established at the very outset.

3. *A new federal political party representing the West should be ideologically balanced.*

In order to ensure that we could draw support from the disaffected members of the Liberals and the NDP as well as the Conservatives, it is important that a new Western political party have a strong social conscience and program as well as a strong commitment to market principles and freedom of enterprise.

A new federal party which embodies the principal political values of the West will transcend some of the old categories of left and right. It will provide a home for the socially-responsible businessman and the economy-conscious social activist. It should be a party whose members and leaders are characterized as people with "hard heads and soft hearts," i.e., people who attach high importance to wealth creation and freedom of economic activity on the one hand, but who are also genuinely concerned and motivated to action on behalf of the victims of the many injustices and imperfections in our economic and social systems.

We need a political party in which Canadian youth—who are presently alienated for the most part from the federal political party system—will feel at home. Canadian youth have special interest in jobs, in the economy of the future, in environmental protection and conservation, and in conflict resolution on a world scale—concerns which once again are not easily classified on the old "left–right" spectrum and which again call for ideological innovation and balance. ...

4. *A new federal political party representing the West should be committed to preserving and strengthening Canada through the institution of needed reforms.*

As has been emphasized by other speakers to this Assembly, most of us wish to believe that the West's future lies within, not without, Confederation. "The West Wants In" should be our motto, and any new federal political party created in the West should be designed to achieve that objective, and not the separation of the West from Confederation.

In this connection, let us attempt to channel the separatist sentiment in the West (sentiments which are perfectly understandable under the present circumstances) into separation of Western Canadians from the obsolete federal political party structures which no longer serve us well. If Western Canadians want to separate from something, let them separate by the hundreds of thousands from the Federal PCs, the Federal Liberals, and the Federal NDP—rather than attempting to separate Western Canada itself from the rest of our country.

The West wants in, and when the West gets "in" in a true and meaningful sense, we will be in a position not simply to advance our own interests but to provide support and stimulus to all the resource-producing regions of the country, and the nation as a whole.

5. A new federal political party representing the West should have "room to grow" into a truly national party.

This brings me to the fifth specification which should be given to the architects of any new federal political party originating from the West.

They should build on a foundation broad enough and strong enough to support geographic expansion, so that the party built on that foundation has the potential to become a truly national party with the passage of time.

The federal Liberal Party is a national party with its roots in Quebec. The federal Conservative Party is a national party with its origin and roots in Upper Canada.

There is no reason under heaven why this country could not support a truly national party with its roots in the resource-producing regions—a party which, unlike the NDP, will remain loyal to its region of origin.

A new federal party, created initially to represent the West, should aspire to become that new national party, and nothing should be done in the early stages of its conception and birth to preclude it from eventually gaining support all across the country, particularly in those regions of Ontario, Quebec, Atlantic Canada and Northern Canada which share many of our concerns and aspirations.

Conclusions and Recommendations

Tomorrow, Delegates to this Assembly will be presented with a ballot/resolution calling for them to recommend to Western Canadians a political vehicle for securing action on the West's Agenda for Change over the next few years, including the next federal election.

The options presented on that ballot/resolution will include:

- Supporting and attempting to reform the Progressive Conservative Party of Canada.
- Supporting and attempting to reform the Liberal Party of Canada.
- Supporting and attempting to reform the New Democratic Party of Canada.
- Supporting and attempting to broaden the Confederation of Regions Party.
- Supporting and encouraging Western separatism as advocated by the Western Canada Concept.

- Creating and supporting a new broadly-based federal political party with its roots in the West, and,
- Pursuing and supporting some other alternative to be suggested by the Delegates.

If, after due consideration to the arguments contained in this presentation, as well as the viewpoints expressed on the other alternatives, the Delegates to this Assembly should decide in favour of creating and supporting a new broadly-based federal political party with its roots in the West, then I would invite your support for the following recommendations which will also be put in the form of a Resolution to be included with tomorrow's ballot.

RECOMMENDATION 1: That this Assembly direct its Steering Committee to begin preparations for the Founding Convention of a new federal political party to be held prior to November 15th, 1987.

RECOMMENDATION 2: That this Assembly direct its Steering Committee and the organizers of any Founding Convention for a new Western-based federal political party as follows:

(a) That the Agenda for the Founding Convention include provisions for:

- Defining the ideological position and platform of the new party.
- Selecting the name and establishing a constitution of the new party.
- Selecting a leader.

(b) That the following guidelines be adhered to in organizing the creation of a new federal political party:

- A positive orientation and vision—not merely negative or reactionary.
- Establishment of high standards.
- Achievement of ideological balance.
- Committed to preserving and strengthening Canada—"The West Wants In."
- Provision of room to grow from a regionally based party to a truly national party capable of forming a national government.

(c) That the immediate objective of the new political party to be created at the Foundation Convention in the fall of 1987 would be to field at least 80 candidates in federal constituencies across the West in the next federal election.

RECOMMENDATION 3: That this Assembly direct its Steering Committee to communicate with all Western Members of Parliament to invite them to provide leadership in Parliament for a Western-based reform movement, by separating themselves from their existing federal parties, sitting as a united bloc together in Parliament, and, if feasible, seeking to enter into a coalition arrangement with the Mulroney Government to better advance the interests and concerns of the West.

Hartz-Horowitz at Twenty: Nationalism, Toryism and Socialism in Canada and the United States

H.D. Forbes (1987)

EDITORS' INTRODUCTION

Donald Forbes is a professor of political science and political theory in the Department of Political Science at the University of Toronto. He, Horowitz, and Wiseman represent the triumvirate of the political theory tradition at the University of Toronto that looks at Canadian political culture. Forbes is best known for his work on George Grant (see George Grant: A Guide to His Thought, *University of Toronto Press, 2007) as well as on nationalism, ethnic conflict, and multicultural politics, but he is also a keen observer of Canadian politics. The essay excerpted here provides an assessment of the utility of the Horowitzian approach to understanding Canadian political culture.*

Any overview of Canadian political thought or political culture must reckon with Horowitz's adaptation of Hartz, for it is one of the few things in the field that practically everyone has read and remembers.[1] But what exactly is the Hartz-Horowitz theory? What was the original and why did it need adaptation?[2] How does the adaptation differ from the original? What are its strengths and weaknesses?

This article highlights a simple fact: Hartzian analysis flourishes in Canada, while it languishes in the United States. Different adaptations of Hartz compete for the attention of Canadians. The most successful of these is now required reading in innumerable university courses on Canadian politics. It has provoked continuing debate: there are historical studies of the Loyalists and of conservatism generally, content analyses of the Confederation Debates as well as more conventional studies of the political thought of the Confederation period, systematic comparisons of the political parties and their electoral support, even rigorously empirical studies of student attitudes, all designed to test the Hartz-Horowitz theory. Horowitz's 29-page article has eclipsed a 360-page book published the same year on roughly the same subject; it provides the framework for the most widely used textbook of parties and ideologies in Canada;[5] and it has been mentioned in popular books by leading journalists.[6] How has Hartzian analysis fared in the United States? Any broad generalization about the thinking and scholarly output of America's tens of thousands of Political Science and History graduate students and professors must, of course, ignore some detail. But plainly

Source: Excerpted from *Canadian Journal of Political Science*, vol. 20, no. 2 (June 1987). Some notes omitted. Reprinted by permission.

there is nothing like ten times the volume of controversy about Hartzian questions in the United States that there is in Canada. Hartzian scholarship shows little vitality in the United States. The Hartzian approach does not eclipse other approaches; it has been eclipsed. Indeed, it is practically dead.

How are we to account for this striking difference in the fortunes of Hartzianism in two very similar societies? Can we claim to understand Canadian or American political culture before we have interpreted this hard fact? ...

The Essential Argument

Horowitz objected to the tendency of Hartzian analysts to treat English Canada and the United States as essentially the same: "In North America, Canada is unique," he insisted ("CLS," 143; CLP, 3). Hartz had allowed that "it would be a blind traveller indeed who did not sense the difference between Ottawa and Kansas City, Kansas City and Cape Town" (FNS, 34). The difference he had sensed between Ottawa and Kansas City was Ottawa's "Tory streak coming out of the American Revolution" (FNS, 34). This "streak" or "touch" must be noted in any description of English Canada, but it does not distinguish English Canada *fundamentally* from the United States or South Africa. "In the case of the bourgeois fragments the unifying themes are even more marked than in the case of Latin America and French Canada" (FNS, 34). In particular, there is the same dynamic of fragmentation in English Canada as in the United States, the same ideological immobility, and the same atrophy of the future. "There may be a Tory touch in English Canada, but the fragment, despite the Cooperative Commonwealth Federation of recent times, has not yielded a major socialist movement" (FNS, 34).

McRae, charged with the detailed presentation of English Canada, had also stressed similarities rather than differences. "The central figure of the English-Canadian tradition [is] the American liberal" (FNS, 234). English Canada began with the arrival of the Tories or Loyalists after the American Revolution, but they were not "a genuine Tory aristocracy or a privileged class" because the American Revolution was not a genuine social revolution (FNS, 235). Their "convictions" may have differed in some respects from those of the Americans they left behind, but the differences were "subtle, minor" (FNS, 238–39). Toryism or Loyalism is "a differentiating quality that distinguishes the Canadian fragment from its American origins," but its importance should not be exaggerated; "for many historians it has obscured the all-important parental relationship between them" (FNS, 239). Their most important family resemblance is their common reaction to industrialism. The American liberal fragment developed a powerful labour movement without being significantly attracted to socialism, and "in broad terms, Canada has done the same" (FNS, 269).

How important is the "touch" or "streak" of Toryism that all agree distinguishes Canada from the United States? Horowitz plainly wanted to stress what Hartz and McRae implicitly denied—the legitimacy of socialism as an element of Canadian political culture derived from Canada's Tory past. His essential argument was that "non-liberal British elements [had] entered into English-Canadian society together with American liberal elements at the foundations" and that consequently liberalism today "is accompanied by vital and legitimate streams of toryism and socialism which have as close a relation to English Canada's 'essence' or 'foundations' as does liberalism" ("CLS," 156; CLP, 19).[13]

Horowitz began his paper by insisting on the strength of socialism in Canada: "In the United States, organized socialism is dead; in Canada socialism, though far from national power, is a significant political force" ("CLS," 143; CLP, 3). The problem was to explain this difference. Many relevant hypotheses could be considered. For example, Canada is more British than the United States and Canada's "organized socialism" is the best imitation of the British Labour party that can be managed in the circumstances. Or Canada's cabinet-parliamentary system of government requires stricter party discipline than the American presidential-congressional system and is thus more likely to spawn third parties. Or immigrants with Marx in their luggage arrived later in Canada than in the United States and have not yet been assimilated. Or the Canadian political culture is touched by toryism and thus naturally produces and welcomes socialist ideas. Horowitz favoured this last hypothesis. He drew a sharp contrast between English-Canadian and American political culture—but also carefully conceded that others would be within their rights to describe things differently.

> [T]he United States is the perfect bourgeois fragment, the "archetype" of monolithic liberalism unsullied by tory or socialist deviations, [while] English Canada is a bourgeois fragment marred by non-liberal "imperfections"—a tory "touch," and therefore a socialist "touch." The way Hartz and McRae would put it is that English Canada and the United States are "essentially" alike; differences are to be found but they are not "basic." Surely, however, whether one describes the differences as delicate, subtle, and minor or as basic, significant, and important depends on one's perspective, on what one is looking for, on what one wishes to stress ("CLS," 148; CLP, 7).

Horowitz was looking for a political-cultural, rather than a more strictly "Hartzian," explanation for the "differing weights of Canadian and American socialism" ("CLS," 149; CLP, 8). Horowitz rejected the Hartz-McRae contention that English Canada's Tory touch is so delicate, minor, subtle, and generally unimportant that one can say of Canada, as of the United States, "no toryism in the past; therefore no socialism in the present" ("CLS," 148; CLP, 7). Hartz and McRae are right about the ideological climate in which socialism grows, Horowitz seems to have thought, but wrong about the Canadian climate.

Toryism Explains Socialism?

Since 1776 liberalism has become entangled with American nationalism in complicated ways, so that today any basic criticism of liberalism smells of treason to Americans. In adapting Hartzian analysis to English Canada, Horowitz did not simply turn this Hartzian argument around. There is remarkably little about nationalism in Horowitz's paper, given its provenance, and a great deal more than one would expect about "toryism" and "corporate-organic-collectivist ideas." The heart of its argument is the claim that "the tory and socialist minds have some crucial assumptions, orientations, and values in common, so that from certain angles they may appear not as enemies, but as two different expressions of the same basic outlook" ("CLS," 158). Both tories and socialists reject the liberal idea of society as merely "an agglomeration of competing individuals," and both reject, therefore, "the liberal idea of equality," which is "equality of opportunity" ("CLS," 144). A political culture with a touch of toryism will be more receptive to the characteristically socialist concern for "the good of the community as a corporate entity" ("CLS," 154; CLP, 16), according to Horowitz, and the demand for equality there will tend to take a socialist form, namely, "equality of condition rather than mere equality of opportunity" ("CLS," 147; CLP, 6). Socialist parties will tend to flourish there—at least by comparison with their untimely death in purely liberal political cultures.

A full analysis of the Hartz-Horowitz model would involve a lengthy investigation of its central but obscure notion of "corporate-organic-collectivist ideas." Does tory collectivism have very much in common with socialist collectivism, or do they resemble each other only very loosely, like sandbars and snack bars? Such a digression is fortunately unnecessary here, since both Horowitz and his critics have taken a different tack. Horowitz presented his interpretation of Canadian political culture as an explanation for the greater strength of socialism in Canada than in the United States. His critics have disputed the factual basis of this explanation rather than its conceptual intricacies. Are the relevant ideologies found in Canada and do they co-exist or follow one another historically as the theory claims?

The simplest objections of this sort rest on the mismatch between feudalism/toryism and socialism in the different regions of the country. The problem of feudalism without socialism in French Canada (or Quebec) has already been mentioned. A similar problem comes to light if the Maritimes and the West are compared. Toryism is said to be strong in the Maritimes, but socialism seems to be stronger in the West.[16] Two prairie provinces equally lacking in feudalism or toryism, Alberta and Saskatchewan, have had very different experiences with socialism.[17]

Notes

1. Gad Horowitz, "Conservatism, Liberalism, and Socialism in Canada: An Interpretation," *Canadian Journal of Economics and Political Science* 32 (1966), 143–71, reprinted with some additions and slight modifications in *Canadian Labour in Politics* (Toronto: University of Toronto Press, 1968), 3–44, 57. Quotations from these sources are hereafter acknowledged parenthetically in the text, using the abbreviations "CLS" and CLP, respectively. If the quoted material is the same or practically so in both sources, references to both will be given. If there is a significant difference between them, only the first will be quoted and cited.

2. See Louis Hartz, *The Liberal Tradition in America* (New York: Harcourt, Brace and World, 1955), and Louis Hartz et al., *The Founding of New Societies* (New York: Harcourt, Brace and World, 1964). References hereafter to these sources will be parenthetical, using the abbreviations LTA and FNS, respectively.

5. William Christian and Colin Campbell, *Political Parties and Ideologies in Canada: Liberals, Conservatives, Socialists, Nationalists* (2nd ed.; Toronto: McGraw-Hill Ryerson, 1983).

6. Charles Taylor, *Radical Tories: The Conservative Tradition in Canada* (Toronto: Anansi, 1982), 114–15, 175, 182–83; Richard Gwyn, *The 49th Paradox: Canada in North America* (Toronto: McClelland and Stewart, 1985), 169–71; and Ron Graham, *One-Eyed Kings: Promise and Illusion in Canadian Politics* (Toronto: Collins, 1986), 128

13. Compare McRae, "Hartz's Concept of the Fragment Society," 21–23, and Horowitz, "Notes," 387–88.

16. Compare Preece, "Liberal-Conservatism and Feudalism," 136–37.

17. Compare Wiseman, "Pattern of Prairie Politics."

Elites, Classes, and Power in Canada

Leo V. Panitch (1995)

EDITORS' INTRODUCTION

Leo Panitch is the Canada Research Chair in Comparative Political Economy and Distinguished Research Professor at York University, Toronto, and the co-editor of the Socialist Register. *He is a prominent scholar in the leftist political economy tradition. Much of his scholarly work, based on Marxist political analysis, examines global capitalism and global finance and the role the United States plays in creating and managing a capitalist world order. He is also a political theorist in the Marxist tradition. The essay excerpted here examines class power structures in Canada and the role those power structures play in creating class (and implicitly racial, ethnic, and sexual) inequalities.*

"*In Toronto there are no classes ... just the Masseys and the masses.*" This little ditty, perhaps reflecting a centralist bias characteristic of Canadian politics itself, captures graphically the way political scientists have often approached the study of power in Canadian society. Inequalities of political and economic power are rarely denied and indeed are frequently a direct object of study. In general, however, political scientists have operated with a somewhat impoverished—and misleading—set of concepts in trying to understand these inequalities. As in the case of "the Masseys and the masses," they have tended to categorize society in terms of a gradation of rich, middle, and poor, and to examine politics in terms of elites with power and masses without. In employing such imprecise and over-simplified generalizations, social scientists have obscured and mystified the real links between social, economic, and political power in Canada.

Who, then, are these "elites" and "masses"? Occasionally, and most usually in the context of voting behaviour studies, the "masses" are divided into statistical classes grouped together on the basis of income, occupational status, or the "common-sense" self-perception of individuals themselves in class terms. Insofar as actual socioeconomic collectivities of people are dealt with, this has usually been done in terms of the concept of "interest groups"—formal organizations of farmers, workers, business-people, and the like. Those who lead such organizations are usually designated as "elites" and differentiated from the "non-decision-making" mass of their members. In this view, *power* is seen in terms of *relations among elites.* It is extended to the study of relationships between elites and masses only through the highly structured contexts of elections, opinion polls, and interest group "demands."

The problem with this approach is not that it sees politics as isolated from socioeconomic structure. On the contrary, the behaviour of elites is very much seen as conditioned by the

---

Source: *Canadian Politics in the 1990s*, 4th edition, edited by Michael S. Whittington and Glen Williams. Scarborough, ON: Nelson, 1995. Some notes omitted. Reprinted by permission of the author.

socioeconomic "background" of the individuals who compose them, and by the highly structured demands coming through voting or interest groups from society. As in the celebrated political system approach, which serves as a conceptual framework for Canada's most widely used introductory political science text, the determinant of politics is seen as "demands" coming from the "environment" of politics.

It is often alleged that what is wrong here is that the political system is a "black box" that reveals little of the inner workings of government, where the most salient elites make their decisions. There is something in this argument, but what is even more striking is the "black hole"—the environment. We are told that scarcity prevails here and that demands are generated by conflicts over resources, but a systematic examination of the way in which our economy is structured to cope with material scarcity, of the social relations that result between people, and thus of the concrete material clash of social forces that goes on is seldom undertaken. References to individual competition or intergroup competition, as with rich and poor, elite and mass, may give us clues, but because of their "gross-ness" as categories, because of their abstraction from concrete social relationships between people in a capitalist society such as Canada, they do not contribute enough to our understanding of what is acknowledged to be the determinant element of politics—the socioeconomic system in which politics is embedded.

To properly understand the relationship between society and politics involves taking an analysis of society seriously, which itself entails going beyond categories such as elite, mass, and group. It involves getting down to the material social relationships between people, their common experiences in terms of these relationships, and the actual collectivities they form and the struggles they enter into handling these experiences. This is what a *class analysis*, as opposed to an *elite analysis*, of society and politics is designed to do. In Canada—and even in Toronto—there *are* classes, and it is their history of contradictory relations to one another, and the balance of power that results at given periods and instances, that establishes the foundation of politics, including setting the extent and limit of the power of the Masseys, or that of any other "elite."

Elite Analysis in Canada

There is fairly widespread agreement among political scientists that what is meant by the term "democracy" as applied to a contemporary political system is "that institutional arrangement for arriving at political decisions in which individuals acquire the power to decide by means of a competitive struggle for the people's vote." The people themselves do not decide, and therefore power does not immediately reside with the people, but rather "the people have the opportunity of accepting or refusing the men [sic] who are to rule them." This is an "elitist" conception of democracy that does not require or expect high citizen participation in public affairs beyond the act of choosing between competing teams of leaders. A degree of *elite-pluralism* is guaranteed in this system, at least with a view to elections and formal parliamentary opposition, by a two-party or multiparty system. Moreover, in the case of a federal system like Canada's, the elite-teams compete for votes in various jurisdictions, and this further tends to multiply the extent of elite-pluralism. Finally, insofar as freedom of association prevails, it is recognized that the decision-making elites may be subject to a process of interest-group competition for influence upon them.

This system of elite-pluralism, however much it may be demarcated from broader, more mass-participatory conceptions of democracy, is not to be sneezed at as a minimal description of "actually existing" liberal democracies. It captures, albeit in too formal and nonhistorical a fashion, some of the basic differences between a polity such as ours and an authoritarian regime. Yet serious students of power in Canadian society have understandably not been willing to rest content with minimal descriptions of this sort. They have wanted to know *who* these competing teams of leaders are in socioeconomic terms and the extent to which they reflect in their competition and decision-making a narrow or broad range of approaches to public issues and concerns. They have wanted to know the relationship between the democratically elected political elites and those decision-makers in institutional spheres, such as the private corporations that dominate our economy, that are not democratically elected. To speak of elite-pluralism properly, they have recognized, entails examining the degree of *autonomy* political elites have from, at least, the elites that exercise power (in this sense of decision-making) in the economic sphere. ...

Turning to the tendency for elite analysis to treat social, political, and economic power in relation to equality of opportunity, it should be apparent that problems of domination and subordination are not reducible simply to patterns of recruitment. Even a perfect meritocracy implies a social division of labour, with people in authority and people subject to their authority. Authority positions, positions of control, set structural limits to what individuals can do in occupying decision-making roles within these institutions. If the president of INCO were to change places with a hard-rock miner, the structural position of the *place* occupied by each individual would strongly condition her or his behaviour. Elite analysis, in general, gives too much credence to the autonomous ability of "elites" to make unconstrained decisions. ...

It may be said that the main shortcoming of elite analysis is that it tends to ascribe *too much power*, indeed exclusive power, to those at the top. Restricting the concept of power, by definition, to authority in institutions obscures the fact that *power is a fluid social process* that, if stopped dead and anatomized in institutional terms, constantly evades analysis. The very private property market economy that corporate elite members seem to dominate by virtue of their institutional authority and cohesiveness is at the same time a limit on their authority and cohesiveness. Their positions are dependent on maintaining a rate of profit relatively high in relation to other corporations. Even if corporation executives don't lose their positions by the corporation going bankrupt, capital will flow form the less profitable corporations to the more profitable, and thus those in the less profitable will lose a good deal of their power. It is less institutional control than control over capital, a much more fluid thing, that is the foundation of the power of the corporate elite.

Similarly, by looking for power only among the elites one is forced to treat the masses as inert political clay, without self-activity (except perhaps in the highly structured context of elections). Yet the ways in which collectivities outside the "confraternity of power" engage in struggles to further their interests both limit and influence the decisions of institutional officeholders. Indeed, in the very definition of democracy that introduced this section it may be noted that the political elites' power finds its source in "the people's vote." This already implies that the power in question cannot be atomized only by examining the elites but must instead be seen in terms of a relationship between masses and elites. This would mean paying attention to the social collectivities that make up the "masses," inquiring whether these have modes of activity, of exercising power, outside of the electoral process—as indeed they do. If would also mean examining whether and where the relations between the collectivities intersect and overlap within and between the spheres of economy, state, and culture that the elite theorists look at only in terms of those at the top.

It is one of the ironies of elite theory that it often takes its intellectual root in the argument that Marxist class analysis assumes an all-powerful ruling class that does not fit 20th-century reality. Yet elite theory ends up seeing power much more monolithically than class analysis ever does, for class analysis entails seeing power as a *relational* concept, involving the necessity of tension, conflict, and struggle between social classes. ...

Class Analysis

The concept of class which finds the significant determinant of social and political behaviour in the ability or inability of labour—one's own and others'—demonstrated its value in nineteenth-century historical and sociological analysis, but has been rather scorned of late years. No doubt it is inadequate in its original form to explain the position of the new middle class of technicians, supervisors, managers, and salaried officials, whose importance in contemporary society is very great; yet their class positions can best be assessed by the same criteria: how much freedom they retain over the disposal of their own labour, and how much control they exercise over the disposal of others' labour. Nor is this concept of class as readily amenable as are newer concepts to those techniques of measurement and tabulation which, as credentials, have become so important to modern sociology. Yet it may be thought to remain the most penetrating basis of classification for the understanding of political behaviour. Common relationship to the disposal of labour still tends to give the members of each class, so defined, an outlook and set of assumptions distinct from those of the other classes.

This does not necessarily mean that the members of a class, so defined, are sufficiently conscious of a class interest to act mainly in terms of it in making political choices. Nor need it mean that their outlook and assumptions are a conscious reflection of class position or needs as an outside observer or historian might see them.

These words by C.B. Macpherson, from *Democracy in Alberta*, are as relevant today as when they were written 30 years ago. The central notion here is that it is people's *relationship* to property, to the ownership and control of the means of production, that is the main guide to the social composition of society and to the power relations that pertain therein. Macpherson has noted in another context that a "somewhat looser conception of class, defined at its simplest in terms of rich, middle or poor, has been prominent in political theory as far back as one likes to go." It is this looser definition of class that is employed in elite analysis in Canada. Insofar as the object of attention is the elite and its characteristics, the 80–90 percent of the population that is excluded from the upper or middle class (defined by elite family backgrounds, private-school or university education, fathers with professional occupations, or an income above a certain level) remains an undifferentiated "mass." ...

A class analysis always begins with *social relationships* that people enter into, or are born into, in producing their material means of livelihood. For production to take place in any society—and without it no society can exist—three elements are necessary: producers—the people doing the work themselves; objects of labour—the natural materials to work on (land, mineral, fish, etc.); and means of labour—instruments to work with (hoes, nets, tractors, boats, machines, computers, etc.). These elements may be owned by the producers themselves (collectively as in many primitive tribal societies, or individually as in the case of the family farm or the craftsperson's workshop) or by someone else who is a nonproducer. In a slave society, all the elements—including the producers— are predominantly owned by slaveholders. Under feudalism, the most important object of labour—the land—is predominantly owned by landlords. In a capitalist society, the means of labour—the machines, factories, offices, etc.—are predominantly owned by capitalists, individually or as groups of capitalists (as in the modern corporation).

Thus, the relationships between owners and nonowners, producers and nonproducers, vary in different modes of production. Under slavery, the direct producers are in a position of servitude to the nonproducers and can be bought and sold or born into servitude. Under feudalism, the peasants are not themselves owned and possess their own tools, but are legally tied to the land and required to pass over a portion of their produce to the landlord. Under capitalism, the producer is free, in the sense of having a proprietary right over his or her own labour, but is disposed of proprietary holdings of the objects and means of labour. In order to obtain the wherewithal to exist, therefore, the producer must sell his or her labour for a wage or salary to those who own the means of production and who control this labour directly—or indirectly through managers—in the production process. On this basis we can locate the predominant social classes of each society.

> *Classes are large groups of people, differing from each other by the places they occupy in a historically determined system of social production, by their relation (in most cases fixed and formulated in law) to the means of production, by their role in the social organization of labour, and consequently by the dimensions of the share of social wealth of which they dispose and the mode of acquiring it. Classes are groups of people one of which can appropriate the labour of another owing to the different places they occupy in a definitive system of social economy.*[12]

It will be seen immediately that classes thus approached are not ordered in a higher and lower fashion, as rungs on a ladder, but rather in terms of people's *relationship* to one another. While it is a multidimensional relationship in that people are dependent on one another (the elements must be brought together in order for production to take place), it is unequal dependence in that one class appropriates the labour of another. Because the mutual dependence is therefore one of dominance of one class and subjection of another by the appropriation of labour, the social relationship is a *contradictory* one, entailing the potential of antagonism, of conflict, between the classes. This is not to say that the permanent condition of society is one of strikes, demonstrations, revolts, and revolutions. These are but the more explosive outcomes of the contradictory relations in question. But in the sense of an irreconcilable *basis* of conflict, over how much and under what specific conditions labour will be appropriated from the direct producers, the system is a conflictual one. This has historically been expressed in struggles over control of the labour process, over the length of the working day, and over remuneration, over new machines that displace labour and/or require labour to work more intensively.

But if these kinds of struggles have been more common than struggles to "change the system" itself, this reflects the balance of power between the classes. Class analysis is precisely about assessing that balance of power. This does not mean that those who sell their labour to others—the working class in capitalist society—have power only at the moment of social revolution. For it will be seen that what is operating in the relations between classes is never all power on one side and the lack of it on the other. Because the classes are constituted in terms of their mutual, contradictory dependence on one another, both sides always have power. The balance of power may be unequal, and may structurally favour those who own and control the means of production, but depending on given economic, cultural, and political conditions, the balance may change. This may alter the terms and conditions of the appropriation of labour, and it may give rise to struggles over changing the historically structured relations between classes themselves. But all this is the object of inquiry within a class analysis.

It should be stressed that in talking about classes in this way, we are talking about actual historical groups, real collectivities of people, who therefore cannot ever be examined in terms of economic categories alone. Classes, as societies, are constituted on a material basis in terms of producing the material means of livelihood, but they exist simultaneously in terms of culture, ideology, politics, consciousness. Insofar as we speak of classes in terms of statistical economic categories (so many owners, so many workers, etc.), we miss the point that we are dealing with real men and women. This is usually seen to be important—and it is—in terms of assessing the degree to which class relations as defined above are expressed in cultural, political, and ideological differentiations and conflicts. But it is important as well in terms of understanding the basis of social cohesion and stability of a society in the face of the inherently contradictory relations between classes, since the maintenance and reproduction of the relations of production is itself dependent not only on economic relations but on the degree of cultural, political, and ideological homogeneity that keeps these contradictory relations in check. This too, then, is part of the balance of power, which means that to undertake a class analysis of society we do not just map out economic relations, but rather examine the totality of cultural, ideological, and political, as well as the economic, relations between classes as the relevant "variables" in the overall balance of power. ...

Political Science and Social Change

The study of politics is not just the study of parliaments or bureaucracies or even a broader study of the most powerful decision-makers in all spheres of society. It must be a study as well of the social forces "from below." Some will say that is the proper field of sociology, especially insofar as the activities of those below, even if they influence the decision-makers, do not have enough power "to change the system." But this is an impoverished view of political science. Indeed, as Antonio Gramsci wrote half a century ago,

> If political science means science of the State, and the State is the entire complex of practical and theoretical activities with which the ruling class not only justifies and maintains its dominance, but manages to win the active consent of those over whom it rules, then it is obvious that all essential questions of sociology are nothing other than questions of political science.

There is another important dimension to political science, of course, which precisely has to do with "changing the system"; which is not just about analyzing what the state and ruling class do, criticizing it on this basis, or even coming forward on the basis of this analysis with "public policy" proposals for enabling the state to manage the system better. Rather, this other dimension of political science is about developing analyses of the processes and strategies involved in changing the system from one based on class competition, exploitation, and conflict to a different system based on the elimination of classes and the development of as fully a democratic, egalitarian, and cooperative society as possible. Here we begin to raise larger questions about what "science" is really all about. And Gramsci is again a valuable guide:

> Is not science itself "political activity" and political thought, in as much as it transforms men, and makes them different from what they were before? … If science is the "discovery" of formerly unknown reality, is this reality not conceived of in a certain sense as transcendent? And is it not thought that there still exists something "unknown" and hence transcendent? And does not the concept of science as "creation" then mean that it too is "politics"? Everything depends on seeing whether the creation involved is "arbitrary," or whether it is rational—i.e., useful to men in that it enlarges their concept of life, and raises to a higher level (develops) life itself.

We can see, in this sense, the importance of a political science that is trying to know more than how to uncover how the power elites rule the world, but that also has an understanding that the majorities subjected to that rule also have power capacities, and is trying to discover how those capacities might be enhanced—not just to criticize the elites or ruling classes, not just to influence their decisions through struggles "from below," but to "transcend" the present system of power relations entirely. This is less a matter of constructing Utopian visions of a "good society" than of discovering the means whereby the subordinate classes have increased their power historically, and of trying to discover further and better means. Political science has a role to play in demonstrating that most people are not just passive recipients of someone else's power, that they currently exercise some power even if just in relation to the greater power of the dominant classes. It could have a larger and more creative role to play by discovering the limits to the ways in which subordinate classes have organized so far, and by trying to think through and offer advice on how to organize for a fundamental challenge to the powers that be. This will, above all, be a matter of discovering the kind of political organizations that enhance the intellectual capacities of working people themselves, so that they can become leaders and educators in their own communities and develop their capacities to run society and state in a fully democratic manner. To be a political scientist, in this conception, is to be someone who knows how to do more than criticize the power elite. It is to be someone who is orientated to discovering how to help those who have the potential power to change the system to realize that they have that potential—and then actually to act upon that potential. Philosophers, a great social scientist once said, have always tried to understand the world, but the point of this understanding, he appropriately insisted, was to change it.

Note

12. V.I. Lenin, "A Great Beginning" (1919), *Selected Works*, vol. 3 (Moscow: 1971), p. 231.

The Decline of Deference

Neil Nevitte (1996)

EDITORS' INTRODUCTION

Neil Nevitte is a professor of political science at the University of Toronto. He has been a co-investigator on a number of Canadian national election studies and principal investigator of the World Values Survey (Canada) under director Ronald Inglehart. Professor Nevitte's research focuses on political participation and Canadian public opinion and value change. A prolific scholar of many books and articles, his 1996 book The Decline of Deference *coined a new phrase in Canadian political behaviour, and marked a sea change in the understanding of Canadian values and public opinion. Rather than a picture of continuity, Nevitte argues that Canadian values are changing quite dramatically and that these changes are occurring in the context of cultural shifts in a number of post-industrial societies. They thus appear "less isolated, and less idiosyncratic."*

Interpreting Turmoil

There is nothing remarkable about vigorous public debate, the airing of differences of opinion, the competition of interests, or controversies about what future directions a country should take. Indeed, all this is the stuff of political, social, and economic life in any open and vibrant democracy. What is striking about the Canadian experience of the 1980s is just how passionate and widespread those debates were and that the controversies engaged issues so fundamental to communal life. Equally striking is the fact that, at the end of the decade, most of the contentious matters remained unresolved. The turbulence was not confined to politics or to the easily recognizable "big issues" of the era, the Constitution and free trade with the United States; it washed across all spheres of endeavour, dividing Canadians in the home, in the workplace, and in the polity.

What explains the turmoil of the period? This book tries to answer that question, beginning with the observation that, in one way or another, many of the conflicts were battles about fundamental values—about what values divide Canadians, what values they share, and what values make Canadians distinct. If the turbulence erupting during the decade was indeed about values, then one plausible explanation for that turbulence is that the 1980s was a decade of significant value change. This book investigates that theme, and presents a great deal of evidence to show that Canadian values did change in the 1980s, and, as we shall see, were in some respects quite remarkable. It is not enough, though, simply to show that values changed. Taking up the theme of value change raises other difficult questions: Which values changed? In what ways? And what explains the shifts?

Source: Excerpted from *The Decline of Deference: Canadian Value Change in Cross-National Perspectives* by Neil Nevitte. Peterborough, ON: Broadview Press, 1996. Reprinted by permission.

Canada as One Stage

When interpreting change, context is everything. Seen up close, the variety, scope, and depth of conflicts Canadians faced throughout the decade appear to be unique. In their details, of course, they are. But that turmoil can also be viewed from a broader perspective, and from that more distant vantage point the Canadian setting may be seen as a particular stage on which larger forces are played out. The rising levels of support for Quebec national independence and the growing pressures for greater decentralization, for example, may reflect growing concern about autonomy and shifts in communal identities. Those themes featured prominently in other settings during the same period, often with dramatic results. In some instances, shifting communal loyalties culminated in the most tragic and radical of all outcomes, the bloody collapse of the state, as in Yugoslavia. In others it brought equally significant changes in the opposite direction, such as the reunification of Germany. Both instances serve as useful reminders of the fluidity of political life. They illustrate yet again that state boundaries are neither static nor inviolate. Political communities are dynamic; they can fragment and re-combine. The collapse of Meech Lake undoubtedly was the immediate cause of sharply increased support for the independentist option in Quebec in 1990. From a longer historical perspective, though, that surge in nationalist sentiment can be regarded as but another phase in the recurrent cycles of support for national autonomy. Then again, viewing those same dynamics from a broader cross-national perspective reveals striking similarities in the rhythms of nationalist movements throughout the advanced industrial world. As in Quebec, the nationalist identities of the Catalans, the Basques, the Occitans, and the Corsicans in Spain and France, the Welsh, Scots, and Irish in Britain, the Jurassians in Switzerland, Armenians and Ukrainians in the former Soviet Union, and national minorities elsewhere have been remarkably resilient. Despite enormous and sustained pressures to assimilate, minority nationalist sentiments have not disappeared or crumbled under the weight of either authoritarian central planning or advanced industrialism, as some expected they would. Instead, to a remarkable degree communal identities have persisted, and the communal dynamics of these groups continue to shape the politics of many if not most states (Tiryakian & Rogowski, 1985).

In its details, the Canada–U.S. free trade agreement was a unique bilateral economic pact. But the formation of that larger trading bloc has parallels elsewhere. The push to North American free trade can be seen as but one example of a more general theme; most advanced industrial states are seeking to expand their trade environments. The emergence and expansion of the European Economic Community provides the most comprehensive example of economic collaboration, but there are other examples of lowered trade barriers and increased regional economic cooperation, such as the Australia–New Zealand pact and revitalized interest in economic cooperation in Latin America. The concerns raised by partners to these arrangements, particularly by publics in smaller partner states, have a familiar ring; they echo many of the worries that Canadians aired during the debate about Canada–U.S. free trade. In important respects they reflect similar dilemmas. The largely economic logic driving states to pursue such arrangements is clear: the intention is to encourage prosperity by exploiting economies of scale and comparative advantage while securing access to large markets. Canadians and publics elsewhere worried about the effects. They asked: What about autonomy? Sovereignty? Will expanded trade limit the capacity to pursue domestic public policies that reflect the particular collective aspirations of the Canadian public?

The emergence of such novel partisan formations as the Reform Party and the Bloc Québecois undoubtedly reflect a combination of social and structural tensions that are peculiar to the Canadian setting. Shifting partisan alignments, though, is hardly a trend unique to Canada. The fragmentation of party systems, the increased volatility of electorates, and the emergence of parties challenging the status quo have been the hallmarks of political turbulence throughout nearly all advanced industrial democracies since the 1970s (Dalton, Flanagan & Beck, 1984). As the West European experience illustrates, these challenges can come not only from nationalist groups, from the left, or from the right, but also from parties and political formations that have no obvious ideological roots in any part of the traditional left–right spectrum (Dalton, 1988; Muller-Rommel, 1990). Different electoral rules and institutional arrangements shape the opportunities for the mobilization of new political parties in different ways. In some cases, as in Germany, the rules of the game are deliberately designed to stack the deck against the formation of new political parties. In others, the barriers to entry are much lower. But even when these cross-national variations are taken into account, the general pattern of partisan fragmentation is a remarkably persistent one (Kitschelt, 1990).

Challenges to the status quo have come not just from new political parties; they have also come from non-partisan formations, most notably interest groups. Vigorous and increasingly sophisticated interest groups have become a much more prominent feature of political dynamics in Canada since the 1980s (Cairns, 1990; Phillips, 1991). Those very same dynamics also feature prominently in the turbulence experienced in most other advanced industrial democracies during the same period. A mountain of evidence demonstrates that the rise of issue-driven movements, movements employing a host of direct-action strategies, has so altered the substance and dynamics of state–society relations across advanced industrial states that conventional interpretations of normal political contests no longer apply (Keuchler & Dalton, 1990). The surge in activity of groups promoting women's rights, the right to life, pro-choice, gay rights, consumers' rights, the environment, peace, and a host of other concerns relating to "quality of life," "minoritarianism," or the status of historically marginalized groups, all contributed to the turmoil facing Canadians since the early 1980s. Precisely the same concerns pushed their way onto the agendas of other advanced industrial states in the 1970s and have become increasingly prominent since then (Barnes et al., 1974). To be sure, there are cross-national variations in the success of interest group activities and in the organizational forms they take. In some instances, for example, environmental movements have coalesced into political parties, as in the cases of the Greens in West Germany or Ecolo and Agalev in Belgium. But in most cases, as in Canada and the United States, ecology movements have pursued their goals through non-partisan strategies (Kitschelt, 1984). There are also significant national differences in the successes of some groups and in the dynamics surrounding those successes. In some settings, as in Canada and the United States, the emergence of an organized pro-choice formation sparked a powerful reaction on the part of pro-life forces. At issue, in both cases, was not just the legality or morality of abortion. The abortion debate spilled over to a larger set of questions; it polarized publics around the status of women and became a battleground for competing definitions of "the family" and competing values about "family life." In other settings, the reactions have been much less robust and much less organized. There are significant variations too in the goals of movements bearing the same generic label. The goals of feminists in Britain, for example, are not precisely the same as those of feminists in the United States, and neither are identical to those preoccupying feminists in Sweden (Gelb, 1990). Far more striking than the national differences in organizational form and precise focus, though, are the common impacts of these movements; all have changed their respective domestic political agendas.

Most advanced industrial states have some historical record of tension between racial majorities and minorities. With the exception of the United States, few advanced industrial democracies have sustained experience of open racial conflict. During the course of the 1980s, racial issues and the politics of immigration became more contentious and more salient to both political discourse and social dynamics throughout most of western Europe. Once again, there are very significant variations in the salience of race and in the extent to which and how racial issues shape domestic political life. In Portugal, perhaps the most multiracial of all West European societies, the politics of race has remained all but irrelevant. But in Germany, France, Belgium, Austria, Italy, Denmark, and Norway parties of the far right exploit fears about the social and economic consequences of immigration and the "invasion of foreigners." In the process, they have made striking electoral gains during the latter half of the 1980s.

Understandably, Canadians are absorbed in the details of their own lives. But when we step back from the precise details of Canadian political, social, and economic turbulence of the last decade, when the transformations are placed in the broader context of changes taking place elsewhere, Canada's recent experiences with fracturing parties, surging interest group activism, increasing public irritation with the status quo, declining satisfaction with the political classes, rising communal tensions, and increasingly abrasive relations on other social fronts all appear less isolated, and less idiosyncratic. And if the turmoil Canadians faced has much in common with the uncertainties experienced by citizens in other advanced industrial states, it may well be that the causes of the turmoil have more to do with the structures and rhythms of late industrialism than with the particular quirks of Canadians or the peculiarities of the Canadian institutional setting.

Three Perspectives on Canadian Value Change

1. Canada as an Advanced Industrial State

First, advanced industrial states have crossed a series of significant thresholds.[1] Typically, all have experienced unprecedented levels of affluence; all have economies that are increasingly driven by the tertiary sector; all have undergone massive expansions in the educational opportunities available to their populations; each has experienced the "information revolution" and a corresponding growth in communications-related technologies. The social consequences of these changes have also been dramatic: they include the expansion of social welfare networks and dramatic increases in the social, geographic, and economic mobilities of the populations. Moreover, from a broad historical standpoint, these developments have taken place in a relatively short time frame—in about the last twenty-five years.

The second observation ... is that these structural transformations are linked to fundamental shifts in the value systems of publics. Again, observers do not all agree about the emphasis to place on the various aspects of the value changes. Some characterize the shifts as change from group solidarity to self-actualization; they see a greater importance attached to "inner goals" as central (Huntington, 1974). Others describe the changes in terms of "individualization" (Ester, Halman and deMoor, 1993). ...

2. Canada as a North American State

A second plausible explanation for Canadian value change works from a narrower frame of comparison; it fixes attention on Canada's position as a North American state. The United States serves as Canada's most important reference society, and there is a long tradition of interpreting Canadian values through the optic of Canadian–American comparisons. For example, there is a wealth of accumulated historical wisdom explaining the distinctiveness of contemporary Canadian values in terms of differences in "founding circumstances." These historically informed accounts emphasize the sharp contrasts between Canada's counter-revolutionary past and the revolutionary catharsis of the United States. Unlike the United States, Canada experienced no civil war, and the trajectory of Canadian sociopolitical development was shaped decisively by the presence of dual, European, founding fragments (Clark, 1962; Lower, 1964; Morton, 1961; Underhill, 1960). ...

3. Canada as an Immigrant Society

A third possible explanation for Canadian value change is even more narrowly focussed; it draws attention to changing patterns of population replacement. The dynamics of population replacement are affected by a host of factors, including fertility rates, longevity, immigration, emigration, changing attitudes to the family, the place of women in the economy, and education. ...

The significant shift in country of origin [of immigrants to Canada] has had several obvious consequences. One is that Canada has become a less European society than ever before, and the introduction of Canada's policy of multiculturalism in the 1970s reflected that changing reality. Another is that communal relations have become more complicated. To the already difficult relations between the three primary groups with historic claims grounded in founding status—Canada's First Nations and English and French settlers—have been added "new Canadians" who come from extraordinarily diverse backgrounds and make claims for social, economic, and political inclusion.

Note

1. See Huntington (1974) "Post-Industrial Politics: How Benign Will It Be?" *Comparative Politics* 6: 147–77.

Fire and Ice

Michael Adams (2003)

EDITORS' INTRODUCTION

Michael Adams is a co-founder of Environics, a Toronto polling and market research firm, and president of the Environics Group of research and communications consulting companies. He is the author of multiple books on Canadian and North American social values and social change using public opinion survey research. The excerpt below is from his 2003 Donner Prize–winning book on Canadian and US social values. He disputes the argument that Canadians and Americans are becoming more alike and he notes that distinct differences in public opinion are still in evidence.

Introduction

I don't even know what street Canada is on.

 —Al "Scarface" Capone

While Americans are benevolently ignorant about Canada, most Canadians seem malevolently informed about the United States.

 —Merrill Denison, "4,000 Miles of Irritation," Saturday Review of Literature, *7 June 1952*

The Americans are our best friends, whether we like it or not.

 —Robert Thompson, national leader of the Social Credit Party (1961–1967), malapropism *quoted by Peter C. Newman in* Home Country, *1973*

The World has long watched the United States with a mixture of envy, admiration, resentment, fear, and disgust. Perhaps nowhere are these feelings more potent—or the watching more constant—than in Canada. We are under no illusions about our neighbour's accomplishments: America is the economic engine of Western capitalism; it is the source of astounding technological innovation; it is the matrix of popular culture; it is a military power like no other in history.

We take pains to remind ourselves, too, though, that America's crime rates in all categories are triple those in other industrialized nations; that its carnivalesque displays of wealth cannot conceal the rage and despair of its poorest; that Canada strives to be an upstanding citizen of the world while the United States has, under George W. Bush, reaffirmed its commitment

Source: Excerpted from *Fire and Ice: The United States, Canada and the Myth of Converging Values* by Michael Adams. Toronto: Penguin Canada, 2003. Reprinted by permission.

to brash unilateralism; that Canada consistently outranks the U.S. in the United Nations' Human Development Index, the planet's de facto annual quality-of-life ranking.

It is perhaps this last difference in which Canadians take the greatest comfort: on a personal level, Canadians sense that although Americans may make the more impressive living, Canadians have better gotten the hang of how to live. Looking south, we feel that even many of those who are ostensibly successful seem unable to savour their success, to enjoy the happiness promised in Thomas Jefferson's Declaration of Independence. And as the temporary cohesion engendered by the tragedies of 11 September continues to weaken, Americans seem to be returning to business as usual—lives that appear (from above) relentlessly competitive, perilously chaotic, perennially unfulfilling.

For all of our pressing our noses up against the glass of American prosperity and achievement, we cherish our separateness—our unassuming civility, our gift for irony and understatement in a world of exaggerated claims and excess, the myriad "intangibles" we are certain set us apart—and wring our hands over what will become of our quirks and idiosyncrasies as the leviathan to the south continues to thrash its ever more powerful tail and the self-declared prophets of globalization augur the death of difference.

This book is about Canadians and Americans. It offers up the results of the pulse-taking that Environics has been performing on both sides of the border during the past decade and elaborates, through the lens of social change, the national histories that have brought Canadians to their current uneasy coexistence with their Yankee neighbours. It discusses the trajectories the two societies seem to be following—trajectories that, contrary to Jeffrey Simpson's views in his book *Star-Spangled Canadians*[1] and echoed by Michael Bliss in a January 2003 series of articles in the *National Post*[2] on the evolving Canadian identity, are not ineluctably drawing together but actually diverging in subtle but important ways.

To be fair, Simpson and Bliss are certainly not alone in their belief that Canada and the United States are becoming more similar. When Ekos Research asked Canadians in May 2002 whether they thought Canada had been becoming more or less similar to the United States during the preceding ten years, a majority of respondents (58 per cent) replied that they thought Canada was becoming more American. Thirty-one per cent thought there had been no change in the two countries' similarity or difference, and a mere 9 per cent thought Canada was becoming increasingly distinct from the United States. When asked whether they wanted Canada to be more like or less like the U.S., a majority of Canadians (52 per cent) reported that they would like Canada to be less like its neighbour. Thirty-four percent wanted the two countries' identities and relationship to remain the way they are now, and only 12 per cent of Canadians desired greater convergence with the U.S.

In this book I advance the rarely heard, and even more rarely substantiated, thesis that Canadians and Americans are actually becoming increasingly different from one another. Canadians are everywhere confronted with the claim that our southern border is rapidly becoming irrelevant: our health care system will soon cease to differentiate us as a nation; our beloved Queen Elizabeth will not be able to hold out much longer against George Washington on the battleground of international currency; we may have to hand the controls of our immigration and refugee systems over to Uncle Sam in the name of continental security; and our ongoing gobbling of American media and popular culture will soon endanger any differences that may yet linger even in our very minds. The left chants these supposed omens of convergence in grave tones, while the right brightly trumpets them as signs that rational markets are at last poised to triumph over the illogic of national borders. What I propose to show in the following pages is that the rarely disputed prognosis of Canada–U.S. cultural convergence is, in important ways, false. At the most basic level—the level of our values, the feelings and beliefs that inform our understanding of and interaction with the world around us—Canadians and Americans are markedly different, and are becoming more so. ...

North America's Two Distinct Societies

In the days and weeks following 11 September, Canadians' feelings of sympathy for and solidarity with the United States were expressed again and again. Canadian firefighters and medical professionals travelled to New York City to offer assistance to those affected by the terrorist attacks. Families in Newfoundland opened their homes to fearful and distraught Americans whose planes had been diverted into Canada after news of the disaster had spread through airline communication systems. On 14 September, 100,000 Canadians gathered on Parliament Hill to express their grief over the tragedies that had befallen their neighbours.

The reaction was more immediate and heartfelt than in any other nation. It brought to mind a child in a schoolyard tearfully rushing to the aid of an older sibling in serious distress, affection and fellow feeling blotting out all the usual resentment over quotidian bullying or petty squabbles. Certainly, after things had settled down somewhat, some of the usual fault lines between the two countries began to reappear: Canadians began to wonder about what the U.S. response to the attacks would be, and some eventually began to fret openly (if gingerly) about how Canadians would be drawn into the conflict. But for a short time, the differences between Canada and the United States seemed to dissolve.

As the horror receded and daily life slowly resumed, the differences that had seemed so trivial as to be almost non-existent on that Tuesday morning began to reassert themselves little by little. As 2001 wound shakily down and 2002 began, many Canadians once again found themselves beginning to roll their eyes at phrases like "axis of evil" and shake their heads at George W. Bush's repeated references to the women of Afghanistan as "women of cover." Without losing any of our sympathy for the lives lost or irrevocably altered on 11 September, Canadians began to regain some of their sense of distance and difference from the United States and its worldview.

This slow, tentative process was accelerated very suddenly on 17 April 2002, when news of the deaths of four Canadian soldiers in Afghanistan reached North America (or at least, the news *seemed* to reach North America, but for all the attention it received south of the border it might as well have been lost in transit). The four soldiers were killed (and eight others injured) by "friendly fire"; a U.S. fighter pilot dropped a bomb on the Canadians (whom he mistook for enemy soldiers) as they were carrying out a training exercise on the ground.

"Accidents happen in wars," all voices seemed to concede sadly. "Nobody wanted this to happen." But as President Bush made his first, second, third, fourth, and fifth public appearances the next day without ever mentioning the incident—and even ignoring a question shouted by a Canadian reporter as Bush scuttled away from one press conference—sadness turned to anger. Was it really too much to expect that the United States might have been saddened at having killed and wounded a group of young Canadians who were doing their best to help America fight its war? Was it too much to expect that the American president would at least *pretend* to be dismayed, expressing at least some modest words of empathy and regret? Or that the *New York Times* might have spared a little space somewhere ahead of page fourteen on the day following the incident?

Now Canadians were beginning to recall the old simmering resentments of life in Uncle Sam's backyard. Though the feeling of fraternity that had permeated the country in the period immediately following September 11 had been entirely genuine, this familiar feeling of ill use was no less so. Canadians seemed to recall, in April of 2002, that although it may sometimes seem that Canada and the U.S. are "on the same page," that's usually because we're reading over their shoulder.

Because the cultural differences between Canada and the United States tend to exist beneath the consciousness of our daily lives, it is sometimes possible to imagine that those differences do not exist. After all, on any given day, most Canadians, like most Americans, can be spotted in their natural habitats driving cars, consuming too much energy and water, spending a little less time with their nuclear families than they would like, working a little more than is healthy, watching television, and buying some things they could probably survive without. But differences—both subtle and marked—do exist, and do endure. Some are external (gun control, bilingualism, health care), but many exist only inside the minds of Canadians and Americans—in how they see the world, how they engage with it, and how they hope to shape it.

In the foregoing chapter, I gave a broad outline of the direction of social change in the United States. In this chapter, I will offer a closer look a Canadians' and Americans' responses to individual survey questions—responses that attest, one by one, to a broad trend of cultural *divergence*. Subsequently, we will place Canada and the United States in the same sociocultural mapspace, so that we can see how the two countries' trajectories of social change appear relative to one another when they're placed in the same graphic territory.

But before the big picture, I'd like to share some raw numbers. We begin our portrait of these two neighbours with a comparison of their religious convictions. Canadians are by now quite familiar with evangelists Jerry Falwell, Pat Robertson, Jimmy Swaggart, Jim and Tammy Faye Bakker (who are slowly getting back to the business), and even William Jennings Bryan, who defended creationism in the famous Scopes Monkey trial in the 1920s. We know that Christian fundamentalism has far deeper and more enduring roots in the United States, particularly in the Bible Belt, than here in Canada. What we sometimes fail to remember is that not so long ago, Canadians were more conventionally religious than Americans. In the mid-1950s, 60 per cent of Canadians told pollsters they went to church each Sunday; the proportion in the U.S. at that time was only 50 per cent. Today, only a fifth of Canadians claim weekly church attendance (22 per cent, according to Ekos), whereas the proportion in the U.S. is 42 per cent. A 2002 Pew Research Center poll found religion to be important to 59 per cent of Americans—the highest proportion in all the developed nations surveyed—and to only 30 per cent of Canadians, a rate similar to that found in Great Britain and Italy. Nearly four in ten Canadians do not consider themselves to be members of a religious faith. In the U.S. the proportion of atheists, agnostics, or secular humanists is only 25 per cent. In less than a generation, Canadians have evolved from being much more religious than Americans to being considerably less so.

Canadians have not only rejected in large numbers the authority of religious institutions, but have brought this questioning of traditional authority closer to home. Our research shows Canadians to be far less likely than Americans to agree with the statement, "The father of the family must be master in his own home." In 1992 we found that 26 per cent of Canadians believed Father must be master (down from 42 per cent in 1983). In 1992, 42 per cent of Americans told us Dad should be on top. Since then the gap has widened: down to 20 per cent in Canada and up to 44 per cent in the U.S. in 1996, and then down even further (to 18 per cent) in Canada in 2000 and up further still (to 49 per cent) in the U.S. in that year. The widening gap between the two countries now stands at an astonishing thirty-one points, with Canadians becoming ever less deferential to patriarchal authority and Americans becoming more and more willing to Wait Till Their Father Comes Home to find out if it's okay to watch *The Simpsons*.

Paralleling this differing orientation to patriarchal authority are the two populations' attitudes toward the relative status of the sexes. In a word, Americans are more predisposed to male chauvinism than Canadians, and here again the gap is widening. In 1992, 26 per cent of Canadians told us that men are naturally superior to women, while 30 per cent of Americans felt the same way. Four years later in 1996, the proportion of Canadians believing in the innate superiority of men declined to 23 per cent while the U.S. proportion rose to 32 per cent. By 2000, the proportion in Canada stood at 24 per cent while that in the U.S. shot up to 38 per cent. It only stands to reason, many Americans seem to be telling us, that if God-fearing men are the superior beings on this planet, then they should certainly be the bosses in their own homes.

Canadians' more egalitarian views regarding the status of women and the structure of the family, plus a more skeptical view of traditional institutional authority, also seem to lead them to a more relaxed view of what constitutes a family Over the past decade, Canadians have consistently felt that two people living together, what we used to call living common-law, in fact constitutes a family. In 2000, 71 per cent of Canadians felt a couple that shared a home were a family, up from 66 per cent in 1992. Only 54 per cent of Americans shared this view, albeit up from 49 per cent in 1992. It is almost impossible to imagine a governor of any U.S. state daring to brazenly "live in sin" with his or her "life partner" as can Ontario Premier Ernie Eves. When in 1942 the Conservatives added the adjective "Progressive" to their party name, I doubt they had common-law cohabitation in mind.

What emerges so far is a portrait of two nations evolving in unexpected directions: the once shy and deferential Canadians, who used to wait to be told by their betters what to do and how to think, have become more skeptical of traditional authority and more confident about their own personal decisions and informal arrangements. Americans, by contrast, seeking a little of the "peace and order" that Canadians hoped "good government" would provide, seem inclined to latch on to traditional institutional practices, beliefs, and norms as anchors in a national environment that is more intensely competitive, chaotic, and even violent.

Attitudes toward violence are, in fact, among the features that most markedly differentiate Canadians from Americans. In the year 2000, 50 per cent of Canadians told us they felt violence to be all around them, a high figure to be sure, but nowhere near the 76 per cent of Americans who felt the same way. Americans' responses to our questions about violence suggest that they may even be becoming inured to the violence they perceive to be ubiquitous. In 1992, 9 per cent of Canadians and 10 per cent of Americans told us that violence is a normal part of life, nothing to be concerned about. In 1996, the figure in Canada was still

9 per cent, but had grown to 18 per cent in the U.S. In 2000, 12 per cent of Canadians felt that violence in everyday life was normal, but in the same year 24 per cent of Americans felt the same way. For one American in four, representing 70 million people, violence is perceived as a normal part of one's daily routine. The other three-quarters of the population, presumably, are doing all they can to avoid those 70 million, particularly if alone on the street after dark.

We found further evidence that violence is becoming more, not less, normative in America when we asked Americans to agree or disagree that when one is extremely tense or frustrated, a little violence can offer relief, and that "it's no big deal." In 1992, 14 per cent of Americans agreed with this sentiment, as did 14 per cent of Canadians we polled. In 1996, the proportion was 10 per cent in Canada but zoomed to 27 per cent in the U.S. By 2000, the proportion in Canada was back up to 14 per cent, but had surged further to 31 per cent in America, nearly one-third of the population. Again, you might not want to confront one of these folks when they're feeling a bit on edge, particularly when you remember that many of them (including the U.S. Attorney General) believe their Constitution guarantees them the right to bear firearms.

America is and always has been a very competitive society, nurtured by the myth of the American Dream, which suggests that anyone with a little vision and a lot of hard work can achieve material success. Sociologist Seymour Martin Lipset points out that in all categories, crime rates in America are about three times higher than they are in other industrialized countries. Lipset suggests as an explanation for this phenomenon the following: the American Dream, and the concomitant imperative to achieve material success, are so strong in America that many people pursue the goals of wealth and status in reckless, sometimes even criminal, ways. The end is of such monumental importance that the means become almost irrelevant.

Our polling found some interesting results in this area. In 1992, we asked Canadians and Americans whether they would be prepared to take "great risks" in order to get what they want. That year, nearly equal proportions of Canadians (25 per cent) and Americans (26 per cent) reported that they would indeed be prepared to take great risks to get what they wanted. The same in 1996. But by 2000 still only a quarter of Canadians were prepared to take great risks while the proportion in the U.S. increased to 38 per cent—a full eleven points higher than in Canada.

Americans are prepared to put a lot more on the line than Canadians to achieve their version of the American Dream, including personal risks to life and limb. They are also, as it turns out, more willing than Canadians to risk the lives and limbs of others to achieve the same ends. In 1992, 10 per cent of Canadians and only 9 per cent of Americans told us that it is acceptable to use violence to get what you want. In 1996, 11 per cent of Canadians felt this way, but the proportion of Americans rose to 17 per cent. By 2000, 13 per cent of Canadians felt the use of violence, presumably on or off the ice, was an acceptable way of achieving one s objectives, while the proportion in the U.S. was 23 per cent, nearly one in four and almost double the figure in Canada.

Lipset's hypothesis about the possible relationship between crime and the deep-rooted imperative of the American Dream illuminates an interesting contradiction: frustrated by their inability to achieve the Dream by socially acceptable means, those who obtain the trappings of success unlawfully exercise excessive individualism precisely *in order* to conform.

The idea that America's ostensible commitment to individualism may mask a deep impulse toward conformity is borne out in our polling data. We find that Americans are in fact more prone to conformity than their neighbours to the north, who reside in a land that not only tolerates but actually celebrates linguistic, ethnic, and regional group identities. We track three items that shed light on this intriguing question: do people mind changing their habits, do they relate to people who show originality in dress and behaviour, and do they relate to people who repress rather than show their emotions. Our findings are surprising. In 1992, 51 per cent of Canadians and 56 per cent of Americans reported that they did not like changing their habits. In 1996, 48 per cent of Canadians reported being stuck in their ways—a decline of three points—and 58 per cent of Americans said the same thing, an increase of two points. By 2000, we had a widening and quite significant gap: only 42 per cent of Canadians said they don't like changing their habits while 54 per cent of Americans reported the same, now a gap of twelve points showing Canadians to be less conservative and more flexible than Americans in their day-to-day routines.

Notes

1. Simpson writes, "Canadians, whether they like or acknowledge it, have never been more like Americans, and Canadian society has never been more similar to that of the United States. If the two countries are becoming more alike, and they are, this drawing together does not arise because Americans are changing. Canadians are the ones whose habits of mind, cultural preferences, economy, and political choices are becoming more American—without being American" (p. 6).

2. In a dialogue with *National Post features* writer Brian Hutchinson, University of Toronto historian and author Michael Bliss is quoted as saying: "But what strikes me is that we are becoming more similar to the Americans in our culture and in our values" (*National Post*, 18 January 2003, p. B1).

77

While Canada Slept

Andrew Cohen (2003)

EDITORS' INTRODUCTION

Andrew Cohen is an author, journalist, and professor of journalism and international affairs at Carleton University. Among his books are A Deal Undone: The Making and Breaking of the Meech Lake Accord; The Unfinished Canadian: The People We Are; *and* Extraordinary Canadians: Lester B. Pearson. *In 2009, he was appointed president of The Historica-Dominion Institute. This is an excerpt from* While Canada Slept: How We Lost Our Place in the World, *his controversial critique of Canada's ebbing internationalism, which was a finalist for the Governor-General's Literary Award for Non-Fiction in 2003. Although Cohen challenges deep-seated myths about Canada abroad, he also proposes ways in which Canada, if it summons the political will, can once again do great things in the world.*

Introduction

A few weeks after the calamitous events of September 11, 2001, John Manley, who was then minister of foreign affairs, mused about Canada and its place in the world. More advocate than diplomat, Manley was artlessly and unusually frank. "We are still trading on a reputation that was built two generations and more ago," he complained in a newspaper interview, "but that we haven't continued to live up to. You can't just sit at the G8 table and then, when the bill comes, go to the washroom. If you want to play a role in the world, even as a small member of the G8, there's a cost to doing that." Citing "the glaring inadequacy" of Canada's capacity in areas of foreign and defence policy, he worried that our weakness is compromising our traditional commitments overseas.

Manley, who has now been in Cabinet for nine and a half years, is no amateur. But he has a penchant for making direct, provocative remarks. Over the next few months, after he was named finance minister and deputy prime minister, he would cause a minor tempest by musing aloud about the future of the monarchy in Canada during a visit by Queen Elizabeth. To his credit, though, he never withdrew his comments on Canada's decline, even when his candour was greeted coolly in Cabinet. Indeed, the day after his interview he reiterated that "a lot of things changed on September 11. And one of those is that the burden that we are going to have to be asked to bear internationally is going to become greater. And we're not going to have an option, if we intend to play the influential role we have in the past … without shouldering that burden."

Source: Excerpted from *While Canada Slept: How We Lost Our Place in the World* by Andrew Cohen. Toronto: McClelland & Stewart, 2003. Reprinted by permission of the author.

As the country's chief diplomat, Manley was refreshing. Amid the puree of platitudes which passes for truth in Ottawa these days, his lament had a ring of authenticity. It was a clarion call to a country that has stepped away from its spirited internationalism. As columnist Jeffrey Simpson of the *Globe and Mail* puts it, "Never has the world meant more to Canada; never has Canada meant less to the world."

While Canada Slept tries to show why. It argues that our vision is less broad today than it was in the past, especially in the decade or so after the Second World War. We are no longer as strong a soldier, as generous a donor, and as effective a diplomat, and it has diminished us as a people. Our decline isn't a secret, but it seems more acute in 2003, amid rumours of war, calls to arms, pleas for moderation and negotiation, threats of terrorism, and laments for the poor and victims of disease, all of which have stirred Canadians at different times in different places.

This is a good time to rethink Canada's place in the world. Things are moving. In January 2003, the minister of foreign affairs and international trade invited Canadians to consider the great questions of our internationalism and register their views in writing and in public forums across the country. He calls this "a dialogue" on foreign policy rather than "a review" and it will not deal with defence or aid, per se. But he promises to report shortly thereafter on what he has heard from the people and to make recommendations to the government. At the same time, the Liberal Party is choosing a new leader and prime minister. If the leadership race is a contest of ideas, it will surely generate discussion about the responsibilities and opportunities for Canada beyond its shores, where the world is in the midst of upheaval.

A re-examination of our foreign relations, limited as it may be, is welcome. Up to now, the debate on Canada's place in the world has been generated by ad hoc groups or government watchdogs or parliamentary committees, usually confined to one area, such as aid or trade. What remains missing is an assessment of all the elements of our internationalism, together rather than separately, and how they affect each other.

This book tries to address that, examining the principal arms of our foreign relations: defence, aid, trade, and diplomacy. Each chapter begins with a review of what Canada did in the world in the past. This has a purpose. In an age of ignorance, it is important to know that we did not just arrive here fully formed, tumbling from the heavens. We did things abroad. We went to war, we kept the peace, and we died doing both. We fed, taught, and treated people in hard places, we brokered and proselytized in international councils. We bought goods from the corners of the earth and sold them there, too, and we became rich. We have a past. We come from somewhere else.

Decline? Decline from what? Canadians ask the question with incredulity, as if things were always as they are today. They weren't. Here, history is our reference. Our guides are Hume Wrong, Norman Robertson, and Lester Pearson, Canada's three most eminent diplomats who represented Canada when it began asserting itself in the world in the post-war era. Such was Pearson's impact that no prime minister since has failed to evoke his legacy or tried to escape his shadow. It is through his experience and that of his two colleagues that we see where our soldiers fought and kept the peace, how our diplomats helped create the international trading system and the architecture of the post-war era, how our benefactors laid the foundation of the world's first aid program.

But this isn't an elegy for Canada. Decline doesn't mean despair or disintegration, much as the chorus of Cassandras, bond-traders, currency speculators, continentalists, and self-hating

Canadians have predicted for most of our 135 years. The issue here isn't the country's survival; it is more the kind of country that we will be in the world—with what means and what ends, with what authority and what ambition, with what self-image and what self-respect.

So, beyond recalling the triumphs of the past and cataloguing the ills of the present, we look to the future. It is true that Canada cannot recover the influence it had in a smaller community of nations a generation or two ago. But as we found dignity and pride in what it did abroad, we can do so again. *While Canada Slept* challenges Canada to reinvent itself, and it makes some modest proposals.

A cautionary note. While this study draws on experts, it makes no claim to be written for them. It isn't a diplomatic history, an economic or trade analysis, or a philosophical treatise. It does not claim to cover all those things Canada does in the world, only the most important of them. There are many other parts of the picture, just that they are smaller parts. In the interest of clarity, there are no footnotes.

At root, *While Canada Slept* is a commentary based on a personal assessment of our standing in the world and the common misunderstanding that surrounds it today. Its purpose is to illuminate the face of Canada abroad, to encourage Canadians to think imaginatively about their country. Along the way, we touch on some of the enduring themes of our nationhood—sovereignty, maturity, memory, identity. We also revisit the warm mythology around Canada as a peacekeeper, donor, trader, and diplomat, a mythology which continues to shape the popular, if mistaken, view of Canada as it ponders its identity abroad. ...

A Potemkin Canada: Appearance and Reality

Much as Wrong, Robertson, and Pearson might think that Canada remains a formidable presence in the world, they would be mistaken. Indeed, what they might find is something of a Potemkin village. When Empress Catherine made a ceremonial tour of Russia's southern provinces in 1787, her minister Grigory Aleksandrovich Potemkin wanted her to see a happy, prosperous kingdom. Because such a Russia didn't exist, he invented it—erecting brightly painted false facades on Catherine's route along the Volga River. If Wrong, Robertson, and Pearson were to pay twenty-first century Canada a visit, their impression would be an illusion. We have created a Potemkin Canada.

The truth is that Canada is in decline in the world today. It is not doing what it once did, or as much as it once did, or enjoying the success it once did. By three principal measures—the power of its military, the generosity of its foreign aid, the quality of its foreign service—it is less effective than a generation ago. In other areas—such as the relative strength of its economy, the diversity of its trade, the persuasiveness of its diplomacy, the quality of its foreign intelligence, and the awareness of the world among its people, and of its people among the nations of the world—it is also in retreat.

What is the scope and nature of this decline? In some ways, such as the size of its armed forces and the volume of its international aid, it can be measured. In other ways—such as the deterioration of its foreign service—numbers and graphs tell only part of the story; reports, studies, and surveys tell the rest, and the weight of the evidence is damning. In still other ways, such as Canada's loss of stature in Washington or its influence in the councils of the world, conclusions are necessarily more nuanced. Any rush to judgement is shaded by real diplomatic successes here and there, by senior diplomats no less talented than their predecessors, their work often unrecognized. Ultimately, though, what emerges is a sad, general decline.

That decline is not the product of one party, one politician, one policy, or one period. It has been going on for decades—slowly, often imperceptibly, sometimes accelerated, sometimes arrested, under both the Liberals and the Conservatives. To some observers, such as the rueful Arthur Andrew, a diplomat of thirty years, it began in the 1960s. To some the 1950s, at the end of the golden age. To others the feckless 1970s. Many blame years of austerity. More likely, it is the accumulation of many forces, including continentalism and globalization, the Constitutional Wars, an ignorance of the past among Canadians, and a failure of vision among their leaders. To argue that Canada has abandoned or diluted its traditional roles in the world isn't terribly new. The argument has been made in different ways at different times. It is just that now—with the country's leadership in play, the war on terrorism in train, and the military in eclipse—the sense of loss has become more acute, gathering a momentum of its own.

At root, it is about values. The deterioration of Canada's social services, especially health and education; the lethargy of its politicians, personified by the most parochial prime minister since an early Mackenzie King; a soft, irresponsible media, which covers the world fitfully; an education system which doesn't teach history. As Canada has become a lesser country at home, it has become a lesser country abroad.

Michael Bliss, one of Canada's leading historians, recalls growing up in the 1950s in a country which he believed would have a higher standard of living than the United States, better social programs, a stronger civic and social order, more livable cities, more responsive political institutions, and "a balance of power and professionalism in world affairs." He believed all that was possible until 1967, which historian Pierre Berton calls "The Last Good Year." It was the hundredth anniversary of Confederation, before separatism and stagflation in the 1970s, and Canada still looked forward with optimism. Since then it has been downhill. "Yes, Virginia, there was a time when we could envisage Canada as being on top in North America," Bliss writes. "Now it has become evident that when we write the history of the last 30 years of Canadian national life, it will be in substantial part a sad story of squandered opportunities and decline. It will be a story of ill-conceived national economic and social policies, of onanistic obsession with Quebec, of the mindless parochialism of provincial governments, of the decay of civic spirit, of the full flowering of our national penchant for self-delusion, complacency, and mediocrity."

You don't have to accept all Bliss's evidence; had there not been that "onanistic obsession" with Quebec there might be no Canada today at all. But his lament, which has been expressed more harshly by newspaper magnate Conrad Black, who renounced his citizenship and left Canada, does speak to a growing sense of aimlessness.

"In nearly all dimensions of national life, we Canadians are falling behind both our southern neighbours and our own potential," Bliss says. "The fact that from certain perspectives we remain such a wonderfully successful country has the tendency to mask our weaknesses. But these weaknesses are becoming so numerous and glaring that a moment of national truth is approaching, a time when we have to face up to the implications of Canadian decline."

Bliss speaks as a conservative born in the 1940s, perhaps nostalgic for a disappearing past. Progressives see the same thing. "We haven't woken up to the fact that what makes us distinctive is that we're the 'public good' country—we have great airports, great public transport, great urban services, great welfare state, great health care," says historian and social critic Michael Ignatieff. "And we're underfunding our identity. There's better public-good investment in the United States. I have a sense of a country living off the capital of the post-war era, the King–St. Laurent–Pearson–Trudeau years, which built this independent Canada. And that capital's running down."

Whether it is Ignatieff's underfunded identity or Bliss's "flowering of self-delusion," the conclusion is the same: Canada is losing its stature and its promise. Curiously, when Bliss or Ignatieff make that point, few challenge them. Indeed, few seem to care. A senior cabinet minister in the present government likens today's Canada to 1950s America, a period of material prosperity but social paralysis: "We're coming to the end of the Eisenhower era," he says. "Canada is drifting."

Values follow each other as the long dash of the national time signal follows ten seconds of silence. In the 1990s, as the government became less generous in social services, it became less generous with the world's poor. It was easy; they don't vote here. As the government reduced the civil service, it reduced the foreign service, and the military, too. As it refused to invest in itself at home, it refused to invest in itself abroad. O, Canada. The unfinished country has become the diminished country. ...

More Than a Whisper

... Canada is content with a foreign policy largely driven by the imperatives of trade and economic development, instead of the other way around. It salutes free trade except with the developing nations, which need it most. By and large, it cleaves to the priorities of a foreign policy it established nine years ago. While Britain, Australia, and the United States are increasing spending and reviewing defence policy, Ottawa wants only a superficial re-examination of defence, aid, and foreign policy, each independent of the other. It promised reviews in the Throne Speech in September 2002, but has been slow to initiate and publicize the one on defence, and has ordered not a review, but a "dialogue" with Canadians to guide its deliberations. The result is a Canada more responsive than inventive on the international stage, given to a kind of lofty ad hockery, inclined to embrace the next fashionable idea, be it soft power or human security, as long as it doesn't cost too much.

For all its history and geography, for all its energy and diversity, is this the best that Canada can do in the world? In 2003, it appears so. Canada's failure to invest in itself—its "pinchpenny diplomacy," as political scientist Kim Nossal puts it—has turned a thrusting cosmopolitan into a timid provincial. "This rich, safe and well-endowed community has grown to begrudge international activism," Nossal laments, "to constantly cry poor, and to whinge (quite implausibly) that it cannot afford to spend more on international affairs." Without real resources, it is harder for Canada to be taken seriously these days in London and Washington, in NATO, and at the UN. It no longer speaks with the same authority in the international community. That [American statesman] Dean Acheson could write the polemic he did a generation ago [*Neighbors Taken for Granted*] suggests that he took Canada's complaints seriously and felt them personally. Today, he'd probably just ignore them.

Is it influence lost, then? Can Canada recover the stature and spirit it had? The answer is yes. Canada can reclaim its *locus standi* in the world, or at least a good part of it, and create a new role for itself. ...

The challenges are great but not insurmountable. Nations make choices, and certainly Canada can: to renew its international citizenship, to make its foreign policy distinctive, to project a new sense of identity. In each of the arms of foreign policy examined here—defence, aid, trade, and diplomacy—there are things Canada can do. Some are modest, some are ambitious. Some are being examined and even adopted by Ottawa, slowly and incrementally. Most, though, mark a break with the status quo, which is the point. ...

Seize the Day

... At the end of the day, we can have the world's best small military, its most efficient, generous aid program, and its most imaginative foreign service. We can reject mediocrity. For we can re-equip ourselves to assume meaningful roles—in mediation, peacekeeping, or reforming the United Nations; in alliances with like-minded Nordic countries on regional and environmental questions; in bringing ideas and innovation to international financial institutions, as we already have; in addressing the illicit diamond trade or the proliferation of small arms or the evil of child warriors.

What we do abroad will enrich us at home. For a country forever wondering if it has a future, indeed doubting if it has one, the new Canadian internationalism could become an instrument of pan-Canadian unity, taking us beyond the boundaries of language and race and region, drawing on all elements of a truly diverse society. Our diplomacy, our aid, and our military (the national institution which has most successfully accommodated language and culture) reflect a broader purpose. In time, with courage and will, the world will become our mission again, and it will give us pride and purpose, again.

For Canada, it is time to awake, and seize the day.

78 "Defence, Diplomacy, and Development"

Paul Martin (2004)

EDITORS' INTRODUCTION

In recent years, Canada has had to confront complex issues as it attempts to forge an identity on the international stage in a post-9/11 world. In addition to being in the thick of a complicated (and, many believe, unwinnable) war in Afghanistan, Canada has sought out an institution-building role in various troubled countries around the globe. Although Prime Minister Paul Martin's speech represents the partisan perspective of a Liberal prime minister, it offers a good example of the "exporting Canadian values" theme in recent Canadian foreign policy. Andrew Cohen strongly questions Canada's current ability to play an important role in the world (see reading 77), but Martin promotes the potential of "the three D's," although he readily acknowledges the hurdles that exist within current international systems. At the same time, Canada has had to acknowledge US security demands. "The best protection we can have at home," Martin tell his American audience, "is a world that works."

It is a privilege to discuss with this distinguished audience, Canadian perspectives on some of the most important issues facing the global community.

Tomorrow, I will be meeting with President Bush. We will be talking about bilateral trade issues like our softwood lumber exports, where our producers and your consumers continue to be hurt by the inability to solve the dispute once and for all. We will discuss the BSE—Mad Cow issue, where the highly integrated North American cattle industry requires open borders as soon as possible to enhance confidence at home and abroad, based on sound science.

Frankly, we are continually astonished at how quickly the border can be closed when pressures erupt in the United States. Fifteen years after the Canada–US free trade agreement, ten years after we trilateralised it with Mexico under NAFTA, we should be able to do better. We have to recognize that ours is a North American economy; Canada is the largest export market for 37 of your states. You are our largest export market. Protectionism benefits no one.

We will consider other areas as well where a North American perspective benefits both countries, for example energy, the electricity grid and the environment, where we are looking at ways to intensify bilateral co-operation to maintain clean air and water for both countries.

Source: Address by Prime Minister Paul Martin at the Woodrow Wilson Center, on the occasion of his visit to Washington, DC, April 29, 2004. Reprinted by permission.

We will also be talking about international issues, including our shared commitment to promoting democracy and human dignity, our resolve to combat the scourge of human trafficking, and the steps both countries are taking to promote security at home, on our shared continent, and around the world. And it is this last subject that I want to talk to you about today—Canadian perspectives on how to build greater security for us all.

The ultimate human right is the right to personal security, and so the first duty of government must be to protect its citizens. That responsibility is being tested by an array of threats that is unprecedented in our times: rogue states, failing and failed states, international criminal syndicates, weapons proliferation, and terrorists prepared to act with no concern for the cost in human lives, including their own.

Once protected by oceans, today's front line stretches from the streets of Kabul, to cities in the United States, from the rail lines in Madrid, to cities across Canada. Our adversary could be operating in the mountains of Afghanistan, in the cities of Europe, or within our own borders. There is no home front. The conflict is not "over there." Our approach to security must reflect this reality. ...

A good defence also means taking the fight to where it's needed. Canadian soldiers are there, in some of the hottest of the hot spots. We have almost 2000 troops in Afghanistan, and the current commander of the International Security Assistance Force is a Canadian. We have just recommitted ourselves to extending our tour in Afghanistan beyond the August 2004 date originally set for withdrawal, and we still have major deployments in the Balkans, the Persian Gulf and Haiti.

The fact is, Canada currently ranks second among NATO nations when it comes to the percentage of troops deployed abroad in multi-national operations. Ahead of the French, the British, the Italians, the Spanish and everyone else except the Americans. Nor do we foresee an early end to the kinds of security challenges we face. That is why, recently, we announced major new procurement decisions to ensure our military has the equipment it needs to get the job done.

In describing our approach, it is immediately clear that there are many areas of common cause with American policies. There are also areas where we disagree. It has always been so, and it is a remarkable—perhaps the most remarkable—feature of Canada–US relations over the years, that our differences have served to distinguish us, but they have never divided us. In the specific case of Iraq, we did not join the coalition forces. I believe this was the right decision for Canada, and Canadians supported it. But there is no disagreement at all with what has to be done going forward.

To this end, Canada has pledged $300 million to assist the Iraqi people to rebuild their country and establish responsible and democratic governance. We are already providing training in Jordan for Iraqi police. And as circumstances permit, we are prepared to do significantly more in this and other areas of institution building.

We are also ready, in concert with our Paris Club partners, to forgive Iraqi debts to Canada of around $750 million. We agree as well that the sooner the UN can move back into Iraq, the better. Now so far, the policies I have described, including the need to send troops abroad, are primarily defensive, designed to counter threats against us.

There is however, another dimension to the debate as well, one that arises from the need to deal, at the same time and on many different fronts, with the challenges arising from globalisation. Economically, the benefits have been enormous. But they have been far from even, and too many countries are being left behind. Even if more people are better off than ever before, the absolute gap between rich and poor is growing.

We all agree this cannot continue. Much ink has been spilled in trying to come to grips with this, the world's greatest moral issue. Where much less analysis has been forthcoming, however, is on another aspect of globalization, one that touches directly upon our need for greater security.

The information revolution has helped spread ideas about human rights and political freedom that have transformed entire regions, but it has also created tensions—ethnic, religious, cultural—within many traditional societies. These tensions within failing or failed states or within those that cannot match the world's pace of change, are the equivalent of a tinder box waiting for a match.

True security is much more than simply defence against attack. It is a conviction that we will be most secure when citizens in all countries are able to participate fully in national life, when they can see clearly that their own well-being and freedom require a functioning state that listens to them and, ultimately, is accountable to them. The key ideas here are "functional" and "accountable."

If we have learned one thing over the decades of foreign assistance it is this: countries will not work—cannot work—unless they have public institutions that work; and the best way to make sure those institutions do work is to have them accountable to the publics they serve. Foreign aid is important but its benefits are clearly circumscribed when functional and accountable institutions are not in place. ...

[A]s a specific thrust of our role in the world, we intend to focus our international effort much more on helping countries to build the institutions of modern government they need to provide security and the means to a decent life for their citizens.

In Canada, we refer to the three D's—defence, diplomacy, and development. This means we are integrating our traditional foreign policy instruments more tightly, especially when responding to the need of vulnerable states to build up their own capacity to govern themselves. As Afghanistan has demonstrated, even the presence of foreign troops cannot guarantee security unless there is also progress towards a political settlement. But, equally, there will be no political settlement unless security is established. And proper economic development needs both—security and political stability—if it is to work.

The common thread in the three "D's" is capacity building in all areas of governance. Too often, people focus only on one dimension, and neglect the rest. We see this approach occasionally in discussions of public security; experts tell us to do some police training, build a prison or two, and then, once the situation settles down, pack up and leave.

This isn't good enough. The three D's means building public institutions that work and are accountable to the public for their actions, "not just policing" but also government ministries, a system of laws, courts, Human Rights Commissions, schools, hospitals, energy and water and transportation systems. It means working on many levels at the same time, and doing so in ways that reinforce each other. It also means a vibrant private sector. ...

In terms of today's headlines, the need for institution-building is seen most graphically in Iraq. But it is also true in countries where, although there has been no recent conflict, there is still a need for us to help create the requisite institutions, or prevent the erosion of existing institutions of government. Africa is an example where leaders are acting to build institutional capacity, both nationally and regionally. They are doing so through their New

Partnership for Africa's Development (NEPAD)—an initiative Canada, the United States, and other G8 partners are supporting through the Africa Action Plan.

Institution-building sounds straightforward, but it is in reality a very difficult proposition. There is a fine line to be walked between assistance and interference. There is a need to promote modern methods without dismissing valued local traditions.

There is no one blueprint but, as in so many other areas, there is the old advice: play to your strength, and it is because of this that we believe Canada can and will play an important role, as countries in stress come to grips with the need to build the institutions of modern governance. When I think of Canadian strengths, I think of the very beginnings of our country.

The British North America Act of 1867, our first constitution, granted to Parliament the power to legislate for the "peace, order and good government" of Canada. This is not a phrase to set the pulse racing but that is not such a bad thing when you are building for the long haul. As the times have changed, Canadian expectations of government have changed as well but "peace, order and good government" have always served as clear standards by which to measure the performance of our institutions.

We have I believe another strength in this endeavour that goes back to our founding. When we began as a country, we managed to bind together in one political community, two linguistic groups and two major religious denominations. Over the years, we have added a rich tapestry of other languages, ethnicities and religions, and have striven to address the concerns and claims of our aboriginal peoples. Some like to say that Canada was one of the first "post-modern" states, one of the first countries to explicitly reject the notion that a state consists of one people, one ethnic group with one language and culture. Canada has never described itself as a "melting pot"; instead, we have always talked of ourselves as a "mosaic."

Perhaps, that is why Sri Lanka has turned to Canadian experts for help in developing a federal solution to its inter-communal strife. Thus, as a major industrialized nation, but never a colonial nor a super power, we have certain unique advantages, as we focus much more than we have in the past on institution building as the essential foundation of a secure, modern state. Advantages we intend to exercise as a major foreign policy thrust.

So far, I have talked about institution-building and better governance within countries, but that is only part of the story. There is also an urgent need to make international systems and multilateral institutions work more effectively. The fact is we need better international governance to help spread the benefits of globalization more equitably while also helping countries offset some of its inevitable costs. We need multilateral institutions that work because, despite their many frustrations, they carry a legitimacy that no one country can muster on its own. They stand for the principles that every country deserves a seat at the table, has legitimate interests to be met and values to be respected. Now it is easy to complain that this or that institution isn't working, but let's stop the buck-passing. Multilateral institutions are us, the sovereign member states. We are accountable for whether they work or not. Most of us would agree that reform of many institutions within and without the UN family is necessary and I won't take the time today to belabour the obvious.

There is, however, one proposal I would like to raise. The responsibility for good international governance falls ultimately upon the shoulders of the political leaders of the world's sovereign governments. But there is a real problem here; many of today's international organizations are not designed to facilitate the kinds of informal political debates that must occur between politicians.

In short, leaders cannot make the bold decisions required if international fora remain focused only on ratifying the product of bureaucratic negotiations. The most fruitful exchanges between leaders often take place in the corridors of great meetings, one on one, far removed from the actual agenda. When leaders do meet in international fora, it is difficult to break free of the "briefing book" syndrome and get down to brass tacks, to thinking outside the box. Bureaucrats and diplomats can take an issue so far and no further; only political leaders can make the leap so often required to break an intellectual, emotional or historical impasse.

Photo ops are no substitute for political will. We have to find ways for political leaders to work with each other internationally, the way they work with different political constituencies at home—debating, exploring, and searching for value-driven solutions that are inclusive rather than divisive, stabilizing rather than destructive, pragmatic rather than ideological.

How do we get there? An approach I believe to be worthwhile would be to look at the lessons learned from the Group of 20 Finance Ministers that was formed in the wake of the Asian financial crisis that began in 1997. We foresaw an informal gathering of finance ministers, representing established and emerging centres of influence and coming from very different political, economic, cultural and religious traditions. We wanted to bridge the "us versus them" mentality that bedevils so many international meetings, and it has worked remarkably well—because peer pressure is often a very effective way to force decisions.

We believe a similar approach among leaders could help crack some of the toughest issues facing the world. We need to get the right mix of countries in the same room, talking without a set script. We are not proposing a new bricks and mortar institution, but we do believe a new approach directly involving political leaders could help break a lot of logjams. I would suggest we should convene a select group of countries from North and South tackling just one issue, and see where that takes us—it could be global terrorism or global public health. For instance, the United States, Canada and other G8 countries, working with the UN, have done much to develop a humane response to the AIDS crisis in Africa.

In Canada, our Parliament is legislating changes to allow Canadian companies to provide generic anti-HIV/AIDS drugs to African countries at low cost. We are the first industrialized country to bring forth groundbreaking legislation of this kind. I am very proud of this.

But the need for cheap medicines goes beyond AIDS and beyond Africa. Can we not find a balance between the clear need for the intellectual property rights that underwrite much of our medical research and the equally clear need to help alleviate suffering among people who cannot afford the fruits of that research? There are other issues a leaders' G-20 could deal with as well, such as rescuing the current round of multilateral trade negotiations, where the biggest stumbling block is agriculture. Agriculture is not simply a trade issue that will be decided solely on its economic merit. ...

In much of the discussion about good governance, both within countries and internationally, we assume that most governments would prefer to work well on behalf of their citizens rather than remain apart in wretched isolation. But as we know this is not always the case. What of those countries that are unwilling to take the first steps towards responsible national or global citizenship? What do we do when their populations face humanitarian catastrophe? What do we do when people are confronted by a culture of hate or violence spawned by their own government as occurred in Rwanda?

If a nation violates all accepted standards of responsible behaviour, the question is: do we, the international community, have a responsibility to protect—in this case, to protect a country's people from their own government? A recent international commission reported to the United Nations that we do have that responsibility, and it set out various types of acceptable interventions, including measures such as sanctions and military action under certain conditions—including acting under "the right authority."

We in Canada find ourselves very much in agreement with UN Secretary-General Kofi Annan when he said: "Surely no legal principle, not even sovereignty, can ever shield crimes against humanity." We believe that humanitarian intervention, under compelling circumstances such as a Rwanda or a Kosovo, is warranted. We reject the argument that state sovereignty confers absolute immunity. As Nobel Prize laureate Elie Wiesel has said: "Neutrality always means coming down on the side of the victimizer—never on the side of the victim."

What is required is an open discussion about the need for intervention in situations that offend the most basic precepts of our common humanity. We need clear agreement on principles to help determine when it is appropriate to use force in support of humanitarian objectives.

Now some may say that all of this takes us far from the security agenda that we in North America must have in place to protect our own citizens. I don't believe this to be the case. I suspect neither do you. The points I would make are quite straightforward.

First, in terms of North America, we must protect our borders. I can assure you Canada will do more than its share.

Second, the best protection we can have at home is a world that works. Here the capacity and hence the responsibility of each of our countries varies. We are not a superpower. That is true. But as I mentioned, this can also be an advantage. Seen holistically rather than piecemeal, the decisions we make as a world will determine whether all the advances we have made in recent decades can work for everyone, or whether hundreds of millions—perhaps billions—of people will be left behind forever.

We have to demonstrate to people around the planet that international systems can be made to work for everyone. We have to give every person a stake in good governance, at home and internationally.

We have a duty to protect our citizens. Day by day, it becomes clearer that our long-term security requires the spread of freedom around the world, freedom from oppression, freedom from corruption, freedom from hunger and ignorance and hopelessness. Freedom for everyone to live a secure, prosperous, and productive life.

We cannot ignore the very real threats to our security posed by terrorists and political thugs who find their genesis not in poverty but in hate. But equally, we cannot ignore the long-term security imperative to build a more equitable and safe world for everyone on this planet.

Thank you.

Atlantic Canada in the Twenty-First Century: Prospects for Regional Integration

Robert Finbow (2004)

EDITORS' INTRODUCTION

Robert Finbow is professor and chair of Political Science at Dalhousie University with a cross-appointment in Canadian Studies. He has published on labour and environmental aspects of NAFTA, comparative health care and social policy, comparative North American political cultures, and Atlantic Canadian regionalism.

Canada's Atlantic provinces are often treated as an afterthought in academic texts. Robert Young refers to the dearth of inquiry about the Maritime provinces—Nova Scotia, New Brunswick and PEI—as analysis is replaced by stereotypes of patronage, with "petty princelings" fighting for the "spoils of office." Traditional attitudes of "distaste, fascination and disdain," which extend also to Newfoundland, give the region's critics a "soothing sense of bemused condescension." For many scholars, it is often easiest to lump these provinces together, despite the risk of over-generalization. This chapter will criticize these superficial analyses by looking at the institutional, economic, cultural and historical forces that distinguish these four provinces. It will assess the feasibility for greater integration or even outright union in the region, which is often advocated by outside observers as a simple panacea for regional dependence and underdevelopment. It will consider current common challenges that may force them to seek greater integration, cooperation or political union in the future. Finally, it will note the institutional constraints that will limit the prospects for integration and union, however desirable.

Observers are divided on the merits of referring to Atlantic Canada as a "region." There are similarities among these provinces, notably proximity to the sea and the maritime orientation to economic activity. They also share a population with fewer recent immigrants, mostly old-stock British and Acadian, with First Nations and African-Canadian minorities. In addition all four provinces share marginal resources, limited economic prospects, and regional disparities, marked by high unemployment and reliance on federal transfers for provincial and individual incomes. But diversities are also evident between them which are

Source: Excerpted from "Atlantic Canada in the Twenty-First Century: Prospects for Regional Integration" by Robert Finbow. In *Regionalism in a Global Society: Persistence and Change in Atlantic Canada and New England*, edited by Stephen G. Tomblin and Charles S. Colgan. Peterborough, ON: Broadview Press, 2004. Notes omitted. Reprinted by permission.

reinforced by the institutions of federalism and their inducements to province building, "parochialism," and "competitive statecraft." Murray Beck referred to a single Atlantic political culture as a "chimera," as citizens express provincial, not regional loyalties. ...

Some observers suggest that, despite the persistence of nineteenth-century provincialism, a weaker transcendent regionalism has developed in Canadian federalism, which created similar grievances, political marginalization, and dependence on federal programmes. As Jim Bickerton phrases it, "Atlantic Canadian regionalism in a very real sense can be considered a *creation* of the federal government or at the very least a socio-political phenomenon that exists, and has always existed, in symbiosis with the federal government." Initially, Atlantic Canada produced the federal regime's fiercest critics, including the first separatists in Nova Scotia in the late 1880s. Decreased economic and political influence in the federation induced transitory movements for regional cooperation, such as the Maritime rights agitation of the 1920s or the Maritime union discussion in the 1960s.

Subsequently, the region supported use of the federal spending power for cost-sharing in post-secondary education and health care, for equalization grants to provinces facing fiscal shortfalls, and for unemployment insurance to individuals with benefit duration tied to local unemployment rates. Ottawa poured millions into regional development to address disparities in incomes and unemployment by attempting, largely unsuccessfully, to create industrial "growth poles." Despite initial intentions, federal governments diluted these policies, caving in to political pressures from more populous regions. Bickerton notes that: "Regional development, which had originally been conceived and designed as a targeted, tightly controlled, rationally planned diversion of industrial growth from the over-heated and inflation-prone industrialized core to the chronically underdeveloped periphery, had become instead a pork-barrel accessible to federal and provincial politicians in every region." This dependence on federal programmes, alongside resentment of declining political and economic power, induced a dual conception of confederation, balancing central authority in redistribution with provincial control of economic destiny.

As the Atlantic provinces enter the new millennium, they retain historical characteristics in their cultures, economies and societies. These distinctions make their treatment as a single region questionable, and hamper any move toward union or coordination of policy and institutions. These differences are accentuated by the institutions of federalism, especially electoral fetishism and institutional structuring associated with province building, which augment provincial distinctions. However, Atlantic Canadians also confront economic and political forces that may force them to consider cooperation or even union, notwithstanding their differences. Fiscal crisis has caused the federal regime to reduce its contributions via transfers to provinces and individuals, leaving token programs for political purposes, while orienting major national policies towards more populous provinces. The small regional caucus in Parliament has limited influence on policy, though occasionally regional ministers do secure high profile expenditures, often with limited long-term benefits. Globalization and technology require more efficient use of public monies, and cause some to question the viability of four small, competitive provinces. In this chapter I will briefly survey political life in each province, and I will assess how difficult it will be to bridge the gaps between them in search of integration or cooperation in the common interest.

Newfoundland and Labrador

Newfoundland's dominion status and late entry into Confederation, and the isolation and lifestyle of its dispersed outport communities, separate it from the Maritimes. This province is overwhelmingly British and Irish in social origin, and dependent on fishing, forestry, and mining. The indigenous Beothuk were entirely wiped out by conflict with settlers and European disease; Innu peoples remain in isolated, impoverished towns in Labrador. French influence is felt in the traditional fishing concession known as the French Shore on the west coast, but this is a small element of the contemporary population. ...

Newfoundland was led into Confederation by the charismatic Joey Smallwood after a referendum in 1948, in which only 52 per cent preferred union with Canada. Smallwood convinced this slim majority that Newfoundland would benefit from Canada's social programs and from integration into the national economy. The province experienced an increase in living standards, as many took advantage of new economic opportunities and federal employment and income support. Smallwood spoke expansively of the "miracles ... as the benign air of Confederation breathed over us ... [as] our poor, downtrodden, backward Newfoundland ... was launched at last upon her astonishing career as a Canadian province."

But while the post-confederation period improved conditions, the province never achieved the expected economic miracle. ...

Dissatisfaction with Confederation lingered as some harked nostalgically to Dominion status, and blamed Ottawa for poor conditions. Federal and provincial development efforts both failed and forced reliance on overproduction in fisheries, with disastrous consequences for fish stocks. Sean Cadigan argues that the failed development policies merely continued a pre-confederation pattern that inadequate social welfare measures could not rectify:

> Together, Newfoundland and Canada established a ruinous cycle. They relied in the short term on social programs to deal with the dislocation caused by the failure of modernization programs, while in the long term turning even more to modernization, especially overexpansion in the fishing industry, to minimize the need for social programs. Overexpansion led to fisheries collapse and dependence on even more social programs, such as the fisheries moratoria program ... TAGS."

A "neo-nationalist" movement emerged in response to the economic "trump" of oil, with the discovery of the Hibernia oil field in the early 1970s. This cultural revival was compared with peripheral nationalism in Western Europe. Under the leadership of Brian Peckford, Newfoundland challenged Ottawa on constitutional reform and fiscal federalism. Peckford sought control of the offshore to allow the province to set the pace of development and maximize local benefits and linkage development from offshore oil and gas. Newfoundland joined Quebec and Alberta in opposing Pierre Trudeau's centralist vision. But the province lost key legal decisions on offshore jurisdiction. Liberal Premier Clyde Wells emerged as a defender of Trudeau's centralism against the decentralist proposals of Brian Mulroney's Meech Lake Accord. His successor, Brian Tobin, who served in the federal cabinet, defended Ottawa's role in setting national standards for social policy. ...

Tobin looked to Ireland for a model to reinvigorate the provincial economy via new technologies, manufacturing, entrepreneurship and tourism. His success in diversifying the economy remains uncertain, but statistics indicate that the provincial workforce is now shifting to the service sector, with merely 15 per cent left in primary industries. The collapse of the cod stocks, which was the mainstay for hundreds of isolated outports, was a profound economic and cultural blow, and contributed to alienation from Ottawa, which was accused of mismanaging this resource. The people of Canada's poorest province were forced into even greater dependence on federal social assistance, as plans were devised to retire fishermen and retrain the young. ...

Nova Scotia

Nova Scotia was a reluctant entrant into Confederation, and produced the country's first open secessionists with Joseph Howe's opposition to union in 1867 and the Repeal movement led by W.S. Fielding in 1886–87. Confederation corresponded with (and perhaps contributed to) economic eclipse as the province, once home to the world's fourth largest merchant navy, experienced decline. National policies, notably tariffs and railway construction, were blamed for Nova Scotia's predicament, generating tensions with Ottawa, as provincial politicians sought "better terms." After the Diefenbaker victory in 1957 and the start of equalization payments, regional development programmes and health care cost-sharing, federal-provincial relations improved. ...

Nova Scotia was a divided society at the time of Confederation, with those favouring union looking to integration around railway towns and industries, and those opposing confederation seeking self-determination as a global trading and shipping centre. Deep socio-economic divisions persist, with continued effects on governance. The province's agrarian, fishing, mining, forestry and urban communities are distinct worlds, making it curiously difficult to govern. Historically, ethnic fragmentation among Gaelic Scots Catholics in Cape Breton, Pictou Scottish Protestants, Loyalists and Englishmen, German speakers in Lunenburg, francophone Acadians, African-Canadian settlers, and indigenous Mi'kmaqs created political diversity. As Miller has noted, these regions "might unite for specific political action" particularly "to assault the political, economic or religious privilege of Halifax but there was no fusion." Religion dominated political discourse, with Catholic–Protestant divisions in education and services. This has receded, but the effects can still be seen in the plethora of small colleges serving different constituencies. ...

Recently, the two major parties have alternated in power. These centrist clones focus on issues of public management and leaders' personalities, not distinct policies. Governments are forced to compromise provincial interests with particular concerns of diverse constituencies in order to govern. This contributes to a patronage culture, with questionable public management and numerous scandals over the use of public funds. Patronage is an important political motivator in this have-not society, as supporters of each party routinely secure government contracts and employment. ...

More recently, the province has fragmented into three competing political zones: Cape Breton, where the Liberals and NDP compete for seats; Metro Halifax with a three-way competition where the NDP made inroads; and the rural mainland, where the Tories remain strongest. This creates a competitive three party system. The province's regionalized party system may produce an enduring period of three-way competition and minority government, depending on the NDP's durability and potential expansion. [*Editor's note: In the June*

2009 election, the Nova Scotia NDP won a majority, marking the first time the NDP has formed a provincial government in the history of Atlantic Canada.]

Nova Scotia remains among the worst provinces in the area of public management. The province has failed to balance the budget, and has one of the highest per capita debt loads in Canada. The Conservative government of John Hamm has borrowed rhetoric from Mike Harris's common sense revolution, declaring in its 1999 Throne Speech that "self-reliance and personal responsibility are the keys to building strong families, strong communities and a better province." It is unclear if Hamm's downsizing efforts will be sufficient to restore fiscal balance. But the current conflict between urban and rural municipalities over fiscal equalization indicates that old divisions are still evident.

New Brunswick

New Brunswick takes pride in its status as the only officially bilingual province. The francophone Acadians, returnees from the expulsion from Nova Scotia in 1755, settled mainly in the north and northeast of the province, adjacent to Quebec. The anglophone community originated with Loyalists in the Saint John River valley, with later arrivals of Yorkshiremen and Irish Catholics. New Brunswick is closer to continental markets than its Maritime cousins. The potato industry spawned the McCain's frozen food empire; the Irvings built on car dealerships and gasoline to become a provincial giant spanning numerous sectors (including a near media monopoly). Forestry is the largest primary industry, and the mining industry is diverse, led by zinc, lead and silver. Politics has centered on ethnic and geographic divisions, with the Liberals supported mainly in the rural, poor, Acadian north and the Conservatives in the largely English, more urban, prosperous south. This split has affected most elections, with important swing ridings of mixed ethnicity in the centre of the province near Moncton making the difference between Conservative and Liberal victories. Periods of long Conservative rule alternated with Liberal regimes, though early governments included coalitions of both parties, which were themselves loose associations of county parties, reflecting traditions of localism and patronage. ...

After sweeping all 58 seats in 1987, the Liberal government of Frank McKenna adjusted to fiscal constraint and the telecommunications revolution. McKenna was remarkable as perhaps the only leader in the region to impose severe restraint measures and still retain popular support (winning three majority governments before retiring in 1997). To balance the books, he closed hospital beds, laid off nurses, froze civil-service wages, consolidated government departments and cut up to 3700 jobs from the public service. Somehow McKenna managed to inspire confidence from New Brunswickers about their province's potential. He attracted many new businesses to the province, like courier services and telemarketing, with up to 7000 jobs in call centers and big name investors like Purolator Courier, United Parcel Service, Federal Express Canada, and CP Express and Transport. He was accused by other provinces of using unfair, costly subsidies and tax breaks to lure these firms from away. ...

Despite his achievements in fiscal discipline, welfare reform, and economic and entrepreneurial cultures, unemployment, debt and dependence on federal transfers still limit prospects. McKenna's job creation programme, using tax concessions and grants to lure firms from away produced short-term benefits but left an uncertain legacy for permanent and balanced economic development.

Some policies initiated in the McKenna years, such as an ill-fated scheme for an American company to build private prisons and construction of a toll road linking some of the province's largest cities, created problems for his successor, Camille Theriault. Discontent also emerged over school closures, elimination of elected school boards, hospital wait lists, workfare, and other austerity measures. Theriault soon lost to the youthful Conservative leader Bernard Lord.

Lord, 33 when elected in 1999, ran on promises of tax cuts, health spending and elimination of the highway tolls. He hoped to be the latest in a pattern of young, energetic leaders —from Robichaud to Hatfield to McKenna—to win multiple elections for both parties, which contributes to the province's reputation for vigour and innovation in governance. Despite protests from farmers and labour, Lord carried forward with his election promises of restraint and tax reductions, and limited new spending to address pressing needs in education and health care. It remains to be seen if Lord can sustain the tradition of multi-term premierships by young, bold, reformist premiers. ...

The demise of the Confederation of Regions party (a libertarian party of popular protest) does not spell the end of ethnic politics in the province; while the majority continue to support bilingualism, former COR supporters returned to the Conservative ranks to campaign against Theriault and may have contributed to Lord's surprise win. Some suggested that the COR's collapse could allow the Canadian Alliance to make inroads at the federal level in the province, but they did not win a seat here in the 2000 election. Despite occasional reactionaries, New Brunswick has bridged its linguistic differences, though violent confrontations with Mi'qmaks over lobster and forest resources have flared recently.

Prince Edward Island

Prince Edward Island, the "garden in the gulf," is an insular community, where the birthdays of children are noted on the provincial website. Its government operates like a municipality, with local concerns predominant. The province relies on farming (especially potatoes) and fisheries (notably shellfish) and its bourgeoning tourism industry (featuring its remarkable beaches and gentle countryside). Its politics initially revolved around the issues of absentee landlords, who won much of the island in a 1756 lottery; the reversal of this situation after Confederation instilled a fierce loyalty to the land on the Island.

Insularity is another enduring theme, as this small colony resisted confederation at first. Contact with the mainland was by ferry for over a century after Confederation. Politicians often promised a fixed link to the rest of the Maritimes, but some citizens resisted this possible disruption of island life. The construction of the Confederation Bridge, an engineering marvel, in the 1990s brought new prospects of economic integration, but rekindled fears. In a community where everyone knows your name, and where a murder a decade is the norm, the intrusion of the North American mainstream is resisted, even though young people often migrate elsewhere to find it. The fixed link project was opposed by environmentalists and community activists fearful of the loss of the Island way of life, but 59 per cent supported it in a 1988 plebiscite. ...

Confederation, entered reluctantly in 1873 because of railway debts and the end of reciprocity with the US, is still perceived as a mixed blessing. Some considered it a conspiracy of the British colonial office and Ottawa, imposed against the will of the majority. This province carries little weight in federal politics, though it is over-represented in population terms, with its four seats in the House of Commons protected by the Senate floor rule. Like its Maritime neighbours, it relies heavily on federal transfers, though the levels of federal support have dropped from 60 to 40 per cent of the provincial budget. ...

Political participation is the highest in the land, with over 85 per cent voter turnout in provincial elections. Politics is intensely contested, and the province is given to political extremes, with frequent landslides multiplied by the small chamber, where the opposition is often minimal (one member only after the 1999 election). While some families vote according to inherited loyalties or on patronage lines, the voters are well informed and a few votes can decide an election. In 1996, a mere 2,108 votes produced a majority for Pat Binns' Conservatives. ...

Though often accused of traditionalism, PEI was the first province to elect minority and female premiers (Joe Ghiz and Catherine Callbeck, respectively). Ghiz, of Lebanese origin, withstood racial slurs in the legislature to win the confidence of the population. He gained credibility on the national scene with his reasoned, moderate interventions in the Meech Lake debate. For a brief period in the 1990s, women simultaneously served as premier, lieutenant-governor, opposition leader, and Speaker of the House, an unprecedented circumstance in any province. ...

Outsiders often question PEI's viability and the expense to the nation of preserving a separate province for such a small population. However, there is a fierce commitment to autonomy here, reflected in the concern about the cultural impact of the fixed link to the mainland completed in the 1990s. Although often depicted as a virtual "ward" of Ottawa because of its small size and fiscal dependence, the Island has shown some independence. For instance, it is the only Atlantic province not to harmonize its sales taxes with Ottawa's GST.

Prospects for Atlantic Cooperation

Many observers suggest that these four historical units are no longer effective as self-governing provinces. The existence of 4 governments for 2.25 million people, versus one province for 12 million in Ontario, is considered wasteful. Critics speak of "overgovernment" and urge Atlantic or Maritime union as a potential solution to dependence and underdevelopment. Cooperation, including closer integration of policies and services, may be a necessary response to fiscal crisis and decentralization of authority. While Quebec sovereignty has faded as an immediate threat, it remains a possibility, which would isolate Atlantic Canada physically. Asymmetry, decentralization, fewer transfers, and more provincial powers are also possible. The fiscal and ideological climate in other regions has reduced support for interprovincial transfers, which could threaten the ability of these small provinces to provide essential services to their people.

Interprovincial cooperation has achieved some results, but many important elements of industrial development have not been included. And these arrangements can be undermined or abandoned by these provinces, in response to internal electoral pressures. Essential regional cooperation can only progress so far without political integration because of provincial sovereignty, which encourages both governments and societies to orient on provincial, not regional, lines. Union advocates believe that these provinces need to go beyond creating a single economic space, to creating shared facilities, services, and programmes if the citizens of this region are to retain services of national quality.

Political union could promote consolidation of government resources, and give the region a more coherent position in national forums. It could reduce expensive legislative and bureaucratic duplication and permit economies of scale in programmes. It could reduce spending on administration, while directing more revenues to services like health and education. It might allow cooperation in tourism, resource management and economic integration. And it could promote region-wide development and end competition for limited investment through costly tax concessions, loans or grants. Finally, a larger unit might simply be more credible as a voice for regional interests in the federation, even facilitating changes like Senate reform. Acadians outside New Brunswick might favour union to secure some of the benefits of their brethren in that province.

However, political union would be difficult if not impossible to implement. There is no constitutional means to force provinces together, given their veto power over changes to their jurisdiction and borders. In addition, there would be losses for the region, including the constitutional veto under the 7-of-10 provinces rule, and an end to the protection of the Senate floor rule for smallest provinces prompting a decline in the number of MPs from the region. Furthermore, these provinces could face the loss of distinctive identities, which are especially important to residents. For instance, PEI might reject submersion in a larger, less personal unit, in which its distinctive entity would disappear. New Brunswick's Acadians would become more of a minority in a united province. Newfoundland also feels little sense of identity with the Maritimes. There could be more tangible costs, like the loss of government employment, which would affect the health of the regional economy in the short run. There would also be the loss of experimentation with better approaches by different regimes. Public opinion on union remained divided in 1990s polls, with 35 per cent supportive of union, 38 per cent opposed and 26 per cent undecided.

These figures could indicate the need for slower integration to bring population onside and to demonstrate the benefits of closer cooperation in the preservation of services and standard of living. This could include the use of constitutionalized agreements between provinces, to enshrine cooperative arrangements and to allow for the merging of key institutions and bureaucracies. It could also permit the creation of a single economic space, tax and expenditure coordination, enshrined procurement rules and durable agreements to reduce interprovincial competition via costly investment incentives and tax breaks. The provinces could create innovative pools of investment capital using merged public sector pension funds. They could create self-sufficient interprovincial agencies with their own sources of revenue independent of individual provincial regimes (for example, a regional transportation agency funded by fuel taxes).

Eventually, the region might create joint bureaucracies in key areas such as health, post-secondary education, or create a common federal court for the region. An agency like the Council of Atlantic Premiers could direct the process and assign the major institutions to different provincial capitals to share employment benefits equitably. Ottawa could contribute to this process by promoting greater certainty in cost-sharing arrangements and by making some transfers to regional agencies. This level of cooperation could become an end in itself or a possible first step towards political union.

It may be in the region's interest to coordinate policies trans-provincially while retaining separate provinces, with four votes in constitutional and federal-provincial forums. How-ever, any scheme of integration or cooperation would have to be implemented carefully to maximize savings and minimize costs. Some economists warn the benefits of economic inte-gration without full union would be minimal. There would also be concerns about how to keep interprovincial institutions democratically accountable without a joint assembly. Careful steps will be needed to ensure that these institutions do not become a super-government that fails to reduce the cost or size of bureaucracy. It would be difficult to balance community input into policy from all four provinces, and debates over the degree of influence (or even location of new agencies) could be anticipated. It may be hard to promote cooperation in government services if independent provincial bureaucracies persist, with their own inter-ests at stake. And politicians will always be tempted to pull back from cooperation for their own electoral purposes.

Current experience with cooperation is mixed. Maritime initiatives in higher education, and municipal training and development, lottery corporation, and veterinary and police education have existed for years. Newfoundland joined in Atlantic agreements on procure-ment and internal trade in the 1990s. Integration of some economic regulations, taxation, and insurance legislation has progressed more recently. A Council of Atlantic Premiers was formalized in 1989 to promote Atlantic concerns. Despite this progress, the continued exis-tence of four sovereign provinces has created continual problems of competition which the region can ill afford. There has been infighting such as Nova Scotia's threatened withdrawal from the Atlantic Lottery Corporation and the police academy, PEI and Newfoundland's conflict over shrimp quotas, and Nova Scotia and Newfoundland's arbitration case on off-shore boundaries. Intense economic need makes these provinces competitors, not coopera-tors; substantial institutional integration may be required to overcome this parochialism and encourage durable, mutually beneficial cooperation.

But long-time advocates of union see it as a costly and distant prospect, which is unlikely to materialize. This is not surprising in light of the distinct historical trajectories and very different cultural, economic, and social conditions affecting contemporary politics in the four Atlantic provinces. While outside observers tend to lump them together into a residual category, as parochial political and economic backwaters, this brief survey reveals profound variations in these political systems. These different traditions and contemporary practices constitute a significant barrier to intra-provincial cooperation, let alone political union. It is not easy for people accustomed to provincial loyalties and cultural identifications, and especially provincial-level organization in civil and pressure groups, to reorient on a regional basis. If anything, global homogenization encourages peoples to hold ever more strongly to particularities, even while integrating with distant nations. Therefore, it may not be easy for Atlantic Canadians to dispense with provincial symbols and cultures or to accept a new homogenized bureaucratic regionalism, however efficacious for expenditure and services.

Indeed, it is difficult to imagine how union or cooperation will occur within the Can-adian federation as it is currently constituted. Observers of Canadian politics have long argued that the institutions of federalism interact with social forces to create durable pro-vincialisms, which are resistant to any trans-provincial regionalism. Institutions set the boundaries for political conduct and provide incentives and constraints for political actors, limiting and shaping their behaviours. In the current constitutional context, political leaders in Atlantic Canada have little incentive to cooperate across borders, even to improve the cost-effective delivery of services and programmes. As long as they are accountable only to their own electors, Atlantic governments will often undertake policies that place them in destructive competition.

Whatever will to cooperate may exist, it will require a restructuring of federal institutions to provide sufficient rewards for cooperation. Such restructuring may not occur at all unless a crisis of sufficient magnitude (for example, Quebec sovereignty or radical decentralization of powers) forces these provinces to collaborate. Whether the costs of such a crises can be mitigated by intra-provincial cooperation short of union is uncertain. Meanwhile, analysts can do no more than to urge creation of trans-provincial institutions and funding arrangements to limit the damage of decentralization, duplication and under-funding of essential public services.

This brief survey of provincial politics in Atlantic Canada indicates that portrayals of the homogeneity of this region are misguided. The distinctive political histories and trajectories of these provinces, coupled with very diverse and distinct socio-cultural bases, indicate why it has been so difficult to create a sustained movement for unification. Newfoundland's neo-nationalism and cultural revival are clearly oriented along provincial lines, with provincialist tendencies at times approaching Quebec's in intensity. Nova Scotia is a regional leader in commerce, education and economics, yet it is plagued by internal diversities and fragmentation which make its own governance problematic, and which undermine its ability to cooperate with its neighbours. New Brunswick's unique accommodation of bilingual communities and vigorous public policy innovation could suffer in a homogenized Atlantic entity. Prince Edward Island retains a distinct, insular identity that will be challenged via increased contacts with mainland North America, let alone by submersion in a unified region.

Yet necessity is the mother of invention: challenges of globalization, Quebec sovereignty, decentralization, hemispheric integration, and technological innovation could still require greater integration and cooperation among these four small, vulnerable provinces. The challenge will be to get leaders here to look beyond electoral interests and parochial sentiments and accept durable cooperative arrangements in the interest of retaining world-class public services. This may be the fundamental challenge confronting the region, as it seeks to improve its competitive position in the integrated global economy of this new century.

Suggested Reading

Beck, J. Murray. "An Atlantic Region Political Culture: A Chimera" in D.J. Bercuson and Phillip Buckner, eds. *Eastern and Western Perspectives*. Toronto: University of Toronto Press, 1981.

Bickerton, James and Alain-G. Gagnon. "Regions and Regionalism in Canada" in James Bickerton and Alain-G. Gagnon, eds. *Canadian Politics* (5th edition). Toronto: University of Toronto Press, 2009.

Forbes, E.R. *Challenging the Regional Stereotype: Essays on the 20th Century Maritimes*. Fredericton: Acadiensis Press, 1989.

Smallwood, Joseph R. *I Chose Canada*, Vol. II. Scarborough: Signet, 1975.

Tomblin, Stephen. *Ottawa and the Outer Provinces*. Toronto: Lorimer, 1995.

80 Political Action on Stage West

Roger Gibbins (2009)

EDITORS' INTRODUCTION

Roger Gibbins is the president and CEO of the Canada West Foundation, whose ethos is "a dynamic and prosperous West in a strong Canada." Prior to assuming that role, he was a professor of political science at the University of Calgary, with which he is still associated, and is a past president of the Canadian Political Science Association. He has written extensively on western Canadian themes and issues, including his contribution to Canada by Picasso: The Faces of Federalism *(by Roger Gibbins, Antonia Maioni, and Janice Gross Stein, published by the Conference Board of Canada in 2006).*

The following op-ed piece appeared in the fall of 2009, as Canadians waited to hear if they would be thrust into a fourth election in just five years. In considering this piece alongside Preston Manning's 1987 speech (see reading 72 in this volume, "The West Wants In"), one gets a palpable sense of the West's emergence over the last two decades into an increasingly important player in Canadian political life. In addition to the West beginning to take on a leadership role on policy matters, Gibbins also notes a new tone to the political discourse of western Canadian leaders.

As Ottawa becomes increasingly paralyzed by a dysfunctional Parliament, the centre of Canada's policy conversation has shifted west.

Some of the most interesting action in well-written plays takes place out of the spotlight. Although the main action appears to be unfolding on centre stage, much of the richness is found on stage left or stage right. This is increasingly the case on Canada's political stage.

A good example was last week when all the focus was on election fever in Ottawa. Story after story, and conversation after conversation, was filled with speculation whether the Liberals would pull the plug on the minority Conservative government and, if they did, whether the NDP or Bloc would shove it back in. Commentators stormed to the microphone to predict who might win or lose an election about nothing. Nobody outside Ottawa wants an election; voters are hunkered down riding out the recession.

Meanwhile, on stage west and out of the spotlight, something of potentially great long-term significance was taking place. Meeting in Calgary, the premiers of British Columbia, Alberta, and Saskatchewan signed the Western Economic Partnership. This interprovincial trade agreement will create the largest barrier-free trade and investment market in Canada.

Source: First published in *The Calgary Herald*, September 21, 2009. Accessed from *The Mark*, September 30, 2009 (www.themarknews.com). Reprinted by permission of the Canada West Foundation (www.cwf.ca).

Nor did the premiers stop with this milestone. They went on to address pension reform, gang violence, and the Canadian production of medical isotopes. They also signed a memorandum of understanding on carbon capture and storage technology and policy. It was a busy day!

These developments are also important because they mark the further westward drift of the national economy and Canadian policy leadership. Unencumbered by the national policy paralysis induced by minority governments, the western premiers are determined to make their regional economy work.

The developments mark a huge evolutionary change in the tone and character of intergovernmental relations. In the not-too-distant past, the western premiers met annually to play golf, get to know one another, and draw up a list of grievances against the federal government. Now the meetings are intensive policy discussions with a focus on what the premiers and their governments can accomplish together.

Although the premiers are vigilant in pointing out how federal policy might be improved, Ottawa bashing is a thing of the past as the premiers focus on better things to do. Ottawa is the target only when it comes to constructive policy initiatives that might engage the federal government.

The interprovincial trade agreement marks the de facto extension of the earlier B.C.–Alberta agreement—The Investment and Labour Mobility Agreement (TILMA)—to include Saskatchewan. Premier Wall of Saskatchewan had promised in the election campaign that brought him to power that he would not sign the existing TILMA. Last week he signed a similar agreement and as the child of TILMA marches east, the regional economy will be better for it.

TILMA, it should be noted, was the first successful initiative to reduce interprovincial barriers to trade. The premiers of B.C. and Alberta were able to go where their provincial counterparts were unable to go, and where Ottawa showed no interest in going, and now Saskatchewan is on the same path. Meanwhile, the rest of the provinces wrestle with economic barriers designed for the 19th century.

Now some might argue that the Western Economic Partnership is incomplete because Manitoba is not on board. However, Manitoba's exclusion was more by circumstance than by design. The Calgary meeting took place just after the announcement that Manitoba Premier Gary Doer would shortly become Canada's new ambassador in Washington, and thus he was in no position to engage his government in regional initiatives. The doors and windows have been flung open, and the welcome mat is in place for when a new premier and cabinet are in Winnipeg.

So, while the national political system struggles with an increasingly dysfunctional Parliament and minority government, the policy initiative shifts west. The western premiers are no longer criticizing from stage west, they are leading the national debate.